THE BUILDINGS OF ENGLAND

BE26

WILTSHIRE

NIKOLAUS PEVSNER

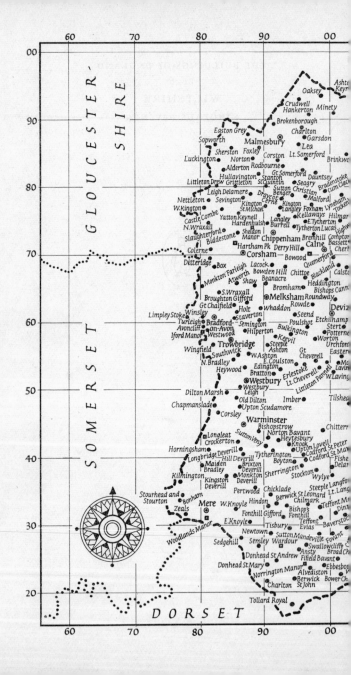

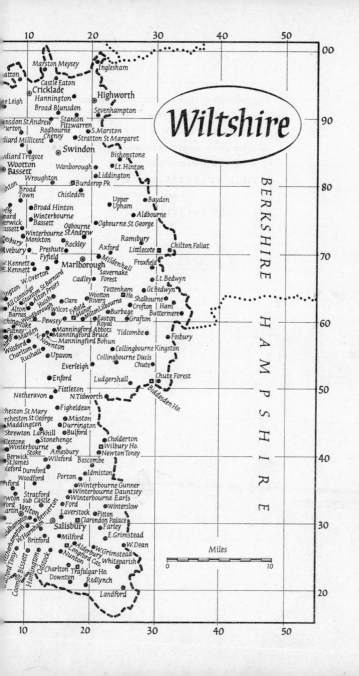

*The publication of this volume has been made
possible by a grant from*
THE LEVERHULME TRUST
*to cover all the necessary research work and
by generous contributions from*
ARTHUR GUINNESS, SON & CO LTD
and
ABC TELEVISION LTD

THE BUILDINGS OF ENGLAND

Wiltshire

BY

NIKOLAUS PEVSNER

★

WITH NOTES ON THE PREHISTORIC
AND ROMAN ANTIQUITIES

BY

DEREK SIMPSON

PENGUIN BOOKS

Penguin Books Ltd, Harmondsworth, Middlesex
U.S.A.: Penguin Books Inc., 3300 Clipper Mill Road, Baltimore 11, Md
AUSTRALIA: Penguin Books Pty Ltd, 762 Whitehorse Road,
Mitcham, Victoria

—

First published 1963

—

—

Made and printed in Great Britain
By William Clowes and Sons, Limited London and Beccles
Gravure Plates by Clarke and Sherwell, Limited
Set in Monotype Plantin

CONTENTS

★

Map References

*

The numbers printed in italic type in the margin against the place names in the gazetteer of the book indicate the position of the place in question on the index map (pages 2–3), which is divided into sections by the 10-kilometre reference lines of the National Grid. The reference given here omits the two initial letters (formerly numbers) which in a full grid reference refer to the 100-kilometre squares into which the country is divided. The first two numbers indicate the *western* boundary, and the last two the *southern* boundary, of the 10-kilometre square in which the place in question is situated. For example, Chisledon (reference 1070) will be found in the 10-kilometre square bounded by grid lines 10 and 20 on the *west* and 70 and 80 on the *south*; Luckington (reference 8080) in the square bounded by grid lines 80 and 90 on the *west* and 80 and 90 on the *south*.

The map contains all those places, whether towns, villages, or isolated buildings, which are the subject of separate entries in the text.

FOREWORD

Wiltshire is not one of the best-researched-into counties. The Victoria County History *is the most important source of information for this book, the* Wiltshire Archeological and Natural History Magazine *(especially the late C. E. Ponting's papers) the next-best. I have tried to see more than I was guided to by existing literature, but must still have overlooked much, especially among the innumerable, always attractive houses of Cotswold type in the north-west and north of the county, and of course among interiors of houses in general. What existing literature would yield has been prepared very well for me by Mrs Hall, then Helen Davey. I want to thank her in the first place, my wife and my secretary, Margaret Tims, in the second. Immediately after them I want to pay my debt of gratitude to all those incumbents who have answered questions I had put to them and later read proofs, and all those owners of houses who put up with my visits, extended hospitality to us, and again consented to reply to intricate questions or questionnaires. Among the most helpful were Lord Methuen and Lady Radnor. The editor of the* Victoria County Histories, *Mr R. B. Pugh, allowed us access to unpublished material, and Miss Elizabeth Crittall and Mr. K. Rogers put their specialized knowledge at our disposal. At the museum at Devizes I was most kindly helped by Mr R. E. Sandall, at the Swindon Library by Mr H. Joliffe. At Salisbury my principal benefactors were Mr Hugh Short and Mr B. C. Parsons, Clerk of the Works to the Cathedral. For Marlborough College I had the support of Mr Kempson, for the area round Marlborough, Devizes, Swindon that of Geoffrey Grigson, for churches around Wroughton that of Mr J. A. Finch. Mr Harry Ross kindly gave me information on castles, and this is marked* HR *in the gazetteer. Moreover Mr Pugh, Miss Crittall, Mr Rogers, the Rev. C. Blunt, Miss J. Burnett Brown, Mr N. Davey, Lt-Col Floyd, Mr Kempson, Mr Lansdown, Lord Methuen, Lord Moyne, Mr Panzetta, Lady Radnor, and Mr Short all read proofs of the parts their specialized knowledge was specially valuable for.*

The Introduction to Prehistoric and Roman Remains and all paragraphs in the gazetteer referring to them are written by Mr Derek Simpson, the Introduction to Geology by Mr Terence Miller. The Ministry of Housing and Local Government (here abbreviated MHLG*) have a statutory duty to draw up lists of buildings of architectural or historic interest and have again very kindly put at my*

*disposal the lists compiled by the Chief Investigator and his staff.
For the districts not covered yet by the Ministry my most valuable
source of information as regards secular architecture was the National
Buildings Record (NBR). For Victorian churches my own material
was greatly increased by Mr Peter Ferriday's Index of Restorations
which he most generously gave on permanent loan to The Buildings
of England (abbreviated PF) and by the Goodhart-Rendel Index at
the Royal Institute of British Architects (abbreviated GR). Sir
Thomas Kendrick's Index of Stained Glass I have, thanks to his
kindness, also had access to (abbreviated TK), and the same is true
of Mr E. Croft-Murray's volumes on decorative painting.*

*The principles on which the following gazetteer is founded are the
same as in the twenty-five volumes of The Buildings of England
which precede it. I have myself seen everything that I describe. Where
this is not the case the information obtained by other means is placed
in brackets. Information ought to be as complete as the space of the
volume permits for churches prior to c.1830 and all town houses,
manor houses, and country houses of more than purely local interest.
Movable furnishings are not included in secular buildings, though
they are in churches. Exceptions to the latter rule are bells, hatch-
ments, chests, chairs, plain fonts, and altar tables. Royal arms, coffin
lids with foliate crosses, and brasses of post-Reformation date are
mentioned occasionally, church plate of after 1830 only rarely.
Village crosses are omitted where only a plain base or a stump of the
shaft survives. As for churches and chapels of after 1830, I had to
make a selection, and this is dictated by architectural value or by
significance otherwise in the light of architectural history. The same
applies to secular buildings of the C19 and C20.*

*Finally, as in all previous volumes, it is necessary to end the fore-
word to this with an appeal to all users to draw my attention to errors
and omissions.*

INTRODUCTION

WILTSHIRE, as one travels in the county, seems larger than it is. Being seventeenth among the counties, it comes nearly half-way down the list. The illusion of distances is due to the solitude of the downs, but also to so many changes from character to character and from landscape to landscape. Most people, if Wiltshire is mentioned, just think of Salisbury Plain, but that is unfortunate considering how the military have treated it. The Marlborough Downs have preserved their solemnity far more nobly and there 2a are stretches of unspoilt downs also s of the Nadder between Wilton and Tisbury. The most characteristic feature of Wiltshire is indeed the alternation between the villages and the downs. The two Avons run N–S, the Bristol Avon in the county from Malmesbury to Bradford, the Salisbury Avon from Upavon to Downton. The other valleys, small but in their scenery very telling, run W–E: the valley of the Kennet, the Vale of Pewsey, the valleys of the Wylie, the Nadder, and the Ebble. And in addition to the prettiness of the valleys and the majesty of the downs, there are the generously wooded stretches towards Hampshire and Dorset 1 and towards Somerset, and there is of course the North Wiltshire plain, between where the Marlborough Downs end and where the Cotswolds start.

All this is experienced in terms of landscape, but can only be understood in terms of the history of the earth and this particular piece of it. A special introduction about Wiltshire geology is therefore appended (p. 69). Here it is only necessary to look at geology in terms of building materials. The best English stone, jurassic oolitic limestone, runs in a diagonal band through the country, from South Yorkshire into Dorset. It touches Wiltshire in the corner near Bradford-on-Avon and Corsham. Another good jurassic building stone comes from the Portland and Purbeck beds round Tisbury. The famous stone of Chilmark from which Salisbury Cathedral and Wilton House were built is also Portland. In the Marlborough Downs they had that unique material, Sarsen stones or Grey Wethers, lumps of sandstone on the chalk which were left over when the rest of the sandstone cover weathered away. Flint is distributed in all the chalk parts of the county. But cottages in these parts are also quite often built of blocks of pugged chalk. And brick rules round Swindon and made more and more inroads into the flint and sandstone areas, as time went on. With so many building materials so close together, combinations were thought out which are visually specially pleasurable: flint and brick in bands, flint with brick dressings, flint and stone in bands (in the Avon valley N of Salisbury) or in chequerwork, and even bands in which sandstone and limestone alternate. At Longford Castle there are bands of greenish grey alternating with bands composed of alternating little squares of flint and buff stone.

It has been said that Wiltshire in size is seventeenth; in population it is yet lower: it comes thirty-first. For Wiltshire is not an industrial county. Swindon is the only industrial town, and even Swindon has only about 70,000 inhabitants. Wiltshire is a county of small towns; that is architecturally more characteristic of it than anything else. Salisbury has only about 35,000 inhabitants, and yet what a variety of town, close, and cathedral – the town hardly taken in by most visitors. Trowbridge has under 16,000, Bradford under 6,000. With Melksham and down s to Westbury and Warminster they form almost what is now called a conurbation, though admittedly in a modest way. Then there are Chippenham and Calne NE of it, and Devizes E of it, and there is Tisbury in the sw. Tisbury, Melksham, and Westbury have little to make them remain architectural images in one's mind, but the image of Trowbridge remains, compact with no wide spaces, of Bradford rising on both sides of the Avon, steeply to the N, more gently to the s, of Chippenham's wide market place, of Calne's factory as the hub of the town, of Warminster's long street with the historical centre almost unnoticed off its s end, of Swindon's division into the old town and the new, and so on.

All these towns lie in the valleys; not one of them grew on the downs. Yet it is on the downs that prehistoric Wiltshire lived and worked. Why the county is infinitely the richest area of all England in prehistoric remains, and one of the richest areas in Europe, cannot be fully explained. The subject is of supreme interest, and for many visitors Wiltshire means Stonehenge and Avebury rather than even Salisbury. So a special introduction to Wiltshire prehistory and Roman Wiltshire was called for, and this will be found on pp. 56–68. What attracted the early Britons to the hills is that they were dry,* whereas the valleys were swamps. The move from Old Sarum to New Sarum, even if made many centuries later, remains symbolic. The hills were certainly

* As they still are – cf. the six villages called Winterbourne.

already left by the Romans, and the Anglo-Saxons followed suit.

Wiltshire is poor in ANGLO-SAXON REMAINS, but what there is, is in valley-villages and valley-towns. St Lawrence at Bradford-on-Avon is the only major and the only early monument, now that it has been proved to be in its plan and part of its structure St Aldhelm's *ecclesiola*, i.e. a building of the late C7. With its two porticus, the narrow archways into them and into the straight-ended chancel, and its high, narrow proportions, it is typical of Anglo-Saxon architecture at its most idiosyncratic. The external enrichment by pilaster strips, blank arches, and blank triangle-heads instead of arches, however, is the result of a remodelling of probably the C10. The monumental angels originally flanking a rood such as that preserved at Romsey in Hampshire belong to this remodelling. They, a little-known Virgin and Child at Ingle-sham, and the tympanum at Knook are all that need be mentioned of Late Saxon sculpture, the tympanum actually belonging to the so-called Saxo-Norman overlap, i.e. quite probably to after 1066. But the great age of sculpture in this part of England was the C9. To this are assigned the strange archway into a former porticus at Britford, with its slabs in the jambs decorated with rather hard, metallic foliage scrolls as well as interlace, the parts of cross-shafts and gravestones at Ramsbury in a similar style and the one, more thrilling unquestionably, with a Viking dragon in the so-called Ringerike style, the part of a Viking-looking cross-shaft at Colerne, perhaps by the same carver, and the mysterious slab at Codford St Peter with the agile figure of a man bending back-wards and holding up a branch. What does it represent? The figure is not at all small, and the piece is in every respect unique in Europe. Its date cannot perhaps be regarded as finally settled.

Hardly anything else need be referred to: Netheravon with its quite substantial former crossing tower, two heads of wheel-crosses, one at Ramsbury the other at Amesbury, occasional windows (Avebury, Mildenhall), and occasional long-and-short quoins (Alton Barnes, Bremhill, Burcombe, Upton Scudamore); that is about all.

For the NORMAN STYLE in Wiltshire the key building must of course have been the cathedral of Old Sarum. Nothing of it stands above ground, but the foundations have been excavated, and they show two stages: St Osmund's building begun after the see had been transferred from Sherborne in 1072 and completed in 1092, and Roger's building of before 1139, the year in which he died. St Osmund's was quite small, only 173 ft long, and dis-

tinguished by the feature of two towers standing on the whole
squares of the transepts. This feature at the time was, as far as our
knowledge goes, completely new for the whole of Europe. It was
repeated in the late C12 at Exeter and recurs in the first quarter
of the twelfth century at Angoulême Cathedral and in the late
C12 at Lyons and Geneva. Roger enlarged the cathedral by a W
front with twin towers and by a longer and different E end bringing
the total length to 316 ft – not very large when compared to
Norman Winchester or Ely or Norwich or several others. His E
end is interesting. He let his high choir end straight (like Anglo-
Saxon chancels), placed a rectangular ambulatory round it, and
made his three chapels face E, two small ones in continuation of
the chancel aisles and a big one in the middle. All three were
apsed inside but straight outside. The motif of the straight wall
of an apse he took from Osmund's E end, but the idea of the
ambulatory with three chapels is French Romanesque standard,
only with the ambulatory semicircular and the chapels radiating.
This scheme was current in England as well and was indeed
represented by Malmesbury Abbey, but the English were never
happy about two of the three chapels not pointing E and tried all
sorts of things to amend the fault (Norwich, Gloucester, etc.).
Roger's way of amending it is historically important, as the straight
E end was to become the rule in Gothic England.

Roger was a great man in his time, chancellor and justiciar.
He was the uncle of the bishops of Ely and of Lincoln, and he
enlarged at Sarum not only the cathedral but also the castle. Here
excavations have shown a most remarkable feature – namely not
a keep but instead a main building with four ranges round a quadrangle. The only parallel in Europe to this is Roger's other castle
at Sherborne, also known only from excavations. Roger was hostile
to Stephen, and his CASTLES were confiscated. Of the only other
major royal castles in Wiltshire one has disappeared – Marlborough, where only the mound remains; of the other – Ludgershall, there survives only an impressive but unenlightening cliff
of the former keep. Roger's other two castles, Devizes and
Malmesbury, have again completely gone.

9   But Malmesbury has the nave of a major Benedictine abbey.
The E end has disappeared. Its plan has already been described.
The most interesting motif of its elevation is the pointed arches
of the arcade. No date is documentarily known for Malmesbury,
but the nave must for stylistic reasons belong to c.1160. So the
pointed arches ought not to be explained as a reflection of Gothic
innovations but as inspired by the Cistercians, who had begun

to use pointed arches in England already in the 1130s, under
the influence of the Romanesque pointed arches of Burgundy.*
The rest at Malmesbury, the round piers, the gallery, the
decoration, and – far more important – the sculpture are all
Norman, i.e. Romanesque. The sculpture of the Malmesbury
porch has many French sources, in the Middle West as well as
in Burgundy. The two lunettes with the excessively elongated 8b
seated figures of the twelve apostles and the angels flying horizontally above them are among the best work of the time in
England. So must have been the outer portal of the porch, when 10a
the small figures and scenes in the medallions could still be read
and appreciated.

Other NORMAN SCULPTURE in Wiltshire is very minor,
though enjoyable: two small figures at Ivychurch (Alderbury),
two small figures under arches at Landford, a seated Christ at
Stanton St Quintin, some other bits and pieces at Colerne, Ramsbury, and Stanton Fitzwarren, and so to the Virgin with the
Prophet (?) below at Sutton Mandeville, which is of the C13 but
in the Romanesque tradition. In addition there are figured tympana at Highworth, Little Langford, Rodbourne, and Knook, if
the latter can be counted as Norman now. There are about sixty
Norman doorways preserved in Wiltshire. None of them is as
ornate as, say, those of Yorkshire. That there are nearly as many
Norman fonts as well need hardly be said. Their turn in this
Introduction will come later.

To return to architecture proper, next to Malmesbury, St John
at Devizes is probably the most impressive Norman church, 10b
large, with a completely preserved crossing tower and that rare
feature, a rib-vaulted chancel. St Mary at Devizes has this feature
too, and its chancel is altogether similar to that of St John and
probably a little earlier. Another Norman central tower is at
Stanton St Quintin, and the Late Norman arches of yet another
remain at Tisbury. Manningford Bruce has a wholly preserved
small Early Norman village church. There are well over thirty
Norman arcades wholly or partly preserved in Wiltshire churches.
Early among them are those of Longbridge Deverill, Tilshead,
and Winterslow. On the whole signs of an early date are square
piers, unmoulded arches, and capitals not yet decorated with
many small scallops. A little later round piers with square abaci
became the rule. The development then goes from the square

* Bishop Roger's St John Devizes has, however, pointed arches too, and
they are earlier than Malmesbury and not at all suggestive of Cistercian
inspiration.

abacus to the round abacus, from multi-scalloped to trumpet-scalloped and from these to crocketed and stiff-leaf capitals, from the unmoulded to the single-step, to the slightly chamfered, and so to the fully double-chamfered arch, and of course from the round arch to the pointed arch. But while these rules are easily enough deduced from evidence, the actual development was very much more complicated. All kinds of overlap occur. The pointed arches at Malmesbury have already been discussed (p. 16). Some other examples of the ambiguities of actual arcades, as we find them in the county, may be presented. The round, single-step arch ought to be early, as it is at Calne. But at Hullavington (N), Mildenhall, and Sherston it comes with trumpet-scallop capitals, and at Colerne, Crudwell, and Whiteparish the single-step arches are pointed. Of course it was easy to convert a round into a pointed arch when fashion had changed. Then there are the double-chamfered pointed arches at Ivychurch (Alderbury) still on multi-scalloped capitals. Or there are the slender, alternatingly round and octagonal, typical C13 piers of Charlton near Malmesbury, with C12 trumpet capitals and round arches, and the fat, round, Early-Norman-looking piers of Stapleford with dog-tooth, another typical C13 motif, in the hood-moulds. And so it goes on. As a Norman rarity, the circular clerestory windows of Avebury may be appended.

The features just considered have taken us to about 1220. The year 1220 is the year of the creation of New Sarum, that is of Salisbury Cathedral, and Salisbury Cathedral is a building in the purest EARLY ENGLISH STYLE, indeed the purest major E.E. building in the country. The story of the cathedral is told in another place (p. 346). Here only the salient points can be reiterated. The cathedral was begun under Bishop Richard Poore (1217–29). The name of the original designer is not recorded. A mason *Nicholas of Ely* has a good claim. So has *Elias de Derham*, Canon, distinguished churchman, and outstanding craftsman. The cathedral was built very quickly. After five years the Lady Chapel and retrochoir could be consecrated, after thirty-eight years the whole building. It was essentially ready then. The plan had not changed, unless perhaps the W front marks a change. The principal motifs were decided upon in 1220 and adhered to to the end. They are rectangularity in plan, the straight-ended high choir, the straight ambulatory, and the three straight-ended E chapels, taken over perhaps from Roger's Old Sarum, though radically altered in style. The motif of the two pairs of transepts on the other hand was taken from Canterbury, Wells, and Lincoln, the three E.E. cathedrals begun thirty to forty-five years before Salisbury. From Canterbury and Lincoln also came the delight in Purbeck marble. Salisbury uses long, slender, detached Purbeck shafts wherever possible. The contrast of this dark grey, shiny stone with the light, warm, greyish-buff Chilmark stone, and indeed with the cool grey unpolished Purbeck, is one of the two most readily remembered characteristics of Salisbury. The other is less easy to formulate. It is an impression of nothing done to excess. Proportions contribute to that, and the attempted balance between the verticalism of all Gothic forms and the stressed horizontalism of the somewhat squat gallery. A refusal to decorate contributes perhaps even more. Of all the major capitals inside, just two have leaves. All the others are moulded. If you are looking for stiff-leaf on areas more than an odd six inches square, you must lift your eyes right up to the vaulting bosses. The vaults incidentally are quadripartite, i.e. have nothing of the adventurous novelty of Lincoln, and the windows are consistently lancets, also in pairs and triplets, and a little later with some simple plate-tracery. The only prominent place where variety is allowed is the piers. Here divers beautiful shapes have been developed, all by means of the contrast between a core and detached Purbeck shafts. This delightful motif inspired by Canterbury and Lincoln in its turn inspired a number of parish churches, especially Heytesbury, Luckington, and Wilcot.* At Foxley and Wilcot trumpet-scallop capitals still occur with E. E. piers – another proof of how hard the Norman style died.

At Salisbury the restless w façade of the screen type ended the activity on the cathedral proper. It must have been begun under Bishop Robert Bingham (1229–46), i.e. at about the same time as the screen façade of Wells. It cannot be decided which of the two came first. Both of course continue an Anglo-Norman tradition of screen façades. Of the many statues displayed on the Salisbury front none has survived unscathed. To admire Salisbury sculpture one must look at the former rood screen of about 14a 1235–50, and especially its deliciously intimate little heads used as hood-mould stops. The same motif was chosen for the later chapter house, where also biblical scenes were carved in all the 15b spandrels. These however have been restored out of aesthetic existence, and one has to look at the unrestored little scenes on the monument to Bishop Bridport who died in 1262 to get an idea of 16

* The usual E. E. pier shape however is round. Foxley is round with four attached shafts, Netheravon has some quatrefoil piers with thin rectangular shafts in the diagonals.

what they must have been like. Similarly the completely un-
14b restored head found in the excavations of Clarendon Palace is the
best reminder of how far delicacy of carving and human understanding went.

At the time when the façade was being built or furnished,
Salisbury put up a big detached bell-tower or campanile such as
Chichester still possesses and Westminster and Norwich and
other cathedrals and abbeys once possessed. The Salisbury cam-
17a panile was pulled down in the late c 18.* Also the cloister – not a
15b necessity in a non-monastic cathedral – and the chapter house
were built. They must date from about 1270. Here (and in the
Bridport Monument a little before) a new motif appeared in
Wiltshire: bar tracery and all it stood for in the way of a richer,
broader, ampler style. It had been introduced from France to
England at Westminster Abbey in 1245 (and at Binham in
Norfolk c. 1240), and from the Westminster cloister and chapter
house reached Salisbury with a twenty-years' delay. This stage of
Salisbury is reflected in a humble way in the octagonal vestry of
19 Enford and on a much higher level in the s chapel of Boyton
church, founded by an Archbishop of York, probably about the
years 1275–80.

Boyton is a parish church, and it is time to leave the cathedral
and look at the E. E. style in the towns and villages. The finest,
both of them indeed exceptionally fine, are Potterne (which was
18a collegiate anyway) and Bishops Cannings. Both were churches
on manors of the bishops of Salisbury. Both have crossing towers.
Potterne has some of the reticent perfection of Salisbury, Bishops
Cannings much of its elegance and several of its motifs. The low
chancel, the s porch, and the vestry are rib-vaulted. A speciality
of some small Wiltshire parish churches is very heavy, somewhat
overpowering bell-turrets on the w gable, set diagonally. Such
18b exist at Biddestone, Castle Combe (from another church at
Biddestone), and Sevington (from Leigh Delamere). Another
interesting oddity is the church of Wootton Bassett, which was
two-naved with circular piers – circular piers are of course the
c 13 standard – and in this 'hall' appearance perhaps an echo of
the E parts of the cathedral. Similarly the introduction of clerestory windows at Donhead St Mary – simple lancets – may have
been encouraged by the cathedral, as may have been the crossing
towers in other places such as Sherston and Chilmark, though it
must not be forgotten that clerestories as well as crossing towers

* Is it reflected in the originally detached position of the tower of St Thomas
at Salisbury?

had been not at all uncommon in Norman parish churches. The Chilmark tower is rib-vaulted inside, and rib-vaulted also is the N chapel at Amesbury Abbey and, though as late as *c.*1300, the E end of the N aisle at Box.

Amesbury Abbey is the one other major church apart from the cathedral whose principal features, as far as they are preserved, are those of the C13 – sheer walls and lancet windows. The mention of Amesbury is a reminder that a separate survey of the MONASTIC REMAINS in the county is overdue; for Malmesbury has already been given its due prominence among Norman buildings. These two and Lacock are the only three major abbeys of which much survives, and only at Lacock are the claustral quarters preserved.

Amesbury was a Benedictine nunnery, one of the famous nunneries of England. So was Wilton; and a third famous nunnery was just across the Dorset border at Shaftesbury. Shaftesbury was the largest English nunnery, Wilton with up to *c.*80 nuns one of the largest. Lacock was for Augustinian canonesses, and here the C13 E range of the cloister, with the chapter house, all vaulted, can still be seen. The church on the other hand has disappeared completely. The cloister at Lacock lay N of the church, which is unusual, but had been done at Old Sarum Cathedral and at Malmesbury and was also done at Stanley, the Cistercian abbey of Wiltshire, of which nothing survives, at the Augustinian Ivychurch (Alderbury), with one remaining late C12 pier and one respond of the church and pretty C12 double-chamfered capitals of a former cloister, and at the Augustinian Bradenstoke, whose substantial remains, especially the Guest Hall, were sold to America but in the end never shipped and are lying in packing cases somewhere in Britain.* Monkton Farleigh with just one wall with two tall lancets was Cluniac and quite a big house. Maiden Bradley with no remains, and Longleat, also with no remains, were both Augustinian. Kington St Michael with only small bits in the buildings of Priory Farm was another Benedictine nunnery. There was also a small Premonstratensian house at Charlton, a Gilbertine house at Marlborough, a Trinitarian house at Easton (Corsham), and there is a little of walls of the mid-C14 house of the Bonshommes at Edington. That is all, so far as monks and nuns and canons and canonesses are concerned – alien cells and granges excepted.

The friars settled down in the towns as usual, Dominicans and

---

* On the site are only a rather featureless tower and two small vaulted undercrofts.

Franciscans at Salisbury, the former moving to Salisbury from Wilton, and Carmelites at Marlborough. Their churches and houses have gone, except for some dubious remains of the Franciscans at Salisbury. At Ansty the Knights Hospitallers had a preceptory, and a C15 range may be their hospice. Then there were collegiate establishments. Potterne has already been mentioned, Edington will be mentioned later. Salisbury had two important colleges: of one, St Edmund's College, nothing has survived, of the other, De Vaux College, a buttress and some walling. It lay close to St Nicholas's Hospital, an interesting survival of a formerly two-naved building with two chancels, or rather chapels (for the naves of course served as wards). St Nicholas's Hospital goes back to Bishop Bingham, De Vaux College to Bishop Bridport, St Edmund's College to Bishop de la Wyle, i.e. all three were bishops' foundations of the mid C13.

St Nicholas's Hospital was placed close to the bridge that Bishop Bingham built in order to provide a southern access to his cathedral and to his new town from the main road to Wilton; for at that time Wilton was an important town and Salisbury had still to establish itself. Salisbury is an interesting example of a planned C13 town, with the main grid of streets N of the cathedral no doubt laid out about 1220. Wiltshire has some other new towns of the early C13, though on a much smaller scale, boroughs created for economic and administrative reasons (*see* p. 199) by the bishop of Winchester and not consisting of more than one straight street. That at Downton – across the Avon from the old village – is wider than the others and still called The Borough. Salisbury town has no houses left of so early a date, but in the close there remain quite some traces of THIRTEENTH CENTURY HOUSES, those of the bishop and the canons. The Bishop's Palace had its predecessor on the hill at Old Sarum, and the excavations there have shown the existence of a range N of the cloister and running S–N which has been convincingly identified as the hall range. The foundations show a division into nave and aisles and two smaller rooms at the N end. Bishop Poore's Great Chamber at New Sarum has been replaced by the Georgian bishops' drawing room, but its vaulted undercroft is there. So is that below the hall of one of the canon's houses, the so-called North Canonry. Of Leadenhall, the house of Elias de Derham, some windows can be seen, re-set in a garden wall. One of them is of two lights with plate tracery, clearly work of the cathedral masons. Nos 21 and 56 The Close show traces of private chapels, the former of the C13, the latter of the early C14. But the most important survival is one which has only recently come to light, that of the first-floor hall in the Old Deanery. Lancet windows have been found, and the original roof with the only C13 louvre opening in England.

A first-floor hall is also the characteristic feature of King John's House at Tollard Royal, dating, it seems, from *c*.1240. It had twin windows, and other rooms, no longer in their C13 state, adjoined it. King John's is a small house; Clarendon Palace was on a regal scale, the only such royal palace (as against castle) which we know outside Westminster. Excavations undertaken in the 1930s have taught us of the C12 and C13 buildings and brought forth valuable tiles and the beautiful head already referred to, 14b but they have been allowed to disappear in the trees and bushes instead of being exposed as respectfully as those of Old Sarum. So now once again nobody can see what Henry III's palace was like. If to these scanty remains we add the surprisingly big rib-vaulted porch at Sheldon Manor, we have exhausted the C13.

The LATER MIDDLE AGES must for several reasons be considered as one. Wiltshire is not a DECORATED county, and the most interesting developments are C14–15 versus C13 rather than C14 versus C15. Specifically Dec buildings or parts of buildings to remember are, needless to say, the superb crossing tower and spire of Salisbury, not only the tallest in England (404 ft) but also 12 – there is a strong case for saying so – the finest, exquisitely slender and exquisitely detailed, rich, with much ballflower decoration, but not at all showy; then the church of Bishopstone near Salisbury with its tierceron-vaulted chancel and s transept and its strange founder's monument placed outside in a vaulted, open two-bay attachment to the s transept, the nave vault of Malmesbury with its lierne-vault consisting of square bays each with four square panels, the ribs arranged in saltire crosses, the chancel of Urchfont with the same vaulting pattern, the barbed 20b trefoil tracery at Malmesbury, Great Bedwyn, and Downton, the airiness and spaciousness of such chancels as that of Downton, and also of Tisbury with four-light side windows and Dinton with three-light side windows, the octagonal crossing tower of Wanborough (looking odd enough with the Perp w tower so close to it), and some arcades with continuous mouldings (Aldbourne, Longbridge Deverill, Lydiard Tregoze, Maiden Bradley, Winterbourne Bassett).

For the genesis of the PERPENDICULAR STYLE Wiltshire possesses one of the most significant churches in the country,

20a Edington, a collegiate church, built by Bishop Edington of
Winchester in 1351–61 and less an example of transition than of
co-existence. The beautiful chancel with its uncommonly well
21a preserved sculpture is Dec in its character and most of its forms.
But the windows of the church are some entirely Dec and some
entirely Perp. Broad Chalke is under the immediate influence of
Edington, an influence that can be traced in some other churches,
such as Westbury, as well.

Wiltshire, thanks to its sheep, was a prosperous county in the
C15 and early C16, and whole Perp churches were built to demon-
26b strate that, churches such as those of Trowbridge (much rebuilt
since) and Calne, to name two towns, St Edmund and St Thomas
at Salisbury, and Lacock and Steeple Ashton in villages. Calne
24a has a transeptal N tower, and towers in positions other than at the
w end or the crossing are not uncommon in Wiltshire altogether.*
Towers with vaults are also not uncommon, tierceron-stars at
Barford St Martin, Bradford, Bratton (a big church almost entirely Perp), St Mary Devizes, Colerne, Ogbourne St Andrew,
and Purton, lierne-vaults at Cricklade (in the crossing tower built
during the whole first half of the C16)‡ and Bishops Cannings,
fan-vaults at Castle Combe, East Knoyle, Highworth, and Pewsey. Vaulted porches are of course quite a usual thing. The tierceron-star is the most frequent form. Lierne-vaults are at Calne,
Sherston, Steeple Ashton, and Westbury, fan-vaults at Trowbridge, panelled tunnel-vaults at Keevil, Trowbridge, and Urchfont, a plain tunnel-vault with transverse arches at Donhead St
Mary. All these porches are to the s or N of the nave and aisles,
except for Trowbridge, where a porch is placed in front of the w
façade.§ At Westbury a chapel has a tierceron-vault, at St Peter
Marlborough the chancel is tierceron-vaulted. Steeple Ashton
was built to be stone-vaulted throughout even if the actual nave

---

* To enumerate them: N towers at Boyton, Charlton near Upavon (attached
to a modern church), Luckington, Stanton Fitzwarren, Stapleford, West
Harnham; s towers at Bulford, Burcombe, Chisledon, Coombe Bissett, Compton Chamberlayne, Honington, Langley Burrell, Pitton, Salisbury St Thomas
of Canterbury, Winsley; s w towers at Christian Malford, Marlborough St
Peter, Orcheston St Mary, Rodbourne. Most of the s towers are in South
Wiltshire.

‡ Cricklade church is dedicated to St Samson, a Cornish-Breton
dedication. But Wiltshire is poor in unusual DEDICATIONS. Amesbury
is to St Melor, Baverstock to St Edith, Sherrington to St Cosmas and St
Damian.

§ w porches are also at Chapel Plaster near Box, Great Chalfield, Keevii,
Lacock, and Tisbury.

vault was in the end constructed of wood. The vaults are of the
lierne type.*

Steeple Ashton is the most ornate Perp church in the county, 25
though certain chapels added to churches may be on their smaller
scale yet more lavish. This display of prosperity is economically
explained by a look at the jamb of a Perp window at Seend, where
sheep-shearing shears are carved. The N aisle was built by John
Stokes, who died in 1498. At Steeple Ashton the N aisle was due
to the generosity of a Long, the S aisle of a Leucas. The church of 26a
Great Chalfield is Thomas Tropenell's, and he also built a chapel
at Corsham, apart from the manor house of Great Chalfield. John 29a
Webbe's merchant's mark appears at St Thomas Salisbury, and
he built the stately house now called Church House. Also at St
Thomas are donations of a Swayne, a Ludlow, a Nichol. At
Trowbridge we have wills of a Wykes (1460) and a Terumber
(† 1483). William Smyth † 1436 is connected with St Mary
Devizes, Richard Lamb with St John, in the roofs of Tisbury
names of merchants of the C16 and into the C17 are recorded.
Thomas Horton, the clothier of Bradford, built the tower of
Westwood. The dignitaries of the church did not want to be left
behind either – see the Stafford Chapel at North Bradley († 1446)
– nor did the nobility recede. There are Hungerford Chapels at
Chippenham (1442) and Cricklade (? † 1484), and there is the
Tocotes and Beauchamp Chapel at Bromham (1492). This chapel 24b
and the chapel of Devizes also with Beauchamp heraldry have
specially lively openwork parapets, reminiscent of those of a group
of towers, e.g. Fovant, which reach over into Dorset (Shaftesbury). Decidedly Somerset in type on the other hand is another
group of towers, with pretty little buttress-shafts attached to the
buttresses (e.g. Bromham, Calne, Castle Combe, Steeple Ashton).
Altogether Somerset affinities are patent in some of the most
spectacular Perp work in Wiltshire, e.g. the low-pitched roofs of
such churches as St Thomas Salisbury and Tisbury with their
tie-beams and dainty decoration, or the pierced tracery filling the
bell-openings and generally called Somerset tracery, or a type of
bell-opening of two lights but surrounded by two blank ones left,
two right, and four below a transom (Devizes St James, Nettleton,
West Kington, Westwood, Yatton Keynell, and similar Melksham and Colerne). The nearest in Somerset is the Shepton Mallet group and, though on a much grander scale, the crossing tower
of Wells Cathedral.

* Another interesting motif at Steeple Ashton is tracery of straight-sided
lozenges. It is also found at Keevil and North Bradley.

Steeple Ashton was called Steeple Ashton because originally it carried a spire. Spires are altogether quite common in Wiltshire even if, apart from that of the cathedral, none are anything very special. The same is true of the arcades inside. The standard section of the piers is that with the four shafts and the four hollows or four waves in the diagonals, only the shafts carrying capitals. There are few of more complex section. But there are quite a number of arches made more conspicuous by panelling and panelling of the imposts (Bradford, Corsham, Steeple Ashton, Trowbridge, and some eight or ten others). The finest arch is the chancel arch at Castle Combe, with statuettes all along arranged in the French cathedral way. Finally there are hoods on heavy brackets instead of porches. They shelter the priest's doorways at Bishopstone near Salisbury and St Thomas Salisbury, a former priest's doorway (?) at Downton, and the W entrance to the Tropenell church of Great Chalfield.

Great Chalfield church and Great Chalfield Manor House are one visually. The church adjoins the manor house and they both 29a lie inside the moat and the walled enclosure. The manor house is the most complete, unified example of C15 DOMESTIC ARCHI-28 TECTURE in the county. South Wraxall alone can vie with it which is larger and has a finer gatehouse, but is rendered less unified and more varied by considerable alterations of about 1600. Great Chalfield was built by Thomas Tropenell, the clothier, South Wraxall probably by Robert Long. With the gate house of South Wraxall one may compare the outer and the inner gatehouses leading to Place Farm Tisbury, which was a grange of the abbesses of Shaftesbury and not a manor house. Very much is also preserved at Westwood Manor, built by Thomas Horton, yet another clothier. Some of it is C15, but most dates from the time of Henry VIII. Domestic architecture of the C14 is rare. 29b Woodlands Manor has its C14 chapel and hall, the roof with cusped wind-braces, Sutton Veny Old Manor House its C14 hall No. 56 The Close at Salisbury its former C14 porch (with the chapel above), but the most complete piece is the hall, porch, and 22b undercroft of Norrington Manor, begun in 1377. The hall has transomed Perp windows, the porch a simple lierne-vault, the undercroft a rib-vault.

23   A little later, in 1393, licence to crenellate Wardour Castle was given to John Lord Lovel. It is one of the most interesting C14 castles in England. By the second half of the C14 castles as against manor houses had become rare. Wardour with its hall above the entry archway, high up on the upper floor for safety's sake, but

with large windows along both sides for amenity's sake and with
its hexagonal courtyard behind surrounded by even ranges of ^{p.}₄₈₈
buildings must be compared with such compositions as the oblong
courtyard of Bolton Castle of 1379 and the circular courtyard of
Queenborough on the Isle of Thanet of 1361.

The halls of town houses were not necessarily smaller than
that of Wardour Castle. Quite a number are preserved, the best
at Salisbury. There, inside the Close, was Bishop Beauchamp's
hall in the Bishop's Palace of which only the porch remains, three-
storeyed with a yet taller, nicely decorated staircase turret. In the
part of the palace built over two hundred years before by Bishop
Poore, Beauchamp added a chapel with straight-headed windows.
The hall of the Vicars Choral is only represented by its entrance
and the three doorways to kitchen, buttery, and pantry. But No.
54 The Close has its hall roof with cusped wind-braces and even
its wooden screen, though re-set, and the King's House also has
the hall roof with cusped wind-braces and in addition a handsome
fan-vaulted porch. More can be seen of halls in merchants'
houses: the hall of John Halle, with its two large, transomed,
straight-headed four-light windows and its splendid roof with 30b
cusped wind-braces, much admired by Pugin, but now the con-
course of a cinema, and the hall of John Webbe (now the Church
House), with an original polygonal bay window, again a good
traceried roof, and a wide archway into the courtyard. In the
country Hazelbury Manor, Box, has the most impressive c15
appearance. However, the porch as well as the bay window are
recent construction, even if it is likely that the former and certain
that the latter existed. Other preserved hall windows and roofs
are at Bradfield Farm Hullavington, at Brook House Southwick,
and at Maddington Farm Shrewton, preserved windows at Littlecote, a much larger affair from the start with a good deal that goes
back to the early c16, and preserved roofs at Beanacre Old Manor,
Easton Court Farm Corsham, Garsdon Manor House, and Tower
House Malmesbury. A number of good Perp chimneypieces have
also been preserved: at Great Chalfield, at Westwood Manor, and
in Salisbury, at Church House, several, though only one *in situ*.
A specially fine one is at the hall of John Halle, another at No. 12
The Close.

Wiltshire is not a county that glories in timber-framed building. The technique was used quite a lot evidently, but little of
special note has come down to our time. The most perfect house 30a
is no doubt the Porch House at Potterne. Talboys, Keevil, looks
more perfect than it is. At Salisbury the House of John à Port is

the most noteworthy, the Old George Hotel with its two irregular (later) oriels the most picturesque.

For BARNS on the other hand the county is one of the most rewarding. The C15 barn of Place Farm Tisbury is with 188 ft 22a the largest in the land, the early C14 barn of Burton Farm Bradford-on-Avon is only 20 ft shorter, i.e. both are the length of only the most ambitious parish churches. Brokenborough, Hill Deverill, and West Dean have other specially long ones. That of West Dean is of brick and ascribed to the early C16. But brick had at that time hardly left a mark on Wiltshire.*

Finally some buildings for other purposes. Three Hospices (if one does not count the Hospitallers' establishment at Ansty) have survived: at Bradford-on-Avon (St Mary Tory), Chapel Plaster Box, and South Wraxall. The first and third are T-shaped with a domestic and a chapel arm. The dispositions at Chapel Plaster are obscure. Two Market Crosses still stand, that of Malmesbury and the Poultry Cross at Salisbury, and then there is Maud 3b Heath's Causeway, 4½ miles of it, from Wick Hill to Chippenham, provided by this simple but public-spirited old pedlar woman about 1475 to help people on at times of flood (*see* Kellaways, p. 249). She might have spent the money paying for one of those ambitious church monuments with which the rich and the mighty tried to perpetuate their existence. It is a reassuring thought that Maud Heath's memory is fresher than theirs.

CHURCH MONUMENTS – we have to start early indeed if we want to survey those of Wiltshire: in 1099, the year when St Osmund died; for his black marble slab survives, even if the date on it was probably put on only in the C17. The kneeling base that originally went with it may be later. Then follows Bishop Roger's P. slab. He died in 1139, and the slab is Tournai work, with a flat 376 band of foliage round the figure in flat relief. He is followed by Bishop Joscelin who died in 1184. This is of Purbeck marble, the English material that was just taking the place of Tournai marble. The relief is conspicuously rounder and the modelling conspicuously more self-assured. It is an important monument to date this change by. Then follow Bishop Bingham † 1246 and Bishop Giles de Bridport † 1262, both excellent Purbeck effigies very similar to those of the same date in other places, e.g. Ely Cathedral, and both with canopies. That of Bridport has, as has 16 already been said, large arcading with bar tracery just a little earlier than cloister and chapter house. It also has the beautifully

---

* West Harnham Mill has brickwork of about the same time, and the oldest parts of Littlecote are of brick too (*see* also below).

carved little figure scenes in the spandrels of which something has also been said. Bishop de la Wyle † 1271 has yet another Purbeck effigy. Meanwhile William Longespée, who had died in 1226, had received his monument, of freestone, the earliest English effigy of a knight in armour. The change to the specifically English pose with crossed legs seems to have been made about 1250 – see for Wiltshire the effigy of the younger Longespée. There are quite a number of other examples of this type in the county, e.g. Sir Alexander Giffard at Boyton, two at Berwick St John, one at Tollard Royal, etc.

Monuments up to the beginning of the C14 which deserve recording for special reasons are the foliated-cross slab at Broad Hinton with the head of a lady in sunk relief, the incised miniature slab of a forester (?) of c.1275 at Steeple Langford, the miniature effigy of a bishop at Salisbury, the so-called Boy Bishop, the miniature page holding a cup at Britford, and the early C14 lady at Stockton, who lies on her side, not her back. Early C14 monuments of greater elaboration are those of Simon of Ghent † 1315 and Roger de Mortival † 1329 in the cathedral, both with monumental canopies. The Ghent Monument has ballflower decoration, the Mortival Monument on its arch instead of crockets a series of small reclining figures, a charming motif, and culminates in a thin openwork canopy similar to those of the Despensers at Tewkesbury. The later C14 is represented at the cathedral chiefly by the monument to Bishop Wyville † 1375, a brass 7 ft 6 in. long showing the demi-figure of the bishop in a fantastic turreted fortress, guarded by a small knight below. It is a composition without parallel. Otherwise Wiltshire is poor in remarkable brasses. Those at Clyffe Pypard (late C14), Mere († 1398 and † 1426), and Draycot († 1393 and † 1419) are the best.

For the C15 and early C16 the choice of monuments is great, but not many call for special comment. Alabaster effigies in the cathedral are of Bishop Milford † 1407, Robert Lord Hungerford † 1459, and Sir J. Cheney † 1509, in the country of Sir Richard Tocotes † 1457 at Bromham. The most ambitious chantry monument in the cathedral is that of Bishop Audley † 1524. Canopied monuments were erected in the cathedral for Bishops Woodville † 1484 and Blyth † 1499, and in the country for Sir Ralph Cheney † c.1401 at Edington and for one of the Bonshommes also at Edington, where at the time the Bonshommes were in charge. The canopied tomb of Elizabeth Beauchamp of c.1492 at Bromham is of Purbeck marble, as are two recesses at Ramsbury. Specially noteworthy tomb-chests are those of Thomas Tropenell

at Corsham † 1488 and of Sir Thomas Long at Draycot, early
C16.

CHURCH FURNISHINGS can be treated as an appendix to this
summary of the art and architecture of the Middle Ages in Wiltshire. Compared with other counties Wiltshire has not much of
more than local interest. Starting with FONTS, there are over fifty
11a Norman fonts in the county, about eight or ten of them being of
the quantity-produced Purbeck type with shallow blank arches.
They were made square or octagonal, and they went on into the
C13, with pointed and pointed-trefoiled arches. In Wiltshire they
all occur in the southern parts. Of other fonts by far the most
11b interesting is that of Stanton Fitzwarren with the eight figures of
Virtues and Vices. The font at Upavon has an Annunciation (a
curious choice), apart from a flower, a lion, etc., that at Little
Hinton a band of wild irregular knots and animals, that at Castle
Eaton a big leaf trail. Interlaced arches are used as decoration at
Avebury, Donhead St Mary, and Lydiard Millicent, and smaller
at Durnford, scallops on the underside at Etchilhampton, Everleigh, Fifield Bavant, Longbridge Deverill, Nettleton, Norton,
Sutton Benger, and Tockenham. The fonts at Codford St Mary
and North Tidworth are exactly like capitals of arcade piers. Of
C13 fonts by far the most beautiful is the enormously large, round,
and only moulded black marble font of Preshute, regal indeed, as it
is supposed to be royal (Marlborough Castle). Moulded also is the
round font of St Mary Cricklade. The fonts of Berwick Bassett
and Winterbourne Bassett have some stiff-leaf decoration.

14a   Then SCREENS, starting with the former rood screen of Salisbury Cathedral, already mentioned. With its stiff-leaf capitals and
the lively demi-figures of angels in its spandrels (older than the
spandrel angels of Westminster and Lincoln), it is a most beautiful
piece. Up to the same quality, but of much later date, are the
Perp stone screen of veranda type at Compton Bassett and
the stone screen of c.1430 to the Tropenell Chapel at Great Chalfield. The tall stone screen to the Tropenell Chapel at Corsham has
a fan-vaulted coving, as has the stone screen at Heytesbury. Of
wooden screens Mere has indubitably the best, indeed the only
one to stand up to comparison with Somerset and Devon. One
of them has six-light divisions, the other eight-light divisions.
27 Three rood-loft parapets are preserved, at Avebury, Corsham,
and Hullavington, and Bradford-on-Avon has two dado panels
of a screen formerly painted with figures in the East Anglian way,
which, however, occurs occasionally in the South-West.

Medieval PAINTING has altogether little to offer in Wiltshire.

The C13 medallions in the chancel roof of the cathedral are totally Victorian, even if said to represent what went before. That leaves the big Doom in St Thomas Salisbury as the only work of any consequence, and it is aesthetically poor stuff. STAINED GLASS of the C13 is amply preserved at Salisbury Cathedral, but it is all grisaille work in geometrical patterns. Some of it is now at Laverstock. Figured C13 glass is at Wilton church, but it is French and brought in. There is much later glass at Wilton too. At Salisbury there are also some C14 figures and more of the C15 and early C16, the latter Flemish. Of C13 TILES also Salisbury Cathedral has many. The source of this sudden delight in tiles with patterns and figures was again Westminster Abbey. The royal palaces also went in for the fashion. The Chertsey tiles are familiar. At Clarendon Palace C13 tiles have been found in plenty too, and in churches in the country they were used as well. Samples remain at Malmesbury and West Dean. Corsham Court also keeps tiles of the C13 and later centuries. To stay with design in the flat for a further moment, some pieces of EMBROIDERY of about 1500 may be recorded: fragments of chasubles at Hullavington and Sutton Benger and the pieces at Wardour Castle.

Design in the round after the screens needs few words. There is of course a certain amount of PLATE, starting with the chalice and paten at Salisbury Cathedral found, it is assumed, in the tomb of Bishop Longespée who died in 1297, and the C14 pewter chalice at North Bradley, also found in a coffin. Late C15 or early C16 patens of usual types are at Corsley, Melksham, Orcheston St Mary (1506), and Teffont Magna, chalices at Manningford Abbots, Codford St Mary, Highworth (1523), and – gilt and uncommonly fine – at Wylye (1525). This is the place also to record the stately brass LECTERN at St Martin Salisbury, one of a type which occurs in such distant places as Bovey Tracey in Devon and Wiggenhall St Mary, Norfolk. Beyond that, however, nothing: no Perp fonts, no Perp pulpits,* no sculpture.

This scarcity of survival may also be responsible for the fact that, unlike other counties, Wiltshire has no contribution to make in its church furnishings to the fascinating problem of when and how the Italian RENAISSANCE arrived and spread. The earliest preserved record of this important change is in the field of CHURCH MONUMENTS, and so we must return to them after having left them in their state of the 1520s only a page or two earlier. The crucial monument is that to the fifth Lord Stourton

---

* West Kington though has quite a good wooden pulpit. So has Potterne. Others are of stone (e.g. Berwick St James, Bremhill, and Nettleton).

at Stourton, and he died in 1536. The monument is a Gothic
tomb-chest, but it has pilasters at the angles and candelabra motifs
on them. On the other hand the monument to William Geoffrey
in Salisbury Cathedral has no indication of the Renaissance,
although he died in 1558, and that to Thomas Bennett, also in the
cathedral, who died in 1558 too, again has no Renaissance motif,
unless one counts the fact that the dead man lies on a half-rolled-
up straw mat, and that that is a motif of the Netherlandish Early
Renaissance appearing for the first time in the monument to the
Count of Nassau at Breda of about 1535.*

32a   Then follows Sir William Sharington's monument at Lacock.
He died in 1553. Here the impression is one of pure Early Renaissance, i.e. of Italian forms taken, as was usual in the first half of
the century, from the Quattrocento rather than the High Renaissance, and from North Italy or North Italian work in France
rather than Rome. Only the basket arch is a reminder of Late
Gothic customs – French and English. The use of strapwork on
the other hand is emphatically c16. It was only created as a new,
really anti-Renaissance, form of ornament in the 1530s, at Fon-
tainebleau. The Netherlands took it over at once, and it became
their most characteristic contribution. On what paths these
various forms had reached Sharington no-one can say. A drawing
for a chimneypiece made by Holbein for Henry VIII for example
combines Quattrocento decoration with strapwork, and Holbein
had died only in 1543. Nonsuch, Henry VIII's pleasure palace,
may also have combined the two. Moreover, Sharington was one of
Lord Protector Somerset's protégés, and Somerset was intensely
interested himself in architecture. Sharington about 1550 also
built for himself at Lacock Abbey, but in his DOMESTIC ARCHI-
TECTURE he was not as assured as in the design for an individual
piece such as a monument. A chimneypiece at Lacock is indeed
Early Renaissance, but the octagonal tower which he added to the
nunnery buildings is not a Renaissance conception, even if the
balustrade on its top and the chimneystacks in the guise of Tuscan
31   columns are. But inside the tower he placed two stone tables which
with their grotesque caryatids carrying baskets of fruit would be
up-to-the-moment whether at Antwerp or in Florence. Moreover,
they are, especially one of them, of extremely fine craftsmanship.
Sharington's hall at Lacock is not preserved.
    Nearest to this work in historical position if not in style comes
33a the wrongly-called Holbein Porch at Wilton, work clearly of

* The same motif occurs in the so-called Sydenham Monument in the
cathedral. He died in 1524; so it can hardly represent him.

*c.*1560–70. Its parallels are in Northamptonshire, that is the circle of Thorpe Senior, rather than in Wiltshire. It has two orders of fluted columns, round arches, frontal busts in medallions, and at the top a shell gable like Sharington's tomb. It is indeed funerary monuments to which we have to return in order to see the step-by-step development during these extremely interesting decades. Sir Richard Brydges died in 1558, and his sumptuous monument 32b at Ludgershall with its fat baluster columns and its busy foliage is still Henry VIII in motifs, though it is Elizabethan as a composition. In the middle, however, is still a four-centred arch. Sir William Wroughton died in 1559. His monument at Broad Hinton is more conservative in its dominant Perp elements, but it displays a strapwork cartouche. Sir Francis Choke † 1562 at Shalbourne has columns but also a four-centred arch. Completely Early Elizabethan are – again a type more frequent in Northamptonshire – three monuments of the following twenty years, all three with fleshy, prominent foliage, big, a little bare ornamental motifs, and no effigies or figures at all: John Ernele † 1571 at Bishops Cannings, John Berwick, 1574, at Wilcot, and William Ernele, 1581, at All Cannings.

This style is represented also, and with the greatest accomplishment, in a chimneypiece at Longleat. Sir John Thynne, who was also a confidant of Somerset, built Longleat for himself over a long period. The house as we see it now dates from after a fire which occurred in 1567, but the chimneypiece in question may well be of before the fire. It has been shown to be very probable that it is the work of *Allen Maynard*, a Frenchman who worked at Longleat. Another similar chimneypiece is at Woodlands Manor. Longleat itself is a milestone in English c16 architecture. It is the first completely Elizabethan house, large, self-assured, all of a piece, built round two courtyards with unified fronts to all sides, displaying most prominently its grid of large mullioned- 33b and-transomed windows and confining to a secondary role the (originally French) orders of pilasters and the medallions for busts. The top is a balustrade, and above it reach only the columnar chimneystacks and the lead-covered caps of inner stair-turrets. The principal masters are known by name: *John Chapman*, who had been in the King's Works from *c.*1541, *William Spicer*, later surveyor of the Queen's Works, and *Robert Smythson*, who was sent by Humphrey Lovell, the Queen's Master Mason. Smythson seems to have been the architect of Sir Thomas Arundell at Wardour Castle too. There a doorway is convincingly similar to the Lord Protector's style, but the new windows are not, as one

2

might expect, mullion-and-transom-crosses but still of the low
mullioned type with arched lights which belongs to Henry VII
and not to the 1570s.

34a   Side by side with Longleat, Longford Castle grew up to it
fantastical shape. It was begun about 1580 and completed in 1591
Sir Thomas Gorges was fascinated by astronomy, as his monu
ment in Salisbury Cathedral implies. He gave his house the shap
of a triangle, a shape representing the Trinity in the hands of Si
Thomas Tresham of Rushton, the fanatic Catholic, and at Long
ford interpreted as such by John Thorpe, the surveyor who drev
it later. The corners of the triangle at Longford are marked by fa
round towers, a piece of medievalism no doubt appreciated at th
time in a Spenserian way. They may derive from Gripsholm ir
Sweden, as Gorges's wife was Swedish. To the façade of Long
ford, well if not quite correctly rebuilt by *Salvin* about 187c
Gorges gave arcading on ground floor and second floor, a moti
not used anywhere else as far as we know and very different fron
the remorselessly uniform rhythm of Longleat. Also on th
top floor and in the dormers there are numbers of little termin
caryatids such as one expects on chimneypieces and screen
rather than façades. Inside, Longford has only a few chimney
pieces, Longleat a big one in the hall and the wooden hall screen

Then there is Corsham Court begun in 1582, but there toda
only the porch and the adjoining bays are in their original form
Littlecote is a large house too. It dates, as we have seen, partl
from the early C16, but largely from the 1580s and 1590s, and i
of brick – the first prominent appearance of this material that w
have to register. The long gallery is 110 ft long and has window
with two, three, and even four transoms. Such enormous window
28 are also externally the chief contribution of the years about 160
to South Wraxall. Inside, the room with these windows has wha
36 must be one of the biggest chimneypieces in all England, carve
with wild Netherlandish figures and ornament, and opposite
mysterious big projection in the wall with shell-headed niches t
look at or sit in. These niches occur often in Wiltshire: at Long
ford, where they belong to the original portal, at Wardour Ol
Castle (i.e. in work of *c*.1575), at Longleat in the W range, at Keevi
Manor, at Erlestoke (now in the village), at The Hall Bradford
also inside, and, oddly enough, outside Edington church. Ther
are other chimneypieces at South Wraxall, one dated 1598
and there is one specially attractive carved plaster ceiling witl
the typical thin ribs forming interlacing geometrical patterns
Such stucco work is found in many houses in the county: a

Avebury c.1601, at Boyton c.1618, at Keevil Manor (where there 37
is also the wooden hall screen), at Stockton House, and at Westwood Manor. At Stockton one ceiling has broad bands instead
of thin ribs, a sign usually of later design. At Westwood one ceiling
has deeper, broader ribs, and this is also as a rule a sign of later
design. Another ceiling of this type is at No. 91 Crane Street,
Salisbury. Altogether, in Salisbury houses several Elizabethan or
Jacobean plaster ceilings have been kept: at No. 17 The Close,
at No. 21 The Close, at the King's House in The Close, and at
Church House. No. 17 The Close and this particular part of the
King's House are incidentally of brick, an innovation probably
for Salisbury. At the same time the Joiners' Hall is timber-framed
with a lot of Netherlandish decoration. It is the most ornate
timber-framed house in the county. The next in order of display
is at once quite subdued, a house to the s of Porch House at
Potterne, just with the concave-sided lozenges so much more
frequent in the black-and-white counties.

The external carving on the Joiners' Hall is much the same as
that on wooden overmantels. Both are rustic in the extreme. The
comparison can be made at Charlton Park near Malmesbury, at
Westwood Manor, at The Hall Bradford, at College Farm Purton,
to name only a few examples. Some more really massive stone
chimneypieces ought to be recorded too: one at Cottles outside
Atworth, one at Boyton, one at Marlborough College, one (from
Bristol) at Lake House Wilsford near Amesbury, and several at
Stockton House.

Lake House, built probably shortly after 1578 (and since re- 35b
built), and Stockton House belong to an Elizabethan and Jacobean
type characteristic of Wiltshire. They have completely flat fronts
with symmetrical fenestration and gables like saw-teeth on top,
Keevil Manor four by three, Boyton three by three, Stockton
three by three, and so on. The type goes back a little further, as a
Pembroke estate map of 1562 shows just such a house, with four-
ight mullioned and transomed windows and as many as nine of
the saw-tooth gables, as the predecessor of the present Ramsbury
Manor.

These houses were again as a rule built for rich clothiers, e.g.
Stockton House for John Topp. Their MONUMENTS tell us as
much as the interiors of their houses of their pride and their desire
to show off. John Topp's († 1640) at Stockton church has columns,
arches, and a recumbent effigy. That is one current type which
appears frequently, though with variations, not only in Wiltshire
but everywhere. Examples in Wiltshire are the Mompesson tomb 38a

in Salisbury Cathedral († 1627) and monuments at Westbury († 1629), Edington († 1630), and so on. The other most current type is that with kneeling figures facing one another across a prayer-desk (e.g. Lydiard Tregoze † 1594, Chippenham † 1627 West Dean † 1627). If yet more money was to be spent, the structure to contain the effigies could be built up to prodigious heights. This is what was done in Westminster Abbey, and also at Salisbury Cathedral in the monument to the Protector's son Lord Hertford, who died in 1621. Or else the monument could be made a four-poster, a six-poster (Broad Hinton † 1597; note the crazy arches), or an eight-poster (Charlton near Malmesbury † 1598, Collingbourne Kingston † 1626, Lydiard Tregoze, 1634). Another variation on one of these themes is the frontally kneeling figures at Aldbourne (two monuments of c.1615). Monuments of just before and just after 1600 at Bromham († 1593) and Durnford († 1607) still have traces of Perp – a Gothic cresting or a four-centred arch. Quite on its own stands the monument of c.1615 at Lydiard Tregoze which is in the form of a painted triptych with an elaborate pedigree (but cf. Burford in Shropshire).

Of the CHURCHES themselves in which these monuments were erected nothing can be reported. The medieval buildings still served their purpose. Hardly any new ones were built before the 1620s – in Wiltshire just one: Easton Royal, in 1591. This was paid for by Lord Hertford and is a humble affair, of nave and chancel only, with straight-headed Perp windows and a roof with tie-beams and kingposts. The font is apparently of c.1591 too and is also quite plain and not at all novel.

But CHURCH FURNISHINGS altogether do deserve a paragraph or two to themselves for the century after the Reformation. PLATE must come first. The Elizabethan Settlement brought a whole glut of new cups and paten covers, because of the decision to let the congregation partake of the wine. The glut came in some counties just before 1570. In Wiltshire, for reasons which ecclesiastical historians ought to know, it came in 1576–7. Before that there are few new pieces: one paten of 1553 (?) at West Grimstead, one cup of 1564 at Bradford-on-Avon, a few of 1570, 1571, 1572 etc., and then of 1576–7, counting cups and patens as separate pieces, nearly fifty in the two years. How could silversmiths cope?

Just about as many new PULPITS were provided in the century at present under consideration. But they are spread out and nearly all came much later anyway. In the gazetteer they are called Jacobean, though some may be a little earlier and many no doubt are Carolean. None recorded is before 1607 (Westwood). This is followed by probably 1613 (Steeple Langford), before 1619 (Stratford-sub-Castle), 1619 (Durnford), and then by ones dated 1626, 1627, c.1628, 1628, 1630, 1630, 1631, 1633, 1637. The best are those at Minety (1627) and Wylye (1628). Often these pulpits go with LITANY DESKS. One Jacobean LECTERN also deserves mention. It is at Durnford, and has a chain to attach the book by. PEWS are frequent, including family pews; the most rewarding are at Mere (1638–41). Then there is one rustic FONT COVER (Tisbury) with Gothic blank tracery, there are COMMUNION RAILS (with uncomfortable spikes on the rail at Edington, with balusters instead of knobs at Berwick St James and Durnford), and then there are the SCREENS at Westwood, with openwork ovals spiked to the inside of the oval, and at West Harnham, with the sort of decoration that one knows from domestic woodwork. In fact, a great deal of woodwork was brought into churches in the C19, and some of this came quite patently from furniture in the houses.

HOUSES we have left about 1600. The Jacobean record is varied and interesting. Three jobs need all the emphasis. Not one of them is firmly dated. Charlton Park near Malmesbury is sup-34b posed to be of 1607. It is indeed in the tradition of the Elizabethan 'prodigy houses'. Three ranges round a courtyard with the fourth originally an open colonnade. A big porch in its middle. Towers in the corners with ogee caps, and much strapwork. But the large mullioned and transomed windows display prominently the motif known as the Ipswich motif, i.e. an arch instead of the transom in the middle one of a group of three openings, and this motif is characteristic of c.1660–75 and completely surprising for 1607. The Hall at Bradford-on-Avon is one of the 'more-window-than- 35a wall' houses familiar in Derbyshire and Yorkshire and not down in the South-West. It is a compact, monumental, somewhat forbidding composition, and good chimneypieces and plasterwork are inside. The hall is placed exactly in the middle of the front and entered in its own middle – an early case of such symmetry. Finally there is Wyke House near Hilperton. This is distinguished by large shaped gables to front and side, and below that on the side a porch with a top frieze of pierced strapwork – again not at all Wiltshire in style.

To these a few oddments must be added: the two triangular gatehouses of Amesbury dated 1600 and 1607, Eyre's Folly Whiteparish, an octagonal look-out tower or standing of 1606, and Newhouse Whiteparish, of before 1619, which was built by

Sir Thomas Gorges of Longford Castle to a shape as unusual as that of Longford and also playing on the number three. The house has a hexagonal centre and three wings radiating out from it. It is of brick, as is Eyre's Folly.

Sir Thomas Gorges's monument in Salisbury Cathedral, erected in 1635, is eminently representative of one trend in MONUMENTS during these years. It has Baroque barley-sugar columns (like Nicholas Stone's portal of St Mary Oxford), any number of intellectually fascinating inscriptions, and astronomical and mathematical paraphernalia. The only thing in the county one can compare with it, though very different in kind, is the stucco
38b DECORATION applied to the walls of the chancel of East Knoyle church by the rector, Wren's father, in 1639. There again are the stories not easily read and the many inscriptions including Greek words. The ornament is still entirely pre-classical. The earliest classical monuments in the country are two tablets in Salisbury Cathedral recording deaths in 1639 and 1641. They are neither Jacobean nor Baroque, i.e. they show awareness of the radical change brought about in English architecture by INIGO JONES.

The date of the change in London is 1616–19, the beginnings of the Queen's House at Greenwich and the Banqueting House in Whitehall. But these buildings took some years to emerge, and then it took some years for their message to be recognized, let alone heeded. In Wiltshire *Inigo Jones* himself worked in his
43 last years. His is the design of the s front of Wilton House. It dates from 1649 and was intended to be twice its length, but even what is there has Inigo's new calm, his spaciousness and indeed classicity. Inside, however, he provided the most sumptuous suite of rooms of the mid C17 in the whole of England, the one job to vie with the best of French decoration of that time, and as a matter of fact inspired by it. The shapes and proportions of the
44 rooms – one a cube, another a double cube – are on the other hand, like the exterior, the proof of the lessons learned by Inigo from Palladio. Individual motifs used here gained currency in the late C17 and the C18, e.g. the Venetian window and the open pediment, triangular, segmental, or double-curved.

45b   Inigo may have done another job in the county, the grand gates of Fonthill, built by Sir Francis Cottingham after 1631, and traditionally ascribed to him: a triumphal arch composition with pilasters with intermittent rocky rustication (a Serlio motif) and a heavy pediment. Also, Inigo's work was immediately continued
p. 83 by his second-in-command *John Webb* at Amesbury in 1661. The house was thoroughly remodelled in the C19, but the giant

portico rising above a rusticated ground floor is still a reminder of the classicity of this house as well.

But such classicity in a county like Wiltshire was still for some time beyond the grasp of the masons. The normal job in town and country remained in its motifs pre-classical. It is not without interest to investigate this. In CHURCHES the record is as follows. At Dauntsey the W tower was rebuilt Gothic in 1630, at Upton Lovell in 1633 and at Chippenham (including the spire) in 1633 too, and so was also the tower of St Edmund Salisbury in 1653–5. Upton Lovell has nave windows of 1633, and they have the arched lights of the time of Henry VIII. The same windows appear in the chapel attached to Stockton House and assigned to the mid C17. Standlynch (now Trafalgar House) got a new little church in 1677 and, though it is much altered, it clearly was Gothic too. On the other hand the St Johns, about 1633, gave their new family chapel at Lydiard Tregoze church classical columns. 42a Classical columns were also put into the crossing at Calne, after the tower had fallen in 1638 (but how long after?), and tall classical columns were used most impressively for the arcades of St Mary Marlborough after the town fire of 1653.*   42b

In HOUSES the ambiguity is the same. The traditional mullioned windows and gables go on e.g. at 46 High Street Malmesbury dated 1671, at Fitz House Teffont Magna dated 1700, and even in a house at Donhead St Mary dated 1712. But here the unmoulded string-course shows the real date. The fenestration replacing this was by mullion-and-transom cross-windows, not an innovation of course either, as Longford Castle had used them consistently in the 1580s. They now appear much in local work, e.g. in 1657 at Jaggards Corsham, an E-shaped manor house with two identical porches, and in 1658 at Eastcourt House Crudwell. Oval windows set vertically are typical in all England of the latter C17, and we find them in Wiltshire in Borough House Downton in 1673, the Manor House of Stanton St Bernard in 1677, and Thorne Farmhouse at Donhead St Andrew in 1700. At Borough House and Thorne Farmhouse they appear side by side with two-light mullioned windows. The more progressive yet not quite metropolitan taste of the later C17 was for stone or brick fronts with quite even cross-windows and hipped roofs. Examples are Bathampton House Steeple Langford of 1694, Norton Bavant House of 1700, Roche Old Court Farm Winterslow, Odstock Manor House, and Great House Kington Langley. These houses

---

* The tall columns in Avebury church look much the same, yet date from as late as 1812.

reflect what might be called the WREN STYLE, although Wren
neither created it nor often used it. It was created by Hugh May,
it seems, in the early 1660s, and Wren did not take much notice
of it, because being Surveyor General to the King he did work
for private people only occasionally to oblige a friend. One of his
friends was Seth Ward, a fellow mathematician and astronomer
and a fellow of his also in the founding of the Royal Society. He
became bishop of Salisbury in 1667 and may well have consulted
Wren on work he decided to do. The new staircase in the Bishop's
Palace with is strong turned balusters hardly qualified for con-
sultation. But did the new STALLS in the cathedral? They were
replaced by Wyatt's and then by Scott's. But some simple panels
remain inside No. 9 The Close and some poppy-heads with symmetrical juicy leaves at Ansty. Seth Ward also founded the
Matrons' College in the Close. This is dated 1682. It is of brick,
low, with projecting wings and still has two-light windows –
though also circular windows in the dormers, the only motif
which is early for Salisbury at that moment. More likely still is
46a advice from Wren for the almshouses and the church begun at
Farley in 1681 and 1688 respectively by Sir Stephen Fox, who was
on the commission for Chelsea Hospital. Both buildings are of
brick. The church is a Greek cross with added w tower and chancel
and the entrance through the s transept – a Wren conception,
even if the execution was not supervised by Wren. The interior
makes a fine ensemble perfectly in keeping with the façades. The
almshouses have wooden cross-windows as well as still two-light
mullioned windows. Other almshouses founded in those years
are the Hungerford Almshouses and School at Corsham (1668),
still with gables and mullioned windows, but also with decidedly
Baroque external decoration and some windows whose Gothic
forms are more probably Revival than Survival, and the Somerset
Almshouses at Froxfield, a much simpler job, built in 1694 and
then only half their present size. Schools built in these years
are those of Cricklade (1651, small and pre-classical), Crudwell
(1670, square with cross-windows and a hipped roof), Box
(early C18, three-storeyed, of six bays and plain), and the more
ambitious school of Lord Weymouth at Warminster. This dates
from 1707, and in its disposition and motifs again comes near the
Wren style.

46b Houses in the pure Wren style at its best are Ramsbury Manor
of c.1675–80 and Urchfont Manor of c.1685.* The latter has a
staircase with strong twisted balusters, a motif typical of the late

* To these can be added the Theological College in The Close at Salisbury.

C17 and recurring for instance at Compton Bassett Manor Farmhouse in 1699, the former still some traces of the so-called Artisan Mannerism of the mid C17 (not otherwise represented in Wiltshire) but also an overmantel in the most luxuriant Grinling 47 Gibbons style. A whole room in that style, though perhaps somewhat later, is at Compton Park Compton Chamberlayne. The equally luxuriant stucco work, also of flowers and fruit, that goes with such wood carving can be seen in Wiltshire at Gifford Hall Broughton Gifford, Boyton House, No. 17 Market Place Devizes, and at Poulton House Marlborough (1706).

To study in detail the development, the fashions, and the resistances during the second and third third of the C17 one ought to go once again to the CHURCH MONUMENTS. We have seen them just go Baroque in 1635 and classical about 1640. Some more stylistic and typological notes are now required. The twisted columns of the Gorges Monument of 1635 are repeated in a tablet at Garsdon († 1643), and Inigo Jones's open scrolly pediments inside Wilton House in a tablet at Hannington († 1657). The frontal bust is a fashion of the second third of the century. A poor monument at West Dean with a date of death 1629 shows it already. It was taken up by the two sister monuments at Berwick St Leonard († 1647) and Ogbourne St Andrew (1655), where couples are seen in a circular recess together holding a skull. The full freedom of the C18 in the treatment of the frontal bust is already reached in the Evelyn Monument at West Dean († 1689). The bust is in a large niche, and the niche can be closed by metal doors. Metal doors also close the black marble niche against which 41b kneels the white marble figure of Robert Pierrepont at West Dean († 1669). The figure is a maturely Baroque re-thinking of the Elizabethan motif of the kneeler and could well be by *Bushnell*. The recumbent effigy becomes the semi-reclining effigy of † 1636 at West Lavington, the more elegantly semi-reclining effigy of † 1654 also at West Lavington, and finally the eloquent, self- 41a important semi-reclining effigy of Sir William Jones († 1682) for whom Ramsbury was built. To end with, two uncommon types both created in the early C17 but not much favoured before the end of the century: the seated figure and the standing figure. The seated Mompessons († 1633) at Lydiard Tregoze are movingly 39 pensive, the standing St John (1645) also at Lydiard Tregoze is psychologically and sculpturally inferior. That becomes fully clear when one compares him with Col. Glanville at Broad Hinton († 1645), also standing, but in the composition and all the para- 40 phernalia vastly superior.

Funerary monuments of the EIGHTEENTH CENTURY are more conveniently arranged by sculptors than by type, but a few typological remarks may still be helpful. The bust in the roundel comes still at Tockenham in a monument commemorating a death in 1726. The free-standing bust is more up-to-date: 1706 at Great Bedwyn, and † 1725 at Stourton, and, in front of an obelisk, †1716 at East Kennett and † 1728 at Collingbourne Kingston. Two free-standing busts also are in a monument († 1753) at Urchfont which is by *Peter Scheemakers*. He did two less ambitious monuments at Broad Blunsdon († 1733) and Downton († 1741), and another at Downton with a standing figure by an urn († 1755).* But standing figures are rare in Wiltshire. The only one of the type established about 1700 is the Spackman at Clyffe Pypard by *John Devall*, and he died in 1786. One characteristic type of the second quarter of the century is the architectural tablet or monument, noble, restrained, and without any figures. Examples are at Durnford † 1710 already, and then e.g. at All Cannings c.1729, Lyneham † 1731, South Wraxall † 1733, Bradford-on-Avon † 1737, Lydiard Tregoze † 1749.

The latter two are by *Rysbrack*, and he did one more without any effigy, though a little more light-heartedly – at Alvediston in 1746 – and two more ambitious monuments. They are Sir Edward Seymour at Maiden Bradley (1728) with a semi-reclining figure against a sumptuous architectural background, and Thomas Lord Wyndham († 1745) in Salisbury Cathedral with a seated allegorical figure.

The most classical monuments of the mid century are the Clarke Monument in Salisbury Cathedral († 1757), not completely preserved, and the Long Monument († 1767) at Draycot, which is – no wonder – by *Wilton*. A *Thomas Scheemakers* (1784) at Downton, a *J. F. Moore* (1775) at Ramsbury, and two *van Gelders* († 1786, † 1801) also at Ramsbury are nothing special. In Salisbury Cathedral is a good *Bacon* († 1780), in Wilton church a *Rossi* with a delicate relief (1793). That takes us to about 1800.

Other CHURCH FURNISHINGS can be quickly disposed of: the rather wild and Mannerist STAINED GLASS in the E window of the chancel of Salisbury Cathedral designed by *J. H. Mortimer* in 1781, the several brass CHANDELIERS of the Dutch type (Cherhill 1702, Cricklade 1733, Minety 1748, Ramsbury 1751, Wootton Bassett 1782, Ogbourne St George given 1788, Wylye 1814), the City-churchish WOODWORK at Stratford-sub-Castle of c.1710–15, the fine reredos of 1724 at St Thomas Salisbury,

52

54b   * Also a chimneypiece at Corsham.

and the ORGANS of St John Devizes, late C17, Chippenham, *c.*1730, and Warminster (from Salisbury Cathedral), 1792 – which is Gothick. The delightfully chock-a-block interior of Mildenhall is mostly the work of the years 1815–16 and is Gothick too. So here we must stop.*

Wiltshire is not a county for GEORGIAN CHURCHES. The only two buildings to be referred to are Hardenhuish of 1779 by *John Wood* of Bath, not carried out quite according to his design, and the much larger chapel of Wardour Castle by *Paine*, of the 1770s, enlarged by a beautifully composed E end with shallow transepts, their ends segmentally curved, as is the E wall. This is by *Soane* and dates from 1788. Both architects got amazingly 59b well the no doubt desired effect of the Catholic church as an *ecclesia triumphans*: giant pilasters and giant columns and much stucco decoration. The house to which it is attached is, as we shall see, the grandest of Wiltshire C18 houses too. Otherwise, in the field of churches, there are the plain Gothic Survival tower of Stratford-sub-Castle of 1711, the Gothic Survival tower of Kington St Michael of 1725, and then, also Gothic, the Neale Chapel of 1775 at Great Chalfield church, and that is Gothic Revival, and a remarkably correct piece too, and therefore again must be looked at later and in a different context. The shades of Gothic in the C18 and their relation to the Georgian Classical can only be fully understood when we discuss houses, and before that can be done a few sentences must be devoted to the NONCON-FORMISTS. Wiltshire actually possesses the earliest of all Non-conformist chapels in the country, but unfortunately not a feature of the original building has been allowed to remain. It is the chapel at Horningsham which Sir John Thynne of Longleat built for his Scottish workmen in 1566–7. Outside Corsham is a C17 chapel (Monks Lane), at Bradford is quite an ambitious Presbyterian chapel of *c.*1698 (now Zion Baptist) with two large arched windows in the middle and two cross-windows l. and two r. above the two doorways. Then there are the Quakers at Melksham with a meeting house of 1734, and quite a few more chapels of the late C18 and early C19, though none very noteworthy. Certainly note-worthy, on the other hand, is the Moravian Settlement at East Tytherton, with its quiet brick buildings of the 1790s.

So now the way is clear for HOUSES of the C18. The century was one of prosperity in the country. The nobility and the squires had a good time on their estates, and trade, thanks to the expand-ing and more thoroughly exploited Empire, flourished. Defoe

* Another very complete and nicely crowded interior is at Old Dilton.

writes: 'They told me at Bradford that it is no extraordinary thing
to have clothiers in that county worth £10,000 to £40,000 a man',
and he calls Bradford and Trowbridge 'the two most eminent
cloathing towns in that part'. Architectural evidence bears that
out. The houses of the C18 at Bradford and Trowbridge are up
57a to the best of Bristol, and at least two at Trowbridge (now Lloyds
Bank and the Midland Bank) are grander than any and would
make quite notable additions to the *palazzo* architecture of, say,
Verona. Complementary to the entrepreneurs' houses are the
weavers' houses, terraces of three storeys up the hillside of Bradford and a characteristic part of the pattern of this remarkable
little town.

The merchant class was also among the patrons for whom mansions were built in the country, though they were rather London-
ers than local men: a Hoare of Hoare's Bank at Stourhead, Alderman Beckford at Fonthill (the house preceding Fonthill Abbey),
Sir Peter Vandeput, a London merchant, at Standlynch (later
called Trafalgar House). The nobility also enlarged or rebuilt,
the Seymours (Lord Hertford) at Marlborough, the St John
Bolingbrokes at Lydiard Park, the Arundells at Wardour,
the Earl of Suffolk and Berkshire at Charlton Park near Malmesbury (inside), the Earls of Shelburne at Bowood. They employed many of the leading architects: *Colen Campbell* at
Stourhead, *Roger Morris* perhaps at Lydiard Park and certainly
at Wilton, *Paine* at Wardour, *Revett* and *Wood* of Bath at
Standlynch, *Keene* and *Robert Adam* at Bowood, and finally
Soane at Wardour.

But it is the evolution of architectural style we are here chiefly
concerned with, and this must now be outlined. First there is the
continuation of the Wren-type house, a specially beautiful exam-
48b ple being Mompesson House in The Close at Salisbury, dated
1701. This type goes on with much more modesty – brick, five
bays, two storeys, hipped roof – at The Moot Downton, of *c.*1700,
Poulton House outside Marlborough of 1706, and so on. Mompesson House has l. and r. of the doorway two windows narrower
than the others. That was a William and Mary and a Queen Anne
fashion.* Shell-hoods over the doorways are another, though
examples in Wiltshire are not only of 1715 (Bratton House), but
also of 1736 (a cottage at Monkton Farleigh).

The most interesting houses of the Early Georgian years, however, are those reflecting the rather more massive grandeur of

---

* Cf. Malmesbury House Salisbury, Nunton House, Fittleton Old Rectory,
and a house of *c.*1730 in The Parade at Trowbridge.

Late Wren and the Baroque perversities of Vanbrugh, Hawksmoor, and Archer. The façade closest to Vanbrugh is that of Netherhampton House. Rather more Archerish is Ivy House 49b Chippenham of *c*.1730. Also in the spirit of Vanbrugh and Hawksmoor is the way in which at Biddesden in 1711–12 a massive, 49a quite unfanciful design suddenly turns medieval in a castellated tower. Rather more from Late Wren come the heavy, solid, tall façades of the Marlborough mansion of Lord Hertford, begun 48a just before 1700, of the Wyndhams' mansion, now Council House, at Salisbury altered *c*.1715 etc., of Landford Manor and No. 68 The Close, the latter perhaps of 1718. Also in The Close at Salisbury is the former choir school (now called Wren Hall) in the same style, one-storeyed and completed in 1714*, and the adjoining one-storeyed addition to No. 56 The Close of 1727. Its quoins of blocks of even, not alternating, length are typical of Late Wren and the early C18. Other typical motifs are segment-headed windows. We find them at Biddesden, at Netherhampton House, at Landford Manor, and also still at the rectory of Alton Barnes of between 1728 and 1737 and at No. 21 St John's Street Devizes of 1740 and Baydon Farmhouse of 1744. Windows with a kind of basket arches are a variation (cf. Council House and Wren Hall, Salisbury). Fully round-arched windows are favoured for grander occasions, and so appear at Marlborough, the biggest mansion of these years in Wiltshire, and also at Biddesden. Giant pilasters on the other hand (e.g. at 1 Castle Street Salisbury) are relatively rare in Early Georgian Wiltshire, although frequent in Early Georgian England.

In the weaving towns about 1730 a type of design was favoured in which the doorway and the windows above it on the first floor or the first and second floors were emphasized by columns or pilasters in tiers. The type comes from Bristol, where it occurs at No. 29 Queen's Square in 1709–11, and Bath, where one finds it in General Wolfe's house in Trim Street of shortly after 1707. Druce's Hill House and Westbury House at Bradford belong to 50 this type – it is no distance from Bradford to Bath – and also houses in The Parade at Trowbridge, that short stretch of street which on one side has *palazzi* only, at Devizes (Greystone House, 1731), and at Corsham (The Grove).

No more can be said of the houses of these and the other towns of Wiltshire, but they are full of enjoyable Georgian architecture. Just one example deserves recording as a postscript, because it

* The SCHOOL interior is preserved, with benches and the headmaster's chair.

comes from a town usually left aside: Swindon. The house in question (Cricklade Street) is dated 1729 and has the liveliest assembly of motifs: giant pilasters, a Venetian window, grotesque keystone heads.

The reaction against the Baroque tendencies of the early c18, overcrowding, or massiveness, or licence of motifs and composition, began already in the second decade. It was led by Lord Burlington, and Palladio and Inigo Jones were the guiding stars. It has in fact been shown recently that the very first essay in revived Inigo goes right back to 1710. It is Wilbury, designed for himself by *William Benson*, who followed Wren for a short time as Surveyor General when the grand old man of English Baroque Classicism had been dismissed. Wilbury has been much altered, but it still has a detached portico and pediment as its central motif. Stourhead comes next, designed by *Colen Campbell* and of the purest Palladianism, then *Burlington*'s own remodelling of Tottenham House of the 1720s and 1730s, long since changed entirely, and after that, still purely Palladian, Lydiard Park of 1745–9, perhaps by *Roger Morris* – the Palladian Bridge at Wilton is by him too, unless it was designed by the able amateur *Lord Pembroke* – Fonthill Splendens, built after a fire of 1755, very grand, with quadrant links to pavilions and almost entirely gone, and finally Wardour Castle by *Paine*, built in 1769–76 and the largest c18 country house in Wiltshire. Its exterior is somewhat bleak, but its circular staircase hall is, next to Inigo's rooms at Wilton, the most beautiful room in the county. Wardour has the same quadrant links as Fonthill, a motif taken from Palladio's villas, and a motif that was also used in the sixties at Standlynch to enlarge the house of 1733. The architect for this was the *younger Wood*.* The *elder Wood* had built Belcombe Court outside Bradford in 1734 with giant pilasters, in the style he used so successfully in and outside Bath. Palladian also, or at least utilitarianly classical, one must call the extensive stable range round two courtyards at Bowood. This is by *Henry Keene* and of 1754. *Adam*'s spectacular additions have alas been allowed to disappear. They were of the 1760s.

The interiors are more to be regretted than the exteriors, even if some of them have been re-installed in other places. Of INTERIORS altogether, some more must now be listed, excellent classical ones of c.1748 at Lydiard Tregoze, excellent Rococo ones at Malmesbury House Salisbury, the Old Deanery Salisbury,

---

* But the porch with the fine tentatively Greek Doric columns is by *Revett*, who had returned from Athens a few years before.

Mompesson House Salisbury, and Little Durnford Manor, a series of hidden-away back rooms in Salisbury houses, all worth searching out: No. 45 Castle Street of *c.*1750, No. 1 Castle Street, The Hall New Street, and No. 38 St Ann Street, all three of *c.*1775, and No. 40 St Ann Street of 1812, particularly richly stuccoed. In the country the Adam style is represented by the dining room of Compton Park Compton Chamberlayne and work at Charlton Park near Malmesbury, some of *c.*1772–6 but some, it seems, of the C20. And then there is the Chinese Rococo of the entrance hall at Standlynch (Trafalgar House) of *c.*1765–70 and the delicious Gothick Rococo of the library of 54a Malmesbury House, The Close, Salisbury, hardly possible later than the 1750s.

Those were the years of the equally spirited GOTHIC REVIVAL of the hall at Lacock Abbey designed by *Sanderson Miller*, with 55 statue niches filled by iconographically enigmatic terracotta figures, the work of a wholly obscure German or Austrian called *Sederbach*. Only a little more than forty years after, Rococo Gothic had made way for Romantic Gothic, and Wiltshire saw with amazement the most daring piece of Gothic Romanticism grow to the skies: William Beckford's Fonthill Abbey, designed for 60a him by *James Wyatt*. It must have been wonderful when it was new, however ostentatious and preposterous it was. It lay in the woods on top of the hill at the foot of which the preceding Font-hills had been. It spread out cruciform and had a tower 225 ft high (which very soon collapsed) and vast vaulted (stucco-vaulted) halls. The fragment that alone remains of it is miserable and sordid, and perhaps there is poetic justice in the fact that Wyatt's classical masterpiece in Wiltshire, Bowden Park Bowden Hill, 59a completed in 1796 (when Fonthill was begun), stands perfect out-side and perfect inside.*

Gothicism and Romanticism lead us naturally to the land-scaped GROUNDS of the country houses and their architectural furnishings. Old Wardour Castle got a Gothic Banqueting House in 1788 and one of the craggy grottoes in which Mr *Josiah Lane* of Tisbury specialized. He also did the grotto at Bowood, where in addition quite a creditable cascade was made and where *Adam* in 1765 built an exquisite and monumental Mausoleum in the form of a Greek cross. Amesbury, Bowden Park, and Wilbury have small grottoes too. Fonthill has several, and a spacious boathouse in the form of a nave with aisles. Wilbury has a classical octagonal

---

* One almost unknown surviving piece from Fonthill Abbey is the chimneypiece at Bathampton House Steeple Langford.   60b

pavilion, Wardour Castle a temple, Amesbury a once very charming Chinese Temple (1772, by *Chambers*), and Wilton, apart from the Palladian Bridge, several loggias, a triumphal arch by *Chambers*, and a column, the latter (with bands of rocky rustication) and
45a at least one of the loggias going back to the Inigo Jones or John Webb period. But the best place in all England to enthuse in landscaped grounds and garden furnishings is, side by side with
56 Stowe, Stourhead. The buildings are of the 1740s and 1750s and are placed with great visual cunning along or above a lake of varied outline: a large grotto, the larger Pantheon, a (later) rustic cottage, and several temples, including one designed on the pattern of the Temple of the Sun at Baalbek. The church of Stourton was made part of the picturesque plan, and its Gothic appeal reinforced by the re-erection of the Gothic High Cross (of 1373) from Bristol Green. Further away from the house there is another original Gothic canopy (St Peter's Cross), and Alfred's Tower, a triangular medievalizing tower like that in Windsor Great Park.

An appendix must be devoted to what might be called PUBLIC BUILDINGS of the Georgian century. Most of them were presented by the nobility and the rich. TOWN HALLS must start with Wootton Bassett of 1700, given by Laurence Hyde, first Earl of Rochester, and, with its open ground floor with fifteen stumpy
51b columns, extremely conservative. Then comes the New Hall, not town hall, of Devizes, a pure Palladian building of 1750–2. Compared with that, the market house of Wilton of 1738 seems quite insignificant. Corsham, given by the Methuens, is of 1784, and then the Salisbury Guildhall of 1788 etc. This was designed by *Sir Robert Taylor* and built with modifications by *W. Pilkington*. It was given by Lord Radnor and is the first grander town hall, grey brick with rocky rustication, large windows, and a spacious assembly room. It was followed by the town hall of Devizes of 1806–8. This is by *Baldwin* of Bath, and the finest of the Wiltshire town halls. Westbury is of 1815, Warminster of 1830, Melksham of as late as 1847, and this indeed has the typical elongated Italianate Victorian windows. Wiltshire has quite a number of LOCK-UPS, polygonal or square with stone domes or caps (Box, Bradford, Bromham, Heytesbury, Hilperton, Lacock, Luckington, Shrewton, Steeple Ashton, Trowbridge, Warminster). The centre range of the HOSPITAL of Salisbury is by the *younger Wood* of Bath of 1767–71 and a purely utilitarian brick building. Further ALMS-HOUSES were built at Salisbury too, in 1702 (Trinity Hospital, with a small, attractive courtyard and a chapel) and 1750 (with a lantern and an arcade at the back). The Heytesbury almshouses of

*c.*1769 are quite sizeable and look as though they were designed about 1680–1700, the Somerset Almshouses at Froxfield were doubled in size in 1775 and given their monumental gateway and chapel in 1813. And one SCHOOL at least was built which, if not large, is sufficiently original to be placed on record. It is at Mildenhall and was designed in 1823 by *R. A. Abraham*. Its plan is cruciform. Abraham must have liked geometrical plays of planning, for he submitted plans to the Earl of Radnor to double the size of Longford Castle by converting the triangle into a hexagon with a free-standing seventh tower in the middle of the courtyard. Of this only a certain amount was carried out, as we shall see. One HOTEL should be added, the White Hart at Salisbury with its early C19 portico, and also the passion of the C18 for SPAS. Seend is mentioned as a spa by Aubrey as early as 1684. There were Georgian spas at Purton, Middlehill (Ditteridge) near Box, Holt, and Melksham. Only at Melksham can one still get a faint impression of the buildings. They are of *c.*1815.

And one more equally novel type of architecture, though for work and not for recreation: FACTORIES. The conversion from home-weaving to factory-weaving took place in the late C18. The documents in Derbyshire, Shropshire, the Cotswolds, and Yorkshire are familiar. The Wiltshire ones ought to be studied more closely. The best data are at present available for Trowbridge. They show that these brick (or sometimes stone) ranges of three or four storeys with segment-headed windows and a few minimum Georgian details belong to *c.*1812, and then *c.*1815–30. But at Devizes one such factory remains firmly dated 1785, and at Westbury two attributed to 1772 and 1784. The former is said to have iron columns, iron beams, and shallow brick vaults. The Malmesbury mill is of the late C18 too, the only dateable one at Bradford (now Spencer & Moulton's) of shortly after 1802, and the Wilton Royal Carpet Factory certainly does not look later.* As a postscript to this, the Watt beam engine of *c.*1812 in the Crofton Pumping Station must be given a place here, a splendid piece.

It served the Kennet and Avon Canal. For these were the years of the CANALS. The Kennet and Avon Canal was begun in 1786. It was completed in 1810 and connected Newbury with Bath. It was designed by *John Rennie* with, in the preparatory stages, *Robert Whitworth*. It is 57 miles long and it has 106 locks. Twenty-nine of these are grouped close together just outside

* The tradition of unselfconscious monumentality in factory buildings turned selfconscious in the Victorian age – see e.g. the rubber works of 1875 63b at Bradford-on-Avon.

Devizes. Near Limpley Stoke and Avoncliff are remarkable aqueducts. It goes past Hungerford, Great Bedwyn, Burbage, Pewsey, Devizes, and Bradford. The canal is now disused. Earlier than the Kennet–Avon is *Robert Whitworth*'s Thames-Severn Canal, built in 1783–9 and connecting Inglesham with Stroud by Cricklade, Latton, and Sapperton (in Gloucestershire, where it has the famous tunnel, nearly 4,000 yards long). It is 29 miles long. The Wilts and Berks Canal is much narrower, or was, as it is in many places now almost unrecognizable. It starts from the Kennet–Avon Canal at Sevington outside Trowbridge and goes by Melksham, Dauntsey, Wootton Bassett, and Swindon to Abingdon. It was designed by *William Whitworth* and built in 1796–1810. It is 51 miles long. The only other canal in the county, the North Wiltshire Canal, is only 9 miles in length and connects Swindon on the Wilts and Berks with Letton on the Thames–Severn. It was completed in 1819. The most worth-while buildings connected with the canals are the Crofton Pumping Station and the pretty Honey Street Wharf at Alton Barnes.

Twenty years later the canals were doomed and the RAILWAY AGE had begun. In Wiltshire the railways arrived in the late 1830s, and the London–Bristol railway, *Brunel*'s railway, was only completed in 1841. It is important for Wiltshire architecture; for it made Swindon. The station was built in 1842, the railway works in 1843, and the original, humbly-planned bit of new town in *c.*1850 etc. The station was famous for its sumptuousness, both of ashlar-faced architecture and of appointments inside the waiting-room and the short-lived hotel on the upper floor. The railway also provided a church in 1843–5, and the old town got itself a new one too in 1851. Both these CHURCHES are by *Sir G. G. Scott*. He had been active in the county before, and it may be assumed that he did not look back with pleasure to his neo-Norman church at Swallowcliffe built in 1842–3, when he was still in partnership with Moffatt.* The neo-Norman, or indeed the *Rundbogenstil*, as the Germans say, for it can be Romanesque, Early Christian, or Byzantine, was the great fashion just at that moment. Charlton near Donhead St Mary is neo-Norman and of 1839, Grafton by *Ferrey* is neo-Norman and of 1844. And then 61b there is the church of Wilton, neo-Italian Romanesque on a grandiose scale and of 1843. This was paid for by the Rt Hon. Sidney Herbert and cost £20,000.‡ It made the reputation of

---

* He also designed the church at Zeals in 1843–6, and St Paul at Chippenham, on which see below.

‡ The little church at Axford in 1856 cost £425.

Thomas Henry Wyatt (in partnership with *David Brandon*). He had already in 1836 been made consulting architect to the newly founded Salisbury Diocesan Church Building Association, and for them built ten new churches, partly rebuilt thirty, and restored another twenty. In 1835 he had still built Grecian – the Assize Court at Devizes – but later he built Gothic. Only two more of his churches in the county are Norman and they are, characteristically enough, again of 1843 (Crockerton) and 1844 (Dilton Marsh). Most of Wyatt's churches are naturally small, but he could go all out at St John Bemerton of 1860–1, again for the Pembrokes of Wilton, and at Semley of 1875 for the Marchioness of Westminster. Even earlier, some new churches in or near villages, paid for by pious and wealthy patrons, were remarkably impressive, especially Everleigh by *Morlidge* of 1813 and Teffont Evias of 1824–6 by *Fowler*, with a proud steeple. But mostly churches of this size were provided for the growing villa suburbs of the towns: Christ Church Sambourne, outside Warminster, of 1830–1 by *Leachman*, St James Devizes of 1834, a remarkably credible piece of neo-Perp, Holy Trinity Trowbridge by *Livesay* of Portsmouth, 1838, with plaster vaults on iron columns, Christ Church, Bearfield, Bradford by *Manners* of Bath of 1841, and St Paul Chippenham of 1854–5 by *Scott*, already mentioned. Apart from Scott, there is not one of the London Gothicists among the providers of these churches.

But some of them had quite a good connexion in the county. *Butterfield* restored Amesbury Abbey in 1853 and left as his mark a remarkably perverse stair-turret. Much later he built Foxham (1880, with a chunky screen) and Baverstock (1883). But he was mostly busy as a restorer. *Street* also did much restoring, if no original work, *Brooks* built Marston Meysey in 1876–9 with a rib-vaulted chancel, and *Pearson* Sutton Veny in 1862, also with rib-vaults in chancel and crossing, and the very beautiful Chute Forest church in 1875.

For CHURCH FURNISHINGS of the Victorian Age nothing needs listing except STAINED GLASS. *Pugin* designed some of course for his own house, St Marie's Grange at Alderbury, and also the glass for the grand window at Bishopstone near Salisbury – an undeniably uninspired design. Early *Morris* glass is at Sopworth (*c.*1870), at Rodbourne, and at Salisbury Cathedral (*c.*1875–80) and early *Kempe* glass at Patney (1873), Bemerton (1878), Stratford Tony (1884), and Pitton (1886). Later Kempe glass cannot be summed up, nor indeed could it all be put into the gazetteer. Wiltshire was his county. He lived at No. 17 The Close, and so did his partner *Tower* later.

FUNERAL MONUMENTS for the first third of the century come to an index by artists. Only few need enlarging upon. *Flaxman* at Market Lavington, 1797, Ashton Keynes † 1800, and Salisbury Cathedral † 1796 and 1807, *King* of Bath, the indefatigable, especially good at Great Somerford † 1794 and especially large, ambitious, and Grecian at Whaddon † 1807. *Westmacott Senior* at Devizes St John († 1784) and Wilton († 1794), *Sir Richard Westmacott* with an excellent relief of the Holy Family and a shepherd at Wilton † 1827, with very Grecian, rather stolid figures at Nunton † 1831 and other monuments at Whaddon († 1814) and North Wraxall († 1837), his son *Richard Westmacott* with a sensitive relief of Charity at Farley († 1802), *John Bacon Junior* at Britford (1820), *Chantrey* with the ambitious half-Grecian, half-Gothic memorial to the first Earl of Malmesbury in the cathedral (1823), a life-size relief at Edington († 1815) and a minor monument at Longbridge Deverill († 1837), *Baily* with the Crabbe Monument at Trowbridge († 1832) and others, the little-known *T. Denman* at Figheldean † 1818, *R. C. Lucas* with the seated figure of Colt Hoare, the Wiltshire historian, again in the cathedral (1841), *Lough* with the sleeping Methuen child at Corsham († 1829),* *Gaffin* of Regent Street with a still entirely Georgian tablet in the cathedral commemorating a death in 1861 – an almost unbelievably late date; and so to the Gothicists. In Salisbury Cathedral correct and ambitious neo-Gothic monuments start with that to the Poore family, with a proper canopy. This is of 1817 and was designed by the Rev. *Hugh Owen* and made by *John Carline* of Shrewsbury. This seems to have set off *Osmond*, who became one of Pugin's craftsmen. But he did the canopied monument for Bishop Fisher in the cathedral in 1828, when Pugin was only sixteen. After that, especially in the mid thirties, he did many Gothic stone tablets, quite small and quite commercial – Mrs Stanton tells me that Pugin spoke of them as Osmond's blisters. *Pugin* designed another of the grand canopied Gothic tombs, that to the Rev. George Augustus Montgomery at Bishopstone near Salisbury already referred to. This is of 1844 and ends the record of the first half of the century. Of the second half – apart from some stately and stodgy bishops' monuments with recumbent effigies in the cathedral – nothing needs special attention except the fabulous monuments to J. H. Thynne † 1887 at Longbridge Deverill and to the Marchioness of Ailesbury † 1892

64

* The same motif at Chilton Foliat († 1861) by *Popham*.

at Savernake Forest, both by *Alfred Gilbert*. Finally there is a tablet by *Eric Gill* at Wilsford near Amesbury († 1922).

This leaves only VICTORIAN DOMESTIC ARCHITECTURE unsummarized; for the Victorian public buildings do not deserve to be in this Introduction. We must for a moment go back to about 1800, as we had left country houses in 1796 with *Wyatt*'s Bowden Park and Fonthill. In 1801 he was called to Wilton to gothicize much of the house and make it more convenient. Chilton Lodge Chilton Foliat of 1800 by *Pilkington* is still Palladian with a giant portico, and Palladian also rather than Grecian must be called *Cundy*'s grand and spacious remodelling and enlarging of Tottenham House (1825). Grecian with giant porticoes are Pyt House Newtown of 1805 etc. designed, it is said, by its owner, and Philipps House Dinton by *Sir Jeffry Wyatville*, built in 1813–16. Wyatville was responsible too for the early C19 alterations at Longleat, especially the big staircase. A big staircase was the chief internal alteration also which *Bellamy* made at Corsham, but he worked here (in 1845–9) in the Italian Renaissance and outside in a rather bleak simplified Jacobean. *Barry* gave Georgian Bowood an incongruous Italianate tower (1840) and the picturesquely asymmetrical Golden Gates (1834–57). In the same years (1835) *Pugin* built for himself and his wife St Marie's Grange at 61a Alderbury outside Salisbury, a small house of brick, asymmetrical, with two towers, a chapel larger than any other room, and Gothic chimneypieces and stained glass. It was not like any real Gothic building and had much romanticism in its outline, but it was sensibly planned and not for show. Again in the same years *Hopper* made Amesbury Abbey rather freer and less disciplined 62 than Webb had left it (*c*.1830 etc.) and made Rood Ashton for the Longs gloriously baronial (1836). The castle at Devizes was given that baronial cachet still as late as *c*.1860–80, after *Goodridge* had built the first castellated round tower in 1842. That Abraham had planned to double the size of Longford Castle and give it seven instead of three round towers has already been said. Later, about 1870, *Salvin* restored the façade from its Georgian back to its Elizabethan state and did it remarkably skilfully. He also did much to the interior. At Longleat the interior was thoroughly Italianized by *Crace* about 1875.

By then Norman Shaw was busy in London and *Philip Webb* was as busy as he wanted to be in the country. Wiltshire has his largest country house, but one in which the astringency of his style comes out more intensely than in any other. Clouds, East Knoyle was first built in 1881–6 and then rebuilt after a fire in

1889–91. It has been ill-treated recently, and was originally even more ruthless and disjointed than it is now. Webb advised a much younger man, *Detmar Blow*, on his restoring of Lake House Wilsford near Amesbury in 1898, and Blow also built, rebuilt, enlarged, or altered Heale House Woodford after 1894, Fonthill House in 1904, Wilsford House near Amesbury in 1904–6, and Hatch House Newtown in 1908.

So we are in the TWENTIETH CENTURY, and not much need be said about it. Architecturally it has called for little effort. There is no new industry except at Swindon, that is no council housing worth speaking of, that is not much school building activity, that is not a County Architect's office architecturally as enterprising as those of many other counties. At Swindon alone, where industry is growing fast, the architecture is more interesting. The new factories are acceptable, there is a nice shopping precinct in a new housing area, the new Technical College is highly creditable, and *Powell & Moya* have built the one outstanding building of recent years in the county, the new Princess Margaret Hospital.

Otherwise Wiltshire would be as wonderful as it must have been in Hardy's, in Hudson's, and in Jefferies' days, if the Army, and more recently the Air Force, had not got hold of it. As it is, the Army is up in Salisbury Plain with towns of barracks and genteel soldiers' housing and with all the mess of tin huts and tank tracks, and the Air Force is down in the northern plain with the mess of the airfields and the noise of the planes. Meanwhile the delightful towns, not forced to expand substantially, could remain delightful, even if architecturally nibbled at by indifferent new shop fronts, fascia-boards, and council houses, if it were not for the A-road traffic roaring through them and making them intolerable. The situation is perhaps no worse in Wiltshire than anywhere else but it is felt to be more incongruous.

And so, in conclusion, FURTHER READING. The best we have is the Victoria County History, consisting at the time of writing of volumes I, part I, III to VII (1953–62).* The local antiquarian journal is the *Wiltshire Archeological and Natural History Magazine*. This contains many papers on individual churches, the best of them mostly by C. E. Ponting. Of county guide-books the *Little Guide* (by F. R. Heath, revised by R. L. P. Jowitt) is familiar. So is the *Shell Guide* (first edition by Robert Byron 1935, second edition by David Verey 1956). Less known (and less known than it deserves) is Geoffrey Grigson's *The Wiltshire Book*, 1957. The

---

* We have also most generously been allowed to make use of the materials for volume VI.

volume of the *Cambridge County Geographies* (by A. G. Bradley, 1909), though in many ways out of date, is still to be recommended. The same is true emphatically of the *Memorials of Old Wiltshire* (ed. A. Dryden, 1906). The old county histories, i.e. John Aubrey's *Topographical Collections* (edited and enlarged by J. E. Jackson 1862) and Sir Richard Colt Hoare's *History of Modern South Wiltshire* (5 vols, 1822–37, plus a sixth volume on Salisbury, written after 'the estimable Baronet' had died, by R. Benson and H. Hatcher, 1843) remain indispensable. In addition for houses there are of course the many articles published in *Country Life*. Wiltshire church plate is collected in J. E. Nightingale's book of 1891, Wiltshire brasses in Edward Kite's book of 1860. That one would also consult such national collections as that of brasses by Mill Stephenson, of screens by Aylmer Vallance, of stalls by Bond, and so on, goes without saying. They can obviously not all be named in each of the introductions to the volumes of *The Buildings of England*.

INTRODUCTION TO THE PREHISTORIC
AND ROMAN REMAINS

BY

DEREK SIMPSON

FOR many people the archaeology of Wiltshire means Stonehenge and Avebury. These two monuments have achieved a popular recognition granted to few in the whole of European prehistory. This fame has perhaps overshadowed the many other sites in which the county abounds; for it is one of the most richly endowed areas in Europe. Within its borders lie Windmill Hill (Avebury), the type site of the earliest farming culture in Britain, and many fine long barrows, including the magnificent monument at West Kennett. On Salisbury Plain the barrows of the builders of Stonehenge have produced a wealth of finds of the brilliant Wessex Culture of the Early Bronze Age, whose centre was in Wiltshire. In the Iron Age again one has the type site of the first iron-using culture in these islands and the farmstead of Little Woodbury (Britford), which has thrown so much light on the economy of the period. Later still the Wansdyke represents one of the most spectacular post-Roman field monuments in Britain. All these monuments present a kaleidoscope of man's achievement and progress in prehistoric and early historic times. Their importance stretches far beyond the borders of the county, and it should be a cause for no little alarm that this heritage is menaced by agriculture and building developments – a threat which increases from year to year.

Wiltshire's natural pre-eminence in the field of prehistory has been magnified by the intensive field work and excavation of three centuries of antiquarians and archaeologists. The tradition, begun in the C 17 by John Aubrey, who was primarily concerned with the great ceremonial monuments of Stonehenge and Avebury, was maintained in the following century by William Stukeley, who supplemented field work with the opening of a number of the many barrows on Salisbury Plain. Towards the end of the century large numbers of the Wiltshire barrows were excavated by William Cunnington and his patron Sir Richard Colt Hoare. Their work is recorded in Hoare's two great volumes, *Ancient Wiltshire*. The finds from these excavations still form the bulk of the material evidence for a study of the Late Neolithic and Early Bronze Age cultures of the region. In 1853 the Wiltshire Archaeological and Natural History Society was formed to foster the growing interest in Wiltshire's past. Throughout its life the descendants of William Cunnington have played an important part in its development and in the study of Wiltshire archaeology: many important excavations were conducted by Maude and Ben Cunnington, including those at Woodhenge (Durrington), The Sanctuary on Overton Hill, and the Early Iron Age settlement at All Cannings Cross. The last three decades have seen an intensification of the work of excavation, field work, and study. One may mention Professor Piggott's recognition and study of the brilliant Early Bronze Age Wessex Culture, the field work and many excavations conducted by the late J. F. S. Stone, Alexander Keiller's work at Avebury and Windmill Hill, the Stonehenge excavations directed by Professor Piggott, Professor R. J. C. Atkinson, and Dr Stone, and the many excavations sponsored every year by the Ministry of Works. In the recording of field monuments outstanding work has been done in recent years by Mr L. V. Grinsell, culminating in the gazetteer of Prehistoric, Roman, and Saxon sites published in the *Victoria County History of Wiltshire*.

The earliest human cultures of the PALAEOLITHIC (Old Stone Age) period are represented in Wiltshire by flint hand axes of Acheulean type. These axes have been found in the gravels of the Avon near Salisbury and at the important site of Knowle Farm, Savernake Forest, which has produced enormous quantities of these tools, many having a peculiar surface gloss. So far no material of the final (upper) Palaeolithic phase, such as is found in the Cheddar caves, has been recorded in the county.

Following the final retreat of the ice the warmer climate encouraged the spread of birch and pine forests. The changing environment produced a corresponding change in material equipment and the emergence of the MESOLITHIC cultures. Two main groups are recognizable in Britain. One, related to the French Sauveterrian industries, is characterized largely by microliths – small flint blades, blunted on one side for incorporation in arrow or javelin heads, and frequently of composite form. These microliths are generally found in sandy heaths and uplands and are almost the sole surviving objects of this group. The second group, linked with the Northern Forest Cultures of Denmark and the Baltic, is mainly concentrated in river valleys and estuaries, fishing, hunting, and the collection of wild fruits and berries being the basis of the economy. The large flake axe, with its tranchet point, was developed as an effective tool against the encroaching forests, and barbed bone or antler points and wedge-shaped flint arrowheads were used for fishing and hunting. The evidence for Mesolithic settlement in the county is not extensive, although microliths have been found at sites near Chippenham, and other industries of Mesolithic form occur on Windmill Hill (Avebury) and Hackpen Hill (Wroughton) on the Marlborough Downs. All these sites are represented by a mere scatter of worked flints and waste flakes unassociated with any structure such as the wind shelters found at Farnham in Surrey.

By about 3000 B.C. the first NEOLITHIC communities had settled in South Britain, introducing the knowledge of agriculture and stockbreeding to these islands. The first Neolithic culture, the Windmill Hill Culture, belongs to an extensive group of Western Neolithic cultures whose antecedents can be traced in the West and Central Mediterranean. The culture takes its name from the hilltop camp on Windmill Hill, near Avebury, where it was first recognized. Other similar camps occur in the county at Whitesheet Hill (Kilmington), Knap Hill (Alton Barnes), and Robin Hood's Ball (Shrewton), the type being confined to South England. These camps are roughly circular enclosures surrounded by one or more concentric banks and ditches broken by numerous unexcavated areas forming causeways between the ditches. The very low banks and numerous entrances make it clear that their purpose was not defensive, and it is probable that they served as corrals or stock enclosures to which the herds of the Windmill Hill folk would be driven in the autumn.* The large quantity of animal bones found in a number of the causewayed camps shows that a considerable proportion of the stock must have been slaughtered at this time of the year, due no doubt to the impossibility of providing sufficient fodder for the winter. After slaughter

* Recent work however, largely at Windmill Hill, has shown in fact that there is no preponderance of young animals among the skeletal remains from the ditches, nor, as had previously been supposed, is there any evidence for the pole-axing of oxen. The practice of carefully burying the animal bones after a feast (and of burying whole animals in an articulated condition) by covering them with material from the bank implies some form of ceremonial or ritual gathering – very few of the bones show signs of having been gnawed by rodents or dogs, for whose presence on the site there is ample evidence. The occurrence of numerous axes of foreign stone and of pottery tempered with grit unobtainable in the vicinity of the camp again imply the congregation of peoples drawn from a considerable area. In the light of this new evidence it has been suggested (1962) that the causewayed camps represent communal gathering places, which, like medieval fairs, served as social, religious, and economic centres.

the hides were prepared with flint scrapers, and combs made from red deer antlers. Picks for excavating the ditches were manufactured from deer antlers, and shoulder-blades of oxen served as shovels.

The new agriculturalists still appear to have engaged in hunting, as many leaf-shaped arrowheads of flint have been recovered from sites of the culture. In addition to scrapers, arrowheads, and other small tools, flint was used for the production of axes and adzes, some of which may have served as hoes in addition to being employed to clear areas of forest for sowing. So important was flint as a raw material for tools that it was deliberately mined, vertical shafts being sunk into the chalk to locate the beds of superior flint which were then followed laterally. The best known Neolithic flint mine is that at Grimes Graves, Norfolk, but one extensive mining area has been investigated at Easton Down, near Salisbury. Associated with the shafts were numerous finished and partially completed tools and an enormous quantity of waste flakes and cores showing that implements were manufactured on the site. The pottery of these Early Neolithic colonists is generally well fired and thin walled. The characteristic forms are bag-shaped or carinated with rounded bottoms, any decoration being confined to cord impressions or incision on the upper part.

Occasionally burials are found in the ditches of causewayed camps and in flint mines, but the characteristic funerary monument is the earthen long barrow, of which many fine examples occur in the county. A particularly well preserved and accessible specimen is that at the Winterbourne Stoke cross-roads. Normally wedge-shaped in plan, the burials, often of twenty or more individuals, generally occur at the broader end of the barrow, lying on the old land surface beneath it. There is evidence to suggest that corpses were stored in a timber mortuary enclosure until a sufficient number had accumulated to warrant the erection of a barrow. Mortuary enclosures have been encountered beneath a number of long barrows, including one under a recently excavated example at Fussell's Lodge, near Salisbury.

A second tomb type found in Wiltshire and introduced by later Neolithic immigrants is the chambered long barrow. A group of these tombs, with stone-built burial chambers in the form of elongated galleries beneath mounds of earth or stones, is concentrated in the lands bordering the Severn Estuary and in the Cotswolds – the chambered long barrows of Wiltshire representing outliers of this group. The finest example in the county is undoubtedly that at West Kennett, with its slightly crescent-shaped façade of great sarsens behind which a passage leads to the two pairs of side chambers and the single terminal chamber. A succession of skeletons accompanied by Windmill Hill pottery lay on the floors of the chambers, and material belonging to later cultures occurred in the soil and occupation material which filled the chambers to the sarsen capstones.

The hunter-fisher communities continued to exist after the arrival of the Windmill Hill culture, and by the end of the third millennium B.C. had adopted agricultural techniques, pottery, and other traits from the primary Neolithic colonists. The resultant fusion brought about the formation of SECONDARY NEOLITHIC cultures – Neolithic in the sense that they were stone-using agriculturalists and herdsmen but still maintaining features of the old hunting and gathering economy. The two most important of these groups, recognized largely by their distinctive ceramic forms, are the Peterborough and Rinyo-Clacton Cultures. Peterborough vessels are generally bowl-shaped with everted rim, the body being decorated with impressions made with a short length of cord or bird bone, frequently arranged in a herringbone pattern. Rinyo-Clacton forms are generally straight-sided, bucket-shaped vessels ornamented with shallow grooves and stab marks forming geometrical designs. Both wares are noticeably coarser and thicker than Windmill Hill vessels. The underlying Mesolithic tradition of these cultures is reflected in their flint tools. Flake axes with tranchet cutting edges and arrowheads developed from Mesolithic types are the most characteristic. Many of the ground and polished stone axes in the county discovered casually during ploughing or picked up from the surface may be attributed to the Secondary Neolithic cultures. The majority of these axes are of foreign stones manufactured at the source of the stone, which may be as far away as Cornwall, Wales, or even Cumberland. They must have found their way to Wiltshire by a widespread bartering and exchange system. There are few field monuments of these cultures. Rinyo-Clacton and Peterborough pottery was found in a secondary position in the West Kennett chambered long barrow, and vessels have recently been discovered in round barrows of the Lake and Earls Farm Down cemeteries. One important new form of ceremonial monument however is the henge. The best known examples are of course those of Woodhenge (Durrington) and the first phase of Stonehenge. The characteristic henge of the Secondary Neolithic cultures is a circular area bounded by a bank and ditch, the bank generally lying outside the ditch (an exception is the Phase I Monument at Stonehenge), broken by a single entrance. At Woodhenge the central area has a complex setting of concentric post holes which probably supported a roofed structure. A similar building may have occurred at Stonehenge, but all traces have been obliterated by later structures. At the centre of the Woodhenge monument was found the dedicatory burial of a child with cleft skull, and cremations were discovered in the ring of Aubrey Holes immediately within the area of the bank at Stonehenge.

About 1800 B.C. or a little before, further Late Neolithic immigrants settled in Wiltshire. They came from Holland and the lands at the mouth of the Rhine, and are called BEAKER FOLK after the characteristic pottery which they buried with their dead. Two principal groups are recognizable in the county. The Bell Beaker Culture, with its smooth profiled pots decorated with horizontal zones of impressions made with a blunt-toothed comb or length of cord, appears to be the earlier. The makers of this pottery must have entered Wiltshire when it was still possible to gain access to the chambered tombs, as a magnificent bell beaker was found in the filling of the West Kennett tomb. The classic assemblage of this culture is the grave goods accompanying the crouched skeleton of a man beneath a round barrow on Roundway Down. In addition to a fine beaker, a large copper dagger with projecting tang for attachment of the hilt, a copper pin of Central European type, a barb and tang flint arrowhead, and a stone bracer to protect the wrist of the archer were placed beside the body. Another important find from the county is the burial at Mere associated with a bell beaker, small tanged copper dagger, stone wrist guard, and two small discs of sheet-gold decorated with a cruciform pattern (possibly button covers).

The second, later, group, with its long-necked beakers – i.e. beakers which have a pronounced neck separated from the lower part of the body by a marked constriction – entered the county from the region of the Upper Thames valley. Characteristic grave goods of the culture include copper daggers with rivets for the attachment of the hilt, beautifully worked flint daggers modelled on the metal forms, and stone battle-axes with perforated shaft holes. A fine example of the latter weapon was found with a long-necked beaker beneath a ploughed-out round barrow near Woodhenge, and another in one of the barrows of the Lake group S of Stonehenge. Thus although a few copper weapons are associated with the Beaker cultures, these cultures are still basically Neolithic, and flint implements were still widely used. The Beaker Folk continued to work the flint mines at Easton Down, and stone

axes were imported from the factory sites. They also introduced a new burial monument – the round barrow. Those which cover long-necked beaker burials are noticeably larger than bell-beaker barrows. The barrows are surrounded by quarry ditches from which the material of the mound was obtained, and are termed bowl barrows from the resemblance of the mound to an inverted bowl. Many of the Beaker barrows occur on Salisbury Plain, with a lesser concentration on the Marlborough Downs round Avebury. The henge monument was developed by the Beaker communities, the peak of the tradition being reached in the monuments at Avebury and Stonehenge. The Avebury group consists of an enormous henge, partially enclosing the modern village, linked by an
4b Avenue of paired standing stones to a second site, the Sanctuary, on Overton Hill, $1\frac{1}{2}$ m. to the S. Beaker burials were found at the bases of two of the Avenue stones, and a third, possibly foundation burial, was found at the Sanctuary. At Stonehenge the Beaker contribution lay in the quarrying and transport of the bluestones from Pembrokeshire and their erection in a double circle within the earlier Secondary Neolithic henge.

The inception of the BRONZE AGE saw in Wiltshire the rise of the brilliant Wessex Culture. As the county lay on an important trans-peninsular route from Ireland to the Continent, its strategic position was quickly appreciated by communities in North Germany, which traded ore and amber with the great Mycenaean civilization in southern Greece, and groups from that area settled in Wiltshire, establishing themselves as overlords over the native population. They were able to control the flow of Irish gold and copper to the Continent, acting as middlemen between the Irish miners and the Continental merchants. Their wealth and the widespread commercial links which they established are reflected in the magnificent series of objects they buried with their dead, a number of which, including faience beads and gold-bound amber pendants, are evidence of direct contact with the Eastern Mediterranean. The bowl barrow, introduced by the Beaker Folk, continued to be erected, but new barrow types were also developed. The bell barrow, consisting of a circular mound separated from its surrounding quarry ditch by a flat area or berm, is generally associated with male burials, while the disc barrow, a low mound at the centre of a flat platform surrounded by the ditch and external bank, and the saucer barrow, again a low barrow but spread over the whole area encompassed by the ditch, appear most frequently to have covered female graves. The main concentration of barrows is on Salisbury Plain, and particularly in the region of Stonehenge, around which they cluster in cemeteries.

Stonehenge represents the only field monument, other than barrows, which can be ascribed to the Wessex Culture; the grandiose sarsen circle and horseshoe and the final bluestone settings were erected by Wessex chieftains. The culture can be shown to have flourished from c.1600 to 1400 B.C. and is divisible into two periods, each of about a century in duration – a division originally based on dagger forms but recently extended to cover many tools, ornaments, weapons, and pottery types. Inhumation, generally in a crouched position, was the standard burial rite in the first period, but it was replaced after 1500 B.C. by an almost universal preference for cremation. A number of the burials are remarkable for the richness of the objects buried with the dead and must rank as the interments of chiefs or kings. Perhaps the most magnificent is that beneath Bush Barrow, a bowl barrow belonging to the Normanton barrow cemetery, s of Stonehenge. At the centre of the barrow, on the old ground surface, lay the extended skeleton of a man accompanied by two very large copper daggers, a copper axe, a breastplate and belt fastener of gold, a ceremonial stone mace-head, and a wooden wand inlaid with dentated bone roundels. Behind the head was a large number of copper rivets which may originally have formed part of a wooden or leather shield.* Women of rank were accorded equally magnificent burial, as is attested in the Golden Barrow at Upton Lovell, where the body of a woman was accompanied by an armlet and other gold ornaments, and a necklace of amber beads – the latter an import from the great commercial centres of North Germany. Less rich burials, such as those beneath barrows in the Ashton Valley (Codford St Peter), s of Chitterne, of males accompanied by bronze daggers and stone battle-axes, suggest a similar warrior aristocracy, while the very large number of graves containing only a few amber, shale, or bone ornaments, small knife daggers, or bone pins must represent the native peasantry subject to the warrior-merchants. This native element is apparent too in the form and ornament of the urns in which the cremated bones of the dead were placed for burial in the second phase of the culture. The small accessory vessels, termed incense cups although their purpose is obscure, have a similarly Neolithic ancestry.

By 1400 B.C. the Wessex Culture as such had ceased to exist. Copper ores were now being extensively worked in the eastern Alps, and the importance of the Irish deposits, on which the wealth and power of the chieftains depended, had decreased, as the bulk

* Or perhaps more likely a helmet.

of 'international' trade shifted from west to central Europe. In Wiltshire, however, the native peasantry, with its roots in the Neolithic, survived to contribute to the MIDDLE AND LATE BRONZE AGE cultures of the area. Cremation was still the standard burial rite, and the cinerary urns continued in use with biconical forms, often ornamented with applied horseshoes or finger-impressed ornament. The practice of burying rich grave goods with the dead was abandoned, and this tends to create the impression of a considerably impoverished population following the Wessex Culture. The population however appears to have increased and prospered, although the picture is that of a less markedly stratified society than in the preceding period. Connexions were maintained with northern Europe, and it was largely as a result of these contacts that the flanged axe of the Early Bronze Age was replaced by the more efficient bronze palstave, often with a cast loop to hold it more securely to its haft, and the rapier was developed from the dagger. Bronze was becoming more abundant, and small hoards of tools and weapons, the products of itinerant smiths or merchants buried in times of unrest, now appear. Bowl barrows continued to be erected over the dead, although urn burials were frequently inserted in existing Beaker or Wessex Culture barrows, or, more rarely, formed cemeteries of flat graves, as at Easton Down.

By 1200 B.C. a new culture – the Deverel-Rimbury Culture – had emerged in southern Britain. Two of the three pottery forms, the bucket and barrel urns, have their roots in Secondary Neolithic pottery tradition, while the third type, the globular urn with rounded body and vertical neck decorated with geometric grooved ornament, has no native antecedents and must represent an intrusive element, possibly from north-west France. The dead, invariably cremated, were buried in urns or deposited as simple heaps of bones in existing barrows, in low barrows, or in flat cemeteries. Associated with the culture are rectangular or sub-rectangular field enclosures surrounded by boundary ditches, five of which occur on the Marlborough Downs, a single example near Woodhenge, and another in the s of the county, on Boscombe Down. On Thorny Down occurs a small compound enclosing eight or nine small huts grouped around a central rectangular house. Weaving is attested by loom-weights on the site and corn was ground on saddle-shaped querns. Bronze was now much more abundant and was employed for manufacturing a wide variety of tools and weapons. The bronze-smith may by now have become a specialized craftsman peddling his wares across the countryside and collecting worn or broken bronzes to be re-smelted. A number of these bronze-smiths' hoards, containing broken and obsolete tools as well as unused articles, have been found in Wiltshire, including one with nine socketed axes from Manton Down near Marlborough, the Donhead St Mary hoard with its eleven axes, bronze gouge and hammer, and bronze mould, and the hoard of torques and bracelets found between Amesbury and Salisbury during road-mending operations.

By the beginning of the C5 B.C. fresh waves of settlers were arriving in Wiltshire from the Continent, bringing with them tools and weapons of iron. These newcomers, the IRON AGE 'A' culture, represent an expansion of Celtic-speaking peoples from the Low Countries and Northern France. Wiltshire, with its well drained soil, was attractive to these agriculturalists, who settled in large numbers and quickly absorbed the aboriginal Bronze Age population. The classic site for this culture in Wiltshire, and indeed in Britain, is that of Little Woodbury (Britford), $1\frac{1}{2}$ m. SW of Salisbury. Here excavation revealed a large circular wooden house with entrance porch surrounded by a group of grain storage pits, corn-drying racks, and barns, all contained within a palisaded enclosure. Cereal production appears to have been the main economic activity, the land being divided into small square fields cultivated with ox-drawn ploughs, although cattle, sheep, and goats were also reared. Another very important site in North Wiltshire, which was unfortunately only partially excavated, is at All Cannings Cross, and other settlements of the period which have produced large quantities of finds occur on Swallowcliffe Down and Fifield Bavant Down. Numerous clay and chalk loom weights, spindle whorls, and bone weaving-combs frequently decorated with concentric circle ornament from Iron Age 'A' sites attest to the importance of cloth manufacture. The pottery consists of coarse, generally bucket-shaped cooking vessels and finer wares with angular profiles often coated with a haematite slip, giving them a bright red, glossy surface after firing. The characteristic ornament was the La Tène I brooch of safety pin design in bronze, used as a dress fastener. A large series of knives, hoes, hammers, and other tools were manufactured from iron.

The pattern of sites and small finds in Wiltshire at the inception of the Iron Age is that of a relatively stable peasant society living peacefully in open farmsteads, but by the middle of the C3 B.C. many of the farmsteads were fortified and hill-forts constructed on eminences. This development may in part have been due to the increasing pressure of population on the land, but was certainly

3

accelerated by the threat of invasion by warlike tribes from across the English Channel. The invasion threat passed so far as Wiltshire was concerned, and the population lived in peace for a further two centuries. Caesar's campaign against the Veneti in Brittany in 56 B.C. led to the flight of a number of refugees from Brittany, and some of these displaced groups appear to have reached Wiltshire, where they established themselves as overlords over the Iron Age A peasantry. The culture of these chieftains – Iron Age B – is characterized by fine, bead-rimmed pottery copying metal forms, countersunk handles, and rotary querns. Yarnbury Castle (Berwick St James) and a number of the other existing hill-forts were reconstructed and defended by multiple ramparts – a reflection of the sling warfare practised by the Iron Age B peoples. This wave of hill-fort building may be the result of pressure from Iron Age C people, the Belgae, displaced from Gaul by Caesar's campaigns. Settling initially in south-east Britain, Belgic invaders gradually pushed westwards until, c. A.D. 10–25, Wiltshire was occupied by Comodius, a prince of the Atrebates. Some hill-forts were again occupied and remodelled by the new overlords, and further sites were constructed. A feature of a number of the Belgic earthworks (e.g. Stockton) is the tendency for the ramparts to extend down the hill slopes, contrary to the dictates of strategy. These forts may represent more permanent settlements and tribal centres, in contrast with the earlier forts, which were only temporary refuges occupied in periods of unrest. Another remarkable monument of the Atrebates, just over the border at Uffington, Berkshire, is the figure of a horse cut in the chalk on an escarpment below the hill-fort of Liddington Castle. The stylized treatment of this horse compares closely with representations on Belgic coinage. On the other hand the white horses of Wiltshire are comparatively modern – most of them were cut in the C18 and C19.* A number of the Belgic forts are unfinished, as the brief domination of the area by the Belgae was brought to a swift end when in A.D. 43 the Second Augustan Legion under Vespasian advanced from the SE, crushing all resistance and quickly establishing Roman authority in the district.

The roads were probably constructed in the first decades of the ROMAN occupation both for military purposes and to enable the produce of the downland farms to be distributed; for Wiltshire and its neighbouring counties served as the granaries of Britain in the early Roman period. Many of the settlements, such as that

* They are at Alton Barnes, Broad Town, Cherhill, Pewsey, Preshute, Westbury, and Wroughton.

on Fifield Down, continued to be occupied by Iron Age peasantry whose material culture, with the addition of a few Roman forms, remained relatively unchanged. Important town sites occur at Sorviodunum (Old Sarum) and Cunetio (Mildenhall), both lying 8a on important road junctions from Aquae Sulis (Bath), Calleva (Silchester), and Venta Belgarum (Winchester). Little remains of the Roman town at Old Sarum, but at Mildenhall air photography has revealed street plans and a large town house, and recent excavations have disclosed a large gateway with paved entrance at the s of the town. The majority of the villas in the county occur on its borders, with an important group in the neighbourhood of Box strung out along the road from Mildenhall to Bath. Those near Verlucio (see Calne, p. 143) may be connected with iron-smelting, as the fields are still strewn with iron cinders. The house at Okus quarries near Swindon on the other hand was possibly that of the overseer in charge of the working of the Purbeck and Portland stone there. Another minor industry is represented by the recently discovered series of pottery kilns in Savernake Forest, not far from Mildenhall. These were probably constructed in the c I A.D. A number of the products of the kilns have bead rims, which emphasizes the importance and continuity of the pre-Roman Iron Age traditions. The earliest villas appear to have been small structures with only a few rooms, but by the mid c3 a larger form, the corridor villa, had appeared, based on an arrangement of rooms along a connecting corridor. The sequence is well represented at Atworth, where the house began as a simple structure to which a corridor was added and finally, in the c3, a bath suite. The corridor villa might be further enlarged into a courtyard villa in which the rooms are arranged round a central open court, as at Box, where over forty rooms, a number having mosaic floors, were discovered. The evidence from Atworth and other villa sites points to a decline in villa life in the second half of the c4, when their wealthy tenants were replaced by peasant farmers who converted many of the fine rooms and bath suites into stables and outbuildings. Other signs of unrest are the hoards of coins and other valuables such as the deposit of pewter from Manton near Marlborough buried at this period, and the fortification of towns (e.g. Mildenhall). The cause of this unrest was the pressure from Saxon raiding parties on the east coasts. Their attacks were intensified towards the end of the c4, and early in the c5, under the weight of these attacks and unrest in other parts of the Empire, the Roman legions were withdrawn from Britain.

By the end of the C5 SAXON penetration had extended to the Upper Thames valley, and it may have been in an attempt to check their advance that the Wansdyke was constructed by the Britons. The final defeat of the Britons in Wiltshire, however, was inflicted by another group of Saxons under Cynric, advancing northwards from the New Forest. After a victory at Old Sarum the whole county was overrun by the southern bands, who united with the Saxon tribes of the Upper Thames. There are few surviving monuments which can be ascribed to this pagan Saxon period. The dead were occasionally buried under round barrows, the most notable being at Coombe Bissett, where a male skeleton was accompanied by an iron sword with bronze studded hilt similar to that from Sutton Hoo (*see The Buildings of England: Suffolk*, p. 20). More frequently burials were inserted in existing Bronze Age barrows. A particularly rich female grave of this type is that discovered in a barrow on Roundway Down. The grave goods included pendants, beads, and a chain and medallion of gold. The dead were also buried in flat cemeteries which have left little or no surface indication. Important cemeteries in the s of the county have been discovered at Harnham Hill and Petersfinger (Clarendon Palace), near Salisbury. Male and female inhumations were found, many of the former accompanied by iron swords and shields and bronze saucer brooches. The pagan Saxon period ends in the county with the establishment of a Christian mission at Malmesbury by Maildubh in the first half of the C7.

INTRODUCTION TO THE GEOLOGY
BY
TERENCE MILLER

WILTSHIRE, to the geologist, is pre-eminently the county of the English Chalk. But, although it is impossible to avoid the impression of great space on the Chalk uplands, in fact a good third of the county is occupied or underlain by pre-Chalk rocks. These Lower Cretaceous and Upper Jurassic strata form a kind of composite lower layer to a two-layered cake, of which the Chalk forms the upper part. The contrast between the rocks of the two layers underlies the contrast between the two strikingly distinct types of Wiltshire scenery.

The county has a conveniently rectangular shape, 30 miles broad and almost 50 miles long from N to S. Very roughly, the geological dividing-line runs up from Shaftesbury (in Dorset), through Warminster, then to the W of Devizes, and curves round to pass a mile or so S of Swindon. To the E and SE of this line is 'Chalk Wiltshire'; to the W and N the lower layer of the cake emerges from below the Chalk. However, the line is not continuous and unbroken, for there are two major easterly embayments – the Vale of Wardour in the SW corner of the rectangle, and the Vale of Pewsey near the centre. These two vales, cut down through the upper layer, allow the lower layer to be exposed in two tongues, bounded N and S by chalk ridges.

The Jurassic rocks of north-west Wiltshire are physiographically part of the dip-slope of the Cotswolds. They form an eastward-slanting upland along which runs the ancient Fosse Way down towards Lugbury. The rock – of the Great Oolite formation – much quarried about Corsham and Box, is one of the most famous building stones of England. John Aubrey, in his *Description of Wiltshire*, records the legend of its discovery by St Aldhelm, by whose name a variety is still known – St Aldhelm Box Stone. The Great Oolite slope, with its thin upper veneer of Cornbrash limestone, disappears eastwards below the much more easily eroded Oxford Clay. In this clay have been cut the two main valleys of west and north Wiltshire – the Bristol Avon, which runs through Chippenham, Melksham, and Bradford; and the Upper Thames or Isis, whose southern tributaries rise along the Vale of the White Horse, NE of Swindon. The watershed between these two river systems, one draining to the Bristol Channel and the other to the North Sea, is the low ridge between Charlton and Lydiard Millicent.

Next in stratigraphic order above the Oxford Clay comes another limestome formation, the Corallian. This has a rather patchy development in a curved line from Calne, along the Bremhill–Tockenham ridge, to Wootton Bassett and Highworth. The stone is less compact than the older Box freestone, and has not been quarried so extensively. Nevertheless it provides a local source, and is not unlike Cotswold stone in appearance.

E and S of the Corallian comes the last of the Jurassic clays, the Kimeridge, again forming a vale, although a narrower one than that of the Oxford Clay. This Kimeridgian vale is in many places continuous with the mid-Cretaceous Gault Clay which forms the low ground immediately in front of the main escarpment of the Chalk. The separation of limestone-based upland from clay-vale is well displayed in the western approach to the Vale of Pewsey, where the Corallian limestone forms a plateau, carrying the villages of Hinton, Keevil, and Steeple Ashton, above the heavy lower ground of Kimeridge Clay on the E towards Great Cheverell and Urchfont. A similar but 'inverse' relationship can be seen in the Vale of Wardour. Here the open W end of the valley is based on Kimeridge Clay, while in the E part between East Knoyle and Tisbury another group of limestones – the Portland and Purbeck divisions of the uppermost Jurassic – make a prominent ridge that falls away southwards to make the l. bank of the river Nadder. These rocks have been worked from very early times as Chilmark Stone, which was used in the C13 in the fabric of Salisbury Cathedral. Small isolated patches of the same limestones occur s of Devizes, between Potterne and Great Cheverell, and again in the s parts of Swindon, where they have been quarried.

Soon after the Jurassic rocks had been deposited they were gently folded, elevated, and slightly eroded. The next set of deposits produced sedimentary rocks of a rather different kind – the sandstones, instead of limestones, of the Lower Cretaceous, in two main subdivisions, the Lower and Upper Greensands, separated by a thin clay formation, the Gault.

The Lower Greensand, which is usually yellowish or buff-coloured (and occasionally, as at Seend, a deep brown ironstone), like the top Jurassic strata, occurs in isolated patches. Such a patch, NW of Devizes, makes the spur of hill that runs out from Roundway, on the Chalk, to Sandy Lane (suggestive name), on which may once have stood the Roman station of Verlucio, mentioned in the Antonine Itinerary. The Upper Greensand, a delicate pale greenish-grey colour, and often carrying concretions (called locally 'burrs'), has a much more extensive and continuous outcrop. It forms the bedrock of almost the whole of the Vale of Pewsey, from Devizes (where it has been quarried, at Potterne) to the s edge of Savernake Forest. In the Vale of Warminster the Upper Greensand forms a distinct step in the topography below the main Chalk slope around Maiden Bradley and towards Zeals and Penselwood.

The rest of Wiltshire, as we have seen, lies upon and is made of the Upper Cretaceous Chalk. This is the upper layer of our model layered cake – a mass of over a thousand feet of pure, soft, white limestone, constructed almost entirely of the accumulated remains of minute animals and primitive sea-plants between seventy and a hundred million years ago. The extreme porosity of the rock has enabled it to resist (or avoid) surface erosion, so that its outcrop-area forms an elevated table-land with only a few deep valleys. The thin limey soil, and the sandy deposits that occasionally lie spread on the Chalk surface, combine with their upland position to give Salisbury Plain and the Marlborough Downs their peculiar character and atmosphere. 2a

The Chalk itself is too soft to make a good building stone apart from minor interior work – with the exception of the lower part, close above the Upper Greensand, which has been worked a little as Chalk Stone. But in spite of this, the Chalk uplands, being open and well-drained, provided excellent camping places for the early inhabitants of the region, as has already been said.

In the extreme E and SE of Wiltshire thin remnants of post-Cretaceous (Eocene) strata lie upon the Chalk. These are soft, almost uncemented sands, and plastic clays. They occur in the low ground SE of Salisbury between the Avon and Test valleys; and in the SE part of Savernake Forest. Although these are now only small patches, it is clear that they once stretched farther w over the Chalk. Traces of this former extension are found in the spreads of grey sandstone 'boulders', originally irregular well-cemented patches within the Eocene sands, which now lie scattered over the Chalk – as around Salisbury itself, and again near Marlborough. These easily movable blocks of hard stone were used to construct the main parts of the great monuments of Avebury (where there are over six hundred of them) and Stonehenge, and in minor ways in buildings of all ages. They are known variously as 'greywethers' or 'sarsen stones'.

WILTSHIRE

*

ABLINGTON see FIGHELDEAN

ADAMS GRAVE see ALTON PRIORS

ALCOMBE see DITTERIDGE

ALDBOURNE

St MICHAEL. A large and interesting church which must be
presented chronologically. The original church was Norman
and had three-bay arcades. Of these one circular capital with
scallops remains on the N side – re-used – and the three S
arches also remain, with zigzag at r. angles to the wall surface
and billet. They were re-used in the C13, when the arcades were
rebuilt with double-chamfered pointed arches. At the same
time the N arcade was lengthened to the W by one bay. The
former W wall is still recognizable. Norman also are the S doorway, which has zigzag at r. angles like the S arches, and the
traces of a SW crossing pier appearing in the E respond of the S
arcade. The chancel is E.E. with lancets. The three widely
spaced lancets in the E wall are of 1867. The S chapel seems of
c.1300, see the continuous double-chamfered arches to N and
W and also, if one can trust them, the windows with Y-tracery
and the doorway. After that came the Perp additions. The W
tower is the most conspicuous, a splendid piece of big, not over-
ornate elements, ashlar-faced with a four-light W window with
niches l. and r., a tall tower arch, a projected vault inside, tall
transomed three-light bell-openings with Somerset tracery,
diagonal buttresses with attached buttress-shafts with pinnacles, panelled battlements, and incomplete pinnacles intended to be very large. Perp also the N chapel (a niche inside next
to the E window), most of the windows, the transepts with their
arches, the chancel arch, the embattled two-storeyed S porch,
the chapel E of this with battlements and panelled arches inside
to N and E, and the embattled clerestory. The tower was linked
up with the S arcade by a Perp arch. But the story here is more

complicated. The s arcade has five bays, the N arcade four. Why did they never tally? And why has the w bay of the s arcade an arch very similar to the w arch of the N arcade which linked up with the former w wall? The same cannot have been true on the s side. Was this a re-used arch, and when was it inserted? Good Perp roofs with moulded beams in nave, aisles, transepts, and chapels. – FONT. Octagonal, with lozenges on square panels, most probably of the 1660s. – PULPIT. A lavish Jacobean piece, said to come from Speen, Berkshire. – SCREEN to the s chapel; Perp. – PLATE. Paten, 1663; Flagon, 1678; Chalice and Paten Cover, 1684; Chalice, 1694. – CURIOSUM. Two Fire Engines of 1778. – MONUMENTS. Brasses to Richard Goddard and his wife who died in 1492, 25-in. figures (s aisle). – Brass to Henry Frekylton, chaplain, † 1508, c.12 in. (chancel w end). – Tomb-chest with shields in encircled quatrefoils. On it incised alabaster slab of John Stone, vicar, c. 1510. – William and Edward Walrond † 1614 and 1617. Both kneel frontally in arched niches. Much strapwork. – Richard Goddard. Very large. Six frontally kneeling figures. Much strapwork and flower decoration. No name, but Richard Goddard who died in 1615 is likely, as the monument is evidently by the same carver as the Walrond Monument.

The church dominates the GREEN. It lies above and along one of its sides. Plenty of pleasant cottages along the other sides. To the w of the church the SCHOOL, very Gothic, brick and stone, and indeed by *Butterfield*, 1857–8. He restored the church in 1868 (PF). To the NE of the church, yet higher up, COURT HOUSE, partly of the C16, with two mullioned windows with arched lights. In the Green the VILLAGE CROSS. Steps and shaft are complete. From the s side of the Green two streets lead s to the present village centre with its round pond. Here the other principal house of Aldbourne, an C18 brick house of nine bays. Doorway with Doric pilasters.

LEWISHAM CASTLE, s of Stock Lane. A motte and bailey, possibly the stronghold of the troops of Louis the Dauphin in 1215–17 (HR).

ROMANO-BRITISH SETTLEMENT. *See* Upper Upham.

1020

ALDERBURY

ST MARY. 1857–8 by *S. S. Teulon*. Flint, with a w tower embraced by the aisles and with transepts. Geometrical tracery. The bell-stage of the tower has four gables. Spire with broaches

between the gables. Inside, brick bands around the arches. –
PLATE. Elizabethan Cup and Paten Cover.

IVYCHURCH, $\frac{3}{4}$ m. N. Founded in the C12 for Augustinian
Canons. What remains *in situ* is a round pier and a W respond
to its W, both with many-scalloped round capitals of the late
C12. The arches were double-chamfered. A part of the W front
also stands, with an added buttress. The front was no doubt
that of the church. In addition the W side of the adjoining farmhouse has three double capitals, also Norman, and no doubt
from the cloister. More of these in the gardens. In the W front
of the house also smaller Norman fragments, two figures,
a pope frontal and a saint in demi-profile holding a book,
and a bigger Perp panel with three large quatrefoils and eight
small ones over. The cloister lay to the N of the church, which
had a S aisle only.

FOUNTAIN, on the A-road, N of the church. The fountain is
early C20, but incorporates several of the double shafts of the
cloister with their capitals, including a kind of merlon design.

ALDERBURY HOUSE, SW of the church. Said to be built of
materials from the campanile of Salisbury Cathedral, after
Wyatt had pulled it down in 1789. Of this nothing can be seen.
The house is just a quiet ashlar-faced late C18 building. Basement to the S and W with rocky rustication. To the N two canted
bay windows and a tripartite doorway. To the W also tripartite
windows under blank arches.

(GEORGE AND DRAGON INN. Inside, a Perp chimneypiece with
an ogee arch on the lintel and big roses in the spandrels. NBR)

THE CASTLE, Castle Lane. Possibly a motte and bailey (HR).

ST MARIE'S GRANGE, 1 m. NW, on the A-road. 1835, built by 61a
Pugin for himself after he had got married. He was only twenty-
three, and his house is a romantic dream come true, but made
to come true with highly reasonable means. It carries an inscription 'Laus Deo' and another 'Hanc domum cum capella
edificavit Augustus de Pugin, 1835'. Pugin left St Marie's
Grange in 1837, and soon after the house was enlarged. That
confuses the issue. The later and the earlier details are too
similar to distinguish between them by style. Pugin's house
was L-shaped, the enlargement made it oblong. The material
is red brick with diapers, Ms, crosses, etc. in blackish vitrified
headers. The house is not big, but it has three towers. The most
picturesque of them, the circular one at the SE angle, belongs
to the post-Pugin addition. The tall square tower at the NE
angle was Pugin's principal accent. It contained the entrance

and was connected with the road by a bridge. The entrance now is one storey lower. This present ground floor was at first service rooms. In the tower a spiral staircase ascends. To the W of the tower is the parlour, followed by the library. In the library is an original fireplace. Its main window is set in so as to allow for a view of Salisbury Cathedral. It has a turret towards the river. The windows are mullioned with lights with four-centred arches. The other arm of the L contained the chapel. Its doorway is now re-used in the addition at the landing of the new staircase. The chapel went through two storeys and had an open timber roof and a tall window of three lights. The embrasure is visible on the present second floor. On the second floor also Pugin's former bedroom. The fireplace has an A and a P. Off the bedroom is a garderobe in the turret mentioned above – a case of extreme medievalism. The original external appearance of the house is doubtful. What roofs had it for instance? Had the N tower a pyramid or a saddleback roof? Ferrey's illustration in his Life of Pugin cannot be trusted, but Mrs Stanton very kindly tells me that an unpublished Pugin drawing has the large tower ending square and the library turret with a pyramid roof. – STAINED GLASS. On the first floor some original Pugin glass, on the second floor some early C16 glass from Ivychurch.

In 1874, while digging out a ferret, a gamekeeper uncovered a SAXON BURIAL. It was the extended skeleton of a man accompanied by a sword, spearhead, and knife of iron and a shield boss ornamented with silver-headed rivets.

8080

ALDERTON

St GILES. A Neeld church, see Grittleton, p. 233. By J. Thompson, 1845. N tower with spire recessed behind battlements. Imitation Norman N doorway, imitation C13 S arcade. Sumptuous chancel E wall with two figures in niches. Old the tower S wall with the blocked doorway to the former rood-loft. – STAINED GLASS. Crucifixion of c.1845. – PLATE. Sweetmeat Dish, 1639; Chalice given in 1663. – MONUMENTS. Thomas Gore † 1532. Tomb-chest with shields in quatrefoils. No effigies. They were of brass. – Charles Gore † 1628. He kneels, small, and though he died aged six, he is dressed like a man.

SCHOOL. 1844–5. Heavily picturesque. With Italianate tower and wooden oriel windows. The doorway and one C13 three-light window come from the old church.

Also Neeld cottages, gabled, often with windows with basket

arches. But some houses are original, e.g. one of five bays with upright two-light windows, and the MANOR FARMHOUSE, with gables and mullioned windows. The VICARAGE, E of the church, is again a Neeld job, i.e. probably by *Thompson*.

ALL CANNINGS

oo6o

ALL SAINTS. A large church with a tall crossing tower. It followed on its site a Norman predecessor which was also cruciform; all that survives of it are two short semicircular responds, one with a trumpet-scallop capital, the other a decorated capital of the same type. They show that the Norman crossing was actually bigger than that of the C14. This has two continuous chamfers and seems not too late in the century. The tower, however, is Perp, and so is all else outside the church, except the N porch entrance, which must be early C14 (cf. Bishops Cannings), and of course the chancel, which is of 1867 and by *Weaver* (PF). Inside, the arcades (three bays) are E.E. Circular piers, octagonal abaci, tall double-chamfered arches. Of the Perp exterior features the only ones deserving special notice are the S chapel and S transept, which were specially embellished with decorated battlements and pinnacles and large windows. The chapel has the arms of Sir Richard Beauchamp, Lord St Amand, who died in 1508. But the most prominent thing inside is no doubt the High Victorian chancel, elaborately decorated in every respect, including detached shafts of pink granite and a wooden vault. It ought to be stone. The nave roof is the very opposite, a tie-beam roof with very thin members, and indeed dated 1638. – FONT. Octagonal, Perp, with quatrefoils enclosing shields and flowers. – FONT COVER. Of Jacobean type, simple, dated 1633. – STAINED GLASS. Small original bits in several windows. – Chancel glass by *Lavers & Barraud*. – MONUMENTS. William Ernele, 1581. Standing wall monument. Lush arms with stylized rose trails l. and r. Above initials and delightful knot-work. Curved gable with three eagles. An original and impressive piece. – Ernle family, probably *c.*1729. Doric pilasters and an open pediment. No figures; no foliage.

RYBURY CAMP, 1 m. NE of Allington, is a bivallate earthwork. It has not been excavated, but probably dates from the Iron Age.

ALL CANNINGS CROSS, $\frac{3}{4}$ m. ENE of Allington. An Iron Age A settlement site, part of which was excavated in 1911–22. Seventy-five pits were discovered, some serving as drying ovens, others lined with wattle and daub as storage pits. A very large quantity of small finds was made. Among ornaments may be mentioned swan's neck and ring-headed pins of iron and La Tène I bronze brooches. In addition to iron knives and gouges there were numerous bone and antler scoops, awls, and other tools. Large quantities of animal bones – ox, sheep, goat, and a few pig – were also found. The many complete or restorable vessels included haematite-coated wares.

0060   ALLINGTON

St John Baptist. 1851. Flint and rubble. Low s tower with pyramid roof. The tall nave looks hunchbacked by the side of the tower. Lower chancel. Old parts have been re-used in the new building, e.g. some of the Norman abacus of the chancel arch, a length of Norman zigzag at r. angles to the wall (nave N side), a lancet window (chancel N), the hood-mould of the E window. – plate. Cup, 1576.

(Barn, on the road to Chippenham, beyond Bulidge. The remnant of a house built for Sir Gilbert Prynne † 1627. On one side a blocked transomed window, on the opposite side a doorway. The knocker of the back door has the date 1612. Inside two fireplaces. *See* J. Badeni: *Wiltshire Forefathers*)

Rybury Camp, *see* All Cannings, p. 77.

All Cannings Cross, *see* All Cannings, p. 77.

1060   ALTON BARNES

St Mary. The church lies less than ¼ m. sw of Alton Priors. It is an Anglo-Saxon church, as is proved most emphatically by the enormous long-and-short quoin stones at the w end and also, once one has noticed them, by the tall, narrow proportions of the nave. The impost moulding of the chancel arch is also in all probability Anglo-Saxon. Evidence in the nave is obscured otherwise; for it is over-restored and externally rendered. The chancel moreover is rebuilt in brick. It is dated 1748. w window probably altered in the c17. Nice nave roof with tie-beams and wind-braces. – font. Big, c18, with baluster stem. – pulpit. A three-decker. – stained glass. One heraldic panel to W. Lamplugh † 1737. – plate. Chalice and Paten Cover, 1757.

Rectory. Built some time between 1728 and 1737. Vitrified brick and red brick. Two storeys, five bays. The first-floor windows segment-headed. Doorway with straight hood on very involuted brackets.

CHANDLER'S HOUSE, ¼ m. N. Early C18; five bays and two storeys; brick. Flat quoins, hipped roof. Doorway with pediment on brackets.

HONEY STREET WHARF, ½ m. SW. On the Kennet and Avon Canal. A minor, but the best, bit of canal scenery in Wiltshire. Weatherboarded buildings, one with a clock turret. A brick warehouse as well. On the clock-face the date 1854.

WHITE HORSE. 166 by 160 ft. Cut in 1812, a copy of the Cherhill White Horse.

KNAP HILL, 5 m. SSE of Windmill Hill, on a commanding eminence overlooking Pewsey Vale. A Neolithic causewayed camp of univallate construction, broken by a number of causeways. Much of the material of the bank has slipped down the hill, and the ditch is visible only as a shallow depression. The site was excavated in 1908 and again in 1961. Windmill Hill sherds were found in the primary ditch silting, with later Beaker fragments stratified above them. The paucity of finds in comparison with Windmill Hill suggests that Knap Hill was occupied for only a brief period of time. At the NE end of the camp is a ROMANO-BRITISH ENCLOSURE.

ALTON PRIORS

ALL SAINTS. Perp W tower with panelled arch towards the nave. Nave and low brick chancel. The nave is wide, because a s arcade was at some time taken out. This is proved by the position of the Norman chancel arch. The imposts with small pellet frieze. The arch is completely unmoulded. To its l. bits of an arch moulding with small saltire crosses. – STALL FRONTS. Jacobean, with tall blank arches. – COMMUNION RAIL. C18. – BOX PEWS. – PLATE. Chalice, 1577; Paten, 1638. – MONUMENTS. Big tomb-chest; plain. – Above it brass plate to William Button † 1590, provided by his grandson. Conceitism at its best. The deceased rises from his tomb, his naked body turned to the background where the gates of heaven have opened and the angel with the last trump appears. Below, to the l. and r. of the sarcophagus, others also rise. Plenty of inscriptions.

ADAMS GRAVE, I m. NNE. A chambered long barrow with prominent side ditches. Part of the burial chamber is exposed at the SE end. The barrow, which is of the classic wedge-shaped plan, is supported by a retaining wall of upright sarsens and oolitic dry stone walling (the latter feature now buried beneath the barrow material). Excavated in the C19, when skeletons and leaf-shaped arrowheads were found.

ALVEDISTON

St Mary. Mostly of 1866 (*T. H. Wyatt*). Only the tower seems older, and the windows of this, including the twin bell-openings with quatrefoils in plate tracery, look c17. In the nave on the s side one more c17-looking small window. The tassel-like brackets for the tower arch are the most convincing c17 evidence. – PLATE. Elizabethan Cup; c17 Paten. – MONUMENTS. Later c14 Knight, perhaps John Gawen (*see* Norrington Manor, p. 320). Angels at his head. Displayed in the s transept behind heating pipes. – Quite a number of sizeable tablets. Wadham Wyndham † 1668. Black columns and an open segmental pediment with arms. – Mrs Wadham Wyndham † 1704. Grey column and broken segmental pediment with urn; also four cherubs' heads. – Ann Wyndham † 1748. White columns and segmental pediment with urn. – John Wyndham † 1724. No columns, but urn at the top and fine Rococo cartouche at the foot. This monument is by *Rysbrack*, 1746. It was placed on behalf of John Wyndham's son Thomas, † 1745, whose monument in Salisbury Cathedral is also by Rysbrack. – Thomas King † 1787. By *Brown* of Sarum. Delicate shafts instead of columns. The other detail thin too.

Manor House, less than ¼ m. sw. Of brick, in a stone country. Five bays, two storeys. Doorway with shell-hood on carved brackets. Segment-headed window above. Nicely curved garden walls.

AMESBURY

St Mary and St Melor. An unusual dedication. Amesbury Abbey for Benedictine nuns was founded in 980 and re-founded as a priory of the Order of Fontevrault for men and women in 1177. At the time of the refoundation there were about thirty nuns, in the early c14 there were over a hundred, apart from a small number of chaplains and clerks. In the c13 and c14 the priory was much favoured by royal and noble ladies. The male religious are not heard of after the end of the c14. Of the domestic parts traces have been found on the site of the mansion, especially tiles. However, the mansion is so distant from the church that it must either have been a northern outlier, or the church must have been the parish church and not the priory church – which is improbable considering the dimensions of the building.

The church is of flint. The nave, cut short at some later date, is basically Norman, as is proved by the corbel table on the N side, two blocked clerestory windows on the S side, and also the NE respond, exposed in the solid later wall of what can only have been an aisle, though one is tempted to consider it the major exit from the church into the former cloister. But the noble appearance of the church, as we now see it, is essentially E.E. The crossing tower has three widely-spaced single bell-openings, the chancel long single lancets – interrupted by two early C14 windows of much larger size, one with cusped inter-sected tracery with a big pointed quatrefoil spread out at the top, the other with reticulated tracery. They are not in line. The E window is by *Butterfield* who restored the church in 1853 and is responsible for the strident colours of tiles inside against the E wall, now mercifully hidden by curtains. The transepts have three stepped lancets in the end walls and single lancets otherwise. Against the E sides of both, the outline of a chapel can be seen which stood against the chancel. The N transept has in addition a second, outer E chapel, and that has remained intact, except that the pretty late C13 twin window in the gable with its shaft, its leaf capital, its pointed-trefoiled light, and its quatrefoil above is said to be re-set. *Butterfield* provided, concealed from the eye of the passer-by, one of his most violent designs as a turret in the NE corner of the crossing. The heavy top ought to be studied in detail. The nave has a Perp S aisle and a W end by *Butterfield*. The windows on the N side high up above the cloister (or the former Norman N aisle) are also Perp. The jambs of a richly shafted early C13 doorway, just W of the NW corner of the truncated nave, is re-set. It is not known what it belonged to.

The interior bears out the evidence of the exterior. The cross-ing tower rests on triple-chamfered arches. Thin triple-shaft responds with moulded capitals. This looks a little later than the N transept. The entry into the demolished N chapel has been left standing. Its substantial moulded capitals and its hood-mould on stiff-leaf stops are early C13, as the exterior suggests. The same features at the entry to the outer N chapel. This is rib-vaulted inside. The ribs spring from slender angle-shafts. The two E capitals have stiff-leaf, the ribs fine triple-rolls. Double piscina with hood-mould on stiff-leaf stops. In the W wall of the N transept a small doorway to the former cloister. In the S transept no interior C13 features. In the chancel a small doorway with hood-mould on stiff-leaf stops and a tall, rather crude arch with openwork cusping, crocketed gable, and buttress-shafts. It must be of *c*.1300, and was most probably a substitute for an Easter Sepulchre. The S aisle is Early Perp, see the two-bay arcade with pier of the well-known section of four shafts and four hollows. Decorated capitals, arches of two hollow chamfers. The crossing pier in the SW corner, i.e. the corner of the aisle, is panelled just a little to link up in style S and W with the Perp work. Good roofs nearly everywhere. In the nave low pitch, tie-beams on arched braces, tracery in the spandrels and above the tie-beams,* in the transepts and aisle ceiled wagon roofs with many bosses.

FONT. Square, Norman, of Purbeck marble, with the familiar very shallow blank arches. – SCREEN. A stately piece of five-light divisions. The door is preserved. – SCULPTURE. In a showcase C9 cross-head of a wheel-cross (cf. Ramsbury). – Supporting a shelf in the chancel two angel corbels from a roof. – STAINED GLASS. Some C13 quarries and some C19 remains in a N window. – PLATE. Flagon given *c*.1677 and remodelled in 1853.

AMESBURY ABBEY. The house is the successor to the priory. The premises were granted to the Lord Protector Somerset and later his son the Earl of Hertford, who lived at Amesbury and died in 1621. Of this period are the two curious gatehouses to the E, on the Pewsey road, the nearer now called KENT HOUSE and enlarged by an C18 range, the farther called DIANA'S HOUSE. This is dated 1600 ('Diana her hous'), the other 1607. They are both irregularly triangular in shape and have a higher stair-turret. Both house and turret carry ogee caps. In the wall next to Diana's House arch with a strapwork cresting. Then, in 1661, *John Webb* built a house in the Inigo Jones style for the Duke of Somerset. It was a noble edifice of a kind yet very rare in England, purely classical, of nine bays, with a pedimented giant portico of two columns and two angle pillars rising above a rusticated ground floor. The first floor was rusticated too, and there was an attic storey above. The house had a hipped roof and a domed belvedere on it. This house was illustrated in *Vitruvius Britannicus* in 1725. In that year it went to the third Duke of Queensberry, who held it till 1778. *James Paine* added wings to the l. and r. of the façade.‡

About 1830 the then owner, Sir Edmund Antrobus, found that the house was in too bad a state to restore it, pulled it down,

* Good stone head corbels.
‡ I owe this information to Mr. John Harris.

and had a new one built on the old lines by *Thomas Hopper*. Hopper kept to the nine-bay front but made a portico of six instead of four columns. He made the ground floor of the portico a porte-cochère, kept the rustication extending over ground floor and first floor, but increased the height of the second and altered the roof completely. The heavy window surrounds on the top floor are also his. So are the giant attached porticos on

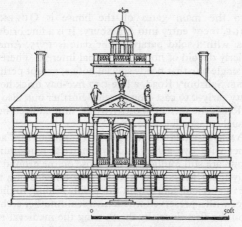

Amesbury Abbey, as originally built by
John Webb, 1661

the E and W sides with their heavy attics, and of course the big middle tower. Under this the stone staircase runs up to the 62 first floor. The proportions of the hall are dramatic, the forms monumental. Two tiers of arched galleries, and high up the light coming in through the tower windows. The ballroom has been divided up, but the big dining room remains, with a plaster ceiling again in Hopper's heavy forms, not in the simple geometrical circles, oblongs, or ovals of Jones and Webb, and the back stairs, with a wrought-iron balustrade.

The grounds were originally landscaped by *Charles Bridge-man*, but it is hard to see whether anything of his layout survives. In the grounds some buildings of the C18, namely the GROTTO half-way up the hillside across the river to the W of the house, the so-called CHINESE TEMPLE on a bridge across

the river, also to the W of the house, and the BALUSTER
BRIDGE to the N, which is dated 1777. The temple is by
Chambers and was built in 1772.* It is a square flint structure,
with circular windows and surrounded by a wooden veranda.
Also Georgian the GATEPIERS, next to Kent House, with
alternating rocky rustication and the higher GATEPIERS next
to the church. These have pairs of Tuscan columns and niches
between. The columns are nearly entirely kept in a kind of
sheaths.

Close to the main gates of the house is QUEENSBERRY
BRIDGE, the W entry into Amesbury. It is a fine bridge of five
arches, with a solid parapet. The date is 1775. Amesbury is
singularly devoid of houses of special interest. There is really
not a single one that needs special notice, except perhaps RED
HOUSE, Salisbury Road, a late-C17 five-bay brick house with
a pretty early-C19 cast-iron porch.‡ Further out, also in Salisbury Road, the former WORKHOUSE, flint and red brick with
the usual octagonal centre.

WEST AMESBURY HOUSE. A later C17 front of flint and stone
chequer with two gables and symmetrical fenestration. The
windows are still mullioned, but those on the ground floor are
already tall. (Behind this front are the remains of a medieval
house: an arched doorway in the W side leading to the screens
passage with a preserved wooden screen. Another arched doorway on the first floor. In the W wing the medieval roof with
arched braces and wind-braces. *Country Life*)

ANSTY

ST JAMES. A small church with transepts. The arches to chancel
and transepts look older than Perp, the transepts however are
Victorian (*see* Buckler's drawing). – FONT. Round, Norman,
with a band of something like stylized drops hanging down. –
STALLS. With symmetrical poppyheads of rich stylized leaves.
Said to come from Seth Ward's stalls of *c.*1670–5 at Salisbury
Cathedral.

Ansty had a Preceptory of Knights Hospitallers. It seems to have
been to the N of the church, and traces of it may survive in the
MANOR FARMHOUSE (base moulding on the W side). To the E

* But the Rev. Richard Woodyeare in a letter of 1750 writes: 'Ambrosbury
... Saw the Duke of Queensberry's: a Chinese House and Bridge', etc.
(*W.A. & N.H.M.*, x, 1867, p. 84).

‡ Next to it ANTROBUS HALL, a public hall, *c.*1924, by *Geoffrey Fildes*.

mullioned windows and one very big Venetian window. Inside, of the latter date, staircase with Chippendale fretwork balustrade.

Across the village pond another old building, probably the actual hospice of the preceptory. It has tall straight-headed windows with arched lights of the early C16 type, one of four lights and several of one light.

ASHCOMBE see TOLLARD ROYAL

ASHTON KEYNES

0090

The village of four crosses.

HOLY CROSS. The stately church stands away from the village, by the manor house. It possesses a Norman chancel arch with two orders of shafts, decorated capitals, and zigzag in the arch, also at r. angles to the wall plane.* A little later, say *c.* 1190, the E pair of arches of the N arcade, which have octagonal piers, capitals with single flat leaves, and double-chamfered arches. The W bays must have followed immediately. Circular piers, capitals with crocket-like leaves, circular abaci. Then, and now certainly in the C13, the S arcade followed, of four even bays with circular piers, moulded capitals, and circular abaci. Late C13 N chapel, see the lancet lights with pointed-trefoiled heads (E stepped, N flat-headed) and see the two arcade arches towards the chancel. Moulded capitals, double-chamfered arches, as before. Dec N aisle. One window has round-arched lights and a quatrefoiled circle over, a slightly perverse form. Dec S aisle and S and N porch entrances. Perp W tower with battlements and gargoyles, and Perp S doorway with leaves in the spandrels. In the end came *Butterfield*, who restored the church in 1876–7 and left his mark in the geometrical decoration of the E wall inside. But what is the date of the clerestory, with its alternatingly upright and diagonal quatrefoils in circles? Wagon roof with tie-beams. – FONT. Norman, of drum-shape. Big palmettes upside down below, zigzags above. – REREDOS. Perp, reset in the E wall of the N aisle. A triptych with three plinths for statues to the r. and l. under nodding ogee arches, in the middle in a cusped almond shape. – STAINED GLASS. Some in a S aisle

---

* The arch was widened and raised by *Butterfield* in 1877 (PF). In the N wall of the chancel, now inside the organ chamber and the vestry, are three shallow, i.e. early, buttresses. They could be Norman. Mr F. Longland drew my attention to them.

window. – PLATE. Chalice and Paten Cover, 1732. – MONU-
MENT. Mrs Charlotte Nicholas † 1800. By *Flaxman*. Long inscription, and above small relief of the dying woman surrounded
by her family. – CHURCHYARD CROSS. E of the church. With
complete shaft.

MANOR HOUSE, SW of the church, across a field. C17. Gateposts
on the road. Good group with the farm buildings.

The village is to the E, and we may profitably start looking at it
from the S end of the HIGH ROAD. The first house here is
ASHTON HOUSE, C18, stone, of five bays and two storeys with
an arched central window. In front a brook, which now accom-
panies us as we walk northwards. S of the White Hart Inn a
second CROSS, base, steps, and shaft. In GOSDITCH the CON-
GREGATIONAL CHAPEL, probably *c*.1800, with arched windows. Also the truly horrible Gothic SCHOOL of 1870. Further
N in the High Road a house with six curious medieval heads
under the eaves. Then the third CROSS, again base, steps, and
shaft. To the E towards FORE STREET, to the BETHESDA
CHAPEL of 1838 and the fourth CROSS, base, steps, and stump
of shaft. To the W across the street two-arch BRIDGE to a
delightful group of houses at the end of a lane which continues
as a footpath to the church: ASHTON MILL, BROOK HOUSE,
and others, most emphatically 'group value', as the MHLG
calls it.

At CHURCH FARM is a motte and bailey EARTHWORK (HR).

ASHTON VALLEY *see* CODFORD ST PETER

8060
ATWORTH

ST MICHAEL. Low Perp W tower, now detached to the N of a
church of 1832, designed by *H. E. Goodridge* of Bath. The
exterior has merits, the interior hardly. Crisply carved small
trefoil friezes, handsome E and W gables, or rather pediments,
though they are pierced by pinnacles, which makes one expect
internal aisles. But the interior is undivided. – WEST GALLERY
on iron columns.

(BARN, S of the church. Of cruck construction. NBR)

From the church to the A road one passes first POPLAR FARM-
HOUSE, early C18, with a symmetrical arrangement of mullioned windows, a later doorway with Tuscan columns and a
pediment, and a mansard roof behind a parapet – twelve tall
poplars in front of the front – and then the CONGREGATIONAL

CHAPEL of *c.*1790–2, with pointed windows and a hipped roof. Opposite, on the A road, the WHITE HART INN, a nice C18 house of three widely-spaced bays with a mansard roof. On the way to Cottles MANOR FARMHOUSE, early C18, of five bays with segment-headed windows, two very slim ones to the l. and r. of the doorway.

COTTLES itself is early C19 Gothick. Two canted bays and all the windows with four-centred heads. Doorway on thin grouped shafts. Inside, a splendid Elizabethan stone chimneypiece, much too big for the house. Caryatids l. and r., overmantel with coat-of-arms and l. and r. frontal faces in cartouches.

ROMAN VILLA. N of the village a Roman villa of winged corridor type. Excavation revealed four periods of construction. It was begun *c.*200, a corridor was added *c.*250, and *c.*300 the N side was reconstructed and baths added at the S end. The site appears to have been occupied for a further century, although the villa fell into decay and the bath suite was converted to farm purposes. Traces of mosaics were recovered, though most of the floors seem to have been of lime concrete.

AVEBURY

1070

The earthwork at Avebury is perhaps the most impressive pre-historic monument in Wiltshire, and in scale and conception ranks among the foremost works of prehistoric man in Europe. The site is less widely known than Stonehenge, and the visitor approaches it with fewer preconceived ideas of its appearance. As a result the initial impact is frequently greater than that of the better-known monument. Undoubtedly the outstanding feature of Avebury is its size. There are no vantage points from which it may be seen completely: the various features of bank, ditch, and circles have therefore to be studied as individual structures.* The feeling of unity and order which one gets at Stonehenge is absent at Avebury, and the broken nature of the site, divided into four quadrants by roads and houses, the large gaps in the circles of stones, and the rugged forms of the un-dressed sarsens suggest a work of nature rather than the hand of man.

The bank and ditch enclose an area of 28 acres. The crest of the bank originally rose 55 ft above the bottom of the ditch. The circle of bank and ditch is broken at four points by opposed entrances now utilized by modern roads. All four are probably

* The best view is probably that at the entrance from the Devizes road.

original, although the E causeway has not yet been proven by excavation. Immediately within the area enclosed by the ditch was a circle of approximately a hundred undressed sarsens, those flanking the entrances on the N and S being noticeably taller than the average. Towards the centre of the site lie two further stone circles. Near the centre of the N inner circle are two stones which, with a third destroyed stone, formed a three-sided enclosure called the Cove by William Stukeley, the C18 antiquary. In the C18 many of the stones were broken up to provide building material for the village, and Stukeley's observations and plans are invaluable for a picture of the site before this destruction. Although all surface indication of the destroyed stones has disappeared, the stone holes cut into the chalk survive, and the position of vanished stones is now marked by concrete obelisks. Moreover, many of the stones were simply buried, and these have since been re-erected in their original positions.

4b   From the S causeway of the earthwork, the AVENUE of approximately 100 pairs of standing stones runs for $1\frac{1}{2}$ m. to a second site on Overton Hill. Like the stones of the Avebury circles, those of the Avenue are undressed sarsens obtained from the Marlborough Downs, but here the builders appear to have preferred two distinctive shapes, one tall and pillar-like, the other broad and rectangular. Stones of the two types are arranged in opposed pairs in the Avenue and may represent male and female symbols. Dedicatory burials occurred at the bases of four stones, in two cases accompanied by bell beakers and in a third by a vessel allied to Rinyo-Clacton Secondary Neolithic ware.

At the SE end of the Avenue, on Overton Hill, is a second ceremonial site known as the SANCTUARY. It consists of two concentric stone circles and four post circles. Invisible on the ground, the site was excavated in 1930, when the plan of post and stone holes was recovered. The setting of posts and standing stones represents at least two and possibly three building periods, the posts probably supporting some form of roofed structure. The position of the posts and stones is now marked by low concrete pillars. Against one of the stones of the inner circle was a foundation burial of a bell beaker inhumation, and further sherds of Bell Beaker and Peterborough ware and fragments of Niedermendig lava, from the quarries near Eifel, were found in the post holes.

About 1 m. S of the earthwork, and immediately N of the Bath

road, lies SILBURY HILL. This enormous earthen mound is 4a
550 ft in diameter at the base, 100 ft across its flat top, and
125–30 ft high; it is surrounded by a ditch and covers an area of
approximately 5½ acres. In 1777, the Duke of Northumberland
employed Cornish miners to sink a shaft into it, without result,
and later investigations were equally unfruitful. It is presumed
to be of pre-Roman date, as the Roman road from Bath (Aquae
Sulis) to Mildenhall (Cunetio) was diverted to avoid it. A
human skeleton and a Viking* bridle bit were discovered on the
top in the C18, but the circumstances of the find are obscure.
Little is therefore known as to the builders or the date of the
site. Its resemblance on a gigantic scale to a round barrow and
its proximity to the Avebury group, however, suggest that it is
to be connected in some way with that other remarkable feat of
prehistoric engineering.

¾ m. SE of Silbury Hill is the WEST KENNETT LONG BARROW.
This is the finest example of a chambered long barrow in
Wiltshire. The site, which can be approached from a footpath
off the Bath–Marlborough road, is 340 ft long by 75 ft wide,
with the burial chambers at the broader E end. Entrance to the
chambers is gained by a passage leading from the slightly concave façade of upright (restored) sarsens. The passage, the two
lateral chambers, and the one terminal chamber are roofed with
enormous capstones, and the gaps between the upright sarsens
of the walls are filled with dry-stone walling. All the stones are
undressed, although areas of some appear to have been used for
grinding and polishing stone axes. The passage and terminal
chamber were excavated in the C19, but the lateral chambers
remained undiscovered until excavation by Professors Piggott
and Atkinson in 1955. On the floor of the burial chambers were
twenty skeletons, the majority disarticulated, associated with
Windmill Hill pottery which was also found in the body of the
mound and on the old land surface beneath the barrow. The
chambers and passage were later filled with soil and occupation
debris in which were found numerous Secondary Neolithic
sherds and artefacts, and also Beaker pottery including a
magnificent bell beaker.

1½ m. N of Avebury is the causewayed camp of WINDMILL
HILL, which gives its name to the earliest Neolithic culture in
Britain. It consists of three concentric ditches, the outer enclosing an area of 20 acres. The ditches are interrupted by numerous
causeways of unexcavated chalk, each ditch serving as a quarry

* Or more probably Saxon.

for material to build the bank which stood on its inner side. Most of the bank has been obliterated by ploughing, although a portion of it can be discerned within the outermost ditch on the N face. Excavations were begun in 1925 by the late Alexander Keiller, and since the war further work has been directed by Dr Isobel Smith. These excavations have shown the occupation of the site to be seasonal; herds were assembled there in the autumn for slaughter, as it was impossible to keep more than a fraction of the animals alive through the winter. In addition to large quantities of animal bones (mainly cattle with lesser deposits of sheep, goats, and pigs), antler combs, flint scrapers, and bone awls show that the hides were also prepared on the site.

Between the inner and the middle ditches are Bronze Age ROUND BARROWS, and further barrows lie on the slope SE of the camp.

More ROUND BARROWS 1 m. NE of Avebury, on South Farm and Overton Downs. Many are almost ploughed away, but there are a number of very fine bowl barrows on South Farm Down.

Finally, immediately N of the Beckhampton roundabout, two STANDING STONES close together,* and 1 m. SW of the roundabout, on the l. side of the Devizes road, more BARROWS. The group comprises a single unchambered long barrow and a number of bell and bowl barrows. Three of the barrows lie in a wood and are in good condition; the others are ploughed regularly and are fast disappearing. ¼ m. SW of this cemetery, on the opposite side of the road, are three very fine bowl BARROWS.

The PRESENT-DAY VILLAGE of Avebury lies inside the stone circle. It has no specially enjoyable buildings in the main street, but would anybody therefore wish it to disappear? The question sounds ridiculous, but it came up when it seemed likely for a while that the splendid thatched BARN, E of the church and the manor house, would be allowed to disappear, because saving it would mean the saving of an intrusion into the purity of the circle.

ST JAMES. The church forms a perfect group with the house. In addition, the church is archaeologically uncommonly interesting. The arcades inside are continued to the W in pieces of solid wall, and in this two Anglo-Saxon windows are preserved, one N, one S, both with slightly tapering sides. Then, in the C12, aisles were built. Proof of this are the S doorway with two orders

---

* A third stone was destroyed in the C18. A crouched inhumation with a bell beaker was found at the foot of one of the stones.

of colonnettes, and a keeled roll and a big zigzag in the arch,* and the W and E responds of the arcades. Of these only the angle-shafts remain, but their message is eloquent enough. The arcade itself, of two bays only, is now of tall Tuscan columns, a surprise, but not an unpleasant one. They were put in in 1812 by Mr *Button*, a builder of Calne (PF), to replace the Norman ones. The single-chamfered arches high up could be medieval but, if so, must be a little later than the responds. The small W lancet of the N aisle could belong to them. The circular clerestory windows, of which three are exposed on the N side, however, seem to be Norman too. Late C13 chancel, see the low, broad chancel arch and the bar tracery of the windows. The chancel was rebuilt in 1879. Perp W tower, ashlar-faced, with a stair-turret higher than the battlements, and with pinnacles. The S aisle front of flint and stone has an ashlar-faced upper part, also with battlements and pinnacles, and this no doubt belongs to the time of the tower. – FONT. Norman, of cylindrical shape. The bottom third has intersected arches. Above big scrolls and also two big serpents with twisted tails, their heads turned towards the figure of a saintly bishop holding a crozier. His pleated cassock is a typically Norman feature. – ROOD SCREEN. Perp. The lower parts heavily restored and the coving C20. But the parapet of the loft is original and a rare survival. One-light divisions with little trefoil arches carrying steep crocketed gables. Friezes of leaves and grapes below and above. – STALLS. With C17 parts. – TILES. A number at the E end of the N aisle, and some also at the E end of the S aisle. – PLATE. Paten, 1636. – MONUMENT. Susanna Holford † 1722. Good tablet in the chancel.

AVEBURY MANOR. Built on the site, or close to the site, of a small Benedictine cell founded in the early C12 and dissolved *c.*1414. Of this fragments have been found and are now in the house, e.g. a double capital of twin Norman colonnettes perhaps from the cloister. The house itself was built *c.*1557 and much enlarged *c.*1600. The oldest part is the E range. Its S part however belongs to the enlargements and forms a projecting wing to the new S front, a fine, not quite symmetrical piece, dated 1601. Large mullioned and transomed windows, with two transoms on the ground floor. The porch is a C20 addition, but its entrance is the original doorway. Fluted pilasters, round arch, and a strange tall, arched top gable. The porch leads into an

* Among the built-in architectural fragments in the porch are also Norman ones.

entrance passage, made about 1730 out of the original screens passage. To its r. is the hall, also converted c.1730. Pedimented doorways and a good fireplace. The hall was always only of ground-floor height. The drawing room in the projecting wing and the bedroom above it both have ceilings with thin plaster ribs in geometrical patterns. Both rooms also have good contemporary stone chimneypieces. Above the hall the former great chamber, with a coved ceiling with restrained plasterwork of c.1730. In 1907 etc. a large library was added. It was built with a number of C18 pieces brought in, e.g. the pedimented doorcase and the elaborate chimneypiece. – The house has a number of delightful enclosed GARDENS with topiary work, a number of fine GATEPIERS,* a circular DOVECOTE, and STABLES, rebuilt in the C20 with an open curly pediment over the door and a lantern.

From the churchyard a footpath leads across the OLD BRIDGE, only 7 ft wide and with one only of its four small arches preserved in stone, to TRUSLOE MANOR, a fine later C17 stone house with a big hipped roof. Two storeys, mullioned and transomed windows, and a porch with pilasters. Further on the lane called BRAY STREET. Here, on the N side, more or less opposite Trusloe Manor, BANNINGS, C18, of chequered brick, five bays wide, and at the end of the lane, on the same side, WESTBROOK FARMHOUSE, thatched, and with some mullioned windows.

AVONCLIFF
1 m. NW of Westwood

8050

Right down in the valley. The big, blank building with three ranges round a courtyard, and no redeeming feature save a heavy debased-Grecian doorway, is called the OLD COURT and was the WORKHOUSE. It is said, however, that it was built as a weaving establishment in the C17. How is one to understand that? The most likely thing is that they were weavers' cottages, built at one go, and even then they would be extremely interesting. At the back the CHAPEL, also early C19, and behind this the domed weavers' DRYING HOUSE, with a top chimney.

(The CROSS GUNS INN, C17, of three bays, with gabled dormers and mullioned windows, is picturesque. MHLG)

AQUEDUCT. Of the Kennet–Avon Canal, which was built by *John Rennie* shortly before 1804. Bath stone, Georgian in style.

* The pair on the Swindon road comes from Cumberwell House, between South Wraxall and Bradford, and dates from the early C18.

AXFORD

ST MICHAEL. 1856 by *William White*, at a cost of £425 (GR).
Low; nave and chancel in one; no bellcote. Brick and flint
bands. W and E lancets, the sashed side windows later. A comfortable interior.

PRIORY FARM, 1 m. E. Attached to the house, which lies immediately by the river Kennet, is a C14 CHAPEL, a plain oblong of
which some windows with Y-tracery, the priest's doorway, and
the cinquecusped ogee-headed piscina survive. To the W the
chapel must have been two-storeyed, see the one Perp upper
window.

BAPTON MANOR *see* STOCKTON

BARBURY CASTLE *see* OGBOURNE ST ANDREW

BARFORD ST MARTIN

ST MARTIN. E.E. chancel with paired lancets, and on the E side
a stepped group of three. Inside the paired lancets are framed
by tall and wide, thin single-chamfered blank arches. Then the
crossing. The piers start with heavy semi-octagonal responds,
perhaps E.E. too. But they continue with Perp mouldings and
a Perp tierceron-star vault with a big circle for the bell-ropes
and also with extremely slender corner shafts. The vault was
put in when the tower was completed. Perp also the straight-
headed N and S windows, on the N side placed curiously at
different levels. Perp finally the N transept N window. But the
W front is C17; see also the NW window on the N side. – PULPIT.
With early C16 linenfold panels re-used. – Chancel PANEL-
LING. Jacobean. – So is the ALTAR TABLE, made up, it seems,
of Jacobean pieces. – SCULPTURE. In the chancel a small stone
panel with a kneeling woman holding a basket of loaves (?). –
PLATE. Silver-gilt Chalice, 1611; Flagon, *c.*1658; Paten; Almsdish. – MONUMENTS. Brass plate to Alis Walker † 1584, kneeling, with many children. – Also a most interesting monument
to an unknown Elizabethan or Jacobean young woman. This
is in the chancel. Recess with four-centred arch. Tomb-chest
on which three shields in framed fields. Painted effigy of a young
woman in a transparent shroud. On the frame: Ego scio quoad
morti trades me. Constitua est domus omni viventi. Job 30.
Behind the cadaver:

O mortal man   Forsee thy fatall fall
How when or where thou knowest nothing at al
No sooner past the wofull mothers wombe
But subiect straiet unto the desert tombe
Like as you are I lived Latlye here
Lyke as I am you shortlye shall appeare
from earth I came and so to dust do yielde
All fleshe must fade as dothe the flowers in fylde
No stately   But death doth soone devoure
What then preveyles our pomp or puissant power
Lyke as we fall right so we ryse again
The just to Joye the rest to Endless payne
Use then the time so that when lyfe doth sease
Though corpses consume y^r souls may lyve in pease.

CROSS. Near the church the base and part of the shaft of the
village cross.

HURDCOTT HOUSE, 1 m. SW. Five-bay, two-and-a-half-storey
ashlar front of 1809. Closed-in Tuscan porch.

BATHAMPTON HOUSE see STEEPLE LANGFORD

BATTLESBURY CAMP see WARMINSTER

0030
BAVERSTOCK

ST EDITH. Small W tower. Dec chancel. Perp otherwise. –
Butterfield restored the church in 1883 and introduced in the
chancel his favourite geometrical patterns of tiles of many
colours. The floor is affected too. – SCREEN. Tall, wide open,
reaching up to the roof. This also must be *Butterfield*. – MONU-
MENT. John Henry Leech † 1900. A remarkable cartouche of
generously high relief and with a large cherub's head at the top,
remarkable as an example of early William and Mary Revival
in sculpture.

2070
BAYDON

ST NICHOLAS. Two-bay Norman S arcade of chalk. Square, only
slightly chamfered piers, round arches also only with a slight
chamfer. The imposts of the chancel arch are the same, the
arch was altered later. N arcade of three bays, E.E., with round
piers, moulded capitals, round abaci, and double-chamfered
arches. Bases with spurs. The N clerestory of single lancets
seems to be E.E. too.* The S clerestory is Perp, as is the W

* But if so, is much renewed. The N aisle was rebuilt in 1858 (PF).

tower, at least in its upper parts. The tower arch may be early
C14. – FONT. Circular, but at the top octagonal. Plain blank
arch-heads to effect the transition. Most probably late C13.

BAYDON HOUSE FARMHOUSE. The date-stone 1744 is not in
figures of that date, but may well represent the truth, see the
blue brick with red-brick trim and the segment-headed ground-
floor windows. Steep one-bay pediment over the centre.

BEANACRE
2 m. N of Melksham

9060

ST BARNABAS. 1886. – In the church plain Norman FONT from
Melksham.

OLD MANOR. A most interesting survival. L-shaped and consisting of an early C15 hall with its original roof, and the rest,
of the early C16, with windows with round-arched lights. Part
of the house is the chapel, which was originally detached. The
surround of its large SE window remains. Two doorways with
four-centred arches. The hall roof has collar-beams on arched
braces and two tiers of wind-braces. Next to it the solar roof,
at r. angles.

BEANACRE MANOR, S of the Old Manor. E-shaped, of c.1600.
Gabled, with a gabled two-storeyed porch, added a little later.
Two good chimneypieces inside, one very big for its position,
but restrained, with fluted columns and on lintel and entablature only geometrical motifs, including the revivalist motif of
intersected arches, the other brought in from a cottage at
Easton, with single animals and fruit in high relief, rather oddly
arranged. In the centre a cherub's head surrounded by a fat
wreath. The staircases are in two symmetrically placed projections at the back.

BECKHAMPTON see MILDENHALL

BEECHINGSTOKE

0050

ST STEPHEN. Nave and chancel; bellcote. The masonry perhaps
medieval; the detail not. Especially the W front is entirely
Victorian. Above the priest's doorway the date 1791. The Vic-
torian work is by S. B. Gabriel, 1860 (PF). – STAINED GLASS.
E window by Wailes, 1848; NW window by Powell, designed by
Holiday, 1871 (faded).

BEECHINGSTOKE MANOR. Thick thatch; yet an E front of brick
with two symmetrical bows and a doorway with a pretty cast-
iron porch, i.e. quite a townish design.

BEMERTON

ST ANDREW. Small, with tile-hung bell-turret. Nave and chancel in one. On the S side two small windows which may be genuinely Dec. The rest all over-restored. However, in the N wall a blocked Norman doorway. – SOUTH DOOR. Handsome, C17.

ST JOHN. 1860–1 by *T. H. Wyatt* for the Pembrokes of Wilton. Lavishly done. The church, seen from the N, looks indeed the sort of church one finds on its own in the parks of great mansions. Large, of stone, with N tower with twin two-light bell-openings with Geometrical tracery and a higher stair-turret with spirelet. Interior with a multitude of well carved naturalistic foliage capitals. Ornate E wall with five windows, those l. and r. in pairs with detached shafts in front. – REREDOS and handsome mosaic and gesso frieze below of medlar trees. This is probably of the time of *Ponting*'s restoration, i.e. of 1896. It was all designed and made by Miss *Nellie Warre*, daughter of the then rector. – STAINED GLASS. E and W windows from about the time when the church was built. In the N aisle one early *Kempe* window: 1878.

RECTORY, S of the church. George Herbert's rectory, which he repaired and in which he died. Original of the whole façade only one mullioned two-light window.

Along, or close to, the Nadder quite a number of Salisbury villas of *c*.1830–50, e.g. RIVERSFIELD, white brick, with a long veranda.

ROMAN ROAD. *See* Salisbury, p. 347.

BERWICK BASSETT

ST NICHOLAS. Small, with a recent S porch tower. Early C18 brick chancel. But is the C13 group of three closely-set stepped lancets an original re-used piece? According to *The Builder* 1857 nearly all the church is by *T. H. Wyatt* (PF). – FONT. E.E., octagonal, with trefoiled arches on colonnettes and sprays of stiff-leaf emanating to the l. and r. from each of the little capitals. – SCREEN. One-light divisions. The top with a frieze of foliage and a cresting. – BRASS. William Bayly † 1427, demi-figure of a priest.

OLD MANOR HOUSE. A picturesque and mysterious house. The main stone range seems C15. It has its arched doorway from the side of the church and the entrance to the porch opposite. But the doorway inside the porch has been taken to Vasterne

Manor, Wootton Bassett. The upper floor is timber-framed with pretty brick-nogging. Lengthening to the E.

NEW MANOR HOUSE, to the SE. The main part seems to be of the later C17, with symmetrical fenestration of mullioned windows.

BERWICK ST JAMES

0030

ST JAMES. Norman N doorway with one order of shafts carrying scallop capitals. The lintel has a regular all-over pattern of slanting lozenges. Tympanum with bands of green and white stone (cf. Stapleford). Arch with zigzag at r. angles to the tympanum. Blocked remains of a S doorway. E.E. chancel with lancets including 'low-side' lancets S and N. Why should they have the little ogee-headed recesses? In the E wall three stepped lancets. The chapels off the nave are both baffling. They have one wide arch each, round and single-chamfered to the S, pointed and single-chamfered with coarse nailhead decoration to the N. Are they both E.E. too? Next to the N arch a nice Perp doorway, probably to the upper floor of the N porch. The porch is attached to the chapel, and both have straight-headed Perp windows. The W tower has a date 1670, and the round-arched lights of the window confirm such a date. Good nave roof on big head-corbels. Low pitch and tie-beams. – PULPIT. Of stone; Perp. – COMMUNION RAIL. Jacobean or later. With tall, quite unusual baluster-shaped knobs on the posts.* – PLATE. Flagon by *Gabriel Sleath*, 1739.

N of the church two attractive houses, MANOR FARM, of brick with a front of chequer brick, and GODWINS, of stone, with mullioned windows.

YARNBURY CASTLE, 2 m. WSW of Winterbourne Stoke. One of the finest hill-forts in Wiltshire. Its situation on relatively low-lying country in an uncommanding position is in contrast to the majority of the forts in the county. The site was first occupied in Iron Age A times, when a single bank and ditch, roughly circular in plan with entrance on the W, was constructed. Excavation in 1932 proved the bank to have been revetted with upright timbers, and post holes of a possible gateway were also located. Leading from the entrance to the interior were two parallel rows of flint kerbing – apparently the remains of a roadway. From the lower ditch silting came many sherds of Iron Age A pottery. Later the site was enlarged by Iron Age B peoples, who added two further banks and ditches and an

* Cf. Durnford.

elaborate entrance outwork on the E, considerably increasing the size of the enclosed area. Finally this structure was encircled by a fourth rampart, which yielded Belgic (Iron Age C) pottery.

The ENCLOSURE consisting of a slight bank and ditch on the W side of the fort is probably of Roman date.

BERWICK ST JOHN

9020

ST JOHN BAPTIST. Everything over-restored in 1861 (by *Woodyer*), except the crossing tower, which is Perp. Three-light bell-openings with Somerset tracery. Decorated parapet and battlements; pinnacles. Of a former roof or ceiling several bosses and shields are preserved in the chancel. – PAINTING. Demi-figure of William of Wykeham. Assigned to *c*.1600. – STAINED GLASS. Uncommonly good glass of *c*.1862 in the W, E, and S transept windows. – PLATE. Flagon, 1754–5. – MONUMENTS. Two cross-legged Knights, one of the late C13, the other early C14. The earlier has his head on a pillow placed squarely, the later diagonally. The earlier lies under a Dec canopy with nobbly leaf crockets, the later in a plain recess.

FERNE HOUSE, 1 m. W. Built, according to Colt Hoare, in 1811. But the stately present house must be later. It has rainwater heads dated 1903. To the W a lower wing which seems Georgian. The house itself looks *c*.1850, classical with balustrade and a big porte-cochère. (In the dining room linenfold panelling.)

WINKLEBURY CAMP, ¼ m. SE. A univallate Iron Age hill-fort. Within the fort were a number of disused storage pits filled with occupation debris. An unfinished Belgic earthwork was begun, to encircle the earlier site.

BERWICK ST LEONARD

030

ST LEONARD. Blocked Norman S doorway. Lintel with rosettes. The church was rebuilt in 1860. Nave and chancel only. – PLATE. Chalice, Paten Cover, and two Flagons, 1674. – MONUMENT. George Howe † 1647. Large tablet. In a circular recess relief demi-figures of husband and wife, one hand of each on a skull. In oval recesses below demi-figures of three children. At the top an open segmental pediment.

BERWICK HOUSE. Late Georgian. Blue vitrified brick with red-brick trim, five bays, two and a half storeys. Porch with Tuscan columns and a pediment. Bow window on the W side.

BEWLEY COURT *see* BOWDEN HILL

BIDDESDEN HOUSE

1½ m. E. of Ludgershall

Built in 1711–12 for General Webb, whose equestrian portrait by 49a *John Wootton* hangs in the entrance hall. It is a very remarkable house, even from the point of view of English, not of Wiltshire architecture. It belongs to the Vanbrugh–Hawksmoor–Archer group and can hold its own in it. Its architect is unknown. The house is of brick, chequered in red and dark blue. It is of seven bays by seven bays with a bold projection of the centre on the entrance (S) side. It has two storeys and a half-storey above the cornice. The windows are all round-arched below, segment-headed above, the cornice. On the W and E sides the aqueduct rhythm of three closely-set arched windows is particularly impressive. The centre of the S side is a high entrance hall, and so above the ground-floor arches there are here round windows. This centre is also made more prominent by a big, somewhat heavy segmental pediment. Trophies l. and r., arms at the top. The only element which breaks the symmetry of the façades is the most remarkable of all – a castellated round turret at the NE corner, built, it is said, to house a bell brought home from Lille by the general. One is at once reminded of Vanbrugh Castle, but Biddesden is just a little older. So one has to go back to Hugh May's castellated work at Windsor and the castellated brick work of the Wren office at St James's Palace and the summer house at Hampton Court. On the same E front blank windows painted recently with Regency people behind glazing bars. They are by *Roland Pym*, 1935.* The rooms inside are mostly altered, but the entrance hall remains, and the staircase with three twisted balusters to the step – two clockwise, one anti-clockwise – and carved tread-ends.‡

In the grounds a recent TEMPLE to the NE, and a recent GAZEBO (by *George Kennedy*) to the W, which has mosaics by *Boris Anrep* inside. In the walled garden a lead STATUE by *Stephen Tomlin*.

BIDDESTONE

8070

ST NICHOLAS. Norman S doorway with one order of colonnettes with one scallop and one similar capital. Plain arch. Tympanum

---

* A *trompe-l'œil* window on the W side by *Dora Carrington*, 1932.

‡ In the dining room a large carpet designed by *Marion Dorn*.

with cross in a beaded circle. Also two Norman windows in the chancel. Dec another chancel window and the chancel arch. Also Dec, or say of *c.*1320, the s porch and the w window with its intersected tracery. But the only really remarkable feature of the church is the bell-turret on the ridge of the nave by its E end, C13 work and very similar to Leigh Delamere: a square set lozenge-wise with corbels carrying nook-shafted posts. The arches seem lost, but the spire is there. – FONT. Norman, circular, with just one big band of flat zigzag. At the four corners of the foot defaced heads. – BOX PEWS and WEST GALLERY. Late Georgian. – PLATE. Chalice and Cover, 1577; small flat Cup, 1672; Paten, 1705. – MONUMENT. William Mountjoy † 1731. Simple tablet signed by *M. Sidnell.*

ST PETER. Pulled down. Part of the tower in the grounds of Castle Combe Manor (p. 145).

A very handsome GREEN with a pond. Several grey houses with mullioned windows, especially POOL FARMHOUSE on the s side with a GAZEBO on the garden wall. On the N side WILLOW HOUSE, Early Georgian, of five bays and two and a half storeys, with even quoins and segment-headed windows. The centre window round-arched, and on top of the centre a miniature pediment. Doorway with open pediment. At the E end of the Green a three-bay house of the early C18 with mullioned windows, but a doorway with a shell-hood on volutes. Further E still the MANOR HOUSE, a flat C17 front with three gables and symmetrically set mullioned windows. On the garden wall a GAZEBO of brick, with a canted front to the road. BARN and outbuildings at r. angles to the front.

BINCKNOLL CASTLE *see* BROAD TOWN

BISHOPS CANNINGS

ST MARY. That the church is of such uncommon size and nobility is not, as at Potterne, due to its having been collegiate. It was a parish church, but on a bishop's, the bishop of Salisbury's, estate. The church is cruciform and E.E. almost entirely, not as pure as Potterne, but more lively. The spire on the crossing tower and the excessively high stair-turret are a C15 addition. Otherwise here are the E.E. features: the two lower stages of the tower, the first with simply chamfered lancets, the tall second, i.e. the bell-openings, with elaborately moulded lancets. Trefoil frieze and corbel table, and then the Perp addition.

The nave and chancel roof were much higher than they are now, as one can see from the marks against the tower. The aisle and clerestory windows all Perp. The transept fronts with five stepped groups of moulded lancets and small doorways asymmetrically below (that on the N side blocked). To the E single lancets, except for the S E bay, which has a one-bay chapel attached to it. The E wall of this has again a group of stepped lancets, but a smaller one. To the S one window with Y-tracery. The chancel is considerably lower than the rest, which is a pity. Its S windows have Y-tracery, those to the N are single lancets, almost overdone in the internal mouldings. The E window is again a group of stepped lancets, but much simpler in the mouldings; evidently somewhat later than the W parts. Attached to the chancel on the N side is a two-storeyed vestry. Lancets on the lower floor. The nave ends to the W again in a group of three stepped lancets. It is worth comparing the mouldings of all these lancets. It has already been said that those of the chancel E window are the plainest and latest. The N and S transepts, upper tower, and vestry E window all have external multiplied rolls, as have the chancel side windows internally. Only the nave W window is again plainer.

But two features have so far not been mentioned, because they break the continuity of the rest. The N aisle W window is a small Norman window; so we must be prepared for Norman work. The S doorway is indeed not far from Norman. It has a single-stepped round arch, though also shafts with stiff-leaf. Perhaps the window too is still possible towards the end of the C 12. We shall have to see about that. Meanwhile the S porch has a fine quadripartite rib-vault with a stiff-leaf boss and an entrance which was renewed in the early C 14. Triple shafts, ballflower decoration, and a crocketed gable.

On entering it becomes at once patent that this is indeed a Late Norman church developing into E.E. Four bays, round piers, square abaci, single-stepped arches. The capitals are mostly of the trumpet-scallop variety, but one and the neighbouring S E respond are definitely developing towards stiff-leaf and leaf crocket types, and the arcade arches are pointed. The church at that time already had a clerestory, as the marks above the spandrels, not the apexes of the arches, show. The W window is shafted inside, as are the transept S and N windows and the chancel E window. We must move into the transepts now. Their E walls are a puzzling sight. They consist of two splendid arches, deeply and elaborately moulded with capitals in which vestiges of trumpet-scallops can easily be overlooked because of the displays of stiff-leaf, but the arches, two in the N, two in the S transept, are blank, except for the one outer S chapel whose exterior has already been described. In the other cases there is no more than a lancet under the arch. The blank S arch is narrower than the S chapel, and no chapel could have been built to extend it E; for the clasping buttress of the tower would have interfered. The N arches are of even width. The W arches, i.e. those from the aisles to the transepts, are of the same kind and similar details. What is one to assume? Looking at the walls above the E arches, one can clearly see a disturbance. To be in line with the crossing arches, the wall had to be set back. There must have been a change of plan here, i.e. the crossing must be later than nave, aisles, and transepts. The crossing arches have sturdy octagonal responds and triple-chamfered arches. The lierne-vault is of course a Perp addition. The details in the S chapel are the same as those in the S transept. The piscina in the S transept should not be overlooked either: it has a cusped trefoiled head, and the hood-mould has cusps too.

Entering the chancel now, we can see, though not approve of, the reason why it was kept low. It is vaulted, and the mason (or patron) did not want to take the risk of higher walls. Three bays, quadripartite rib-vaults, the mouldings with three fine rolls. The transverse arch between bays one and two is of the same details, that in front of the altar is enriched by a number of mouldings. The capitals are moulded too; no stiff-leaf here, except for the two in the E corners. The arch from the crossing into the chancel deserves notice. It is an odd compromise between the needs of the vaulted chancel and the wish to preserve just one capital (three scallops) of a respond of the Norman crossing. One must assume that that capital went with a crossing smaller than the present one and still extant when the transept E wall was built. The double-chamfered, pointed arch of course must be a rebuilding link with the W arch of the chancel. In the chancel an E.E. pillar piscina. Trefoiled hood on head corbels. One can see that the trefoiled arches were continued to the W as sedilia arches. These sedilia are gone, and gone also is a former trefoil-headed priest's doorway. Instead new sedilia were put in in the C14, and they are also damaged. To the N of the chancel the vestry, with a plainly vaulted ground floor. Single-chamfered ribs on corbels.

PENITENTIAL SEAT. A great oddity. On the back wall a gargantuan hand is painted, and a large number of inscriptions refer to sin and death, e.g. on the thumb: Nescis quātū; Nescis quoties; deum offendisti. Also (fourth finger): Nescis quo devenies; Nescis qualiter morieris; Nescis ubi morieris; Hora mortis incerta est. And (fifth finger): Cito oblitus eris a charis; Status tuus est miser; etc. It all seems to be C17 work. – ORGAN. Presented in 1809; Gothick. – POOR BOX. Plain; handsome. – PAINTING. The much renewed large scrolls in the chancel vault look C17. – STAINED GLASS. E window 1860 by *Wailes*. – PLATE. Chalice, 1660; Paten, 1712. – MONUMENTS. John Ernele † 1571. A good, characteristically Early Elizabethan piece; i.e. no figures, not much ornament, but very fleshy foliage round the central coat of arms. This is at the top under a curved cornice. Below, the back wall has the inscription set in strapwork, and the tomb-chest has three shields also set in strapwork. – A HELM near by.

In the village little to note, perhaps really only the two thickly thatched, timber-framed COTTAGES, 1 m. SE of the church. The windows project as little oriels, each on one bracket.

KITCHEN BARROW, 2 m. ENE. Long barrow on a spur overlooking the Kennet valley. The side ditches curve slightly inwards at the NE end. A large sarsen projects from the mound at this end and probably forms part of a buried chamber. The site has not been excavated.

BISHOP'S FONTHILL   9030

ALL SAINTS. A complete little E.E. church with a crossing tower, though over-restored (*T. H. Wyatt*, 1879) and with a rebuilt chancel. The tower stands on triple-chamfered arches and has single-light chamfered bell-openings. The capitals of the responds are of different kinds. Several had foliage and one is preserved with enough to show a delightful display of deeply undercut trails and stiff-leaf. The tower must have been, or have been meant to be, vaulted – see the springers of single-chamfered ribs standing on good moulded capitals. In the S transept an altar recess with a single hollow chamfer. – PEWS. Two Jacobean pews remain.

BISHOPSTONE   2080
2½ m. ENE of Wanborough

ST MARY. In the chancel an extremely ornate, small, re-set Norman doorway. Two orders of colonnettes. In the arch zigzag, also at r. angles to the wall surface. The N porch entrance, simple but dignified, of *c*.1200, must also be re-set. Steep, un-moulded arch on the simplest imposts. The s aisle E window *See* p. 577 with its reticulated tracery is the only sign of the Dec style. The rest is Perp, i.e. all other windows, the low W tower, and especially the pretty quatrefoiled and pierced s aisle parapet and the arcades inside of a typical profile, the same as at High-worth. Projections without capitals to the nave and aisles, shafts with capitals to the arch openings. The N arcade is shorter to the W than the s arcade, because the N porch is attached to its W end. – FONT. Norman, of basin shape, with little decoration. – SCULPTURE. Small Norman bits in the s doorway. – STAINED GLASS. Assembled bits in the s aisle E window, some of it C14 like the window. – PLATE. Chalice and Paten Cover, inscribed 1627; Flagon, 1634; Paten, 1719; Alms-bowl, 1761. – MONUMENT. Edetha Willoughby † 1670. Good big tablet.

0020

BISHOPSTONE

4½ m. SW of Salisbury

ST JOHN BAPTIST. A big church and mostly Dec. Cruciform, with a crossing tower and without aisles. In the crossing alone evidence of an earlier date. The arch towards the s transept is lower than the others and, above it, a Norman arch and a win-dow with a Norman head now looking into the crossing. For the rest it is all of a piece, and we can start at the W end. The W window has three stepped lancet lights with pointed trefoils in the head, the side windows have arches upon arches (cf. e.g. Wells, Lady Chapel, also Edington*). The s and N doorways are Dec in their mouldings too. Only the two-storeyed porch is Perp. On the upper floor two small windows and a niche between. The window to its E and that opposite are also a Perp alteration. Transepts and chancel with tall two-light windows with very simple flowing tracery (the top part of a fleur-de-lis). s transept with parapet with pretty quatrefoil decoration. s win-dow of three lights with reticulated tracery and an ogee sur-round which carries as its finial a window in the form of a spherical triangle, cusped. Below the s window the strangest of additions: two vaulted bays open to W, s, and E, with heavy buttresses, and inside low tomb-chest with ballflower decora-tion – perhaps the MONUMENT to the patron who built this part of the church. The arch mouldings again Dec, the vaults

---

* Bishopstone is so called because it was a living of the bishops of Winchester, and Edington was of course rebuilt by a bishop of Winchester.

quadripartite. In the N transept nothing of this kind, but, as we shall see, an uncommonly large monument inside. The chancel is the same as the S transept, except that the parapet is decorated with plainer quatrefoils. Priest's doorway under a deep hood with an ogee gable. Vault inside, with ridge-ribs and a boss. Also a niche in the W wall. Chancel E window of four lights, just duplicating the tracery motif of the two-light windows. Again a spherical triangle interpreted as a gable finial. In the reveals of the window inside two niches. The N corner of the E wall contains a stair-turret. Small N vestry; turret and vestry just with small pointed-trefoiled windows. Perp crossing tower, embattled.

The sumptuousness of the E parts of the exterior is exceeded in the interior. Both S transept and chancel are rib-vaulted. Tierceron stars in two bays with bosses. They are decorated with leaf except for some in the chancel, where there are a Coronation of the Virgin and the Signs of the Evangelists. The vaults rest on shafts with excellent heads as brackets below. In the chancel between the two bays there are crouching little figures instead of heads, decidedly reminiscent of Edington. Extremely ornate sedilia with three little vaults with bosses. The seats are separated by coarse tracery. Gables with crockets and finials. Pinnacles behind and above them. To the l. and r. of the altar niches, niches also in the N transept E wall and (over-restored) the S transept E wall. Vaulted chancel piscina, piscina with ballflower in the N transept, piscina with a rich canopy (all but Victorian – *see* below) in the S transept. Nave roof with moulded beams.

FURNISHINGS. FONT. Octagonal, Perp, all re-tooled. With St Andrew's crosses, cusped. – WOODWORK. Much assembled from Britain and abroad. Panels with Perp tracery from chest fronts, panels with saints from bench ends, Early Renaissance panels of domestic origin, Baroque bits and pieces, etc. – STAINED GLASS. Original fragments in the vestry windows. – The glass in the S transept S window, which is certainly nothing at all special, was designed by *Pugin* and made by *Wailes*. – PLATE. Set made at Cologne and presented in 1663. – MONU-MENTS. In the N transept, taking up the whole width of the N wall, a tomb recess with a wide depressed round arch cusped and subcusped and much ballflower. Under the arch and in front of the monument coffin-lids with incised crosses. – An unknown Divine (N transept), *c.*1630, frontal demi-figure between pilasters. – The Rev. George Augustus Montgomery

† 1842. By *Pugin*, 1844.* A super-Gothic tomb-chest and canopy fitting the position in the s transept s wall extremely well. Above it the Pugin window, to its l. the piscina canopy, which might well be Pugin's too.

BISHOPSTONE HOUSE. Built in 1820. Commodious square house of grey brick, five by three bays.

THROOPE FARMHOUSE, ¼ m. SE. The original house Georgian, of five bays and two storeys. Doorway with pediment. Much recent enlargement.

FAULSTONE HOUSE, ⅞ m. WSW. Probably late C17. Mullioned windows, hipped roof. DOVECOTE, quite possibly pre-Reformation, round, with bands of flint and stone and a conical roof.

NETTON FARMHOUSE, I m. WSW; NW of the above. 1637. Flint and stone chequer. Three bays, mullioned windows.

CROUCHESTON METHODIST CHAPEL, 1¼ m. SW. Brick, in chequer of red and dark blue. Arched windows and doorway. The front has a pediment. Probably late C18.

8040   BISHOPSTROW

ST ALDHELM. C14 W tower with recessed spire. Odd narrow, tall, two-light bell-openings, straight-headed. Nave rebuilt in 1840, but radically victorianized by *W. Scott Champion*, 1876–7 (PF), who also rebuilt the chancel. – LECTERN. With a twisted stem on four lions' heads and paws. Openwork desk. Probably C19. – STAINED GLASS. E window by *Hughes*, 1879, terrible. – NE window by *Kempe*, c.1892. – PLATE. Two Chalices and Patens, 1797.

BISHOPSTROW HOUSE, ⅜ m. N. 1817 by *John Pinch* of Bath (K. Rogers), with a wide bow in the centre of the façade. On the other side porch with unfluted Ionic columns *in antis*. In the garden a round TEMPLE of 1770 (K. Rogers), a summer house, etc.

In the grounds to the E of the house a MOTTE AND BAILEY known as THE BURY (HR).

0060   BLACKLAND
                           1¼ m. SE of Calne

ST PETER. Small, with a bell-turret. Modest Dec E window. On the s side of the chancel one lancet. – STAINED GLASS. E window by *Kempe & Tower* (date of death 1906).

---

* The accurate date was kindly communicated to me by Mrs Stanton. He received £52 for it.

BLACKLAND PARK. Later Georgian mansion of five bays and
three storeys, ashlar-faced. The centre has a Venetian window,
a tripartite lunette window over, and a pediment. In the centre
of the garden front a porch on Tuscan columns. The GROTTO
belonging to the house has alas collapsed.

BLUNSDON ST ANDREW

1080

ST ANDREW. Mostly by *Butterfield*, 1868, see especially the odd
W front. Bellcote with spirelet, just one big buttress to the r.,
then the aisle W window – an elongated sexfoil – and round the
corner a tall chimney. Original plain early C13 N doorway. Inside a re-used plain doorway of c.1200, now a niche in the W
front. Original, low C13 three-bay arcade. Round piers, round
abaci, double-chamfered arches. The responds probably not
original. – STAINED GLASS. A N window by *Kempe*, c.1896. –
E window and S aisle E window by *Lavers & Barraud* to *Butterfield's* design. – PLATE. Set inscribed 1815.
BLUNSDON ABBEY. Built about 1860 by a Swindon man. Gothic
and many-gabled. The house is now a dramatic ruin towering
above a sea of caravans.
CASTLE HILL, ¼ m. NE of Broad Blunsdon church. Univallate
Iron Age hill-fort with a second bank and ditch on the S.

BOLEHYDE *see* BULIDGE, HARDENHUISH

BONHAM

7030

½ m. SW of Stourton

MANOR HOUSE. On the ground floor an Elizabethan plaster
ceiling. Attached to the house the former CHAPEL OF ST
BENEDICT (R.C.). The W doorway and the one small lancet
on the N side are medieval. Bell-lantern on the roof.

BOREHAM *see* WARMINSTER, p. 494

BOSCOMBE

2030

ST ANDREW. Flint and rubble. Nave and chancel and shingled
bell-turret with pyramid roof. Big N chapel added probably in
the C17. Five-light N window with transom. The chancel N and
S windows of the same time or a little earlier. Single-framed
roofs with tie-beams. Between nave and chancel a plaster tympanum. – PULPIT. A three-decker, with tester, dated 1633. –

The pulpit goes with the FAMILY PEW and the BOX PEWS, and also the solid wooden boarding instead of a transept SCREEN. – STAINED GLASS. Small C15 bits in the W and E windows. – PLATE. Chalice, Paten, and Flagon, 1708.

IRON AGE SETTLEMENT, ½ m. ESE. Extensive Iron Age settlement, excavated in 1950; five pits containing Iron Age A pottery and a single Belgic sherd.

BOWDEN HILL

ST ANNE. 1856, by *Gabriel* of Bristol. NE tower with a German Romanesque roof. Norman details. The nave and chancel however imitation E.E. – MONUMENTS. Medievalizing brass plates to John N. Gladstone † 1863 and his wife † 1862.

Opposite the church the CONDUIT HOUSE built by Sir William Sharington for the Lacock Abbey water supply. A small oblong with steeply pitched roof. Plain classical (later) doorway, and above it a medallion with foliage decoration.

BEWLEY COURT, ¾ m. NW. An uncommonly interesting medieval house. Work of the C14 preserved in the fireplace corbelled out of the E front, the timber-framed W wall of the hall, and the hall roof with wind-braces and with carved circles. The hall faces N. The S side and the SE parts are of the C15. The porch adjoins the projection of the E wing and runs flush with it. The odd thing is that the porch does not lead straight into the hall, because the C15 placed a 6-ft layer of minor rooms in front of the S side of the C14 hall. To the W of the hall the former parlour and guest chamber with a C14 timber-framed W wall. The N end of the E wing is later C17 work.

BOWDEN PARK. Built for Barnard Dickinson of Bristol, heir to Jamaican riches. By *James Wyatt*, completed in 1796 and an exceptionally perfect example of its date. Ashlar-faced S front with a bow against which stand four giant unfluted Ionic columns. To the l. and r. one tripartite window with a blank segmental arch over. Above these, crisply carved symmetrical foliage panels. The S side of the house was continued to the E by an orangery, which was replaced about 1850 by a wing entirely in keeping with the reticence of the Georgian work. To the N there were further Victorian additions, and these have been pulled down in the 1950s and replaced by more work in keeping with Wyatt (*Kenneth J. R. Peacock* of *Louis de Soissons & Partners*). Inside, an oval room behind the bow. In it statues of *Coade* stone dated 1796. Behind the hall the staircase, with a discreet iron handrail. To the l. of these two principal rooms and to the r. two. The decoration is exquisite throughout, and very sparing. The most it goes to is oval relief panels on walls. The fireplaces also have no caryatids, just small reliefs or not even these. On the first floor above the oval a smaller circular room. In the grounds to the SE a GROTTO, very rocky outside. The WEST LODGES are classical, the EAST LODGES castellated. The latter were in existence in 1806 (Buckler drawing).

Opposite the latter the GATEHOUSE to Spye Park, an excellent early C16 piece with an oriel to each side. Arms of Henry VIII. The gatehouse comes from Bramham House, the mansion built by Edward Baynton and burnt in the Civil War.

SPYE PARK. 1865–8 by *William Burn*. (The stables may be of the late C17.)

BOWER CHALKE

HOLY TRINITY. The only features which seem pre-Perp are the arches into the two transepts, single-chamfered with continuous mouldings, and the nave with windows of one and two lights which look *c.*1300. The N porch tower is Perp (top rebuilt recently), and the transept windows are Late Perp. *T. H. Wyatt* added the S aisle and rebuilt the chancel.

BINGHAM'S FARMHOUSE, ½ m. NE. C17. Symmetrical three-bay front of stone.

Other attractive houses.

BOWOOD

The house is no longer what it was; but the grounds of 1,000 acres are more beautiful than ever. The history of the HOUSE starts with a house of moderate size built by Sir Orlando Bridgeman about 1625. This was bought in 1754 by the first Earl of Shelburne, who employed *Henry Keene* to alter and enlarge it and add extensive stables round two courts to the NW. Only their E range was from the start for domestic use. It has always been known as The Little House. Keene also worked for the earl at High Wycombe. Then the earl died, and his son, in 1760, called in *Robert Adam*. Adam gave the C17 house its S portico and, in 1768–70, connected the house by a new dining room with Keene's much larger block and closed Keene's two courtyards to the S by a range with a centre portico and an orangery and a library inside. This is how the house remained, except that *C. R. Cockerell* in 1824 made a chapel N of the centre of the long Adam range, and *Sir C. Barry* added the Victorian tower. Then the reverse process began, and in 1955–6 the Bridgeman–Keene–Adam house was pulled down. The dining room is now the Board Room of Lloyd's. The stable courts were converted into flats. So what the visitor is now faced with is the extent of the former stable courts and the Adam work in its s range. The stables are simple and dignifiedly utilitarian, two-storeyed with pedimented three-bay angle pavilions. The s front is a fine composition between two of these, arched and articulated by a raised central accent with attenuated coupled columns and a pediment, and two sub-accents, raised a little less and with single columns. The capitals of a typical reeded Adam form. The friezes reeded too. Inside, the centre is separated from the rest by screens of two Ionic columns. In the library a later c18 chimneypiece formerly in the house and a charming coved ceiling with medallions of poets and philosophers.

Cockerell's chapel, N of the centre of the Adam range, is entered by huge iron gates. The architecture is simple, with three arched windows either side. Restrained Grecian detail. ORGAN CASE, probably of the time of the chapel. To stress the chapel *Barry* added his tall Italianate tower. It is dated 1840 and perched awkwardly on the roof.

The GROUNDS of Bowood are superb, with the long lake to the E of the house. As *The Beauties of England and Wales* put it, they 'may be ranked under each of the three distinguishing classes into which the agreeable objects of nature have been divided: the sublime, the picturesque, and the beautiful. The latter may be seen in the lawn and pleasure grounds, the picturesque in the lake and its artless, wild and broken accompaniments; the sublime in the extensive prospects, the rich wood, and the massive rock, worn into furrows by the rush of falling waters. Here the minutiae of landscape is never perceptible; it is absorbed in the striking grandeur of the surrounding scenery.' The grounds of Bowood were laid out first with the advice of the Hon. *C. Hamilton* of Pains Hill in Surrey, then by *Capability Brown* in 1761–8, and before 1803 *Repton* had also done things (*see* his *Theory*). At the foot of the lake the CASCADE, quite a spectacular display, due to Mr Hamilton and his enthusiastic study of Gaspard Poussin and other Franco-Italian landscape painters. Later, *Josiah Lane* of Tisbury built a GROTTO interweaving it with the cascade. The grotto was long and elaborate but has largely collapsed. A grotto recess survives at the end of the lake. Also by the

lake a TEMPLE with a front of four Roman Doric columns
and a pediment.

But the principal garden ornament is *Adam*'s MAUSOLEUM,
a design of exceptional purity and nobility. It was complete in
1765. It is a square with four projections like short cross-arms,
one of them being the portico of two pairs of Tuscan columns.
Dome over the square. Inside, the arms are tunnel-vaulted,
the true tunnel-vault being a form of greater gravity than the
segmental tunnel-vault which Adam usually preferred. The
arms are divided from the centre by screens of two Tuscan
columns with nothing solid above their entablatures. – MONU-
MENTS. First Earl † 1761. White marble sarcophagus with
straight sides and, in the centre, a medallion with a mourning
woman. By *Carlini*. – Life-size seated figure in ideal drapery,
called Mercury. By *Alexander Brodie*, 1862.

In front of the house TERRACES, laid out, in contradiction
to Capability Brown's principles, in 1951 (by *George Kennedy*).

GOLDEN GATES. By *Barry*, 1834–57. Tripartite entry as in
a triumphal arch, and to the l. a square Italianate turret, to the
r. a big square Italianate tower. Barry had an Italianate taste,
as he had a Gothic and a Jacobean. Among his buildings Mount
Felix is perhaps the nearest to these gates. The contrived asym-
metry is characteristic.

Outside the Golden Gates an ESTATE of neo-Tudor housing including the Lansdowne Arms.

OBELISK on Cherill Down, *see* p. 150.

WHETHAM HOUSE, 1¼ m. SSE. C17. Of six bays and two storeys
with two gables. The windows rhythmically alternating; originally mullioned but now mostly sashed.

BOX

ST THOMAS OF CANTERBURY. Mostly of the C14. Central
tower with spire. The S aisle is of 1840. The N aisle entrance is
of 1713, arched, with Tuscan columns and a broken segmental
pediment. The earliest tracery is in the N aisle E window (cusped
intersected). To this corresponds inside the highly unusual
motif of a rib-vaulted E bay. Nice Perp W doorway with leaf in
the spandrels. Original two-storeyed NE vestry. The W and E
tower arches clearly C14. The C14 N arcade is of four low bays.
Octagonal piers, the arch mouldings convincingly C14, except
for the W bay, which seems a renewal of the date of the N doorway. The straight-headed Gothic windows to the l. and r. of

the latter have been recognized by Brakspear as of 1713 too. One feature in the church is earlier than all the rest, a mysterious recess in the E wall of the N aisle. This is in a reredos position, but may well be a re-set E.E. tomb recess. Short detached shafts with moulded capitals, richly moulded depressed two-centred arch standing on short vertical pieces. – FONT. Simple, with quatrefoils, octagonal. Perp. – PLATE. Set, 1707. – MONUMENTS. Anthony Long † 1578. Bearded effigy, placed in a low C14 (?) tomb recess. – Margaret Blow and her late husband who died in 1754. An exceedingly charming large hanging monument with a garlanded big urn in front of a grey obelisk. Three cherubs' heads at the foot.

SCHOOL. 1874 and 1894. Gothic, with a terrible, spindly tower.

TUNNEL ENTRANCES to the small tunnel W of Box and the Box tunnel proper E of Box. Both are classical, the former more ornate. The BOX TUNNEL was built in 1837–41 and is, with its 3,212 yards' length, an engineering feat of *Brunel*'s.

Immediately W of the church the OLD SCHOOL, a substantial building of three storeys, six bays wide, with regular flat-mullioned two-light windows, and string-courses all along above the windows, i.e. early C18. Four dormers on top. Then up to the MAIN STREET (for the church lies in a dip) and to the LOCKUP, a little square with a domed stone roof. A little to the W MANOR FARMHOUSE, C17, three storeys, three gables, symmetrical fenestration, as if it stood in the country and not facing the High Victorian Gothic POYNDER FOUNTAIN of 1878 with its pink granite columns. From here down quite steeply to the MARKET PLACE, not a *place* in the French sense at all. FROGMORE HOUSE still has mullioned windows but already a shell-hood over the door.

CHAPEL PLASTER, 1⅛ m. ESE. A small C15 hospice and chapel, probably for pilgrims to Glastonbury. Nave and chancel. W porch with a niche above the W entrance, N transept. In the E wall of the chancel a reredos with three niches. The chancel had transverse arches across to support a stone roof. Very soon the nave and probably also the transept were made two-storeyed. The porch is also ascribed to this second build. It is not at all certain how the space originally available was used. Was the nave the hospice, the transept the priest's room, and only the chancel reserved for services?

HAZELBURY MANOR, just NW of Chapel Plaster. Externally the most spectacular features of Hazelbury Manor are the hall bay and the two-storeyed porch, both C15-looking. In fact they are

BOX 113

both C20, but there was evidence for their building, evidence of a staircase and thus the upper storey of the porch, evidence of the large bay by its panelled entrance arch. The hall itself survives and has a screen which was brought from a house at Barnstaple, and its original roof with collar-beams on arched braces and two tiers of wind-braces. An interesting feature is the panelled back arch into a small extension with a straight-headed four-light window from which access was by a smaller panelled arch to the C15 newel staircase. Of this indications remain on the first floor. The present staircase is, however, Jacobean and comes from a house at Shrewsbury. It has flat cut-out balusters. Windows with two transoms. This staircase lies at the corner of the front and the W range. The range is arcaded (with segmental arches) on the ground floor and has regular three-light mullioned and transomed windows. To the W the range has a row of five even gables and again regular windows, mullioned only. Two of the gables are original, three C20. Round the corner, back to the front, two more gables, though the masonry of the corner is said to be C15. Jacobean plaster ceiling with thin ribs in a room on the first floor. The adjoining room handsomely Queen Anne. Jacobean also an excellent stone chimneypiece, all small geometrical motifs. This comes from the STEWARD'S HOUSE, now joined to the manor house by a passage. The Steward's House has two steep gables and mullioned windows. To the N of the house Jacobean archway with strapwork above standing out against the sky. At the time the house belonged to Hugh Speke. To the N of the house a raised terrace with pretty corner bastions and an odd corbelled-out seat. What date may they be?

WARNCLIFFE HOUSE, ¾ m. WSW. In the garden a garden house with a small C13 lancet.

RUDLOE MANOR, 1¾ m. NE. A very attractive late C17 house with a big hipped roof. Four bays, three-light mullioned windows. The centre axis just two upright ovals one on top of the other. Central chimney. To the r. a buttressed medieval BARN.

ROMAN VILLA, 100 yds NW of the church. Of courtyard type, excavated in the C19 and early C20. The passage surrounding the courtyard had a tessellated floor, and there were similar floors in several of the rooms, forty of which were located. A number of the rooms lay above hypocausts, and included in the complex was a bath suite and fountain. A moulded capital bearing the relief of a huntsman, and a figure holding a trident were among the small finds.

There are two further supposed villa sites at Ditteridge and
Hazlebury.

BOYTON

ST COSMAS AND ST DAMIAN. Stone and flint chequerwork; a
picturesque group from the N. The church has a N porch tower,
and attached to it on the E, the N transept, on the W, a lean-to
ending in a Victorian chimney (*T. H. Wyatt*'s restoration of
1860). The tower entrance is by a sumptuous E.E. arch with
many mouldings, no doubt not *in situ*. The doorways inside
with continuous mouldings look rather later. Under the lean-to
a small Dec window.* The N chapel is Dec, see the reticulated
tracery of a N window, and the arch to the nave with two sunk
quadrant mouldings. But the chancel is E.E., and the S chapel is
quite ambitious E.E. The chancel has a Victorian E window and
single lancet windows. Sedilia and piscina with trefoil arches.
But the chancel arch is a Dec remodelling, just like the N
chapel arch in its details. Now the S chapel – which makes it
certain that no architectural traveller will forget Boyton. It has
a fine E window of three stepped lancet lights, the middle one
with a short arch on vertical pieces and circles above the lights.
The mullions and tracery are moulded. The S windows are
small lancets. But the W window is a tour-de-force, a little
showy perhaps but certainly powerful. It is an exaggeratedly
large circular window with three quatrefoiled spherical triangles
and between them three circles each filled by three small circles.
Bar tracery appears at Salisbury Cathedral only about 1270,
and the tracery here is a little in advance of Salisbury. One
might date the chapel *c.*1280, and that date agrees with the fact
that Walter Giffard, archbishop of York, obtained the church
before he died in 1279, and that his brother, Godfrey, bishop
of York, in 1279 made elaborate liturgical provisions for the
chapel. It was probably founded to commemorate their brother
Sir Alexander. The chapel has a two-bay arcade with a pier,
octagonal with four attached shafts and boldly moulded capitals. The arch has one chamfer and one roll. Trefoil-headed
sedilia and piscina with small, awkwardly placed gutter. The
lancet windows to the S have trefoiled rere-arches. – (SCULPTURE.
St Martin and the Beggar; early C14; stone. What was it
originally? NBR) – STAINED GLASS. Old bits assembled in the
E window. Some of them C13 and probably from Salisbury
Cathedral (cf. Laverstock, p. 263). – In the S chapel two panels

* The lean-to was originally two-storeyed; see the remaining corbels.

of German glass, with a date 1484; the w window by *Horwood* of Mells, the E window by *Alexander Gibbs*. – PLATE. Chalice, 1660; Paten and Flagon, 1694; Paten, 1728. – MONUMENTS. In the Giffard Chapel probably Sir Alexander; late C13 effigy, cross-legged. The tomb-chest much later. – Probably Lady Margaret † 1338. No more than the tomb-chest with little canopied arches. Both monuments have been treated unkindly.

BOYTON MANOR. Built by Thomas Lambert and completed in 1618 (MHLG). A fine square house, three by three gables, with regular windows of three lights with a transom. In the centre of the entrance (E) side two-storeyed porch. On the ground floor Ionic columns, on the first floor Corinthian pilasters. No gable or balustrade. The s side of the house received a new doorway about 1700. At the same time a new staircase was provided. The plan of the house is such that two staircases lie symmetrically in the middle of the s and N sides. One has Jacobean balusters, the other twisted ones of *c.*1700. Above this latter is a fine plaster ceiling with an oval wreath and ample garlands in the coving. The principal room on the first floor, including the upper storey of the porch, has its original panelling with pilasters, a fine, large stone chimney-piece with columns l. and r. and geometrical patterns on the lintel, and a plaster ceiling with thin ribs.

BRADENSTOKE CUM CLACK   *9070*

ST MARY. 1866 by *C. F. Hansom*. Almost on the village street. Nave and chancel and bellcote. Dec forms. The interior spacious and lavish with much carving. – FONT. 'Exhibited at the Great Exhibition of 1861' (Jackson's Wiltshire Collections. Does he mean 1851 or 1862?). Small, with the Signs of the Evangelists, the Dove, and the Cross.

Just s of the church, between it and the street, a CROSS, with its shaft preserved.

Along the street w of the church several timber-framed cottages.

PROVIDENCE CHAPEL of 1777. Brick. Segment-headed windows. Half-hipped roof with a little lantern. The minister's house attached.

BRADENSTOKE PRIORY. Founded in 1142 for Augustinian canons. Little is left on the site, but excavations have revealed the plan, and substantial buildings were purchased in the 1930s by William Randolph Hearst and taken to St Donat's Castle. They were the guest house and the prior's lodging, the latter with a splendid late C15 chimneypiece, and the tithe barn, which stood to the SE of the precinct and was 104 ft long. On the site there is now no more visible than a square C14 tower which once marked the NW corner of the W range and part of the undercroft of the W range, with octagonal piers and heavy single-chamfered ribs, also C14. The church lay to the S of the cloister, an uncommon arrangement, but one also to be found at Ivychurch, Malmesbury, Lacock, and Stanley, all in Wiltshire. The church was *c.* 250 ft long and had transepts but no aisles. A S aisle was added in the early C13, and a W tower in the C15. Against the N side of the cloister stood the refectory, which once had a very fine and interesting, very steeply pitched open timber roof of the early C14 with arched braces forming complete round arches below the collar-beams. They were decorated with ballflower.

CLACK MOUNT has a MOTTE AND BAILEY with water moats of which considerable traces remain (HR).

BRADFIELD FARM *see* HULLAVINGTON

8060

BRADFORD-ON-AVON

The excitement of Bradford-on-Avon is its position, with the hills rising steeply to the N, houses appearing on top of houses and steps connecting the streets. Moreover, there is a wealth of excellent houses, especially of the early C18, reflecting the affluence of the clothiers and architecturally the nearness to Bristol and Bath, and there are still factories in the valley contributing business. They do not spoil the picture at all. Machinery invaded the cloth-making trade towards the end of the C18. A riot against installing a scribbling machine occurred in 1791. In the early C19 Bradford had thirty-two cloth factories.

HOLY TRINITY. Evidence of the Norman church the long round-headed windows in the chancel, the re-set smaller Norman window above the S porch, and the flat buttresses. The chancel was lengthened about 1300–10, see the E window, five lights, the first and last taller than the others, and a big circle with three pointed trefoils between. Perp W tower, though the mouldings of the W doorway seem to indicate an earlier beginning. Short recessed spire. A tierceron-star vault inside with a big circle for the bell-ropes. Panelled tower arch. Perp N and S aisle windows, embattled. Perp also the S porch (with a niche) and the embattled S chapel with straight-headed windows and a four-centred arch inside. The N aisle arcade is partly Victorian (1864 by *Gill*; PF) with inscribed ribbons wrapped round the piers, partly Perp re-done. The section of the piers is four thin shafts and four times three hollows in the diagonals. In the N aisle a curious panelled Perp recess. Is it *in situ*? It may have been the reredos of the western of the two chapels, which originally made up the whole N aisle. They were indeed separated by a cross-wall. The eastern chapel was that of the Horton family (*see* below). Squint from N aisle to chancel of the (unique?) length of 20 ft. – FONT. Perp, perhaps re-cut in the C17. – SCREEN. Two panels from the dado painted with Fathers of the Church, writing. They may once have been very good (nave W). – PAINTING. N of the E window: The Virgin being taught to write. – In the N aisle E: The Virgin, the Child, and St Joseph, oil-painting by an Italian Mannerist. – STAINED GLASS. In a S window many Netherlandish roundels, C16 and later. – N aisle E, *c.*1877, quite acceptable. – PLATE. Cup, 1564; Chalice and Paten, 1634; Paten, 1705; Flagon, 1723; Spoon, 1756; Set, 1764. – MONUMENTS. In the chancel S and N walls two big tomb recesses of *c.*1300–10, that on the N side simply with continuous mouldings, the other more elaborate. Cusped arch and crocketed gable. Buttress-shafts on heads. In the N recess effigy of a Lady, in the other a cross-legged Knight.– At the W end of the nave bust from another effigy of a Lady, also *c.*1300. The rest has disappeared. – Brasses to Thomas Horton † 1530, the great clothier, and his wife (N aisle E wall). Two 12-in. figures with scrolls and a Trinity at the top. – Charles Steward, 1701 by *Nost*. Standing figure in front of a blank arch. Mourning putti l. and r. – Anthony Methuen †1737. By *J. M. Rysbrack*. Noble standing monument with a grey sarcophagus framed by Ionic columns carrying a pediment.– John Thresher, father and son, *c.*1741. Architectural tablet, but with two putti outside holding draperies.

ST LAWRENCE. Now that Messrs Jackson and Fletcher have 6 proved the two dates of St Lawrence it can safely be called one of the most important Early Anglo-Saxon and at the same time one of the most important Late Anglo-Saxon churches in all Britain. It is recorded by William of Malmesbury that St Aldhelm built an *ecclesiola* at Bradford. A monastery at Bradford, no doubt the one to which the little church belonged, is mentioned in a deed of 705. To this church belongs the plan and the ground-stage of the church as it is today, except that the pilaster strips were made by cutting back the walls to their l.

and r., when the upper parts were rebuilt. For this we have no date, but the late C10 has much probability. Yet a little later, in the C11, the single-splay windows were remodelled into double-splays.*

The church is very small and consists of nave, two *porticus* N and S, of which the southern one has mostly disappeared, and a square-ended chancel. The nave is 22½ ft long, the chancel 13 ft. The church in its final form is excessively high in proportion to its width. The relation in the nave is 13 ft 2 in. by 25 ft 3 in., in the chancel 10 ft by 18 ft 4 in. The external walls are divided horizontally into three tiers plus gables in the nave, two plus gables in the chancel. The W wall was rebuilt in 1875. Otherwise the lowest tier has the pilaster strips already referred to, the next blank arcading of short, broad, flat pilasters, with flat, big capitals which are just blocks with tapering sides. The details of the N *porticus* are a little different. The second tier here has the short pilasters, but no capitals or arches, and there is another fragmentary tier of pilaster strips in the gable.

Inside, the steep, narrow proportions are even more impressive. While they belong to the C10, the equally impressive narrowness of the openings between nave and chancel and nave and *porticus* belongs to Aldhelm. The chancel arch is about 3 ft 6 in. wide, the *porticus* arches have a width of less than 3 ft. The arches are slightly stilted. Capitals and abaci are reduced to a single block. Rough roll mouldings are kept away from the edges and run as an illogical outer accompaniment to the whole opening.

SCULPTURE. On the nave E wall high up two horizontally floating angels in shallow relief, originally no doubt connected with a rood such as the one at Romsey. – Also part of a CROSS with interlace ornament.

CHRIST CHURCH, Bearfield. 1841 by *Manners* of Bath, chancel 1878 by *J. O. Scott*. Big, prosperous church with W tower carrying a recessed spire. Flying buttresses support the spire. Tall Perp three-light windows. No aisles. Chancel a lengthening of the short chancel still usual in 1840. A chapel was also added.

ST MARY, Tory. The chapel of a hospice, the two together T-shaped, just as it is preserved at South Wraxall Manor Farmhouse. At St Mary the house is altered, and the chapel was rebuilt all but the E wall (with niches l. and r. of the window)

---

* Proof of this is in the N *porticus* W window, whose outer splay cuts into one of the late C10 pilaster strips.

in 1877. Aubrey calls it 'the finest Hermitage I have seen in England, several rooms and a very neat chapel of good free-stone'. Leland states that it is placed on the highest point of Bradford.

NONCONFORMIST CHAPELS, *see* Perambulation.

TOWN HALL, Market Street and Church Street. 1855, by *Thomas Fuller* of Bath. Large, with an angle turret, Jacobean with shaped gables and mullioned and transomed windows, irregular and picturesque, but on a scale excessive for Bradford. The building is indeed no longer the town hall. The centre is now the ROMAN CATHOLIC CHURCH.

PERAMBULATION

We start at the TOWN BRIDGE. Nine arches, plain parapet, essentially C17, though there are still two C13 arches. In the middle, set on a cutwater, the so-called CHAPEL. It was no doubt a chapel in the Middle Ages. But as it is, with its domed roof and bell finial, it is C17, and as it is also known as the BLIND HOUSE, which is a current name for a LOCKUP, it was no doubt that. How Pugin would have revelled in this contrast!

N of the bridge we can turn W via Market Street into Church Street or N E into Silver Street. We choose the former. CHURCH STREET has a fine sequence of houses, starting with the SWAN HOTEL, Later Georgian, of three bays with a central Venetian window and a one-bay pediment at the top. White and black on ashlar. Then on the other side CHURCH HOUSE, stately Georgian, of three wide bays and noble proportions, with a big arched door surround of alternating sizes of rustication and a Venetian window over. Top pediment. Opposite the RUBBER FACTORY. The five-storeyed, dominant part with the giant 63b pointed arches up the façade and the pointed corbel-frieze dates from 1875 and is by *Richard Gane*. The other, three-storeyed part, with broad segment-headed windows, looks early C19. Back to the other side for the OLD CHURCH HOUSE (Holy Trinity Church Hall). Built by Thomas Horton, the clothier (*see* above); so Leland tells us. T-shaped, buttressed, of two storeys, with the part at r. angles to the street of only one storey. Windows mullioned, the heads of the lights four-centred. In the two-storeyed part original ceilings, the upper one with moulded beams. In the one-storeyed part one original wooden gallery. The two Tuscan columns are said to come from a pulpit. Then a widening and a delightful loose group. Facing

us DUTCH BARTON, Georgian, ashlar-faced, of five bays. Up
50 a little, above, on the r., DRUCE'S HILL HOUSE, an Early
Georgian front of Bristol type. Three storeys with a balustrade
occasionally curving up a little. The centre bay is flanked by
pilasters with sunk panels on the ground floor, by Corinthian
fluted pilasters on the first. Segment-headed ground-floor windows. Nos 20 and 21 gabled, C17. Back to Church Street, where
the side of Dutch Barton reveals itself as C17, gabled, with
mullioned windows. Another interruption: ABBEY HOUSE,
again facing W. Later C18, five bays, doorway with pediment
on Tuscan columns, two pedimented first-floor windows, three-
bay pediment. (At the back a C16 range with good ceilings with
moulded beams, and also moulded doorways and fireplaces.
MHLG) Then N of Holy Trinity another nice row, including one
house of the late C17, with two gables and upright two-light
windows. Later doorway with Tuscan pilasters and a metope
frieze. Then, detached, NW of the church, a three-bay Early
Victorian Tudor house,* and across, facing E, LITTLE CHAN-
TRY, a five-bay house with three-bay pediment and one-bay
lower attachments l. and r. In fact this house is only part of
THE CHANTRY, reached up a passage on its r. The elevation
one sees from the passage is C17, irregular, with mullioned
windows. The W side is the earlier façade proper, c.1700, of
seven bays and three storeys with, on the first floor, cross-
windows. Doorway with segmental pediment; arched window
over. The façade is spoiled by unsightly additions taking the
place of former projecting low wings. Immediately above the
house BARTON ORCHARD, an C18 terrace of three-storeyed
weavers' houses (the fourth storey seems later). The rhythm is
two windows, two doorways with blank wall over, seven windows with a doorway below in the middle, and again two
windows with blank wall over and two more windows. From
here, steep up, one can get up to Newtown (*see* below).

Back to the Town Hall and up MARKET STREET. Several smooth
ashlar fronts, one house with gables and mullioned windows.
No. 27 of only two bays, typical early C18. At the top of Market
Street was THE PRIORY, a great estate of the Methuens, now
in decay. Gloomy Gothic wall to the street. The prettier Gothic
house inside is partly demolished. Fragments of the original
medieval house in the grounds. The house stands at the corner
of NEWTOWN, and here, on the l., is a BARN belonging to the
estate. Late medieval, looking low from the street, much more

* Until recently a school.

commanding from the s. A little further on, on the other side, the BELL INN, dated 1695, with a square porch and no special features. To its w Nos 54–9, late C17, gabled, three-storeyed. Now up a steep lane to MIDDLE RANK with the ZION BAP-TIST CHURCH, formerly Presbyterian Church. This was built c.1698. Windows with slightly stepped-back mouldings, entrances with bolection mouldings. To the w again terrace of gabled houses of the late C17. Upright ovals are as characteristic of this date as is the semicircular hood on brackets over the door of No. 9. The next tier, yet higher up in this steep growth of Bradford, is TORY. Here, on the way to St Mary, Nos 27–32, a Late Georgian terrace of three storeys, very townish. The end bays have canted bay windows. The windows are still of two lights with broad, flat mullions. Nos 33–37 are a little earlier. Doorways with Tuscan columns and pediments, window surrounds a little moulded.

Back once more to Market Street. On the e THE SHAMBLES, a pedestrian lane, connecting the street with Silver Street. In The Shambles two timber-framed houses with renewed bargeboards and one house with a C15 doorway.

SILVER STREET starts by the bridge with the RUBBER FACTORY. The Co-op shop has ruined a monumental Early Georgian front. Giant pilasters, windows with Gibbs surrounds. Top cornice, half-storey above. Then BROWN'S shop, the w part Victorian, all glass, except for the piers with alternatingly vermiculated rustication and fancy Gothic gables. The e part Georgian, of five bays. Then on the l. COPPICE HILL. Many gabled cottages, e.g. No. 9 with windows with C17 mullions but a doorway with a bolection moulding. At the top a good group facing down, with No. 19, Georgian, and Nos 20 and 21, C17. A cast-iron gate leads up to the WESLEYAN METHODIST CHURCH of 1818. Five-bay front with three-bay attic. Arched windows. Doorway with Tuscan columns and metope frieze. Grecian details. From the bottom of Coppice Hill Silver Street forks l., KINGSTON ROAD r., into the FAC-TORY of Spencer Moulton & Co. At the entry No. 3, Georgian, of seven bays, doorway with partly blocked columns. Then No. 9, lower, with a pedimented three-bay centre. The ground-floor windows also pedimented. To the l. The Hall in its grounds, see below. Near the end the factory, big, with broad segment-headed windows and a bell-turret. It is known that The Hall and its grounds down to the river were sold in 1802 to one Thomas Divett, who thereupon built the mill.

Continuing SILVER STREET, on the l. SILVER STREET HOUSE, rendered, three storeys, of five bays, with, on the first floor, a nice alternating rhythm of window pediments and niches to the l. and r. of the centre window. The pediments form part of a string-course. Up on the l. WHITEHEAD'S LANE. The corner house, SUN DIAL HOUSE, with a typical, often recurring rhythm of two-one-two windows. Pedimented doorway and window over. At the top the OLD MANOR HOUSE, five bays, two storeys, moulded door surround with pediment.

On in SILVER STREET. EASTERN HOUSE must be Early Victorian. One bay wide, but on the ground floor a three-arched loggia. The street is now called WOOLLEY STREET. Several more good Georgian houses. First AUDLEY'S, No. 5, with the two–one–two rhythm of windows and a Tuscan porch. Then, opposite, OLD HOUSE, dignified, simple Georgian. With No. 15 a fine group starts. LYNCHETTS has a doorway with delicate Adamish detail, but some rather bleak Venetian windows. MOXHAMS, No. 17, is mid-Georgian. Doorway with fluted pilasters and a metope frieze. Door pediment and window pediment over. No. 19, ST OLAVE'S, is Early Georgian. Ground floor and attic windows with a kind of basket arches. On the first floor pedimental hoods. Doorway with Gibbs surround and pediment. No. 21 is early C19 and has a veranda in front.

Opposite the entrance to THE HALL, the one nationally major mansion of Bradford, not a town house but a country house in character. It was built by John Hall, a clothier, about 1610. The S front* is short, tall, and almost entirely glazed. It has windows with two transoms on the lower as well as the upper floor, with the one exception of the porch doorway in the middle. To the l. and r. of the porch there is just enough space for a three-light window. Three projecting bays, each with a further narrow semicircular projection in the middle. The whole of a bay has thus twelve lights. Small medallions in the sill zone of the upper floor. Top cresting with open rings and little obelisks and, lying back behind bays and porch, three plain, even gables. The N front has projecting wings, and in the middle the course of the former staircase marked by rising windows. The original kitchen seems to have been in the NE corner. The E and W sides are plainer but also have two-transomed windows. They are in their original state. The E front is not ashlared. The hall lies in the middle of the house and is entered in its middle. Originally however the room to its W

35a (margin)

* Almost entirely renewed *c.*1850.

formed part of it. This explains the odd placing of the sumptuous fireplace. It now seems pushed out of true by the doorway
to its l. The doorway has large foliage scrolls up its surround
and an arch at the top with foliage spandrels. The fireplace has
coupled columns l. and r., Doric below, Ionic above, and a
large lintel with an absurdly big guilloche frieze, about 2 ft
3 in. high. Handsome square panel with egg and dart, and a
coat of arms in the overmantel. In the hall itself no original
Jacobean features are left. The room to the E of the hall has
panelling with giant pilasters and a stone chimneypiece with
triple supports and strapwork. Above the entrance hall is the
Great Chamber. Its plaster ceiling is of c.1850. In the main w
room on the first floor some niches with shell apses similar to
those at South Wraxall and outside Edington church, and also
at Montacute in Somerset and Cranborne in Dorset. The main
E room has a wooden fireplace with two tiers of little caryatids
in the overmantel and panelling with giant pilasters. In the
garden, in the SE corner, an octagonal DOVECOTE. In addition
two TEMPLES: the one to the E with four bulgy Tuscan
columns may be Victorian, the other, to the W, of the same type
looks trustworthily Georgian. The last Hall left the estate to
Rachel Baynton of Great Chalfield, and from the Bayntons it
went by marriage to the first duke of Kingston. He died in 1726,
the second duke in 1773, his dubious duchess in 1788. The sale
of the estate in 1802 has already been reported.

Let The Hall be the end N of the river. Now S of the bridge. At
once a fine sight: WESTBURY HOUSE, on its own, Early
Georgian towards the bridge, with a Palladian garden alcove
to its r., four Tuscan columns carrying a pediment and opposite
a blank bit of wall with three Gothick arches, now the back wall
of the public conveniences. The house itself has angle pilasters
or rather strips in three orders, i.e. interrupted by two string-
courses, segment-headed windows on the ground floor, and a
top balustrade. Doorway with alternatingly blocked pilasters.
An open stair with iron handrail leads up to it. To the side the
house is much more swagger, in the Baroque style of Bristol.
The centre marked by Ionic pilasters and a broken segmental
pediment on the ground floor, Corinthian pilasters and a broken
triangular pediment on the first floor. Staircase with thin turned
or twisted balusters, three different patterns for each step. To
the E a few more good houses, THE THREE GABLES, C17,
gabled; its l. neighbour of five bays, Georgian, doorway with
Tuscan columns; the l. neighbour of this again gabled.

From the side façade of Westbury House St Margaret's Street begins. Opposite the Liberal Club, Early Georgian with a curly open pediment. Then some nice Early Victorian Tudor work (No. 7). Opposite, lying back, a range said to have been a dye-house or a weaving-shed. It looks early C19. Higher up No. 46 again has a doorway with open curly pediment. Then, opposite, lying back, through an archway the Baptist Chapel of 1798. Pointed windows with Y-tracery. Doorway with Tuscan columns and a pediment. To the r., at the fork with the Frome Road, the Men's Almshouses of 1700. Seven bays, four doors, two storeys, low, hipped roof. Two-light windows with stepped-back mullions. In the middle coat of arms. Front parapet with vases. A little further out, opposite Junction Road, to the w is Barton Farm. The house is of various dates and has a Perp porch entrance in the form of a four-centred panelled arch and a window with arched

22a lights. To the s the Tithe Barn of the nunnery of Shaftesbury,* 168 ft long, that is, longer than Edington church, with two porches, each long side and a roof with collar-beams on arched braces and three tiers of wind-braces. The N porches are much bigger than the s porches. Big buttresses all along walls and porches, with many-stepped set-offs. The barn seems to be early C14 and is as monumental as a monumental church.

Back to St Margaret's Street and on the l. the Congregational Church of 1798, also approached by an archway. Flat five-bay front with pedimental gable. Minister's house attached to the l. Higher up, round the corner, in St Margaret's Place No. 4 with a semicircular door-hood on volute brackets, No. 5, Early Georgian, with three pedimented dormers and a pediment over the middle window.

OUTER BRADFORD

To the NE Woolley Grange, dated 1665, but much altered. Main front with gables carrying finials and a porch with a balcony.

To the N, in the Bath Road, Old Ride (formerly Frankleigh House), C17, but now mostly of c. 1848.

To the w, in the Winsley Road, Budbury Castle, a folly, tall, with an Italianate roof, dated on a plaque 1850, and in the Turleigh Road first Well Close, low and gabled to the street, but with its front to the s, in two parts. The w part has a square porch of c.1730. Then Wellclose House, Georgian, of five

* Cf. Tisbury for another barn of the same nunnery.

bays with a five-bay pediment and on the first floor pediments
alternating between triangular and segmental. Finally, after a
bit, BELCOMBE COURT. Belcombe Court ought really to be
across the border in Somerset. It belongs to Bath, is in fact by
the *elder John Wood*, and, what is more, was praised by him as
having 'the best tetrastyle frontispiece in square pillars (of the
Ionic order) yet executed in or about Bath'. This refers to the
s front of the wing which Wood added to an older house for
Francis Yerbury, a Bradford clothier, in 1734. For pillars we
must read pilasters. They are unfluted and have Ionic capitals
and carry a big pediment. The ground-floor windows have
pediments too. The small upper windows touch the entablature. Inside, the finest rooms are the octagonal study and the
drawing room. The study has a coved ceiling with garlands in
the cove and putti on clouds in the centre. In the drawing room
between two niches a big aedicule niche with pediment. The
windows in both rooms have surrounds standing on decorated
little volutes. (In a bedroom overmantel with a garland and an
oval relief. NBR) The w side has slightly projecting pedimented
wings and a shallow bow window in the middle. Above this a
tripartite window. To the l. an extension also with tripartite
windows. That on the ground floor has pilasters and a pediment
over the centre. The E side faces a courtyard open to the s.
There is a big pediment here as well, and the doorway has a big
pediment too, carried on unfluted Ionic columns. At r. angles
a lower five-bay range with a bust in a circular niche. Facing
the main doorway an archway through the third range of the
courtyard. Above the archway a round turret with a stone
dome, obviously older, though no date is recorded. Outside
this courtyard an older one with a C15 BARN and STABLES.
The w window of the latter has Dec tracery, probably not *in
situ* or not genuine. According to Wood, Francis Yerbury and
his father and forefathers used the outbuildings 'for offices and
Work Houses'. In the garden, facing the main façades, a domed
ROTUNDA (and also, according to *Country Life*, 1950, an imposing GROTTO).

BRATTON

9050

ST JAMES. Above the village, just under the downs. If it were
not for the E walls of the transepts and the chancel, the church
would be entirely Perp. It is a short, compact building, ashlar-
faced, with battlements on nave, aisles, and crossing tower. The
tower has a higher stair-turret. Only the chancel is low,

rebuilt in the C19 (E.E. style) and disappointing. S porch attached to the S transept, a very unusual arrangement. The W window, equally unusually, has its jambs inside continued to the ground. Two-bay aisle arcade. The piers with a section of four shafts and four wave-mouldings. The details of the crossing piers are the same, but the mighty octagonal bases might well be a survival of the pre-Perp church. Tierceron-vault inside the tower, with a large circle for the bell-ropes and with bosses. In the E wall of the N transept four large, even niches. – FONT. Norman, entirely re-cut, circular, with scallops and a band of horizontal V-shapes above. – STAINED GLASS. E and W windows by *Gibbs*.

BAPTIST CHAPEL. 1734. Externally a gem. Brick with stone dressings. Arched doorway with a round window over and arched windows l. and r. Lower attachments of 1786 l. and r.

BRATTON HOUSE. 1715. A most impressive building of brick (unfortunately rendered) with stone dressings and with a doorway in each of its fronts, though the whole back has been replaced by a Regency façade with very large windows. The Early Georgian façade is of seven bays, quite unadorned, except for the doorway with an open pediment. The sides are of five bays, and their doorways have shell-hoods on brackets. Original panelled entrance hall and staircase with slim balusters, three to a tread, one of them twisted, and carved tread-ends.

MELBOURNE HOUSE, W of Bratton House. 1768. Brick, with stepped tripartite windows; late C18.

A three-bay house E of Bratton House has a pretty iron porch.

COURT HOUSE, at the NW corner of the village. Dated 1626. Big timber-framed house with one stone part. The timbers are narrowly-spaced uprights and the infilling is partly brick.

A little to the E of this YEWTREES, a nice Georgian pair; brick.

BREMHILL

ST MARTIN. The NW angle of the nave ought to be observed. Anglo-Saxon long-and-short quoins. Arcades of *c*.1200, terribly re-done at the restoration of 1850 (by *Butterfield*). Three bays, circular piers, capitals with decorated trumpet-scallop capitals, circular abaci, double-chamfered pointed arches. Also one stiff-leaf capital on the S side, two moulded capitals on the N. The chancel is E.E., but also much renewed. Lancets on the N and S sides, one on the N blocked, one on the S originally a 'low-side' window, but lower part blocked. This was wider than the upper by way of shoulders. The E window has detached shafts inside. The chancel arch is variously moulded. The leaves of the capitals can hardly be trusted. E.E. also the lower part of the tower. But the w window in the Dec style is by *Butterfield*, 1864. Above, the tower is most probably C14. Top with two twin bell-openings with Somerset tracery. Perp aisles and two-storeyed s porch. Gargoyles and battlements. The porch has a tierceron-star vault with big bosses. – FONT. Norman, circular, with a motif of semicircular scales, some very re-tooled. – PULPIT. Of stone, Perp, the side of the stair like the side of a throne. Is this by *Butterfield*? – BENCH ENDS. With mid-C16 panels. – STAINED GLASS. Original bits in the head of the N aisle NE window. – w window by *Hardman*, 1864. – s aisle w windows by *Kempe*, 1903. – PLATE. Chalice, 1662; Paten, 1726. – MONUMENT. George Hungerford † 1698. Erected between that date and 1712. Demi-figure, thin round the waist, hand on his heart, wig on his head. Pilasters with emblems of the arts of peace (violin, drawing tools) and of war (cannon, pistols). Twisted columns outside. Putti on the ledge and at the top.

CHURCHYARD CROSS. Base and shaft.

CROSS by the entrance to the churchyard. Steps and rather heavy, strongly tapered shaft.

BREMHILL COURT. The former vicarage. An old house of which a gable with mullioned window appears behind the present façade. The old house was given generous Gothic trim by the Rev. William Bowles, the poet and frightened eccentric who was rector during the years 1805 to 1844. He gave it its openwork parapet (on the pattern of Stourton) and its turrets and pinnacles. One turret carries the date 1820. In the garden he went all out to create another Leasowes. But Shenstone's Leasowes was some sixty years old when Bowles started his garden and entirely out of date. Thomas Moore understandably said that Bowles had 'frittered away its beauty by grottos, hermitages and Shenstonian inscriptions'. Not many of these furnishings survive, but some do – urns, an obelisk commemorating the peace of 1814, a little rocky cave, and a few fragments from STANLEY ABBEY, 2 m. w. This was a Cistercian nunnery founded in 1154. The fragments now flank the path at the back of the house. Thomas Moore also says that the sheep bells were tuned in thirds and fifths.

WICK HILL. On the hill the MAUD HEATH MONUMENT, created in 1838 at the expense of the Marquess of Lansdowne and William Bowles. Square pillar turning into an octagonal shaft, and high up the rustic seated figure of Maud Heath, looking towards Kellaways (*see* p. 249). The inscription reads:

Thou who dost pause on this aerial height
Where MAUD HEATH's Pathway winds in shade
   or light,
Christian Wayfarer in a world of strife
Be STILL and ponder on the path of life.

The quality of the poetry matches that of the statue.

BREMILHAM *see* FOXLEY

BRIMSLADE FARMHOUSE *see* BURBAGE

0080

BRINKWORTH

ST MICHAEL. The church is Perp, with a chancel of 1889.* But the chancel arch itself is old (Dec?) and has continuous chamfers. Perp W tower with battlements, earlier than the nave, see the asymmetrical position of the tower arch in relation to the nave and S aisle. Arcades of five bays with tall octagonal piers and arches with two hollow chamfers. Much colour preserved. Aisle roofs with bosses. Embattled aisle parapets. Embattled S porch in the middle of the aisle, with two three-light windows l., two r. The same arrangement without a porch on the N side. S doorway with a four-centred arch. Wagon roof in the nave, with tie-beams. – PULPIT. 1630, with back panel and tester. R. and l. of the back panel upright lion and unicorn. – WEST GALLERY and stair; C18. – Towering ORGAN CASE of *c.*1905. – PLATE. Chalice, 1630; Flagon, 1637; Paten, 1718. – MONUMENT. Exceptionally fine, very delicately carved tablet to John Weeks, set up in 1748. By a master who worked at Lydiard Park?

1020

BRITFORD

ST PETER. Cruciform church with a crossing tower. The tower and also the W wall (of 1767, *see* below) are ashlar-faced. The crossing arches are clearly early C14 (two continuous chamfers dying into the imposts). The chancel E window is Dec too (reticulated tracery). The other windows renewed. The tower was rebuilt in 1767. The nave is tall and has the windows un-

---

* In the E wall of the S aisle is a fragment of a Norman arch, not *in situ* (J. Lee Osborn).

usually high up. This gives it an Anglo-Saxon flavour, and the sensation of the interior is indeed the low entrances from the nave to the N and S into *porticus*. The S arch has voussoirs of Roman tiles, but the N entrance has a decoration unique in English pre-Conquest work. In both entrances the deep reveals have two tall stone slabs as upright posts and square slabs connecting them like rungs of a ladder. All this is plain on the S side, except for one of the square slabs having interlace decoration. But on the N side in the E reveal the upright slabs are [7a] decorated with vine scrolls developed from the Ruthwell–Bewcastle stage, i.e. English decoration of *c*.700. The carving is harder here and the most probable date is the C9. The connecting slabs have interlace. Above the imposts two stone corbels. What can they have been meant for? The arch above them would make the display of images impossible.* – PULPIT. Late C17. Blank arches with palm-trees. Above heads of cherubs, and the dove with the olive branch. At the angles big balusters. All rather rustic. – BENCH ENDS. Some in the chancel.–PEWS. In the S transept. Late C17 panelling with fluted pilasters. – CHEST. Small, heavily iron-bound, C15 probably (N transept). – PLATE. Set, 1749–50. – MONUMENTS. Miniature effigy of Purbeck marble of a young Civilian holding a cup. In the other hand he holds a scroll with the inscription: 'Orate pro anima Nickolaus qi gist ici'. Probably of *c*.1300. – Duke of Buckingham † 1483 (?). Tomb-chest with small figures in niches with nodding ogee canopies. Very decorated arch with ogee top and buttresses. These upper parts of the monument are not in their original position. – Jervys family, 1820. By *Bacon Jun*. Open white marble book with pedigree. – Mausoleum of the Earls of Radnor. The mausoleum was built in 1777, but completely gothicized or rebuilt probably about 1873, when *G. E. Street* restored the church. Shrine-like stone roof.

THE MOAT. Early C18 garden front of five bays with segmentheaded windows. The entrance side Gothick, early C19, with ogee-headed windows. This side is longer, too. It has two canted castellated bay windows.

HOUSE, NW of the church. C17, of brick, with a symmetrical threebay front. Below four lights with transom – doorway – four lights with transom. Above four lights – two lights – four lights.

COTTAGES on the main road, to the SW. Simple symmetrical estate cottages (Longford Castle) in a plain Georgian, of grey brick.

* In the S transept W wall an oblong opening with bars (NBR).

5

LITTLE WOODBURY, ½ m. WSW. Site of an Iron Age A farmstead consisting of an enclosure, house, barns, corn-drying
racks, and storage pits.

BRIXTON DEVERILL

ST MICHAEL. Good C13 chancel arch, with triple shafts, the
main one keeled. Short W tower, C13 and C15. Then, of *c.*1730,
the nave ceiling, the eaves outside the nave, and probably the
responds of the tower arch. The rest of 1862. – FONT. Norman,
circular, with a band of arrowheads. Transferred from Imber.
– Modest C17 FONT COVER.

Pleasant group of thatched stone cottages by the church, and the
MANOR FARMHOUSE with C17 mullioned windows, but one
in the front gable which looks *c.*1730. (An inner doorway is
supposed to be C15 work.)

COLD KITCHEN HILL, I m. W. On Cold Kitchen Hill has been
found gradually an enormous quantity of small things pointing
to extensive occupation of the hill, beginning in Iron Age A
times (sherds of All Cannings Cross type pottery, La Tène I
brooches) and continuing through C (bead-rimmed pottery,
bronze penannular brooches, etc.) to the Roman period. The
Roman finds are remarkable for the very large number of
brooches and other ornaments, suggesting some form of votive
deposit. With the Roman material is associated a settlement
from which fragments of painted stucco walls and hypocaust
flues remain.

BROAD BLUNSDON

ST LEONARD. Mostly by *Butterfield*, 1872, but the S arcade of
four bays with circular piers, circular abaci, and double-chamfered arches is late C13. To this belongs the one S window
with two pointed-trefoiled lights and a circle in plate tracery.
Perp W tower, but the parapet probably of 1872. Of 1872 emphatically the arcade to the S chapel. – PULPIT. Simple, Jacobean. – TOWER SCREEN. Jacobean, with balusters, and a good
strapwork top. – PLATE. Paten, 1723; Chalice, inscribed 1764.
– MONUMENTS. Thomas Haydock † 1612 and family. Brasses
(nave W end). – John Potenger † 1733, signed by *Peter Scheemakers*. Tablet of white and grey marble. Two cherubs' heads
l. and r., one at the foot, excellently carved. – (CROSS SHAFT
in the churchyard.)

(MANOR FARMHOUSE, SW of the church. Late C16. Irregular.

Gabled. Some windows with odd gable-shaped hoods. A good staircase with vertically symmetrical balusters. NBR)

(UPPER BURYTOWN FARMHOUSE, ¾ m. NE. C16. L-shaped. Mullioned windows of three lights. NBR)

CASTLE HILL, *see* Blunsdon St Andrew, p. 107.

BROAD CHALKE

ALL SAINTS. Big, ashlar-faced church with transepts and a crossing tower. Essentially it dates from two periods, the late C13 and *c.*1360–70. The late C13 work is as follows. First the N transept with E lancets and an unusually fine N window. This is of three lights with three quatrefoiled circles in bar tracery. The window is shafted, but the lights are just single-chamfered. The mouldings of the upper part are relatively flat too. Nice aumbry with pointed-trefoiled head. The single-framed wagon roof has also been assigned to the late C13. Secondly the W doorway, with shafts and many mouldings in the arch. Thirdly the chancel, with pointed-trefoil-headed lancets and a nicely moulded priest's doorway. The lancets have rere-arches. Sedilia with cinquecusped arches. The work of *c.*1360–70 is similar to Edington (and Bishopstone near by). The nave windows are entirely Perp, rather broad and with simple, big panel tracery. The W window is of five lights, the others are of three. W front with fleurons below the battlements. It is the mouldings of the S doorway (with blank tracery in the spandrels) and of the crossing arches which show the C14 date. In the crossing tierceron-star vault with a big hole for the bell-ropes. The E end of the nave has to the l. and r. of the crossing arch half-arches to buttress the tower. They are also simple in their mouldings. The N one is single, the S one double like a bridge arch. Do they presuppose the existence of aisles, either in the C13 or at least as a project in the C14?* The bit of frieze of the outer wall of the N transept showing here is a sign that this was once outer wall. But there can still have been in the C13 either no aisles and a narrower nave or low aisles. Later Perp the S transept S window and the top of the tower and the two-storeyed S porch with fleurons below the battlements. Nave roof with angel-brackets. – FONT. Octagonal, Perp, with amply cusped quatrefoils enclosing roses, leaf, shields, and on the side a quatrefoil of shells. – PULPIT. Early C17. – PEWS (in the transepts). Plain, C17. – SCULPTURE. Small piece of Anglo-Saxon interlace, probably

* As Mr Robert Potter points out, the springing of the arcade arches from the tower piers can still be seen.

from a cross-shaft (nave N side). – MONUMENT. S of the S porch, in the churchyard, simple inscribed slab to *Christopher Wood*, the painter, † 1930. He lived at Reddish House.

OLD RECTORY, W of the church. The archway with adjoining pedestrian entrance could well be of before the Reformation. The wall here is in fact continued to the W with buttresses. But the earliest surviving windows are mullioned and probably of Elizabethan date.

REDDISH MANOR, SW of the former. Very lively early C18 brick front of four bays, not at all correct or polite. Two-bay centre with a pediment on giant pilasters. In the pediment a horizontally placed oval window with a wreath as a surround and a mask at the top. Doorway with segmental pediment on brackets. The bust on top may be a recent addition.

GARSTON HOUSE, 1 m. W, below the road, by the river. C16–C17 with mullioned windows. The MHLG points out that the walls are *c*.3 ft thick and may be older than the C16.

KNIGHTON MANOR HOUSE. The doorway is C16, with a four-centred head. At the back five-light mullioned and transomed windows, late C16 or early C17.

On KNIGHTON HILL a Saxon FORTIFIED PLACE (HR).

BROAD HINTON

ST PETER AD VINCULA. An E.E. church, much restored by *Ponting* in 1879. The earliest-looking motif is the (re-set) priest's doorway, round-arched and single-chamfered. But this may be contemporary with the (re-set) organ chamber lancets, and the group of three stepped lancets close together in the chancel E wall. Probably late C13 the nave doorways. W of the S doorway a small lancet with a shouldered rere-arch. The nave is aisleless, but aisles were probably removed in the C17 (*see* below). The chancel arch was shifted in the C19 to be the connexion between chancel and organ chamber. Narrower than the present Victorian one, it has semi-octagonal responds and, instead of capitals, just curious twin hanging lobes at the angles. Double-chamfered arch. The W tower is Perp, ashlar-faced, and has a tall arch towards the nave, and a stair-turret rising above the battlements. The C17 alterations are datable by the date 1634 on the roof, which has tie-beams and, higher up, hammerbeams, and plenty of pendants, a rough but stylish piece. Of the C13 aisles evidence may be provided by some fragments now built in at the E end of the nave. There is the base of a semicircular respond

and a capital of a respond with naturalistic foliage. Also at the
E end of the nave some small Norman fragments. – PULPIT.
Gothic of 1843, but with C18 parts. – STAINED GLASS. E window by *Clayton & Bell*, probably of the time of the restoration.
– PLATE. Set, 1676. – MONUMENTS. A remarkable number,
and at least two of remarkable quality. C13 coffin lid in the
chancel. Foliated cross and above it a lady's head in relief sunk
in a quatrefoil. – Low tomb recess with coffin, re-set in the s
chapel. – Sir William Wroughton † 1559, an extremely fine
example of the Early Elizabethan style, still linked closely to
the Perp tradition. Of the canopy type, open towards the s
chapel. Tomb-chest with inscription in a fine strapwork cartouche. Canopy with an arch consisting of a straight top on
quadrant bits. Inside the jambs of the canopy incised cross and
hands, feet and heart of Christ. Above the arch inscription
referring to Queen Elizabeth I. – Sir Thomas Wroughton †1597
and wife. Large standing monument, of the six-poster type.
Two kneeling figures facing E, she with a big widow's hood.
The two front arches of the canopy are of a crazy design. Each
is two-thirds of a trefoil arch, the missing thirds being the outer
ones. The corner columns are therefore taller than the middle
column. – Col. F. Glanville, killed fighting for the king at
Bridgewater in 1645. Standing alabaster figure in an oblong
niche with semicircular top and bottom. He is in armour and
holds the metal staff of a standard. His own real ARMOUR is
displayed above. All along the niche runs an inscription engraved in a band of slate, and on a panel of slate below it says:

> Nec dedit aut Marti Invenē Dabit Anglia pugnax
> Maiorem: sat erit progenuisse parem.

In the sides of the niche excellent small alabaster reliefs of
Victories, and at the foot the small, reclining figure of a woman
in her shroud. Her agonized features are not easily forgotten. – 40
John Glanville, 1673. Inscription tablet with open scrolly pedi-
ment and garlands along the sides. – Mrs Frances Stone † 1715.
Good, simple marble tablet.

BROAD TOWN

CHRIST CHURCH. 1844 by *W. Hinton Campbell*, at the expense
of the Marchioness of Ailesbury (cf. Savernake). In the lancet
style, with a w bellcote. The detail quite seriously and generously done. – STAINED GLASS. In the middle of the three E
lancets medallions by *T. Baillie* (TK). – PLATE. Paten, 1782.

The WHITE HORSE on the hill above Little Town Farm was cut out of the turf as late as 1863. It is 78 by 57 ft, and at the time of writing poorly kept up.

BINCKNOLL CASTLE, 1½ m. NE. Motte and bailey castle on a chalk promontory. The top was scarped off to form the motte.

BROKENBOROUGH

9080

ST JOHN BAPTIST. Low, by a low farmhouse. Bell-turret of timber at the E end of the nave. Early C13 N arcade of four bays. Circular piers and circular abaci. Double-chamfered round arches. Later C13 chancel arch. Dec chancel windows. The rest Perp. – FONT. Octagonal, Perp, with quatrefoils; bad. – PULPIT. Small, Jacobean. – READER'S DESK. A panel dated 1641. – PLATE. Chalice, 1651.

BARN, ⅛ m. s. Very large, with two porches and angle buttresses. Collar-beams on arched braces inside. But alas, alas roofed with corrugated iron (at the time of writing).

BROKENHAM see NUNTON

BROMHAM

9060

ST NICHOLAS. Remains of the Norman predecessor of the church small blocked windows in the N wall and a doorway in the W wall. E.E. chancel (rebuilt accurately by *Slater & Carpenter* in 1876) with three stepped E lancets, internally fully shafted, and N lancets. The central tower was also begun at that time, see the arches to W and E with two big hollow chamfers. Its recessed spire is Perp. C14 s arcade of four bays with octagonal piers and moulded arches. Two-storeyed Perp s porch, much restored. Inside, against the church wall above the doorway a fan-coving, as if for a former balcony. Simple Perp N windows. But the feature which makes a visit to the church memorable is the s chapel or Tocotes and Beauchamp Chapel, for which licence was granted in 1492 to Sir Roger Tocotes and to Sir Richard Beauchamp, son of Tocotes's wife by her first marriage. Later it became the Baynton Chapel. The chapel is very similar to the s chapel at St John, Devizes. It is three bays long and exceedingly ornate. Buttresses decorated with thin buttress shafts and pinnacles. Five-light window with angel-busts at the apex. Small doorway with an ogee gable, treated in pierced work inside. Battlements with quatrefoils, pinnacles with their

24b

own decoration. Inside, the middle of the three bays is singled out by arches with fleurons to the W and E and a tierceron-vault with a large, oddly shaped pendant surrounded by a ring of liernes. Similar arches to the chancel, two bays only, as the W bay was the S transept of the E.E. church. Image niches in the S wall and to the l. of the E window. Excellent painted ceiling. – FONT. Octagonal, Perp, with little pendants and simply panelled fields. – SCREEN. To the S chapel. Simple, of one-light divisions. – DOOR. To the tower. C15. With tracery. – STAINED GLASS. In the S chapel SE window original canopies and figures in the tracery heads. – E window, c.1870, excellent, by *William Morris*, i.e. the figure-work from *Burne-Jones* cartoons (A. C. Sewter). – W window by *Constable* of Cambridge, 1879. – MONUMENTS. Sir Richard Tocotes † 1457. Alabaster effigy on tomb-chest with twin arches framing quatrefoils. Free-standing. – Excellent monument of Purbeck (?) marble to Elizabeth Beauchamp, c.1492. Tomb-chest with cusped quatrefoils containing shields. Canopy arcading merging into the heavy top. Against the back wall kneeling image of brass. – Brass to John Baynton † 1516. A 3-ft figure. – Sir Edward Baynton † 1593. Tomb-chest with shields in lozenges. Gothic cresting still, though supported on two columns. Brasses against the back wall. – Three HELMS and GLOVES in the S chapel. – In the churchyard tall Celtic CROSS to commemorate Thomas Moore, who lived at Sloperton Cottage (*see* below) and is buried at Bromham. Erected in 1906.

A few nice houses close to the church. Immediately to the S a cottage with a cruck-truss in the centre (NBR), to the NE at the corner of the churchyard the LOCKUP of timber, and further NE a timber-framed cottage with narrowly spaced uprights. To the SW a timber-framed house with a square porch on Tuscan columns. The l. and r. sides of the porch have Jacobean balusters. W of this another cottage with narrowly spaced uprights and then, down the hill, the COLLEGE OF THE POOR, almshouses dated 1612. Six gables of timber-framing. Stone ground floor. Decayed at the time of writing.

At WESTBROOK, ½ m. NW of Bromham, NONSUCH, a fine house of c.1700. Seven bays, two storeys, three-bay pediment, hipped roof. Doorway with segmental pediment, carved below the pediment and on the lintel. The windows and the doorway have bolection-moulded surrounds. One good fireplace of c.1760 inside, with caryatid maidens in profile.

SLOPERTON COTTAGE, to the SW of Nonsuch. With pretty

Gothic trim, including a porch and a bay window. Early C19. Thomas Moore, the poet, lived here.

WANSDYKE. Wansdyke has been regarded until recently as a continuous earthwork, but work by Sir Cyril and Lady Fox and Mr Anthony Clark has shown that it consists of two lengths separated by a gap extending from the region of Bath to Morgan's Hill, N of Devizes. It is the E portion which lies mainly in Wiltshire. The two segments are linked by the Roman road from Bath (Aquae Sulis) to Mildenhall (Cunetio). At Morgan's Hill the Roman road and Wansdyke diverge and at this junction a section was cut across the two in the C19 showing the Wansdyke to be superimposed on the road. From Morgan's Hill the dyke runs E to All Cannings Down, and at Red Shore cuts across the Ridgeway; it then swings NE through West Woods, where it becomes more broken, and in Savernake Forest large gaps occur – probably undefended because dense forest would provide a natural barrier. SE of Chisbury Camp a short stretch is visible, followed by a further gap, until it reappears N of Shalbourne. The precise purpose of the earthwork is uncertain. It is of Late Roman or post-Roman date and referred to as the Wansdyke in C10 Saxon charters. Throughout its course the ditch faces N, and so it was possibly constructed by Britons against Saxon penetration from the Upper Thames region.

WEST PARK FIELD, ½ m. N, on the r. of the Chippenham Road. A ROMAN VILLA was excavated here in the C19, when several rooms were found, two with tessellated pavements – hypocaust and bath house.

MOTHER ANTHONY'S WELL, 1 m. NW of Roundway. Site of a ROMAN VILLA with traces of wall foundations which produced many fragments of mosaic flooring.

OLIVER'S CAMP. *See* Roundway.

BROOK HOUSE *see* SOUTHWICK

8060

BROUGHTON GIFFORD

ST MARY. E.E. N arcade of four bays with round piers with round abaci and double-chamfered arches. E.E. priest's doorway in the chancel with trefoiled head. About 1300 the S chapel of two bays was built (octagonal piers, double-chamfered arches). The chancel arch corresponds to the chapel arches. One small window with a pointed trefoiled head in the chapel,

another in the nave W of the porch. The porch itself is attached
to the chapel. It is Perp and was originally two-storeyed. Flat
niches with supporter angels in relief to the sides of the entrance. Perp W tower with a small recessed pyramid roof. –
STAINED GLASS. Some Perp glass in a N aisle window. –
PLATE. Cup and Paten Cover, 1576; Almsbowl, 1731.

RECTORY. Built c.1850 by *T. H. Wyatt*. Gabled, in the C17
style.

MONKTON HOUSE, ⅝ m. SE. Dated 1647. Irregular, with gables.
Pedimented early C18 doorway. The door with a large central
oval is C17. Inside a chimneypiece, partly stone with three big
quatrefoils, partly stucco and C17.

On the way to Broughton Common at the junction of MILL
LANE the MANOR HOUSE, dated 1622, L-shaped, with gables
and mullioned windows. Porch with round-arched entrance.

BROUGHTON COMMON, ¾ m. NW. The BAPTIST CHAPEL was
built in 1806. Round-headed windows in two tiers on the front,
long ones divided by a mullion in two on the side. Between it
and the Manor House HOLLYBROOK HOUSE, late C18, of
three bays, with the familiar rhythm of two–one–two lights.
Flat, broad mullions. Lower, one-bay wings. Overlooking the
Common on the N side GIFFORD HALL, c.1700, five bays,
two storeys, hipped roof. Middle pediment. Doorway with
segmental pediment carved on the underside. The staircase has
a beautiful plaster ceiling with detached flowers in the bands
framing the panels. Thin turned balusters.

BROUGHTON HOUSE is on the S side of the Common. It is dated
1673 and has two gables and symmetrical fenestration of three-
and two-light windows.

BRUNTON HOUSE *see* COLLINGBOURNE
KINGSTON

BULFORD

1040

ST LEONARD. Flint. Very big, squat S tower, with its pyramid
roof no higher than the nave. Elizabethan entrance. The date
of the tower itself cannot be verified. The proportions make a
Norman or E.E. date likely. Norman the round-arched inside
of a N window, the chancel arch (with a pretty, cinquefoiled
altar-niche to its r.), and the round-arched insides of chancel
windows. E.E. the one lancet in the S wall of the nave, the S
doorway with one order of shafts carrying stiff-leaf capitals and
an arch with a roll moulding, and the lancet to the N wall of the

chancel. The chancel corbel-table also rather E.E. than Norman. Single-frame roof with tie-beams; in the chancel they are
moulded. The E window is Perp and has, again inside, panelled
reveals and little canopied niches. Long N transept, built in
1855. – FONT. Square, plain, of Purbeck marble (?). – COM-
MUNION RAIL. C17, with flat balusters. – PAINTING. Traces
of much wall painting, including a St Christopher E of
the nave NW window and something now unrecognizable W
of the same window. – PLATE. Chalice, 1570; Flagon, 1636.*

MANOR HOUSE, SW of the church. With four even gables. Mullioned windows, replaced by sash windows on the first floor.
Apsed hood above the doorway.

BULFORD BARRACKS. Started in the first World War, but mostly
built in 1935–9 and now covering an area of one square mile.
The impression is of a garden suburb, tree-planted streets,
Neo-Georgian houses, and bigger buildings. Hutments look
as if tomorrow they also will have turned Neo-Georgian. However, the most recent housing is one stage further in architectural fashions, rather like pretty new council housing.

ST GEORGE, Garrison Church. By *G. L. W. Blount & William-
son*, 1920–7, large, Perp, spick and span and smug. Rock-faced.
Crossing tower, five-light aisle windows, W, N, and S rose
windows.

BULIDGE *see* HARDENHUISH

9050   BULKINGTON

CHRIST CHURCH. 1860 by *T. Cundy*. Nave with bellcote and
chancel. Rubble walls. Tracery of *c.*1300.

2060   BURBAGE

ALL SAINTS. Flint with a stone pattern. Built in 1854 by *T. H.
Wyatt*; S aisle 1876. Only the low W tower is old. Arch towards
the nave with two continuous chamfers. Spreading façade with
the two aisles embracing the tower and having their own pitched
roofs. The W porch entrance is old too, with its big leaf stops
– probably Dec. – STAINED GLASS. By *Powell* S aisle 1859,
1863. – PLATE. Chalice and Paten Cover, 1624; Flagon, 1733;
Paten, 1739.

CANAL WHARF, 1½ m. NNW. Group of brick buildings.

WOLF HALL, ¾ m. ENE. Opposite the present Victorian house
in a dip a red-brick house with one Tudor wing with mullioned

* The vicar communicated the dates 1577–8 and 1576 to me.

windows and a group of tall Tudor chimneyshafts (polygonal with projecting tops) and one wing refronted *c.* 1740.

BRIMSLADE FARMHOUSE, 2 m. NW. C17 S front with three gables, symmetrical, of two storeys with a three-storeyed porch. The ground floor of brick in chequer pattern, the rest tile-hung. All windows sashed. (Inside panelling, especially, in one upper room, C16 panelling. MHLG)

ROMANO-BRITISH BURIAL. At Southgrove Farm a male skeleton accompanied by crossbow, whetstone, bronze tweezers, iron hammerhead, and knives was found in 1893.

BURCOMBE   *0030*

ST JOHN BAPTIST. Anglo-Saxon chancel, see the unmistakable long-and-short E quoins. Short S porch tower, the top of 1667. N aisle of 1858, and all other external details C19. – SCULPTURE. Defaced Crucifixion on the sill of the W window; probably from a cross-head. – PLATE. Chalice and Paten, 1629.

UGFORD FARMHOUSE, ¾ m. E. The l. part timber-framed with thatch, the r. part stone, of two storeys with a dormer and mullioned windows. This part is dated 1635.

BURDEROP PARK   *1080*
1¼ m. W of Chisledon

A square, stone-faced Early Georgian block of two and a half storeys, three to five bays in size and rather forbidding externally. The only more ornate front to the E. Here the doorway and windows on the ground floor have pediments (segmental and triangular) and frames of the Gibbs type. To the S doorway with segmental pediment on carved brackets. Also to the S two detached service wings at r. angles to the front. In spite of the external appearance, the house is much older. Two rooms on the ground floor have Jacobean (or earlier) plaster ceilings with geometrical patterns of thin ribs.* On the first floor above a chimneypiece a large painted coat of arms surrounded by garlands and dated 1663. Also at the back a formerly detached service building with windows with wooden crosses and the old leaded glazing, i.e. later C17. Of the time of the façades the whole top storey (which is of brick, stone-faced) and also one splendid fireplace with a head in the lintel and the spacious staircase in the middle of the house (former courtyard?). This has three turned balusters to the tread.

* In one of them initials and the figure 36.

BURTON *see* NETTLETON

BURY HILL *see* PURTON

0070

BUSHTON
¾ m. NW of Clyffe Pypard

MANOR FARMHOUSE. Brick with stone trim. Five bays, two storeys. Hipped roof. In the middle of the façade doorway with semicircular hood on brackets. Arched window above it. Another almost identical doorway on the side. The house has a datestone 1747 on the façade, a late date for a house which looks more like 1725.

3060

BUTTERMERE

ST JAMES. In perhaps the most tucked-away position of any Wiltshire church, and also perhaps the smallest of all.* Nave and chancel in one. The spirelet has been taken down. Simple late C13 windows, mostly of one light. – FONT. Norman, of tub-shape, with a band of flat zigzag. – PULPIT. C18.

CADLEY

2060

Savernake Forest, 2 m. SE of Marlborough

CHRIST CHURCH. 1851 by *T. H. Wyatt*. Big cypress-trees nearly hide the one distinguishing feature of an otherwise dull church, the naughty w front consisting of a tall two-light window on the l. of a middle buttress, a small, low projecting baptistery on the r. of it, a window above this in the form of a spherical triangle (and filled with three spherical triangles), and a circular window in the gable (filled with three trefoils and three small circles).‡

9070

CALNE

24a ST MARY. The proud church of a prosperous clothiers' town. Nearly all Perp outside, the great age of Calne. Transeptal N tower with set-back buttresses decorated in four tiers with buttress shafts and pinnacles in the Somerset fashion. This tower is however not Perp but Perp Survival (rather than Revival). The crossing tower of the church collapsed in 1638 and was replaced by the present one. The w doorway also looks an alteration of the C17. The windows, curiously enough, have

* But cf. Fifield Bavant.

‡ Outside, against the E wall tablet to Robert Byron, who died in 1941 aged thirty-five.

intersected tracery. Everything W of this is embattled and pin-nacled. Five-light W window, three-light clerestory windows. Spacious N porch datable to *c.*1470, with a lierne-vault and pendant. A C14 chapel between the porch and the tower. S porch, S chapel, and S transept are a rebuilding of 1864 (by *Slater*; PF). Inside, the church makes quite a different picture, equally grand but much earlier. The Norman nave already had the full width of the present nave. Five-bay arcades of *c.*1160–70. Circular piers, multi-scalloped capitals, also with decorated scallops, square abaci, single-step round arches. The first bays from the W on the N side come first, the third and fourth next, then the first four on the S side. The last arches belong to after 1638. The crossing tower must have fallen to the N and E; for at the E end of the S aisle the Norman arch from the aisle into the Norman transept remained intact. The rebuilding was done with classical Tuscan columns. The arches, imitating medieval mouldings, include those of the nave E bay. C17 two-bay ar-cades to the chancel chapels. Of the Norman church the only other remaining piece is a part of a doorway, now re-set inside the N doorway. Zigzags meeting at r. angles; hood-mould with billets. Good nave roof of low pitch with tie-beams and tracery over. – FONT. Octagonal, Perp, with quatrefoils. – REREDOS. Designed by *Pearson*, 1890. – The ALTAR in the chapel W of the S transept and the very large and sumptuous ORGAN CASE, both decidedly Arts and Crafts, are by *C. R. Ashbee*, made by his Campden Guild *c.*1905. – CHEST (N aisle). Uncommonly big. – STAINED GLASS. S chapel E window by *O'Connor*, 1866. – MONUMENTS. William Norborne †1659; nice tablet. – Bene-dict John Angell Angell † 1856. With a circular relief with two angels and a portrait medallion above.

FREE CHURCH, Church Street. 1867 by *Stent* of Warminster. Rock-faced, Gothic, with (ritually speaking) NW tower. Geo-metrical tracery. Terrible.

ZION CHAPEL, Pippin Road. 1836. Straight-headed windows and a steep pediment. The minister's house is attached.

TOWN HALL. 1884–6 by *Bryan Oliver* of Bath. Tudor with Gothic touches. Asymmetrical tower. Not much can be said in its favour. – REGALIA. Loving Cup of 1741–2 or 1756–7; silver-gilt Snuff-box of the early C18.

SCHOOLS, *see* in the Perambulation below.

PERAMBULATION

The hub of Calne is without any doubt HARRIS'S BACON

FACTORY, founded about 1770. The nice two-storeyed office building of stone, Tudor, with Baroque motifs, is dated 1901. Towering over it the big utilitarian main building of five storeys, built in 1923 and 1930. Across Church Street the addition of 1953–4, more severe, but also more stylish. The factory faces the Town Hall across THE STRAND. The best building here however is the LANSDOWNE ARMS HOTEL (formerly the Catherine Wheel), Late Georgian, long and low, thirteen bays with an unbroken parapet. Round the corner of the Town Hall in PATFORD STREET one pretty C17 (?) cottage with two canted bays, and one early C19 ashlar-faced house with two bows and a doorway with Tuscan columns and a pediment. In the HIGH STREET to the N nothing of importance. Halfway up it MARKET HILL, a turfed triangle, not now at all market-ish. Nice houses around, especially one of 1705, pink-washed, of five bays. Pedimented canopy of wood. From here to the S the short CASTLE STREET to the interesting CASTLE HOUSE, on the site, it is said, of a castle (of which nothing is known). The house seems to be Jacobean. It has an even street front of four wide bays with mullioned and mullioned and transomed windows. The back range is of c.1800, ashlar-faced with a central bow. The two ranges are connected by a recessed range again with mullioned windows. (Inside a stone chimneypiece of the mid C17. Above the mantelshelf a roundel with two putti holding cornucopias.) From the N end of the High Street CUR-ZON STREET turns W. Right at the beginning a fine double house with the date 1741 on a rainwater head. The house appears earlier. Segment-headed windows in moulded frames, even quoins, doorways with open segmental pediments. One would say c.1710–20. To the l. and r. a projecting ashlar-faced bay, evidently Late Georgian. Then ST MARY'S SCHOOL with a big range of 1932. (Reliefs by Mrs *Birnstingl*.)

But the principal walk is to the SE and S, starting unpromisingly under the bridges of Harris's factory, that is down CHURCH STREET. Facing the church some stately ashlar-faced early C19 houses, e.g. one with Venetian windows without the divisions between the three parts. To the N of the church the former CHURCH HOUSE, one-storeyed, with a mullioned window under the gable, to the SE of the church DR TOWNSON'S ALMSHOUSES, founded in 1682. Very modest. Four pairs built on a curve. Rendered, with mullioned windows under hood-moulds. On in Church Street, passing the Youth Hostel (C17 with a canted bay window with mullions and transom), to the place where The Green, the London Road, and Silver Street meet.

In SILVER STREET at the start HARRIS'S SOCIAL CLUB, formerly Woodlands, the Harris mansion, an atrocity of 'free Renaissance', i.e. vaguely Italianate, details. Built in the late 1860s.* A good deal further out VERNLEAZE, early C19, ashlar-faced, with a veranda of coupled unfluted Ionic columns with rather inelegant capitals. At the corner of LONDON ROAD and The Green the WHITE HART HOTEL, c. 1800, with a porch of two pairs of columns. Then THE GREEN, a spacious triangle with the wealthiest houses of Georgian Calne. Opposite the White Hart the BOYS' SCHOOL of 1829, with a pretty Gothic stone front. A second front to the E, and an almost identical one a little further N for the GIRLS' SCHOOL – see the statuette of a girl in the gable. The principal houses are on the S and E sides. On the S side No. 19 with a datestone 1758, but with its two-light windows with flat frames a good deal earlier-looking. On the E side ADAM HOUSE, C18, of three bays, the central window a low Venetian one. The parapet rises above this. It has four pineapples. Two more C18 houses with pediments on brackets over their doorways. No. 9 lies back and is of four storeys. Five widely spaced bays, three-light windows. Was this a mill? No. 5 is similar, though of only three storeys. It has a central archway. No. 4 is of three bays and two and a half storeys with Venetian windows on the ground floor. It is ashlar-faced, whereas Nos 5 and 9 have coursed rubble walling.

VERLUCIO. On the S boundary of the parish, on the Roman road between Bath (Aquae Sulis) and Mildenhall (Cunetio), is the supposed site of the Roman town of Verlucio. So far no structural remains other than tesserae have been found to support this attribution.

NUTHILLS ROMAN VILLA, NE of Sandy Lane. Of corridor type. One large room and parts of others have been excavated. The large room contained a fountain and drain. The walls were plastered and painted with geometric designs in red, blue, and black. Small finds included Samian and coarse wares, a bronze brooch, glass, and a large quantity of horse, sheep, and pig bones.

STUDLEY ROMAN VILLA, ¾ m. W of Calne and E of Studley Brooke Farm. Remains of bath, hypocaust, and pillars were discovered in the C18.

* Opposite, in the garden of SOUTH PLACE is an C18 GROTTO, at the time of writing in poor condition and likely to disappear soon.

CALSTONE
2½ m. SE of Calne

ST MARY. Small, on the slope of the downs. Nave and chancel and W tower with parapet. – FONT. C18. Simple, octagonal, with part-fluting. – STAINED GLASS. A panel of fragments of old glass in the S chancel window. – PLATE. Chalice and Paten, c.1728.

CAN COURT see LYDIARD TREGOZE

CASTERLEY CAMP see UPAVON

CASTLE COMBE

ST ANDREW. Essentially a Perp church, except for the fine chancel E wall of the late C13 with four pointed-trefoil-headed lancets and one small quatrefoil over, except for the Dec N chapel E and N windows with flowing tracery, and except for the fact that in 1850–1 much of the church was pulled down and faithfully rebuilt. Proud W tower with diagonal buttresses, decorated with buttress-shafts and pinnacles in relief, in the Somerset fashion, panelled battlements, pinnacles, and the spire of the stair-turret reaching up higher than the rest. Three-light bell-openings. Tall arch to the nave and fan-vault high up. The tower was begun in 1434. Embattled N and S aisles, the S aisle with a small E doorway. Arcades of three wide bays with piers of the familiar Perp four-shafts-four-hollows section and capitals decorated with leaf and angel-busts. The climax is the chancel arch, on which, as in the voussoirs of a French cathedral, portal statuettes stand under canopies and lean up the arch. The chapels are separated from the aisles not by arches but by half-arches, i.e. flying buttresses. – FONT. A C14 bowl with eight blank ogee arches, demi-figures against the bottom of the bowl, and a fine, C13 support of short piers and big openwork four-petalled flowers, or should one say ornamental dogtooth? – SCREEN. To the N chapel. Simple, Perp. – PULPIT. Simple, Perp. – STAINED GLASS. E, W, nave E (rose), and N chapel E windows by *Ward & Nixon*. Others by *Gibbs*. – PLATE. Flagon, 1721; two Patens, 1774; Chalice and Cover, 1775.– MONUMENTS. Tomb-chest with effigy of a cross-legged Knight, two angels by his pillow. Six mourners under thick, almost vegetable ogee arches. Early C14. – Walter Fisher, erected 1764. Urn against grey obelisk. – Scrope Family Monument, 1850. Big, Victorian Gothic, with tomb-chest and triple canopy.

MANOR HOUSE. Low, gabled, 1664 (date on the panelling of the staircase hall), but too much victorianized to be judged (large new wing 1873). In the grounds the BELL-TURRET of the demolished church of St Peter, Biddestone. Square with spire. The four stone posts carry twice-shouldered lintels. Also in the grounds a big Gothic ARBOUR. The ice-house has been filled in.

CASTLE. N of the house on rising ground, about ½ m. away. Earthwork and scanty remains of masonry.

MARKET CROSS. The four heavy stone posts now carry timber beams and the roof. Inside, the cross on a tall base decorated with quatrefoils. Pinnacles at the apex of the roof. S of the cross MOUNTING BLOCK. A HOUSE to the l. of the entrance to the churchyard has a Perp three-light window, probably re-set.

The Cross is the hub of Castle Combe. The church is to the E, 2b the Manor House to the NE. The village is famous and indeed unspoiled, except by over-restoration and tidying up of the houses, especially the bigger ones. The best of them is perhaps the DOWER HOUSE to the N, of c.1700, with four gables, cross-windows, and a doorway with a shell-hood on volutes. To the S close row of gabled cottages.

VICARAGE. 1848. In the traditional local style, copied largely from Leigh Delamere rectory.

SHRUB HOUSE, ½ m. SW. The house has an unusually long BARN with two porches, unfortunately largely pantiled.

CASTLE EATON ₁₀₉₀

ST MARY. Very attractively placed by the river Thames. Two Norman doorways, the southern one with one order of colonnettes and zigzag in the arch. Hood-mould with pellet decoration on two beasts' heads. Late C13 chancel, see the chancel arch and the shafted E window of three trefoil-headed lancets. The nave on the S side has a corresponding window, the others are by *Butterfield*, who restored the church in 1862. To this period belongs the one memorable feature of the church, the heavily corbelled-out bell-turret with spire.* Pretty N chapel with a N window whose reticulated tracery is interrupted by a circle at the top, a piscina, and next to it a charming corbel with a little man, upside down. Blocked crypt below. Perp W tower, in vain

* Inside an original early C14 BELL, rediscovered in 1900.

trying to compete with the spire and the turret. Inside, the remarkable thing is the timber posts on stone plinths (made for stone piers?) to separate the N aisle. – FONT. Norman, drumshaped. With a big leaf trail. – PULPIT. Sumptuous Jacobean piece, but at the foot part of the top frieze of a Perp screen. – WOODEN SUPPORT. Dated 1704. Twisted shaft and top with arms. Was it for a w gallery? – PAINTING. Good Virgin and Child (N arcade, E respond). – STAINED GLASS. In the E window glass of 1862. – PLATE. Paten, 1708. – CHURCHYARD CROSS. Base and part of the shaft.

RED LION INN. Georgian. Brick. Of three wide bays with a stone-slated hipped roof.

CHALCOT HOUSE see DILTON MARSH

CHAPEL PLASTER see BOX

8040

CHAPMANSLADE

ST PHILIP AND ST JAMES. By *Street*, 1869. Nave with square bell-turret set diagonally, and chancel. Lancets and windows with plate tracery. 'A model of its kind' (GR).

BAPTIST CHAPEL. 1788. Segment-headed brick windows in a stone building. Hipped roof.

WHEELWRIGHT'S ARMS. C18, brick, low, of five bays and two storeys.

No. 54. Of three bays and three storeys. Early C18.

DEAD MAIDS, ½ m. NE, at the main crossing. Of three bays, with an apsed door-hood.

9020

CHARLTON
1¼ m. s of Donhead St Mary

CHAPEL. 1839 by *William Walker* (GR). Neo-Norman, a plain oblong, but with a two-tower façade, the towers sensibly short. They are castellated, as is the piece between them. w gallery on Norman posts. – PLATE. Chalice, 1734.

(COOMBE HOUSE (St Mary's Convent), 1 m. w. Neo-Tudor, 1886.)

1020

CHARLTON
1¾ m. SE of Nunton

ALL SAINTS. By *T. H. Wyatt*, 1851. Brick, E.E., with bellcote.

SCHOOLHOUSE. 1622. Brick, of three bays with mullioned windows, later altered. Symmetrical front of two storeys. One bay added.

CHARLTON

2 m. NE of Malmesbury

ST JOHN BAPTIST. Much restored, and the windows called 'all new' by Aubrey in 1670. Even so, the W window of the un-buttressed W tower with good tracery of c.1300 seems convincing.* So does the N chapel E window with pointed trefoiled lights and a quatrefoil in plate tracery, i.e. late C13. However, this window, if old, must be re-set, as the W arch of the N chapel inside cuts into the N arcade, which is the main feature of the church. Four bays with slim circular piers, decorated trumpet-scallop and in one case horizontal stiff-leaf capitals, octagonal abaci and round double-chamfered arches – i.e. c.1200. The N aisle NE window, a small lancet, would go with that. On the S side Perp windows, though one Dec 'low-side' window, and battlements. – FONT. Norman, circular, with a band of pellets and two bands of rope. – PULPIT. One panel of the C17 pulpit above the present one, dated 1630. That may also be the approximate date of the TOWER SCREEN with long, slender balusters and of the SCREENWORK round the organ with columns and little figures at their tops and re-used tracery from the Perp screen. All this belonged to the Suffolk Pew (see below). – Of a stone PARCLOSE SCREEN to the N chapel a little remains next to the altar. – PLATE. Chalice, 1734. – MONUMENT. Sir Henry Knyvett† 1598 and family. An eight-poster with columns carrying a straight entablature (except at the W end, where there is an arch). Very restrained decoration, especially at the top. Only the tomb-chest or base below has plenty of strapwork. Balusters in front to support the columns above. Recumbent stone effigies and kneeling children at the head and foot ends.

Handsome village street with divers attractive houses and, at the E end, a little outside, VILLAGE FARMHOUSE. This must be late C17. Three steep gables with small horizontal oval windows in them. Five bays and two storeys below with stone cross-windows. No projection.

CHARLTON PARK. Though not as large as Longleat or Longford, i.e. what Sir John Summerson calls the prodigy houses, Charlton Park is a prodigy house all the same. It has the fantastical character, the exuberance, the certain heaviness, and to the full the unexpectedness of the prodigy houses. It was built by the Countess of Suffolk, wife of the first Earl of Suffolk, builder of Audley End and the palace near Charing Cross later

* The tower top is probably C17.

known as Northumberland House, and later Lord High Treasurer. She was a Knyvett, and Charlton was Knyvett property.
Four ranges round a courtyard with four corner turrets carrying
ogee caps. Parapets with gay little strap cresting, even up and
34b   down gables. The w side has the entrance. Here two lower
gabled wings project. The façade itself has a projecting middle
porch and is open in a loggia on the ground floor. Attached
sturdy Tuscan columns. The back wall of the loggia was originally open to the courtyard. It was closed when the courtyard
itself was closed. This took place in 1772–6, under the twelfth
earl. The architect was the younger *Matthew Brettingham*. He
also re-did the s and e fronts. The other original front is to the
N. This is of the E-type with the outer strokes higher than the
middle one. The original work has ground-floor windows with
one transom, first-floor windows with three, and a second floor
of varying height. In the turrets the windows at that level have
two transoms, in the bay windows on the N side one, otherwise
none. The most characteristic motif of Charlton Park is a way
of raising in the middle of a big window the transom or lowest
transom to form an arch. This is a motif much favoured about
1670 but very unexpected at the early date of Charlton Park.
But what is that date? It is usually given as 1607, but the source,
a letter of the countess mentioning the house, may just as well
be interpreted as referring to the predecessor of the present
house. The earl fell from grace in 1618 and was rehabilitated
in 1621, though not to his former glory. He died in 1626, she
in 1633. The interior is mostly Georgian and after. The most
important Jacobean survival is the long gallery above the loggia.
This has a square bay (above the porch), a central chimneypiece with a stone lintel with excellent strapwork and a wooden
overmantel with caryatids, two ornate doors with caryatids, and
a ceiling with complicated geometrical patterns of broad ornamental bands of stucco work. As for the later interior work,
the evidence is ambiguous. It was certainly begun about 1772–6,
but not completed until early in the c20. The hall which replaced the courtyard was begun, according to the *Beauties of
England and Wales* (published in 1816), after 1783 and still incomplete when the book came out. The style is perfectly convincing of the last quarter of the c18. Large apse containing
the entrance from the loggia and a second facing the entrance.
Galleries in two tiers along the sides. Glazed oval dome over
the centre. Other rooms with elegant stucco decoration, especially the former dining room, which is entered by the door

in the far apse of the hall. Staircase with simple iron
balustrade.

GARDEN PAVILIONS and WALLS. The pavilions are Georgian; the convex colonnade linking them, however, belongs to
the early C20.

LODGES, on the Malmesbury Road. Neo-Jacobean, of un-
recorded date.

STABLES. Late Georgian, with lantern.

ANDOVER HOUSE. Attached to the stables. Late Georgian,
Gothick façade. Windows with Y-tracery and quatrefoil windows.

VILLAGE FARMHOUSE. Late C17. Excellent flat five-bay front
with cross-windows and three even gables with horizontally
placed oval lucarnes in them.

CHARLTON

1½ m. NW of Upavon

1050

ST PETER. 1858 by *Pearson* (PF). Nave and chancel in one. But
by the side of the nave Perp N porch tower and, attached to its
E side, an embattled one-bay Perp chapel. Straight-headed
windows with angel-busts as hood-mould stops. Angel-busts
also l. and r. of the E window inside. Panelled four-centred arch
towards the church. Ceiling with moulded beams. – In the
chapel BRASSES to William Chancey † 1524 and wife (18-in.
figures), probably the founders of the chapel. – SCREENS. Rood
screen of one-light divisions, the tracery unusual, with straight
diagonals crossing. One foliage band at the top. – The chapel
screen is simpler. – PLATE. Chalice, Paten Cover, and Flagon,
1706.

A Premonstratensian Cell may have existed at Charlton, but this
is by no means certain, and in any case no architectural evidence
remains.

CHERHILL

0070

ST JAMES. Church and manor house are oddly in line, the house
W of the church. Perp W tower with battlements and small
pinnacles, and Perp E window of five lights, inside with shafts,
head stops, and, in an arch moulding, fleurons. On the N side
one Transitional doorway. Perp S aisle arcade of three bays.
Octagonal piers and four-centred arches. – WEST GALLERY.
Early C19 Gothic, on cast-iron columns. – CHANDELIER.
Brass, with the – in England – uncommonly early date 1702.

Probably by *John Spooner* of Bristol († 1703), who signed the chandelier of 1701 at Cirencester. – PLATE. Chalice, 1631; Paten, 1717; Chalice, 1749.

The MANOR HOUSE has mullioned windows with hood-moulds and is much renewed. The famous Cherhill BARN was demolished in 1956. It was 110 ft long, of timber-framing, with nave and aisles, massive timbers, and a huge roof of stone slates.

To the SE, against the face of the downs, the Cherhill WHITE HORSE, 130 ft long, cut into the grass in 1780, and the LANSDOWNE OBELISK, erected in 1845 (41? 43?) by the third Marquis to commemorate his ancestor Sir William Petty, the C17 economist. The outline is heavy, owing to the high base, Victorian proportions as a matter of fact as against the more elegant Georgian proportions.

OLDBURY CASTLE, ¾ m. SE. Univallate hill-fort excavated in the C19, when Iron Age A pottery was found in storage pits within the ramparts.

CHICKLADE

9030

ALL SAINTS. Small, of 1832. Nave and chancel in one: oblong bell-turret. Long two-light windows with transoms, probably an alteration. – SCULPTURE. Small Pietà; wood; German? early C17? – PLATE. Chalice and Paten, 1698.

CHILMARK

9030

ST MARGARET. A handsome cruciform church of generally E.E. appearance. But the earliest part is a re-set doorway of *c.*1200, now in the W wall of the N aisle. Round arch and a goodly roll moulding. Then the chancel with lancets, small to the N, larger to the S; corbel-table. The crossing tower seems Dec from outside – see the bell-openings – but the crossing arches of three chamfers may well be before 1300. Quadripartite rib-vault with single-chamfered ribs rising awkwardly in the spandrels of the arches. The tower has a recessed broach-spire which was rebuilt *c.*1760. The S window of the S transept (three-stepped, cusped lancet lights under one arch) is apparently of the same date as the crossing. The N side is of 1856 throughout, including the aisle arcade. Perp S doorway with hood-mould on primitive busts. – PULPIT. Jacobean. – PLATE. Cup, 1576; Set, 1743.

CHILMARK MANOR, S of the church. C17, with mullioned windows. Three sides of a small court, which is closed by a wall with a gate and gatepiers. The wall curves up to the sides of the house. Attached to the house an earlier range with one pre-Reformation doorway.

CHILMARK HOUSE. Early C19. Three bays, two storeys, with a porch of elongated Greek Doric columns. A C17 terrace opposite, with mullioned windows.

CHILTON FOLIAT

3070

ST MARY. The S arcade is E.E., with round piers and round abaci. But are the triple-chamfered arches all right? The exterior of the S aisle is all the result of *Ferrey*'s restoration of 1845. He also made the E window. The W tower is probably of *c.*1300, see the mouldings of the doorway and the chamfered lancet windows. Above the bell-openings the odd motif of re-used bits of a Norman billet-frieze. Battlements and pinnacles Perp. One N window (cusped Y-tracery) of *c.*1300, the N chapel Perp with three-light windows. Handsome Jacobean nave roof, a semicircular wagon roof on carved wall-posts. – SCREEN. Jacobean, with baluster colonnettes but also (re-use or revival?) Gothic tracery. – FONT. Octagonal, with naively carved sacred scenes, no doubt by *Thomas Meyrick* (*see* Ramsbury). – PLATE. Chalice and Paten on foot, given in 1699; Plate and two Goblets, given in 1796. – MONUMENTS. In the chancel in a low recess effigy of a cross-legged Knight. – Above white marble baby asleep: Francis Hugh Leybourne Popham † 1861, by *E. I. Popham.* – In the churchyard MAUSOLEUM to the Pearse family; heaviest Grecian. Mentioned in *The Beauties of England and Wales* in 1814. By *W. Pilkington* (*see* below).

CHILTON LODGE, ¾ m. E (actually in Berkshire). 1800, by *W. Pilkington.* Monumental five-bay façade of ashlar, only one and a half storeys high but generously spaced with a giant Composite portico to which a wide staircase leads up. Pediment over the portico. The ground-floor windows l. and r. of the portico are set under blank arches. On the E side a porte-cochère, on the W side an attached wing, both said to be by *Sir Arthur Blomfield.* STABLES of brick behind.

CHILTON HOUSE, NW of the church. Red brick, of five bays and three storeys. Late Georgian. To the W canted bay in which the entrance. The entrance hall is octagonal. Behind it, in the centre of the house, a spacious staircase with a cast-iron handrail, lit from above by a circular glazed lantern which appears as a little dome outside.

RECTORY, just E of the church. Georgian. Five bays, two storeys, hipped roof.

VINE COTTAGE, in the village, i.e. further E. Of c.1700. Four bays with a hipped roof. The first-floor windows still with wooden crosses.

BRIDGE HOUSE, by the bridge of the Hungerford road. Rain-water heads 1766. They can only refer to the curious river front, with six tall arched upper windows above a much lower ground floor. To the r. another identical bay added. The gabled house behind apparently older. Can it have been an inn which was given an assembly room in 1766?

₉₀₇₀

CHIPPENHAM

ST ANDREW. Quite an impressive church, and at first acceptably medieval. However, the upper parts of the tower and its open-work parapet and recessed spire are of 1633 – remarkably Gothic indeed, by way of Survival or of Revival? And the in-terior with its Perp arcades (five bays, very thin piers) is of 1875–8, when *R. Darley* rebuilt the nave and chancel and added the N aisle. What then is earlier? First of all the Norman chancel arch was re-used as the arch to the N chapel. It has shafts with multi-scalloped capitals, and zigzag, also up the jambs, and also at r. angles to the wall surface, and to the E of the arch a re-set Norman window appears. The window comes from the nave N wall. Then the lower part of the W tower, with the triple-chamfered arch to the nave. This is Dec. Dec also the N chapel E window, formerly the chancel E window. After that the ornate Perp S (or Hungerford) Chapel built in 1442 by Walter Lord Hungerford, Lord High Treasurer to Henry VI. The buttresses have applied buttress-shafts with pinnacles, and the buttresses themselves have pinnacles too. Battlements. In addition an outer transeptal-looking Perp S chapel with similar details. This was originally two-storeyed. In the chancel re-mains of the original Perp sedilia above the present one. – ROOD SCREEN. By *F. E. Howard*, 1921. – Bits of a Perp SCREEN with closely intertwined branch-work in the spandrels (in the entry to the NE vestry). – ORGAN CASE. A superb piece of c.1730 with turrets and a big segmental centre pediment. – COMMUNION RAIL. C18, with slender twisted balusters. – CHEST. In the S aisle. A very remarkable piece. C13, with two panels flanked by geometrical ornament. Each panel has three animals, one beneath the other, namely the lamb between two doves, a pair of unicorns, a fox and fowl, and two leopards, a hound and stag, and a mobbed owl. – STAINED GLASS. In the outer S chapel a window by *Christopher Whall*, 1918, in a kind of Pre-Raphaelite Expressionism. – PLATE. Set, 1766. – MONU-MENTS. On the E wall of the Hungerford Chapel C13 stone effigy of a Lady; inscription in Norman script. Very flat carving. – In the same chapel plain, badly preserved tomb-chest of Andrew and Sir Edward Baynton; 1570. Shields on the chest. – Sir Gilbert Pryn † 1627 (the date written on later). Big hanging monument with kneeling figures, the couple facing one another across a prayer desk. Obelisks l. and r. Slate inscription plate below l., and r. a plate with three engraved standing couples separated by trees and inscriptions, separated also by dainty branches. The inscriptions are:

> Eche mans a plant: and every tree
> Like man, is subiect to mortalitie.

> These bravnches dead & fallen away are gone
> From vs vntill the Resurrection.

> These grafted thus, by wedlocks sacred dome
> (God gravnte) may flourish, till those other come.

– Many tablets; a recurrent type with inscription plates and very flat ornament comes from the mid and late C17.

ST PAUL. 1854–5 by *Sir G. G. Scott*. Tall and big, with a broach spire 176 ft high. E.E. Geometrical style, handled consistently, but internally not of C13 proportions.

CONGREGATIONAL CHAPEL, Emery Lane, off St Mary's Street. 1750. Three by three bays, plain, with a one-bay pediment.

TOWN HALL, *see* Perambulation.

POST OFFICE, *see* Perambulation.

ST ANDREW'S HOSPITAL, the former WORKHOUSE. Tudor style, 1858. Two parallel ranges connected by a bar. The place where this meets the back range is raised (with an octagonal lantern) as usual.

PERAMBULATION

We start at the W exit of the churchyard and find ourselves in the SE corner of the MARKET PLACE, which consists of an irregular open space and an island of buildings which is pierced in a N–S direction by a pedestrian lane. The island was known as the Shambles. It was started in 1580. Until then the OLD YELDE HALL, probably of the C16, had stood alone. It is timber-framed and, at the time of writing, not too attractive-looking. A plaster coat of arms with the date 1776 in one gable. (In the upper room an oak bench and the bailiff's chair. Built on to the town hall and now a store the former COUNCIL CHAMBER. Timber-framed interior; roof with tie-beams, collar-beams, queenposts, and wind-braces. MHLG) Now round the Market Place. First at the exit from the churchyard to the N a long house of six bays with even quoins and hipped roof (No. 34), probably Queen Anne. To the S CAUSEWAY continues here. Near its start No. 53, timber-framed, with a middle oriel and bits of humble pargetting. No. 39 is a double house, each unit just one bay wide with a big arched upper window. Mansard roof. The continuation of Causeway is LONDON ROAD with some typical early C19 villas, very restrained, ashlar-faced, detached or in pairs.

Close to the same SE corner of the Market Place to the N No. 38, with two canted bay windows and a doorway with pilasters and pediment. The house is however not C18 but C17 remodelled (see the top storey of the bay windows). Then past the corner of St Mary's Street with the new POST OFFICE (1959 by *C. G. Pinfold*) which rounds the corner, a nice, if far from enterprising, design. Opposite a group of tall Georgian houses with canted bay windows (Nos 44–49). One of them has an archway with a Venetian and a lunette window over and a pediment at the top. Facing the western space of the Market Place the stately ANGEL HOTEL, Georgian, of seven bays and three storeys. Porch of pairs of Tuscan columns. Off by a passage to the E to a recent MOTEL on a staggered plan (1959 by *R. J. Brown*). Back to the Market Place and, to the l. of the Angel Hotel, the OLD PALACE, with pedimented doorway and Venetian windows on the ground floor, set under blank basket arches. What date is this? About 1800? Then a seven-bay rubble house with an asymmetrical doorway with Tuscan columns and pediment. Opposite the BEAR HOTEL, thoroughly Tudor Gothic, with a porch and gables.

That is the Market Place. By the Post Office ST MARY'S STREET starts with No. 65, a gabled cottage with rendered wall. No. 61 is of five bays, ashlar-faced, Early Georgian with even quoins and a one-bay pediment. Doorway with pediment on corbels. Then the street hooks round and runs parallel with the Market Place. This stretch is the best at Chippenham. First on the E side THE GROVE with, in its garden, the remains of the SPA started in 1694. Of it some columns and a lintel with a large asymmetrical shell and frond design remain as part of a garden pavilion. No. 54 is of eight bays with a Tuscan porch and stables on the l. No. 53 is of brick for a change, and a handsome early C18 design. Pedimented doorway, slender windows, the middle one arched. Even quoins. Next to it one of the two timber-framed houses of Chippenham worth mentioning. This one has narrowly spaced uprights. Opposite is the E end of the parish church. More Georgian houses. Then opposite an L-shaped C17 house (No. 15), and again on the former side a typical major ashlar-faced Georgian house, five bays, three-bay pediment, pedimented doorway on Tuscan columns. No. 41 is a gabled cottage, No. 18 (on the other side) an irregular seven-bay house with Tuscan doorway, No. 19 (again opposite) the five-bay ashlar-faced type.

St Mary's Street is a quiet backwater area at times when the HIGH STREET is a roaring stream of traffic. We must now walk down this from the Market Place and see what is worth seeing. It is no good looking at ground floors; they are altered by shop windows. At the S end of the island site No. 54 lies across it, ashlar-faced, of four bays. The first interesting house is on the W side: Nos 17–18, timber-framed, with a nicely irregular sky-line. It ought to be preserved. Off to the W here, into RIVER STREET. At its foot, beyond the tear made by a car-park, a tall three-storeyed later C17 house with stone cross-windows, quite impressive but at the time of writing derelict. Opposite the entrance to River Street in the High Street a four-storeyed house of 1908, as if it stood in Mayfair. Again on the W side the TOWN HALL, built by *J. Thompson* in 1848 at the expense of Joseph Neeld, M.P. (*see* Grittleton, p. 233). Arched ground floor. First floor with groups of thin-arched windows or window-lights, a feature typical of the 1840s. Opposite the NATIONAL PROVINCIAL BANK, a small five-bay *palazzo*, slightly debased in the details. 1876 by *G. M. Silley*.

The High Street is continued by the BRIDGE, widened from the medieval form in 1796. Eight or nine round arches. Good balustrade. Then to the l. into BATH ROAD. The oldest part of NESTLE's factory was originally a 'manufactory of cloth' and dates from before 1830. Then in its own grounds by far the most interesting if not the most perfect house of Chippenham: IVY HOUSE.* Its most impressive part is the NE part. This 49b was built, it seems, about 1730 and is in the English Baroque style, say the style of Archer.‡ The main front has a recessed

---

* Its closest competitor was pulled down *c.*1930 and re-erected at Bath (*see The Buildings of England: North Somerset and Bristol*, p. 131).

‡ Mrs Rooke kindly told me that the house was bought in 1725 by John Norris, whose crest is above the front door.

centre and short projecting wings. The centre is of two storeys and three bays with arched ground-floor windows and a doorway with paired columns. Arched window above it provided with volutes at the foot and rising into a broken pediment. The wings are two bays wide and rise to a third storey. This has low arched windows and curving-in sides to support big segmental pediments. The E side has two bows, the S side a doorway with a shell-hood and an arched window over. Fine entrance hall with pilasters, a niche, and other early C18 motifs. Staircase with slim twisted balusters. Long W wing, older than the house but remodelled in 1758 when the pediment was added.

Back to the end of the High Street and up to the r. past the station to MONKTON HOUSE, lying entirely on its own and facing the river. It is of seven bays and three storeys with a three-bay pediment and a doorway with a pediment on detached Ionic columns. (A rainwater head at the back has the date 1757. MHLG) Back again and through the RAILWAY VIADUCT of 1839 with its impressively bare arches. Then up NEW ROAD, with ashlar-faced early C19 villas similar to those in London Road, a typical ribbon development along the arterial roads. Continue up Pew Hill to sample PEW HILL HOUSE (now part of the Westinghouse Brake Company), by *Silcock & Reay*, 1895, in the local Tudor and Stuart style.

LANHILL LONG BARROW, 2 m. W, on the l. of the A420. A fine chambered long barrow, of E–W orientation, 185 by 90 ft. Towards the E end is a false entrance, and there are two burial chambers on the N and one on the S. The N chambers, roofed with flat slabs, produced only unaccompanied skeletons. In the S chamber, which had a corbelled roof, were eleven inhumations associated with Windmill Hill pottery.

0050   CHIRTON

ST JOHN BAPTIST. Lavish Norman S doorway, with one order of colonnettes and continuous zigzag. Also continuous outer beakhead, if the stylized forms up the jambs can be called that. In the arch, interspersed with the beaks are odd motifs: a hand, a head, a little man. But the immediate door surround is Dec. Much else of interest is Dec, especially the S aisle SE window, but it seems to be the work of the restorer of 1850 (*Butterfield*, as GR notes with a question-mark). Low Perp W tower. Late C12 arcade of three bays, terribly scraped. Round piers, square abaci, big capitals with trumpet-scallops, singly placed upright leaves and leaf crockets. Single-framed roof, believed to be the original one of *c*.1200. – FONT. Norman, circular, with statuettes of the twelve apostles under arches. Once apparently an excellent piece. – STAINED GLASS. In the porch window, heads etc. of the C15. – E window signed by *Wailes*. – By him no doubt also the N and S windows.

CONOCK MANOR. A Georgian house of great charm. The oldest piece is the E doorway with an open segmental pediment. That looks *c*.1700 or a little later. Did it perhaps belong to the W front, which has giant angle pilasters and may well be Early Georgian? However, the rest of this front, i.e. the windows (five bays), the pediment over the centre bay, the semicircular porch with fluted Ionic columns, and the single-storey wings to the l. and r., of which one forms an open loggia to the E, are all Later Georgian and may well be part of the same campaign as that to which the STABLES belong. They are of brick and carry a date 1765 on the central lantern. Fine iron RAILINGS in front of the stables and the r. wing of the house. The windows of the E side were gothicized about 1820. Inside there are several nice late C18 fireplaces (brought in from outside), a staircase with a pretty iron handrail, and one exceptionally fine room. This lies in the r. wing, is low, of two bays, and has shallow, coffered groin-vaults. One of the two is of *c*.1820, the other is C20. Of *c*.1820 also the two rustic LODGES with treetrunk porches and some estate COTTAGES, especially one very ornate pair with heavy clustered chimneystacks, and ornate bargeboards to gables and dormers.

CONOCK OLD MANOR, $\frac{1}{2}$ m. W of the Manor. Of *c*.1710. Brick with stone quoins, seven bays, two storeys. Arched windows, doorway with bolection surround. The windows were originally of the cross-type, see the side.

CHISENBURY PRIORY *see* ENFORD

CHISLEDON

HOLY CROSS. Quite a big church. The oldest fragment the top of a small Anglo-Saxon window built into the SW pier of the arcade. This arcade is of five bays and dates from *c*.1200. Round piers, round abaci, pointed arches with one chamfer and a chamfered hood-mould. The capitals go from foliated varieties still dependent on the motif of trumpet scallops to stiff-leaf proper. The W bay is separated from the others by the thickness of the earlier w wall, but seems all the same no later than the rest. The chancel arch is of the same style and date. The E wall of the chancel has a close group of three stepped lancet windows. Below it, outside, a niche with an inset blank panel trefoiled at the top. Originally in it a relief with Crucifixus, Virgin, and St John. Externally the church is mostly Perp. s porch tower. The majority of the windows straight-headed. – STALLS. Some re-used Early Renaissance panels with, e.g., heads in profile. – SCREEN. Two panels in the s aisle probably from the dado of the former screen. – PULPIT. A thickly carved Jacobean piece. – COMMANDMENT BOARDS. C18. In the s aisle, formerly above the chancel arch and originally probably used as a reredos. – SOUTH DOOR. With big iron hinges. – PLATE. Chalice and Paten Cover, 1625; Paten, 1768; Almsdish, dated 1808. – MONUMENTS. In the chancel Perp tomb-chest with shields in cusped panels. – Francis Rutland † 1592 and wife, 13-in. standing brass figures (also chancel). – Edward Mellish † 1707. Tablet with a large family, the man kneeling to the w, the woman to the E. – Many tablets to Georgian members of the Calley family of Burderop Park.

CHISLEDON MANOR. Georgian house of red brick, three bays wide. Close by a TOLLHOUSE with a polygonal front.

ROMAN BUILDING, w of the Plough Inn. A hypocaust, fragments of columns, and Romano-British sherds were found in 1930.

CHITTERNE

9040

ALL SAINTS. 1863 by *T. H. Wyatt*. The w tower faces the street. The church is quite large, with a polygonal apse. Perp is the style chosen, the material flint and stone, used in a rough chequer, as is usual hereabouts. – FONT. Circular, Norman, plain, except for a band of blobs at the foot of the bowl. – PULPIT. Jacobean. – PLATE. Almsdish, 1734. – MONUMENT. Large tablet to Matthew Michell † 1752. Excellent, with trophies l. and r. and a ship sailing along in the 'predella'.

ST MARY, ¼ m. SW, by the manor house. This is the chancel of the destroyed church of St Mary. Chitterne had two parishes. The old All Saints stood somewhat N of Chitterne House. The chancel is Perp, of flint and stone chequer. Inside, bits of STAINED GLASS and a fragment of a MONUMENT. Tomb recess in the N window, its ogee arch outlined against the window. Shafts l. and r. with tops for images or candles. Or was it an Easter Sepulchre and not a monument?

MANOR HOUSE. Brick, L-shaped, though perhaps formerly larger. The ground-floor windows altered, the upper windows with mullions and transoms. C17.

CHITTERNE HOUSE, N of the parish church. Late C17 house of two storeys, flint and stone bands. Symmetrical fenestration, a continuous string-course above the ground-floor windows. The date 1635 appears too early. The back of the house is C18 brick, five bays, plain. To the SW of the house a C17 gateway, round-headed and with a top semicircular on short fluted pilasters. Attached on the l. to this the so-called CHAPEL, an oblong building not orientated. Its windows are mullioned with arched lights and hood-moulds. The roof inside could indeed be earlier than the stonework. Tie-beams, collar-beams, and arched braces. There is no evidence that it was a chapel. Opposite this, a nice group of a timber-framed gable and a stone attachment of two bays with cross-windows.

ASHTON VALLEY BARROW GROUP, see Codford St Peter.

CHITTOE

9060

ST MARY. 1845 by *T. H. Wyatt*. Nave with bellcote, N transept, and chancel. Minimum Dec. Porch in the angle of transept and chancel. – STAINED GLASS. E window by *Wailes*, signed with his monogram.

SANDY LANE, 1 m. NE. WANS HOUSE is of shortly before 1821. (Mainly two storeys; cemented. Three widely-spaced bays, plain parapet. One-storey projecting wings with canted bay windows. Between the wings two-storeyed veranda with iron columns and balustrading. MHLG)

The GEORGE INN at Sandy Lane has on its side a good, quite substantial early C18 doorway with open curly pediment.

CHOLDERTON

2040

ST NICHOLAS. 1850 by *Wyatt & Brandon*. Flint. Nave and chancel in one, and tall polygonal NW turret with spire. Tall two-light windows.

CHOLDERTON HOUSE, opposite the church, i.e. ¼ m. N of the village. Flint and red-brick dressings. Seven bays, two storeys, a flat front. Doorway with carved surround and straight hood.

The centre of the village is on two banks of a little stream.

MANOR HOUSE. Early C18. Vitrified brick with red-brick dressings. Five bays, two storeys, hipped roof, segment-headed windows. To the l. and r. attachments. That on the l. is dated 1732, i.e. it is older than the house in its present appearance, that on the r. is of *c.*1920.

CHRISTIAN MALFORD

9070

ALL SAINTS, by the River Avon. Late C13 work in nave, chancel, and s aisle, i.e. one N lancet in the nave, in the chancel windows with plate tracery, badly treated outside, and inside shafted with some dog-tooth and an untouched piscina, in the s aisle the arcade of four bays with octagonal piers and double-chamfered arches starting out of vertical pieces. The arcade corresponds with the chancel arch. Also a s aisle window shafted inside. This however looks *c.*1300 rather, and the s doorway with its slight ogee at the top and a cinquefoiled arch must be yet a little later. One order of shafts, hood-mould on head-stops. Inside, the doorway has many fine mouldings. Fully Dec indeed the E window, new outside, but all right and shafted inside. Niches l. and r. of it, and a good little piscina close to it. In addition a number of Perp windows, and the SW tower, which is clearly post-Reformation and perhaps C18 rather than C17. Clasping buttresses. Windows with Y-tracery. A second glance, however, will show that the lowest stages are early C14 – see the s doorway and a window looking into the church. The s aisle has a single-framed roof, probably still the original one, the nave a Perp wagon roof. – FONT. Circular; Norman. At the bottom short scallops; above, arches. Drastically re-worked. – SCREENS. The rood screen of narrow one-light divisions. Very finely cusped entrance arch. Perhaps still C14. – The s aisle screen is finer. Also one-light divisions, but coving as well and three top leaf friezes. – STAINED GLASS. In the N aisle, the chancel N, and the s aisle SW windows, some Perp fragments. – PLATE. Almsdish, 1690. – MONUMENT. William Willes † 1815. By *King* of Bath. A big hanging monument with cornucopias l. and r. of the inscription. Above tall standing woman, elegantly draped, by an urn.

SHEKANIAH CHAPEL. 1836. By the Avon, $\frac{1}{2}$ m. N. With pointed windows with Y-tracery and a pedimental gable.

CROSS. Base and shaft. On the green, to the NE (not the N) of a gabled C17 house with mullioned windows.

CHURCH END RING *see* STEEPLE LANGFORD

2050

CHUTE

ST NICOLAS. 1869–72 by *J. L. Pearson*. Flint and red brick. Nave and chancel and SW porch tower with slate-covered broach-spire. Geometrical tracery. Not as interesting as Pearson's neighbouring church at Chute Forest. – FONT. Circular, Norman, with rather disorderly decoration of triangles, lozenges, etc. – PLATE. Chalice and Paten, 1710; Salver, 1726.

STANDEN HOUSE, ¾ m. E. Late C18. Of grey brick. Centre of three bays and three storeys with a pediment and a lantern. Two-storey wings of three bays, making an impressively spread façade. The window surrounds of alternatingly raised bricks, a kind of minimum rustication.

CONHOLT HOUSE, 1¾ m. ENE. Until a few years ago the house consisted of a later C17 part with wooden cross-windows, and at an obtuse angle a later range facing s. The latter remains, the former has been almost entirely pulled down. The obtuse angle is covered over by a semicircular porch of Ionic columns. The remaining range is of seven bays and two storeys with a spacious added bay window to the r. It is of grey brick. Its date is not known. 1810–11 is the most likely: this date is recorded (Kelly), but not precisely what it stands for. In the re-entrant angle an oval staircase was made, with a simple cast-iron handrail. – STABLES with a middle two-bay pediment.

CHUTE FOREST

3050

ST MARY. By *Pearson*, 1875, and a very fine building. Flint and red brick outside, red brick inside. s tower with a tall shingled pyramid spire. Low narrow aisles with lean-to roofs and transverse arches. The nave also has three bold transverse arches. Single-framed roofs. The windows in deep reveals.

CHUTE LODGE. A square brick house of c.1775.* Five bays. Rusticated ground floor, principal floor, and attic floor. On the entrance side a pedimented three-bay projection. An open staircase leads in two arms from l. and r. to the upper entrance. Arches with rocky rustication and half-hidden keystone heads carry the landing. The roof unfortunately altered – see the deep eaves, probably Early Victorian. On the garden side the centre is a big canted bay, and the main windows have Gibbs surrounds. The other two sides have central canted bays too. Inside three principal rooms on the *piano nobile*. Delicate stucco work. The middle room is an octagon, the l. room has a canted bay, the r. room (formerly the library), however, has a segment-headed shallow apse fitted into the external canted bay. In the middle of the house an oval 'flying' staircase, i.e. with

* Chute Lodge is attributed by Mr Colvin to *Sir Robert Taylor*.

steps supported only in the wall. Above a gallery of Ionic columns. Glazed oval dome.

CLACK see BRADENSTOKE CUM CLACK

1030

CLARENDON PALACE

Clarendon appears in a document as a military gathering-place as early as the 1070s. By 1130 or earlier it must have been a royal habitation. Henry II and then Henry III made it into a palace – a palace, not a castle; for even at the time of its greatest extension it was not fortified. A Council was held at Clarendon in 1164, à propos of which Herbert of Bosham calls it a 'nobilis et praeclara regis mansio', and 1166 is the year of the Constitution of Clarendon. Henry III enlarged the palace considerably, and the surviving Liberate Rolls tell of the great hall, the king's and the queen's apartments, several chapels, the kitchen, various offices, and more. Wall-paintings also, mostly secular, are not infrequently mentioned. The palace was much in use throughout the C14 and to the later C15. What remained in the C18 was engraved by Stukeley in 1723. In the C20 nearly all was gone or smothered in trees and undergrowth. In 1933 Professor Tancred Borenius began excavations, and these were continued to just before the Second World War. The area explored was about 750 by 300 ft. The great hall was located with its porch, with the familiar three doors leading out of its lower end wall to buttery, pantry, etc., and by a corridor to the kitchen. The hall was aisled, and beyond its upper end followed the living quarters, a complicated group. Moreover, a large C13 tile pavement of 1250–2, made for the Queen's Chamber, was 14b found* and an exquisite carved head of a young man, no doubt a label-stop and no doubt of *c*.1230. It is similar to those on the screen in the transept at Salisbury Cathedral. The war and the death of Professor Borenius cut excavations short, and today Clarendon is a tragedy. A footpath leads into the wood. One threads one's way through elder and wild clematis. A solitary iron notice-board of the Ministry of Works indicates that one has arrived. One crag of walling stands up. All the rest is back to its sleeping beauty. Surely, out of respect for English history if for no other reason, these remains ought to be as clearly visible as those of Old Sarum.

GATE LODGE. By *Pugin*. White brick with a shaped gable. 1837. He would not have done that later.

---

* This is now in the British Museum.

PETERSFINGER SAXON CEMETERY. Sixty-three pagan-Saxon burials, both male and female, were excavated here in 1949–51. From the male graves came remains of eight shields, spear-heads, and a single iron battle-axe. Large quantities of amber and glass beads, saucer brooches, and a Roman fan-tail brooch were found in the female graves.

CLATFORD BOTTOM see PRESHUTE

CLATFORD HOUSE see FYFIELD

CLEY HILL CAMP see CORSLEY

CLYFFE HALL see MARKET LAVINGTON

CLYFFE PYPARD   *0070*

ST PETER. In a lovely position below a wooded stretch of the cliff. Perp W tower, ashlar-faced, stair-turret higher than the battlements. Pinnacles. Perp nave and aisles and S porch. All over-restored in 1874 by *Butterfield*, who also rebuilt the chancel in 1860. This is evident from his colour effects with painted and inlaid geometrical motifs. Nave arcades with thin octagonal piers. Arches with two hollow chamfers, perhaps interfered with. Nice wagon roof with tie-beams. On the easternmost of them the base for the former rood. – FONT. Carved by the Rev. *F. Goddard* in 1840; and very crisply carved it is. – PULPIT. An exceptionally splendid piece, dated 1629. With an attached pierced iron lectern. – SCREENS. Rood screen and N and S parclose screens, all of the same pattern, with one-light divisions and one carved band along the top. – STAINED GLASS. Old bits in the heads of N and S windows. Also Swiss and Netherlandish panels of the C16 and C17. – Funeral HELM (N aisle). – PLATE. Paten Cover, 1576; Chalice and Paten, 1682. – MONUMENTS. Tomb recess in the N aisle with cusped and crocketed ogee arch. The effigy below is of the later C14, still cross-legged. It is very damaged. – Brass of a Knight, later C14, 4 ft long and very good. – Elizabeth Goddard, 1605. A painted board with a coat of arms flanked by pilasters. – Two kneeling figures from an Elizabethan or Jacobean monument. They are all that remains, and they peep incongruously out of the rood-loft doors. – Thomas Spackman, carpenter, † 1786. By *John Devall Jun.* White marble. He stands on a pink marble base, dressed in ideal clothes with a long flowing mantle and holding an eloquent pose. Below to his l. and r. two children reading and writing. The inscription tells that Thomas Spackman left £1000 for the purchase of Bank three per cent consolidated annuities, largely to pay for a master to teach the poor children of the parish reading, writing, and arithmetick. The monument displays plenty of the tools of the carpenter's trade, a gratifying sight in an age of such snobbery in monuments.

MANOR HOUSE, N of the church. Largely rebuilt c.1880 for Horatio Nelson Goddard. Brick, gabled.

VICARAGE, s of the church. 1839–40. Stone, gabled.

LONG BARROW, ¼ m. SW of Corton. Much reduced by ploughing. Excavation in the C19 revealed a deposit of eight skeletons beneath a cairn at the E end. At the w end, a Later Bronze Age cinerary urn burial has been inserted.

COATE see SWINDON, p. 460

9030

CODFORD ST MARY

ST MARY. Norman stones from a corbel-table kept in the s porch. Also a stone from another place; specially good. E.E. chancel arch, rather coarse, with arched capitals and fat shaft-rings. C14 W tower, not too late in the century, see the deep mouldings of the doorway and the semi-pre-Perp tracery of the window, quite similar to Edington. The rest mostly Victorian. *T. H. Wyatt* worked here in 1843, but the present E.E. s arcade is not his, but replaces his. It must belong to the restoration of 1878–9 by *E. H. Lingen Barker* (PF). – FONT. Norman, circular, just with rolls top and bottom of the bowl. – PULPIT. Jacobean, with two back panels and a later tester. – PLATE. Chalice, c.1500. The original bowl has been replaced (*Ant. J.*, vol. XI). – MONUMENT. Fragmentary. The architectural parts said to belong to the tomb of John Mompesson, rector from 1612 to 1645. A good composition. Fluted Corinthian columns, framing arches with diamond-cut voussoir-stones. Big, well-decorated entablature. The bases of the columns have ribbon pattern, the fields between them shields in simple strap cartouches. Inside broken parts of an effigy of the C14 (?).

9040

CODFORD ST PETER

ST PETER. Along a roaring main road. Tiny Norman bits re-used in the N wall (scale pattern) and the s wall E of the porch (zig-zag). E.E. chancel, though nearly all Victorian, by *T. H. Wyatt*, 1864 (PF). The lower part of the three stepped E lancets is

original. Perp w tower and s aisle. Rebuilt s porch. N aisle and
arcade of 1864. – FONT. Norman. Round base with scallops.
The base shaped like a Norman capital, i.e. round below, square
above. Decoration with rosettes, stars, and saltire crosses. –
Jacobean FONT COVER. – ROOD SCREEN. Neo-Jacobean, by
Eden. – STAINED GLASS. Chancel windows and w window
apparently by *Powell*'s, 1860s and 1870s. – PLATE. Paten, 1717;
Set, 1761. – SCULPTURE. This is of course what matters at 7b
Codford. A piece of a tapering shaft, about 4 ft tall and showing
a man with a mallet holding on to, or raising, a stylized branch.
The man wears a crown or a fillet and his head is violently
thrown back, as in ecstasy. His clothes are rendered with nar-
rowly-set parallel incisions, hard and poignant. The representation is framed by odd thin shafts with many bands, as if
turned in wood. The sides of the pieces have foliage scrolls.
It is probably part of a cross shaft and is universally ascribed
to the C9. But what can it really be compared with?

WOOLSTORE, E of the church, on the main road. Seven bays and
three storeys, brick, with a hipped roof. Arched ground-floor
windows and two small doorways.

ASHTON VALLEY BARROW GROUP. Small cemetery of bowl
barrows, ¾ m. sw of Chitterne. Two of the barrows covered the
graves of warriors with magnificent polished stone battle-axes.

COLD KITCHEN HILL *see* BRIXTON DEVERILL

COLE PARK *see* MALMESBURY, p. 296

COLERNE

8o7o

ST JOHN BAPTIST. Colerne is a hill village. Approaching it from
the s one may picture oneself in the Tuscan hills. The church
stands out with its slender w tower against the sky. This – to
change the picture – and the actual lane up from the s, are
Cornish rather than Wiltshirish. The tower is tall and done
con amore. Set-back buttresses, stair-turret higher than the
tower top and crowned by a spire. Four-light w window, and
the same repeated blank to the N and s. Then a stage of very
tall plain blank panelling but with a canopied niche to w, N,
and s. Then the bell-openings, two of two lights, lengthened
below a transom, but blank. Somerset tracery, and indeed
Somerset affinities. Parapet with a frieze of cusped trefoils in
triangles. The tower and the aisles are ashlar-faced. Inside the

tower tierceron-star vault with an octagon of ribs for the bell-rope hole. The aisles have large Perp windows too. Only the E view, with two Victorian E.E. windows, is disappointing.* As so often, the interior is much earlier than the exterior. Four-bay arcades of *c.*1200–10, unfortunately over-restored. Round piers, octagonal abaci. The S arcade has decorated trumpet capitals and one-step pointed arches. The N arcade is a little later. The arches are double-chamfered, and among the capitals

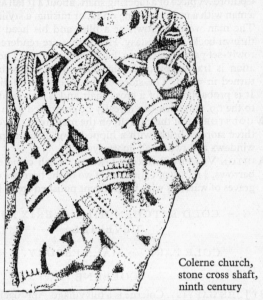

Colerne church,
stone cross shaft,
ninth century

are two with stiff-leaf. The N chapel of two bays goes with the N arcade. In the chancel elaborately vaulted sedilia niches, banished to the N side by Victorian E.E. sedilia. In the S wall a plain C14 tomb recess with ogee top and fleurons. A tomb recess of *c.*1300, with finely moulded arch, in the N chapel N wall. – SCREEN (under the tower). Perp. Of one-light divisions. Traceried dado. Fleuron frieze at the top. – SCULPTURE. Small bearded saint under an arch with colonnettes. The arch is pointed. The style of the arcade and the drapery suggest a date *c.*1200. – CROSS SHAFT. Two large fragments of one of the best C9 crosses in the West Country. The motifs, wildly intertwined

* Restoration 1875 by *Wilson, Willcox & Wilson* (PF).

dragons, flatly carved, are very similar to the Danish Jellinge style. – STAINED GLASS. In a N window old grisaille glass. The E window by *Bell* of Bristol, *c.*1850. – PLATE. Porringer, Cover, and Salver, *c.*1680, parcel-gilt. All three with chased decoration. – MONUMENT. Richard Walmesley † 1893. Tomb-chest with very realistic white-marble figure asleep holding a bible.

MANOR HOUSE, NE of the church. A datestone 1689. In the garden two good small archways in line. On the top open segmental pediments with a ball between the shanks.

W of the church in the Square houses Nos 4–6 have together an awkwardly reassembled shell-hood.

LUCKNAM, 1¼ m. N. The S front Late Georgian with two big bows and between them seven bays. Porch of two pairs of Roman Doric columns with metope frieze. On the top a Victorian neo-Jacobean excrescence. By the side big square Victorian water-tower. The NORTH LODGE is half Latest Classical, say of 1830, half heavily Victorian Italianate, an extraordinary instance of Victorian self-confidence.

ROMAN VILLA, W of Lucknam Lodge. Partially excavated in the C19, when twelve rooms (some with plastered and painted walls), a hypocaust, and two mosaic floors were uncovered. One of the mosaics bore the representation of a chariot with rider drawn by four horses. Romano-British burials and a coin hoard have been found in the same area.

SHIRE STONES, 1¼ m. SW of Colerne. An C18 'megalith' probably constructed from a demolished chambered long barrow.

COLLINGBOURNE DUCIS

2050

ST ANDREW. Flint and stone. The chancel seems to represent the late C13, but was rebuilt in 1856 (by *Street*; PF), and all detail has lost its validity. Oblong Perp W tower. To the W three-light bell-openings, straight-headed with a hood-mould. Inside, three-bay arcades of *c.*1200, i.e. round piers, still square abaci, but C13 bases and arches which have only slight chamfers but are pointed. The capitals have trumpet scallops or are fluted. One has at two corners stiff-leaf, at the two others heads.

CHURCH FARMHOUSE, ENE of the church. The house has big Victorian bargeboards. Belonging to it a long BARN, weather-boarded and thatched, and inside with one aisle and tie-beams on arched braces and collar-beams.

COLLINGBOURNE KINGSTON

St Mary. Four-bay arcades of *c*.1200 with round piers and double-chamfered pointed arches. The capitals and the abaci vary. The abaci are octagonal on the N side, round on the S. The capitals are of the trumpet-scallop type. On the N side, moreover, the fourth bay is later altogether, probably C14, i.e. the Norman church was shorter, and the N arcade first made to that length. Then a decision was taken to lengthen the church, but the E bay was not at once provided. Probably there was a transept here which was only demolished in the C14. To the arcades belong the two flat buttresses in the W walls of the aisles and the small lancet in the W wall of the N aisle. Victorian chancel arch*. The late C13 chancel windows look Victorian too, but may be only renewed. One blocked and therefore – *see* below – definitely original window is a little later: two ogee-headed lights and a quatrefoil over. The rest Perp, especially the W tower with three-light, straight-headed bell-openings. The clerestory windows, however, are Victorian, of an oddly playful kind, quite out of keeping with the church or Wiltshire – pentagon and hexagon surrounds and cinquefoils and sex-foils. They replace circular C18 brick windows (*see* Buckler's drawing). – STAINED GLASS. E window by *Hughes*, 1865. – PLATE. Chalice and Paten Cover, 1687. – MONUMENTS. Brass to Joan Darell; the husband, who died in 1495, is missing; 18½-in. figure. – Thomas Pile † 1560/1 and wife and Sir Gabriel Pile † 1626 and wife. A very big composition of stone, blocking the SE window of the chancel. The two recumbent effigies of the parents on a sarcophagus under the transverse coffered arch. Three detached Corinthian columns in front. To head and foot lower loggias, as it were, are added. They are connected with the main structure by arches and have flat ceilings and each their own crowded columns, two front, two back. In the loggia at the feet of the recumbent effigies the younger couple kneel frontally. Children by the side of the old couple (not *in situ*?). Big top structure above the centre with a second order of colon-nettes and an achievement. – Gertrude Pile † 1630. Tablet with kneeling figure. – Edward Richards † 1728. Bust in front of an obelisk.

Brunton House, ⅜ m. NE. Seven-bay brick house of *c*.1700. Two storeys, hipped roof. Later porch with Tuscan columns and a straight entablature.

* By *John Colson* who restored the church in 1862 (PF).

COMPTON BASSETT

ST SWITHIN. Quite a big church, a little elevated. Externally all
Perp except for the chancel, chancel chapels, and N porch,
which are of 1866 (by *Woodyer*). W tower with a stair-turret
higher than the tower. Embattled aisles. The interior, as so
often, is much earlier. Late C12 N arcade. Circular pier, capitals
with a variety of trumpet-scallop capitals, square abaci, and
double-chamfered pointed arches. The S arcade must have
followed soon. Round abaci and moulded capitals. Ceiled wagon
roof in the nave, the wall-posts on big heads. The Victorian
chancel is flanked inside by chapels divided off by three very
narrow arches. But the finely moulded chancel arch is Perp. –
FONT. Octagonal, Perp, with quatrefoils. – ROOD SCREEN.
What remains in one's memory of Compton Bassett is the
swagger screen of veranda type. The front has three four-
centred arches on posts with small (new) figures under nodding
ogee arches. The arches carry a lacy frieze. Leaves in the spandrels, foliage band, fleuron band, top battlements. The roof
inside is panelled and slopes down to the screen proper. This
is of one-light divisions, three l. and three r. – WEST GALLERY.
With traceried panels, probably from a screen. – STAINED
GLASS. E window by *Hardman*, c.1866. Has faded badly.–
HOURGLASS STAND.– PLATE. Chalice and Paten Cover, 1638;
Paten, before 1700; Flagon, given in 1700. – MONUMENT.
Alan Walker Heneage † 1828, aged two years. By *Baily*. A sprig
and a rosebud broken off.

SW of the church are the STABLES of the former Compton House.
The house was rebuilt c.1932–5 by *George Kennedy*. The stables
date from c.1665–70. To the S the range is of one storey, to the
N of two. Stone cross-windows, big hipped roof. In the middle
two archways, with an upright oval window between. At the
W end doorway with steep pediment.

MANOR FARMHOUSE, 1 m. N. Dated 1699. Five-bay front of
two storeys with a two-storeyed porch. Hipped roof, central
chimneys. Staircase with strong twisted balusters.

DUGDALE'S HOUSE, N of the former. Of red brick, early C18.
Quoins. Ground-floor windows with flat stone lintels. Doorway
with open segmental pediment containing an urn.

COMPTON CHAMBERLAYNE

Church and house lie close together and share the embattled
character. The church is small, the house large.

St Michael. Late c 13 s tower with Perp top. Late c 13 N transept with two lancet windows. The arch inside has the original triple-shafted l. respond and is double-chamfered. Perp chancel and Perp nave. – PLATE. Paten, 1684 or earlier; Flagon, 1752; Chalice, 1780.

COMPTON PARK. An extensive house belonging to the Penruddock family from the c 16 to the c 20. It is all ashlar-faced, all castellated, and externally all late c 18-looking. Its flat, seven-bay E façade overlooks a long lake, a superb setting. The only medieval evidence is one buttress on the w side. Then there is some evidence of the house built according to Colt Hoare before 1612, namely one doorway with a four-centred head in the forecourt on the N side and, at the back of the front range close to its s end facing w, a spiral staircase with two-light windows on three levels and a three-light window at the top. Otherwise all is sashed and even. The lake front has on the ground floor flat wooden Venetian windows, without any pilasters or columns. Inside, behind this façade, is the most glorious proof of an earlier date. Drawing room, s of the entrance hall, with wood-carving in the *Grinling Gibbons* tradition, brilliantly done, with fruit, flowers, and leaves deeply undercut. The whole panelling is original too and the fireplace also. The ceiling makes a date not before 1725 likely. To the s of this room another with a similar ceiling. To the N of the entrance hall the dining room with excellent Adamish decoration of coving and ceilings. Chimneypieces with measuring instruments etc. Staircase with two twisted balusters to the step and carved tread-ends. This goes in date with the drawing room.

CONHOLT HOUSE *see* CHUTE

CONKWELL GRANGE *see* WINSLEY

CONOCK MANOR *see* CHIRTON

COOMBE BISSETT

1020

St Michael. Norman s doorway with double-chamfered, round arch. Norman two-bay s arcade. Double-chamfered round arches supported on a round pier with square abacus. The capital has angle-leaves and decorated scallops. The w respond has many trumpet scallops. The E respond was remodelled in the c 15. Stop-chamfers with Perp flowers. Arch across now used to help to support the Perp s tower but originally probably leading into a s transept; for the s respond of the arch is Norman again. Perp N arcade of three bays with thin piers of the usual four-shafts-and-four-hollows section. Moulded arches. Perp clerestory. Externally the chancel appears C 13 (see the N lancets – and also the small double piscina inside), but has a Perp E window. The embattled N and s aisles are Perp. They are clearly cut short by a Victorian w front. The date of the reduction seems to be 1845. The s tower has big buttresses and is ashlar-faced. Higher stair-turret. To the tower corresponds a short N transept with a Perp N window. – FONT. C13. Moulded basin. On five supports.

BRIDGE. A typical example of the commodious new Wiltshire bridges of c.1780.

(PACKHORSE BRIDGE, 40 ft downstream from the new bridge. 6 ft wide; three pointed arches, new wooden parapets. At the end an original mounting stone.)

CORSHAM

ST BARTHOLOMEW. A large church with a commanding s tower with spire. It looks as if it were all built for the great house and the estate in the days of Victorian prosperity. In fact *Street* only restored an old church, but he did it unfortunately thoroughly, and he added the tower. He did this after pulling down the existing crossing tower. The church to which this belonged was a Norman church. Its arcades survive, though in a state of Victorian freshness. Three bays plus a separate w bay, a lengthening done, it seems, immediately. Circular piers, multi-scalloped capitals, one with trumpet scallops, square abaci, unmoulded round arches. That the crossing tower was Norman too is proved by the responds with trumpet capitals. The Norman N doorway with a zigzag arch is a complete restoration or replacement. The N aisle was work of c.1300. The w window with its curious tracery of radial arches upon the arches of the three lights (cf. Wells Lady Chapel) is characteristic enough. The N windows are similar. Late C17 w doorway with basket arch and hood. Dec s aisle, the w window with flowing tracery. Perp s porch of two storeys with niches. Tierceron-star vault inside. The boss has a king's head. Perp s chapel (Tropenell Chapel) with four-light windows. Hood-moulds on charming busts. Panelled arches to the chancel. Good moulded ceiling beams.* Good Perp chancel arch, also panelled. The E end wall

* The E half of the chapel was later divided into two storeys.

new. Tall Perp N chapel with a wide C14 arch to the nave. The
Methuen Chapel on the N side was added in 1874. – FONT.
Octagonal, Perp, with quatrefoils. – REREDOS. Ornate, of the
1870s. – SCREENS. The loft parapet of the former rood screen
now in a screen to the S chapel. It had painted decoration. –
Fine, tall stone screen to the N chapel, with fan-vaulted coving.
– BENCHES. Some Perp ends with simple tracery in the S aisle.
– STAINED GLASS. E window by *Kempe*, 1892; N chapel E window, 1878, copied from the Flemish C16 glass in the Lady
Chapel of Lichfield Cathedral. – Methuen Chapel E window by
Kempe, 1899 (with his trade-mark, the wheatsheaf). – PLATE.
Almsdish, 1719; Flagons, 1757 and 1764. – MONUMENTS. In
the S chapel two Perp tomb-chests with shields in cusped
quatrefoils, one of them uncommonly tall and big. This is
probably to Thomas Tropenell of Great Chalfield who rebuilt
the chapel. – Alice Cobb † 1627. Standing wall-monument with
kneeling figures. Strapwork and obelisks at the top. – Constance
Methuen † 1829, aged two, by *J. G. Lough*. A sleeping child,
in the Banks and Chantrey tradition. – Lady Methuen. Designed by *Lord Methuen* and carved by *F. T. Kormis*, 1960.
Alabaster recumbent figure; a small angel sits at the foot, writing. Good reliefs along the sides of the tomb-chest.

CORSHAM COURT. The impression is of a big Elizabethan house,
although in fact little of the outside and hardly anything of the
inside is Elizabethan. The house was built in 1582 by Thomas
Smythe, haberdasher and Collector of the Customs of London.
The estate then passed through the hands of the Hungerfords
and Thynnes and was bought by Paul Methuen of Bradford-
on-Avon in 1745. It is still the property of the Methuens.

Elizabethan the centre of the S front, i.e. the porch with
Tuscan columns, the bays to its l. and r. with thin pediments,
and the inner halves of the two projecting wings. Mullioned
windows with one transom. Straight-sided gables. Inside, two
Elizabethan rooms on the top floors. Then Paul Methuen's
enlargements and remodelling. Its purpose was to house the
extensive collection of pictures collected by his cousin Sir Paul
on the Continent and bequeathed to Paul Methuen in 1757.
However, even before then, the N front of the Elizabethan
house had been replaced by a simple classical one of nine bays.
It carried the date 1749. In 1760, *Capability Brown* was called
in. He widened the two wings on the S side to twice their original
width or thickness, keeping their Elizabethan character, and
changed the E range into a grand Picture Gallery with an ante-

room. The exterior is oddly bare, with the functionally sound
but visually unsatisfactory small gallery windows high up. The
gallery is 72 ft long and has a coffered ceiling on a splendid,
deep, fluted coving. The fireplace here, which was made by 54b
Scheemakers, has somewhat phlegmatic female figures to the
l. and r. The anteroom, called the Cabinet Room, has a very
dainty fireplace, also by *Scheemakers*, with, in the frieze, figures
from the Lysikrates Monument; they were apparently introduced after the fireplace had been made. To the w of the Picture
Gallery Brown made an octagonal room, but of this only the s
part remains; the rest has been pulled out to the N. Brown also
worked in the w wing. Here one can recognize his hand in the
circular windows with quatrefoils and the Venetian window.
Inside, the plasterer *Thomas Stocking* of Bristol did the charming armorial Rococo ceiling in the Breakfast Room. This was
originally the Library and had delightfully playful Gothick
bookcases and a Gothick overmantel. The porch on the w side
with its tierceron-vault is a puzzle. It was originally a butler's
pantry with a muniment room over, but seems too archaeologically correct not to be some original work transferred from a
church. It can hardly be Brown's or indeed his successor's.

For changes to the house were by no means over yet. In 1800
John Nash was asked to enlarge it once again, to house further
Methuen pictures. His main contribution externally was an
ornately Gothick N front with a gay, quite inventive polygonal
centre. The front, as we shall see, is all changed. But it is continued to the r. towards the octagonal Dairy. This and the
passage is all steep gables and pinnacles. The interior of the
dairy with the butter basin in the centre is very pretty. Nash
also castellated Brown's E front and gave it its pretty oriel window, a much needed embellishment. The hood-moulds above
the windows replacing Brown's pediments are perhaps less
justifiable. By Nash also the polygonal buttress turrets. On the
w side only the polygonal s w buttress or turret is Nash's. Inside, the new main N rooms had skylights for the pictures. To
their s Nash formed a Grand Hall behind the centre of the
Elizabethan façade with two monumental staircases l. and r.
He also provided a new library in the w wing, in a more restrained Gothic. The ends are separated by compound shafts.
The beautiful chimneypiece, perhaps by *Cheere* (Mrs Webb),
was originally at Highclere. It has young caryatids with lovely
features.

The house now had its present size, but its vicissitudes were not at an end yet; for about 1845 *Bellamy* pulled down Nash's N range, which turned out to have been badly built, and replaced it by the present structure, in a rather heavy-handed Jacobean. Big, solid, square middle erection, four storeys high. Bellamy's work was completed by 1849. It has concrete foundations and iron girders. Inside, Nash's Entrance Hall was again subdivided.* Bellamy made a new, monumental, Italianate principal staircase. It is placed in the square tower just referred to, has a tunnel-vault, and looks as if it belonged to a public building. The Organ comes from the Assembly Rooms at Bath. ‡

The grounds of the house were laid out by *Brown* (plan dated 1761) and completed by *Repton*, who started in 1799. The COLD BATH opposite the N front, a little to the W, a charming little building, is by *Brown* in a half-Gothic, half-Elizabethan style. It opens in three Gothic arches, the middle one with a four-centred head. The bath inside is small. On the upper floor a window with Y-tracery between two niches. Behind was the changing room. The STAINED GLASS in the Changing Room is characteristically blue and yellow. Also some C15 bits.

Corsham Court is approached from the S. The two long ranges l. and r. were STABLES and RIDING SCHOOL. Hipped roofs, cross-windows, and to the N rows of steep gables with finials. The most likely date is the late C16. The rusticated ARCHWAY and GATEPIERS look *c.*1700. The archway reaches up into a broken segmental pediment.§

LAKE COTTAGE. By *Nash*. At the E end of the lake, in the wood to the E. A plain oblong. The eaves rise in the middle of the long sides to house an upper window – a traditional motif.

PERAMBULATION. Corsham has no match in Wiltshire for wealth of good houses. There are in fact no bad ones, and there are a few of really high merit. We start by the church. In CHURCH STREET immediately the theme of Corsham, low, gabled cottages on the S, a stately ashlar-faced five-bay Georgian house on the N. The cottages have curved hoods on volutes, and

* But *Nash*'s Gothic chimneypiece, in what is now the Dining Room of the Bath School of Art, remains.

‡ Furniture otherwise is not here referred to. This is a principle of *The Buildings of England*, though with so much furniture actually made for the house and completely documented it is hard to keep to it. Medieval TILES were recently found in a loft in the timber-yard, and they include late C13 pieces of the same designs as at the Salisbury chapter house and Clarendon, tiles with cockerels probably early C14, C15 tiles of the Malvern School, with circles and trefoils, etc.

§ Big GATEPIERS also at the S end of the avenue opposite the Almshouses, and at the NE entrance.

behind the Georgian house rises a Methuen folly, a tall artificial ruin displaying church windows and even a precariously placed Norman respond with part of its arch.

Facing Church Street the TOWN HALL, dated 1784. Ashlar; arched windows on the ground floor. The arches were originally open, in the usual town-hall fashion. Three-bay pediment. In 1882 the building was heightened and certain details added. The building belongs to the HIGH STREET. We turn N first, S second. To the N a wide pavement of setts on the E side. Also on the E side a tall late C17 house of three storeys with symmetrical three-light windows. Then a long group of gabled C17 cottages, some with canted bay windows. On the W side we turn off by the MAYO FOUNTAIN of 1897 into PRIORY LANE to look at THE PRIORY, 1776, standing on its own, five bays, two and a half storeys, Tuscan doorway.

Now S of the town hall. The street now winds slightly. No. 76 (E) with a nice humble open curly pediment above the door, PORCH HOUSE (W) C18, with a square arch and a Tuscan doorway, No. 33 (W) C17, with mullioned windows and gables, No. 29 dated 1703, but still gabled and with two-light mullioned windows in the gables, No. 40 (E) set back, late C18, with the typical conservative two-light windows with broad, flat mullion and No. 19 (ALEXANDER HOUSE), a fine early C18 house of three storeys with parapet and segment-headed windows. Simple doorway with straight hood on carved brackets. No. 17 is three-storeyed, late C17, with mullioned windows. No. 13 has an open curly pediment over the door, No. 12 (E) an Early Victorian shop-front with columns. No. 11 is low and gabled, C17, and the end on the E side is the METHUEN ARMS HOTEL, built c.1805 and with a porch of paired columns.

Across the S end of the High Street THE GROVE. Built in 1737. Five bays, two storeys, hipped roof, even quoins, doorway with Ionic pilasters and carved segmental pediment. The first-floor centre Corinthian pilasters and a triangular pediment. (Original panelling and fireplaces inside.) Stables with hipped roof, two-light windows, and a pedimented archway. Staircase with thin twisted balusters. To the E to the HUNGERFORD ALMS-HOUSES AND SCHOOL. Built in 1668. L-shaped. The N range is the almshouses. Seven gables, mullioned windows, Baroque pediment above the coat of arms and inscription. The W range has a gabled porch, and to the r. the schoolroom, the latter with three large two-light windows with remarkable posthumous-Gothic detail. Basket arch over the two arched lights. The porch has bulgy Ionic columns and a segmental arch on the ground floor, arms between pilasters under a broken segmental pediment on the first floor. Mullioned and also upright oval windows. Little lantern. Inside, the schoolroom has its original seating, the master's pulpit chair at one end, a gallery with termini pilasters at the other.

To the w on to Lower Pickwick.

OUTER CORSHAM

LOWER PICKWICK, ¾ m. w. The *clou* of course is PICKWICK MANOR, an unusually impressive example of the late C17 manor house with cross windows and big gable-like dormers, and in addition the possessor of a wing of the C14, as one surviving window proves. The C17 part has a shell-hood above the door. Good houses in the street to the NE, e.g. No. 25 etc. and Nos 20, 22, 32, all cottages with mullioned windows, but all with door hoods showing how relatively late they were built. No. 40 has a nice scrolly open door pediment, No. 53 two canted bays and a one-bay pediment. This house is Late Georgian.

EASTON, 1 m. E. Several gabled houses with mullioned windows, and in the village street C18 cottages stepping down to EASTON HOUSE, C18, ashlar-faced, of four bays and two storeys. Pedimented doorway. Good stables. (EASTON COURT FARM, according to Brakspear, has a C15 chimney and a C15 open timber roof.)

MONKS LANE, 1¼ m. s, w of Monks Park. CONGREGATIONAL CHURCH, probably a 'five-mile chapel'. C17, a plain oblong, with two-light windows and one five-light dormer-like upper window placed under the eaves, which curve up from it. The interior is intact, with a gallery on three sides, box pews, and the pulpit.

GASTARD, 1½ m. SE. The church of ST JOHN BAPTIST is of 1912, Gothic, with a broad w tower. GASTARD COURT has C17 mullioned windows, but the buttresses point to the survival of medieval masonry.

NESTON, 1¾ m. SSW. ST PHILIP AND ST JAMES is of 1866, by *Hakewill* (nave with bellcote and chancel, Geometrical tracery). NESTON PARK was built shortly after 1790. It had then five bays with a tripartite doorway and a good spacious staircase with thin iron handrail. About 1840 an addition was built to the l. and an ambitious giant portico of Corinthian columns with pediment was put in front of the house so that the doorway was no longer in the middle. To remedy this, two open stair-cases lead up to the portico. Giant Corinthian angle pilasters were also added.

JAGGARDS, Moor Green, $1\frac{1}{2}$ m. sw. A date 1657 on an excellent stone fireplace inside. The house has a symmetrical façade, of E-shape, but with the middle bow not a porch but the former hall chimney. The projecting wings are two identical porches, an interesting anomaly which seems here not to be the work of later addition. The l. porch led into the hall (or screens passage), the r. one direct to the main staircase, preserved, with flat cut-out balusters. Cross-windows. Gables. The room with the fireplace also has thin-ribbed plasterwork.

CORSLEY

ST MARGARET. 1833 by *John Leachman*, and altered by *F. W. Hunt* in 1891. But the w tower, which is quite tall, is Perp. The church is aisleless, and the chancel was apparently never built. Tall windows with Y-tracery. w gallery on cast-iron columns. – PULPIT. Nice; Georgian. – PLATE. Paten, late C15 or early C16; Cup, c.1574; Flagon, 1700; Almsdish, 1742. – MONU-MENT. Nathaniel Barton † 1828. Grecian. White against a black background. Extinguished torches l. and r.

ST MARY TEMPLE, $1\frac{1}{2}$ m. s. 1902–3 by *W. H. Stanley* of Trow-bridge. Arts and Crafts Gothic. Polygonal bell-turret over the E end, with cross-windows as bell-openings, and a spire. Aisle-less nave; exposed brick. Open timber roof. Low side windows, two transomed E windows.

MANOR FARMHOUSE. Said to have been built by Sir John Thynne about 1545. That can hardly be. The house itself is brick, with three cross-gables and mullioned and transomed windows of three and four lights. This is Elizabethan proper. The archway into the front garden can also not be c.1545, but may well have connexions with Sir John and be an advanced piece of c.1560. Pilasters l. and r. of a straight-headed doorway. Above, an attic, and in relief on it an upper aedicule of pilasters supported by volutes and a top pediment.

CORSLEY HOUSE, $\frac{3}{4}$ m. s. Grecian. Five bays, with a three-bay pediment. Greek Doric porch of unusual shape. Vertical bands with incised (Soanian) ornament along the corners. Bow win-dow round the corner. Staircase with cast-iron handrail. Gre-cian iron garden railings and gates.

(CORSLEY MILL FARM, $\frac{3}{4}$ m. WNW. C17. Brick, of two storeys.

Five four-light mullioned and transomed windows on the first floor. Doorway with curved hood on brackets. Opposite a former CLOTH MILL, brick, of five bays and three storeys. MHLG)

CLEY HILL CAMP, ¼ m. E of Sturford. Univallate Iron Age hillfort on Cley Hill.

CORSTON

9080

ALL SAINTS. Impressive bell-turret with a spire on four heavy stone posts. Said to be Perp work. The s porch entrance is Perp too. But the church is of 1881 with a chancel of 1911. – SCREEN. Perp, of one-light divisions. – STAINED GLASS. Two Flemish roundels.

CORTON LONG BARROW see CLYFFE PYPARD

COTTLES see ATWORTH

1090

CRICKLADE

ST SAMPSON. A Celtic, i.e. Cornish–Breton dedication. The distinguishing feature of the church is its proud and self-certain, somewhat heavy and certainly not elegant, crossing tower, built at the expense of the duke of Northumberland and the Hungerfords (see coats of arms) at the time of the Reformation. It resembles that of Fairford in Gloucestershire. In a will of 1512–13 20 shillings are left towards the rebuilding of the tower, but heraldry points to completion in the early fifties. The tower rests on mighty piers and is inside decorated almost like a Spanish piece of the time of the Reyes Catolicos – only more bleakly. Plenty of shields, and also niches with canopies, crosses, vases. Ornate lierne-vault with well over sixty bosses. Outside, the first stage has big windows with intersected tracery, a curious anachronism, the second stage just very tall panelling and small windows. Sturdy polygonal buttresses, tall openwork battlements, and very big pinnacles. But chronologically the tower is the end, not the beginning of the story of the church. A detail at the NE corner, outside, indicates an earlier crossing tower, as indeed one would presuppose. The beginning of the story of the church is Anglo-Saxon, the s wall of the nave. There is here *in situ* a complete lesene or pilaster strip from the time when this was outer wall. Then Late Norman arcades were pierced through the Saxon walls, see two bays of the N arcade and one of the s arcade. Piers, or rather pieces of wall left standing, and responds. Capitals with big stylized leaves.

The triple-chamfered arches are late C13, i.e. of the time when the W bay was added on the N and the W bays on the S side. Moulded capitals. The W wall of the nave was built at the same time, with an interesting W window of three stepped lancet lights with two niches above the outer lights. The W, N, and S doorways all belong to this phase. So does the beautiful W part of the N aisle wall, which has lancet windows, nobly shafted inside. The S aisle wall and its windows are too renewed (in 1864 by *Ewan Christian*) to be relied upon. The W window is like the nave W window, but the lights are pointed-trefoiled. Finally C13 also, though of uncertain date, the E wall of the N transept. Contemporary with this phase but by a different mason the rebuilding of the chancel. Windows with three lancet lights, the middle one lower, and a big (cinquefoiled) circle above. The E window is Victorian, as is of course the internal decoration of the E wall. In the style of the chancel the N aisle N windows. Perp, besides the tower, the transepts, embattled and pinnacled, and the S (or Hungerford) chapel, probably built by Sir Edmund Hungerford, who died in 1484. It is also embattled. The buttress was added in 1569. Niches inside l. and r. of the E window.

FONT. Octagonal, Perp. – STAINED GLASS. W window by *Kempe*, 1888. – SCULPTURE. In the porch pieces of Anglo-Saxon interlace. In the S aisle N wall reset pieces, among them two fine Norman animals. – CHANDELIER. In the chancel. Brass, not big, of two tiers. 1733. – PLATE. Chalice and Paten Cover, 1615; Flagon, 1680; Chalice and Paten Cover, 1701. – MONUMENTS. In the N aisle Dec tomb recess with cusped and crocketed ogee arch flanked by buttress shafts. In the cusping ballflower. In the recess tomb-chest with quatrefoils and on it a defaced effigy. – In the churchyard NE of the church a Perp tomb-chest with quatrefoils. Foliage decoration above them. – HIGH CROSS. A complete piece, but without the sculpture in the head. It originally stood in the main street and was taken to the churchyard *c.*1818, when the old town hall was taken down.

ST MARY, High Street. A small church, its E wall bordering on the street. The church is basically Norman, see the good chancel arch. Scalloped capitals, arch with zigzag at r. angles to the wall surface. Fragments of another Norman arch with zigzag on the N chapel window (and in the Rectory garden). Small W tower, C13 below, Perp above. The church is much restored. Divers windows. Arcades inside of three bays with octagonal piers and moulded four-centred arches, i.e. Perp. Perp also the arch into the N chapel. Nice roof with moulded beams. The nave roof is single-framed with tie-beams. – FONT. Circular; C13. An unusual piece with a many-moulded base, a Victorian shaft, and a moulded bowl. – PULPIT. Jacobean. – CHANDELIER. Brass, of two tiers, late C18. – PLATE. Chalice and Paten Cover, 1577. – CHURCHYARD CROSS. A complete C14 cross with all the sculpture in the four-sided lantern head.

PERAMBULATION. We start by the church. To its E the TITHE BARN, stone, thatched.* Overlooking the churchyard and fronting on BATH ROAD is ROBERT JENNER'S SCHOOL. He was a London goldsmith and founded the school in 1651. The porch, now facing N, formed the middle of the S front. This was thus symmetrical, of three bays, as the first floor still is. Mullioned windows, and not an inkling yet of the Inigo Jones revolution. Bath Road leads into the HIGH STREET. The best houses lie at its S end, i.e. as one turns r., and the best of all overlooks the churchyard. It is dated 1708 on its doorway. Steep open curved pediment on brackets. The house is of stone, two storeys high and five bays wide. Hipped roof. The windows may originally have had wooden crosses, as they still have at the back. Opposite a four-bay house with a clumsy early C19 Tuscan porch. On the same side as this further N LLOYDS BANK, C18, of five bays, the ground floor altered. Then an early C19 house, naive, with, on the ground floor, Venetian windows under big segmental arches. Again on the W side, facing down Calcutt Street the VALE HOTEL, three bays with a porch; early C19. Then an uneventful stretch of low cottages. At the N end No. 72, C18, of four bays with big gatepiers, and the METHODIST CHAPEL of 1810, with lancet windows, and, opposite, THE PRIORY (Nos 1–3), a group of houses containing the slightest remains of the Hospital of St John Baptist, a *xenodochium* or guest house for poor travellers founded before 1231, namely a tall blocked arch facing the street,‡ a blocked doorway inside an entrance to the r. of the former, and traces of external stairs to the W of this.

FORTIFICATIONS. A square enclosure surrounds the town; excavation in 1952 revealed a dressed stone footing on both sides of the walls and, incorporated in the rubble core, fragments of Roman tile. Sherds of Saxon pottery were also found. The

* The NBR records a cruck-trussed barn. Is it this barn?

‡ This is perhaps the chapel E window mentioned by Aubrey as being like that of St Ebbe at Oxford.

fortifications appear to be those set up under Alfred's direction. A portion of the stone footing of the W sector of the fortifications has been left exposed in the town cemetery.

CROCKERTON   *8040*

CHURCH. 1843 by *Wyatt & Brandon*. Quite sizeable. Norman, like Wyatt's Wilton and Dilton Marsh. Nave and chancel in one, apse, NW porch tower. The apse has internal arcading. Open roof. – FONT. Also imitation-Norman. Large, round, with the twelve apostles under arches.

BAPTIST CHAPEL, Crockerton Green. Chapel and house in one. Arched front windows, straight-headed back windows. It looks early C19.

JOB'S MILL, 1 m. NE. Pretty early C19 Tudor house of three bays with a steep-pitched roof, a porch with a steep-pitched roof, and lower attachments.

HOUSE, Low Ridge, on the slope of the hill, ¼ m. NE. By *Peter Wingfield*, 1956. L-shaped, single-storeyed.

CROFTON   *2060*
1½ m. NNW of Grafton

PUMPING STATION at the summit of the Kennet and Avon Canal. This part of the canal was completed in 1811. The pumping station was needed because Crofton is 401 ft. above the source of the Kennet. It is a brick house of four bays and two and a half storeys. Next to it a round chimney which has lost 20 ft of its height. The engines have recently ceased to work. They are a pair of beam engines, the older having been supplied by *Boulton & Watt* about 1812. The cast-iron beam is an enormous piece. The future of the engine certainly ought to be secured.

CROUCHESTON see BISHOPSTONE, p. 106

CROWOOD HOUSE see RAMSBURY

CRUDWELL   *9090*

ALL SAINTS.* N aisle of two bays with circular pier, trumpet capitals, and a prettier capital to the E respond. Pointed one-step arches. The N doorway belongs to this, of which a round

* Miss Vernon has pointed to the high, narrow shape of the nave as perhaps indicating the proportions of a Saxon predecessor of the present church.

hood-mould with dog-tooth remains – i.e. late C12. The one N lancet could also be contemporary. Late C13 N chapel, see the pointed-trefoil-headed windows. The chancel has on the one hand a priest's doorway probably of the late C12, on the other an E window of the same type as the chapel windows. The S aisle has an arcade also of two bays. Octagonal pier, starved capital, arches of early C14 moulding. Are the two E lancets of the very wide aisle original?* The W tower was started in the C14 (see the mouldings of the arch towards the nave) and completed in the C15. The aisles embrace it. Bell-openings with Somerset tracery. Parapet with openwork quatrefoils. Pinnacles. Perp also the embattled, two-storeyed S porch with its pinnacles and the many-moulded S doorway with four-centred arch. N aisle roof Perp, with tie-beams and collar-beams on arched braces – rather a domestic motif. – SCREENS. In the N chapel parts of a Perp screen with one-light divisions and top friezes. To the S chapel screen with Early Renaissance panels. – BENCHES. With linenfold and Early Renaissance panels. Aubrey says they were given by one Walton, and Waltons appear in the parish in the mid C16. Another end has the arms of Henry VIII, i.e. dates from before 1509. On yet others a stag, a Tudor rose, etc. – READER'S DESK. With panels of the same time. – STAIRS to the tower. Some stairs starting in the NW bay of the aisle and with a Jacobean handrail. – STAINED GLASS. In a N window late C15 representations of the Seven Sacraments, an excellent set, even if incomplete. – PLATE. Chalice, inscribed 1628; Patens, 1687 and 1732.

By the church an exceptionally fine group of stone buildings. To the S a C15 BARN with buttresses; to the SW a house with mullioned windows; to the W the SCHOOL HOUSE of 1670, a square with hipped roof and widely spaced cross-windows with mullioned windows over, three bays to the side; to the NW the OLD RECTORY, with an E front of the early C18 (segment-headed windows), but otherwise irregular of the C17 and C18; to the W of this a circular DOVECOTE, and yet further W CRUDWELL COURT, Georgian, of three bays and three storeys with a porch whose pediment stands on Tuscan columns. Tripartite windows.

EASTCOURT HOUSE, 1½ m. ESE. Dated 1658 outside and 1662 on a quaint wooden overmantel inside which shows the front of the house not quite as it is now. The windows now are more regularly placed. They all have stone crosses. Lower projecting

* Former transept?

l. wing with mullioned windows. To the r. a bigger C18 (or
C20?) wing. The original staircase has turned balusters, a
string decorated with flowers, and a handrail decorated very
charmingly with little animals. Fine big drawing room in the
big newer (or new) wing, with decoration of c.1750.

MURCOTT FARMHOUSE, ¾ m. S. Late C17. Of seven bays, with
cross-windows. In the gable two small upright oval windows.

DAUNTSEY

ST JAMES. Norman S and N doorways with polygonal shafts
standing quite a bit outside the door opening. The shafts have
decorated single-scallop capitals. The lintel has a segmental
bottom edge. Early C14 E window; but the most interesting
contributions are of the C17. The W tower was rebuilt by the
first Earl of Danby in 1630 in the Gothic style – see especially
the gargoyles and pinnacles. The same patron built the N chapel,
whose windows are remodelled but whose round-arched entrance to chancel and aisle remains. This is dated 1656. For the
C17 furnishings see below. Low Perp four-bay arcades with
octagonal piers and double-chamfered arches and big vertical
pieces. – ROOD SCREEN. The tracery C14 (ogee heads and trefoiled spandrels), but the lower parts are Laudian (tall balusters
and dado). – TOWER SCREEN. With bits of a Perp foliage frieze.
– STALLS. Partly Perp, partly C17, but largely Victorian. –
BOX PEWS. Jacobean, nice, with knobs. – PULPIT. With carved
panels. C16? From the Netherlands? – SCULPTURE. Four
white and gold Catholic figures; foreign, and probably C18. –
PAINTINGS. Tympanum painted with the Last Judgement,
early C16, of poor quality. – Murder of the Innocents, in oils,
Italian Baroque. – STAINED GLASS. Chancel N and S, C15 and
early C16 fragments. – MONUMENTS. Sir John Stradling and
wife, incised slab, early C15 (chancel floor). – Sir John Danvers
† 1514 and wife. Tomb-chest with shields in cusped quatrefoils. On the lid brasses, 28 in. long. – Ann Danvers † 1539.
Ornate monument with a tomb-chest with shields in richly
cusped quatrefoils, polygonal buttresses with concave mouldings, low arch with leaves in the spandrels, leaf top frieze.
Angels above the top. Against the back wall brass plate with
kneeling figure, Trinity, etc. – First Earl of Danby † 1643. In
the family chapel. Enormous tomb-chest of white and grey
marble without any figure-work or ornament. – Anne Creed

† 1772. Graceful tablet. Two cherub's heads at the top. – Fifth
Earl of Peterborough † 1819. Black floor-slab with a white
crown in relief. – George Bisset † 1828. Standing stone monument; Gothic.

DAUNTSEY HOUSE. Absolutely plain Georgian ashlar front. The
terrace borders the river Avon. At the back four bays with a
central Venetian window. The GATEWAY is tripartite and also
absolutely unenriched. The parapet is raised over the centre.

DAY FARM STONE CIRCLE *see* SWINDON, p. 460

9070

DERRY HILL

CHRIST CHURCH. 1839–40 by *Wyatt & Brandon*. Perp. w
tower with recessed spire. Tall straight-headed two-light Perp
windows. The chancel still short and never lengthened.

LITTLE ZOAR. Chapel of 1814, little indeed. Windows with
Y-tracery.

0060

DEVIZES

Devizes originated from the castle. This was established by the
bishop of Sarum in a suitable place belonging to their estate of
Cannings, but soon became royal. St John was the church inside
the castle, St Mary the town church. The centre of the town lay
there. The Market Place could only be developed after the castle
had lost its sense and its outer fortifications. The shape of the
outer bailey is still clearly recognizable in the half-oval of New
Park Street–Monday Market Street–Sheep Street–Bridewell
Street. The Market Place is on the chord, just below the castle.

CHURCHES

ST JOHN. A major Norman church, dominated by a mighty
crossing tower with round stair-turret higher than the tower.
Big Norman windows with decorated arches. Twin bell-openings flanked by blank arches, also all decorated. The tower is
oblong; so there are three arches altogether to the N and S, five
to the E and W. Norman work also appears outside in the transept fronts, in the shape of half-destroyed pairs of windows and
a small window in a gable. The arches are again decorated. The
chancel has Norman buttresses and a small window in the E
gable. The other Norman windows are Victorian. Externally
mostly Perp, except for the w front, which looks Perp but is

in fact of 1863 (by *Slater*; PF). The S or Beauchamp Chapel, so named because of the occurrence of Beauchamp heraldry, is very similar to the Beauchamp and Tocotes Chapel at Bromham, licensed in 1492. Like the chapel at Bromham, it is extremely ornate. Two bays, four- and five-light windows, closely decorated battlements, pinnacles. On the E side instead of the middle pinnacle a tall niche with canopy. The N or Lamb Chapel (in the moulding of the E window was an inscription: Orate pro bono statu Ricardi Lamb) is ornate too, but less so. Battlements and pinnacles and buttress-shafts with pinnacles in relief on the buttresses. Simple Perp aisles. Perp transept N and S windows. Perp porches, that on the N side two-storeyed.

Entering the church, one is at once attracted to the E: Norman crossing; responds with capitals, tampered with, fat roll mouldings, arches round to the E and W, but pointed to the N and S, a remarkably early example in England. Norman chancel, low and fully rib-vaulted. Two bays, low wall-shafts with scalloped and also stylized foliage capitals. Fat roll mouldings in the ribs. The E bay has wild blank arcading of intersected 10b arches with zigzag. Scale pattern in the spandrels and above the arches. The corbel-table of the Norman chancel appears inside the S chapel, and of the Norman S transept too. Monster faces and grimacing human faces. All this display can be attributed to Bishop Roger of Sarum, who also rebuilt the castle. The nave arcades are disappointingly scraped. Six bays, square piers with semicircular shafts, polygonal abaci, i.e. late C14. No clerestory. The westernmost bay of the nave is of 1863, as is the W front also. The Beauchamp Chapel is as ornate inside as outside. It was lengthened to range with the E wall of the chancel. The Norman intersected arcading of the S wall thus becomes a screen wall. Two bays, panelled arches. A niche between them, two (renewed) niches by the E window, one between the S windows. Gable of the priest's doorway reaching up in front of the lower part of the SE window. A strainer arch across below the W arch of the chapel. Ceiling with traceried panels – it is said, 288 of them. Panelled ceiling in the Lamb Chapel too. – PULPIT. Perp, with meagre gabled blank arches. – ORGAN CASE. The upper part with rich acanthus is late C17. – PLATE. Flagon, 1702; altered. – MONUMENTS. George Heathcote † 1768 (S transept). Britannia seated, one hand holding an anchor, the other the medallion with the portrait of the deceased. By *King*. – Several women by urns, e.g. *c.*1762 by *Prince Hoare*, † 1788 by *King*, † 1784 by *Westmacott Senior*, finer, larger, and more classical. – James Sutton † 1801. Woman by a column. By *Westmacott*, the future Sir Richard. – William Salmon † 1826. Grecian youth by a column. By *Baily*. – In the churchyard obelisk to record the drowning of four people on Sunday, 30 June 1751. One of the inscriptions reads: 'Remember the Sabbath Day to keep it holy.' The four people had been out enjoying themselves.

ST MARY. St Mary also has a Norman chancel. It dates from the same time as that of St John, and may well be due to Bishop Roger's liberality too. Externally the Norman work is recognizable by the flat buttresses, the corbel-table, and the square stone blocks. The E window is Victorian.* Internally again one has the surprise of a two-bay rib-vault. The same fat rolls, the same intersected arches, though only a fragment on the S wall is original. The stretch on the E wall is wholly renewed. The details seem a little earlier than at St John, i.e. less wild (no scale pattern, thinner zigzag). Norman also, and evidently re-used, the zigzag bands up the arch of the S porch entrance. Apart from this arch and the chancel, the church is Perp. There is an inscription in the roof recording the rebuilding of the church by William Smyth, who died in 1436 ('qui istam ecclesiam fieri fecit', etc.). Tall w tower. Diagonal buttresses, with buttress-shafts and pinnacles in relief. Pinnacles. Pairs of two-light bell-openings. Four-light w window with transom; niches l. and r. Aisle and clerestory windows of three lights. Gargoyles, battlements. The clerestory has pinnacles too, and the middle one of the E wall, as at St John, is a tall canopied niche instead. Its plinth has William Smyth's initials. Two-storeyed embattled S porch. Inside, arcades of five bays with octagonal piers and double-hollow-chamfered arches. Low panelled chancel arch. The niches l. and r. look all Victorian. Tall tower arch and tierceron-star vault in the tower, with a big circle for the bell-ropes and bosses. Nave roof of low pitch with tie-beams and tracery over. Good corbel heads. – FONT. Octagonal, Perp, with tracery pattern. – ORGAN. Gothic; early C19. – WEST DOOR. Traceried. – SCULPTURE. Pelican of wood over the S door. Was it a roof corbel? – WEATHERCOCK (under the tower). Brass. – PLATE. Set, 1789. – MONUMENT. John Garth † 1761. Portrait bust in an oval medallion hanging from an obelisk.

ST JAMES. Fine Perp w tower, the stair-turret not at a corner. The bell-openings of two lights, continued down blank below a transom. The whole repeated to the l. and r., entirely blank.

* Above it a late medieval STATUE of the Virgin.

Decorated battlements, pinnacles. The body of the church 1832 by *Pennistone*. Competently Perp, with four-light and five-light windows, pinnacles in relief on the buttresses, battlements and pinnacles on aisles and chancel. Arcades with piers of four shafts and four hollows. Four-centred arches. Can all this archaeological exactitude really be of 1832? Only the short chancel betrays the early date. – STAINED GLASS. E window by *Wailes*, 1849. – N aisle NE window by *Kempe*, c.1900. – MONUMENTS. Bridget Keynes † 1752. Big standing wall-monument without any figures. White, grey, and black marble. Inscription triptych; columns l. and r. – Edward Colston † 1859, aged nine. He lies on a couch. Smaller children mourn him. Putto angels lift him by his hand. By *E. Hancock*.

IMMACULATE CONCEPTION, St Joseph's Walk (R.C.). 1865, by *Charles* (?) *Hansom*; new chancel 1909 by *A. J. Scoles* and *Raymond*. The style of c.1300. Nave and chancel, but the arcade for a s aisle built. Polygonal apse.

ST PETER, Bath Road. 1866–7 by *Slater & Carpenter*. s aisle 1884. Nave and chancel and polygonal apse. Simple C13 style. The capitals of the arcade and the corbels for the roof cannot have been intended to remain just cut blocks. Was carving intended? It is true that starkness characterizes the church throughout, e.g. no cusping at all in the windows. Only the bellcote is busier. – PLATE. Chalice, made in Amsterdam, 1649.

BAPTIST CHAPEL, Sheep Street. 1851–2 by Mr *Hardick*. E.E., rather gaunt, with lancets and tall pinnacles. The OLD BAPTIST CHAPEL is almost opposite. This is of 1780, was enlarged in 1818 and later, and has no special features.

PUBLIC BUILDINGS

TOWN HALL. By *Thomas Baldwin* of Bath, 1806–8, using parts of the preceding C17 building. A fine, elegant, accomplished little building. Ashlar stone. The front of five bays has as its centre an ample bow and faces down St John's Street. Rusticated ground floor with the windows in arched fields. In the bow the arches are segmental. Above, tall unfluted Ionic columns. The windows in the bow on the first floor pedimented. The building is rounded at the back as well. The ground floor was originally open. Inside, Assembly Rooms with nice, restrained Adamish plasterwork. – REGALIA. Loving Cup, 1606; Pair of Maces, c.1660; Staves, c.1709.

ASSIZE COURT, Northgate Street. By *T. H. Wyatt*, 1835, when he was still Grecian and not Victorian. Dominant four-column portico of unfluted Ionic columns, pediment, lower wings l. and r. Inside, square hall with a coffered ceiling, partly glazed. The stairs go up l. and r. between solid walls.

ROUNDWAY HOSPITAL. Opened in 1851. By *T. H. Wyatt*.

PERAMBULATION

The origin of Devizes, as has already been said, is the CASTLE. It was an Early-Norman motte-and-bailey castle and was extensively improved by Bishop Roger of Sarum. It played a prominent part in the struggles between Stephen and the Empress Maud and belonged to the Crown for the rest of the Middle Ages. On the mound was a stone keep, and there was an aisled hall, 70 ft long, of which foundations are supposed to exist. But nothing medieval is recognizable. It has all been buried under the extensive castellated pile of picturesque outline begun by *Goodridge* of Bath in 1842 with a new keep, and massively enlarged (rock-faced) in the sixties and seventies. The so-called St John's Gate incorporates Norman bits from St John's Church. Arch with zigzag, also at r. angles to the wall. Hood-mould on monster-heads. Jambs with two orders of colonnettes. Capitals with scallops and upright crocket-leaves. The mighty gatehouse, picturesquely asymmetrical at the front, was the last of the new buildings. Lanes lead down to the MARKET PLACE, and here we start properly. It is spacious and funnel-shaped with, at the narrow end, the big brick brewery of 1885. In the middle the handsome MARKET CROSS, by *Benjamin Wyatt*, 1814. Square base, and above a transparent canopy with flying buttresses. An inscription tells a story worth reading. To its s the FOUNTAIN, commemorating T. H. S. Sotheron Estcourt, 1879, a typically mixed Victorian affair, with a kind of Renaissance basin but Gothic shafts. The inspection of the houses starts in the NE corner with the BEAR HOTEL, two separate buildings, the l. polite, the r. homely. Ashlar on the l., black and white paint on the r. The l. building is Georgian, but its decoration may be imitation-Georgian.* At its back, in the yard, three big Tuscan columns. The r. part is lower and has a deep porch with a bear on. Bold Egyptian lettering. Sir Thomas Lawrence, the painter, was the son of the inn-keeper of the Bear. The CORN EXCHANGE is of 1857 (by

* It was done, however, before 1900 (Devizes Museum, R.84).

W. Hill of Leeds), with the usual giant columns and Ceres on the attic. Cast-iron arches with tracery inside. After that plenty of nice, unassuming Georgian houses of three storeys, the best on this side being early C18: No. 16, which lies back and has a shell-hood enriched by branches, and No. 17, a fine six-bay brick house with a hipped roof. Moulded window- and door-surrounds, open door pediment; gatepiers. (Inside a very rich stucco ceiling. NBR) Then on the other side PARNELLA HOUSE (No. 23) of *c*.1740–50, evidently a doctor's house, as the statue in the niche with Gibbs frame represents Aesculapius. Ashlar-facing, rusticated ground floor, two canted bays above with Venetian windows. The BLACK SWAN HOTEL is dated 1737. Six bays, three storeys, rendered. Pilasters in three orders. LLOYDS BANK is dated 1892. It is of brick, and very typical of the coming of the neo-William-and-Mary or neo-Early Georgian of *c*.1900–10. Then – an illuminating comparison – No. 40 of 1866, stone and sweetly debased, really still Early not High Victorian. Note the Gothic shafts, but the oddly shaped and framed arches, things hard to describe. The MARKET HOUSE (Butter and Poultry Market) is of 1835, by *Pollard* of Frome. Three bays, arched rusticated ground floor, square centrally placed turret on top. Long passage with stalls l. and r. behind.

Now first to the NW, because it will not take long. Down NORTH-GATE STREET, with No. 3 on the l., three bays, three storeys, late C18, with canted bay windows, then the turn to New Park Street, which will be described on p. 192, and, again on the l., SANDCLIFFE HOUSE, early C18, stone, with giant pilasters, and NORTHGATE HOUSE, mid-Georgian, of brick, with a pedimented Ionic porch. It is mentioned as a coaching inn in 1771. Added bay window on the r. (Late C18 chimneypieces. NBR) Then the CANAL BRIDGE, with a canal house by the side, noticed as such by its canted front. In THE NURSERY early C19 brick terraces; also a stone terrace. So to the BATH ROAD, with late C18 and early C19 houses and terraces. RED HOUSE is three-storeyed and of brick, THE CEDARS two-storeyed, of stone (with giant Ionic angle pilasters and a two-bay pediment). TRAFALGAR TERRACE dates itself. So on to SHANE'S CASTLE at the fork, small and generously castellated. Hood-moulds over the windows. It was a toll-house and is probably Early Victorian.

Back to the Market Place and now to the S. THE LITTLE BRITTOX is a pedestrian passage; St John's Street takes the traffic. At its start at once, facing down on to the Market Place, the

51b NEW HALL, built to be a public hall, a noble stone building of 1750–2, four bays with a rusticated ground floor, five unfluted Ionic columns over, and a pediment. The ground floor was originally open. The house is really in Wine Street. The architect was called *Lawrence*. Then in ST JOHN'S STREET the NATIONAL PROVINCIAL BANK, three-storeyed, ashlar-faced, with a ground floor with smooth rustication and recessed fluted Ionic columns above. Probably of *c.*1820–30. Nos 37–38 are of five bays, stuccoed, with giant fluted angle pilasters. The POST OFFICE is an imposing early C18 brick house, red brick laced with blue brick. Doorway with open pediment on brackets; otherwise plain. This is followed by an Early Georgian three-storeyed brick house dated on a rainwater head 1749. The centre window is arched, with pilasters and a Gibbsian arch. The parapet curves up in the middle. Across the street and into ST JOHN'S ALLEY to see the best display of timber-framing at Devizes – quite a long stretch, all with oversailing upper floor and closely set verticals. Original doorway with four-centred head. The house is probably Elizabethan or Jacobean. Back to St John's Street and on: a five-bay rendered Georgian house with giant angle pilasters, a Tuscan porch with metope frieze, a pedimented window with pilasters over. (Nos 23–24 have a pre-Reformation ceiling with moulded beams and bosses, one carrying the monogram of Christ. *W.A. & N.H.M.*, XLI). The Town Hall is in prominence now (*see* p. 187). The DISTRICT CLUB to its W has fine early C19 cast-iron gatepiers with over-throw. No. 21 is dated 1740 and has segment-headed windows and giant pilasters. On into ST JOHN'S CHURCHYARD. Some timber-framing on the l. On the r., at the corner to the church-yard (with its handsome cast-iron entrance), the ALMS-HOUSES, single-storeyed, of *c.*1842. There are only sparse houses facing the churchyard, chiefly two: the SEXTON'S HOUSE, W of the church, one of the few at Devizes with the mullioned windows and dormers of the C17, and a brick house dated 1733 to the E of the church. The latter has really no dis-tinctive features.

The New Hall belongs, as has already been said, to Wine Street. The continuation of this to the E is THE BRITTOX. On the r. a long, even early C19 ashlar front of eleven bays. Giant pilasters. Opposite a good early C18 brick house with a ground floor destroyed by a shop front, but above stone quoins, carved medallions, and a hipped roof. Back to the other side with an ashlar-faced three-bay house with widely spaced paired fluted

angle pilasters. The end is an Early Victorian ashlar-faced building. From the start of The Brittox s along the HIGH STREET.
Nothing of note before GREYSTONE HOUSE, built in 1731.
Ashlar-faced, five bays, three storeys, rather a confused design.
The centre has a Tuscan doorway with metope frieze and a
window over with Ionic columns and a pediment. But squeezed
in to the l. and r. of these are narrow arched windows. The whole
centre carries a big segmental pediment. (Good staircase with
thin turned balusters and better plaster ceiling with trophy.
NBR) Opposite the WILTSHIRE FRIENDLY SOCIETY, Vic-
torian-Jacobean. The continuation of the street is LONG
STREET, with the best sequence of Georgian houses, if not the
best houses. First No. 8, dated 1737, a good building of three
storeys with rusticated stone ground floor and brick above; five
bays below, two with Venetian windows above; parapet. Adjoining No. 9, with a tripartite archway. No. 10 is brick, of five
bays, No. 11 (facing the church) stuccoed white. It was the
town house of the Lansdownes and Late Georgian. Nice window balconies. Big porch of two pairs of Ionic columns; laurel
frieze. Opposite the MUSEUM, again a five-bay brick house,
this time with a one-bay pediment. Then an Early Georgian
front with segment-headed windows, opposite another five-bay
brick house and No. 37, Early Georgian with arched ground-
floor windows and a doorway with Tuscan columns and metope
frieze. Bridewell Street leads off here, but that is to come later.
We go on to the end of Long Street with more such houses:
No. 36 with two Venetian windows, No. 32 again with two
Venetian windows, and so on. At the end HILLWORTH
STREET to the W. HILLWORTH HOUSE is Early Victorian,
rendered, symmetrical, with two gables and a simple veranda
between. Octagonal conservatory with Tuscan columns on the
l. In the garden to the SE square C18 brick SUMMER HOUSE
with domed stone-slated roof.

Now off Long Street into Bridewell Street, the whole arc ending
at the junction of New Park Street and Northgate Street. Not
much here. No. 28 BRIDEWELL STREET is another five-bay
brick house just like those in Long Street. Then in SHEEP
STREET new urban housing, not attractive, and built with concrete blocks in 'Cornish Unit Construction'. At the fork first
MARYPORT STREET for a glance at the THREE CROWNS
INN, an Early Victorian front with hood-moulded windows
and bargeboards, and at the MASONIC HALL of 1834 (originally National Girls' School), High Victorian Gothic with large

twin windows. Then the r. fork, along Monday Market Street
(Nos 6–8 are timber-framed and belong to the C15) to reach
the s end of NEW PARK STREET. The CASTLE HOTEL is
handsome with its mansard roof and Tuscan porch, long, low,
and of brick. Soon the best house in Devizes, BROWNSTON
HOUSE, dated 1720. Brick and stone dressings. Seven bays,
two storeys and basement, three-bay projection, no pediment,
hipped roof. A one-bay addition on the l. Doorway with segmental pediment. Staircase with sturdy twisted balusters.
Original gatepiers and iron gate. After that, on the other side
the TOBACCO FACTORY, built as a silk mill by John Austie in
1785 (rainwater heads). Yellow brick, three storeys, plus a later
fourth. Eleven bays. One big upper lunette window, another
in the gable end. The side towards New Street was rebuilt in
1831. (The interior has oak beams and elm joists. *W.A. &
N.H.M.*, LV) Again opposite Wharf Street, which leads to the
WHARF of the Kennet and Avon Canal with its early C19 brick
WAREHOUSE. At the corner of Wharf Street a terrace of early
C19 stone cottages with incised (Soanian) ornament. Nothing
more in New Park Street, and now finally into SIDMOUTH
STREET from the s end of Monday Market Street, turning E.
At the corner HANDEL HOUSE, early C19, ashlar, with Greek
Doric columns dividing shop windows from each other. Then,
part of the same group, lying back a little, ALBION PLACE,
with a stone veranda of segmental arches and an iron balcony
over and at r. angles a house with Tuscan porch and iron
veranda over. Then turn l. up GAINS LANE for a view of
ST JAMES'S HOSPITAL, the former WORKHOUSE, red brick
and cruciform with raised centre, as usual. Built in 1836. So
to ESTCOURT HOUSE, plain, but ashlar-faced and of seven
bays with a three-bay pediment. Here the street ends in the
Common, a nice wide green opening. At the far end St James;
to the r. down SOUTHBROOM PLACE, modest red cottages
and between them a townish ashlar-faced three-storey terrace
with balconies on the first few – and across the green two larger
houses, HEATHCOTE HOUSE, of three bays, two lights, one
light, two lights, with a hipped roof and a doorway with a base
on the entablature, and SOUTHBROOM HOUSE (now part of
the Secondary Modern School), built in 1773, ashlar, of seven
bays with a three-bay pediment and low wings leading to
earlier wings (mullioned windows).

A ROMANO-BRITISH SETTLEMENT SITE in PANS LANE
produced many fragments of Samian and coarse wares, and

iron tools. Two burials, accompanied by Romano-British vessels (New Forest ware), were found on the same site.

DILTON see OLD DILTON

DILTON MARSH   *8040*

HOLY TRINITY. By *T. H. Wyatt*, 1844. Resolutely Norman. Big apse, transepts, crossing tower, nave, and zigzag doorway. The crossing has, rather surprisingly, a rib-vault. – FONT. Square, imitation Norman, presented by the architect.

BAPTIST (PROVIDENCE) CHAPEL, Penkney. 1810. Brick, two tiers of pointed windows with Y-tracery.

CHALCOT HOUSE, ¾ m. SW. An unusually animated early C18 front. Brick and stone dressings. The windows flanked by pilasters (which is an unusual thing) and surmounted by pediments alternatingly triangular and segmental. On the top floor pilasters too, but no pediments. Doorway with thin Ionic columns.

PENLEIGH, ¾ m. NE, the other side of the railway. Dated 1710. Seven bays, plain. But the doorway with its bolection moulding is now the garden gateway.

TAN YARD, by the railway station, originally a woollen mill. A penny of 1806 was found embedded in a window frame.

APPLE TREE INN (no longer an inn). Opposite the Baptist Chapel. An excellent Adamish stone front of five bays. The side bays have outer angle pilasters and inner angle half-pilasters. Doorway with columns with fluted capitals. Fluted frieze over. Pedimented middle window, and a panel and garlands above the three middle windows.

DINTON   *0030*

ST MARY. A dignified church with the crossing tower as its centre, essentially Dec, but with older and younger parts. The oldest feature is the N doorway. One order of shafts with a trumpet capital on the l., a crocket capital on the r. Double-chamfered pointed arch, i.e. *c.*1200. Late C13 transepts. In the E wall of the S transept a lancet, in that of the N transept three stepped lancets. Then the Dec style. The nave has a three-light W window of stepped cusped lancet lights. The crossing has arches of two chamfers dying into the imposts and a vault with diagonal and ridge ribs. In the corners the Signs

7

of the Evangelists. The top of the crossing tower is Perp. The light and airy chancel has a five-light E window with cusped intersected tracery and a blank pointed quatrefoil in the gable connected with the window below as if it were the finial of an ogee arch. The N and S windows are large, of three lights, with reticulated tracery. Double piscina with ogee arches. Wagon roof, ceiled, with bosses. – FONT. Square, of Purbeck marble, with the usual shallow blank arches. On the W and N sides they show that they are Norman, on the S and E sides they have been re-cut about 1300. – STAINED GLASS. Original fragments in the chancel NE and SE windows. – PLATE. Cup and Paten Cover, 1576; Paten and Flagon, 1730. – MONUMENTS. A number of worth-while tablets from 1695 to 1773.

PHILIPPS HOUSE, ⅜ m. NW. 1813–16 by *Sir Jeffry Wyatville* for a branch of the Wyndhams. Nine-bay front of ashlar stone, two storeys, with a four-column giant portico of unfluted Ionic columns and a pediment. No ornament, hardly any mouldings. The doorway has two very slender, elongated brackets. To the E five bays, the first tripartite with a blank arch. To the W the same but cut into at the N end by the curved W wall of the former kitchen. In this an apsed alcove. The interior also is very sparing in decoration. Mostly just thin friezes. The details, e.g. the roses in the Drawing Room friezes, on the way to the Victorian style. The same is even truer of the frieze of cornucopias and shields in the entrance hall. The room has a coved ceiling and shallowly apsed side walls. The only more ornate room is the staircase hall. The staircase rises in one arm and returns in two. The iron balustrade has the simplest pattern. On the upper floor in the walls of the staircase columns of brown scagliola. They form an open screen to the N and S, but are blank to the E and W. Shallow vault and big glazed lantern. Again very little stucco enrichment.

HYDE'S HOUSE, NW of the church. The oldest part is probably the big square DOVECOTE, which seems pre-Reformation. But parts of the house are also C16. The front however is a remodelling of the early C18. Five bays, with a pedimented three-bay centre. Quoins. Doorway with unfluted Ionic columns, a pulvinated frieze, and a pediment. Behind, mullioned windows.

SCHOOL. A rustic cottage, just S of the stables of Hyde's House. Several more houses and cottages with mullioned windows, e.g. LAWES COTTAGE, ⅜ m. E, with a symmetrical front, a cottage to the w of Lawes Cottage with three dormers, and also LITTLE CLARENDON, to the E of Lawes Cottage. This is bigger and has a gabled two-storeyed porch and a bigger gable on the r. Round the r. corner a buttress, sign of an earlier period.

MARSHWOOD HOUSE, ⅝ m. WNW. Early C19 front, but the centre of the house no doubt older. Three bays, castellated. Deep porch with Tuscan columns. Taller one-bay additions with hipped roofs.

DITTERIDGE
¾ m. NW of Box

8060

ST CHRISTOPHER. Nave and chancel; bellcote between them. Interesting Norman s doorway. The imposts of the jambs with a dragon and a quadruped. Head-corbels for the lintel. Tympanum interfered with, but a frieze of lyre-shaped leaf motifs around it. Remains of an altered Norman N doorway. Also a Norman s window. The chancel is E.E. It stands on moulded corbels. One Dec s window and two low Dec recesses in the s wall. The church was restored in 1860 by *Edward Godwin*, and the rounded stone PULPIT is no doubt like. – FONT. Circular, Norman, with an unusual motif of long rolls, as if in a wrong perspective making their tops and ends visible. – STAINED GLASS. Some designed by *Godwin*, i.e. probably chancel s, nave one N, one S. – PLATE. Chalice, 1627.

CHEYNEY COURT, 200 yds SW. A C17 house with an odd façade, flat, with three even gables, but the fenestration as if at the l. as well as the r. end there were staircases, i.e. large rising mullion-and-transom cross-windows. The other windows mullioned only.

COLE'S FARM. Dated 1645. Three storeys, gables, mullioned windows. (Inside some contemporary plasterwork. MHLG)

ALCOMBE MANOR, ½ m. W of Cheyney Court. To the r. of the entrance a small two-light C14 window, the only evidence of the medieval part of a much modernized house.

SPA HOUSE, Middlehill, ⅝ m. S of Ditteridge church. The house is connected with a spa which had its pump-room, boarding-house etc. in 1786, but failed. Spa House is of that time, three-storeyed with two canted bay windows. A house attached on the l. has a Venetian window. Could that be the boarding-house? However that may be, mind the rhinoceros which, at the time of writing, stands in the trees opposite facing the house and you.

9020

DONHEAD ST ANDREW

St Andrew. Of the local green sandstone. The puzzle of the church is the tall narrow Norman arch leading N from the E end of the N wall of the nave, E of the end of the N aisle arcade. To the w of it in the arcade E respond some stonework is exposed which, however, does not help to explain the arch. Otherwise, the church has little of special interest. Low w tower, rebuilt in 1893. Perp tower arch. The bell-openings look c17, the pinnacles are c19. Most of the windows Perp and straightheaded. Embattled aisles. The arcades are of three bays; Perp. Section of the piers four shafts and four hollows. The capitals simply a block set lozenge-wise. Good nw respond with a shield held by angels and a mask as the support of the shaft on which the shield stands. The chancel arch goes with the arcade arches. The rest of the chancel rebuilt in 1838. In the tower N wall built-in fragments, including what appears substantial parts of a stone screen. – STAINED GLASS. In the chancel much of c.1845–55. – MONUMENTS. John Cummings, later c17 tablet, delightfully rustic. – Sir James Pender † 1921. Edwardian-looking sarcophagus in the churchyard.

Thorne Farmhouse, ¾ m. NE. Dated 1700. Mullioned windows, but also the upright ovals in oblong frames which are so typical of the later c17.

(Leigh Court Farmhouse. Probably c16, with a gabled porch. MHLG)

9020

DONHEAD ST MARY

St Mary. There was an aisleless Norman church here in the c12. This is witnessed by the small detail of a length of frieze once below the eaves. It can be seen on the s wall of the N aisle, close to its E end. In the later c12 this church was given aisles. The s aisle came first. Three bays, sturdy round piers with octagonal abaci. One capital has trumpet scallops, others stylized leaves on the way to stiff-leaf. The w respond has a head too. All the details robust. The arches are already double-chamfered and pointed. The N arcade piers have round abaci and capitals left uncarved. Of the same time the arches to the transepts, which have on their underside two demi-rolls. In the course of the c13 the nave was given a clerestory – an uncommon thing in Wiltshire. The windows are of one light only. Rere-arches to the inside. Dec s doorway. The attached s porch has a pointed tunnel-vault with transverse arches. Perp w tower, though its ground stage is perhaps earlier. The top has eight pinnacles, the middle ones on corbels. Perp chancel chapels of two bays. Piers with four thin shafts and four wide diagonal hollows. Plain blocks set lozenge-wise instead of capitals. Double-chamfered arches. Perp chancel arch, or at least its S respond, with foliage and small figures. The chapels have straight-headed windows. W of the S aisle was once an attachment of which traces remain. – FONT. Norman, circular, with arcading and a top band of interlace. – PULPIT. Jacobean, with arabesque. – PAINTING. Virgin and Child and two Saints. Italian; Trecento. – PLATE. Cup, 1633; Paten on foot, 1734.

OLD RECTORY, to the NW. Early C18 S front of ashlar. Quoins of even length. Three bays. One-bay pediment over the centre. Doorway with pediment on brackets. To this period of the house belongs the staircase with two turned balusters to each tread and carved tread-ends. But the house must be much older. In the recessed part to the N facing E was an early C16 window which has recently been re-set. The occasion was the adding of a new porch, which actually incorporates in its doorway a window surround from Bowood and also a length of frieze – both pieces of course designed by *Robert Adam*.

COTTAGE opposite Glyn Farmhouse, ¼ m. SE. Dated 1712 on an ornate tablet. The windows are still mullioned, but the unmoulded string-course is indicative of the C18.

DONHEAD HALL, ½ m. S. Once the property of Sir Geoffrey Kneller's grandson. The house is Early Georgian. Five bays, two storeys, ashlar-faced. Doorway and windows with Gibbs surrounds. The centre projects by means of quadrants. The doorway is in this projection. It has a pediment on brackets. The projection culminates in a raised attic with pediment – restless but effective. The room behind the projection is apsed at the back as well. Pilasters and a Rococo stucco ceiling. Also several C18 fireplaces.

DOWNTON

ST LAWRENCE. A large and interesting church with transepts and a crossing tower. Externally the nave and aisles are mixed, but predominantly Perp and Victorian.* Early C18 panelled brick parapet on the S aisle. The S doorway is Perp, and the oddly placed secondary doorway on the same side under a hood is Dec. The transepts are clearly E.E., with the superstructure

* Alterations 1812–15 by *Asher Alexander*, according to the Ferriday Index. Is anything of these still visible?

an ambitious Dec remodelling. The transepts have lancet windows, the most trustworthy being N transept W and S transept E, the latter with an external and an internal continuous roll moulding. In the chancel a priest's doorway with a hood has been removed. A second N doorway has continuous E.E. mouldings. But the chancel windows are tall and Early Dec, of two lights with, in the head, a trefoil with three barbs. The westernmost S window has one light extended downward as a low-side window. Similar, but straight-headed windows in the transept E walls as well. The crossing tower has the same kind of walling as the transepts but applied more regularly, i.e. flint with bands of brown stone. But the details are all C 17. So much rebuilding must have gone on. Inside, the story looks different. The nave turns out to be Norman, or at least the three W bays. Circular piers and square abaci. Multi-scalloped capitals with decorated scallops. The S arcade renewed. The surprising thing is that the single-step arches are pointed. On the N side indeed they reach up higher than the original roof-line of the aisle, i.e. are clearly a later heightening. The two E bays were added when it had been decided to enlarge the church to its present size. The two bays have slim circular piers with circular abaci and double-chamfered arches. The arch from the N aisle into the transept is similar, that from the S aisle has triple responds with fillets and excellent stiff-leaf capitals, the leaves still arranged in one tier. The arches are again double-chamfered. The crossing piers to N, S, and W have the same triple responds with fillet as we have just seen. Only the chancel arch proper has richer shafting and also a more richly moulded arch, whereas the crossing W arch is double-chamfered, and the arches to the N and S have double hollow-chamfers. The chancel has the two N doorways clearly also in the E.E. style, the one further W with a depressed two-centred arch on short vertical pieces (cf. Salisbury Cathedral). The upper parts are all Dec, the sedilia nearly entirely Victorian. Only the two E vaulting-shafts and the traces of corresponding ones in the W corners may refer to the E.E. chancel.

FURNISHINGS. – FONT. Square, with chamfered corners. Of Purbeck marble, C 13. With the usual shallow blank arches. – PULPIT. The excellent Early Georgian sounding-board is in use as a table in the transept. – STAINED GLASS. In one N aisle window two C 15 figures and some fragments. – PLATE. Chalice, 1620; Flagon with Cover, 1624; Paten, 1628; two Salvers, 1778. – MONUMENTS. In the N transept damaged tomb recess, cusped arch with an ogee top. – Sir Charles Duncombe † 1711. Tablet with two columns. Below it a marble wall screen or part of another, late C18, monument. Fluted pilasters and, in relief, arms and cherubs' heads, trumpets, skulls with bats' wings, etc. – In the chancel Georgian Feversham monuments. The floor of the chancel with the black marble ovals was put in with the monuments. Lady F. † 1755. By *Peter Scheemakers*. Large standing figure by an urn, in front of a grey obelisk. Below twenty-five special lines of description of her character. – Lady F. † 1757. Simple, with grey obelisk and without figures. – Lord F. † 1763. Signed by *Thomas Scheemakers* and dated 1784 (Gunnis). Similar but bigger. – Also George Duncombe † 1741. Big sarcophagus on very large lions' feet. Again in front of a grey obelisk. This is by *Peter Scheemakers*. – CHURCHYARD CROSS. Base and shaft with a knob at the top.

VICARAGE, NE of the church. C18, brick, six bays with a two-bay pediment.

PARSONAGE FARMHOUSE, NW of the church. Gabled E front with a gabled porch and, to its r., mullioned and transomed windows. C16 to C17.

THE MOOT, Moot Lane, S of the church. A very fine house of moderate size of *c.*1700. Five by five bays; brick, with stone quoins, also to the pedimented one-bay middle projection. Hipped roof. Doorway and window above it of stone. The doorway has an open segmental pediment, the window side volutes. Staircase with thin twisted balusters. Fine iron garden gate, and a finer one yet, brought in, as the gate to the principal garden across the road. This was made by taking advantage of an EARTHWORK, the place where the moots had been held of old. Thus a dell was created and two mounds, ascended by steep paths. On one of them a hexagonal C18 TEMPLE, i.e. Roman Doric columns, metope frieze, dome. Six seats and ornamental cobble floor. View down the mound and down a number of ancient terraces supposedly used for the moots. Also view to the W to the lily pond and the Avon.

HIGH STREET. Many nice cottages, often with C18 numbers on small stone panels, but no single house of importance.

THE BOROUGH. This is the continuation of the High Street across the Avon to the W. In fact it is not an extension but a made New Town, created by Peter des Roches, bishop of Winchester, probably *c.*1205. The name Borough applies to it by rights. Such New Towns were made, before the great age of the French *bastides*, because burgesses paid their dues in cash whereas on all manors with their villages the lord of the manor, that is here the bishop, had all the trouble with feudal labour and marketing of products. Of course, such New Towns – and there were many of them throughout the C13 – could only be successful in an age of expanding population and economy. Two long rows of houses are placed at an uncommonly wide distance. A broad strip of (untended) grass between them. No special houses, the most interesting perhaps the WHITE HORSE INN with two niches in which Perp heads. Opposite this the remains of the BOROUGH CROSS. Round the corner to the S BOROUGH HOUSE, dated 1673. Brick with stone dressings. Two-light windows. Doorway with moulded surround. In the N gable two vertically placed oval windows in oblong slabs. Eaves with brackets at the ends.

COURT FARMHOUSE, ½ m. N. H-shaped, of brick, with two-light windows, late C17. It is odd that both arms of the H have to the outside, i.e. in their long walls, a centre doorway with amply moulded surround and open segmental pediment. Flint and brick BARN, nine bays long, with aisles.

GREAT YEWS, 3 m. W. Eighty acres of yew trees, the largest with girths up to 18 ft.

ROMAN VILLA, 200 yds S of the castle mound. The villa consisted of seven rooms with front and rear corridor and bath house. One of the rooms had a tessellated floor. The site, which was excavated in 1955, is datable to c. 300–50 A.D.

DRAYCOT CERNE

9070

ST JAMES. E.E. chancel with lancet windows, a group of three (all renewed) at the E end and a priest's doorway with a shouldered lintel (later replaced). E.E. S doorway, single-chamfered with a hood-mould. At the four corners of the nave pairs of heads supporting the eaves. W tower with an Early Perp window, but otherwise apparently C17. Perp S porch, deep, with pairs of three-light side openings. – FONT. On a step decorated with quatrefoils. – STALLS. Jacobean fronts with the familiar blank arches. – BOX PEWS and PANELLING. All this seems Early Victorian. It is Gothic, no longer 'Strawberry Hill', but not yet 'archaeological'. – PLATE. Set, 1702. – MONUMENTS. An unusual number. – Cross-legged Knight of the late C13 under an arch with pierced cusping and a crocketed gable. – Brass to Sir Edward Cerne † 1393 and his widow † 1419. They hold hands. The figures are 3 ft long. French inscription. – Sir

Thomas Long, early c16, excellent tomb-chest with shields in amply cusped fields. Traceried bands between. Very similar to the Tropenell Monument at Corsham. – HELM and GLOVES above. – James Long † 1728. Good cartouche. – Sir Robert Long † 1767. An excellent work, with an eloquent bust but architectural and decorative motifs already cool and restrainedly neo-classical. The monument is indeed by *Joseph Wilton*. – Sir James Tylney † 1805. A flying putto holds the inscription scroll. – Lady Catherine Tylney Long † 1825. By *King*. Urn and weeping willow. – Adelaide Cowley † 1843, bust of a sleeping child. Unsigned. – Fifth Earl of Mornington † 1863. Two standing angels l. and r. of the inscription. Arrangement of cornucopias below.

UPPER DRAYCOT. A brick cottage, looking nothing in particular (two-window front, hipped roof), yet in 1864 it gained its designer, Mr *Brick* of the Adelphi, London, a prize and medal of the Society of Arts.

DURNFORD

1030

ST ANDREW. A Norman church, remarkably spacious and remarkably rich in furnishings. Both doorways are Norman; so the present width of the nave is that of the c12. Both doorways have shafts with scalloped capitals. Both have tympana of green and white stone alternating. The s doorway imposes on this a basket pattern. The N doorway has around it a band of a kind of shuttlecocks. Both have bands of zigzag set at r. angles. On the s side the doorway has to the l. and r. a patterned frieze on a short length of wall. On the N side there is instead inside a vertical band of what might be described as lozenge-flowers. One Norman s window can be seen inside. It is blocked and – a curious fact – outside partly hidden by a buttress which, like the buttresses of the church, is characteristically Norman too. So there are two Norman building campaigns. Norman chancel arch as well, with shafts, re-cut capitals, and in the arch zigzag, again at r. angles. c13 lancets and a group of three under one relieving arch in the chancel. One lancet on the N side is a 'low-side' window. The w tower looks c13 too, but the circular windows are surprising. They would suggest an earlier date. Perp s porch of timber. Single-framed nave roof. – FONT. Circular, Norman; short, primitive interlaced arches; band of volutes over. – PULPIT. 1619. With blank arches as usual; not over-rich. – LECTERN. A fine Jacobean piece. Strong baluster

and the original desk with a chain for chaining a book to it.
– FAMILY PEW. Jacobean, with little balusters below the top.
Now parts of the pew are set against the E wall of the nave. –
COMMUNION RAIL. C17. With an alternation of turned balusters and flat openwork balusters. On the rail instead of knobs
tall balusters (cf. Berwick St James). – WEST GALLERY on
columns; C18. – BENCH ENDS. Many, Perp, with simple tracery
patterns. – SCULPTURE. Small, good, Flemish early C16 Pietà.
– PAINTING. A remarkable amount, though much of it desperately badly preserved. Doom or Rood (?) above the chancel
arch; St Christopher E of the S door; large red scrolls, some with
grapes, in several places; C13. The scrolls run over the blocking
of the Norman window. Also in the chancel ashlar pattern with
flowers set in. – STAINED GLASS. Some Perp glass in a nave
N window. – PLATE. Tankard, 1654; Chalice and Paten, inscribed 1674; Salver, 1689. – MONUMENTS. Two tomb recesses in the nave S wall, one with an ogee arch, the other with a
basket arch, both probably Perp. – Edward Younge † 1607. The
monument has a four-centred arch. Against the back wall brass
plate. — Col. John Younge † 1710. Fine stone aedicule with
Tuscan columns and pediment.

MANOR HOUSE, N of the church. Brick. Late C18 front of five
bays and two and a half storeys. For the upper one and a half
thin giant Ionic angle pilasters. Tripartite doorway with a pediment on elegant brackets, almost identical with that at Wilbury
House. Tripartite windows above. Towards the river big bow
window in the middle. Additions of 1913 to the l. and r.

LITTLE DURNFORD MANOR. Six-bay mid-C18 front of flint
and stone chequer with grey brick trim. Brick e.g. the plain,
flat window surrounds. The ground-floor windows have big
pediments alternating between triangular and segmental. The
front round the corner is late C18, with slender windows and a
pedimented porch of Tuscan columns. The dining room is
a splendid mid-C18 room with a proud chimneypiece and
wall panels of tapestry framed in plaster. Rich plaster frieze,
but no enrichment of the ceiling. (The library has late C18
bookcases.)

DURRINGTON

1040

ALL SAINTS. 1851 by *J. W. Hugall* of Pontefract. Knapped flint.
Many old parts re-used externally, especially the Norman S
doorway (one order of shafts, capitals with leaf, arch with roll
moulding), the Norman gable faced with a kind of diaper or

scales, the chancel s lancets of the c13, the Perp w window. Inside, the old church is essentially preserved. Three-bay late c12 s arcade, circular piers, circular abaci, moulded capitals, round arches with two slight chamfers. Alternation of grey and green stone. The n aisle is c19, but outside to the r. of the porch the base of an octagonal early c13 pier has been re-used. The corbels of the chancel arch are of 1851 – extraordinarily shapeless and covered with poorly copied stiff-leaf. – PULPIT. Jacobean; under the usual blank arches the figures of the four Evangelists, an unusual motif. – READER'S DESK. Faith, Hope, and Charity are also Jacobean, but they are re-used pieces. – TOWER SCREEN. Jacobean, with small balusters at the top. – BENCHES. Simple, Jacobean too. – PLATE. Elizabethan Cup; Paten, 1691.

VILLAGE CROSS. By the church corner the enormous base of the village cross.

The village street of Durrington is preserved; but s of it for a mile all is suburb, suburb presumably of the army camps of Larkhill and Bulford.

WOODHENGE, ½ m. s, on the r. of the road. Henge monument 250 ft in diameter with external bank and ditch and single entrance on the NE. Recognized by air photography, and then fully excavated in 1926–8. Within the bank and ditch were six slightly oval settings of post holes, the timbers of which probably supported a roofed structure. Near the centre was the foundation burial of a child with cleft skull. Finds included Windmill Hill and Rinyo-Clacton pottery from the primary ditch silting and, sealed beneath the bank, a large number of bone points, flint scrapers, and two axes of chalk copying stone examples and probably votive. The position of the post holes is now marked by low concrete pillars.

DURRINGTON WALLS. A second and much larger henge monument immediately N of Woodhenge. Circular in plan with external bank and ditch and entrances on the E and W. The diameter is c.1700 ft. Sherds of Secondary Neolithic ware, flint arrowheads, and a bone pin were found during excavation of portions of the bank and ditch.

EASTCOTT MANOR HOUSE see EASTERTON

EAST COULSTON 9050

ST THOMAS BECKET. A small church close to the downs. Nave with bellcote and chancel, and, in addition, a big N transept.

The chancel is Dec, of 1868. S doorway of the late C12. The
capitals Norman with little volutes, the arch round with a roll
moulding. Contemporary imposts of the chancel arch with
nook-shafts with Norman capitals. C14 arch to the N transept.
Two continuous chamfers. Most of the windows seem to be of
the C17. – COMMUNION RAIL. Part of a rail of the C17. –
LECTERN. With a pierced foliage panel of c.1700, probably
foreign. – PLATE. Chalice and Paten, 1683; Almsdish, 1731. –
MONUMENT. Tablet to James Meredith † 1746. Very restrained. Two cherubs' heads at the foot.

BAYNTON HOUSE, W of the church. Of shortly after 1796. With
a hipped roof. A composition of one–three–one windows plus
a two-bay l. extension.

COULSTON HOUSE. Georgian, ashlar, five bays, with a porch on
Roman Doric columns.

EASTCOURT HOUSE *see* CRUDWELL

0050

EASTERTON

ST BARNABAS. 1875. Nave with bellcote and chancel. Brick, with
lancet windows and tiny dormers.

At the W entry to the village the MANOR HOUSE, timber-framed,
also with double-curved braces. Cross-gable with mullioned
windows. Victorian bargeboards. Up the lane by the Manor
house on the l. the ROYAL OAK INN, timber-framed with brick
infilling, thatched roof. Up another lane by the Royal Oak, on
the l. KESTRELS, early C18, brick, of five bays with hipped roof.
Doorway with open curly pediment. Nicely panelled gatepiers.

In WHITE STREET, a no through road, on the r. FAIRFIELD
FARMHOUSE, stone ground floor, timber-framed upper floor
with narrowly spaced uprights. On the l. WILLOUGHBY'S.
Mullioned ground-floor windows under hood-moulds. Upper
floor timber-framed. The windows project a little and have a
bracket under.

EASTCOTT MANOR HOUSE, ½ m. NE. Timber-framed with
closely spaced uprights and diagonal braces. Brick gatepiers
with pineapples.

2020

EAST GRIMSTEAD
1 m. NE of West Grimstead

HOLY TRINITY. By *F. H. Pownall*, 1857. Nave and chancel.
Bellcote on the nave E gable. Elaborate timber S porch.

EAST KENNETT

CHRIST CHURCH. 1864 by *Gane*. Small, with a w tower and spire. Mostly chequered stone and flint. – MONUMENTS. Charles Tooker † 1700. Good simple tablet. – Ann Tooker † 1707. Inscription below pediment. A grey obelisk above with a profile medallion. – Charles Tooker † 1716. Good portrait bust in front of a grey obelisk. Putto heads at the foot.

MANOR FARMHOUSE, E of the church. With mullioned windows. Dated 1630.

MANOR HOUSE, at the E end of the village. Late Georgian, of brick, five bays and two and a half storeys. Two-storeyed one-bay additions l. and r.

LONG BARROW, ¼ m. s. A magnificent long barrow 350 ft long and 20 ft high. It is unexcavated, but the sarsens projecting from the SE end suggest that it covers a chamber. ¼ m. SSW of the barrow is a damaged rectangular enclosure which has produced Middle Bronze Age pottery.

LONGDEAN BOTTOM STONE CIRCLE, 1 m. s of the Long Barrow. A small circle of undressed sarsens 33 ft in diameter. E of the circle is a short avenue of standing stones.

EAST KNOYLE

ST MARY. The chancel is Norman in its bones, see the traces of an outer arcading on the N side.* It is E.E. in its fenestration. Internally it has a terrible imitation Norman chancel arch. What else it has – *see* below – ought to be the purpose of a visit from every Wiltshire tourist. Of the late C13 the N transept chapel, doubled in 1829 and now with two cross-gables. It has Y-tracery with a quatrefoil in a circle in the spandrel and a deeply moulded pointed trefoil window to the w. Dec s porch entrance. The porch is attached to the s chapel, doubled in 1845 and also with two more gables. Inside, the chapels have continuous double-chamfered arches. Perp w tower with battlements and pinnacles, two niches, and a fan-vault inside. Otherwise there is nothing much of interest inside (apart from furnishings), until one enters the chancel. Its plaster decoration is a surprise and a delight. You see Jacob's Dream on the E wall with the angels ascending and descending ladders, you see remains of an Ascension of Christ on the w wall, on the s wall the Sacrifice of Isaac, and on the N wall a kneeling man below 38b

* The Rev. B. C. D. Palmer kindly tells me that there are also two Norman capitals in the ringing-loft of the tower.

a dove and the verse: Oh that I had wings of a dove, added to which απτερος and αποτερος. Many more verses and inscriptions. Also Jacobean-looking strapwork, in bold forms, and fine decidedly Gothic-looking vertical friezes of little intersected arches. All this is interesting enough iconographically and aesthetically, 'a strange and quaint performance', as Colt Hoare writes. What makes it twice as exciting is that the scheme was worked out by Dr Wren, Rector of East Knoyle from 1623. Christopher Wren was born at East Knoyle in 1632. Dr Wren lost his living in the Civil War, and during his trial this scheme of plasterwork was held against him. The trial was in 1647; the plasterwork was eight years old then; so it can be dated 1639. – FONT. Octagonal, with big fleshy leaves on the bowl and the coving connecting it with the shaft. The most likely date is the C17. – PULPIT. Simple; C17. – (CHANDELIER. Brass, one tier of brackets, c.1800.) – PLATE. Paten, presented 1637; two Chalices with Covers and a Paten, presented 1677; Flagon, 1681.

OLD RECTORY, W of the church. C18. Ashlar, five bays, with a wooden porch of two pairs of attenuated Tuscan columns.

WINDMILL. A tower mill without sails, ¼ m. W.

CLOUDS. By *Philip Webb* for Percy Wyndham. Designed in 1879, the designs soon after reduced, e.g. by omitting the spacious inner courtyard and replacing it by a smaller hall. Built in 1881–6 for £80,000, burnt out in 1889 and largely rebuilt in 1889–91 for another £35,000. In 1938 the house was deplorably ill-treated. It lost its towering vertical accents, three dormers with gables (a weak parapet was put in their stead), two bay windows on the W front, and large parts of the service wing. The house is of ashlar stone, four-square, massive, and with motifs reminiscent of the Gothic (polygonal shafts), the Georgian (windows), and vaguely the Renaissance or perhaps Elizabethan (round arches). The motifs were handled ruthlessly – bloody-minded is the term that comes to mind, but must be discarded, as one remembers Webb's sterling character. But it is certainly without concession to grace. The rhythm of the W side is perhaps the most curious. Inside, the great hall has been thoroughly ruined with green pantiling in a Noddy-land way, but the staircase and the big drawing room remain. Excellent brick service wing, including a lodge with an enormous chimneystack.

BROOKLANDS CLOSE, Milton, NE of Clouds. Ashlar, of five bays, still with wooden cross-windows. Probably of the early C18.

EASTON *see* CORSHAM, p. 176

EASTON GREY

CHURCH. Humble w tower. The rest of 1836. Nave and chancel. The Gothic windows with their four-centred arches seem to be later. – FONT. Moulded bowl of the C13. – PULPIT. Jacobean, with back panel and tester. – PLATE. Chalice and Paten Cover, 1728. – MONUMENTS. Rustic tablets of † 1680, † 1684, † 1713, and others.

MANOR HOUSE. Late C18. The E front of ashlar, seven bays and two storeys, with three-bay pediment. Arched niches l. and r. of the middle window. The semicircular porch round the corner with Tuscan columns looks a little later. Staircase with wrought-iron railing.

A nice group of houses by the BRIDGE. The latter is probably C16. It has five almost pointed arches. The doorway of BRIDGE HOUSE has shafts which seem to be C13 to C14 and are no doubt imported.

ROMAN SETTLEMENT, ¼ m. s. Mosaic pavement, wall foundations, and a large number of coins were found here in the C18. In 1810 a stone slab depicting in relief three standing male figures before a seated female was discovered; another find from the site is a stone female head carved in the round. Pipe-laying operations in 1931 produced numerous Romano-British sherds, Samian and coarse wares, glass, and an iron knife.

EASTON ROYAL

Easton Royal had a Trinitarian friary, founded in 1245 by Stephen of Tisbury, archdeacon of Wiltshire. Its purpose was to serve as a hostel for poor travellers. It was dissolved in 1538. Seymour family monuments were in the church and then were transferred to Great Bedwyn.

HOLY TRINITY. After the Dissolution and the demolition of the friary church in 1590, Sir E. Seymour, Earl of Hertford, built the parish church in 1591. It has Late Perp straight-headed windows, the lights being four-centred and uncusped. They have hood-moulds. One such window even above the w doorway, a curiously secular touch. The chancel and the Perp E window are Victorian; so is of course the SE tower with its pyramid roof. This was added in 1853. Roof with tie-beams and kingposts up to collar-beams and above them. The roof runs through from W to E without any distinction between nave and chancel. – FONT. Octagonal, of goblet shape, plain, also no doubt of c.1591. – STAINED GLASS. E window by *Lavers & Barraud*, 1864. – PLATE. Chalice, 1682; Paten, given in 1728.

EASTON TOWN *see* SHERSTON

⁹⁰⁷⁰

EAST TYTHERTON

MORAVIAN SETTLEMENT. Founded in 1745. The front range is of brick, three units in line. The centre is the chapel, dated 1792. Middle doorway with Tuscan porch and an arched window each side. Attached the sisters' house and the minister's house. Modest, with two-light windows. The chapel has inside the original WEST GALLERY and ORGAN-CASE. Behind the SCHOOL HOUSE, dated 1785; a bigger, more severe affair. Three storeys, stone, of three bays, with three-light windows l. and r. and the doorway and single windows in the middle. The settlement faces an open space with some attractive houses and the aesthetically disastrous village hall.

EASTWELL *see* POTTERNE

⁹⁰²⁰

EBBESBOURNE WAKE

ST JOHN BAPTIST. Nave and chancel of flint, W tower of ashlar and Perp, see the tierceron-star vault inside with shafts on demifigures of angels; see also the decorated capitals of the tower arch and the three-light straight-headed bell-openings. Shield below that to the W. The nave and chancel windows are of c.1300 in style but all Victorian in execution. They can be trusted, as they are visible in Buckler's drawing of 1805. But were there aisles? The proportion of the nave is very wide, rather an early C19 proportion. But in the chancel a small late C13 piscina and an early C14 piscina and sedile with crocketed gables. – FONT. Square, Norman, of Purbeck marble, with tapering sides. Against the sides the usual shallow blank arches, but also scallops and big leaves. The five-shaft stem is C13. – PLATE. Chalice, early C16.

⁹⁰⁵⁰

EDINGTON

^{20a} ST MARY, ST KATHERINE, AND ALL SAINTS. A wonderful church and a highly important church. It is so varied in its skyline and so freely embattled that it looks like a fortified

mansion, and the solemn lines of the downs rising immediately
s are the perfect foil. There had been a parish church on the
site to which nothing now testifies but the base of a Norman
s w respond. In 1351 William of Edington, bishop of Winchester since 1345, decided to found a college for a dean and twelve
priests and to erect for them a church and living quarters. At
the desire of the Black Prince the foundation was transferred
to the Bonshommes in 1352. They were canons, and their only
other house in England was Ashridge in Hertfordshire. Building, wholly the responsibility of the bishop, proceeded very
rapidly, and the church could be consecrated in 1361. It is
about 150 ft long and consists of nave and aisles, transepts, a
crossing tower, a chancel, and a three-storeyed s porch. The
building is for the whole of England one of the major demon-
strations of how the Perp style replaced the Dec style. At
Gloucester fully Perp work had been done in the 1330s, and
the chancel was complete by 1357. But assimilation of the new
style took a long time, and at Edington we can watch it. When
the bishop began the rebuilding of the nave at Winchester there
was no hesitation left between the old and the new, but we do
not know when that was. He died in 1366.

EXTERIOR. As building usually started at the E end, it is remarkable that the E window of five lights, arranged two-one-two,
is Perp in so far as the middle mullions reach up perpendicularly
to touch the main arch, but Dec in the details of the side-pairs
of lights and even in the very top unit of the centre light. The
chancel side windows and transept windows are typically a
transition. Arches upon arches in the tracery are a Dec motif
(cf. e.g. the Wells Lady Chapel), but the verticals of the upper
arches are here particularly stressed, and the top unit is completely Perp. The slender w window of the s transept is a
specially inventive design. It is not strictly transomed, but it
has in each of its two lights a lower arch on which stands an
arch upside down. A concave-sided lozenge is formed by these
four arch forms instead of a transom proper. In the N wall of the
chancel a shallow niche, perhaps for a Crucifix. In the N wall
of the N transept four little shell-headed niches, a purely secular
C17 motif, so far unexplained. Could the garden of the mansion, formerly the canons' quarters, have gone right up to the
church? The E parts of the church have pinnacles as well as
battlements. At the w corner of the transept that changes, and
battlements alone seemed enough. Nave and aisles were in fact
parochial.

The aisles have three-light windows gently stepped under shallow segmental arches. On the N side they are short and placed high up to allow for the former cloisters. The E doorway into the cloister survives, with a four-centred arch and fleurons in one moulding of jamb and arch. The W windows of the aisles and the clerestory are purely Dec, of two lights and simple. The W front, however, is grand again. A double portal, i.e. with a trumeau, and a short but broad eight-light window above, entirely Perp. The portal has busts on hood-mould stops, the window has heads, a foretaste of the beautiful sculpture inside. The crossing tower, to end with, has two-light bell-openings Dec in style (see the motif of the four-petalled flowers in the tracery).

The church is entered by the S porch. The entrance arch and the S doorway still have early C14 mouldings: two sunk quadrants and a deep hollow between. Tierceron-vault with a centre lozenge of liernes divided into four cusped lozenges which, owing to the curvature of the vault, appear unexpectedly folded.

INTERIOR. The interior is entirely of its period, except for the charming plaster roofs, that in the chancel white, of c.1789, and with the sparsest Gothick decoration, those of the tower (a fan-vault) and of transept and nave of c.1663 (date in the S transept), also very self-consciously cusped and Gothic and reminiscent of the earlier C17 roof of Axbridge in Somerset.

The chancel is an exquisite composition, not over-decorated, yet of the finest craftsmanship in the manifold but subdued enrichments. The ensemble is entirely Dec in mood and details and as distant from the Gloucester choir as possible. Niches to the l. and r. of the E window with such a tall, thin, and transparent canopy that one is reminded of the monument of Edward II at Gloucester, i.e. work of the 1330s. Outside these niches in the NE and SE corners more niches of a different design. They repeat in the middle of the generous stretches of sheer wall between the windows. In two of them – what a rare and fortunate survival – two of the statues have escaped destruction, though not damage. They are wonderfully tender in their draperies, again reminiscent of the 1330s (e.g. the Rochester Synagogue). Moreover the niches are supported by small figures of the liveliest kind, and the carvers have found opportunities for more figures, busts, and heads in many places (e.g. the string-course of the transept W walls and the springing of the tower vault). Small doorway in the S wall with basket arch and ogee gable, and another, a little simpler (or defaced?) in the N wall. The sedilia are two-thirds destroyed. What remains shows a little vault and panelling with an arch-head upside down on an arch-head.

The crossing arches are all of the four-shafts-and-four-hollows variety, with the shafts still substantial, but the abaci already polygonal. The arch mouldings are simpler in the E arch towards the chancel than in any other. Nave arcade of six bays. The details are the same.

FURNISHINGS. FONT. The base is Perp, panelled, the cover Jacobean, dated 1626. – PULPIT. C17. With back panel and tester, simply panelled. Nice early C18 stairs with slender twisted and column balusters. – SCREENS. The rood screen is so drastically restored that it cannot count any longer. It is of the veranda type, closed, with a high dado and single-light openings to the W, but open in wide arches to the E. Coving and gallery with parapet. – STALLS. A few in the chancel, and the transepts. One in the chancel has a MISERICORD, a dragon, one in the N transept a griffin. – COMMUNION RAIL. Jacobean, flat, openwork balusters alternating with normal turned ones, but the top as spiky as a stockade – a design not accommodating to communicants. – SCULPTURE. Two wooden figures, the Virgin and St John, C17, probably German. They come from another Wiltshire church. – STAINED GLASS. In the N transept E window a nearly complete original Crucifixion, in the N and W windows less. – Smaller fragments in the S aisle, some of them from Imber church. – PLATE. Chalice and Paten, 1738. – Also from Imber Chalice, 1576; Paten, 1680; Salver, late C17 (probably domestic).

MONUMENTS. In the S aisle at the W end two early C14 effigies of Knights, cross-legged, one of them in an ogee-headed recess. His head is on a pillow laid diagonally, the pillow of the other is supported by angels. Both also come from Imber. – Sir Ralph Cheney † c.1401 and wife. Tomb-chest with shields in generously cusped fields. On the lid indents for brasses. Straight canopy. Vault with pendants. Angels and angel-busts at the top. – To the W a small doorway, panelled inside, and with an ogee gable, i.e. the whole must have been a chantry chapel. – Monument to one of the Bonshommes, his initials being I.B. and his name ending in ton (see the tun as a rebus). Tomb-chest with quatrefoils and tuns with sprigs growing out of them. Canopy with spandrels of openwork tracery. An angel-bust at the top. Effigy in long robes, badly defaced. His feet

against the tun with the initials. Little vault inside. – Sir
Edward Lewys † 1630 and wife. Big alabaster monument. Two
recumbent effigies, she behind and a little above him. An angel
or naked putto hovering above them. Black columns l. and r.,
curtains looped round them. The children kneeling below, two
standing angels to their l. and r., one praying, the other mourning, and above them an inscription:

> Since children are the living corner stone
> Where marriage built on both sides meetes in one
> While they survive our lives shall have extent
> Upon record in them our monument.

– Sir Simon Richard Brissett Taylor † 1815. White marble
monument by *Chantrey*. Life-size relief group of the dead man
and two no doubt allegorical women. He was a bachelor. –
Many minor tablets with allegorical figures, e.g. two by *King*
of Bath.

THE PRIORY. The house stands on part of the site of the college.
Whether the present house is pre-Reformation or post- must
however remain doubtful. To the front two square embattled
projections with mullioned and transomed windows. The recessed part between has mullioned windows only, set irregularly.
Porch with four-centred door-head. Another inside the house.
(Two C17 plaster ceilings. VCH) Behind a long stretch of WALL,
no doubt of the college. It has semicircular buttresses.

MONK'S WELL, in the overgrown hollow by the W entrance to
the college, inaccessible at the time of writing. (A small stone-
vaulted cell with two ribbed supports. C14. MHLG)

BECKETT'S HOUSE, ¼ m. NE of the church. Stone house of
L-shape with, set in the angle, a timber-framed enlargement.
Inside, a modest plaster ceiling with a few small motifs. In the
garden wall doorway with a four-centred head.

LONG BARROW, 1 m. SE, on Tinhead Hill. Skeletons and Windmill Hill ware were found at the E end in the C19.

ENDE BURGH *see* SALISBURY, p. 347

ENFORD

1050

ALL SAINTS AND ST MARGARET. Flint and stone. Quite a large
and a very interesting church. The evidence starts with the
impressive arcades, Norman, cut out of the pre-existing walls.
Square piers with four nook-shafts. The round arches repeat
the motif as a thin roll moulding. Otherwise they are unmoulded. The capitals of the shafts are scalloped on the N side,

concave-fluted on the s side. The chancel arch is still Norman
too, but later. The arcades may be mid-c 12; the chancel arch
is late c 12, as is proved by the trumpet capitals. The pointed
arch on the other hand, with its two slight chamfers, is probably
an alteration. It seems later than the responds, but earlier than
the chancel. The chancel is astonishing. Its s wall unfortunately
is a Georgian rebuilding. It is of brick with stone bands and
two big arched windows. The chancel roof carries a date 1804.
But the N wall of the chancel has the boldest blank arcading,
alternatingly higher and lower lancet arches with continuous
mouldings. The last group to the E is narrower than the others.
Interrupting the flow are two doorways, the r. one later (c 14),
but the other contemporary with the arcading. It is a doorway
with a shouldered lintel, and that confirms the late c 13 date
one would in any case have assigned to it. The doorway leads
through the thick wall, by another shouldered doorway, into
the vestry, which is – another surprising fact – octagonal. It
has simple lancet windows and four aumbries. Of the rest of
the church less is to be said. The s doorway with one order of
colonnettes seems c 13 too. In the early c 14 the N aisle was
rebuilt, as wide as the nave. The w and E windows of three
lights with cusped intersected tracery. The w bay embraces
the tower. Pretty piscina, cinquecusped with ballflower surround. Perp E window in the Georgian chancel; still c 14 probably. Perp w tower, ashlar-faced, with a higher stair-turret. It
had a spire which fell in 1817, doing damage to the nave. This
explains some of the obvious Victorian renovations. There remains, however, a minor puzzle in the interior. In the SE corner
of the nave one can see two pieces of Norman work: a length of
straightforward shafting and a length of a nook-shaft with a
bit of straight wall in one piece. Where did they belong, and
how did they come to be built in here? A possible answer is
that they belonged to the chancel arch replaced by the present
one and contemporary with the nave arches. – FONT. Octagonal,
Perp, with key and sword, a rosette, a pointed quatrefoil, a
shield, etc. – TILES. Some, in the vestry. – PLATE. Cup, c.1575;
Paten Dish, c.1716; Almsdish, 1753. – MONUMENT. Ienever
Baskerville † 1615. Kneeling figure on a base with the inscription. Probably not in its original state.

THE GRANGE, Longstreet, ⅜ m. s. A five-bay Georgian brick
house with a hipped roof, the E side and the first floor of the
w side altered later in the Georgian period to three bays with
wider windows. Lower symmetrical wings.

CHISENBURY PRIORY, ⅝ m. N. A C17 house with a fine C18 front of brick, dated by rainwater heads 1767. Five bays, two-and-a-half storeys, parapet with three vases. The ground-floor openings have alternatingly triangular and segmental pediments. The middle window on the first floor is arched and has a Gibbs surround. Behind, the older parts, with mullion-and-transom-cross windows. Front garden with walls and two symmetrically placed sets of GATEPIERS.

BARROW, ½ m. s. An enormous bowl barrow, 150 ft in diameter and 17 ft high.

ERLESTOKE

9050

ST SAVIOUR. By *G. E. Street*, 1880 (GR). In the Perp style, not a usual choice in 1880. s porch tower. In the porch two Norman bases and capitals from substantial round piers; a third inside the church. The capitals are scalloped with small decoration, the bases have spurs. The abaci are square. So this is evidence of a church with aisles of about 1130–50. – PULPIT. Elizabethan, with unusual stylized lily motifs.

ERLESTOKE PARK was built in 1786–91 by *George Stewart* for Joshua Smith. It lay prominently on a hill to the E of the church. The house has been pulled down. Only two wings remain, with characteristically attenuated Ionic pilasters. Also the very fine GATEPIERS by the church, with vermiculated rustication and urns, a classical LODGE to the SE, with a portico of two pairs of unfluted columns, and a delightful LODGE, s of the main road, with a portico of rough tree-trunks. Opposite the church a group of thatched Gothic cottages, from the window details probably a little later.

In the VILLAGE Joshua Smith distributed among the estate cottages a number of architectural and sculptural oddments, coming perhaps from the mansion of before 1786. The oddest of them are stone reliefs of semi-nude deities, four in all. Then there are small Elizabethan panels with heads, a larger Elizabethan panel used as a door lintel, a Perp panel with quatrefoils, and two late C16 or C17 niches, very similar to those at Edington church on the one hand, Keevil Manor on the other.

ETCHILHAMPTON

0060

ST ANDREW. Nave and bellcote; chancel, the latter of 1866. Dec features are the w window with reticulated tracery, the nice s doorway with two sunk quadrant mouldings, and the chancel arch with two sunk wave mouldings, fleurons in the capitals of the responds, and a hood-mould with a kind of simplified ballflower. – FONT. Circular, tub-shaped, Norman. Some scalloping at the bottom. – BOX PEWS, rising at the back of the nave. – SCULPTURE. C14 panel of the Archangel Gabriel under a nodding ogee canopy. – PLATE. Paten, 1675. – MONUMENT. Two late C14 effigies, hers with the typical angular hairdress. Against the tomb-chest twelve mourners.

MONUMENT, 1 m. WSW, on the A road. 1768. To commemorate road improvements. Square rusticated base, square inscription pillar. Garlands down the edges. A seated lion at the top – unfortunately with an iron tail.

EVERLEIGH

2050

The village was rebuilt on a new site in 1810–11.

ST PETER. The church was rebuilt too – in 1813 by *Morlidge* – but curiously enough on a site in the trees, not at all close to the village. It is a typical building of its date, quite dignified in its ashlar facing, Gothic, but of a kind unmistakably early C19, with its narrow, tall proportions and its plenitude of pinnacles. Inside, hammerbeam roofs on head corbels. – FONT. Circular, Norman, with scallops on the underside. – WEST GALLERY. On thin iron columns. – PLATE. Box, C18; Flagon, inscribed 1754; Chalice and Patens, 1813–14. – MONUMENT. Francis Dugdale Astley †1818, the founder of the new church. Enormous tablet, facing you as you enter. White marble frame in Gothic forms and an inscription plate with metal letters. Unsigned.

EVERLEIGH MANOR, ½ m. ESE (R.A.M.C. Laboratories). Georgian, of brick, nine bays wide, with a three-bay pediment and a porch of four Adamish-Ionic columns.

CROWN INN, ½ m. SE. Former Dower House of the manor house. Brick, whitewashed, with two projecting wings and a hipped roof. Probably older than the manor house.

SNAIL DOWN BARROW GROUP, 1½ m. SE. A large cemetery containing all five types of round barrow. Many of the barrows have been damaged by tanks.

EYRE'S FOLLY *see* WHITEPARISH

FARLEY

2020

ALL SAINTS. Built by Sir Stephen Fox and completed by 1689– 90. Fox was on the commission for the building of Chelsea

46a

Hospital and thus acquainted with *Wren*, who may well have
helped to design the church. It was probably built by *Alexander
Fort* (*see* below), who was joiner to the Office of Works and thus
in constant touch with Wren. The church is of brick (still laid
in English bond – which shows the local bricklayer) with stone
dressings, including quoins. W tower; nave with transepts forming a Greek cross; chancel. The main entrance is in the S
transept. Above the doorway a circular window. The S doorway into the tower may well be an afterthought. Round-arched
windows with continuous mouldings. Hipped roofs. The tower
has a parapet with urn pinnacles. The N transept was the family
chapel and has the burial vault under. Brick gatepiers to the
churchyard, with vases. Simple interior with plaster vaults. –
FURNISHINGS. Nearly all of the time when the church was
completed. – FONT. Octagonal, typical of its date. – PULPIT.
With the typical motif of garlands, but also the old-fashioned
motif of short blank arches with diamond rustication. – READ-
ERS' DESKS. The fronts are two panels of the formerly bigger
pulpit. – SCREENS. With tall balusters. – PEWS. Cut down in
size. – REREDOS. By *Salviati*, i.e. mosaic. Of 1875 and rather
gaudy. – PLATE. Set, 1689. – RAILING of iron, to the family
chapel, now close to the N walk. – MONUMENTS. Elizabeth
Fox † 1696. Bust under opened curtain. Columns l. and r. –
Charles Fox † 1704. With columns and a segmental pediment.
Garlands below them. – Sir Stephen Fox himself † 1716 and
his wife, who got a special inscription starting in conscious
medievalism: 'Cy gist' and ending 'Dieu aye merci de leurs
ames'. The tablet is very similar to the previous one; only the
garlands are above the pediment. – Earl of Ilchester † 1802, by
(Sir) *R. Westmacott*. Obelisk, and below it lunette-shaped relief
of Charity. In the spandrels portraits in profile, one l. and two r.
To the l. and r. of the lunette pelicans. – J. G. C. Fox Strang-
ways † 1859. By *Whitehead*. Gothic. With an angel flying up
and holding an inscription.

ALMSHOUSES. In 1681 already Sir Stephen Fox had founded
almshouses at Farley. There is an inscription referring to him
as founder *Scholae huius et Ptochotrophie*, the words incidentally
in a sans-serif lettering. The building was put up by *Fort*, and
the design does not look as if Wren had had anything to do with
it. Fort is called Surveyor to the builder, i.e. he was certainly
in charge. Long, low brick building (Flemish bond), its centre
in line with the churchyard gates. Centre of four bays and two
storeys with wooden cross-windows and hipped roof with

domes. To the l. and r. lower two-storeyed ranges of seven doors each with, on the upper floor, two–four–four–two windows each. They are simply of two lights. In the centre staircase with turned balusters and drawing room with plaster ceiling, both mid-c18.

FAULSTONE HOUSE *see* BISHOPSTONE, p. 106

FERNE HOUSE *see* BERWICK ST JOHN

FIFIELD BAVANT

0020

ST MARTIN. The smallest parish church of Wiltshire,* on its own, on a little hill, facing the downs. Nave and chancel in one; no division at all. Recent tile-hung bell-turret. In the chancel one tiny lancet, i.e. c13. The E window is Perp, one s window c17. – FONT. Circular, Norman. The lower rim of the bowl undulates. It is in fact the top of an underside consisting of trumpet scallops. – PLATE. Chalice and Paten, inscribed 1735.

FIGHELDEAN

1040

ST MICHAEL. Flint and rubble. The tower arch has Late Norman trumpet-scallop capitals towards the nave. Is it re-set? Then the arcades, E.E., with circular piers and double-chamfered arches. The NE pier and the NE respond have some dogtooth decoration. The aisle walls and windows, the clerestory, and the N chapel are Perp. The tower top, rather distressingly neo-Norman, is by *J. W. Hugall*, 1851. The tower arch was then perhaps made lower and narrower than it had originally been. – STAINED GLASS. In the chancel by *Powell & Sons*, 1858–69. – PLATE. Paten, 1787. – MONUMENTS. In the porch two effigies of cross-legged Knights, the head of one on a diagonally-placed pillow, the pillow of the other supported by angels. Both probably late c13. – Edward Poore † 1716. Cartouche with two cheering putti. – Smart Poore † 1747. Good cartouche. – William Dyke † 1818. Grecian, with nicely sentimental motifs of palm-fronds and poppy. Signed by *Thomas Denman*, 83 Quadrant, Regent Street.

Nice group of timber-framed thatched cottages at ABLINGTON, ½ m. SE. Dormers in the thatch. One of the cottages is dated 1665.

* Or must this title go to Buttermere?

SYRENCOT HOUSE, 1 m. SSE. Pale vitrified and red brick. Early
Georgian. Five bays, two and a half storeys. All windows segment-headed. The porch on four Tuscan columns is attached
to a right-hand appendage. The house itself strikes one as
entirely townish.

FIGSBURY RINGS see WINTERBOURNE EARLS

00 30

FISHERTON DELAMERE

ST NICHOLAS. The church was rebuilt in 1833, the chancel in
1862. But there is evidence left of the medieval building. Just
the suggestion of a Norman chancel arch, though the capitals
are partly C19. Bits of Norman zigzag in the S wall. E.E. chancel
with lancet windows, convincing inside. Dec nave S, Perp nave
N windows, S tower with Perp top. – PLATE. Chalice and Paten,
1631. – MONUMENT. Two Crockford children, small tablet,
with at the top one child in bed, the other bundled up in a
shroud. They died in 1622 and 1624.

1040

FITTLETON

ALL SAINTS. Flint and stone, largely rendered. Early E.E. chancel arch, narrow, with two slight chamfers. Early C14 arcades
of three bays (octagonal piers, double-chamfered arches).
Slightly later C14 tower, see the W window. The tower arch
into the nave would not necessarily appear later than the
arcades, but the tower is built into them. The decision to have
a tower must have been made very soon, especially as below
the top cornice there is still ballflower ornament. Recessed
spire and stair-turret higher than the tower top. Nave roof with
tie-beams on arched braces. Bits of tracery in the spandrels.
King-posts alternating with pendants. – FONT. Circular, Norman, with plain sunk panels. – PLATE. Chalice, 1610; Paten and
Flagon, 1720. – MONUMENTS. Thomas Iay † 1623. Small
tomb-chest with two shields in strapwork cartouche. The top
like a shelf, with side and back walls fitted into the window.
Against the back brass inscriptions. The r. one reads:

> The joy of JEAYE is gonne from worlds woe
> To heavenly JOY and happie rest:
> But left some JOYES; her dearest JOY to cheere
> Amidst his cares: in sad and pensive brest.

– Five tablets with urns, ranging from 1790 to 1830.

OLD RECTORY, N of the church. Early Georgian. Seven bays, two storeys, hipped roof. Red brick and, flanking the three middle bays, giant pilasters, stuccoed. The windows l. and r. of the middle one are narrower than the others, an early C18 fashion. The doorway with the broken pediment is later.

FITTLETON MANOR, E of the church. Probably early C18. Flint and red brick. Five bays, two storeys, wooden cross-windows. Doorway with straight hood on carved brackets.

FONTHILL GIFFORD

HOLY TRINITY. Built for the Marquess of Westminster in 1866 by *T. H. Wyatt*, alas to replace a pretty classical church of 1748, built for Alderman Beckford. This had a four-column portico and a small tower behind it. Wyatt's church is bigger of course and, it must be admitted, groups extremely picturesquely from the E, with its NE tower with a spire rising between pyramid pinnacles, an apse, and a round turret to its N. The tower serves for a porch and has short alabaster columns. Inside two-bay transepts, again short, fat piers, and much rich foliage carving by Mr *Sansom*. The chancel and apse are low and rib-vaulted. – Alabaster PULPIT.

FONTHILL ABBEY. Alderman Beckford and the Marquess of Westminster have just been referred to. Fonthill is more famous for William Beckford, author of *Vathek* and nabob of ill repute. But the Fonthill story has yet more principal actors. Beckford's Fonthill estate was of 4,900 acres. It is hilly with beautiful valleys and well wooded throughout, even before Beckford's exotic planting made it what it now is. A major house was first built by Sir John Mervyn, who bought the estate in 1553. It was remodelled by Sir Francis Cottingham, who bought it in 1631 and put up one of the largest stables in England. Nothing survives of the Mervyn time; whether anything survives of Cottingham's work remains to be seen. Later, in 1740, the estate came to Alderman Beckford. He altered or rebuilt, lost the house by fire in 1755, and replaced it by a fine Palladian mansion with giant portico and wings of five by five bays connected with the house by quadrant wings of ten pairs of coupled columns. This *Fonthill splendens* lay immediately to the w of the lake, and all that remains of it is part of one wing transformed into two cottages.* See p. 577

* The situation is near EAST LAWN FARM. There are also inside some wainscotting and several doors probably from the mansion.

Into this mansion young William Beckford moved. But its style did not satisfy him, and so he conceived the idea of a Gothic mansion, not in the valley, where the older houses had been, but on the hill, ½ m. NW. The house grew in his mind and in that of his architect, *James Wyatt*, until it became reality as the most prodigious romantic folly in England. The central tower was 225 ft high to the top of the pinnacles. It was in the middle of a cruciform building *c.* 350 by 290 ft, one wing holding the entrance hall with a straight, wide staircase leading up to the octagon under the tower. In two of the other wings were long galleries, that of Edward III 68 ft long, that of St Michael 112 ft. Beckford began to think of a Gothic folly in 1793, began to build in earnest and to plant 'at a monstrous rate' in 1796, kept up to 500 workmen at a time busy, surrounded the property with a wall 12 ft high, held a three-day-and-three-night party in honour of Nelson and the Battle of the Nile in 1800, moved in finally in 1807, completed the last part of the building in 1812, and moved out and sold out in 1823. He went to live at Bath and in Lansdowne Tower, and his Fonthill tower, negligently built, collapsed in 1825.

It is an eerie experience to visit Fonthill Abbey now. One drives through the woods, once Beckford's grounds and still reminiscent of some of his planting, and finally reaches a ruin of modest size, the N end in fact of the Abbey, with the polygonal end of the Oratory, the walls of the once elaborately vaulted Sanctuary, and corridor to its S, the Lancaster Tower with its higher stair-turret, and just the start of Edward III's Gallery. There is also an embattled, claustral fragment to the E and that is all, except for the Western Avenue which once led to the principal entrance.*

In exploring the grounds to the SW one comes, at about ¾ m. SW of the house, on to two forlorn, though truly gorgeous GROUPS OF STATUES, one of the Four Seasons, the other of the Four Elements. They are clearly Victorian and belong to the mansion built for the Marquess of Westminster about 1847–52 by *Burn*. This house has also disappeared. It was demolished in 1955. Only the LODGE by the Beckford Arms at Fonthill Gifford with its turret is still there. The statuary was bought at one of the International Exhibitions held in Paris, presumably either that of 1855 or that of 1867.

But yet another house was built in the grounds, and this remains. It was built E of the Lake by *Detmar Blow* in 1904 in

* A TUNNEL is under the terraces of the Abbey.

the local Wiltshire C17 style, incorporating as its centre the centre of the manor house of Berwick St Leonard, with its three gables and two spacious oblong bay windows. It was called LITTLE RIDGE and is now called FONTHILL HOUSE.

We must now turn to the accessories of the various mansions so far as they have not yet been mentioned. To start once more in the village of Fonthill Gifford, there is E of the church a GATEWAY with piers with vermiculated rustication, probably of the Alderman Beckford period, though a date in the 1630s is not out of the question. Round the church picturesque COTTAGES no doubt belonging to the Westminster period. The road to the N leads through a TUNNEL.

On the road to Bishop's Fonthill more is to be seen. First on the r., quite close to the road, but not easily seen in the trees, the HERMITAGE, now no more than a small rocky bump. Then on a slope down, with trees l. and r., before the first farm on the l. the DARK WALK, a tunnel under the road, its entrance and exit again not easily seen. It is quite long, with bends and small openings. After that, visible on the far side of the Lake, the LANDING STAGE with vases, and halfway up the wooded slope the GROTTO provided by *Josiah Lane* of Tisbury. All these *divertissements* belong to the Alderman Beckford years.

Finally, of about the same time, at the N end of the Lake the remains of the BOAT HOUSE which, when it was still intact, was really like a crypt of nave and aisles, only of course flooded. Pillars with intermittent blocky rustication carry arches. The front has now alas collapsed.

Architecturally the most important of the remains at Fonthill is the last, the GATEWAY from Bishop's Fonthill. It is on a 45b monumental scale, tripartite, with a big arch in the centre and lower balustraded one-bay side-pieces. The centre has a heavy pediment. The angle pilasters supporting have intermittent rocky rustication. The same motif round the arch. The head in the keystone hardly visible in its rocky surface. To the outside the gateway is continued by retaining walls with vases. They end in big piers. Now all this is attributed by Rutter in 1823 to *Inigo Jones* on the strength of local tradition. If this is correct, it must have been erected when Sir Francis Cottingham owned the estate. He was a diplomat, familiar with the Continent and especially Spain. Other relations with Jones are not recorded. The style of the gateway, however, makes Jones's authorship quite acceptable.

HOUSE by *Peter & Alison Smithson*, 1961–2. By Upper Lawn

Farm, *c.* ½ m. s w of the church. A neat two-storey box glazed on three sides to catch all the sunshine.

FORD

The village lies in the combe. Several worthwhile houses with gables and mullioned windows.

St John Evangelist. 1897 by *C. E. Ponting.* Perp in style. Nave and chancel in one; tiled. Little shingled spirelet. Wagon roof. – The screen reaches right up to the start of the roof. – Stained glass. E window by *Morris & Co., c.*1910, i.e. long after Morris and Burne-Jones had died.

Congregational Chapel. 1815. In the trees above the road. A small oblong. Segment-headed windows. Hipped roof.

FOREST HILL LODGE *see* MARLBOROUGH, p. 301

FOSBURY

Christ Church. Disused at the time of writing. By *Teulon,* 1856. Flint; in the Dec style. s tower with spike and an odd way of introducing the not unusual motif of a frieze of cusped triangles. Nave and chancel in one. No chancel arch, but a distinction between the arched braces of the nave roof and the hammerbeam of the chancel roof, the latter with wilful details. Little otherwise of Teulon's obstinate originality.

Vicarage. The vicarage however displays that originality in the extraordinary gable over the doorway and the triangular oriel. The house is of flint and red brick with asymmetrical gables.

Fosbury Camp. Bivallate hill-fort with inturned entrances on the E; unexcavated, although Iron Age A sherds have been recovered as surface finds. Part of the fort lies within Oakhill Wood.

FOSCOTE *see* GRITTLETON

FOVANT

St George. The feature which matters is the tower, built *c.*1492 (*see* below). It has at the top a frieze of quatrefoils, then an open-work frieze of cusped triangles, then battlements with open-work quatrefoils. The motifs are exactly the same as at St Peter Shaftesbury. Higher, polygonal stair-turret. To the s two niches, the shafts for the images on demi-figures of angels. The windows of the church are mostly renewed. Are the two on the s side with their flat arched tops early c16? On the s side of the chancel an atrocious neo-Norman priest's doorway, made, however, with original Norman parts. Inside the arcades differ, but both now look new, i.e. of the restoration of 1863. The s with its continuous mouldings appears more acceptable. The nave has a ceiled wagon roof with bosses. – PULPIT. Of stone, probably of *c.*1863. – MONUMENT. George Rede † 1492, rector 'tempore edificationis novae turris'. Brass plate with Annunciation and kneeling rector. Inscription scrolls.

OLD RECTORY, s of the church. Georgian. E front of five bays and two storeys. Doorway and attached Tuscan columns and pediment.

CONGREGATIONAL CHURCH, ¾ m. SE, in the village street. Stone, late c18, with arched windows and doorway.

CROSS KEYS INN, on the A 30. Symmetrical c17 front of three bays with three-light mullioned windows.

FOXHAM

ST JOHN BAPTIST. By *Butterfield*, 1880. Nave and chancel in one. The w tower seems half on the roof, like a bell-turret. Small windows all of one sill and apex height, though varied in the grouping. Canted, ceiled wagon roof. Tiled dado in blue and yellow with red. – SCREEN. A tremendous, very chunky piece, far too massive for the small church, which is no doubt the effect Butterfield wanted. The forms of the screen are late c13.

CADENHAM MANOR HOUSE. Later c17 house of five bays with four-light mullioned and transomed windows. (Built into the wall of the c20 porch on the N side part of a cusped window-head of the predecessor of the present house. Inside the house some small panels with delicate Early Renaissance decoration. Not *in situ.*)

FOXLEY

CHURCH. E.E. N arcade, the w bay demolished. Pier circular with four attached shafts, but still capitals with variously decorated trumpet scallops. Moulded arches. The N aisle itself was extended in the later Middle Ages to project so far that it received two cross-roofs. They are single-framed. A N chapel has also been pulled down. In the E respond niche with nodding ogee arch. Low w tower with pinnacles too big for the tower.

Nave roof with tie-beams, collar-beams on arched braces, and wind-braces. C18 s porch and doorway. – Jacobean PEWS with knobs, cut down to make benches. – Jacobean COMMUNION RAIL. – REREDOS, C18, plain panels with moulded frames. – PLATE. Chalice, 1572; Paten Cover, inscribed 1606; Chalice, Paten, and Flagon by *Paul Lamerie*, 1727. – MONUMENT. George Ayliffe; 1722. Standing wall monument of white and grey marble. Twisted columns wreathed round with flower garlands. Rounded top. No figures.

MORTUARY CHAPEL at COWAGE FARM (i.e. the former church of BREMILHAM). Only the nave stands, with its bellcote. – FONT. Octagonal, Perp, with quatrefoils.

FOXLEY MANOR. A five-bay C18 house with a C17 DOVECOTE, the latter square, with four gables.

FRESDEN FARMHOUSE *see* SEVENHAMPTON

2060
FROXFIELD

ALL SAINTS. Flint and stone. Nave and chancel. Wooden bell-turret of the C19. The chancel is E.E., with lancet windows. The nave w window Perp, straight-headed, with a hood-mould. – PLATE. Chalice, inscribed 1619; German or Dutch.

SOMERSET HOSPITAL. Founded by the duchess of Somerset in 1694 and enlarged in 1775. The gateway and chapel 1813. The hospital became in the end a building thirty-seven bays long to the street and with a large oblong courtyard. The chapel stands in its middle. This and the gateway are of ashlar, the rest of brick. The work of 1813 is Gothick, with pretty details. The work of 1694 comprised just under half the present accommodation. It is to the r. (E) of the gateway. The rest is of 1775. The difference can easily be seen: windows with stone mullions and moulded stone surrounds in 1694, wooden windows (and a string-course between ground floor and upper floor) in 1775. The accommodation ultimately provided is for twenty clergy and thirty lay widows. – PLATE. Chalice and Paten, 1695.

RUDGE FARM ROMAN VILLA, 1¼ m. NW. In Rudge Coppice is the probable site of a villa which has yielded a mosaic floor with a central design of a human figure, and a well containing human skeletons, coins, and a bronze vessel inlaid with champlevé enamel in blue, green, and red. This depicts a fortified, crenellated wall above which is an inscription interpreted by Professor Richmond as being an abbreviated version of the names of the towns of Bowness, Burgh-by-Sands, Castlesteads, Birdoswald, and Bewcastle – all on Hadrian's Wall.

FUGGLESTONE *see* WILTON, p. 516

FYFIELD
2½ m. w of Marlborough

1060

ST NICHOLAS. A small aisleless flint church with a Perp ashlar-faced tower. The arch towards the nave is nicely panelled. The chancel is E.E., even if the detail may be largely due to the restoration of 1849. The corbel-table is partly old, and the interesting shafts inside in the E corner, meant to carry a rib-vault, are at least essentially old. In fact the capital now used as a bracket looks more confidence-inspiring than the capitals of the shafts. The C13-looking nave S windows and the whole N aisle belong to 1849. Handsome Perp nave roof of low pitch with tie-beams and tracery over. – PLATE. Chalice and Paten, 1732; Almsdish, 1781.

HOUSE, N of the church. Georgian, of brick, three bays wide, with a Tuscan porch.

LOCKERIDGE HOUSE, ⅜ m. S. Early C18, of brick. Five bays and two storeys. Pedimented doorway. Aprons below the ground-floor windows. Fine stone and brick gatepiers, panelled and with very big pineapples.

CLATFORD HOUSE, ¾ m. E. Brick, gabled, with a few mullioned windows and a few more hood-moulds. Sarsen stone. The N side was sashed later and given a porch with Tuscan columns.

FYFIELD MANOR
⅞ m. ENE of Pewsey

1060

The oldest evidence is in the roof, two moulded beams and wind-braces belonging to a pre-Reformation hall once probably open from bottom to top. Of the same date in the basement on the N side two two-light windows with lights with depressed arches. The basement is of stone, and this stone base runs all round the house. But above the base it is all brick, and all laid in English bond. The date of this must still be the C16, as the beams inside the E half of the S range, with their coarse and curious carving, indicate. The S side of this S range is the façade proper, seven bays and two slightly projecting angle bays in addition. Two storeys and five gables not strictly symmetrical and, judging by the brickwork and the way in which the gables cut into a brick cornice, a later addition. The bargeboards do not allow a date later than, say, 1650, and so the fenestration of the front marks yet another remodelling. The windows in their present glazing are Georgian, but when they were cut in to replace c16 or c17 windows they no doubt had wooden mullion-and-transom crosses such as survive in the w range towards the road. In this form they were probably of *c.*1700, a date borne out by the moulding of the entrance to the forecourt from the road. Again of *c.*1700 the s doorway with a pediment on brackets and the main staircase with slim twisted balusters. The back staircase is older and coarser, perhaps of the time when the gables were set up. To the se of the house square DOVECOTE of bands of flint and brick, with a pyramid roof.

9080   GARSDON

ALL SAINTS. Perp w tower with a parapet of openwork quatrefoils cut down. The hood-mould of the w window on two beasts facing downward. The church by *Coe & Goodwin,* 1856 (GR). Nave and chancel in one, Perp windows. – PLATE. Set, 1684. – MONUMENTS. Sir Laurence Washington † 1643, a younger son of the Washingtons of Sulgrave. Oval inscription plate surrounded by a wreath. Twisted columns support an open segmental pediment. On this two allegorical figures. The inscription says: 'Of known piety, of charity exemplary, a loving husband, a tender father, a bountiful master.'

MANOR HOUSE. The s porch seems mid-c17,* three-storeyed, flat and symmetrical, with mullioned and transomed windows and a parapet with three small gables. But behind this lay a medieval hall range, and the roof of the hall exists still. Four bays with collar-beams on arched braces, kingposts with fourway struts and also with wind-braces. A back wing to the e of the hall range seems to be Elizabethan. Small mullioned windows under hood-moulds. (In a ground-floor room fine stone chimneypiece of before *c.*1630 with pairs of columns below and the overmantel flanked by pairs of termini caryatids. Strapwork cartouche and arms. Also in the same room, broad-ribbed stucco ceiling. NBR)

GARSTON HOUSE *see* BROAD CHALKE

GASTARD *see* CORSHAM, p. 176

* Aubrey: 'Re-edified ... about the beginning of the Civil Warres.'

GIANT'S GRAVE *see* MILTON LILBOURNE *and* OARE

GRAFTON   *2060*

St NICHOLAS. 1844 by *Benjamin Ferrey*. Thoroughly Norman,
down to the lychgate. NW tower with pyramid roof. From the
roof the symbols of the four Evangelists stick out and also
four dogs' heads higher up. Nave with clerestory, aisles, chancel, and apse. The roof altered. The *Antiquarian and Architectural Year Book* for 1844 writes that Ferrey's model had been
Thaon near Caen, Castle Rising, and 'the ruins of the conven-
tual church at Ely'. – STAINED GLASS. W window by *Willement*.
Just N of the manor house a MOTTE AND BAILEY (HR).
WINDMILL. A tower-mill without sails, 1½ m. to the NE.
TOW BARROW, 1¼ m. SE of Wexcombe. Unchambered long
barrow with prominent side ditches on a spur. Windmill Hill
sherds have been excavated on the old land surface beneath the
barrow.

GREAT BEDWYN   *2060*

St MARY. A shapely church with a crossing tower of just the
right height in relation to nave, chancel, and transepts. The
general tenor is C12 or C13, though none of the external details
are. It is inside that one can get an impression of what deter-17b
mined the character of the exterior. The arcades of four bays
are late C12, i.e. they have round piers but square abaci. The
arches are pointed, but have one slight chamfer, then a bold
zigzag at r. angles to the wall surface, and then an equally bold
hood-mould of billets. Flat bases with spurs. Now the capitals,
which are unfortunately atrociously over-restored. The NW
respond is in the best state: trumpet scallops and leaf crockets.
The re-cut SW respond has upright palmettes. Two others have
similar palmettes upside down used as a decoration of trumpet
scallops, and three have decorated trumpet scallops with little
fleurs-de-lis at the top. But one on the S side has stiff-leaf on
stalks arranged in two tiers, the leaves turned horizontal, and
another, also on the S side, crockets with, towards the nave,
three little heads. Long late C13 chancel with, on the N and S
sides, long lancet windows with pointed-trefoiled heads.One
of them is a low-side window, i.e. is continued below a transom.
The E window is Victorian. The piscina is Dec, with an ogee

arch loaded with thick leaves. Below the lancet a bone-hole. The transepts and crossing early C14. The crossing arches of two continuous chamfers, the arches from the aisles into the transepts too. The bell-openings tall, of two lights, the tracery a kind of minimum Dec. Pretty openwork battlements, perhaps later. Transept windows entirely Dec, especially the N and S windows of three lights with ogee trefoils, barbed, i.e. with barbs sticking out between the foils (cf. Malmesbury). The W and E windows have pointed-trefoiled lights and a cinquefoiled circle over, with the foils daintily cusped. The Dec W front however is of 1843. Perp clerestory. – SCULPTURE. In the N arcade E respond shallow niche with a seated figure, probably C14, but almost entirely defaced. – STAINED GLASS. S transept, designed by *Street* and made by *Hardman*. – PLATE. Paten, 1712; two Chalices, 1785. – MONUMENTS. In the S transept two twin tomb recesses with early C14 mouldings. In one effigy of a cross-legged Knight, his head on a diagonally placed pillow. Suggested to be Sir Adam de Stokke † 1313. – John Seymour † 1510, brass, in civil dress (2 ft 1 in.; chancel). – Sir John Seymour † 1536. Removed from Easton Royal Priory. The re-erection took place in 1590. Of that time the tomb-chest with shields and much ribbonwork. The effigy, however, must be of 1536. – Duchess of Somerset † 1674. The monument erected in 1706. Bust at the top; two jolly, almost dancing big putti below. – CHURCHYARD CROSS. Complete, as far as steps, base, and shaft go. Against the shaft one small shallow recess with a defaced statuette. Fleurons below the head. The head is not preserved. The present head is recent, and the polyhedron sun-dial head in the church cannot be original either.

CASTLE. Leland mentions the ruins of a castle still recognizable at his time.

(BEDWYN BRAIL. In the woods, 2 m. WSW of Shalbourne, are the foundations of a mansion begun in 1549 by Lord Protector Somerset and not continued after his execution.)

ROMAN VILLA, in Brail Wood, 1 m. SSE. Partially excavated in the C19, when wall foundations, portions of mosaic and cement flooring, and a cistern were uncovered. Small finds include sherds of Samian ware with a potter's stamp dating it to *c*.A.D. 40–80.

8060

GREAT CHALFIELD

The manor house and the church are an inseparable group. In fact, the church is approached through the gatehouse of the manor.

ALL SAINTS. Small, with a square bellcote projecting a little and crowned by a small crocketed spire. Pretty w porch, really a projecting hood, panelled inside. The most interesting part of the church is the Tropenell Chapel, built by Thomas Tropenell about 1480. Panelled wagon roof, and Perp arch to the nave. The chapel following to the E is that of the Neale family, built in 1775. The arches from this to Tropenell Chapel and chancel are surprisingly accurately Gothic. The blocks above the capitals were no doubt intended to be carved. – SCREENS. To the Tropenell Chapel. Stone. In the heraldry the arms of Thomas Tropenell's second wife. Top frieze and foliage and five shields. Cresting. – Also a Perp wooden screen now used between chancel and organ chamber. – STALLS. With tracery-panelled fronts and poppy-heads. – BENCH END. One is old, with elementary blank panelling. – PULPIT, READER'S AND CLERK'S DESK, a C17 three-decker. – COMMUNION RAIL. Contemporary with the pulpit. – CHANDELIER. The brass chandelier in the nave is thought to be Netherlandish of the C17. It was brought in. – SCULPTURE. As a N window sill a Norman stone re-used with a column and some leaf in the spandrel. – PAINTINGS. Six panels of the Life of St Katherine on the w wall of the Tropenell Chapel. – STAINED GLASS. Some Perp glass in the w window. In other windows mostly C18 fragments. – PLATE. Chalice and Paten Cover and Paten, 1680.

GREAT CHALFIELD MANOR. Thomas Tropenell acquired the estate in 1452, but was in possession securely only in 1467. He died in 1488. Even that is a remarkably early date; for one of the most conspicuous features recurring everywhere is windows with uncusped lights, and this one is used to considering Tudor and rather Henry VIII than Henry VII. However, no-one standing for the first time in front of the house will at once turn to such details. For here is one of the most perfect examples of the late medieval English manor house, mellow in its buff stone and happily balanced in the composition of its façade without being pedantically symmetrical. One enters the precinct by a bridge across the moat which is here, N of the house, at its widest, then turns l. through the gatehouse and finds oneself facing the church and close to the house on one's r. The gateway has a four-centred arch; the upper floor here is not old. Between the gatehouse and the house are subsidiary accommodation and offices.

The façade of the house has the hall windows in the middle, then two gables of the same height and width l. and r., one above

the hall bay window, the other above the porch, and outside
them on either side a higher and wider gable with an oriel window beneath. What breaks the symmetry most effectively is the
hall chimneybreast. There are of course subtler departures
from symmetry as well, for instance in the two oriels. Both rest
on corbels with a kind of fluted panelling. But on the l., which
is the solar side, this rests on a solid buttress with two heads
l. and r., the dado zone of the oriel has blank panelling, here,
and here alone, cusped, and the oriel itself is semicircular and
crowned with fleur-de-lis cresting. The r. oriel is canted and
has no supporting buttress, a blank dado, and no cresting. What
lay behind the r. oriel is not known. It is unlikely that there were
simply buttery, pantry, and kitchen here. The rooms must have
been an extension of the living space. For why otherwise would
there be a four-light window below the oriel? The gables are
crowned by a host of figural finials (knights, griffins, etc.).

The HALL is entered by the porch, which has a tierceron-
star vault with bosses and its original oak door. The windows
are of two lights with four-centred arches and plain Y-tracery.
There are two to the N (plus the fireplace), three to the s. The
hall never reached up into the roof. It was always only of one
storey with an attic or garret above lit from the gable ends. The
hall ceiling has moulded beams with bosses. The high-table
end has a bay window not only to the N, but also to the s, where
it serves as a communicating link to the staircase (which is not
now the C15 staircase, though it has the original doorway).
Both bays are low and have tierceron-star vaults. The opening
of the chimneypiece is many-moulded. In the spandrels are
long leaves, one straight, one wavy. To the l. is the mark of the
arm of a former seat that must have run along the wall. The
wooden hall screen with its dainty buttresses is a copy after the
screen shown in an early C19 drawing. The most curious feature
of the hall is the three little spy windows, two for the rooms
above the hall bays, the third one to the gallery above the
screens passage. They are given the form of masks with open
mouths and eyes – a bishop, the devil, and another face. This
is a feature almost unique in England (but cf. Little Sodbury,
Glos.).

From the hall bay direct to the E lies a vaulted room of two
bays with single-chamfered ribs on corbels. It has small windows, and the outer buttresses were provided less to support
the oriel than the vaulting inside. Probably the room, so close
to the high-table end of the hall, was the strong-room. From

here to the s the wing is rebuilt. To the w of the hall is the present DINING ROOM. The slit to allow observation of the porch with its original shutters should be noted. The room has panelling, remains of impressive figural wall-painting – just one large figure – and a fireplace with interlace work in inlay. From the w end to the s runs a much rebuilt timber-framed wing. Originally the s area was an inner courtyard with ranges of minor building all round.

On the first floor, along the E wing, is the GREAT CHAMBER. Its roof is a copy. The oriel has a lierne-vault with three pendants and a prettily cusped centre. The chimneypiece is reconstructed from original* fragments. The room in the w wing behind the other oriel has an original roof with collar-beams and arched braces and two tiers of wind-braces. It is from this that the roof of the Great Chamber was copied. Small spiral staircases lead up to the little room above the porch and the hall bay to the roof.

To the NE of the church are the remains of a kind of tiny corner bastion or perhaps rather summer house. Further E, across the moat before this joins the lower moat or fish pond, lay the MILL, which may well date from Tropenell's time. The overflow is an upright vertical stone panel pierced by three quatrefoils.

GREAT CHEVERELL

9050

ST PETER. E.E. chancel, much restored c.1867 (PF). Flint and rubble. Original one N, one s lancet, and the single-chamfered recess inside the N wall. Short C14 W tower. Arch to the nave of two continuous shallow hollows. Perp N chapel with battlements and straight-headed windows. The chapel has a N doorway. Two-bay Perp arcade to the chapel, with piers of a four-shafts-four-waves section. Original ceiling with moulded beams and bosses. Wagon roof in the nave, the w bay painted naively with clouds. – FONT. The bowl C13, octagonal, with rough pairs of pointed-trefoiled arches on each side. – PULPIT. Set in it old linenfold panels. – PLATE. Cup, c.1574. – MONUMENT. James Townsend † 1730. Corinthian pilasters and an architrave curved up in the middle. Looped-up baldacchino to reveal the inscription.

MANOR HOUSE. Behind a SUMMER HOUSE of two storeys. Early Georgian. Square, with large windows and a finial on the pyramid roof.

* Probably mid-C16.

GLEBE FARMHOUSE, between the church and the pub. Late
c17, of red and blue chequered brick. Three bays, plus outer
bays with upright oval windows. Hipped roof.

GREAT SOMERFORD
9080

ST PETER AND ST PAUL. Above the Bristol Avon. Early Perp w
tower with battlements and pinnacles. The arch towards the
nave still with c14 mouldings. Nave and aisles with straight-
headed windows. Chancel with big three-light Perp windows.
The sedilia inside is simply one window continued downwards
in blank panelling. N arcade of four bays. Piers with four shafts
and four hollows. Capitals with big coarse leaves and also small
heads. The chancel arch of the same details. Chancel roof
extremely prettily painted with stylized flowers, to the design
of *F. C. Eden*. – FONT. Octagonal, Perp, with quatrefoils, entirely re-cut. – PULPIT. The tester is Jacobean. – STAINED
GLASS. Old fragments in the small window above the pulpit. –
E window, 1865 by *Lavers & Barraud*. – PLATE. Paten, 1735;
Chalice, 1743. – MONUMENTS. Richard Brown † 1687. Tablet
flanked l. and r. by one baluster of unusual shape and one
exceedingly twisted column. – William Pyke † 1794. One of
the most charming works of *King* of Bath. Relief of the Good
Samaritan, exactly as if it came from the centre of a chimneypiece. – Mrs Elizabeth Smith † 1798. With urn and weeping
willow. By *King*. – The churchyard has fine c18 GATEPIERS.
THE MOUNT, SW of the church. Early c19 front of three wide
bays. One-bay pediment. Nice iron porch. Roof and back are
older (late c16?). The name of the house comes from the
former MOTTE AND BAILEY CASTLE close to the river.
RECTORY, SE of the church. At the back canted, two-storeyed
c17 bay with mullions.
BEVIS, opposite the Rectory. Timber-framed, with narrowly
spaced uprights.
(WEST STREET FARM. Built *c*.1700. Built into the front bits of
ornamental stonework of unknown provenance. *See* June
Badeni: *Wiltshire Forefathers*.)
BRIDGE. Late c18. Balustraded parapet.

GREAT WISHFORD *see* WISHFORD

GRITTLETON
8080

ST MARY. Terribly over-restored (by *Arthur Blomfield*, 1865–7;
PF). N and S arcades of four bays, of *c*.1200. Round piers,

capitals with a running scroll attached to the normal trumpet
scallops, octagonal abaci, double-chamfered arches. One capital
has upright stiff-leaf. Unfortunately all s detail and much in
the N is the result of the restoration. Perp w tower, the doorway
under a flat hood (cf. Nettleton). Niches above the w window.
Three two-light bell-openings on each side. All the exterior
features of the church itself again the restorer's. – INSCRIP-
TIONS. In the w porch. 1912 and 1919. Good Arts and Crafts
lettering. By *Walter Rudman* of Chippenham, who died young.
– SCREEN. With Continental oval C18 panels. – PLATE. Paten,
1651 or 1653; Almsdish, inscribed 1667; Flagon without date;
Chalice, 1799.

GRITTLETON HOUSE. By *James Thompson* for Joseph Neeld,
M.P. He was the great-nephew of Rundell (of Rundell &
Bridge), the silversmith who died in 1828 and left nearly a
million pounds to his great-nephew, then aged thirty-nine.
Thereupon Joseph Neeld married the daughter of Lord Shaftesbury, but the marriage went spectacularly wrong from the very
start. This scandal is nearly all that is publicly known about
him. He was made M.P. for Chippenham in 1830, having
become lord of the manor by purchase. The other M.P. was
his brother-in-law. The house was begun in 1848 to *Clutton*'s
design. But Neeld quarrelled with him and Thompson continued. Thompson incidentally complained that Clutton's con-
duct towards him had been 'so thoroughly contemptible that it
fails to prompt me to any retaliation' (J. Badeni: *Wiltshire
Forefathers*). However, the house (illustrated in *The Builder* in
1853) was still unfinished when Neeld died in 1856. It is really a
monstrosity. It has Jacobean gables and a Jacobean central tower,
but windows of a long, thin, Veneto-Byzantine variety, and odd
oriels in unexpected places. Extensive STABLES to the s. Two
equally fanciful LODGES, one with rich wrought-iron gates.

OLD RECTORY, N of the church. Late C18. Three bays and three
storeys. A big tripartite doorway and Tuscan columns. Lower
pavilions with hipped roofs l. and r.

(MEETING HOUSE, s of the village street, on the edge of the
grounds of the house. Early C18? J. Badeni: *Wiltshire Forefathers*.)

FOSCOTE, ⅜ m. s. Two-gabled typical C17 house with mullioned
windows of four, three, two lights.

Neeld estate housing in gabled pairs. Tudor style.

GROVELY CASTLE *see* STEEPLE LANGFORD

HACKPEN *see* WROUGHTON

3060   HAM

ALL SAINTS. Low w tower; nave and chancel. Rendered except
for the s side, which was rebuilt in flint with brick bands and
with round-arched windows in 1733. The windows were made
naively neo-Norman in 1849. What is the date of the roof with
tie-beams and undulating queenposts? It could be about that
on the tower: 1787. – Georgian WEST GALLERY, COMMUNION
RAIL, and BOX PEWS. – PLATE. Chalice and Paten Cover, 1576;
Paten, 1719. – MONUMENTS. John Hunt † 1590 and wife.
Kneeling brasses in a later stone surround with thin columns
and an open curly pediment. – Richard Gillingham † 1719.
Cartouche with putto heads.

HAMPTWORTH LODGE *see* LANDFORD

HANGING LANGFORD *see* STEEPLE LANGFORD

9090   HANKERTON

HOLY CROSS. Two Norman beasts carry the hood-mould of the
s doorway. N arcade of *c*.1200. Four low bays, circular piers,
moulded capitals, circular abaci, double-chamfered arches,
still round. The N aisle wall seems late C13, see the shouldered
arch of the doorway and the E window of three stepped pointed-
trefoiled lancets. C13 mouldings make up the porch entrance.
Perp w tower with battlements and pinnacles. Niches in the
w buttresses. A chapel or w extension of the N aisle has been
pulled down. Miserable chancel of 1906. The chancel arch
looks late C13 or early C14. – PLATE. Chalice and Paten Cover,
inscribed 1577. – MONUMENT. Miles Earle. By *Nollekens*, put
up in 1775. Tablet with urn at the top.
To the sw of the church a house in the Voysey style.

1090   HANNINGTON

ST JOHN BAPTIST. By *Slater & Carpenter*, 1869–71, but re-
using many old parts, e.g. the following: Late Norman s doorway with zigzag at an angle of 90 degrees meeting and forming
broken lozenges. Hood-mould with dog-tooth. The s porch
entrance is Transitional and plain. Early C13 N doorway, with
round arch but E.E. mouldings. Also C13, with a pointed arch,

the priest's doorway. Perp w tower with a very pretty open spiral staircase of timber, the latter of course Slater & Carpenter's. – MONUMENTS. Many tablets, e.g. William Focke † 1657, black columns, open curly pediment, garlands. – Thomas Pile † 1712. Three Corinthian columns carry fragments of a segmental pediment and in the middle an urn. Between the columns busts, each on two cherubs' heads. Good carving.

HANNINGTON HALL. Built in 1653. The E front in its original state, except that the entrance seems to have disappeared. It may well have been in the central canted bay of the symmetrical front. Mullioned and mullioned and transomed windows, in a curious rhythm. Two big gables l. and r. Centre with a balustrade of tapering balusters and an inscription in large letters below. The s side originally had neither the bays nor the porch nor the balustrade and inscription. Behind this front about 1836 – date on the added conservatory – pretty stucco-work in the Jacobean taste was provided, and a staircase, where formerly a courtyard had been. To the E front a range was added on the N side in the late C19.

HANNINGTON WICK MANOR, 1¾ m. NNW. Later C17 house with narrow symmetrical front. Two gables, and a lower gabled porch. Gables on the side elevations as well. But the doorway has a pulvinated frieze and a segmental pediment. Can it be contemporary, i.e. how late can the gabled house be?

HARDENHUISH

9070

ST NICHOLAS. 1779 by *John Wood* of Bath. Small and ashlar-faced. The original plan foresaw a polygonal apse, side walls with one fine Venetian window each, and a polygonal w entrance, that is essentially a central plan. In the event an arched window was added to the w of either Venetian window and a small w tower. It spoils the harmony of the design both outside and inside. The tower has an octagonal top and a little stone dome. The pedimented doorway is in it. Niches l. and r. The windows have columns outside, and the Venetian windows also detached columns inside. In the apse painted Lord's Prayer, Commandments, and Creed. Carved garlands in the frieze above. Pretty lamp BRACKETS. – PLATE. Chalice, 1638; Paten, 1707. – In the churchyard MONUMENT to David Ricardo 63a † 1823. By *William Pitts*. Severely Grecian canopy on four Greek Doric columns with an urn at the top. In the shelter of the canopy things are a little more light-hearted. Four nearly nude maidens round the top half of a Corinthian column.

HARDENHUISH HOUSE. Now part of the schools park of Chippenham, with various modern schools (of no special architectural interest) about. The mansion is Georgian, ashlar-faced, of five bays and two and a half storeys. Three-bay pediment. Curved porch on unfluted Ionic columns. A canted bay round the corner to the l. and further attachment. *Soane* made designs for Hardenhuish in 1829, and the porch seems to be his.

BULIDGE, 1¼ m. NW. To the l. of the porch, wall of the late C13 and the start of a spiral stair behind the dais end of the hall. The rest C17, gabled and with (recent) mullioned windows. The square porch is late C17 – see the moulded door surround and the balustrade. To the r. two square pavilions with hipped roofs; early C18. In front of the W side two oblong pavilions of Elizabethan date framing the original approach.

8070

HARTHAM PARK
1 m. S of Biddestone

The house was built by *James Wyatt* in 1790–5, and much added to c.1858 (date on the stables) and again in 1888 (*MacVicar Anderson*). The former additions are on the SE side and include the porch. They are in conformity with Wyatt's style. The latter additions concern the NW. Inside, the front hall, staircase, and dining room are all of c.1858.[*] In the grounds CHAPEL, built in 1862 to the design of *P. C. Hardwick*, Perp, quite big, with a NW tower.[‡]

In the park also a MOTTE AND BAILEY (HR).

HAZELBURY MANOR see BOX

HEALE HOUSE see WOODFORD

9060

HEDDINGTON

ST ANDREW. Low C13 S aisle arcade. Three bays, round piers and abaci; double-chamfered arches. Taller later N arcade with octagonal piers. Perp W tower with a stair-turret higher than the battlements. Ashlar-faced. Late Perp straight-headed windows in the aisles. Only the chancel E, NE, and SE windows have

---

* I am grateful to Miss Nicholson for detailed information about the house.
‡ PLATE. Flagon, 1716.

Perp tracery. In the s nave roof two dormers. – FONT. Norman bowl and shaft of 1840. The bowl is decorated with blank arches which may well be altogether an embellishment of 1840. – ORGAN CASE. A charming late C18 piece with a carved arrangement of trumpet, horn, and trombone. – PLATE. Chalice, 1577; Flagon, 1602; Paten, 1703.

HEYTESBURY

9040

ST PETER AND ST PAUL. Of flint and stone. A large and impressive church, but an over-restored one (by *Butterfield* in 1865–7) which makes it externally more rewarding from a distance than from near by and internally disappointing in spite of its undeniable grandeur. Heytesbury is also a puzzling church. The story seems to start with the one capital with decorated trumpet scallops which must be of c.1175* and must be re-used. The rest of the interior is fairly unified and belongs to the C13. The chancel has piers of compound shafts including detached ones of Purbeck marble. The arches are triple-chamfered, which puts the date forward to the end of the century. At the E end the lancet window is flanked by two blank ones, all shafted with Purbeck. The decoration with geometrical patterns of red and black tiles is of course Butterfield's. The crossing tower stands on responds with triple-shafts. The SW respond of the nave is the same. Otherwise the nave arcades have very tall octagonal piers and the same triple-chamfered arches as the chancel. The hood-mould stops, however, still have stiff-leaf. Clerestory of lancets in the chancel, of two-light Perp windows in the nave. They are all above the spandrels, not the apexes of the arches. The bell-openings of the crossing tower are Dec, early or mid C14. So that is when the church was completed. The aisle W windows are roundels. The side windows are Butterfield's in their perverse details (the side lights of the groups of three under one arch!). In the S chapel the W arch is also late C13, in the N chapel it is Perp, four-centred and panelled. The N transept was to be given a fan-vault in the C15 or early C16, but this seems never to have been done. Also so late the excellent five-light W window of the nave. It has a transom and panelled jambs. Yet later the S transept S window. Might it be of 1614, the date inscribed on the N transept N side, where Butterfield put in a new Perp window? – SCREEN. Fine stone screen to the N transept, which was the Hungerford Chapel. Early C16, with

* The church became collegiate c.1165.

one-light divisions, depressed rounded arches. Fan-coving to
N as well as S – for a loft. What would a loft have been used for
in this position, i.e. for a screen other than a rood screen? –
STAINED GLASS. Most of the glass of Butterfield's restoration
is good and characteristic. Pale colours, good leading. It is by
Alexander Gibbs.* – PLATE. Chalice, given in 1759; Paten,
given in 1757. – MONUMENTS. Two panels of a Perp tomb-
chest with shields in cusped fields is all the remains of the
interments in the Hungerford Chapel. – Three kneeling figures
are left of the monument to Thomas Moore † 1623 and his
family.

HEYTESBURY HOUSE. A long, severely plain ashlar façade of
1782. Eleven bays and two and a half storeys. Semicircular
porch with elongated Tuscan columns. Their detail is Adamish.
But behind the façade remains the structure of a house of about
1700, known from illustrations. This also had two storeys only,
a hipped roof with nine dormer windows, and a belvedere or
lantern. Yet older bits are visible to the W of the house, notably
one three-light mullioned window of the C17, now in a garden
wall. This may have formed part of the Hungerfords' manor.
The N side of Heytesbury House has two projecting wings. The
centre between them was filled in in 1820, and a Greek Doric
portico *in antis* was set in front of a square entrance hall. Segmental arches of the kind favoured by Soane carry a ceiling
with a glazed dome. Of the rooms of the 1780s the best is the
dining room, with a serving alcove formed by two Roman Doric
columns on uncommonly high pedestals. The Rococo chimneypiece of wood comes from Wardour. Splendid planting in the
grounds.

Behind the church is PARSONAGE FARMHOUSE, with an excellent Jacobean plaster ceiling, not alas entirely preserved. It has
broad bands in geometrical patterns with a central pendant.
The front windows of the house are later, but round the corner
is a mullioned Jacobean window.

In the village street next to the grounds and their tall trees the
HOSPITAL OF ST JOHN AND ST KATHARINE, an old almshouse foundation of the Hungerfords, burnt down and rebuilt
*c.*1769, but much older in style, in fact of a type familiar from
late C17 almshouses. Brick. Three sides of a turfed square. The
middle bay projects, has a pediment, and carries a lantern.
Hipped roof. Sashed windows.

* Who received £105 7s. 6d. for the E window and £77 12s. 6d. for each of
the single-light chancel windows.

In the village on the N side of the main street the LOCKUP, octagonal, with a stone-slated roof, and, further W, old MALT-HOUSES with, to the W, the rounded projection for drying the grain.

HEYWOOD

HOLY TRINITY. 1849. Nave and bellcote, aisles and chancel. Late C13 in style, but the E window of six lights Dec. – STAINED GLASS. E window 1876, especially horrible.

HEYWOOD HOUSE. Proudly neo-Jacobean. Built shortly before 1869. The LODGES are early C19.

BROOK HOUSE. *See* Southwick.

HIGHWAY

4½ m. NE of Calne

ST PETER. By *Butterfield*, 1867. Disused. Nave and chancel in one, with a roof of stone slates. Bell-turret of timber. Single-framed nave roof. The windows pointed-trefoiled lancets. The chancel inside decorated in a typical Butterfield fashion with geometrical patterns of tiles. – The PULPIT has been transferred to St Nicholas, Great Yarmouth.

HIGHWORTH

ST MICHAEL. Of the Norman church on this site only one TYMPANUM survives (S wall). It represents Samson and the Lion, a wild, somewhat unorganized group, surrounded by a band of equally wild trails. The C13 is more fully represented. To it belong the four-bay arcades with their circular piers and double-chamfered arches. The capitals are obviously inter-fered with. The church had at the time a crossing tower. In the chancel one lancet remains, now covered by the Perp two-storey vestry. Perp W tower, tall and with a fan-vault inside. Perp N and S aisles, ashlar-faced, with three-light windows and para-pets with pierced quatrefoils. This motif goes on over the S porch, S transept, and S chapel. The porch has a tripartite niche above the entrance. Perp also the present crossing and the arcade to the two-bay chapels. The piers have concave-sided projections without capitals to N and S, demi-shafts with capitals to E and W (cf. Bishopstone). – FONT. Perp, octagonal, with shields and quatrefoils. – STALLS. Two, with MISERI-CORDS: a mermaid and a bearded head. – PULPIT. With the usual Jacobean blank arches and angle balusters. Much re-cut.

– CHEST. An enormous piece, 9 ft long. – SCULPTURE. The lower halves of two figures in the s chapel, E wall. – PLATE. Hall-marked, silver-gilt Chalice of 1523 with Crucifixus and Man of Sorrows engraved on the foot; C17 Paten; Flagon, 1743; Cup and two Salvers, 1749. – Funeral HELM and SHIRT. – MONUMENTS. Edmund Warneford † 1724 (S aisle E). Standing monument with a very tall obelisk. Cherub-heads and inscription. – William Crowdy † 1838. By *J. Franklin* of Purton. Extremely pretty medallion with an ivy wreath (cf. Purton).

The centre of interest at Highworth is the s end of LECHLADE ROAD. First the JESMOND HOUSE HOTEL, early C18, four bays, two storeys, of brick, with a big doorway. Fluted Doric pilasters, metope frieze, pediment. Then another four-bay brick house, and after that HIGHWORTH HOUSE, also early C18, but much taller. Five bays, three storeys, quoins, segment-headed windows, aprons below them, panelled parapet, plain doorway. A little further N a three-bay stone house with brick trim. Porch on very thin Corinthian posts. Highworth House faces the churchyard, the hotel the HIGH STREET. In the High Street first the ZION CONGREGATIONAL CHAPEL, 1825, of stone, with arched windows and a pedimental gable. Then the finest house of Highworth, again early C18, similar to Highworth House, but more ambitiously done. Four bays wide, three storeys high, with segment-headed windows with aprons. Doorway with Corinthian pilasters and a broken-back segmental pediment. Big top-cornice, panelled parapet. (Excellent staircase with wrought-iron railing. MHLG) Then on the l. the MARKET PLACE. Facing into it the SARACEN'S HEAD, brick, five bays, two storeys, and a central archway. A little further E No. 3, a C17 stone house with two symmetrical bay windows and mullioned and transomed windows.

HILLCOT MANOR FARMHOUSE *see* NORTH NEWNTON

HILL DEVERILL

THE ASSUMPTION. 1843 by *Chapman & Sons* (GR). Very modest. Nave with bellcote, chancel, lancet windows. – The REREDOS, i.e. boards with Commandments, Lord's Prayer, and Creed l. and r. of the E window, still in their original place. – FONT. An C18 baluster. – COMMUNION RAIL. C18. – PLATE. Paten and Flagon, *c.*1700–4; Cup, 1771. – MONUMENT. Tomb-chest with big shields on foiled and cusped fields. Angels holding the shields on the W and E and the middle of the N and S sides. C15.

MANOR FARMHOUSE. Probably late C17, in spite of the archaism of arched lights to the mullioned windows. Symmetrical, identical composition to S and W. Three bays, four-light windows, doorway with hood-mould raised above a very big lintel. An upright oval window over. Top parapet. Attached to the E side of the house an extremely long BARN, fifteen bays, three porches. Across the farmyard on the S side the remains of a stone building of T-shape, C15–16. The surviving window of four arched lights. (Arched timber roof. MHLG)

HILMARTON

0070

ST LAURENCE. W tower of 1840, ashlar-faced. By *Henry Weaver*. Of the same time the S porch. Then, in 1879–80, general restoration by *Street*, who also built the organ chamber. Late C12 N arcade of three bays with round piers, decorated trumpet-scallop capitals, round abaci, and single-chamfered arches plus a last bay with a moulded capital. Nave roof of the wagon type. – SCREEN. Stone screen, Perp, just like wooden screens, with one-light divisions, and crocketed ogee arches. – STAINED GLASS. E and chancel N windows by *Clayton & Bell*, c.1880. – MONUMENT. In the N aisle wall an ogee-headed tomb recess unfeelingly re-done.

The Poynder Estate built cottages in the village first c.1832–5, then c.1874–7, the former of ashlar and quite plain, the latter rock-faced and gabled.

HILPERTON

8050

ST MICHAEL. 1852 by *T. H. Wyatt* (GR). In the Dec style. The only distinguishing feature the dormer W of the porch. Only the W tower with its broach spire is medieval. – FONT. Circular, Norman. With low arches and odd single leaves above them. The font was found in a pond at Whaddon (PF). – SCREEN. Really an iron railing and some gables high up. All quite delicate and of course Gothic. It is said to be by a local blacksmith and as late as c.1894. – STAINED GLASS. In the chancel SE window by *Kempe*, 1890. – PLATE. Cup, 1576; Paten, 1690.

To the E of the church HILPERTON HOUSE, early C18. Of five bays with a hipped roof. The parapet curves up in the middle. Doorway with open segmental pediment.

LOCKUP, opposite the garden of Hilperton House. With the usual domed roof.

WYKE HOUSE, ¾ m. NW. 1865, Jacobean, tall and lavish. With mullioned and transomed windows, shaped gables, and a big bay window in a side elevation crowned by pierced strapwork. The house is a pretty accurate copy of its genuinely Jacobean predecessor and incorporates old materials.

9030   HINDON

ST JOHN BAPTIST. 1878 by *T. H. Wyatt*, a reduced, less success-ful version of his church at Fonthill Gifford. SW tower with spire. Rose window in the W wall of the nave. Lancet windows and windows with plate tracery otherwise, i.e. revived E.E. The windows in the aisles are under small cross-gables.

The village was created by the bishops of Winchester about 1220 and built up mostly between 1220 and 1250. It had over 150 houses then, i.e. more than in 1832. It was built all along the road from Salisbury to Taunton. Behind ran a back lane. A fire consumed much of the village in 1754. The houses and cottages were handsomely rebuilt in Tisbury stone. None calls for special comment.

CONGREGATIONAL CHAPEL. 1810. Windows with plain inter-sected tracery.

HINTON PARVA *see* LITTLE HINTON

8060   HOLT

ST KATHERINE. 1891 by *C. E. Ponting*, free-Gothic, but still pre-Arts and Crafts. Original medieval work the S porch en-trance, apparently Dec, and the W tower, which is Perp. A niche above the W window with two wheels under, and wheels also in the battlements.

CONGREGATIONAL CHURCHES, to the N. The old one of 1810 with pointed windows and a hipped roof, the new of 1880 (by *W. J. Stent* of Warminster), an obtrusive affair with a (ritually-speaking) NW tower and E.E. detail.

THE COURT, ¼ m. to the NE. An early C18 façade of five bays, wildly overdone in all its details, an instructive example of what a vulgar mind can do with promising elements. The windows have on the ground floor open triangular, then open curly pediments, then a niche and the doorway pediment, and then the motifs repeated the other way round. The pediments nearly touch each other, and on the first floor the performance is repeated. Steep middle pediment at the top. Older features at the back. Simple original staircase with slim turned balusters. In other rooms Late Georgian redecoration. The greenhouse in the garden is Neo-Georgian of about 1900.

THE SPA. The scanty remains now inside Sawtell's bedding factory. As an inscription says, the Lady Lisle and the Rev. James Lewis 'patronized this spring and rendered it famous in the year 1720'. The inscription is below an urn in relief set in the blocked portal to the well-house. Tuscan columns and a straight entablature. The well has been sealed, and the lodging house or Great House of *c.*1730 demolished.

THE GREEN. Nice houses around, though none specially noteworthy. One of two windows only has an arched doorway between reached up an outer stair. This seems Early Georgian and was the ASSEMBLY ROOM of the White Hart. Also houses with mullioned windows at the start of the South Wraxall Road (Nos 17–19) and the Melksham Road (No. 71).

HOMINGTON
1020

ST MARY. Externally all of the restoration of 1860. The details of the s tower alone look older and genuine, i.e. C17. But inside, in spite of all renewal, the aisle arcades must be medieval. N arcade of four bays, the first and last arches cut off. Piscina below the last one. Octagonal piers, double-chamfered arches. s arcade of three wider bays with taller octagonal piers. The arch across the aisle, under the tower w wall, is certainly genuine. So are some of the stone corbels for the nave roof.

HONEY STREET WHARF *see* ALTON BARNES

HORNINGSHAM
8040

ST JOHN BAPTIST. Perp SW tower with battlements and pinnacles. The body of the church of 1844, by *Wyatt & Brandon* (GR). The windows are still the tall two-light windows of the early C19, but the arcades are correct Perp. Hammerbeam roof. Big stone PULPIT; Perp. – The STAINED GLASS of the E window is still pictorial; i.e. pre-Pugin in style.

MEETING HOUSE, Chapel Street. The tradition that this was provided by Sir John Thynne in 1566–7 for the Scottish

Presbyterian workmen on the building of Longleat has not been confirmed by the research of the compilers of the VCH. The building is called newly erected in 1700. Windows in two tiers on the sides, two long ones to the – ritual – E. The three-sided GALLERY could be of c.1700. The PULPIT is clearly Georgian, and the chapel was indeed enlarged in 1754 and again in 1816.

Horningsham is a singularly loose village with houses in their own gardens, small or large, and no visual cohesion.

HUISH

1060

ST NICHOLAS. It is said that the church was rebuilt in 1785 and restored in 1879. What we see now seems entirely 1879. Nave with bellcote and chancel. – In the vestry a short length of arcading with ballflower decoration.

OLD RECTORY. Three bays, two storeys, brick, with two shallow bows. The mansard roof follows their curve nicely. The house was under construction in 1812.

HULLAVINGTON

8080

ST MARY. The earliest parts of the church are the arcades, N before S. Three bays, circular piers, trumpet-scallop and decorated trumpet-scallop capitals. The N arches are single-stepped and round, the S arches double-chamfered and pointed. The S porch entrance remains a puzzle. One capital is just like those of the arcade, the other has upright stiff-leaf. Pointed arch. Is the portal *in situ*? The simple S and N doorways are of the time of the arcades. The S doorway has a hood-mould on head-stops. The N chapel arcade is C13. Two bays. Circular piers and circular abaci with some dog-tooth. Double-chamfered arches. The N chapel altogether is a fine C13 piece, very similar to Sherston and Luckington. Long stepped lancet group in the E wall, pair of lancets in the N wall, all inside with detached shafts. Low-side window, one light above, two below a transom. This is probably Perp. Of the later C13 the N aisle W window; two lancet lights and a circle in plate tracery. W tower of Somerset Perp type, by *Blomfield* (PF), built in 1880. Many of the church windows probably also of that time. – SCREEN. The original rood-loft parapet remains (cf. Avebury and Edington). – BENCH ENDS. Perp, with simplest tracery. – PANEL. Big Sacrifice of Isaac, C17, oval, in strapwork and arabesque surround. Does it come from an overmantel? – CHASUBLE.

Beautiful fragment of *c*.1500. With Crucifixus, Saints, and Seraphim. – PLATE. Paten, 1732; Cup, 1735. – MONUMENTS. Simon James Gen † 1616. Plain tablet. The inscription starts:

> O man repent, this world defie
> Remember well that thou must die.
> For as I am so shall thou be
> Dust and ashes [etc.]

– John Jackson † 1739. Outside on the E wall. Metal cross with engraved inscription, set in a stone cartouche with partly arched top.

COURT FARMHOUSE, to the NW. Gabled, C17, with mullioned windows and a good group of barns, etc.

BRADFIELD FARM, ¾ m. N. The rare survival of a C15 hall, 'in the old Gothic fashion', says Aubrey, i.e. with transomed two-light Perp windows, two to one side, one blocked to the other. The roof is also still visible, though only in the attic. It has collar-beams on arched braces. Added in the C17 a tall, tower-like range of three storeys with two- and three-light mullioned and transomed windows, and also simply mullioned windows. Hipped and half-hipped roof.

HURDCOTT HOUSE *see* BARFORD ST MARTIN

IDMISTON

1030

ALL SAINTS. The W tower must be Norman; see the flat but-resses, also inside the aisles; for the aisles now embrace the tower. But before they were built, the chancel was rebuilt. It is E.E. with lancet windows and a group of three stepped closely-set lancets in the W wall. Then the arcades, late C13 most probably. Alternation of grey and green stone. Quatrefoil piers, double-chamfered arches. The tower arch is the same (an enlargement no doubt). The arch from the tower into the S aisle must belong too; for the W respond of the aisle arcade has the same stiff-leaf spray as the E respond of the aisle bay S of the tower. Also the tower arch has the same corbel mouldings as the SW respond. Perp S aisle. Perp two-storeyed N porch with saddleback roof higher than the aisle. Perp N doorway. Perp aisle and clerestory walls; gargoyles and parapet. (Fine ornate roof of Somerset type, i.e. of low pitch with tie-beams. Good roof corbels; Perp. NBR) The bell-storey of the tower is a C19 alteration, as is the steep pyramid roof. – FONT. Plain, but

powerfully moulded. Octagonal; of Purbeck marble. Probably
c14. – MONUMENT. Kneeling figure of Giles Rowbach † 1633.

OLD PARSONAGE. Flint and brick front of the c17. Cross-windows, altered on the first floor into Georgian windows. At the
back gabled and enlarged.

IFORD MANOR

¾ m. W of Westwood

The fine façade of the house must be of c.1725–30. Five bays, two
and a half storeys, even quoins, top balustrade. The windows
are all pedimented, with triangular pediments except for the
middle ones, which are segmental. In the beautiful gardens an
octagonal SUMMER HOUSE of the same time. Unfluted Ionic
pilasters. Pyramid roof. The manor was bought in 1899 by
Harold A. Peto, former partner of Sir Ernest George, and he
gradually furnished the gardens with plenty of statuary and
architectural fragments and also with more buildings, notably
the CASITA with its loggia of very slender Italian columns of
about 1200 and the CLOISTERS, completed in 1913. The sculpture is Roman, Early Christian, and later and came mostly from
Italy, though there are also French Gothic pieces.

BRIDGE. Just opposite the house; of c.1400, but with a statue of
Britannia placed by Harold Peto.

IMBER

The village is in a War Office battle area and half destroyed.

The church of ST GILES is intact, but fenced off by barbed wire,
boarded up, and gutted. Externally Perp, with W tower with an
oblong stair-turret going up a little higher. Arcades inside of
the late c13. Round piers, capitals, and abaci, arches of one
chamfer and one slight chamfer.

INGLESHAM

ST JOHN BAPTIST. A delightful group with the gabled house to
the W. A pity that to the SE stands so townish a three-storeyed
c18 house. The church is very small, but has aisles. Nave with
a late c13 double bellcote with pointed-trefoiled lights and a
circle in plate tracery. The same motif in a chancel S window.
The chancel E window has three such lights stepped under one
arch, the N window plain lancets. c13 N doorway with rounded
trefoiled head. Earlier the S doorway. Round arch with roll

moulding, i.e. *c*.1200. The interior fits these dates. s arcade of two bays with round pier, stiff-leaf capital, octagonal abacus, and round double-chamfered arches. The two responds still have decorated trumpet scallops. The N arcade is the same, but the arches are pointed. The chancel arch goes with the N arcade. In the chancel, preserved only on the N side, fine blank arcading, round-arched, with filleted rolls and leaf capitals. All this is earlier than the chancel E parts. The chancel roof is single-framed with tie-beams and could be of the C13 too. The church was well restored in 1888–9 by the Society for the Protection of Ancient Buildings. An inscription records: 'This church was repaired in 1888–9 through the energy and with the help of *William Morris* who loved it.' The architect was *J. T. Micklethwaite*. – FONT. Perp, octagonal, with quatrefoils. – PULPIT. Elizabethan, with a tester. – REREDOS. Fragments have been discovered, with a pinnacle and a half and small painted figures of *c*.1330. – SCREENS. Perp parclose screens. – PEWS. Jacobean. Box pews and also pews for squire and vicar. – NORTH DOOR. Medieval, with very long hinges. – SCULPTURE. Virgin and Child, and above the Hand of God. Late Anglo-Saxon and would deserve to be better known. A strangely unconventional composition, not of any of the accepted types. Especially odd the Child's legs, pulled up high. – STAINED GLASS. Small bits in several windows, C13 quarries and later fragments. – PLATE. Elizabethan Paten Cover. – In the churchyard base and shaft of a CROSS.

IVYCHURCH *see* ALDERBURY

JAGGARDS *see* CORSHAM, p. 177

JOB'S MILL *see* CROCKERTON

KEEVIL

ST LEONARD. The chancel has two late C13 windows. Otherwise the church is Late Perp and dependent on Steeple Ashton: the w tower e.g. has bell-openings of three lights with the same straight-sided lozenges in the tracery (cf. North Bradley). The deep W porch with a four-centred panelled tunnel-vault on the other hand compares with Trowbridge. This motif recurs in the s porch. s aisle and nave N wall and transepts with battlements and pinnacles. Pier mouldings of four shafts and four big waves.

Only the tower arch has a hollow instead of the wave. Nice nave roof of low pitch with tracery panels above the tie-beams. – FONTS. Both Perp and octagonal with pointed quatrefoils, the one small, the other big. – PLATE. Cup, 1576; two Cups, 1784. – BELL. The Sanctus bell is one of the oldest in the county. It was moulded on a lathe in the C12, not cast in the later usual way (cf. Tytherton Lucas). – MONUMENTS. John Harris † 1657. Tablet with two mourning women on the open pediment. – James Richardson † 1782. Pink and white marble. With a fine profile head in an oval medallion. Sprigs of weeping willow. – Blagden family, c. 1785. Coloured marbles, large and good; no figures. – Mrs Talbot † 1786. By *Ford* of Bath. With the usual standing woman by an urn.

VICARAGE (now Field Head). Built in 1842. With shaped Jacobean-type gables.

KEEVIL MANOR. Built about 1580, with the s porch added in 1611. The house has three gabled fronts and may originally have had a fourth and an inner courtyard as well. The s front has four gables, the others three. All is symmetrical and flat – or was, before the porch was erected which, with its decorated Tuscan columns, adds life. The tiny trefoil-headed windows on the l. and r. sides of the porch must be re-used earlier material. Inside the porch shell-headed niches. The other windows are mullioned and transomed, the mullions concave-sided in section. Doorways and fireplaces all have the same details. Inside the house the hall screen is preserved, with two large round-arched openings with diamond-cut imitation-ashlar surrounds. Modest plasterwork on the hall ceiling. More, of the fine-ribbed variety forming geometrical patterns, in the Dining Room. In the hall also Early Renaissance panelling with the familiar rustic heads in profile. This must be a generation older than the house. In front of the s façade a Jacobean archway into the former front garden, with strapwork on the top and shell-headed niches l. and r.

TALBOYS. A timber-framed house of great charm and value, though some of its features are deceptive.* One of them is the symmetry of the façade. The E part of the house is of 1876; only the centre and the cross-gabled W part are original work of the later C15. The first floor sails over. Closely-set upright timbers and some curved diagonal struts. Excellent bargeboards with

---

* The following is based on a drawing of the house dating from 1866 and information kindly given me by Mrs E. Crawford, who also showed me the drawing.

cusped S-shapes. Also all the window tracery without exception is of 1876 (and no doubt imitated from the Porch House, Potterne). Some of the plain windows at the back however seem to be in order. Inside, the finest features are the hall roof with three tiers of wind-braces and the roof in the cross-wing with collar-beams on arched braces and one tier of wind-braces. The cross-wing is divided into two storeys, and the lower one has a ceiling with moulded beams and bosses. In the hall the gallery seems original, though it is probably in the wrong position.

The village has many enjoyable houses, both timber-framed and of brick.

(LITTLE TALBOYS. Each gable-end shows cruck construction. NBR)

BLAGDEN HOUSE. Late C16 or early C17 house, once much larger. Of stone. The house has three gables like Keevil Manor, but all the front windows sashed. The STABLES are specially attractive, late C17, with three steep gables and upright oval windows. Good GATEPIERS with vases.

PINKNEY FARM. Dated 1684. Rubble. Two- and three-light windows. Stepped-back mullions and little squares at the junctions. Higher Georgian addition.

(LONGLEAZE FARMHOUSE. Dated 1790. Brick. Two- and three-light windows. Scrolled pediment over the door. MHLG) A comparison of the two basically similar houses distant in time by a hundred years is instructive.

KELLAWAYS

9070

1 m. NW of East Tytherton

ST GILES. Small later C18 chapel of three bays with a plain pitched roof. Tiny bell-turret. Pointed doorway with ogee gable, pointed windows. – FONT. Octagonal, with oblong panels. Could be mid-C17. – Original PULPIT with tester and BENCHES.

MAUD HEATH'S CAUSEWAY, towards the bridge across the *3b* river Avon. Maud Heath of Langley Burrell was a pedlar woman who in 1474 left sufficient land and houses to create a road and causeway from Wick Hill to Chippenham and maintain it at a rate of £8 a year. The distance is 4½ miles. The charity was maintained and paid for the present bridge as well. There are sixty-four segmental arches to carry a path along the road. The BRIDGE itself now has an early C19 railing of cast iron with

ogee motifs. At the start of the arches a PILLAR with a ball top, erected to Maud Heath's memory in 1698.
Another such causeway outside Sutton Benger.

KILMINGTON

ST MARY. Good Perp w tower with two big niches to the s and bell-openings of pairs of extremely elongated lights; straightheaded. Openwork battlements, pinnacles. The pinnacles stand on long shafts which grow out of the diagonal buttresses. Big c14 arch from the nave into the s chapel, of a grey stone. Otherwise all 1860s. – PULPIT and LITANY DESK. Made up of c17 pieces not belonging to the church.
NEOLITHIC CAMP, $2\frac{1}{2}$ m. SE, on Whitesheet Hill. A causewayed camp with single bank and ditch broken by numerous entrances. Excavation in 1951 produced Windmill Hill sherds and an ox skull from the ditch silting.

KINGSTON DEVERILL

ST MARY. A curious sight. Nave and s aisle and chancel of 1846 by *Manners & Gill* (GR), but the central tower c15. The square stair-turret rising much above the parapet and crowned by a spire, however, is suspicious.* The c19 parts have tracery from Geometrical to flowing. Inside, the s arcade is Dec. Two bays, low octagonal pier, arches with two sunk waves. The arch from the tower to the nave is double-chamfered and dies into the imposts, that to the chancel has two continuous chamfers. – PULPIT. With Flemish panels of Flamboyant tracery. – SCULPTURE. A fine late c14 seated Virgin, wood, probably German. – STAINED GLASS. In the w window original grisaille quarries. – PLATE. Cup, 1578; Paten, 1704; Paten, 1711. – MONUMENT. Effigy of a bearded Civilian, late c14.
POPE'S FARMHOUSE, $\frac{1}{4}$ m. NW. L-shaped. In one wing, at the back, the head of a two-light early c16 window.

KINGTON LANGLEY

ST PETER. 1855–6 by *C. H. Gabriel*. Nave and chancel and bellcote. Lancet windows. – PLATE. Chalice, 1795.
UNION CHAPEL, on the Common. 1835. With pedimental gable and round-arched windows with Y-tracery.

* It does appear on a picture of 1817.

GREATHOUSE, on the A road. Fine, long, even, nine-bay front of c.1700. Two storeys, parapet, hipped roof. Cross-windows. Doorway with shell-hood.

KINGTON ST MICHAEL

9070

ST MICHAEL. Terribly over-restored (J. H. Hakewill, 1858; PF). Norman chancel arch, very wide. Nook-shafted responds. Arch with zigzag meeting at r. angles and forming lozenges. Norman s doorway with two tall shafts; the rest mutilated. Late C13 chancel. Windows with pointed-trefoiled heads and wide cinquefoiled rere-arches. Piscina of the same date. s aisle also late C13, see the windows to the s (two lights, unencircled cinquefoil) and the E (three lights and a cinquefoiled circle). The arcades are most unhelpful and not enjoyable either. Only the bases seem in order, and the arches. They tell of the C13. The piers are round, the capitals on the s side quite impossible, on the N side at least clearly rebuilt. The N aisle windows could be debased C17 Gothic. They are however said to be of 1755, in which case they are amazingly conservative. The tower is of 1725, an interesting endeavour in the Gothic style. Only the Baroque mouldings of the diagonal buttresses are at once suspicious. The bell-openings have Y-tracery and Somerset tracery and the eight pinnacles look perfectly good. – DOOR. The s door has tracery. – STAINED GLASS. s aisle E 1857, commemorating the antiquarians John Aubrey and John Britton. – PLATE. Chalice, 1570; Almsdish, 1754; Cover, 1791. – MONUMENTS. Daniel Yelfe † 1779. Still a very exuberant Rococo cartouche. – John Hitchcock † 1820, woman by an urn, by S. King of Castle Combe. – Churchyard GATEPIERS. Dated 1760.

LYTE ALMSHOUSES, in the main street. Founded in 1675. Isaac Lyte was an alderman of London. Six houses, six gables, three-light mullioned windows. Almost opposite House No. 23, a little later, with upright two-light windows and a semicircular door-hood.

PRIORY FARM, ¾ m. NW. A Benedictine Priory for nuns was established before 1155. The only range which remains is that to the W and SW of the cloister. Excavations have given some information on the s and E sides. Also, on the s side the w half stands. It is of C13 masonry and has a big fireplace. The church lay on the N. The w range is of the C15 and contained as usual the guest hall and the prioress's lodging. The guest hall now

has two transomed C17 windows under a gable. To its S is a
porch, and inside it a big doorway with a four-centred head.*
To the S of this a C15 two-light window with cusped lights,
and to the N of the guest hall another such window. At the back
a spiral stair.

(UPPER SWINLEY. Farmhouse with a date 1631 on the porch.
J. Badeni)

KITCHEN BARROW see BISHOPS CANNINGS

KNAP HILL see ALTON BARNES

KNIGHTON MANOR HOUSE see BROAD CHALKE

9040
KNOOK

ST MARGARET. Church and manor house lie at the far end of the
village. The church is small. It has a big N porch of two storeys,
meant to carry a tower. The rest is Norman. Interesting S tympanum on Norman shafts. The tympanum has intricate 'inhabited scrolls' with two beasts, essentially symmetrical. The
similarity to illuminated manuscripts is striking, the survival
of Anglo-Saxon motifs too. They are motifs of the early C11.
There is in fact inside, now behind the altar, a short length of
an Anglo-Saxon interlace band. But that is not enough to consider the tympanum Anglo-Saxon, let alone the chancel and
the chancel arch. The chancel windows are single-splayed and
Norman, and the two beautiful and excellently preserved
capitals of the chancel arch can also be nothing but Norman.
The chancel E windows are by *Butterfield*, who restored the
church in 1876. – PLATE. Cup, 1576; Paten, medieval but
altered.

MANOR HOUSE. Delightfully close to the river Wylye. The
range overlooking the river is buttressed and of before the
Reformation. Its S end is reconstruction. The range with the
porch is dated 1637. It has four-light mullioned windows, symmetrically arranged.

UPTON GREAT BARROW. *See* Upton Lovell.

KNOOK CASTLE. *See* Upton Lovell.

KNOWLE FARM see SAVERNAKE FOREST

* Above the doorway a Norman beast's head just like those of the arcades
at Malmesbury.

LACOCK

St Cyriac. An exceptional dedication in England (cf. Swaffham
Prior, Cambs., and South Pool, Devon). Except for the transepts a Perp church, and an impressive one internally and
externally. The transepts are of *c*.1300, the s one rebuilt. Windows with cusped intersected and cusped Y-tracery. For
Perp work, we start with the w tower. It has a recessed spire
and a lower stair-turret with an arched and cusped top. Attached to the tower is a w porch, an unusual arrangement. The
porch has battlements and a tierceron-vault with bosses. The
s aisle and the clerestory have battlements and pinnacles,
and in addition exceptionally inventive gargoyles. Attached to
the s transept is a gabled three-storeyed c17 house. The chancel
was remodelled in 1777, but, with its parapet and pinnacles
remodelled again by *Brakspear* in 1903. And now the NE chapel,
a glorious c15 piece whose date is probably *c*.1430 (arms of
Bishop Neville of Salisbury, who ruled from 1427 to 1437).
Highly decorated battlements; pinnacles; entertaining figures,
one of them undeniably smoking a pipe. Very ornate E window
with most curious tracery: four lights with round arches, four
encircled quatrefoils over, and more above them, just as much
as the pointed arch would allow. Two side windows of four
lights, one of them blocked (*see* below). Now the inside. The
nave is very tall and light. Three-light clerestory windows and
a wagon roof high up. Three-bay nave with wide bays and thin
piers with a section of four shafts and four hollows. The spandrels with some sparse blank panelling. Big crossing space, no
doubt the survival of a crossing which belonged to the church
with the transepts of *c*.1300. Very tall N, S, and E arches. Dec
arch from the s transept to the s aisle. N aisle with springers for
a vault. s aisle with a roof dated 1617. And so again to the NE
chapel. Two bays, in the arch mouldings fleurons. Niches l. and
r. of the E window and between the N windows. Splendid lierne-
vault of two bays, each with a circle of ribs round a pendant.

FURNISHINGS. FONT. Very Gothic, of stone, given by *Sir
Arthur Blomfield* when he restored the church in 1861. –
STAINED GLASS. In the NE chapel E window bits of old glass,
in the N aisle W window typical c18 single-coloured blue, yellow,
violet, green panels. – In the s transept s window typical mid-
c19 glass (date of death 1855). – PLATE. Beautiful mid-c14
Chalice and Cover; small Bowl, 1603; Paten, 1637; silver-gilt
Flagon, 1701. – MONUMENTS. The climax is once more the

NE chapel; for Sir William Sharington (*see* Lacock Abbey)
appropriated it and had his monument erected here. He died
in 1553, and the monument was no doubt made soon after.*
It is one of the finest pieces of mid-c16 decoration in England.
Tomb-chest with exquisitely carved strapwork cartouches, a
very early case of this Netherlandish type of ornament.‡ Pure
Early Renaissance pilasters with arabesque decoration. A depressed segmental arch. A splendid strapwork cartouche against
the back wall. Leaf spandrels. A frieze with knotwork. At the
top a panel with putti holding a shield, the panel flanked by
volutes. Finally a shell top. Everywhere little vases with flowers
take the place of pinnacles. – Brasses to Robert Baynard † 1501
and wife (s transept), 28 in. long. A large number of kneeling
children. – John Talbot † 1713. Good big tablet with an open
curly pediment. – Identical painted wooden tablets to Eward
Bainarde † 1575 and Lady Ursula Baynard † 1623 (s transept).
LACOCK ABBEY was founded by Ela, widow of William Longespée, in 1229. It was for Augustinian Canonesses. At the same
time she founded the Hinton Charterhouse in Somerset. She
retired to Lacock in 1238 and became the first abbess. She died
in 1261. The buildings at Lacock were mainly completed in
1247, though a record referring to work undertaken in 1285
exists. The church consisted of nave and chancel without any
structural division. A s (Lady) Chapel was added in the c14.
The cloister lay to the N (cf. Old Sarum, Gloucester Cathedral,
then of course an abbey, and also Stanley, Bradenstoke, Malmesbury). The abbey was dissolved in 1539 and the premises
bought by Sir William Sharington in 1540. His niece married
a Talbot, and the house belonged to the Talbot family till 1958.
It was at Lacock that W. H. Fox Talbot made his photographic
inventions. As for the buildings, large parts of the nunnery survive, more in fact than of any other English nunnery, but nothing of the church, except its N wall, which is now the s wall of
the house. The NW corner of the church is represented by a
buttress W of the c19 oriels (*see* below). Sharington's octagonal
tower projects into the E bay of the chancel. The best impression
of the medieval remains is obtained when one stands in the
CLOISTER. This is essentially a Perp rebuilding. The two sw
bays are still of the c14, see the finely moulded doorway and

---

* There seems to be no justification for the date 1566 given by Talbot in
W.A. & N.H.M., xxviii.

‡ But it occurs in a Holbein drawing of a chimneypiece, and Holbein died
in 1543.

one window, characteristically different from the others. The vault has a lierne pattern. The corner bays are separated from the others by panelled arches. The vault of the s w bays differs a little. Many bosses, including a lamb, angels, the pelican, a mermaid, a jester, tumblers, birds and beasts. However, there is also plenty in the cloister and even more in the surrounding ranges to take one back, if not to the foundation year, at least to the late C 13. In the w range at its s end the so-called CHAP-LAIN'S ROOM, two by two bays with single-chamfered ribs on a low circular pier. One original s lancet; a C 14 doorway to the w, i.e. out of the claustral premises. To the N of the Chaplain's Room a passage with two rib-vaults and entries from w and E. This was no doubt the main entrance to the nunnery. Then, N again, a room of three by two bays, with circular piers. Doorway to the w with shouldered lintel. Above these rooms were in all probability the abbess's quarters. One can assume that by the end of the Middle Ages they were the most comfortable rooms of the nunnery, and that therefore they became the principal living rooms after the Dissolution, as they are indeed to this day. Nothing remains of the abbess's quarters but two small blocked chapel windows and the narrow spiral stair that led up to them from the s w corner of the cloister. It has bill-hook steps. Further E along the s walk a doorway led to the E end of the nave of the church.* In the E range was first the night stair and then the SACRISTY. This is three bays deep and two bays wide. Entrance with moulded capitals. Arch with one chamfer and one hollow chamfer. The w pier is octagonal (a replacement?), the E pier big, circular, with four attached shafts. Single-chamfered ribs. Corbels with stiff-leaf and two heads. Also two dragons. Piscina with shouldered lintel. Doorway to the chancel of the church pointed-trefoiled with continuous mouldings.‡ To the N of the sacristy is the CHAPTER HOUSE. Many-shafted entrance. The windows l. and r. of the doorway have Y-tracery. Many-moulded arches. The interior is again three bays deep and two bays wide. The w pier is again octagonal (and may again be a replacement). The E pier has a cluster of eight attached shafts. The corbels along the wall are mostly moulded, and the ribs have fine mouldings (in contrast to the simpler sacristy).§ N of the chapter house the PASSAGE which

* Of a second doorway to the church further w only one jamb survives.
‡ In the sacristy some C13 TILES similar to those of the Salisbury chapter house and of Amesbury.
§ In the chapter house some C14 to mid-C16 TILES.

once led to the infirmary. It has a pointed tunnel-vault. To the
N of the entry to this a Perp niche with a canopy, and then two
book recesses with trefoiled heads. In the NE corner is the
WARMING HOUSE, four bays long to the N and two bays wide,
with slim circular piers and single-chamfered ribs.* The room
is entered from the W, i.e. from a passage which forms the E
end of the N range. Doorway into this with a segmental arch.
The ribs are once more single-chamfered. On the upper floor
in the E range the DORMITORY roof is exposed, a very impressive C14 roof with one and a half tiers of lozenge-shaped wind-
braces, with ten-fold cusping. In the N range on the upper floor
the roof is preserved too. This belonged to the REFECTORY.
It dates from the C15 and has collar-beams on arched braces,
and three tiers of wind-braces. Of the fenestration of these two
upper rooms the southernmost dormitory lancet is recognizable; so are the refectory windows. In the N walk the LAVA-
TORIUM, a very wide recess with a C13 arch now overlapped by
two cloister bays. The Perp replacement has a fleuron frieze.
To its l., half-buried in the Perp work, a C13 shaft with capital.
To the W of the refectory, i.e. to the N of the W range, lay the
KITCHEN. Part of its fireplace in the S wall, i.e. the wall towards the present hall (see below), survives. NE of the kitchen
against the N wall of the N range, visible from the N courtyard,
a buttress, evidence that there were medieval buildings here,
though the present courtyard dates from the Sharington period.

Sir William Sharington bought the estate in 1540, as has
already been said. He paid £763 for it. He was an unscrupulous
opportunist, but like several other protégés of the Protector –
William Cecil, John Thynne – an ardent builder and a believer
in the new understanding of the Renaissance style, as demonstrated for the first time in the Protector's Somerset House.
This was begun in 1547, interrupted when the Protector was
arrested in 1549, continued when he was restored to honours
and property early in 1550, and finally cut short by his execution in January 1552. Similarly Sharington, having appropriated much of the proceeds of his job as Vice-Treasurer of the
Bristol Mint, was arrested in 1549 and deprived of his property.
But he managed to get his release, and his wife bought back
his estates for £12,000 in 1550. He died in their possession
in 1553. His monument in the church is testimony of his

---

* In the warming house an enormous CAULDRON of bronze inscribed as
made by *Peter Waghevens* of Malines in 1500. Also in the warming house a
big stone TANK. It was originally outside, and its use is not known.

Savernake Forest

(a) Marlborough Downs

(b) Castle Combe

(a) Marlborough, High Street

(b) Kellaways, Maud Heath's Causeway, after 1474

(a) Avebury, Silbury Hill, pre-Roman

(b) Avebury, The Avenue, *c.*1900–1600 B.C.

Stonehenge, *c.* 1900–1500 B.C.

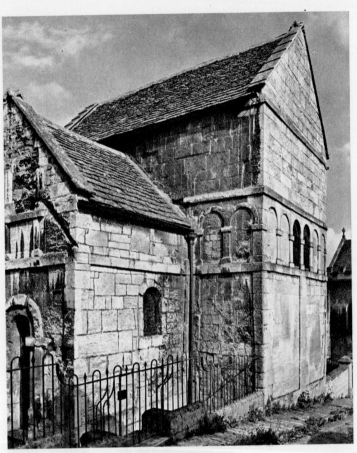

Bradford-on-Avon, St Lawrence, *c.*700 and *c.*1000

(a) Britford church, north doorway,
ninth century

(b) Codford St Peter church,
cross-shaft, ninth century

(a) Salisbury, Old Sarum, Early Iron Age, Roman, and
eleventh–twelfth centuries

(b) Malmesbury Abbey, *c.*1160–70, sculpture in south porch

Malmesbury Abbey, *c.*1160–70; vault early fourteenth century

(a) Malmesbury Abbey, c.1160–70, south doorway

(b) Devizes, St John, chancel, c.1125–35

(a) Avebury church, font, Norman

(b) Stanton Fitzwarren church, font, Norman

Salisbury Cathedral, begun 1220

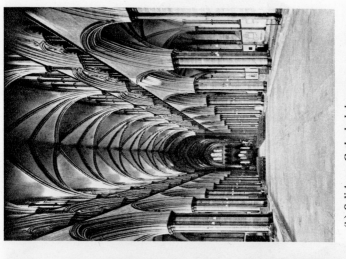

(a) Salisbury Cathedral, begun 1220, Lady Chapel

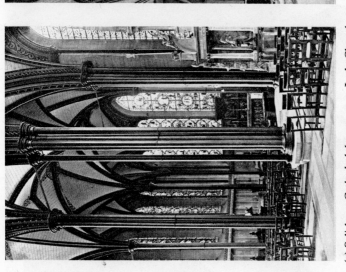

(b) Salisbury Cathedral, begun 1220, nave

13

(a) Salisbury Cathedral, former rood screen, c.1235–50

(b) Clarendon Palace, label-stop, c.1230

(b) Salisbury Cathedral, doorway to chapter house, *c.*1270

(a) Salisbury Cathedral, monument to William Longespée †1226

Salisbury Cathedral, monument to Bishop Giles de Bridport †1262

(a) Salisbury Cathedral, cloisters, begun *c.*1270

(b) Great Bedwyn church, late twelfth century

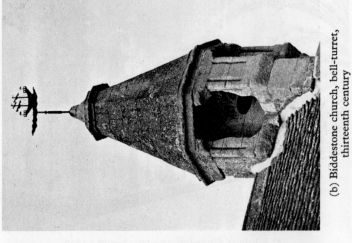

(b) Biddestone church, bell-turret, thirteenth century

(a) Bishops Cannings church, thirteenth century

Boyton church, south chapel, c.1280(?)

(a) Edington church, 1351-61

(b) Urchfont church, c.1325

(a) Edington church, corbel, *c.*1360

(b) Stockton church, monument to a Lady, early fourteenth century

(a) Bradford-on-Avon, tithe barn, early fourteenth century

(b) Norrington Manor, *c.*1377 and seventeenth century

22

Wardour, Old Castle, *c.*1393 and *c.*1578 (*Copyright Country Life*)

(a) Calne church, Perpendicular; tower after 1638

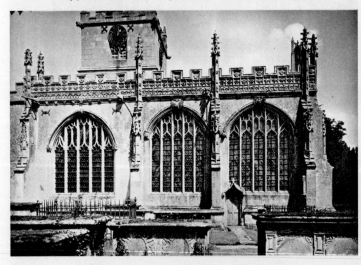

(b) Bromham church, Tocotes and Beauchamp
(or Baynton) Chapel, 1492

Steeple Ashton church, fifteenth century

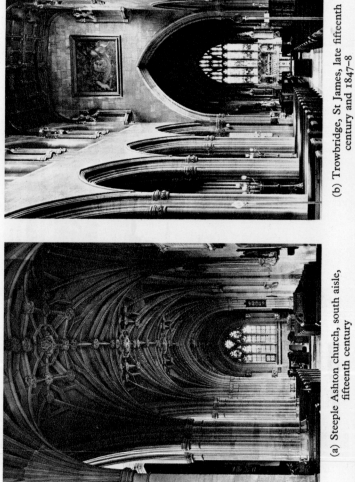

(a) Steeple Ashton church, south aisle, fifteenth century

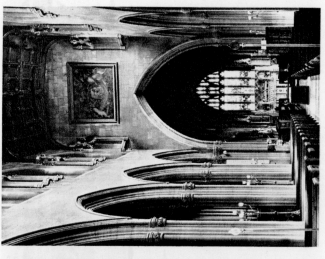

(b) Trowbridge, St James, late fifteenth century and 1847–8

26

Avebury church, rood screen, Perpendicular

27

South Wraxall Manor, fifteenth and seventeenth centuries

(a) Great Chalfield Manor, late fifteenth century

(b) Woodlands Manor, hall, fourteenth and fifteenth centuries (*Copyright Country Life*)

29

(a) Potterne, Porch House, late fifteenth century

(b) Salisbury, house of John Halle, 1470–83, hall

Lacock Abbey, table in Sharington's Tower, *c.*1550

(b) Ludgershall church, monument to Sir Richard Brydges †1558 and wife

(a) Lacock church, monument to Sir William Sharington †1553

(a) Wilton House, Holbein Porch, c.1560-70

(b) Longleat, designed probably 1567-8
(Copyright Country Life)

(a) Longford Castle, completed 1591. From an early
seventeenth century drawing

(b) Charlton Park near Malmesbury, 1607(?)

(a) Bradford-on-Avon, The Hall, c.1610

(b) Wilsford near Amesbury, Lake House, c.1580

South Wraxall Manor, chimneypiece in the drawing room, *c.*1600
(*Copyright Country Life*)

Stockton House, ceiling in the Great Chamber, c.1600

(b) East Knoyle church, plasterwork, 1639

(a) Salisbury Cathedral, monument to
Sir Richard Mompesson †1627

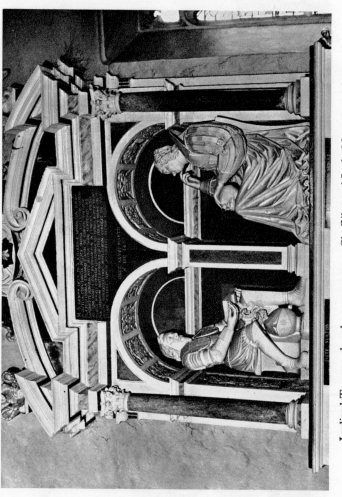

Lydiard Tregoze church, monument to Sir Giles and Lady Mompesson †1633

Broad Hinton church, monument to Colonel F. Glanville †1645, detail

(a) West Lavington church, monument to
Henry Danvers †1654

(b) West Dean church, monument to Robert
Pierrepont †1669, by John Bushnell (?)

41

(a) Lydiard Tregoze church, with seventeenth-century furnishings
(*Copyright Country Life*)

(b) Marlborough, St Mary, south arcade, 1653

Wilton House, centre of south front, by Inigo Jones
and John Webb, c.1650

Wilton House, Double Cube Room, by Inigo Jones, *c.*1650

(a) Wilton House, garden pavilion, seventeenth century

(b) Fonthill Gifford, gateway to Bishop's Fonthill,
by Inigo Jones(?), c.1635

(a) Farley church, designed with the help of Wren(?), built by Alexander Fort(?), complete by 1689–90

(b) Ramsbury Manor, c.1680

Ramsbury Manor, *c.*1680, chimneypiece in the saloon,
by Grinling Gibbons(?) (*Copyright Country Life*)

(a) Marlborough College, C-House, *c.*1700

(b) Salisbury, The Close, Mompesson House, 1701

(a) Biddesden House, 1711-12

(b) Chippenham, Ivy House, c.1730

49

Bradford-on-Avon, Druce's Hill House, Early Georgian

(a) Stourhead, by Colen Campbell, 1721–4, additions by Thomas
Atkinson, 1790–1804

(b) Devizes, New Hall, by Lawrence, 1750–2 (*Copyright Country Life*)

Maiden Bradley church, monument to Sir Edward Seymour, by J. M. Rysbrack, 1728

(a) Trafalgar House, hall, by Roger Morris, 1733 (*Copyright Country Life*)

(b) Salisbury, Malmesbury House, No. 15 The Close, staircase, c.1750

(a) Salisbury, Malmesbury House, No. 15 The Close, bay window in
the library, c.1750–60

(b) Corsham Court, chimneypiece in the picture gallery, by
Peter Scheemakers, c.1760

Lacock Abbey, hall, by Sanderson Miller, 1754–5

Stourhead, gardens, layout decided *c.*1741, cross of 1373

(a) Trowbridge, Lloyds Bank, c.1790

(b) Wardour Castle, by James Paine, 1769-76 (*Copyright Country Life*)

Wardour Castle, by James Paine, 1769–76, staircase
(*Copyright Country Life*)

(a) Bowden Hill, Bowden Park, by James Wyatt, completed 1796

(b) Wardour Castle, chapel, by James Paine, 1776, and Sir John Soane, 1788 (*Copyright Country Life*)

(a) Fonthill Gifford, Fonthill Abbey, by James Wyatt, begun 1796. Now ruined

(b) Steeple Langford, Bathampton House, chimneypiece from Fonthill, c.1800

(a) Alderbury, St Marie's Grange, by A. W. N. Pugin, 1835

(b) Wilton, St Mary and St Nicholas, by T. H. Wyatt &
D. Brandon, 1843

Amesbury Abbey, by Thomas Hopper, c.1830, staircase

(a) Hardenhuish church, monument to David Ricardo †1823, by William Pitts

(b) Bradford-on-Avon, rubber factory, by Richard Gane, 1875

Savernake Forest, St Katherine, monument to the second
Marchioness of Ailesbury †1892, by Alfred Gilbert

advanced tastes in design. How he lived in the nunnery premises it is hard now to follow. The only complete survival is the SE corner tower, SHARINGTON'S TOWER. Such a polygonal tower is not an Italian motif, and the only novel feature of the tower is its top balustrade with vertically symmetrical balusters. The beasts' heads below on the other hand are certainly a memory of gargoyles past. The upper room in the tower has two-light windows with no arches any longer for the lights. This part of the tower can only be reached by a walk along the roof of the gallery below, i.e. the former S walk of the cloister, and the staircase to the top platform starts only in the upper room. The room below this has a vault with eight ribs of square section resting on corbels and with nine pendants. Inside the two rooms are the two most remarkable examples of Sharington's work, the polygonal stone tables. The top of the lower one is supported 31 by squatting fauns each carrying a bucket with big juicy pieces of fruit. The upper table has four niches with allegorical figures and four termini. Above the niches is fruit again. The sources of this display are varied and interesting. Of the Gothic past nothing is left except the little rib-vaults in the heads of the niches. Most of the motifs are derived direct from Cornelis Floris's engravings, i.e. from Flanders, though the upper table is also reminiscent of Benvenuto Cellini, especially the base of his Perseus of 1545–54.

Otherwise of Sharington's activity the following is preserved: a chimneypiece in the STONE GALLERY, i.e. a gallery running above the E range of rooms along the cloister. This has pilasters with dainty decoration in sunk panels, i.e. a North Italian Renaissance rather than a Floris or Cellini motif. In addition there are plenty of stone chimneystacks of Tudor shape, i.e. with twisted fluting or star-shaped sections. Moreover the Brown Gallery and other rooms on the first floor still have their Sharington windows. In the Brown Gallery they are of four twisted fluting or star-shaped sections. Moreover the Stone Gallery and other rooms on the first floor still have their Sharington windows. In the Stone Gallery they are of four lights with one transom and a patera at each meeting of mullion and transom. The lights have shouldered lintels. Sharington's mason had a passion for little corbels to support window-sills.*

Finally the OUTER COURTYARD. This is essentially C16 work, though the masonry of the main gatehouse belongs to the C15. It is of stone, but with half-timbered dormers and a

* Cf. also the corbels of the doorway now in the village school, *see* p. 259.

9

half-timbered clock-turret. Of features there are straight-headed doorways in the N and E ranges, and there is the beginning of a columnar feature close to a C15 buttress at the S end of the E range. That is all.

The HALL, which was in all probability Sharington's hall also (*see* above), is the centre of the work carried out in the new Gothick fashion by *Sanderson Miller* for John Ivory Talbot in 1754–6. His intention to rebuild the principal parts of the house may date back a little further; for S of the hall is the DINING ROOM, and this is purely classical, indeed Kentian, in its details and may well belong to the forties. Ivory Talbot had inherited the estate in 1714 and died only in 1772. The hall faces W. It has two tall ogee-headed windows, a doorway between, and polygonal angle buttresses or turrets with crocketed ogee caps. The doorway is reached by an outer staircase of two arms. Inside is a shallow tunnel-vault decorated with the coats of arms of Ivory Talbot's friends, set in crocketed quatrefoils. Gothic chimneypiece and Gothic doorways, all with cresting. In the walls Gothic niches of various sizes with ogee canopies and little finials. Also brackets for busts. On these brackets and in these niches stands the extraordinary statuary of *Victor Alexander Sederbach*, a pleasant, modest man and a cheap sculptor. Beyond that we know absolutely nothing about him. His Christian names sound North-East German, his surname South German or Austrian, and the statues in Austrian abbeys are indeed perhaps the nearest comparison to these wild, violent, and unrefined mid-C18 pieces. They are made of terracotta, and it has been suggested that Sederbach was perhaps a *Hafner*, i.e. stove-maker, and not a sculptor. Not even the programme which Sederbach followed is recorded. Talbot already in 1753 wanted a statue of the foundress. So she is no doubt the figure above the fireplace. But who are the others? Death is among them, and also perhaps the Seasons. The STAINED GLASS in the hall is a mixture of pieces from the C15 to the C17, partly made for the house, partly imported.

The only notable alteration after Ivory Talbot's time is the three Gothic ORIEL WINDOWS of different sizes in the S wall, i.e. the wall which was once the N wall of the church. They date from about 1830.

In the GROUNDS are a C16 pillar SUNDIAL, a pair of tall Tuscan COLUMNS, formerly a chimney of the house, set up in the C18 in its present position with a sphinx by *Benjamin Carter* on top, and a Gothick archway of the Ivory Talbot years.

THE VILLAGE. Lacock is a square of streets, the High Street with its traffic away from the church. The village is one of the best in the county, compact and without any loss of scale anywhere.

N of the church the TAN FACTORY, early C19, T-shaped, of three storeys, with a total length of eight bays; two-light windows. Then to the W at once a group of cottages, grey stone, but also timber-framing. Along CHURCH STREET, No. 12, brick, C18, with widely spaced windows and a mansard roof. No. 11 has a crazy eaves frieze of full-size capitals of pilasters. Were they made and never used, or bought at a demolition sale? No. 10 is low, C17, with dormers. Opposite the CARPENTER'S ARMS with a broken pediment on brackets over the door. Here branch l. into EAST STREET to see the LOCKUP with its domed stone roof and then a C14 BARN belonging to the abbey estate. This has eight bays with cruck trusses and a four-bay wing. Opposite, No. 4 has a doorway with a four-centred head and a continuous chamfer. That takes us into the High Street, but it is too soon. We continue first in Church Street. No. 8 has an early C14 doorway, one of the next houses a canted C17 bay window (but an upper storey which does not belong). Then the ANGEL HOTEL with a C16 doorway and a timber-framed overhang. No. 3 finally has a cruck truss exposed on the E front. At the end we reach West Street. But first to the W, across the bridge, and to the l. CANTAX HOUSE. Of brick, Georgian, seven bays, two storeys, with a three-bay pediment. Quoins, also to the centre. Gatepiers with vases. Higher up on the r. the CONGREGATIONAL CHURCH of 1783, one by two bays, windows with Y-tracery, hipped roof.

In WEST STREET first nice, even rows of cottages facing one another, those on the E earlier than those on the W side. Then No. 3 (W) with a medieval doorway, and No. 13 (E) of the late C17, five bays, three dormers, two-light windows, porch with pediment. The HIGH STREET announces itself with PORCH HOUSE, timber-framed with closely-spaced uprights and two gables. To the l. the square porch. Then on the other side the SCHOOL. Its r. half is of 1824, Gothic, flat, one-storeyed, with two entrances and two windows between. Inside the l.-hand extension (by *Pritchard*) a stone doorcase taken from the N chapel of the church and stylistically belonging entirely to the Sharington work. It led from the chapel into the transept and is quite a simple but also an elegant piece. In front of the church the village CROSS. The upper part is Victorian. Further on, the POST OFFICE has a nice door-hood on carved brackets, as has No. 11 on the opposite side. The row on this side is dominated by one bigger timber-framed gable with overhang. The end is the RED LION HOTEL, the only bigger building in the village: early C18, of brick, seven bays and two storeys, with a three-bay centre rising to a third storey and ending in a bleak, steeply curved pediment. The windows are segment-headed. There are giant pilasters alternatingly of stone and brick at the angles, also those of the centre.

OUTER LACOCK

NOTTON, 1 m. NNW. NOTTON COTTAGE has two gables and a doorway with a pediment on volute brackets. NOTTON HOUSE must be of c.1840. Three bays, porch on pairs of Tuscan columns, low wings l. and r. LACKHAM HOUSE lies in its own grounds. Sweet LODGE by the entrance with the eaves carried by veranda posts. This lodge must be early C19. Next to it the Victorian replacement – quite an object lesson in C19 history. The house is of seven bays and three storeys with a three-bay pediment. The windows on the first floor are pedimented. Veranda of Tuscan columns on the ground floor. Low wings with pediments. This all looks Late Georgian. At the back, porch of c.1900. In the grounds another house, quite a perfect example of the early C19 Old English *cottage orné*. Two gables with bargeboards. Single-storey porch with bargeboards. Two little bays with Gothic windows.

LADIES BRIDGE see WILCOT

LAKE HOUSE see WILSFORD, p. 513

2020
LANDFORD

ST ANDREW. 1858 by *Butterfield*. Brick with stone bands. Poly-gonal bell-turret on a big W buttress separating two two-light windows. However, the N doorway is a genuine Early Norman piece. Shafts with elementary volute capitals. The abaci and arch (with a roll moulding) may be later. So is the fine piece of Norman SCULPTURE inside. Two figures under tight arches together holding a cross or being busy about it (with cloths?). And what do the regularly distributed square holes in the relief signify? – PLATE. Set, 1758. – MONUMENTS. Eyre tablets of the C18–19.

LANDFORD MANOR, E of the church. The back is of 1599, the front of 1712. Both sides are of brick. The back has a recessed centre and gabled wings and mullioned and transomed windows. The front is taller, of five bays and three storeys, with a panelled parapet. Segment-headed windows. The centre bay has the doorway and the windows above it of stone. Doorway with an enormous mask, the windows above it with smaller masks. (Inside, one Elizabethan ceiling, 53 ft long, one Elizabethan staircase, much panelling on the ground floor, and also a richly carved Queen Anne chimneypiece and a Queen Anne staircase.)

LANDFORD LODGE, 1 m. W. Built shortly after 1776. Brick, two storeys, seven bays, with a three-bay pediment on pairs of unfluted Ionic giant pilasters. Pretty doorcase, not really part of the composition.

HAMPTWORTH LODGE, 1¾ m. WSW. 1910–12 by *Sir Guy Dawber*. A large house in the Tudor style. Genuine timber-framing with brick infilling. All the three main fronts picturesquely asymmetrical. Large hall. Excellent planning of the rooms and relation of the parts of the house to one another. Some genuine Elizabethan or Jacobean overmantels come from Goodrich Court in Herefordshire.

LANGLEY BURRELL   9070

ST PETER. Close to the manor house but wholly surrounded by trees, a delightful church, not neglected, but also not over-restored. The surfaces and textures still tell.* And in addition it is a picturesque church externally as well as internally. Chronologically the church is interesting too – in short there are assets of all kinds. The N arcade dates from c.1200. Three bays, circular piers, capitals with sparse, widely separated stiff-leaf. Circular abaci, slightly pointed, double-chamfered arches. Then much work of c.1300–20. The W front belongs to that date, and the arcade was lengthened for it by a narrow additional arch. W windows of nave and aisle with pointed-trefoiled lancets. The big S tower also seems of c.1300–20. The top stage has a parapet with a ballflower frieze below, the ground-stage a tomb-recess also with ballflower. To the E this ground stage had a two-light window with a barbed trefoil in the head. This was cut into (very soon, it seems) by an arch into the S chapel with three big continuous chamfers. The arch also cut into the

* Restoration 1898 by *Sir H. Brakspear*.

piscina to its r. To its l. a cusped trefoil squint from the nave into the chancel. To the w side of the tower is the s porch. Its entrance arch (two continuous chamfers) and the tiny lancet of its upper storey again go with *c*.1300. The tierceron-star vault inside, however, with its bosses must be Perp. Finally the chancel, according to N lancets and the chancel arch again of *c*.1300. Shafts with moulded capitals, except for some on the l. which have naturalistic foliage. The irregularity of the arrangement is odd. The sedilia are only partially preserved. Cusped arch and crocketed gable. The chancel windows have boldly cinquefoiled rere-arches. On the s side they were abolished by the arch into the Perp s chapel (embattled outside). Perp also the N aisle (battlements and pinnacles). Ceiling with moulded beams. – FONT. An C18 baluster. – COMMUNION RAIL. C18, turned balusters. – SCULPTURE. Several fragments, architectural and sculptural, are to be noted, e.g. the charming little early C14 man, to the l. of the chancel arch, and the architectural piece below the chancel piscina. – PLATE. Two Chalices with Paten Covers, *c*.1660–70; Paten and Flagon, 1702; Paten, 1721. – MONUMENTS. Defaced early C14 effigies, husband and wife, in the outer tower recess. – A number of tablets worth a glance, especially † 1732, † 1810, † 1823.

MANOR HOUSE, E of the church. Ashlar-faced and dignified, if not particularly eventful. Three storeys, five bays, three-bay pediment. Built *c*.1771.

SCHOOL. 1844. Quite nice; Earliest Victorian Gothic, i.e. not yet putting it on thick.

RECTORY. C17, with a w front of 1739. Three wide bays, hipped roof. The doorway and the window above are characteristically Early Georgian. The Tuscan porch is obviously Later Georgian, and the side windows have also been changed. One-bay pediment.

LANHILL *see* CHIPPENHAM

LARKHILL
1040

LARKHILL CAMP. Started in 1920–4, but very largely of 1936–40. Like Bulford, an extensive area and with tree-planted streets, neo-Georgian houses, and larger buildings and a garrison church.

ST ALBAN. 1937 by *W. A. Ross* (chief architect to the War Office). Big; red brick with a short sw tower. Tall, slim, triangle-headed windows. Polygonal apse. The interior also is brick-faced. It has low aisle-passages.

N of the church new buildings are going up at the time of writing, considerably more progressive for their date than the buildings of the later thirties were of theirs.

LARMER GROUNDS *see* TOLLARD ROYAL

LATTON

0090

ST JOHN BAPTIST. Broad w tower, the lower part Norman, the upper Perp, with battlements. The arch towards the nave is Norman. It has two slight chamfers. Norman also the chancel arch, single-stepped with one order of shafts and drastically renewed. Finally Norman too the s doorway. The shafts have bold vertical zigzag, the arch zigzag too, and the hood-mould pellets. Undecorated tympanum on a lintel gently arched at the bottom. The arches to the transepts are round, but double-chamfered. But much here is due to restoration. The transepts on the whole represent a date *c*.1300. Chancel of 1861 by *Butterfield* (PF). It has a pointed tunnel-vault with transverse arches, which is a surprise. – BENCHES. C17; plain. – STAINED GLASS. E window by *Kempe & Tower*, 1911. – At the sw corner of the churchyard two fragments of ROMAN COLUMNS.

VILLAGE CROSS, at the main crossing. Very tapering shaft.

(ROUND HOUSE of the Thames-Severn Canal; cf. Marston Meysey, p. 306. The house lies N of the Cerney Wick Lock. MHLG)

LAVERSTOCK

1030

ST ANDREW. 1858 by *T. H. Wyatt*. Nave and chancel and bell-cote. s side with several gables, to the s as well as the E and w. Norman arch* used for the porch entrance; zigzag at r. angles to the wall surface. – STAINED GLASS. In the w and sw windows genuine C13 grisaille glass, fragments only, reassembled. It was found in the town ditch of Salisbury in 1933 and probably comes from Salisbury Cathedral. Other fragments went to Boyton and to Winchester Cathedral. – In the other s aisle windows broken bits of C18 and early C19 glass very successfully displayed together. – PLATE. Flagon, 1652; Chalice, 1697. – MONUMENT. Gothic tablet by *Osmond*; date of death 1837.

---

* Or parts of it.

9080

LEA

1½ m. SE of Malmesbury

ST GILES. Perp W tower with battlements. Perp five-light E window of unusual design. The rest by *G. J. Phipps*, 1879–80 (GR). – FONT. Octagonal, with quatrefoils. If Perp, then very scraped.

0090

THE LEIGH

2 m. SE of Ashton Keynes

ALL SAINTS. Re-erected ½ m. SE of the old site in 1896. Only the chancel remained (*see* below). So the chancel of All Saints is of 1896 (by *Ponting*; PF). The rest correctly rebuilt. Nave and chancel and bell-turret. Straight-headed Perp windows. Single-framed roof with carved bosses.

OLD CHURCH. The chancel has a late C13 window – three stepped lancet lights under one arch. Nice, finely moulded priest's doorway of the same date. It has a hood-mould on a human head and a beast's head. The E gable of the higher nave also still stands.

8070

LEIGH DELAMERE

ST MARGARET. The very odd Sanctus bell turret is a copy. The original is on Sevington school, *see* p. 419. It must have pleased Mr Neeld (*see* Grittleton, p. 233) so much that he had it copied when he paid for the church to be rebuilt in 1846, by *J. Thompson*. And what is one to make of the equally odd S arcade? Circular piers, double-chamfered round arches, i.e. so far *c*.1200, but no capitals at all, just sparse stuck-on individual stiff-leaf sprigs. That must be Thompson. Thompson entirely is the N aisle or N chapel, the Neeld Chapel. It is separated from the nave by eight arches on a parapet, and inside is a Gothic ORGAN CASE, looking more High than Early Victorian, as also does emphatically the REREDOS in the chancel, which is by *Thompson*. Figures by *Baily* after Thorwaldsen. – STAINED GLASS. All by *Wilmhurst*, and all in the most strident colours. There are copies in it after Michelangelo's Prophets, Overbeck's Virgin, and others. – Even the ALMSBOX is of solid stone and has a relief of the Good Samaritan. – PLATE. Chalice and Paten, inscribed 1577; Paten, 1720.

By *Thompson* for Neeld E of the church the PARSONAGE and the ALMSHOUSES (low, with five gables and projecting wings;

triangular bays on the faces of the wings) and also MANOR FARMHOUSE, W of the church.

LIDDINGTON

2080

ALL SAINTS. E.E. chancel, trefoiled N doorway and N arcade. Three bays, octagonal piers, renewed capitals, double-chamfered arches. In the aisle two fine tomb recesses of *c.*1300. The church was very thoroughly restored in the 1880s (by *Ponting*), and it is uncertain what is original and what is not. The rerearch of the N aisle E window (of three stepped pointed-trefoiled lights) has shafts on stiff-leaf corbels. The W window has a boldly barbed trefoil in the tracery and a cinquefoiled rerearch, i.e. motifs of *c.*1300–20. But are they correct? And is the repetition of the barbed tracery in the S side, or rather S aisle windows, correct? For there was clearly originally a S aisle. The position of the chancel arch proves that. Perp W tower. – FONT. Norman, of tub shape, with tapering sides. Top band of flat zigzag and pellet decoration. – CHURCHYARD CROSS. Only the steps and a stump of the shaft survive.

MANOR HOUSE. Jacobean. Flat front with mullioned and transomed windows and gables.

See p. 577

LIMPLEY STOKE

7060

ST MARY. A small, unrestored, little-known church. Short W tower without buttresses. Parapet and short recessed stone spire decorated with two bands. Short nave and chancel. The N porch entrance is an early C13 arch, round-headed on thin shafts with moulded capitals. On entering, one is met with a surprise: the C20 S aisle arcade incorporates the former S doorway, work of the C11 if not the C10, very narrow and quite undecorated. In the chancel herringbone work was found in 1929. – WEST GALLERY with Jacobean panels. – PULPIT. Stone, with two tiers of blank two-light panels. – PLATE. Chalice and Cover, 1575. – MONUMENTS. Thirteen coffin-lids. Two of them have heads of Ladies above foliated crosses, one a bust with arms joined, also above a foliated cross.

MANOR HOUSE. Three-bay Georgian front to the river (and the railway). Venetian windows. Doorway with Tuscan columns and pediment. Even quoins. The back C17 with three gables and mullioned and transomed windows. (Interior with several Georgian plaster ceilings. NBR)

THE WEIR, N of the Manor House. Late C18, with two bays and several Venetian windows.

DUNDAS AQUEDUCT. It takes the Kennet-Avon Canal across the river Avon. By *John Rennie c.*1805. Three arches, the middle one of a 64½-ft span.

ROMAN VILLA. Fragmentary remains have been discovered at Limpley Stoke.

LITTLE BEDWYN

2060

A lane with estate housing of 1860, brick with diapers of blue brick and with or without gables, leads to the church.

ST MICHAEL. Flint and little stone. Three-bay arcades of the later C12. Circular piers, the abaci still square and the arches round and single-stepped, but the capitals with decorated trumpet scallops as well as one even moulded in a purely C13 way. Maybe this is a replacement. Four capitals have reeding. The tower arch has imposts as simple as if they were Norman, but is triple-chamfered. Recessed spire. All windows Perp and straight-headed. – STAINED GLASS. Old bits in the chancel window to the vestry. – E window by *Barnett* of Newcastle; terrible. – PLATE. Chalice and Paten Cover, 1681.

MANOR FARMHOUSE, across the railway and the canal. C18, of chequer brick with a one-bay pediment. Across the road the octagonal former GAME LARDER, close to the house – the other side a SUMMER HOUSE, square, with two sides wide open in arches. Nice, modest mid-C18 plasterwork inside.

LITTLE CHEVERELL

9050

ST PETER. 1850, except for the low C14 W tower (with pyramid roof), the C14 porch entrance, and the Dec doorway with cusped ogee head in the chancel. – FONT. Octagonal, Perp, with pointed quatrefoils. – PLATE. Chalice and Paten Cover, 1661.

HAWKESWELL HOUSE, S of the church. 1914–20 by *Martin* of Egham (cf. Dauntsey's School, p. 504). Neo-Georgian, brick.

LITTLECOTE

3070

1 m. w of Chilton Foliat

Littlecote is the only major brick mansion in Wiltshire, and very delightful it looks with its long, low, stretching red façade in the lush green of its gardens and the meadows by the river

Kennet. The impression one receives of the house is Elizabethan, i.e. an entirely symmetrical front on the E-plan, though
with only slight projections. Two big gables and the smaller
porch gable. In addition a long w wing in line with the façade.
To the back the house, just as long but mainly flint. Though
the house is not deep, it has an inner courtyard and originally
had a subsidiary courtyard to the w. That side is now open.
In fact the house is much older than the age of Elizabeth I,
though it is not possible now to say how much of its walling
dates back further. The oldest part recognizable is the N W wing,
buttressed to the s and with two-light windows to the back,
with cusped lights – i.e. C15. Then there are in the same wing
and to the N altogether windows with uncusped arched lights,
probably of the early C16. Those of this pattern on the s front,
however, seem a recent alteration, as a picture in the great hall
indicates. The house came into the Darrell family in 1415 and
passed to Sir John Popham in 1589. He later became Lord
Chief Justice. The s front of the main range may be Darrell or
Popham, i.e. it is Elizabethan, and we know no more. It has to
the l. and r. of the porch one enormous four -light window with
three transoms, followed by a yet larger one with four transoms.
On the l. of the porch this represents the hall. On the r. the
windows must always have been a sham, in the sense that a
ceiling cut through them. The GREAT HALL has its screen and
a thin-ribbed plaster ceiling with two pendants. The four-
transom window of course represents the high-table end. The
main staircase must have followed somewhere here, but was
shifted, probably in the C19, to a position immediately to the
r. of the entrance. In the hall and in the rooms good STAINED
GLASS, German or Netherlandish, and C16 and C17, e.g. the
large St Benedict dated 1528 at the N end of the actual screens
passage. Where the present staircase is one would of course
expect buttery, pantry, and such-like rooms, especially as the
large kitchen chimneybreast appears indeed in the E wall of
the range. There are, however, living rooms instead. One of
them has an elaborate overmantel with pairs of caryatids and
the date 1592.*

For the rest of the house comments cannot here be made
room for room. It must be sufficient to mention the following,
all on the first floor, which indeed contained the state rooms,
as is clearly visible on the N side by the size of the windows. The
whole N side of the main quadrangle is filled by the LONG

* The stucco ceiling is probably Victorian.

GALLERY, 110 ft long. This has a C19 plaster ceiling but a wide and fine original frieze with the Darrell arms, i.e. dating from before 1589. It has four four-light windows of two transoms and in the middle a deep canted bay with a total of ten lights. The lights have four-centred heads (though not below the transoms), also a sign of earlier design. Attached to the NE end of the gallery is a CABINET with an original plaster ceiling. Attached to the NW end a big but completely utilitarian STAIR-CASE with a solid newel block. In a number of rooms are overmantels of the time of Sir John Popham, all of plaster. One of them carries the arms of Queen Elizabeth and may commemorate her visit to the house in 1601.

Of the later rooms the most important by far is the CHAPEL. This lies in the NW range, just where it appears at its oldest. It must in fact replace the pre-Reformation chapel; for behind one of the windows with cusped lights is a cusped piscina. The present chapel however is Cromwellian, i.e. with the pulpit instead of the altar in the middle of the E wall. Below it symmetrically the reader's desk and a parapet hiding the steps up. The parapet has (older?) linenfold panels. Three sides of the room have a balustraded gallery carried on slender columns. The W side has a screen of several tiers of balusters. There are original benches as well. Another C17 room is the DUTCH PARLOUR, painted with Dutch genre-scenes, many of them painted complete with frames, and nails and ribbons to hang the feigned frames from. The room to the W of the hall was remodelled in the mid C18 and received a specially fine and unusual white marble fireplace with two young maidens standing on high, urn-like plinths. Finally the conversion of the W wing along the s front into a CONSERVATORY. The thin Gothic windows with Y-tracery can easily be recognized. The conversion took place in 1809.

STABLES. Flint with bands of red brick; C18.

ROMAN VILLA. In 1730 a mosaic pavement was found in the park. It bore a central design of Apollo playing a harp surrounded by mounted female figures. In another portion of the mosaic were depicted leopards and dolphins.

LITTLE DURNFORD *see* DURNFORD

LITTLE HINTON

ST SWITHIN. Small. Small, unbuttressed w tower with pointed, unmoulded arch on the simplest imposts. s doorway Late

Norman with billet motif in the hood-mould. To the same time belongs the s arcade. Two bays, round pier, decorated trumpet-scallop capitals, square abacus, round, double-chamfered arches. The N arcade seems C13, though the arches are round too and have only slight chamfers. Circular abacus, no capitals proper. Early C13 chancel arch with renewed stiff-leaf capitals. Pointed arch with one step and one chamfer, i.e. all this within fifty years or so. Perp s porch and clerestory. Good nave roof of low pitch, with tie-beams and otherwise panelled. – FONT. Circular, Norman, with one band of arcading and one partly of wild knotwork, partly with animals in a disorderly arrangement: a twisted snake with two birds pecking at it and two fishes near by, a quadruped seemingly sitting on its behind, and in fact on a bird. – PULPIT. 1637. With two tiers of the usual blank arches. – READER'S DESK. Goes with the pulpit. – STAINED GLASS. E window by *Kempe*, c.1910, trademark not yet combined with that of Tower. – PLATE. Chalice and Paten Cover, late C16; Flagon, 1634; two Patens, 1719.

LITTLE LANGFORD   0030
1 m. SE of Steeple Langford

ST NICHOLAS. Norman s doorway, primitive but full of zest. One order of shafts with figured capitals, the l. one with animals (a horse?). Roll and zigzag mouldings. Small tympanum with a bishop and a tree of life with three birds. Lintel with a boar hunt. The church was rebuilt in 1864 by *T. H. Wyatt*, but the Dec windows look as if they represented what was there before, and the chancel arch certainly looks Dec. The church is of flint and stone chequerwork. – SCREEN. Bits of the dado re-used in a chancel desk. – SCULPTURE. Panel with the Crucifixus. – PLATE. Chalice, 1660 or 1662. – MONUMENT. Elizabethan tomb-chest with big geometrical and stylized leaf motifs. Effigy of a man.

GROVELY CASTLE. *See* Steeple Langford.

LITTLE PARK FARM *see* WOOTTON BASSETT

LITTLE SOMERFORD   9080

ST JOHN BAPTIST. Thin, unbuttressed Perp w tower. Nave and chancel in one. The details all seem of the C19. Reticulated tracery in the E window, otherwise lancets and windows with

Y-tracery. Single-framed roofs with tie-beams. – PULPIT. 1626, with attached READER'S DESK. The motif of decoration the usual low blank arches. – SCREEN. Fine, solid Perp piece, with, to l. and r. of the entrance, five tall narrow arches. Moulded top-beam with a frieze of quatrefoils in an ogee chain. – BENCHES. Jacobean box pews cut down to make benches. – SCULPTURE. Interesting cross-head, locket-shaped, with Virgin and Crucifixus; C14. – PAINTING. The tympanum above the screen is preserved, and painted on it are the ROYAL ARMS of Elizabeth I. – Also later C17 texts in cartouches. – PLATE. Chalice and Paten Cover, 1714.

LITTLETON DREW

8080

ALL SAINTS. Thin Perp central tower. Otherwise by *T. H. Wyatt*, 1856 (GR). Or is the Perp W window original? – FONT. Circular, C13, undecorated, but moulded shaft, and spurs at the foot. – CROSS SHAFT. Two large fragments of a C9 shaft, among the best in Wiltshire, though not well preserved. Vegetable scrolls on the front, interlace on one side. – PLATE. Chalice with Paten Cover, inscribed 1578. – MONUMENT. Stone effigy of a Lady wearing a wimple; C13.

LITTLETON PANNELL

9050

LITTLETON HOUSE. Late Georgian, white, of three bays with a gable in the middle and on the ground floor tripartite windows under blank segmental arches.
A BECKETTS. 1904 by *E. P. Warren*, including some old remains. Symmetrical late-C17 design with recessed centre and projecting wings. Hipped roof and a lantern on top. Brick.

LITTLE WOODBURY *see* BRITFORD

LOCKERIDGE HOUSE *see* FYFIELD

LONGBRIDGE DEVERILL

8040

ST PETER AND ST PAUL. A varied exterior, thanks to the fact that the N and S chapels have their own pitched roofs. Square W tower without pinnacles, with a higher stair-turret, Dec bell-openings, but a large transomed Perp W window. The rest of the windows of the church straight-headed, Perp, except for the Victorian E window and the NW window, which seems a

C17 substitute. The interior comes as a surprise after this. Early Norman N arcade of three bays with square, slightly chamfered piers and unmoulded arches. C14 S arcade of two continuous chamfers. Tall tower arch with capitals with big leaves, also C14. Chancel and side chapels of *c.*1860. – FONT. Circular, Norman, decorated with enriched scallops on the underside. – PANELLING. S aisle W, *c.* 1700, with Corinthian pilasters, arched panels, and cartouches over. From Hatfield. – WEST GALLERY. A rich piece in the C18 style on the triumphal-arch motif. Straight-headed entry with Ionic columns l. and r. and a segmental pediment, small arched entries with medallions over. Said to be imitation. – CHAPEL SCREENS. 1921–2, neo-Jacobean. – ARMOUR. Under the tower a number of helms, a sword, a bottle, shears, etc.; early C16 to C17. – MONUMENTS. Sir John Thynne † 1580, the builder of Longleat. Simple tablet, low on the S wall of the family chapel. The decoration with cherubs' heads and drapery proves that the tablet is not of the time of Thynne's death. – Isabella Marchioness of Bath † 1830. White marble. A kneeling woman reading in the Bible: 'Blessed are the pure in heart'. Unsigned. – Second Marquess of Bath † 1837. By *Chantrey*. Also white. Grecian pedestal and head in profile on it. – J. B. Thynne † 1887. By *Gilbert*. One of the few things in England that correspond to Gaudí's work in Spain. Tall shaft, alabaster bowl, tall pinnacle. Free-standing, made as a font as well as a memorial. The forms gristly, crustaceous, bossy – how should one describe them? – WAR MEMORIAL. By *F. C. Eden*. In the Comper style.

LONGBRIDGE HOUSE. Of *c.*1840. Brick and stone trim. Tudor, and not quite symmetrical.

THYNNE ALMSHOUSES. Founded in 1655. Stone. Three gables: under each a three-light transomed window. Under the valleys small two-light windows. Doorways with hoods.

BATH ARMS HOTEL, Shear Cross, ½ m. N. The old part late C17 with cross-windows.

LONG DEAN *see* YATTON KEYNELL

LONGDEAN BOTTOM *see* EAST KENNETT

LONGFORD CASTLE

1020

Not much is known of Sir Thomas Gorges, who built Longford 34a Castle. He was born in 1536, became Gentleman Usher of the

King's Chamber, married in 1580 the Swedish-born widow of
the Marquess of Northampton, was knighted in 1586, and died
in 1610. He bought the Longford estate in 1574 and the house
carries the date 1591, probably the date of completion of the
rebuilding. Sir Thomas must have been a curious man – probably one would at the time have called him a fantastical man.
His monument in Salisbury Cathedral (*see* p. 370) has astrolo-
gical connotations. And as he was fascinated by the occult
meaning of the stars, so he may well have been fascinated by
other obscure meanings as well. Longford Castle in any case
was built on a triangular plan, which was a rare thing, and when,
about twenty or thirty years after it had been begun, John
Thorpe drew it, he put into the centre of the triangular court
the sign of the Holy Trinity. So he at least must have assumed
that this is what Gorges wanted to allude to. There is as col-
lateral confirmation Sir Thomas Tresham's Triangular Lodge
of 1593 at Rushton in Northamptonshire, and that, we know,
meant the Holy Trinity in its general form and all its details.
But Sir Thomas Tresham was a fervent Catholic, and of Sir
Thomas Gorges nothing is known that would allow us to believe
him hostile to the Elizabethan Settlement.

It has been said in the literature that the pattern of Longford
is the Danish astronomer Tycho Brahe's country house, Uraniborg. That is wrong, not only because Uraniborg was built in
1576–80 and Sir Thomas's Swedish wife had left Sweden shortly after 1560 and actually settled down in England in 1565, but
also because Uraniborg was a square, developed, it seems, from
Chambord. On the other hand, there is a famous Swedish
castle with three fat round towers set in an irregular triangular
relation: Gripsholm near Stockholm begun in 1537. But to
assume Swedish connexions one would have to assume also
that Sir Thomas did not lay out his new house till after his
marriage, i.e. after 1580. In fact the Rev. H. Pelate, who wrote in
1678, says that little was done till after the Armada, and that
the Marchioness obtained from the Queen the gift of the wreck
of a Spanish galleon off Hurst Castle, which turned out to
contain so much treasure that Longford could be built from it.
The house alone cost £18,000. However, Longford can clearly
not have been built in two or three years, and so one must
assume that the design and the beginning of its execution
belong to *c.*1580.

The triangular shape of Longford Castle was a novelty in
Elizabethan England, as far as we know. Equally remarkable

are the fat round towers, conveying a feeling of the castle, a 'castle air', as Vanbrugh was to say much later, though fortification was hardly in Gorges's mind. The idea is probably, as it were, Spenserian. And highly remarkable also is the façade, facing NW. (One of the three original towers points due N, the other two SW and SE.) It is much more elaborately decorated and much opener to the outside than that of any other of the Elizabethan prodigy houses.* This façade we must first examine.

As we see it now, it is a creditable attempt of *Anthony Salvin* to rebuild it in its original form. Salvin worked for the fourth Earl of Radnor in 1870–8. He found the façade drastically altered. These alterations date from c.1750, when *Robert Taylor* was paid for carvings, and c.1757, when money was paid for 'the logio', and may have been designed either by *Theodore Jacobsen* (on this attribution, *see* H. M. Colvin's *Biographical Dictionary*) or by *Roger Morris*, since he received money in 1742 for the design of a building at Longford. The original state of the façade can be deduced from Thorpe's drawing plus an anonymous drawing of after 1620 which comes from Wilton House and is now at Longford Castle.‡ It tallies with the present appearance except for two or three features. The façade is of three storeys, and between the towers eleven bays wide. The centre is of five bays with a loggia on ground floor and first floor. Loggias to the outside are a rare feature in England, especially before 1600,§ and loggias on two storeys occur nowhere else. The depressed arches on the ground floor may be correct, though Thorpe has round ones. The side parts to the l. and r. of the centre have intermittently blocked pilasters instead, and on the third floor there are caryatids instead throughout the façade. Moreover the second and third bays from outside are projections, or bay windows, and they and the single centre bay carry gables which end in pediments, triangular on the bays, segmental in the centre. This is a noteworthy detail; for such gables ending in pediments, i.e. what is called Dutch gables, were not supposed to exist in England before 1615–20. In the centre gable is the relief of a galleon alluding to the treasure

* Though not opener than Madrid near Paris had been when Francis I built it fifty years before.

‡ This drawing is here illustrated for the first time. It must be of after 1620, because the inscription refers to Lord Gorges, and Sir Thomas's son was created Lord Gorges only in 1620.

§ But the s façade of Burghley had one.

trove to which reference has already been made. The position of the bays is one of the changes which was made by Salvin. They originally adjoined the towers immediately. Salvin's also is the recession of the third floor of the centre. Moreover he did not replace the gorgeous original portal inside the loggia with its crowded caryatids, nor the coupled caryatids carrying obelisks which marked the ends of the five-bay centre. The balustrade on this part of the façade exists only in the Wilton drawing, but both the drawing and Thorpe show the coupled columnar chimneystacks – a demonstratively classical motif, existing earlier at Lacock (*see* p. 258) and contemporarily at Longleat – parallel to the façade, whereas now they are placed at r. angles. All the windows of the façade are of the cross-type.* None are of the large mullioned and transomed type which characterizes Longleat, Burghley, and the other prodigy houses. In the c18, when the house had gone to the Bouveries, later Viscounts Folkestone and later still Earls of Radnor, the façade had been much simplified. As it appeared in 1809 in John Britton's *Architectural Antiquities of Great Britain* it had sash windows, and the Dutch gables were replaced by a plain balustrade all along.

In 1802–17 *David Asher Alexander* was busy at Longford, after *James Wyatt* had made designs for a remodelling. Alexander and the second earl intended to enlarge the castle into a vast hexagon, keeping the NW front with its two towers but letting the third, i.e. the SE tower, stand detached in the middle of the hexagonal court. This ambitious plan did not materialize. Only the N tower was rebuilt and two new sides were started. They run from the N tower E to a new tower and from that tower SE, ending in yet another tower. Between these two a romantic façade was planned and partly executed, with two turrets crowned by conical spirelets. Between them are the stumps of two buttresses. The gap has recently been tidied up, by two utilitarian façades facing each other. Alexander's work was of white brick and remained a shell. So in spite of the ambition of the scheme, the triangular court remained as it had been, with its three round staircase turrets in the corners and their domed caps.

Much more was done when *Salvin* came in. He embellished the S front by two large bay windows with shaped gables and

* Only in the N tower are there remains of a three-light window with a moulded surround and this is, as we shall see, in a place supposedly rebuilt after 1800.

linked it by a one-storeyed new dining room to Alexander's last tower,* which he faced as the old towers had been and emphasized by a higher square tower adjoining it. He would not have been a Victorian if he had not been pining for an asymmetrically placed stronger accent on the skyline than any of the original house had been. In the last twenty years the tower has been reduced in height. But Salvin's most conspicuous work concerned the interior. He covered over the triangular court, giving it a glazed roof and at first-floor level a gallery with a wrought-iron railing in a feeble Dixhuitième taste. He also remodelled most of the principal rooms inside.

There is in fact little left of the time of Sir Thomas Gorges inside. What survives is this: first the shape of the HALL along the façade, to the r. of the entrance, with the r.-hand projection which was originally the hall bay and the first-floor part of the hall. The wooden Elizabethan chimneypiece of the hall is not *in situ*: it was formerly in the NE range. The entrance screen and its repetition to the l. are C20 additions. In the SW tower adjoining the hall is another Elizabethan chimneypiece, this time of stone, with termini caryatids flanking a cartouche with a relief. The Elizabethan-looking panelling however is said to be of Salvin's time. The ground-floor room in the SE tower is the LIBRARY. It has a splendid marble chimneypiece, probably by *Rysbrack*, and a thin-ribbed neo-Elizabethan Salvin ceiling. Genuinely Elizabethan is the shape of the LONG GALLERY in the S wing on the first floor, although the furnishings, and especially the chimneypiece with two caryatids in profile, are of the mid C18 and the meagre stucco ceiling is of Salvin's time. The best Elizabethan ensemble is the circular room adjoining the long gallery in the SW tower, with its columns of black marble and its wainscoting. The room has a stone ceiling with heavy ribs and a big pendant.‡ The stone chimneypiece with the overmantel with a beautiful relief of Orpheus is not *in situ*. It was originally in another room.§ The room next to the other

* But it is not certain whether this link goes back to Salvin, or is later, or was only altered later.

‡ Of the pendant, Henry Lord Coleraine in a poem of 1694 at Longford Castle says:

> Whose Pendant centre is of massive Stone
> Which for this hundred years uncrackt hangs down
> Pointing at harder tasks to Architects
> Then the Pantheon's open round detects.

§ This chimneypiece must not be confounded with that from the Antelope Inn at Salisbury, illustrated in Hatcher's *History*, which is now in a private house in Salisbury. (This information was kindly given me by Mr Shortt.)

end of the gallery, i.e. in the SE tower, is also circular and has an excellent Kentian fireplace and another of Salvin's ribbed plaster ceilings. In the (now internal) NE range are two complete mid-C18 rooms. The DINING ROOM of Salvin's has a specially sumptuous chimneypiece of c.1740, with garlands, an open curly pediment, and an eagle at the top. Many chimneypieces actually went into Longford (according to Mr Gunnis) from 1738 to 1744. The chimneypieces were made by *John Michael Rysbrack*, *Sir Henry Cheere*, the two *Carters*, and *Thomas Cartwright*.

To discuss the furniture and the priceless paintings of Longford Castle would be outside the terms of *The Buildings of England*.

The house is built of Chilmark stone, with the towers faced with bands of flint alternating with bands of small flint and stone squares. As mentioned above, the Rev. Henry Pelate, in the C17, said it cost £18,000, with another £6,000 for the OUTBUILDINGS. At present the outbuildings include a C17 OFFICE BUILDING, rebuilt after destruction in the Civil War, but still entirely pre-classical with its gables and mullioned and mullioned and transomed windows. It is of brick and was restored (and altered?) by *Salvin*. It lies close to the handsome three-arched BRIDGE, which is Georgian in style and by *Gambier Parry*. The ESTATE OFFICE is a Georgian five-by-three-bay brick house with hipped roof.

The GARDENS were done by *Capability Brown*, re-done in 1832, and then simplified after the Second World War, but the four-column MONUMENT with the lead statue of Flora is Georgian. The statue is by *John Cheere*.

8040

LONGLEAT

Longleat is the beginning of the High Elizabethan style, the first of what Sir John Summerson has so felicitously called the Elizabethan prodigy houses. Here the motifs were developed which passed on to Burghley, to Wollaton, to Hardwick and the rest. It would be highly desirable therefore to know when Longleat was built, but the most recent research has left us in ignorance less penetrable than we had thought it was. The plan may belong to 1567–8, the elevation seems to be of 1572 etc. There had been on the site before the Reformation an Augustinian priory, which became Carthusian in 1530. In 1541 the premises were purchased by Sir John Thynne. He had been one of the Lord Protector Somerset's protégés. They were a team of mostly very able men, and he must have instilled into them that passion for building and that faith in a new style of building which he himself possessed. Other protégés of his were Sir William Sharington of Lacock in Wiltshire, a shady character, William Cecil Lord Burghley, the greatest English statesman of the century and the builder of Burghley House and Theobalds, and Sir Thomas Smith of Hill Hall in Essex. Thynne was Somerset's steward in London, while Somerset House was being built in 1547 etc.

Thynne at that time had just finished converting the premises of the priory into quarters for himself and his family to live in. His wife incidentally, whom he had married in 1548, was a sister of Sir Thomas Gresham, another of the knowledgeable patrons of architecture of the generation. Then extension and rebuilding went on gradually in the 1550s and 60s. Among the masons were *John Chapman*, who had been in the King's Works from *c*.1541 and was known to Sharington as well as the Duke of Northumberland, and *William Spicer*, who much later became Surveyor of the Queen's Works, among the sculptors *Allen Maynard*, a Frenchman who was naturalized in 1567. Whatever Thynne may have built with these men suffered greatly from a fire which occurred in 1567. What exactly the fire destroyed we do not know. Anyway, most of what we see now is likely to date from after 1567, and indeed after 1572, as has already been mentioned. Thynne died in 1580, before the house was completed. Among the masons another important name now turns up: *Robert Smythson*. He was sent by Humphrey Lovell, the Queen's Master Mason, who must also have been well known to Thynne; for Lord Hertford, Somerset's son, writes to him about the 'plan' for his – Hertford's – house 'devised by you' – Thynne – and Lovell. In 1576 Smythson worked at Wardour (*see* p. 489), in 1580 he designed Wollaton and yet later probably Hardwick. He first appears at Longleat in 1568.

The greatest innovation of Longleat is that it is a large house with a uniform treatment of all its four façades. Inside, before *Sir Jeffry Wyatville* rearranged it in 1801–11, it had a spacious W courtyard with extruded corners ending in turrets with domed caps, two of them with spiral stairs and, instead of the present E courtyard, a maze of small rooms round two small irregular courtyards and another four turrets with domed caps. Longleat is three storeys high, but seems before Thynne's death only to have had two storeys (plus a basement) and ends in a top balustrade in front of a flat roof. The chimneystacks are paired short Tuscan columns with fancy capitals (cf. Lacock). The entrance is on the s side. The portal is of the c18 but replaces a similar one with coupled columns and a top achievement. Symmetrically to the l. and r. are first two bays of windows, then a two-bay bay window, then another window bay and another two-bay bay window not quite at the corner. The windows are of three or four lights, with two transoms on the ground floor and first floor and one on the top floor. The bay windows are distinguished by orders of pilasters and circular niches in the sill zones of the windows. Originally these had busts *à l'antique*, but not many of them survive. The balustrade motif came from Somerset House, busts in medallions occur *c.*1560–70 on the so-called Holbein Gate at Wilton and recur later at Wollaton. Somerset House was the source of the symmetry and the classical elements of Longleat. Thynne was of course familiar with every detail of it. It had, apart from the orders of pilasters (derived from the 'Loire Style' in France), the double-bay bay windows. The characteristic fenestration of Longleat on the other hand, large, even openings more extensive than the wall areas, which more than anything makes it the fountain-head of the High Elizabethan style, is a development away from the classicism of Somerset House back to the English Perpendicular tradition. Sutton Place in Surrey of the 1520s is the link between the two, still with windows of arched and cusped lights, but already with that rhythm of open and closed which Thynne carried on and so successfully exaggerated. Longleat has very little ornament; apart from the former portal only aprons and little corbels between the windows (cf. Lacock) and some minor strapwork as a cresting on the bay windows. Above this and the balustrade rise the caps of the turrets, curiously out of keeping with the façade and moreover so asymmetrically placed that they seem likely indeed to be a survival of before the fire. How much else is of before the fire cannot be said. Perhaps the disposition of the principal rooms, perhaps even the fenestration, but not the pilasters, it seems, nor the bay windows, nor certainly the balustrade; for we know that gables continue to be mentioned in the documents right down to 1572.

The E and W façades are similar. The rhythm of the E façade is a two-bay window in the centre and then l. and r. three bays and another two-bay window. Again the windows are of three or four lights. The detail measurements are curiously irregular: e.g. the side bay windows differ in their distance from the corners by 4 ft 7 in. The W front is the same as the E front except that there are two instead of three windows between the bay windows. Behind one part of the W façade lay the chapel, apparently not orientated. It was consecrated in 1684 and has now been horizontally subdivided to create new large living rooms. The N front was rebuilt by *Wyatville*.

Wyatville also added the extensive STABLES in the style of the house. They are one-storeyed with two-storeyed corner pieces. Only the windows have Georgian glazing bars. On the S side a higher clock tower.

The INTERIOR of Longleat is rewarding, but not for the survival of features of Sir John Thynne's time. Not a single whole room remains. As one enters one is in the HALL, or rather the screens passage. This element and the position of the hall are still traditional, i.e. medieval and Early Tudor. New ideas on the placing of the hall came only with Wollaton and Hardwick. Thynne's main staircase lay, also as usual, behind the dais end of the hall (to the N). The hall has a hammerbeam roof with collar-beams, arched braces, and pendants. There are also longitudinal beams with pendants, a nice, lively arrangement, probably by *John Lewis*, a joiner who had worked for Somerset before. The upper parts of the roof were ceiled when Bishop Ken's library was built in the 1690s (*see* below). Corinthian columns and pilasters support the ceiling. The Jacobean panels are probably of Wyatville's time. The chimneypiece rises to the whole height of the ground floor. The lower part has pairs of fluted Ionic columns, a very classical frieze, and in the overmantel five caryatids on tapering pilasters. In the middle, figure of a mermaid; the pilaster is replaced by two plaited tails.* The figures carry baskets with very naturalistic fruit, a Flemish motif already used at Lacock about 1550. The Longleat chimneypiece probably dates from about 1575–80. The wooden screen (perhaps by *Lewis*) has fluted Ionic pilasters below, little caryatids again on tapering pilasters above. Facing the screen on the other (E) side is a balcony with openwork scrolls (cf. panels in the churches of Crudwell and East Coulston). This must date from the time of the first Viscount Weymouth, i.e. 1682–4.

The following hints follow the way visitors are taken round the

* The same motif occurs in a drawing convincingly attributed by Dr Girouard to *Maynard*.

house. From the hall one goes through a passage – all the passages round the courtyard are by *Wyatville* – into the Ante-Library with the Green Library to the S, i.e. in the SE corner, and the Red Library to the N. Altogether Longleat has about 100,000 volumes. The ANTE-LIBRARY is the first room we meet with which was redecorated by *J. D. Crace* in the 1870s. The door by which one enters has an Italian marble surround. The ceiling is Italian in style and contains an original painting of the Veronese period purchased by the Marquess of Bath in Venice. In the GREEN LIBRARY are two early C19 English fireplaces, two of many purchased for a total of £750 spent in six years. One of the two fireplaces takes the place of the door from the hall into the library. Another of these early C19 fireplaces, this one less dainty but grander, with a big head in the centre of the frieze, is in the RED| LIBRARY. The ceiling by *Crace* is Jacobean, with broad interlaced geometrical panels of the usual type. N of the Red Library the LITTLE DINING ROOM. Italian marble door surrounds. Another early C19 fireplace, another *Crace* ceiling, and another Venetian painting. In the NE corner the LOWER DINING ROOM, with two early C19 fireplaces and a *Crace* ceiling with many small circles in thick relief.

Up to the first floor to the STATE DINING ROOM above the former room. The decoration again by *Crace*, with more Venetian paintings. The fireplaces have white, life-size maidens and date from Crace's time, but are not by him. Then, in the centre of the E front, the SALOON or GALLERY, 100 ft long. Here *Crace* was responsible for having the cyclopean chimneypiece copied from one in the Doge's Palace in Venice. He provided it with the relief ornament above. Also by Crace the alabaster surrounds of the doors and the ceiling. This however was designed by *George E. Fox* (1873–4), who also worked at Eastnor Castle in Herefordshire. The small paintings are by *Henry Scholz*. The DRAWING ROOM in the SE corner has another ceiling by *Fox* and *Crace* (1873). The paintings were copied by *Caldara* from the Library of St Mark, but the oblong painting in the bay and the frieze are genuine. The other decorations of the room are by *Crace* too, except for the door surrounds which were bought from a dealer. Finally the STAIRCASE made by *Wyatville*. It rises in one flight and returns on itself in two. The design of the balusters is Wrenish, the shallow groin-vault rather Soanian. In the centre a glazed octagonal lantern.

Not seen by the public in general are the following noteworthy features. In the newly formed LIVING ROOM in the W range (*see* above) a very important and impressive chimneypiece has been installed which had been tucked away in a minor position. Its style makes it likely that it dates from *c.*1563–6 and is by *Maynard*, who during those years worked on chimneypieces. It has no figures at all, but ornamental motifs, all decidedly over-sized, complicated swags hanging out of mouths on the wide posts l. and r. and rising foliage scrolls in the frieze. The room has the middle bay window on the W side, and the sides of the bay are provided with niches (cf. Edington). Another chimneypiece, of the time probably of that in the hall, is in the SERVANTS' HALL in the basement. This has two impressive caryatids, i.e. heads on tapering pilasters, and again foliage in the frieze. It seems to be by *Maynard* but may in fact be neo-Jacobean of *c.*1730–40. Finally, above the hall, BISHOP KEN'S LIBRARY, large and quite simple. This was made in the 1690s, when Bishop Ken of Bath and Wells had been deprived of his see.

The GROUNDS of Longleat were remodelled by *Capability Brown* in 1757–62 and again by *Repton* about 1790 etc. His Red Book is kept at the house. ORANGERY of seven bays plus two narrower ones l. and r. It faces the N front. The VASE to the r. comes from the grounds of the Crystal Palace. Close by a COVERED BRIDGE.

SOUTH GATE. Classical. Arched centre with attic and balustrade. One-bay wings of one storey.

BOATHOUSE, N side of Shearwater. Of 1791, part of *Repton*'s work. Four-centred arch, a window on corbels over.

STALLS FARM, ¼ m. from the house. By *W. Wilkinson*, 1859.

LONGSTREET *see* ENFORD

LOWER CHICKSGROVE MANOR *see* TISBURY

LOWER PICKWICK *see* CORSHAM, p. 176

LOWER WRAXALL *see* SOUTH WRAXALL

LUCKINGTON

8080

ST MARY AND ST ETHELBERT. S arcade of *c.*1200. Circular piers with trumpet-scallop capitals, circular abaci, double-chamfered pointed arches. Simple C13 doorway. Later C13 N tower. The two lancets to the N look fine and distinguished. The former bell-openings – two lights and a circle in plate tracery – are blocked; for a Perp top was put on with three-light bell-openings. Equally fine, though terribly over-restored, the E.E. s chapel. E window of three stepped lancets, s lancets, all shafted inside with detached shafts of Purbeck marble (cf. Sherston, Hullavington). Two capitals of the E window have stiff-leaf. To the chancel a two-bay arcade. Pier and responds circular, but hollowed out in four places to take Purbeck shafts. Coarse moulded capitals. Arches with two hollow chamfers. Perp nave and s aisle. C18 N porch, chancel of 1872. – REREDOS of stone. Two bays l. of the chancel arch, with plinths for statues. – PULPIT. Of stone. Is it C18? – STAINED GLASS. E window by *Kempe*. Date of death 1881. Also later *Kempe & Tower* glass. – PLATE. Cup and Cover, 1576; Paten, 1732; Flagon, 1760.

LUCKINGTON COURT. Queen Anne s front. Five bays, two storeys, elongated windows. The semicircular porch with Tuscan columns is later.

Several good C18 houses in the village, especially along the Bristol Road, e.g. PUMP HOUSE. Five bays, upright two-light windows. Door-hood on brackets. Next to it the former village LOCKUP.

LUCKNAM see COLERNE

2050

LUDGERSHALL

ST JAMES. A large, spreading church of flint and rubble. One Norman N window and a blocked Norman N doorway. Wide E.E. chancel, single small lancets to the N and s, three widely-spaced stepped lancets to the E. N chapel Perp, see the entrance arch with (re-set?) big heads. Large s chapel, its entrance arch Perp, but its exterior probably Elizabethan. The w tower carries the two dates 1672 and 1675. – SCULPTURE. A small fragment just E of the s doorway inside. It could be Anglo-Saxon. – PLATE. Paten, 1707. – MONUMENT. The monument to Sir
32b Richard Brydges † 1558 and his wife is one of the most important of its date in England, a date representing in terms of style no longer Early Renaissance, i.e. Henry VIII, and not yet Elizabethan. It is a very large monument and stands between nave and s chapel, with façades to both sides. Tomb-chest with shields to the N, kneeling children to the s. Two recumbent effigies; not specially good. Two bulbous columns l. and r.

Inside them short baluster columns, two to the S, two to the N, supporting a four-centred arch, coffered inside. An angel in relief flat against the soffit of the arch hovering over the deceased. Between each pair of balusters in the reveals of the arch strapwork cartouches, on the E side with the initials RB, on the W side with a shield. Attic with foliage frieze and a medallion with a bust in the middle. Top achievement with short pilasters and cherubs riding sea-monsters. Sir Richard Brydges was a brother of the first Lord Chandos, his wife a daughter of Sir William Spencer of Althorp.

CASTLE. Ludgershall was a royal castle. What remains of it is a crag of flint which was part of the Norman keep, and extensive earthworks. No window shapes can be recognized; only the brick back of a later fireplace.

CROSS, Castle Street. The complete head survives, an unusually big head, but not the shaft. The carvings on the four sides of the head are badly defaced. One can just recognize the Descent from the Cross and the Incredulity of St Thomas.

ALMSHOUSES (?). A row of eight cottages in Castle Street, just S of the castle. Two storeys, of brick, with the rare motif of pilasters in two tiers, i.e. probably later C17. Thatched roof with dormers.

LUGBURY *see* NETTLETON

LYDDINGTON *see* LIDDINGTON

LYDIARD MILLICENT

0080

ALL SAINTS. Dec S arcade, low, with octagonal piers and double-chamfered arches starting on big vertical pieces. Dec S aisle windows (E reticulated tracery). Single-framed nave roof. Perp W tower with Somerset tracery in the bell-openings, a parapet with openwork quatrefoils, and pinnacles. Perp chancel, much restored in 1871. Straight-headed N and S windows; ceiled wagon roof. – FONT. Circular, Norman, with interlaced arches. – PULPIT. Exceedingly elaborate Victorian Gothic. Carved by local boys under the supervision of the curate in 1862. – OVERDOOR. Naive Gothic, dated 1857. – STAINED GLASS. Bits in the heads of the N windows. – MONUMENT. Ferdinand Askew † 1783. Grey and white marble. With obelisk and urn. – CHURCHYARD CROSS. With the whole shaft.

LYDIARD TREGOZE

St MARY. Immediately behind Lydiard Park. Not a big church, but cram-full of enjoyable furnishings, richer than any other of similar size in the county. Externally Perp throughout, except for the simple Dec s doorway and s aisle E window. W tower with Somerset tracery in the bell-openings, a parapet with pierced quatrefoils and pinnacles. Embattled s aisle, s chapel, and s porch. Pretty Sanctus-bell turret at the E end of the nave. In the chancel E wall a three-light Perp window with two plain round-headed windows l. and r. added after the Reformation, perhaps *c.*1633 (*see* below). The arcades inside may both be pre-Perp. N of four bays; piers with four canted projections and no capitals at all, s of three bays with octagonal piers and double-chamfered arches. The nave has a wagon roof, and some of the supporter figures indeed look pre-Perp too. The chancel ceiling however is a coved blue sky with stars, again probably of *c.*1633; for at that time Sir John St John built or re-

42a

modelled the s chapel. The date appears outside. The arcade was replaced by classical columns (one now missing) carrying a straight entablature. Of the monument to him and his family more anon. – PULPIT. Jacobean. – FAMILY PEWS. Partly Jacobean, partly made up of C16 panels, partly Late Georgian (N aisle), partly Victorian. – SCREEN. Jacobean, with the Royal Arms. Surprisingly naive. – REREDOS. Small; C18. Painted with pillars and the figures of Moses and Aaron. – COMMUNION RAIL. A superb piece of luscious wrought iron work, of *c.*1700, and suggested to be Italian. However, clearly made for this position. – PAINTING. Much in various places, mostly defaced. On a N arcade arch C13 ornamental decoration. More in other places in the nave, beneath later work. On the N wall stories of St Thomas Becket. On the N wall of the s aisle St Christopher and a Christ of the Trades. On the nave E wall figures and busts round a former rood above the chancel arch. Also a head of Christ with the Crown of Thorns above the outer doorway of the s porch. – STAINED GLASS. Remains of C15 glass in nearly all windows, especially demi-figures of angels; also saints and small fragments. – Also in the E window large figures of the types and colours characteristic of Flemish work in England about 1633. – W window 1859 by *Alexander Gibbs*. Large figures, strident colours, bad. – PLATE. Chalice and Paten Cover, 1649; Flagon, 1650; Flagon, 1663; Paten, 1669.

MONUMENTS. Nearly all St Johns, and so many that Aubrey said 'it exceeds all the churches of this countie'. Many have their original RAILINGS, several also funeral HELMS. – Nicholas and wife, 1592 (s aisle). The couple kneel side by side, below an arch. Standing monument. – Family triptych, painted, with large figures inside, a family tree ('thirty-two ancestors') outside, an unusual memorial, but not unique (cf. Burford Shropshire, signed by *Melchior Salabuss*, 1588, Besford Worcestershire, 1605, Appleby Castle, 1646). The kneeling couple are Sir John † 1594 and his wife, the standing figure on the l. Sir John, his son, who put up the triptych in 1615 (inscription on the painted sarcophagus). The heraldic display is carried on into the C18. – Sir John and two wives, recumbent effigies, the wives slightly below him. Erected in 1634. All alabaster. Sumptuous eight-poster, the centre part raised in an arch. Top achievement and excellently carved little allegorical figures. Kneeling children in the side pieces at head and foot. More children (those who died) kneeling in medallions and reclining. – Sir Giles and Lady Mompesson † 1633. A delightful piece, full of pensive melancholy. The figures are seated in arched niches, in profile, facing one another. He holds a book, she a skull. Beneath the two we read: 'Siste Viator, Non ut figuras Phidiana confectas manu discutias. Defunctorum mores perlege.' – Edward, killed in the Civil War in the year 1645. Standing, gilt figure in armour below a baldacchino held open by two pages. An impressive composition, but alas bad craftsmanship. – John, Viscount St John, † 1749. By *Rysbrack*. Grey and white marble. Very richly carved arms below a tall grey obelisk. It was this John who rebuilt Lydiard Park.

LYDIARD PARK. Built in 1745-c.9, or rather remodelled from an older building which still appears clearly enough at the back. The remodelling was done for the second Viscount St John, just mentioned. As the architect, *Roger Morris* has been suggested. Stone, of two storeys and eleven bays, the first and last being raised as towers with pyramid roofs, a motif the early Palladians had taken from Inigo Jones's Wilton House and were very fond of (Holkham, Hagley, etc.). The s side is the show-side. Three-bay pediment and balustrade. Doorway with Tuscan columns, well carved metope frieze, and pediment. Otherwise a minimum of enrichment. Pediments above the first and last ground-floor windows, straight architraves above the third and ninth. Similar muted accents on the seven-bay E side. The interior is quite excellently decorated, with equally fine workmanship in stucco, wood, and stone, yet discreet throughout. Entrance hall with coved ceiling. The chief decoration of the wooden wall panels is heads and garlands – in the Kentian style. The climax, as usual, the overmantel. Library on the l. with original bookcases, and library busts in thin open pediments. Again a fine overmantel. Ceiling panels in geometrical patterns with stuccoed frames. Dining Room on the r. with alcove separated by Ionic columns, Drawing Room with a chimneypiece with putto termini in profile. Simple ceiling panels, the frames decorated with fruit. State Bedroom divided in two by a pair of Corinthian columns. The outer part has a ceiling in Rococo, not in Kentian, forms. Above the former bed the head of the Sun in rays. N of the bedroom small apsed chapel. Pretty staircase at the back with three partly twisted balusters to each step.

CAN COURT, 2 m. S. Tall gabled Elizabethan house with mullioned windows. The front symmetrical: only three bays under two gables, the centre being a lower gabled porch.

SAXON CEMETERY, on Basset Down. Discovered when a pleasure garden was laid out in 1922. Finds included iron spearheads, knives, and shield bosses and beads of glass and amber.

0070

LYNEHAM

ST MICHAEL. Immediately by the airfield, but the porch sheltered by an enormous yew tree. Big chancel by *Butterfield*, 1860. Perp nave, much re-done. Short W tower; Perp. The W doorway and also the S doorway indicate an Early Perp, C14, date. Perp N aisle, the arcade with piers with four shafts and four hollows. A very bleak nave roof, probably of 1860. – ROOD SCREEN. Perp, with one-light divisions. – TOWER SCREEN. Jacobean, with slender balusters and little arches. – MONUMENTS. Heneage Walker † 1731. A surprisingly grand and pure piece. Standing wall-monument of white and grey streaked marble. Two tall Corinthian columns and an open segmental pediment with two desperate putti on it. – John Walker Heneage † 1806. By *King* of Bath. With a mourning woman by a broken column.

S of HILLOCKS WOOD the remains of a motte and bailey EARTHWORK (HR).

0040

MADDINGTON

ST MARY. Situated in the middle of Shrewton. Low W tower, Perp above, but Dec – see the arch to the nave – below. Dec S

arcade of five bays, the last two narrower in consideration of a
s transept. Octagonal piers, double-chamfered arches. A small
w lancet indicating the narrowness of the original (pre-Dec?)
aisle. Chancel rebuilt in 1852. The roof was remade in the C17.
On a stone bracket the date 1603, but on a stucco display on the
w wall 1637. – COMMUNION RAIL. Later C17. Alternating
dumb-bell balusters and flat pierced balusters. Now the s
transept screen.

MADDINGTON VICARAGE and MADDINGTON FARM. *See*
Shrewton.

MAIDEN BRADLEY

8030

ALL SAINTS. Immediately w of Bradley House. The earliest
evidence in the church seems to be the N arcade of three bays.
Square, slightly chamfered piers, only slightly chamfered
arches. But there are no positive Norman features visible. Then
the s arcade. This has two bays of continuous double chamfer,
i.e. is probably early C14, and in addition a narrow w bay and
a narrow E bay. The latter is matched by just such an added N
bay. Both have typical early C14 mouldings. The w tower also
seems to have started Dec. The w window is Victorian. Top
parts Perp. Higher stair-turret with openwork quatrefoiled
parapet and pinnacles. Perp s porch with gargoyles. The
chancel E window is still in an early C19 state. In 1845 the
church was called lately restored. – FONT. Square, of Purbeck
marble, of the usual type with very flat blank arches. The
arches are mostly worn away. – FONT COVER. Jacobean,
simple, of light volutes. – PULPIT. Simple; Jacobean. – STALLS
with Jacobean pieces. – BOX PEWS. C17, with little shell-tops
on the ends instead of knobs. – STAINED GLASS. In the SE
window of the s aisle fragments: C14 and C16. – PLATE. Elizabethan Paten Cover; Flagon, 1636; Paten, 1674. – MONU-
MENT. Sir Edward Seymour † 1707. By *Rysbrack*, 1728, but 52
called in the inscription erected 1730. The semi-reclining
figure in contemporary dress is extremely elegant. Sumptuous
architectural background with pediment with reclining putti
and a top pediment of the curly open kind.

BRADLEY HOUSE. The house is a fragment of the great Seymour
mansion illustrated in *Vitruvius Britannicus*, vol. II, i.e. in
1717, and largely pulled down in 1821. The mansion consisted
of three ranges round a forecourt facing E, and wings extending
N and s from the E ends and the w ends of this main composi-
sition, and two extending w. What remains corresponds to the

recessed centrepiece of the composition and the wing going s
from this. The window surrounds would fit an early c 18 date.
The heraldic devices in the ground-floor pediments are of
course Victorian, as is the porch. The wing towards the w is
recent. Fine fireplaces of the late c 18, probably from other
parts of the mansion.

PRIORY FARM. First a Leper Hospital, then, in 1190, a priory
of Augustinian Canons. All that survives is an L-shaped
building of the outer, non-claustral ranges. In the longer range
a gateway near the e end and two upper doorways, and in both
ranges windows and roofs. The date is late medieval.

THE STORES, in the village. c 17. Of three bays, with symmetrical
transomed three-light windows. Inside, a sturdy staircase with
vertically symmetrical balusters. On the ground floor a simple
fireplace, perhaps older than the front, on the first floor a fine,
probably Elizabethan one, i.e. also older than the front. Big
forms, rich foliage, top volutes.

MALMESBURY

9080

A prosperous weaving town until the c 18, but dominantly the
seat of the abbey, which towers over all else, especially as the
town lies on a hill.

THE ABBEY

INTRODUCTION. The abbey of Malmesbury was founded in the
c 7, burnt in the early c 9, rebuilt, and burnt again in 1042.
Then for a hundred years no new building was begun. The
present buildings must be of *c.*1160–70, but we have no docu-
mentary evidence. The chief attraction of the abbey was the
shrine of St Aldhelm. The church was 240 ft long. In its
original form it had nave and aisles, transepts with an e chapel
to each, a crossing with a tower which in the c 14 received a
spire, a 'mighty piramis', as Leland calls it, taller than Salisbury spire, a chancel, and an ambulatory with three radiating
chapels at the e end. They were replaced by an extension with
a small pair of e transepts and a long straight-ended Lady
Chapel in the later c 13. In the late c 14 a big square w tower
was erected on the two w bays of the nave. With these two
towers, and lying so majestically on the hill, Malmesbury must
have looked somewhat as Ely does now. The crossing tower
fell 'in hominum memoria', as Leland says about 1530, the
w tower shortly after Leland's time. With the Dissolution
everything from the crossing eastward was allowed to disap-

pear. The nave however was saved by William Stumpe of the Abbey House (*see* p. 294) and given to the town to become the parish church. The damaged W parts were walled off, and this is more or less as the church presents itself now. It may be added that in 1844 it presented itself very differently. The *Ecclesiologist* writes that the nave is 'a hovel' and 'filthy', and that a horse had been seen feeding out of a piscina. C19 restorers have after all helped things on.

EXTERIOR. Only half of the Norman W front stands. There was only one doorway. It had shafts in two orders and in the arch medallions (see S porch), probably with the Signs of the Zodiac and the Labours of the Months. To its r. and round the corner to the S big frieze of intersected arches at ground level. Flat, nook-shafted buttresses. At the corner a big turret. Along the upper part of the façade and the turret blank arcading, mostly with continuous mouldings, some with decorated shafts. Along the S side Perp aisle windows, mostly in Norman shafted surrounds. They are interrupted by two big three-light Dec windows with curious tracery (an incomplete cinquefoil in the head). Clerestory with very tall three-light Dec windows. Flying buttresses to support the C14 vault. Tall pinnacles. Band of paterae l. and r. of the jambs of the easternmost windows. They went up outside the jambs and seem to have turned the semicircle of the Norman clerestory window heads.

The SOUTH PORCH is the *chef d'œuvre* of Malmesbury, 10a among the best pieces of Norman sculpture and decoration in England. A plain outer arch shelters the Norman arch of eight continuous orders, i.e. without any capitals to separate jambs and arch. Five of the orders have bands of trails or more geometrical running patterns, the second, fourth, and sixth entwined beaded trails forming almond-shaped medallions which contain figure sculpture. The figures are badly defaced, but one can still see what they represented. The scenes on the arch have been set out as follows by the late Professor Saxl:

1. Creation of Adam	God and Noah	Annunciation
2. Creation of Eve	Building the Ark	Nativity
3. God's Warning	Noah in the Ark	Annunciation to the Shepherds and Journey of the Magi
4. Fall	Sacrifice of Isaac	Adoration of the Magi
5. Adam and Eve hiding	Abraham holding the ram	Presentation in the Temple

10

6. God calls Adam	God shows the stars to Abraham	Baptism of Christ
7. Expulsion from Paradise	Burning Bush	Entry into Jerusalem
8. Angel giving the spade to Adam and the distaff to Eve	Moses striking the rock	Last Supper
9. Adam delving and Eve spinning	Moses receiving the tables of the law	Christ crucified
10. Eve with a child	Samson and the lion	Entombment
11. Cain's Murder (or Death?)	Samson and the Gates of Gaza	Resurrection
12.	Samson pulls down the columns	Ascension
13.	David rescues the lamb from the lion	Pentecost
14.	David and Goliath	

The typological relations between Old and New Testament are clear enough in such cases as the Gates of Gaza and the Resurrection, or Moses striking the rock and the Last Supper. On the jambs less is recognizable, but there certainly were Virtues combating Vices. As regards style, the figures were extremely elongated and agile. The drapery folds surround the belly and leave it as a round, oval, or almond-shaped convex area. The medallion motifs seem to be inspired by the west of France, especially such churches as Aulnay. However, the continuous mouldings which occur here and, as will be seen, in other places at Malmesbury are an English, particularly a West Country, speciality. In other countries they do not become usual until the High Gothic period was over, i.e. nearly two hundred years later. Inside the porch, above some uninspired blank arcading, are two lunettes facing each other, each with six seated apostles and an angel flying horizontally above their heads. The figures are again very elongated, but whereas the use of the side walls of a porch for scenes is South-West French (Moissac, Souillac), the style of the figures depends on that of Burgundy about 1130, and the quality approaches that of Autun. In England the nearest parallel is one panel on the w front of Lincoln Cathedral, about twenty years earlier than Malmesbury. Perhaps it ought to be remembered that Roger Bishop of Sarum was the uncle of Alexander Bishop of Lincoln, under whom the figure frieze of the w

front of Lincoln was carved. The inner doorway has a tympanum with Christ in an almond-shaped glory held by two
flying angels, especially Autun-like. The jambs and arch have
three bands of decoration, again continuous, but without
figures. The vault is of 1905. Perp parapet outside with a wavy
line and openwork trefoils inside. Now the N side. The nave
was walled off after the W tower had fallen but received its
dignified W window only about 1830 (designed by *Goodridge*).
The N side of the church here is really the interior exposed and
much stabilized and restored. The cloister lay on this side (*see
below*). Above the cloister shafted Norman windows, interrupted by one tall Dec window not in line with the Dec windows
of the S side. In the tracery big pointed trefoil, barbed. Fine
Norman doorway into the cloister, with a frieze of standing
palmettes. Later the size of the portal was reduced and a cusped
and subcusped doorway set in. The style looks *c*.1300. Of the
N transept hardly anything remains. So to the S transept. Two
tiers of shafted Norman windows. Nothing beyond that
remains sufficiently to help in understanding the outside.

INTERIOR. What little can be said of the E parts is now all
exterior, though it was interior. Three of the huge crossing
arches are upright. On the NE pier the chancel system can just
be recognized. Arcade respond with shafts with two-scalloped
capitals. What the free-standing piers of the chancel were like
we cannot of course say, but there is no reason to assume that
they were different from those in the nave. Decorated frieze at
gallery sill level. Gallery with capitals of several scallops and
zigzag in the arch. Wall-passage above. The crossing received
a later vault (probably C14, *see below*). So did the N and S
transepts. The inner W wall of the S transept shows wall arcading, not intersecting, mast-like shafts to the ceiling, windows,
as we have seen, in three tiers, and a clerestory with a tripartite
arrangement, the side parts lower and with a continuous roll
moulding. Blocked opening (also in the N transept) of the
former aisle. The arch is pointed, and on that more will be said.
Blocked opening into the aisle gallery with round arch. Some
of this is also recognizable in the N transept.

Now we can read on inside. The system remains the same. 9
The responds are like those of the chancel. The piers however
are round, very substantial, and not tall. Circular, multi-
scalloped capitals. Just one capital on the S side has in the abacus
small upright palmettes. The arches are all pointed, and that is
in *c*.1160–70 a remarkably early case. It would be twice as

remarkable if it could be regarded as making Malmesbury Gothic. But that is not so. For one thing pointed arches had already occurred in the Durham nave vaults about 1130. Moreover they are perfectly normal, for arcade arches especially, in the Burgundian Romanesque, e.g. of Autun, and also in other parts of France. And that the general tenor of Malmesbury is Norman, i.e. Romanesque, no one would deny. The arcade arches have roll mouldings with billet and with the zigzag we saw in the chancel. Hood-moulds with billets on stops in the shape of animal heads. At the apexes also heads. The billet of the roll moulding changes to little triangles in the second bay. From the third bay the rolls are plain. The gallery has a sill course with a curious ornament of Ts alternatingly upright and reversed. This goes on for three bays on the s side, only in the first on the N. Then the course is plain. Each bay has a triple opening under one round arch. Decorated scallop capitals. The main arch has zigzag at r. angles to the wall surface. The gallery is replaced in one s bay by an oratory, like a theatre box, perhaps for the abbot to watch services. Or what else can its purpose have been? Brakspear suggests it may have held an organ and refers to the gallery at Exeter with its musician angels. The Norman clerestory is no longer recognizable, and the vaulting-shafts are also probably cut down from the Norman mast-shape to the present indistinctly compound shape.The shafts carry a lierne-vault which must be early, i.e. early C14, because the big bosses still have naturalistic foliage. The lierne pattern is extremely interesting. In plan it is four sub-bays to each bay, each part with diagonal ribs, i.e. basically eight transverse lozenges. This is obtained by running two longitudinal ribs parallel with the ridge rib half-way up. But in reality no one can see that, as it is of course all folded to follow the curvature of the vault. Many foliage bosses, and a few heads. The clerestory windows are very tall, as we have already seen, and they are shafted.

The aisles support the story of the nave in their details. Blind arcading, a flat band of zigzag above it. Windows shafted inside too. Pointed transverse arches. But here we have also rib-vaulting of c.1160–70. Ribs of one main and thin subsidiary rolls.

FURNISHINGS. FONT. Heavy C18 baluster with fluted bowl. – PULPITUM, running between nave and crossing. A solid wall with a middle entrance, now hidden. The fleuron frieze at the top with the arms of Henry VIII is visible. One bay and a little W of it was the rood screen. – STALLS. 1928, in the Early

Renaissance style. – PULPIT. Also neo-Early Renaissance. –
COMMUNION RAIL. Of *c*.1700, with twisted balusters. –
SCREENS. The two Perp stone screens to the E ends of the two
aisles are said to have come from the church of St Paul. –
WOODWORK. In the W wall there are a number of panels of
the Early Renaissance. – TILES. With squirrels, turkey, dog,
rabbit, foliage, arms; in a case on the N wall and on the wall
near by. – PAINTING. Big oil painting of the Resurrection of
Lazarus, by an Italian late-C16 Mannerist. – PLATE. Cup, 1575;
Chalice, 1631; Paten, 1702. – Also Chalice from St Mary
Westport, 1654. – MONUMENT. Perp tomb-chest of King
Athelstan. Plain chest, recumbent effigy, his head below a heavy
traceried canopy. The original head was removed at an unknown date and later replaced.

THE PRECINCT. The CLOISTER lay to the N of the church,
an unusual arrangement, but one paralleled at Gloucester,
Lacock, Stanley, and Bradenstoke. The cloister was remodelled
in the C15 with fan-vaults (cf. Gloucester), and fragments of
the stonework are now assembled in the garden of Abbey
House. The chapter house was oblong. The refectory lay to
the N, and it was, in an entirely uncommon way, continued
to the NE by the dormitory. That is how the reredorter, i.e.
the lavatories, can be where they are (*see* Abbey House, p.
294). The guest house lay to the NW of the W range (*see* Bell
Hotel, p. 295).

THE TOWN

ST PAUL. Only the W tower stands, unbuttressed above. Broach
spire with two tiers of tiny lucarnes.

ST MARY, Westport. Now St Mary's Hall. Rebuilt *c*.1670–80.
Exterior all with gothicized windows, interior entirely altered.
The S arcade of four bays has continuous single-chamfered
mouldings and dates from *c*.1860.

MARKET CROSS. One of the finest in England. Built about 1500.
Octagonal, 41 ft high. Four-centred arches. Spandrels with
leaves. Battlements. Flying buttresses carry a kind of lantern
with statuettes of saints and the Crucifixion. Inside a tierceron-
vault. What was the purpose of such a structure? Leland says
'for poore folkes to stande dry when rayne cummeth'.

PERAMBULATION. Naturally one will start by the Market Cross
and the ABBEY GATEWAY. This is a humble building; of
c.1800, it seems. Windows with Y-tracery. To the NE into a
maze with a few interesting houses, notably ST MICHAEL'S

HOUSE, dated 1796, with a door lintel with a head and two garlands which can hardly belong, the OLD BREWERY, with a ground floor open with coarse columns, and a hipped roof, and the OLD BREWERY HOUSE, dated 1672, but a composite affair. Here access also to ABBEY HOUSE, the large mansion built by William Stumpe (*see* above) who died in 1552. He was a prosperous clothier. His son was knighted; of his great-grand-daughters, three were married to the Earls of Suffolk, Lincoln, and Rutland. The house in its present appearance is no doubt somewhat later than Stumpe's death. Plan with two even projecting wings. Gables and mullioned windows. Inside in the basement, i.e. towards the river still at ground level, the REREDORTER of the abbey with semi-octagonal responds carrying single-chamfered ribs and fine tall windows with cinquefoiled rere-arches. In the house one panelled room with an Elizabethan overmantel with funny caryatids.

To the E from the Market Cross into OXFORD STREET, where, facing us, TOWER HOUSE with a tall square tower of the late C19 (built for star-gazing) and as the garage roof a C15 roof with tie-beams and two tiers of wind-braces. N from here HOLLOWAY, with fragments of the old walls, S from here by Cross Hayes Lane to the opening called CROSS HAYES. The best houses are in the SE corner: No. 28, early C18, ashlar-faced, of three bays with segment-headed windows. Note the arcading on the l. part of the stables. No. 32 is of rubble, C18, of five bays with a one-bay pediment. Further S from here SILVER STREET, where, just where the street starts descending steeply, CULVER HOUSE lies back on the r. Gabled with mullioned windows. All this is parallel to the High Street, which we must now walk down from the Market Cross.

The first good building in the HIGH STREET is No. 10, early C18, of dark brick with stone quoins. Five bays, three storeys. The middle windows arched. Doorway at the r. end with open curly pediment on brackets. Top balustrade. On the other side the KING'S ARMS, with a timber-framed long back wing. No. 46 is dated 1671 and has three steep gables and mullioned windows. Then more Georgian houses, e.g. No. 63, of three bays, rubble and ashlar dressings with a good doorway. Then the High Street turns l. and KING'S WALL starts to the r. It commemorates the town walls. A little way down ATHELSTAN'S HOUSE, a swagger house with an early C18 body and a late C17 wing. The latter is of five bays and has stone cross-windows, the former of three bays, tall, with segment-headed windows, a doorway with a shell-hood, a round-arched middle window, and a top balustrade.

At the foot of the High Street, i.e. by the river, the ST JOHN'S ALMSHOUSE, incorporating a re-set arch of the Hospital of St John. Late C12, pointed, the capitals of the former shafts with leaves, one order of the arch with a Late Norman pattern of hexagons with inserted lozenges. Above a blank arch with late C12 shafts and the arch itself standing on long vertical pieces. The whole probably interfered with. The almshouses were founded in 1694. Simple, gabled, of two low storeys. Through an archway N of the almshouses to the former COURT HOUSE, humble, one-storeyed (with the panelling and balustrade preserved inside; MHLG). Further out a fine big textile MILL. Late C18, L-shaped, of four storeys, with eight bays in each wing, the windows segment-headed, broad and of two lights. A later range detached a little back. Yet further out, on the Chippenham Road, THE PRIORY, Georgian, red brick, of three bays and two and a half storeys. The half storey is probably later – see the position of the pediment. Finally, another bit on, on the other side, BARTON HILL HOUSE, built shortly after 1846. Gabled Tudor.

Back all the way to the Market Cross, and now to the E. First by St Paul's Tower (see above) and the abbey churchyard to the BELL HOTEL, which incorporates some C13 walling of the abbey GUEST HOUSE. The Bell Hotel used to be called the Castle Hotel, and it is here that one assumes the CASTLE of Malmesbury to have been situated which, according to William of Malmesbury, was built by Bishop Roger and lay 'in the very cemetery of the church, hardly a stone's throw away'. Now, past the Bell Hotel, past the BAPTIST CHAPEL of 1802 (pointed windows, but a doorway with a Tuscan porch), and past AVON HOUSE (three bays, two and a half storeys, doorway with fluted pilasters and a broken pediment; attached a nice iron balcony). So to The Triangle and then either on the Bristol Road to the former WORKHOUSE, of 1837–8, twenty-seven bays, the middle three raised by one storey, segment-headed windows, or up St Mary's Street, past St Mary's Hall (*see* above), to HORSEFAIR, where, on the W side, a row of C17 cottages with five gables.

WHITCHURCH FARMHOUSE, ⅝ m. NE. C17. Flat front with nearly symmetrical three- and four-light mullioned windows. The pediment must be an C18 addition.

MILBOURNE HOUSE, ¾ m. ENE. C17. Big, quite irregular, gabled, with mullioned windows.

COLE PARK, 1½ m. s. Probably *c.*1775–6 in its main fronts. To the w five bays, two storeys, parapet, and hipped roof. Doorway with Tuscan columns and pediment. The s elevation with two canted bays. Two humbler brick outbuildings in front at an angle. Gatepost between them.

1050

MANNINGFORD ABBOTS

CHURCH. 1864 by *S. B. Gabriel.* Nave and double bellcote and chancel. In the E.E. style. – PLATE. Chalice of the second half of the C15; Paten Cover, Elizabethan; Flagon, given in 1782.
OLD RECTORY. Under construction in 1812. Brick; two storeys. The front has a big bow window and two windows each side of it. Hipped, slated roof. Ample offices behind, and at r. angles, surprisingly ample stabling, with two coach doors and circular windows above the normal ones. The rector at the time was the Rev. Francis B. Astley.

1050

MANNINGFORD BOHUN

ALL SAINTS, I m. SE of Woodborough Church. 1859 by *N. E. Clacey.* Nave with bellcote and chancel. The facing stone arranged crazy-paving fashion. Windows in the late C13 style.

1050

MANNINGFORD BRUCE

ST PETER. A very completely preserved Early Norman church. Flint laid consistently herringbone-wise. Nave, chancel, and apse. In the apse two original windows, in the nave (N) one. Plain N and s doorways. The w window of three stepped lancet lights C14. Another C14 window in the chancel. Chancel arch Norman, the impost moulding not at all primitive, and the V-joints bonding the two rings of voussoir stones together not at all primitive either. Ponting observed them and called them unique. *Pearson* restored the church in 1882. Due to him is the pretty bell-turret with traceried bell-openings and a lead spire and the round-arched wagon roof of the nave. Due to him also the quite unusual and very successful boarded ceiling of chancel and apse, the pattern being the herringbone pattern of parquet. Did Pearson also introduce the archaeologically correct painted patterns in chancel and apse – or are they original (stylized crockets in pairs, single flowers)? – REREDOS. Designed by *Pearson* (not so happy) and made by *Clayton & Bell.* – PLATE. Chalice, *c.*1574.

MARDEN

0050

ALL SAINTS. Lavish Norman S doorway with one order of shafts, zigzags, an angular chain, a blank tympanum, a kind of crenellation in the hood-mould. Slightly depressed Norman chancel arch. Scalloped capitals, zigzag in the arch, also at r. angles to the wall surface. Tall Perp w tower with higher stair-turret. Rebuilt in 1885 by *Ponting* of Marlborough. Diagonal buttresses with two tiers of buttress-shafts and pinnacles against them in relief. Bell-openings of two lights under a big ogee gable. Nave and chancel externally all Ponting's. Inside good head-corbels for the nave roof. – PULPIT. Jacobean, with back panel and tester. – STAINED GLASS. One N window by *J. & M. Kettlewell*, 1958. St Peter and St Paul. Good, elongated Expressionist figures, strong but subtle colourings. – PLATE. Chalice, given in 1812.

MARDEN MANOR HOUSE. Late C18, of three bays, generously spaced, and two storeys. Rendered. The upper windows are set in segmental arches. Porch of pairs of Tuscan columns.

NE of the village is a large, roughly oval EARTHWORK with external bank and ditch enlosing an area of 50 acres. The ditch has a breadth of 45 ft and lies $3\frac{1}{2}$ ft below the surrounding level of the land. Within the monument was an enormous round barrow destroyed in the C18. The Marden circle, with its external bank, is tentatively included among the British henge monuments, and surface finds of Late Neolithic flint artefacts would tend to corroborate this view, although the problem can only be resolved by excavation.

MARKET LAVINGTON

0050

ST MARY. Mostly of the later Middle Ages,[*] but the chancel E.E., late C13, see the s windows of two lights with bar tracery and the nicely moulded doorway into the vestry. To its r. a square peep-hole. The vestry can also be entered from the w by a doorway with a prettily cinquecusped arch. Dec arcades of three bays, perhaps converted from Norman ones, square, only slightly bevelled piers, double-chamfered arches dying into them. Of the same Dec date the N aisle w window and the charming N windows, straight-headed, of three lights with trefoils above ogee lights. Inside, the piscina and the doorway to

[*] Though small Norman bits have been built into the s porch and the E wall. They were found in 1862, at the time of the restoration by *Ewan Christian*.

the rood-stair are ogee-headed too. A chantry was founded in the church in 1349. This is probably the part of the church it refers to. The s porch entrance, curiously heavy, seems to be Dec as well and so may be the small trefoiled clerestory windows. Perp s windows and w tower. The tower has a shallow giant w niche for doorway and windows. The jambs of the niche are panelled. – PLATE. Chalice with Paten Cover and Paten, 1728; Flagon, 1732; Almsdish, 1741. – MONUMENT. Thomas Sainsbury, 1797 by *Flaxman*. Woman weeping, leaning on a pillar – a moving gesture.

MANOR HOUSE, ⅝ m. WNW. 1865 by *Ewan Christian*. Large, irregular, of brick, in the Tudor style, red with vitrified diapers.

In CHURCH STREET, s of the church, a three-bay stone house with angle pilasters and a handsome classical string-course across. E of the church the VICARAGE, Early Georgian, of five bays, brick, with segment-headed windows.

CLYFFE HALL, ½ m. w. A fine Early Georgian garden front. Five bays, two storeys, and lower later wings. The old part has quoins of even length and the three-bay centre giant fluted Corinthian pilasters and a pediment. Porch of fluted Ionic columns with a bulgy frieze. The other side of the house has been considerably altered by *Sir Ernest Newton* in 1904. By him the entrance motif of porch, Venetian window and oval window over, and perhaps also the three-bay top pediment and the wings.

Opposite a new SECONDARY SCHOOL is being built at the time of writing (County Architect *F. I. Bowden*).

MARLBOROUGH

Marlborough is one spectacularly long and wide High Street running parallel to the river Kennet. The two churches stand one in an elevated position near the E end, the other right at the w end of the High Street. The College is quite separate and not normally visible. The Royal Castle has disappeared; so have the Gilbertine Priory and the house of the Carmelite Friars. There was a great fire in 1653, and no notable domestic architecture exists of before the late C17. Nearly all that matters is Georgian.

ST MARY. In an elevated position E of the E end of the High Street. The church was founded in 1160.* Big re-set Norman doorway in the w tower. One order of colonnettes, zigzag in

---

* Though the churches of Marlborough are mentioned in 1091.

jambs and arch. Norman also was the N arcade which was removed after the fire in 1653. Only the semicircular w respond remains, with scalloped semicircular capital. More Norman fragments in the N wall of the N aisle (corbel-table heads). Perp w tower, ashlar-faced. The N and s sides are also ashlar-faced and have Perp windows. The N side was heightened after the fire of 1653. At the same time the eminently interesting s arcade 42b was built, of five bays, with Tuscan columns carrying free classical capitals which at first sight look early c20. The chancel was rebuilt in 1874 by *Street*. – PLATE. Chalice, 1657; Paten, 1690.

ST PETER AND ST PAUL. w end of the High Street. All Perp. sw tower, ashlar-faced, with bleak polygonal pinnacles renewed in the c18. Aisle windows of three lights. The w bays of the N aisle canted. Five-light nave w window. Tierceron-vaulted s porch and tierceron-vaulted chancel with concave-sided lozenges instead of bosses. It is rare for Perp chancels of parish churches to be vaulted. The chancel was remodelled by *T. H. Wyatt* in 1862–3. Very coloured E wall, tile-paving. – STAINED GLASS. E and s aisle E windows probably of Wyatt's time. – MONUMENTS. Three children of Sir Nicholas Hyde, all † January and February 1626. Tablet with small kneeling figures. – Many Georgian tablets. – Marianne Maurice † 1840. Arrangement of Roman altar, drapery, Bible, chalice, cross, and a hand with lilies. By *Ternouth*, said to be from a design of *Chantrey*.

TOWN HALL. 1901–2 by *C. E. Ponting*. Brick and stone. At the E end of the High Street. Towards it porch, bay, balcony, and fancy gable, all stone-faced. The rest nicely domestic, with hipped roof and cupola. The style generally later c17.*

GRAMMAR SCHOOL, London Road. By *Silcock & Reay*, 1905. Small and in a nice, lively Neo-Georgian.‡

CHILDREN'S CONVALESCENT HOSPITAL (former WORK-HOUSE), Common. Completed 1837 by *Sir G. G. Scott*, when he was young. Two storeys; of stone. Front with five-bay pediment. Two symmetrical courtyards behind. Recent additions by *Stillman & Eastwick-Field*, 1955–7.

PERAMBULATION. It is best to start from St Peter and the College, on which later. The HIGH STREET begins nicely and 3a uneventfully with small houses to the N and s of St Peter. Then

---

* REGALIA. Two Maces, 1652.

‡ A new Grammar School has been built on the hill to the s (end of Orchard Road), 1962 by the County Architect's Department (County Architect *F. I. Bowden*).

the street unites into a broad and long band. The first house of
higher value is WYKEHAM HOUSE on the s side, dated 1761.
Blue brick and red brick trim. Pedimented doorway on Roman
Doric columns. Then the IVY HOUSE HOTEL, very pretty
mid-Georgian. Pedimented doorway. On the first floor two
Venetian and one arched window. The MERLIN TEA ROOMS
have an early C18 front of three storeys, segment-headed
windows, and a prominent centre bay with arched windows
flanked by coupled pilasters in two orders, Doric and Ionic.
(C17 staircase with turned balusters. MHLG) Nos 31–33 are
of the C17, lower and gabled. Opposite the GEORGIAN
RESTAURANT, Georgian, of six bays and three storeys. Nice
porch on thin shafts. The front is tile-hung, and that is now
going to be the distinguishing feature of the Marlborough
houses. A few houses further on another three-storeyed tile-
hung house, of the early C18, long, with quoins of even length.
Then again on the other side the PRIORY, back from the street,
in its grounds. It is of c.1820, and it has Gothick windows.
One window to the E, however, may come from the Carmelite
Friary. Then the POLLY TEA ROOMS, early C18, of brick
chequer, with a hipped roof and slender windows. Nice Late
Georgian bow-fronted shop-window round the corner. Next
to this a house dated 1776, of blue brick with red trim and
all tripartite windows. Back to the N side for the CASTLE AND
BALL HOTEL, C17,* with three gables, tile-hung, and with a
Georgian colonnade along the ground floor. Further on the
MARLBOROUGH GUEST HOUSE with canted bay windows
treated as if they were Venetian windows. On the N side again
some gabled houses with tile-hung fronts. The front of the first
floor of W. H. SMITH's premises is a picturesque assembly of
motifs. (Inside, a good staircase and a panelled room.) Then,
on the s side, the AILESBURY ARMS HOTEL, Late Georgian,
with a porch of four pairs of (recent) fancy columns. On the r.
archway into the yard. Altogether many houses on the s side of
the High Street have archways to yards or lanes down towards
the river Kennet. To the E of the hotel an early C18 house of
four bays with a chequered brick wall, then a group of four
two-bay houses, all tile-hung, and dated 1739. With that the
Town Hall is reached. To its N one more house worth looking at,
of four bays, with all first-floor windows Venetian, all second-
floor windows tripartite. The angle bays are actually canted bay
windows.

* A stone with the date 1750 in the yard.

From the Town Hall the PARADE runs s. At its start the BEAR
INN, by *Crickmay* of Weymouth, late C19, gay, with gables
and a characteristic cartouche. KINGSBURY STREET runs N,
up the hill. First some gabled C17 houses, then across, before
the street narrows, Nos. 10 and 11, a mid-Georgian double
house. Five bays, blue bricks with red trim. The first and last
bays with a pediment and a Venetian window. Two later C18
porches with thin columns. Higher up KINGSBURY HILL
HOUSE. Of chequered brick with quoins. Three wide bays.
Centre bay also with quoins and with a pediment. Originally
the house must have had seven bays. The façade in this form
was probably of *c*.1700. The fenestration seems Late Georgian.
Back to the Town Hall and on to the E to THE GREEN, or
from Kingsbury Street by Silverless Street, a street with plenty
of attractive cottages. The same holds of The Green, but few
houses need special mention. Among them is the COUNCIL
OFFICES, big, along the top side of the sloping Green.
Chequered brick. Seven bays, two and a half storeys, plain,
with a Doric porch with open pediment and an urn. Staircase
with thin twisted balusters. On the E side No. 10 of *c*.1830, of
stone, with a porch of four thin Roman Doric columns. The
SE corner of the Green is closed, which is a good effect. Coming
from the E the attraction of the Green is that it holds no antici-
pation at all of the High Street. Further E nice houses along St
Martin's, and finally, outside the town (and in fact in the parish
of Mildenhall), POULTON HOUSE, the most perfect house of
Marlborough. 1706 is the date. The house is of brick chequered.
Seven bays, two storeys, with a three-bay pediment, a hipped
roof, and quoins. Doorway with an open segmental pediment
on brackets. The end wall of the entrance hall is divided in two.
The staircase with two twisted balusters to the step starts on
the l., an arched doorway on the r., as parts of one composition.
The arch is depressed. The ceiling of the staircase has gorgeous
stuccowork in the late-C17 tradition: an outer frieze of vine,
an inner oval of other fruit, all modelled freehand. Southwards
from the Green BARN STREET. Nos 5–8 a nice group of
terraced houses. At the bottom end on the E side a big early C19
house of five bays with a porch with Tuscan columns. From
here LONDON ROAD, i.e. the A 4, leads E. Along it No. 40,
ALBANY COTTAGE, brick, of three bays, with funny flint
bands round the Gothick windows. Much further out ($\frac{3}{4}$ m.)
FOREST HILL LODGE, probably a lodge of Savernake
Forest, i.e. Tottenham Park. Small, Gothick, and very pretty.

Three by two bays. One and a half storeys. With pointed and quatrefoil windows. Quoins of flint. Cresting with little pinnacles.

MARLBOROUGH COLLEGE

The College is an entirely different story. Though its main entrances are only a few yards from St Peter, the extensive buildings take no part in the town, the very opposite of, for example, Eton. The College was established only in 1845, but it took over an inheritance equally interesting historically and architecturally.

Marlborough possessed a Norman royal castle, first with timber, later – at the latest from 1175 – with stone buildings. Nothing survives of this except the MOUND or motte to the NW of the old buildings of the College. This is 60 ft high. The castle remained in use until the mid C14; then it decayed. Leland in 1541 found 'a ruin' which still included parts of the keep, Camden in the edition of 1610 of his *Britannia* only 'a heap of rammel and rubbish'. Ten years later, Sir Francis Seymour, grandson of the Protector who had acquired the site in 1550, built himself a house near the mound. Charles II visited it in 1663. Of this also nothing remains and nothing is known. At the end of the C17 the sixth Duke of Somerset began to build on a larger scale. In 1699 one and a half million bricks were bought. The house is C-House of the College. Celia Fiennes *c*.1702 saw it go up. In a plan of 1706 its w wing is called Built, its E wing Unbuilt. It must have been complete by 1723 at the latest, when Stukeley drew it. Lady Hertford, daughter-in-law of the sixth Duke, then made the Mound picturesque, by means of a cascade, not preserved, and a GROTTO, preserved. This is on the s side. Lady Hertford in 1739 called it newer and 'prettier than Twickenham', i.e. Alexander Pope's garden with its mound and grotto. However, the pleasure of life in the new house and the landscaped grounds was short. The seventh Duke, formerly Lord Hertford, died in 1750, and the house was sold to become the Castle Inn. Even considering the brisk traffic of the Bath Road, this must have been a uniquely grand inn. It was kept going until 1843, when the College took over.

48a   C-HOUSE is a brick mansion of fifteen bays in a rhythm of six–three–six, with the centre deeply recessed on the N, slightly on the s. Basement and two main storeys. Parapet and hipped roof, originally with a cupola. The wings are of chequered brick with rubbed quoins. The centre is of red brick exclusively and has arched windows on both main floors. Richly carved top cornice with modillions. To the N the area framed by the projecting wings is filled by a colonnade of paired unfluted Ionic columns which is connected by a covered passage with the N doorway. The colonnade comes from Mildenhall Woodlands and was bought c.1800. The interior of C-House poses many problems, too intricate to be tackled here. The back stairs look C17 rather than C18. The main staircase also with its big bulbous balusters one would assign to 1680 rather than the early C18. Also it does not seem to fit the space in which it is set. In one room there is a re-set Jacobean chimneypiece with Moses striking the rock. Strapwork surround. Two flanking figures full of bragadoccio. The chaste, really quite modest decoration of the principal rooms seems to belong to c.1730.

Apart from C-House, the only other pre-C19 building is the former STABLES of the Castle Inn to the NE of C-House (i.e. N and E of the Museum Block).

The COLLEGE started in 1843 with 200 boys. In 1844 *Blore* was called in, and he rose to the occasion by adding two new houses in the William-and-Mary style with windows with brick surrounds. Only his chapel was Gothic, and that has been replaced. He built c.1845–50 s of C-House the MASTER'S LODGE (s extension c.1860–5, the heavy Gothic porch probably of 1861) and E of C-House B-HOUSE. B-House has a pretty white oriel window, a motif we shall find more often at Marlborough It does not form part of the original design. The cheering-up seems to date from the early 1880s (*see* below). The choice of a style of c.1700 was an extremely uncommon thing in the mid C19, though one not unique even in the scholastic field (cf. John Shaw's Goldsmith's College, New Cross, London, of 1843 and Wellington College, Berkshire, of 1856). Blore also started the court* of Marlborough College, by adding to the N of C-House along the W side the DINING HALL which was replaced by a new, ampler and friendlier one, designed by *David Roberts* and called NORWOOD HALL. This is followed to the N by *Blore*'s A-House, again William-and-Mary: with six bays and three storeys with added white first-floor oriels and a recent r. wing. On the opposite, i.e. E, side the following buildings from s to N. First, though not visible from the court, behind B-House and the old stables, the old SICK HOUSE,

* The campus, as it were.

Gothic, of brick, 1863 by *William White*, then facing the
Dining Hall the MUSEUM BLOCK, 1882–3. It is of seven bays,
and has the white oriels in the first and seventh bay, a hipped
roof over the centre, and dormer windows with pediments of
alternatingly triangular and segmental shape. The block was
commissioned from *G. E. Street*, a convinced gothicist, but
Street died in 1881, and the drawings are signed by his son
A. E. Street and *A. W. Blomfield* together, i.e. the future Sir
Arthur Blomfield, also a gothicist. Of A. E. Street the *Journal*
of the RIBA (1930, pp. 203 and 256) says that he entered his
father's Law Courts office in 1878, that the Law Courts were
continued by him after his father's death, in collaboration with
Blomfield, and that his real liking was 'houses of a much later
date'. As for Blomfield, it ought to be remembered that his
nephew *Reginald Blomfield*, a classical man throughout, was in
his office in 1880–3. The Museum Block is connected by a low
Romanesque brick arcade to the plain BRADLEIAN BUILDING,
1873 by *G. E. Street*. Then *Bodley & Garner* were brought in,
and the neo-William-and-Mary spell is broken. Garner in 1893
designed the NORTH BLOCK, a classroom block in a kind of
mixed Tudor style, with projecting polygonal stair-turrets at
the angles, decorated with openwork shields in their parapets
and with mullioned and transomed windows and straight
gables between. The PORTER'S LODGE of 1877 (by *Street*,
allegedly *A. E. Street*) is attached to this block, and across the
Baroque entrance gates rises *Bodley & Garner*'s CHAPEL, a
replacement of 1883–6 of Blore's chapel. For the chapel brick
was abandoned and Bath and Sarsen stone used instead. The
chapel is long and tall with a flèche above the junction of nave
and chancel. Tall buttresses, Dec tracery. The interior has
pointed transverse arches and a panelled ceiling. The chancel
(built entirely of Bath stone) is of two bays, with narrow side
chapels and a polygonal apse. The whole of the E end, including
the REREDOS of 1866, was embellished by *Comper* c.1950. –
PAINTINGS. By *Spencer Stanhope*, 1872–9, taken over from the
old chapel and at that time much repainted. In the Pre-
Raphaelite style. – STAINED GLASS. One window on the S
side by *Morris & Co.*, c.1875–80.

Now for the later and more peripheral buildings. First
immediately W of the area between C-House and the Master's
Lodge the LEAF BLOCK of 1936 by *W. G. Newton*, utilitarian,
Neo-Georgian, and nothing like as interesting as Newton's
other buildings for Marlborough. Then, immediately NE of

the court, on the other side of the road to Preshute and Bath, the first, now the school museum, is in fact a handsome Georgian town-house, converted: the MOUNT INN of 1744. Five bays, two storeys, chequer brick, doorway with pediment on Doric pilasters. Then some smaller buildings: the GYMNASIUM of 1908 in a neo-Hampton Court style (by *Ponting*, incorporating parts of the town GAOL), the RACKET COURTS of 1881 and 1893, and after that FIELD HOUSE, 1910–11 by *Sir Aston Webb*, large, indifferently Neo-Georgian, and connected very effectively to the court by a bridge. Then on the N side of the Bath Road several school houses: BARTON HILL of *c*.1860–5 and LITTLEFIELD and COTTON HOUSE, both of 1872 and largely of blocks of concrete (which was most unusual then). PRESHUTE HOUSE of 1841 or a little earlier with a W extension of 1862, lies behind Preshute church on the S side of the road.

But the main extension of the College premises took place S of these houses and W of the main buildings. Here *W. G. Newton* designed two buildings which, in their stylistic contrast, are most characteristic of the moment when they went up. The MEMORIAL HALL was first designed in 1921 and finally inaugurated in 1925. It stands at the end of an axis from the Bath Road which is crossed by an axis continuing the line of the Chapel to the W. It is of brick with ample stone dressings. The N front has two closed end bays and then, stretching between them, a long loggia with eight giant Adamish columns. The top is a parapet. The back of the building is semicircular. It comes as near to the American Campus style of the same years as anything this side of the Atlantic. Behind the Hall is the other building, the SCIENCE BUILDING, in quite a different mood, because dedicated to a different purpose. This was begun in 1933. It is star-shaped with a central lantern. The walls are of concrete, and there are strips of spacious windows. Here was acceptance of the C20 idiom at a moment relatively early as English architectural history goes, and still only with the qualification that what is good enough for stinks is not good enough for prize-givings. David Roberts's new Dining Hall had still to wait some twenty-five years to become possible in a public school.

ST MARGARET'S MEAD. A flat grave which contained the 'Marlborough Bucket' – a large vat of fir wood, bound with three iron hoops and provided with a top bar and two handles of iron. Three sheet bronze bands bearing relief designs of

human heads and mythical beasts encircle the body of the
bucket. Probably originally a container for some liquid at
feasts, it served as an urn for the cremated bones found within
it. The bucket was imported by the Belgae from Brittany about
50 B.C. It is now in Devizes Museum.

MARSHWOOD HOUSE *see* DINTON

MARSTON MEYSEY
1090

ST JAMES. 1876–9 by *James Brooks* (GR). Nave and chancel in
one, stone-slated roof. On the N side vestry with tall chimney.
Lancet windows. The W front with a sexfoiled circle and the
bell-recess in the gable top, i.e. no bellcote. The surprise of
the church is inside: the fact that the chancel is genuinely
rib-vaulted in two bays. Nave with boarded round tunnel-
roof. – SCREEN. Low stone screen with inset tile panels, and
attached to it the PULPIT, also of stone, and semicircular in
plan.

Nice village. One long street with mostly stone cottages. Several
good bigger C17 houses with barns, especially MANOR FARM-
HOUSE, W of the church, GRANGE FARMHOUSE at the S end,
and the MANOR HOUSE at the N end.

ROUND HOUSE, rather like a tower, with pointed windows. This
is one of several canal houses built along the Thames–Severn
Canal, which was opened in 1789 and is now derelict. This
particular round house is close to a hump-bridge.

MELKSHAM
9060

Of the small towns of Wiltshire Melksham has least character
and least enjoyable buildings. The centre of the town is the
big rubber factory. The church is out of the way, and what is
attractive as a setting is around it and has little to do with the
own.

ST MICHAEL. The church is a Perp church, nothing else matters.
And it is a big church, and so it is all the more remarkable that
its Norman predecessor was just as big; for there is a bit of a
small, flat Norman zigzag frieze on the W wall, and there are
traces of big Norman intersected arcading in the chancel N
wall. With this goes the corbel-frieze outside. Otherwise the
work earlier than Perp is the five-bay arcades of low round

piers with round abaci and a chamfer and a hollow chamfer in the arch, and the pointed-trefoil-headed lancets in the aisle w walls. That is late C13. The W tower is rectangular and has a very pretty composition of the bell-openings with six by seven tall transomed lights of which all the lower parts and the first and last of the upper parts are blank. The buttresses are on the E side, inside the nave, caught up ingeniously by squinches.* Two-storeyed N porch with tierceron-star vault and bosses. Ambitious three-bay S chapel with battlements and pinnacles. Four- and five-light windows. Inside an angel-bust above the E window (cf. Bromham). Embattled three-light clerestory. – NORTH DOOR. With very long iron hinges. – STAINED GLASS. S chapel SW *Ward & Hughes*, 1884; SE *Kempe*, 1897. – PLATE. Chalice, 1571; Chalice, 1576; Paten, 1729. – MONUMENTS. Many worthwhile tablets.

ST ANDREW, Forest. 1876 by *Charles Adye* (chancel restored 1881 by *Street*). Nave with bellcote and chancel. Lancet-style. Dull texture. – STAINED GLASS. E window 1875, quite good. By *Powell & Sons*. – PLATE. Paten of the late C15 or early C16 with the face of Christ; Silver-gilt Chalice, Italian, 1876.

CHAPELS. The whole gamut from the Friends' Meeting House in King Street, now SPIRITUALIST CHAPEL, 1734, two by two bays, with segment-headed windows, and the much bigger but also perfectly simple and businesslike BAPTIST CHAPEL of 1776 (now behind the present chapel), with arched windows and a doorway on Tuscan pilasters with a bulgy frieze over, to the METHODIST CHAPEL of 1872 in the High Street which combines in a showy and somewhat painful fashion giant Corinthian columns and a big pediment with rock-facing and busy foliage decoration round the Italianate entrances.

TOWN HALL, Market Place. 1847. Ashlar-faced, of three bays with a one-bay pediment. Arched windows below, and above windows with lights so extremely elongated as pleased the forties only.

COUNTY LIBRARY, Bank Street. Built for the Capital and Counties Bank probably in the forties. Two storeys, two bays, but the windows even more radically broken up into very elongated lights. The style might be called emaciated classical. Moreover, exceedingly elongated giant pilasters.

The only rewarding part of Melksham is by the church. To its N

* The tower was a crossing tower and was removed to the W end only in 1845.

in the churchyard a huge yew tree propped up by poles. To the s of the church in its grounds MELKSHAM HOUSE, and even this rewarding only with qualifications. Now chiefly accessible from the Market Place and alas so much pulled about that it cannot count any longer as a C17 building. To the w the TITHE BARN, a fine buttressed piece but drastically converted into a schoolroom. To the N of the church CANON SQUARE, and further CHURCH WALK and to the E CHURCH STREET. They are all quite pleasant, especially the first, but what individual houses ought one to single out? Perhaps No. 11 Canon Square, Early Georgian, with segment-headed windows, but a mullioned window round the corner. The VICARAGE in Canon Square is by *Street*, 1877, but nothing special. In Church Street the ROUND HOUSE, a curiosity, used in the later C19 as an ammunition store for the Volunteers.

Church Street leads into the HIGH STREET. The POST OFFICE, No. 14, is an ashlar-faced early C19 house of three bays with giant pilasters. Further N in BANK STREET No. 17, Late Georgian with two shallow bows. Then the late C18 BRIDGE across the Avon with its fine balustrade. s of the High Street the Market Place. Where they join the KING'S ARMS HOTEL, L-shaped, early C19. Opposite PLACE ROAD, a private road to the church, apparently of the 1860s, with some rock-faced gabled villas, detached, semi-detached, and in a terrace. s of the Market Place KING STREET. No. 10 is dated 1705 and has mullioned two- and three-light windows, the mouldings finely stepped back. Attached to No. 42 the FORGE. (Ceiling of *c*.1600 with moulded beams and a central boss. MHLG) Several nice houses opposite, especially Nos 39 and 57, Georgian, with flat-mullioned two-light windows and pedimented door-hoods. Further out CONIGRE FARM, late C17, low, of brick, seven bays, with two-light windows, and WEST END FARMHOUSE, also late C17.

Back to the Market Place and to the SE out SPA ROAD. At the start THE LIMES, Georgian, with a canted bay to the Market Place and a pediment on carved brackets over the door. Nos 8–14 are a charming Regency composition, displaying classical and Gothic friezes, bargeboarding, and iron balconies. No. 14 has a castellated porch. No. 8 was up in 1830, Nos 10–14 must have followed immediately. Nos 16–18 are classical and probably of the same date. Further out on the l. (No. 400) THE SPA. The spring was found in 1815. Buildings were designed on a generous plan. There are three large blocks

of three-storeyed semi-detached houses, each of four bays.
The middle one has a two-bay pediment. (At the back of one
of them, called AGRA, the baths and pump-room.)

On the way to Semington WOOLMORE FARMHOUSE, of brick
with four cross-gables. Symmetrical three-bay front with mullioned and transomed windows. Datestone 1631.

MEMBURY FORT *see* RAMSBURY

MERE   8030

To the NW lies Long Hill, a curiously sudden bump.

ST MICHAEL. A big, solid church away from the main street.
The exterior is mostly Dec and of much visual variety. The
chancel is of C13 date, partly early (buttresses and corbel-table),
partly later (one two-light window with bar tracery which now
looks into the N chapel, and the small single-chamfered doorway below it). Of the C13 also, apparently re-used, the fine
large pointed-trefoiled niche with shafts in the S chapel. The
Dec work is lavish and extensive. The N chapel was built as a
chantry c.1325, but extended later in the C14, the S chapel was
built, also as a chantry, c.1350. The N side has straight-headed
windows of interesting tracery. Towards the W arches standing
upside down on arches, towards the E ogee arches standing upside down on ogee arches. Only the E window is Perp, as is the
chancel E window. The S aisle windows are also straight-
headed, but have the more usual reticulation motifs. The chapel
has flowing tracery to the S and to the E a Perp window replacing a Dec one to which the hood-mould with heads belongs.
Lavish Dec N porch of two storeys. Niche above the entrance.
Vault with a tierceron-star and bosses. The S porch is simpler
and much rebuilt, but has a Dec doorway inside as well, whereas the N doorway is Perp. W tower with the lower part of its E
wall probably of the C11. The rest Perp with polygonal buttresses ending in turret pinnacles (cf. Marlborough). Decorated battlements, three-light bell-openings. Ceiling inside with
traceried panels, over-restored. The total height of the tower
is 124 ft. Now the rest of the interior. Here the arcades of the
chancel chapels have preserved their Dec appearance. Octagonal pier and arches with two sunk quadrant mouldings. The
arch from the S chapel to the aisle corresponds in style; only
the arch from the chapel to the W is Perp. On the E walls of the
aisles one can clearly see that at the time the chapels were built

the aisles were still lower and narrower. The aisle walls were then widened, and in the end the present aisle arcades were built – purely Perp. Five bays, tall piers with four shafts and four hollows, corresponding arches. The clerestory also is Perp. So is the panelled chancel arch. Single-framed nave roof, only the bay above the rood panelled with leaf enrichment in the centre of each panel. The angels along the wall plate are nearly all new. They hold the Instruments of the Passion.

FURNISHINGS. FONT. Octagonal, Perp, of Purbeck marble. Shields in cusped quatrefoils. – ROOD SCREEN. A spectacular Perp piece, very tall, of six-light divisions with transom and tracery below it as well as in the head. The original doors are preserved. Coving and loft are not original. – CHAPEL SCREENS. The finest that to the s chapel Tall, with eight-light divisions, articulated by mullions of different gauge. One arch for the middle eight lights, half-arches l. and r. The N chapel screen was the same, but has been cut down. The s chapel w screen simpler, with one-light divisions, but also good. – STALLS, with MISERICORDS. On the N side four angels, two of them recent copies; on the s side a man putting his tongue out, a flower, a bearded head, a leaf, an angel. – On two of the stall ends are the arms of Gylbert Kymer, rector of Mere in 1449–63. – BENCHES. Simple, of 1638–41, with three knobs at each end, the middle one raised by a semicircle with a shell. – COMMUNION RAIL (s aisle E). C18. – SCULPTURE. Alabaster panel of the Adoration of the Magi; C15 (chancel, N wall). – TILES. Some C14 tiles in the s chapel. – STAINED GLASS. In the s chapel s w window excellent Dec glass, including older figures in their characteristic colours. – The N aisle w window by *Powell's*, 1865, designed by *Holiday*. Excellent, in the Pre-Raphaelite style, but with the big canopies usual in the C14. – PLATE. Chalice, given in 1630; Flagon and Paten, 1699–1700; Chalice given in 1700; Flagon and Paten, 1700; two Patens, 1713(?). – MONUMENTS. Brass to Sir John Betteshorne † 1398, 'fundator istius cantarie', in the floor of his, i.e. the s, chapel, a 4 ft 3 in. figure. – Brass to a Knight, s chapel, half-hidden, probably Sir John Berkeley of Beverstone † 1426. The figure must be c. 5 ft 3 in. long. – Between the chancel and the s chapel tomb-chest with three shields in cusped quatrefoils. Between and at the corners panelled bands. This is supposed to commemorate the first Lord Stourton † 1463. – Nearly all the Georgian tablets have been banished. – Also some funerary ARMOUR (s chapel).

ST MATTHEW, 1¼ m. SE. 1882 by *C. E. Ponting*.

Round St Michael's church a number of interesting or attractive houses. To the SE the CHARNEL HOUSE with a small cusped C15 window, to the S the CHANTRY HOUSE, with a two-light *See* cusped window and a doorway with four-centred head, to the $\frac{P}{577}$ N Georgian houses. The GATEPIERS of the churchyard are handsome.

In the village the SHIP INN, just W of the regrettable Jubilee Clock, has a splendid sign, probably by *Kingston Avery*, who lived at Mere in 1730–63 and was a clockmaker (cf. the fine signs at Wincanton across the Somerset border). The sign is very big and includes grapes and a crown. The house itself is of seven bays and two storeys with cross-windows on the upper floor. Inside the middle archway two (re-set?) doorways with open segmental pediments. All this looks *c.*1700, i.e. of the time when the house was the mansion of Sir John Coventry and not yet an inn. The doorways then were perhaps front and garden entrances. Further W the former WORKHOUSE, 1835 by *G. G. Scott*, in the Tudor style. To the E of the Jubilee Clock a cottage with two canted bays and a Venetian doorway, then a house with some mullioned windows. After that DEWES HOUSE, L-shaped, with cross-windows, a hipped roof, and a doorway with bolection moulding and a segmental pediment, i.e. also *c.*1700.

CASTLE. Mere had a castle built by Richard Earl of Cornwall in 1253. It does not exist any longer, but excavations have shown it to have been a rectangle of 390 by 102 ft with rectangular corner towers and in addition two round towers on each of the long sides.

MIDDLEHILL *see* DITTERIDGE

MIDWAY MANOR *see* WINGFIELD

MILBOURNE HOUSE *see* MALMESBURY, p. 295

MILDENHALL

2060

ST JOHN BAPTIST. This is a perfect example of the small village church of many periods, and, together with its Late Georgian furnishings, preserved completely. Anglo-Saxon windows in the lower part of the tower. The rest of the tower seems to be Norman, because of the twin bell-openings with dividing shafts below the present Perp bell-openings. These have Somerset tracery. The imposts of the arch towards the nave are Norman too, see the tiny pendant double lobes in the corners. The arch is unmoulded and pointed. The W doorway into the tower is E.E. Chronologically next after the tower (minus its doorway) is the S arcade of three bays with round piers, capitals with trumpet scallops, foliage, and heads, square abaci, and single-stepped arches. In the S aisle near the doorway a lancet window. The chancel arch is double-chamfered and pointed, but its brackets, one with a head, are also still Late Norman. The N arcade has round piers and round moulded capitals, but the arcades are still single-stepped. All this is of between *c*.1150 and 1200. The chancel belongs to the same time, see the round-arched, simple priest's doorway. The windows of the church are mostly Perp. The roofs of nave (tie-beams and pendants) and chancel (panelled with charming leaf bosses) seem both to be Jacobean. – In 1815–16 the church was refurnished, and of the charmingly Gothick fitments then put in all seem to survive, namely REREDOS with a nice raised centre, PULPIT with tall back panel and tester and identical READER'S DESK, PEWS in the chancel for incumbent and squire, chancel PANELLING, BOX PEWS, and WEST GALLERY with a backward-curving centre. The FONT of stone is also of that date, and has a wooden COVER. Only the COMMUNION RAIL seems to be a little earlier and is not Gothick. – STAINED GLASS. Remains of the C15 in the heads of the chancel windows. – PLATE. Paten, 1727; two Chalices and Paten Covers, 1733. – MONUMENTS. Thomas Baskerville of Poulton House † 1817. Triptych of white marble, Gothick and with palm trees. By *Harris* of Bath, 1818. – The Rev. Charles Francis † 1821. Also marble, also Gothick, also with palm trees, and also by *Harris*.

POULTON HOUSE, *see* Marlborough, p. 301.

SCHOOL, at the E end of the village. 1823 by *Robert Abraham*. Founded by the Rev. Charles Francis. Cruciform, with an octagonal centre carrying a square lantern. The windows are Gothic, with Y- or intersected tracery. The wings have gables and cross-gables.

BELGIC WAR CEMETERY. Between the church and Black Field were found eight inhumations made haphazardly and accompanied by a La Tène III brooch, part of a bead-rimmed pot, and other Belgic sherds.

ROMAN TOWN. SE of the village is the site of the Roman town of CUNETIO. Air photography revealed a rectangular enclosure with street plans and villa. Mr F. K. Annable has carried out several seasons' excavation on the site, work being mainly concentrated in the area of the fortifications, where a gateway with paved entrance in the W rampart has been discovered. The ROMAN ROAD from Cunetio to Bath (Aquae Sulis) is ill defined in the neighbourhood of the town and is first picked up clearly on Overton Hill, where it crosses the Ridgeway, then runs along the present London–Bath road through West Kennett to Silbury Hill, where its course is altered to avoid the mound. Running W, it cuts the main road to Devizes ¾ m. SW of the Beckhampton roundabout. A short course of the road is clearly visible at this point. At Morgan's Hill it joins the Wansdyke (which is superimposed upon it) and continues due W through Verlucio and finally to Bath. The Road to Old Sarum (Sorviodunum) is clearly recognizable from Cock-a-Troop Lane through the W part of Savernake Forest.

Leaving Cunetio in a NNE direction is the road to Wanborough (Durocornovium), forming a modern roadway or track throughout most of its length.

MILFORD
1 m. E of Salisbury

1020

MILFORD MILL BRIDGE. Attributed to the C14. Really two bridges of two pointed arches each. Causeway with walls between the two bridges. Each bridge has a cutwater.

MILL HOUSE, by the bridge. Of eminent 'group value', as the MHLG calls it. Three-bay brick house, no doubt Georgian. Half-hipped roof and a lawn with weeping willows between house and bridge.

MILSTON
1 m. N of Bulford

1040

ST MARY. 1860. Nave with bellcote and chancel. Flint. Medieval windows re-used, and also the simple C13 chancel arch. – BELL. One bell is of the late C13. – PLATE. Cup, 1576; Paten, 1694.

OLD HOUSE, overlooking the churchyard. Flint, with mullioned windows. It carries the date 1613.

SILK HILL BARROW GROUP, 2 m. NE. A very large barrow cemetery, including some of the largest and best preserved bowl barrows in the county. To the SE, across the Nine-Mile River, is a further barrow cemetery on MILSTON DOWN.

MILTON LILBOURNE

St Peter. E.E. N arcade of four bays: circular piers, circular abaci, double-chamfered arches. The bases of the E respond and the two E piers have spurs, the others have not. The chancel is Dec, except for the imposts of the chancel arch, which were kept from the preceding Norman church. Victorian E window.* Dec also the S porch entrance, though it is much renewed. Perp, ashlar-faced W tower, Perp nave, flint and a regular stone pattern. The S doorway has big heads l. and r. Perp the N aisle too. – FONT. Octagonal, plain bowl, but the base and the five supports typically E.E. – PULPIT. With Jacobean bits. – READER'S DESK. With a simple Jacobean front. – BOX PEWS. C17, a nice, plain, honest job; straight-headed ends. – STAINED GLASS. Bits in the chancel S window. – PLATE. Elizabethan Paten Cover; Chalice, 1655. – MONUMENT. Tomb recess in the N aisle. Remains of the tomb-chest. The back wall with quatrefoils.

King Hall, SE of the church. The house is Victorian, the iron gates Georgian.

Manor House, N of the church. Of blue and red brick chequered. Seven bays with a three-bay projection crowned by a big segmental gable – not strictly a pediment. In the projection vigorously moulded windows with basket arches. Doorway with an open pediment. Parapet and mansard roof. All this is characteristically Early Georgian. The back is later, say *c.*1760–75. Red brick, with a three-bay pediment and a pedimented doorway flanked by Tuscan columns.

Giant's Grave. 2 m. S. Unchambered long barrow. The side ditches are visible. C19 excavation revealed a primary deposit of eight skeletons, one with cleft skull.

MINETY

St Leonard. Entirely Perp. NW tower with battlements and pinnacles. Nave with straight-headed windows and battlements. Chancel also embattled. Only the S porch entrance looks rather earlier. N arcade of four bays. Concave-sided octagonal piers (cf. Chipping Campden and Northleach in the Cotswolds). Moulded, four-centred arches. Excellent head-corbels for the chancel roof. In the N aisle E wall an angel corbel. – FONT. Octagonal, Perp, entirely re-tooled. – PULPIT. A sumptuous piece of 1627, with back panel and tester. – The

* Restoration by *Pearson*, 1875 (PF).

READER'S DESK belongs to it, and the STALLS front. – SCREENS. Both partly Perp. – PEWS. Jacobean, with knobs. – SCULPTURE. Parts of a mid-C9 CROSS, with trails. – STAINED GLASS. Original glass in the vestry door and the head of the w window. – CHANDELIER. Of brass, one tier, of unusually bulbous shape. Dated 1748. – PLATE. Chalice, inscribed 1663. – BRASS. Nicholas Powlett † 1609. Plate with kneeling figures.

THE MANSELLS. The centre dated 1656. With mullioned windows. A late C17 l. wing with hipped roof and a r. wing of *c.*1900 in Gothic and half-timbered fancy work.

MINETY HOUSE, ¼ m. SE. The house early C19 with two lower projecting pavilions. Good recent farm buildings by *Stillman & Eastwick-Field*, 1955.

MONKS LANE *see* CORSHAM, p. 176

MONKTON DEVERILL   8030

CHURCH. Small late C13 w tower. The rest 1845 by *T. H. Wyatt* (GR). Nave and chancel in one. – PULPIT. With panels with scenes from the Bible, German or Flemish, first half of the C17. – PLATE. Elizabethan Cup; Paten given in 1681; Paten, 1711.

MONKTON FARLEIGH   8060

ST PETER. Norman s doorway. One order of shafts. One capital is a big head biting into the shaft. Zigzag in the arch at r. angles to the wall surface. Unbuttressed C13 w tower, the twin bell-openings surrounded by a continuous roll moulding. Corbel table above and a parapet with odd blank battlements. The church was rebuilt in 1844; the SE addition, which looks C17, is said to be of 1829 (VCH). – PULPIT. Jacobean, with the usual blank arches. – PANELLING. Against the w wall unusually good linenfold panelling. Could it come from the Manor?

w of the church the big Gothic RECTORY, 1844–6 by *Hicks*. In the steep village street, a little E of the s gates to the Manor, a cottage (No. 82) which is dated 1736 and has a shell-hood over the door, as a rule a motif of *c.*1690–1700.

MONKTON FARLEIGH MANOR. Monkton Farleigh was a Cluniac priory. It had been founded in 1125, and architectural evidence points to building in the mid C12 and the early C13. That evidence is however very scanty – small fragments of

zigzag and dog-tooth built into the w side of the house, the two
fine tall lancet windows now standing on their own a little to the
w, but once belonging to a building jutting out of the w range
of the cloister to the w, and three stone EFFIGIES of the C13,
two cross-legged Knights with mail-coifs and one lady wearing
a wimple. In addition the coffin-lid of Ilbertus de Chaz, with
very fine Norman lettering. The manor house itself has an E
façade which seems an Early Victorian remodelling of an Early
Georgian front. Inside, the hall on the s side has a ceiling with
moulded beams.

MONKS' CONDUIT, somewhat N of the Manor. A small C14
building with a steep-pitched roof (rebuilt in 1784), standing
all on its own in a field.

BROWN'S FOLLY. Tower on Farleigh Down, looking towards
Bath. It was erected in 1840 by Mr Wade Brown for, it is said,
surveying purposes.

MONKTON HOUSE see BROUGHTON GIFFORD

MOTHER ANTHONY'S WELL see BROMHAM

MURCOTT FARMHOUSE see CRUDWELL

NESTON see CORSHAM, p. 176

1040   NETHERAVON

ALL SAINTS. The most interesting part of the church is the
present w end. It seems to date from the second half of the
C11 and represents a particularly telling case of the so-called
Saxo-Norman Overlap. Although it is a w tower now, it was the
central tower of the preceding church. The nave lay to its w, a
chancel to its E, and to its N and s not transepts but *porticus* in
the Anglo-Saxon sense, i.e. chambers accessible only by small
doorways. These exist, even if now blocked. Small stumps of
the w walls of the *porticus* have been left standing, and their
marks against the tower walls are unmistakable. The E walls
of the *porticus* are now the w walls of the aisles, and exhibit
indeed herringbone flint-laying, also an C11 motif. The tower
arch towards the nave also survives. Its details are mixed Saxo-
Norman: Early Norman volutes, but also busts and leaves
which might be Saxon as well as Norman. The bases are Saxon.
The taller E arch, now towards the later nave, on the other

hand, though capitals and bases seem badly moulded, is with its arrangement of strong shafting and its roll moulding in the arch entirely Norman. The upper parts of the tower look Norman too, and the bell-stage is E.E.* So is the new church replacing the C11 chancel. Arcades of four bays. Round piers, round abaci, double-chamfered arches. Only the E piers and the E responds are different: four round shafts and four diagonally placed square shafts, rather raw. There is a clerestory and this, with its lancet windows, is E.E. too. The chancel also has lancets and an E.E. corbel-table, and there is no saying whether the E bays or the W bays of the arcades came first. Perp aisle windows. – PLATE. Set, 1759.

NETHERAVON HOUSE, to the SW, on an eminence. Late C18. Red brick, of five bays and two-and-a-half storeys, with recent additions. Pedimented Ionic porch. The STABLES are low and have to the outside blank half-oval arches. In two of them half-oval windows, in the middle, below a pediment, a large fully oval window, looking as if one saw it in a distorting mirror.‡

Much suburban military housing.

NETHERHAMPTON

ST CATHERINE. 1876–7 by *Butterfield* (PF). Brick and stone dressings. Only the brick tower is old, i.e. C18. – PLATE. Cup and Paten Cover, 1569; Paten, 1721. – CHURCHYARD CROSS. Only the base and the broken shaft survive.

NETHERHAMPTON HOUSE. A most amazing façade. Behind it a C16 or C17 cottage. The house behind the façade itself may be of the later C17 too (a date 1687 is recorded), but the façade and the addition of the two wings with the two big and higher rooms must be the work of *c.*1710–20, i.e. the Vanbrugh moment. The whole façade is solemnly ashlar-faced. Centre of five bays and three storeys. No parapet or balustrade or visible roof. All the windows have strongly segmental heads and sashes. The glazing seems to be original. Plain doorway with blocks of rustication of alternating sizes. A niche above with the same surround. The wings are two bays wide and one-storeyed, but with taller windows than the others. Their parapet curves up to the centre. Round the corner, clearly not

---

* In Domesday the church is called ruinous. How can that be? Can the overlap still apply to a church begun *c.*1100?

‡ Miss Stroud mentions additions made by *Soane* in 1791.

in situ, a fine porch with slender fluted Corinthian columns.
Good iron gates to the front garden.

WILTON ESTATE COTTAGES, stone-built and gabled, and
neo-Tudor MODEL FARM.

NETTLETON

8070

ST MARY, at Burton, ¾ m. N. The N arcade is puzzling: five bays,
circular piers, octagonal abaci, double-chamfered arches.
Norman W respond and two Norman many-scalloped capitals.
The rest later, perhaps early C14 (ballflower). In the N aisle
one late C13 pointed-trefoiled lancet. N chapel E window with
reticulated tracery. The chancel arch and N chapel arch (two
continuous hollows) might go with that. Priest's doorway
under a heavy hood of stone. Perp W tower, ashlar-faced, in the
Somerset style. Two-light bell-openings with Somerset
tracery, continued below a transom in blank panels and repeated with the lower panels blank to the l. and r. This is not
exactly like any one Somerset tower but similar to the Shepton
Mallet group and the Wells crossing tower (cf. Westwood,
West Kington, and others). W doorway inside a flat porch (cf.
Grittleton). Battlements panelled; pinnacles. Square Perp
Sanctus-bell turret. Perp chancel E window, Perp N porch with
traceried battlements, gargoyles, and a tierceron-star vault
with bosses. Simpler Perp S porch, Perp S transept and S
chapel. A niche in one S window. Ceiled wagon roofs in nave
and chancel. – FONT. Circular, Norman, fluted below, with
scales above. – PULPIT. Perp; of stone. – BOX PEWS. In the
N aisle; Georgian. – COMMUNION RAIL. C17, with vertically
symmetrical balusters. – PLATE. Paten, 1703; Chalice, 1710;
Flagon, 1714; Paten Cover, 1726.

ROMAN BUILDING, ¾ m. S, on the l. of the main road. A rectangular building sunk into the cliff. A sculptured relief of Mercury
has come from it. Other finds include a fine bronze candlestick in the form of a cockerel, a stone relief of the goddess
Diana and her dog, and quantities of Samian and coarse wares.
The site has been interpreted as that of a temple.

LUGBURY, ¾ m. ENE. Chambered long barrow with dummy
entrance portal and four burial chambers along the S side. The
mound has been much reduced by ploughing. Excavation in
the C19 revealed a total of twenty-eight skeletons from the
chambers.

NETTON see WOODFORD

NETTON FARMHOUSE see BISHOPSTONE, p. 106

NEWHOUSE see WHITEPARISH

NEWTON see WHITEPARISH

NEWTON TONEY

2040

St Andrew. 1844 by *Wyatt & Brandon*. Flint; Dec. sw tower with shingled broach-spire. – STAINED GLASS. In the chancel of c.1845. – PLATE. Chalice, 1659; Paten, 1686; Flagon, 1692.
The village develops nicely along two roads separated by a stream.
At the N end FARMHOUSE with three gables, mullioned windows, and Victorian bargeboards.

NEWTOWN

2 m. w of Tisbury

9020

CHURCH. 1911 by *E. Doran Webb*. Small, with fancy Gothic tracery. The chancel arch is taken from the chapel at Pyt House, *see* below.
PYT HOUSE, ¾ m. w. Begun in 1805 to the design of its owner, Mr *John Benett*. The design is curiously similar to Wyatville's Philipps House Dinton, begun eight years later. Also nine bays, also a tetrastyle portico of unfluted Ionic columns with pediments. Also tripartite windows in the side elevation. But the giant recessed loggias in the middle of these sides are not repeated. Very restrained interiors. The staircase is very curious. It rises in one arm and returns in two, and the first, middle arm is supported on iron shafts like those of verandas. Oval glazed lantern. – In two of the principal rooms North Italian chimneypieces, very sumptuous, one of them dated 1553 and referring to the Martinengo family. To the w of the house ORANGERY, earlier than the present house. Five bays with arched openings and Ionic pilasters. Three-bay pediment. Behind and quite high above the house, in the wood, CHAPEL built by Mr Benett for his wife, née Lucy Lambert of Boyton, with a plaster lierne-vault. The chapel is in ruins, with gaping windows and bushes on the roof.
  GATEPIERS. Quite grand, with bands of rocky rustication, a sign that a house of some consequence stood here in the

Early Georgian decades. Colt Hoare reports in fact the building of a new house *c*.1725.

HATCH HOUSE. This was a big C16 or early C17 house most of which was pulled down in 1770. The date 1603 is given on an old map. Original now only the l. gable of the three-gabled W front and two-light basement windows on the N side. The N range has two storeys of four bays with Georgian windows. As for the W front, the other two gables and the three-bay arcade in the middle are part of the alterations made in 1908 by *Detmar Blow*. Garden walls and gatepiers to the S and sumptuous walled garden to the W with a twin-arched loggia at its end. Restored by *Blow*, but a date 1658 on the seat in the loggia.

9020

NORRINGTON MANOR
¾ m. w of Alvediston

22b A lucky survival. The house was probably built by John Gawen, who had bought the property in 1377. Of this house the hall exists, the porch, and one small room to the NW of the hall. The hall has three windows to the S, two to the N, the entrance (by the porch) at the E end, and the fireplace across the W end. The windows are of two lights, transomed, and have simple Perp tracery (just one panel unit). The roof unfortunately has not survived. The porch is entered by an elaborately moulded arch. It has a small two-light window to the W and a fine vault on head-brackets. Diagonal ribs and tiercerons opened out scissor-wise so as to form four lozenges. These and the ring in the centre are quatrefoil-cusped. Of the solar wing nothing remains but a small vaulted undercroft below its N end. It was probably the strong-room (cf. Great Chalfield). Two narrow bays, single-chamfered ribs on corner shafts. The rest of the solar wing was rebuilt in the C17, perhaps only when the Wyndhams bought the estate in 1658. Five-light window below, transomed five-light window above. The same to the back. Good, restrained chimneypiece. The part where kitchen and offices must have been became further living quarters. Three storeys, cross-windows. Round the corner to the E, however, one four-light window which seems to be *temp.* Henry VIII. Long, lower C17 wing to the W of the solar wing, projecting to the S.

8050

NORTH BRADLEY

ST NICHOLAS. A sizeable church, almost rebuilt by *T. H. Wyatt* in 1862. Yet much looks quite trustworthy. Arcades of the C13 inside, three bays with round piers, round abaci, and double-chamfered arches. The outside appears Perp. W tower with considerably higher stair-turret. Tall two-light bell-openings with Somerset tracery and their own tracery, an interesting pattern with saltire crosses (cf. Keevil). Proud three-bay S chapel with a five-light E window and four-light S windows and battlements. Sumptuous one-bay N chapel with two friezes of quatrefoils etc. at the base, nice square-headed four-light windows with unusual tracery and buttress-shafts with pinnacles in relief attached to the buttress. Inside the N window is taken down so as to form a seat as in a manor house, but the seat is a tomb-chest (*see* below). Panelled sides and panelled back below the window. The chapel is behind the third arcade bay, as is the W bay of the S chapel. The other arch is Perp and panelled, as are the W arches of the chapels. The chapel ceilings have moulded beams and panels, those of the N chapel being traceried. – FONT. Good, big Perp piece, octagonal with carved shields in foiled fields. On the shields the Signs of the Evangelists and the Instruments of the Passion. – PLATE. Pewter Chalice and Paten of the C14, found in a coffin (N chapel). – MONUMENTS. On the tomb-chest in the N chapel incised stone slab to Emma, mother of Archbishop John Stafford of Canterbury. That explains the lavishness of the chapel. She died in 1446. Effigy with thin incised canopy. – William Trenchard † 1713. With twisted columns and three putto heads at the foot. – Members of the Long family, erected in 1756. Very pretty tablet of coloured marble with plenty of garlands. Attributed by Mr Gunnis to *Ford*.

BAPTIST CHAPEL. 1775. Big, with a steep pediment. Two tiers of pointed windows, pedimented doorway. Brick.

In the village street some brick MALTHOUSES, NW of the church, a three-bay cottage dated 1713, and ALMSHOUSES of 1810, to the NNW of the church, of seven bays with a middle pediment and two-light windows. Brick, rendered.

NORTH NEWNTON

ST JAMES. Small and on its own, by the Avon and a mill-stream. Short Perp W tower disfigured in the most unexpected way by big warts. They are the projecting beams of the bell-cradle, protected each by a little stone roof. There are eight of these excrescences. May they not be removed. E.E. chancel, see the three stepped E lancets, the single N lancet, and the bases of the

11

chancel arch. E.E. also the piscina with a shelf and the handsome NW window of three stepped, chamfered lancet lights under one hood-mould. The s side of flint and brick, C19, but with one Dec window re-used.*

HILLCOT MANOR FARMHOUSE, 1¼ m. WNW. The r. half of the front late C17, brick, with flat quoins and cross-windows, the l. half Georgian with blue and red bricks mixed and a dentil-frieze between ground floor and first floor. A thatched hipped roof over the whole.

NORTH TIDWORTH

2040

HOLY TRINITY. Flint and stone. Perp. Nave and chancel and w tower. The top of the tower repaired in brick. A niche with a naively carved canopy inside to the r. of the chancel arch. – FONT. Norman, in the uncommon form of a large single-scallop capital. – PLATE. Cup, 1576.

North Tidworth is really part of the Tidworth Barracks area, with much military, suburban-looking housing. On this see *The Buildings of England: Hampshire.*

NORTH WRAXALL

8070

ST JAMES. Norman s doorway (one order of shafts with two-scallop capitals, zigzag in the arch at r. angles to the wall, hood-mould with pellets), but otherwise a C13 church. Chancel with wide continuous chamfers and lancet windows, including a stepped group of three at the E end. Lower stages of the w tower with lancets, bell-openings with Y-tracery, tower arch of three continuous chamfers. Only the big s window in the nave under its own gable has flowing tracery. To the N the Methuen Chapel of c.1793. The ceiling prettily painted with coats of arms. The RAILINGS look decidedly older. – ALTAR-PIECE. Sermon of St John, by a C17 Italianate Dutch painter. – PULPIT. Big, Jacobean, with tester. – MONUMENTS. Paul Methuen † 1837. By *Sir R. Westmacott.* A large white Grecian sarcophagus. In the family chapel.

CHANTRY, s of the church. Small medieval house with a pretty little chimney (and a Perp doorway with four-centred arch and carved spandrels; MHLG).

TRUCKLE HILL, 1¼ m. NE. On the hill was a ROMAN VILLA surrounded by an enclosure 220 yds by 155 yds with a gateway

* The church was much restored in 1864. Can all the windows here described be trusted? Those in the chancel probably, and also the NW window.

on the s side. The house was of long rectangular plan with sixteen rooms, including a bath suite with hypocausts. Some of the rooms were decorated with painted wall plaster. Finds include a bronze statuette, armlets, nails, and Samian and coarse wares.

NORTON

8080

ALL SAINTS. Humble, with a presumptuous bell-turret of 1858. Made for Grittleton House (*see* p. 233), not the church. – FONT. Circular, Norman. Scalloped underside of the bowl. – PULPIT. Jacobean. – Some Jacobean PANELS. – PLATE. Elizabethan Chalice with Cover.

MANOR HOUSE. The old part is dated 1623. It was much enlarged *c*.1900 etc. (by *F. A. Lawson* of Stroud). The old part is gabled and has symmetrically arranged mullioned windows and a two-storeyed gabled porch with Doric columns below, Ionic above. Entrance arch into the front garden.

(MANOR FARM has one C17 gable to the N, BUCKLANDS FARM much more of the C17, but also a part of *c*.1800. *See* J. Badeni: *Wiltshire Forefathers*)

NORTON BAVANT

9040

ALL SAINTS. The church was rebuilt in 1839–41 by *William Walker* of Shaftesbury, except for the C14 tower with a higher square stair-turret,* and the entrance arch to the Benett Chapel, which looks almost C13, but is amorphous in its details. – FONT. An C18 baluster. – RAILING to the Benett Chapel, C17. – PLATE. Bowl, 1696; Flagon, 1710; Paten, 1744; two Patens, C18. – BRASSES to John Bennet † 1461 and wife (25-in. figures, perhaps a reconstruction) and to Thomas Bennet † 1605 and wife.

NORTON BAVANT HOUSE. Seven bays, two storeys, cross-windows, hipped roof. Over the doorway a handsome shell-hood on carved brackets. This must be Queen Anne, but there is a contract of 1641 in existence (K. Rogers).

SCRATCHBURY CAMP, 1 m. NE. Large univallate Iron Age hill-fort, unexcavated.

NORWOOD CASTLE *see* OAKSEY

* On the first floor in the tower is a fireplace with a carved lintel (Rev. D. V. Evening).

NOTTON see LACOCK

NUNTON

St Andrew. 1854–5 by *T. H. Wyatt*, but the s aisle arcade of two bays original, if renewed, c13 work. Circular pier and abacus, double-chamfered arches. The s chapel also of two bays and earlier still, probably of the end of the c12. Square pier, chamfered, pointed arches with one slight chamfer. – plate. Chalice and Cover, 1677; Paten, *c.*1778. – monuments. John T. Batt † 1831. By *Sir R. Westmacott*. White marble; large Grecian relief figures of Faith and Hope, standing side by side. To the l. and r. of the inscription below small relief medallions with reading women; these are very good. – Also several Gothic tablets, e.g. one of 1855 by *Osmond*.

Nunton House, e of the church. Of *c.*1700; brick. Seven bays with a three-bay pediment. Giant pilasters at the angles and the angles of the three-bay centre. Doorway with Tuscan demi-columns and a segmental pediment. The windows to its l. and r. are narrower (cf. e.g. Mompesson House, Salisbury). Stone framing of the window above the doorway. A room with a stucco ceiling of *c.*1740. Staircase with three turned balusters to the tread, probably also of *c.*1740.

New Hall, Brokenham, ½ m. e. The house attributed to *James Wyatt* has been replaced. The brick stables with projecting wings and small clock-turret remain.

House on the road to the river, n of New Hall. Early c18 probably. Brick, five bays, two storeys.

OAKSEY

All Saints. Low c13 s arcade of three bays; circular abaci, double-chamfered arches. Of the same time the s aisle window with two pointed-trefoiled lights and a quatrefoil in plate tracery, and also the chancel lancets and the w tower. But could not the w wall of the nave be Norman? Why should a lancet of the tower have looked into the nave? Perp tower top. Perp clerestory, looking odd on the embattled n side, where there is no aisle. Fine Dec n porch. The entrance has a big ogee arch, cusped and subcusped. Perp s chapel with straight-headed windows and a one-bay arcade. The responds have fleurons in the capitals. – screen. Nice, humble Perp screen. – sculpture. A Sheila-na-gig e of the n porch. – An excellent but defaced seated statuette of the Virgin over the n doorway.

It may be early C14. – PAINTING. S wall of the aisle large St Christopher, large Christ of the Trades. They were discovered in 1933 and left unrestored. They are ascribed to the early C15. – STAINED GLASS. In a N window much of the C15 is preserved, including whole figures. – PLATE. Chased Spanish Chalice.

HOUSE, No. 8. C17. Lintel of one window with a symmetrical pattern of big juicy leaves. The door lintel must have been similar but is half destroyed.

TUDOR HOUSE, NE of the church. With gables and mullioned windows under hood-moulds.

OAKSEY MOOR FARMHOUSE, 1 m. E. C18; rather gaunt. Five bays, two and a half storeys. Porch with thin Tuscan columns and a pediment. Parapet in front of the hipped roof.

DEAN FARM, ⅝ m. NW. Remains of NORWOOD CASTLE, a motte-and-bailey earthwork of the Norman period. Aubrey calls it 'a little cittadel, with a Keepe Hill, both moated round'.

OARE

1060

HOLY TRINITY. By *Teulon*, 1857–8 (GR). It may well be considered the ugliest church in Wiltshire. Red brick with bits of vitrified blue brick. Round-arched with an apse, i.e. probably meant to imply Norman. Nave and chancel in one; bellcote. – FONT. Neo-Norman, with intersected arches, but dressed in glossy white oil-paint (at the time of writing).

OARE HOUSE. An impressive, townish house built in 1740 by Henry Deacon, a London wine merchant. Vitrified brick and red brick dressings. Five bays, two and a half storeys, parapet. Slight three-bay projection with pediment. Wooden porch with fluted Ionic columns and a pediment. The window above slightly decorated. Staircase with slender turned balusters. *Clough Williams Ellis* in 1921 and 1925 added two symmetrical wings, one of them with a large drawing room, and beyond this another wing, facing the front garden with a blank Venetian window above which a tall chimney comes out embraced by two big volutes, a charming and original conceit. The house has a walled front garden with gatepiers and fine original wrought-iron gates and railings and short avenues of lime trees leading to the gates from the village street. In the S garden, in line with the Venetian window of the drawing room, a loggia with a Venetian entrance opening.

COLD BLOW, a little to the NW. Also by *Clough Williams Ellis*. Built in 1922. T-shaped, thatched, with the principal front facing S. In its centre a bow on columns.

At the S end of the village *Clough Williams Ellis* built a terrace of cottages, stuccoed white, and with a central archway. Wooden giant pilasters and a wooden pediment.

RAINSCOMBE HOUSE, N of the village, in a superb position below Oare Hill. Late Georgian, ashlar-faced. Five-bay front. Raised attic above the middle bay. Porch of unfluted Ionic columns. Round the corner a second porch, of two pairs of the same columns. The house is ascribed to *Baldwin* of Bath (Devizes Museum, A87).

GIANT'S GRAVE. Promontory fort overlooking, and $\frac{1}{4}$ m. E of, Oare, on a spur. Unexcavated, but Iron Age A sherds found on the surface.

ODSTOCK

ST MARY. The chancel must have been Norman, see the one N window. It must also have been remodelled in the C13, see the S lancets. As it is, it is a rebuilding of 1870 (by *J. Fowler* of Louth), clearly lower than it had been.* Nave of the C13 with lancet windows, also in pairs, on both sides. Low W tower of flint and stone chequer, oddly attached to the nave. This has a canted W wall. The tower arch is set into the canting. On the N side the canting seems to have a partial justification in the existence of the polygonal staircase projection. The tower arch looks C14. – PULPIT. Jacobean, with flat arabesque carving. The foot, which seems not to belong to it, is dated 1580 and has the inscription: God bless and save our royal Queen, the lyke on earth was never seen'. – PLATE. Elizabethan Cup; Chalice and Paten, 1795. – MONUMENT. Tomb recess in the S wall of the nave. Cusped arch. In the recess low tomb-chest with an incised lid. On it figures of a Civilian, characteristic of *c.*1300–10. He is holding a shield (his heart?). Incised head canopy. Inscription in French. – Elizabethan monument without effigies. Three Ionic columns and two inscription plates. The inscriptions refer to C18 people; so the monument was appropriated.

MANOR HOUSE. The present building, in spite of a nicely decorated tablet with the date 1567, is of the later C17. Brick, with

* The *Building News*, 1870, p. 303, however, mentions only that the E window was preserved and says nothing of the side windows. *See* PF.

stone cross-windows and a hipped roof. Some windows
georgianized; the door surround recent. BARN of the manor
house. Flint and stone, of seven bays; aisled.

PARSONAGE FARMHOUSE, further W. C17. Brick with tile-
hanging. Three wide bays and two short wings.

CHAPEL COTTAGE, yet further W. Cob and thatch, with ogee-
headed windows.

OGBOURNE ST ANDREW   *1070*

ST ANDREW. Not big. Of flint, except for the W tower. This is
ashlar-faced and has a splendid tierceron-vault inside with a
circle for the bell-ropes in the middle and big bosses. The tower
is open to three sides, as the aisles embrace it. It was built into
a three-bay Norman nave of whose arcades now only a little
under two bays survive. Round piers, capitals with crockets
and bits of leaf, square abaci, round arches. One capital now
re-used for the piscina in the chancel. The N doorway has a
simple Norman hood-mould with zigzag, the S doorway is
a little later (still a round arch, but dog-tooth in the hood-
mould). Again a little later the chancel. Round-arched priest's
doorway but lancet windows. The E window may be an early
C14 alteration (reticulated tracery), but was mostly rebuilt 1873. *See*
– MONUMENTS. William Goddard and family, 1655. Hanging $^{p.}_{577}$
monument. Busts in a circular niche; they are together holding
a skull, kneeling children in the 'predella' below. – Anne
Seymour † 1687. Tablet with open double-curved pediment,
and flat leaf decoration down the sides.

Nice village with cottages built of Sarsen stone and thatched.

OGBOURNE MAIZEY MANOR HOUSE, ½ m. S. Jacobean. Bands
of stone and flint. Broad, flat, symmetrical front. Five bays.
Doorway with pediment on thin Ionic columns. Mullioned
windows. The tall arched Georgian windows symmetrically
inserted. The five gables or dormers may be new.

BARBURY CASTLE, 2 m. S of Wroughton. A very fine bivallate
hillfort with magnificent views to the N and W. From the site
have come iron tools and weapons and chariot equipment
including two rings with Celtic 'lip' moulding.

OGBOURNE ST GEORGE   *2070*

ST GEORGE. The S arcade of three bays comes first. Round piers
and stiff-leaf capitals. The N arcade is of two bays plus a third

to the w. Moulded capitals. Both arcades have double-chamfered arches, i.e. all this is E.E. The excellently moulded s
doorway belongs probably to the s arcade. Perp windows,
See Perp w tower. Chancel mostly of 1873. – SCREEN to the N
p. chapel. The top frieze is old. – CHANDELIER. Brass, given in
577 1788. – PLATE. Chalice, 1729. – BRASS. Thomas Goddard
†1517 and wife. Good 18-in. figures (nave E end).

MANOR HOUSE. On the site of a Benedictine priory, founded
*c.*1149. Jacobean house with a flat symmetrical N front. The
date 1619 is on the E chimneystack. Mullioned and transomed
and mullioned windows. The raised window in the middle
lights the staircase, which has vertically symmetrical balusters.
The handsome former entrance door is now in the library. The
s front is also symmetrical, but the window glazing is Georgian.
Of the same remodelling probably the big hipped roof.

OLDBURY CASTLE *see* CHERHILL

8040

OLD DILTON
⅞ m. SE of Dilton Marsh

ST MARY. Small, roughcast white, immediately by the street and
quite unexpected. The exterior is Perp, with a little bell-turret
with spire. The bell-openings like the sound-holes of a flute.
The s porch has a C14 entrance with a two-centred arch. The
fenestration is entertaining. There are all kinds of straight-
headed windows. Lights with two-centred arches cusped,
ogee-headed lights, rounded lights cusped and uncusped, and
even a C17 two-light mullioned window. C17 also the N vestry.
The arcade piers are altered. The arches are panelled. The
FURNISHINGS are entirely unspoilt. Nothing changed since
the C18. Three-decker PULPIT, BOX PEWS, FAMILY PEWS,
WEST GALLERY, even an odd NORTH GALLERY forming the
upper floor of the vestry and looking into the chancel.

OLD SARUM *see* SALISBURY, p. 346

0040

ORCHESTON ST GEORGE

ST GEORGE. Modest w tower with battlements and a pyramid
roof, yet with some embellishments of the w front and even a
panelled arch towards the nave. Embattled chancel. Most of

the external evidence Perp, except for the Norman N doorway
with one order of shafts. One capital is scalloped, the other has
leaf. (Above a N window of the arcade a sad E.E. head.) –
PLATE. Later Cup with Elizabethan base; Flagon, 1721.

ORCHESTON ST MARY
0040

ST MARY. Flint and rubble. SW tower with saddleback roof.
Late C13 doorway with continuous mouldings and S arcade of
two bays with round pier and double-chamfered arches. The
chancel E wall, outside as well as inside, looks early C19. It has
diagonally set pinnacles (as has the S porch) and two lancet
niches l. and r. of the window outside and two blank lancet
spaces, no doubt for Commandments etc., inside. – PLATE.
Paten, 1506; Elizabethan Cup; Flagon, 1729.

OVERTON HILL see AVEBURY and MILDENHALL

OVERTOWN HOUSE see WROUGHTON

PATNEY
0050

ST SWITHIN. Externally entirely Victorian (1877, by *Weaver* of
Devizes; PF). Is anything old? – FONT. Circular; only the base
is E.E. – PULPIT. Simple; C17. – STAINED GLASS. On the
N side an early window by *Kempe*; date of death 1873. – PLATE.
Chalice, 1706; Paten, 1722; Flagon, 1766.

PENLEIGH see DILTON MARSH

PERTWOOD
8030

ST PETER. Nave with bellcote and chancel. No division externally between nave and chancel. N aisle added in 1872. The
piscina in the chancel is the only architectural element of
interest, rather overmoulded; C14. – PULPIT. With Perp
panels. – BELL. Late C13. The oldest bell in Wiltshire with an
inscription. – PLATE. Chalice, 1676; Paten, probably 1676.
MANOR HOUSE. Church, manor house, and cottages huddle
together, sheltered by a wind-break of beech trees to the W.
The manor house seems to be C18, altered into a mildly Tudor
form about 1850.

PETERSFINGER *see* CLARENDON PALACE

PEWSEY

St John Baptist. The architectural story starts with the arcades, which are Late Norman. Four bays, their foundations mighty Sarsen stones. The piers are square, just chunks of the previous side walls, with a slight stop-chamfer. Pointed arches, also with one slight chamfer. Thin hood-moulds. Only the sw bay is different and obviously later. Double-chamfered arch. Then the chancel – later c13 to early c14. The chancel arch is double-chamfered. The s chapel is c19, but its s windows were no doubt those of the chancel. One is a lancet, the other has cusped Y-tracery. In the present chancel in addition another lancet. The e window however has reticulated tracery, i.e. is the end of the work on the chancel (or a replacement). Small two-seater sedilia. Perp w tower with a fan-vault inside. The tower is ashlar-faced and has a fan-light w window. Battlements; pinnacles. Perp aisle walls, the foundations again Sarsen stones. Perp clerestory. – PULPIT and STALLS. By *Street*, who restored the chancel in 1861 and rebuilt the s wall and the w part of the nave. Rather bald. – WOODWORK, e.g. the font cover and the reredos by Canon *Bertrand Pleydell Bouverie*, rector from 1880 to 1910. – PAINTINGS on the spandrels of the nave arcade. Tall lady angels against a background of simple red trails. Also by Canon *Pleydell Bouverie*. – STAINED GLASS. Two s aisle windows and one n aisle window: 1891, 1894, and † 1885. – PLATE. Chalice and Paten Cover, 1679.

There is very little to be seen at Pewsey. The little town has as its centre a little STATUE of King Alfred, 1911, and from this streets run in three directions. The houses are small and self-effacing. The local hotel, the PHOENIX INN, has a cast-iron inn-sign, an unusual thing. Otherwise there is the building of the RURAL DISTRICT COUNCIL OFFICES, formerly the rectory. It lies away from the street and is nine bays long. The two l. and two r. bays are in slightly projecting wings. Chequer brickwork. Hipped roof. Doorway with Doric pilasters and pediment. The staircase has three twisted balusters to the step. The house is probably of *c.* 1700, with the external details Later Georgian. On the way from the Rural District Offices to the church on the l. COURT HOUSE, timber-framed and thatched. Finally, at the far e end of the High Street, BALL, another timber-framed and thatched house. (Opposite this a cruck cottage. NBR)

PEWSEY HOSPITAL, the former WORKHOUSE, lies on the road to Wilton. It is of stone, and has a nineteen-bay front and a five-bay pedimental gable. On it the date 1836. The style is still classical.

WEST WICK FARMHOUSE, under Martinsell Hill, 1¾ m. NNE. Georgian, of five bays and two storeys. One-bay pediment. Doorway with Ionic columns and a broken pediment.

WHITE HORSE, 1¼ m. S. Cut out of the turf in 1785. Almost obliterated before 1900 and re-cut in 1937 to commemorate the Coronation of George VI. 66 by 45 ft.

PINKNEY COURT FARMHOUSE see SHERSTON

PITTON

2030

ST PETER. The single-chamfered round-arched S doorway must be C12. Also Norman a single capital with steep tendril-like volutes, now in the N aisle E corner. The doorway is inside a S porch tower whose lower storey is of the C13 – see the remarkable entrance with a steeply pointed trefoiled arch. One continuous hollow chamfer. In the chancel some remains of C13 lancets. The nave W window of *c*.1300: three lights, cusped intersected tracery. The rest mostly C19 (by *Ewan Christian*; PF). Rainwater heads with the date 1880. – FONT. Norman, circular, with a plaited band. – STAINED GLASS. E window by *Kempe*, 1886. The nobbly-leaf background is characteristic.

PORTON

1030

ST NICHOLAS. 1876–7 by *J. L. Pearson*. Flint; nave with bellcote and chancel. The windows Geometrical to Dec. Nave with a single-frame roof, chancel with a boarded polygonal wagon roof. – FONT. Octagonal; Perp.

POTTERNE

9050

ST MARY. An E.E. parish church of exceptional purity and indeed classicity. This must be explained by the fact that Potterne was a manor of the bishops of Salisbury and that the bishops at least from the later C13 onwards had a manor house at Potterne and held the prebend of Potterne in the chapter of

Salisbury. Moreover, the work of the C13 at Potterne is completely preserved and, except for the very top of the broad, dependable tower, later ages have hardly interfered with it. Nor can the Perp contribution to the tower be considered to do damage to the C13 ensemble. The church is cruciform with a tower over the crossing. All windows except those of the tower are tall lancets, groups of three, stepped and close to each other, in the E and W walls, groups of three, of even height and widely spaced, in the E walls of the transepts. In the tower each side has a pair of tall two-light bell-openings with plate tracery (a quatrefoiled circle), but the Perp mason enriched them with small Somerset tracery and crowned the whole with very elaborate pierced battlements, pinnacles, and a polygonal stair-turret. The crossing arches are of two continuous chamfers, so that in the corners the piers look four-stepped. Their capitals are too small, just a continuation of the mouldings of the string-courses round the window tops. The doorways also have continuous chamfers. The porches may be a slightly later addition. The priest's doorway on the other hand, with so depressed a two-centred arch that it seems segmental, is typically E.E. The Purbeck marble shafts inside the E window, making with two blank lancets l. and r. a stepped group of five, are the only embellishments the C13 allowed itself. – FONT. Tub-shaped, Anglo-Saxon, with a Latin inscription along the rim (cf. Partrishaw, also Little Billing, Northants.).* – PULPIT. Perp, of wood, with two-light blank panels with crocketed ogee gables. – WIND VANE. Of iron, dated 1757. In the porch. – PAINTING. Moses and Aaron from altarpiece given in 1723. – PLATE. Set, 1724. – MONUMENTS. Henry Kent † 1769. Tablet, signed by *Nollekens*. – John Spearing † 1821. By *E. H. Baily*. Large figure of a woman by an urn on a tall pedestal. She leans in an elegant attitude of the van Dyck-Reynolds tradition.

CHURCH HOUSE. Dated 1614. Façade with two symmetrical gables and the lower gable of the two-storeyed porch between. Mullioned windows.

30a PORCH HOUSE, in the High Street. One of the most famous of English late C15 timber-framed houses, remarkably well preserved.‡ The timbering is all uprights, no diagonals and no fancy work. The front has three gables, deliberately asymmetrical and scaled with great sensibility. The smallest is that of

---

* The inscription is, in English: Like as the hart desireth the water-brooks, so longeth my soul after Thee, O God.

‡ During a restoration three French late-C15 coins were found.

the square porch. The house is a hall-house of the simplest plan, with a cross-gabled office part and a cross-gabled chamber and solar part, neither of them projecting. Original roofs are preserved to a large extent. The hall, going up as high as the two storeys in the cross parts, has a hammerbeam roof (with the pendants unfortunately cut off) with three tiers of wind-braces. In the solar appears the cross-roof: collar-beams on arched braces and two tiers of wind-braces. The partition walls are set in independent of the main framework – a very modern conception. The windows also are amazingly intact. The largest is the hall bay. It has a transom and tracery above and below it, above with two little circles between the ogee arches of the lights (a motif popular in Somerset), below with four little panels between them. The latter is the motif repeated in other windows as well, e.g. those of the sides of the porch. To the back the hall has two completely plain five-light windows, the lights being very narrow. Several windows project very slightly, forming little oriels. The chamber oriel seems to carry the solar overhang. The bargeboarding of the gables, with carved quatrefoil friezes, largely in good condition too. From the solar a tiny square spy window with tracery looks into the hall. In 1876 the house was restored for George Richmond, the painter. He put in the mosaic floor of the hall – incongruous but handsome.*

To the s another timber-framed house. The ground floor corresponds to that of Porch House, but the upper floor has the concave-sided lozenges which are typical of the late c16 or c17 and quite uncommon in Wiltshire.

(In COXHILL LANE, off to the E, a CRUCK COTTAGE. NBR)

BLOUNT'S COURT, a little to the s on the hill. A large Victorian Gothic mansion with a porte-cochère tower. Built in 1870–1.

EASTWELL, ½ m. SW of the church. Close to the house a fine late C17 SUMMER HOUSE of brick, two storeys, two by three bays, with a hipped roof.

COURTHILL HOUSE, ¼ m. SW. Of c.1700. Five bays, two storeys, the middle three bays slightly projecting. Hipped roof. The doorway with Tuscan columns and metope frieze seems later.

WHISTLEY FARMHOUSE, 1 m. SW. Early C18. Five bays, two storeys, hipped roof. Doorway with segmental pediment.

* A good deal of STAINED GLASS, C15 and later, is in the windows of the house.

POULSHOT

ST PETER. W tower with pyramid roof 1853. In the chancel windows of the late C13, single-light, pointed-trefoiled, with rere-arches inside. The chancel arch with shafts on head-corbels goes with this date. The E part is Perp. The church is impressive within. Though the arcades of two bays only (octagonal piers, double-chamfered arches) are of the later C14, the narrowness of the aisles tells of an earlier date. The church had indeed had aisles already in the C12; for three capitals are preserved, built into the N wall and the aisle E walls. They belonged to circular piers and are scalloped. – STAINED GLASS. Grisaille quarries with leaf motifs in a chancel s window may well be of the late C13 too. – PLATE. Paten Cover, 1576; Chalice, 1634; Paten, given in 1707.

PRESHUTE

ST GEORGE. W tower, ashlar-faced, with three-light bell-openings and battlements; Perp. The rest of the exterior 1854 by *T. H. Wyatt*. Flint with a stone pattern. Inside, however, late-C12 arcade of four bays. Circular piers, octagonal abaci, the capitals with scallops and decorated trumpet scallops. The arches of 1854. – FONT. A truly amazing piece of black Tournai marble. The date must be the C13. Powerful mouldings and nothing else at all except a quite exceptional size. The font is supposed to come from Marlborough Castle. St George was the parish church of the castle area. – SCULPTURE. Some C14 heads from the old church. – STAINED GLASS. 1854, signed *C.A.G.* – MONUMENTS. Brass to John Bailey † 1518 and wife, 18-in. figures (s aisle E end). – Tablet to Jeff Daniell and his son who died in 1697. Two weeping putti with enormous hankies.
PRESHUTE HOUSE. *See* Marlborough College, p. 305.
WHITE HORSE. Cut in 1804. 62 by 47 ft.
DEVIL'S DEN, CLATFORD BOTTOM, 2 m. W of Marlborough. The remains of the chamber of a long barrow. The stones were erected in their present position in 1921.

PURTON

ST MARY. Beautifully placed, close to the Manor House and separated from the village by trees. An interesting church too, very different inside from what the outside indicates. Inside there are the E responds of the arcades, clearly Norman, flat with many-scalloped capitals. There are then the arcades of three bays, the northern with circular piers, capitals with upright leaves, and octagonal abaci, the southern with round piers, moulded capitals, and circular abaci, the former perhaps c.1200, the latter early c13. The arches throughout are moulded and perhaps late c14. At that time also the piers may have been heightened. Little of the Dec style, i.e. the s chapel with an E window with enterprisingly flowing tracery, the N aisle W window (reticulated tracery), and the s doorway. Perp two-storeyed s porch, s aisle, s transept, chancel with sedilia with one long shallow arch and Easter Sepulchre, much redone,* N aisle, and finally – externally the curious thing about the church – the w tower as well as the crossing tower. The crossing tower came first. It is probably still c14, see the double-chamfered arches into the transepts and the recessed spire. Inside, vault with diagonal and ridge-ribs and a large circle in the middle. The ambitious w tower has a doorway with a four-centred arch, a three-light window with niches l. and r. and above, three-light bell-openings with Somerset tracery, and a parapet with pierced quatrefoils and pinnacles. Niches also in the N and s walls. Altogether the church is curiously rich in niches and corbels for images – see the E gable of the s chapel, the s gable of the s transept, the E wall of the porch, and the N aisle. A squint in the form of a panel with three open quatrefoils between s transept and s chapel.

FURNISHINGS. SCREENS. Two panels, Perp, in the back of the stalls. – SCULPTURE. There are two good c14 heads in the arch of the N transept. – PAINTINGS. On the s transept s wall good Death of the Virgin, late c14. Also other paintings, less clearly visible, i.e. less restored, e.g. Crucifixion above the s transept E arch. – In the reredos, oil painting of the Last Supper, Flemish, influenced by Rubens. – STAINED GLASS. Original fragments in the N aisle W and E windows. The s chapel 's window is quite filled with fragments. – PLATE. Chalice and Paten, given in 1666; Paten, 1708. – MONUMENTS. Nevill Maskelyne † 1679. Tablet with two ugly putti growing out of garlands. – Matthew Vivash † 1839. By *Franklin* of Purton. Medallion with a wreath of ivy, a charming sentimental conceit (cf. the identical tablet at Highworth).

* The E wall with the two gorgeous niches is by *Butterfield*, who restored the church in 1872.

MANOR HOUSE, W of the church. Built about 1600. Symmetrical front with three gables, four-light windows, and a two-storeyed porch. To its W a big L-shaped BARN, the E end of stone and gabled, the rest timber-framed with brick infilling on a stone base.

About ½ m. NW is the HIGH STREET. Its start is an Early Georgian four-bay house of brick with bold stone trim and a two-bay pediment. Then on the other side a four-bay stone house with a pedimented porch on Tuscan columns. Further on COLLEGE FARM, built in 1662, but still quite pre-classical. Symmetrical five-bay front, the windows with hood-moulds. (Inside a wooden overmantel of 1626 with a florid coat of arms and small figures l. and r. in front of pilasters.) At the W end the NORTH VIEW HOSPITAL, former WORKHOUSE,* brick, of eleven bays and two storeys with a five-bay pediment. Built c.1840.

From the start, i.e. the E end of the High Street, N along STATION ROAD, past COLLINS LANE GATE, a toll-house with polygonal front jutting into the street and a panel with a table of fees. So on to PURTON STOKE, where at the S end BENTHAM HOUSE, Early Victorian Tudor with bargeboarded, sharply pointed gables and dormers and in the garden a summer house of stone and flint decoration.‡ Finally, E of the NE end of the village the PUMP ROOM of the minute Purton Spa, an octagon like a garden pavilion, built in 1859. Slate roof with wooden awning similar to those of railway platforms.

RESTROP, I m. W. Fine Elizabethan house with an E-front. Two-storeyed porch, mullioned and transomed windows of four and three lights.

SAXON BURIALS. ¼ m. E of Purton House Saxon burials have been discovered from time to time. Three, excavated in 1912, were accompanied by an iron short sword, spearhead, knife, and a glass bead.

RINGSBURY CAMP, ½ m. SW. A bivallate Iron Age hill-fort with entrance on the E.

BURY HILL, 2½ m. NW. Iron Age hill-fort, the ramparts considerably reduced by ploughing.

PYT HOUSE see NEWTOWN

* ROMAN BUILDING. 350 yds W of the workhouse gate were found fragments of a mosaic pavement.

‡ Mr G. Spain tells me of a tender for additions dated 1867. Architect T. S. Lansdown.

QUEMERFORD

0060

1 m. SE of Calne

HOLY TRINITY. 1853. Nave and chancel. Bellcote with little spire. Geometrical tracery.

MILL. Probably early C19. Stone. Built for flax-spinning. Of nine bays and five storeys, with segment-headed two-light windows.

ROUND HOUSE, ¼ m. E. An elongated octagon of brick with stone dressings and a shingled pyramid roof.

QUIDHAMPTON

1030

¾ m. N of Netherhampton

THE GRANGE. 1677. Ashlar-faced house with picturesque timber-framed insertions and additions. Quite irregular. Mullioned windows and one gabled front with windows in four storeys.

WILTON ESTATE MODEL FARM. Probably of *c*.1850. Italianate windows, an arcaded kind of cloister. The buildings faced with a terrible crazy-paving. Circular DOVECOTE.

RAINSCOMBE HOUSE *see* OARE

RAMSBURY

2070

HOLY CROSS. An E.E. chancel, now recognizable by the form of the buttresses, the chancel arch, the angle piscina with a Purbeck shaft, the blank trefoil arches to the l. and r. of the chancel arch facing into the chancel, and the very odd traces of giant blank arcading on the N wall. The middle arch goes less low down than the others, because a semicircular door-head cuts into it. The chancel windows are Perp, and it is likely that the chancel was lengthened then, and the piscina shifted. The priest's doorway lies in a solid projection or closed-in porch, with its own little lean-to roof. Dec W tower with mighty buttresses, a three-light window with cusped intersected tracery, and a Perp top (see the bell-openings). Dec or earlier the simply single-chamfered S doorway and possibly the aisle windows on both sides (two ogee-headed lights below a shallow, four-centred, as it were cambered arch). Both aisles are embattled. Perp N chapel (Darrell Chapel) of one bay with a six-light N window. Ornate Victorian S porch. The most important Perp contribution is the arcades. Four bays, the piers with four projections which instead of being simply canted have a flat front but wavy sides. The tower arch is the same, and the entrance arch into the N chapel too. In the N chapel two corbels with foliage and, in the jambs of the E window, two canopied circles of differing design. The clerestory of straight-headed three-light windows in line with the spandrels, not the apexes, of the arcade arches is also Perp, as is the low-pitched roof with arched braces on grotesque faces carrying tie-beams. Traceried spandrels.

FURNISHINGS. Quite an uncommon wealth. FONT. Of goblet-shape with a diaper pattern. The scenes carved in relief against the stem are the work of a local gentleman, Mr *Thomas Meyrick*. He did them in 1842. – ORGAN. A very large, very pretty Gothick piece; probably early C19. – CHANDELIERS. Of brass, two tiers, dated 1751. Both together cost £20 10s. 6d. – TILES. A few at the W end of the N aisle. – Here also the most important of the furnishings of the church, the fragments of a late C9 CROSS.* The lowest part has a dragon, intertwined and biting its own tail, in the early Viking style and very similar to the piece at Colerne. On the sides close interlace of a Carolingian or Italian kind. The higher part represents quite a different tradition, that of the Early Christian and the Northumbrian so-called inhabited scrolls. The sides are interlace again. – Displayed in the same place a SEPULCHRAL SLAB with a Latin cross raised in relief and on it a lion *passant*, a strange conceit. – Also two COPED STONES of the C9 with rounded ends, one with interlace, the other with less tight vegetable scrolls, reminiscent of illuminated manuscripts. – Also an interesting fragment of a Norman FIGURE, showing characteristic C12 drapery. – PAINTING. Christ taken from the Cross, large C17 painting, probably Flemish with strong Italian influence. – STAINED GLASS. In the S aisle at the E end by *Casolini*, made by *Powell*, 1861. – PLATE. Apostle Spoon, 1661; Flagon, 1707; Set, 1718.

MONUMENTS. The earliest, after the two Anglo-Saxon coped stones, is the slab on the chancel floor with a Norman French inscription and the indent of a brass. It is to William St John, rector of Ramsbury, † 1322. – Then a number of Perp monuments, all in a fragmentary state. In the Darrell Chapel a big Purbeck-marble tomb-chest with indents of brasses, a second completely plain tomb-chest, and a badly preserved Purbeck recess with decorated tomb-chest. The recess has a

* Or two crosses?

panelled ceiling and panelled jambs. The brasses of the back
wall are all gone. The monument may originally have been
where the organ now is; for two buttress-shafts with pinnacles
remain there. – In the chancel a better-preserved Purbeck
monument. Tomb-chest, colonnettes with lozenge decoration
on the shafts, four pendant arches with ogee gables. Solid
superstructure with cresting. In the E wall of the monument a
little niche. The brasses are looted here as well. – Then a gap
in time and the swagger monument to Sir William Jones of
Ramsbury Manor † 1682. White and grey marbles. Semi-
reclining effigy, one hand demonstrating, the other holding a
scroll. Superstructure with an open book and a skull. – Next
Jonathan Knackstone † 1745 (N aisle E). Exuberant cartouche;
two cherubs at the top. – William Jones, 1775. By *J. F. Moore*.
A very large tablet of coloured marbles. Profile bust in a
roundel, the curtains in front of it held open by two putti.
Short sarcophagus at the top; the whole in front of a grey
obelisk finished with a pediment. – Mary E. Burdett † 1797.
By *King* of Bath. With an urn, a lamb, a baby, and this poem:

> Not formal duty prompts these mournful Lays
> No painted shew of Grief these lines impart,
> No cold unfeeling, stale, insipid Praise,
> But Sorrow flowing from the o'er fraught heart.
>
> No need hast thou of monumental Verse
> Lamented Maid; to prove thy worth was high;
> The Widows tear adorns thy modest hearse,
> Thy name is honored with the poor Mans sigh.
>
> Alas! they cry, that feeling heart is cold,
> That lib'ral hand which gave to all relief;
> That tongue, whose sweetness never can be told,
> Which charm'd our ears, and soothed our sharpest Grief.
>
> If thou canst look, bright Angel from above
> As to thy God thou bend'st th'adoring Knee
> Accept this tribute of a Brother's love
> And in thy Orisons remember me.

– In the S aisle two monuments by *P. M. van Gelder* to members
of the Read family, one † 1786, the other † 1801. The comparison is enlightening. Instead of the fulsome young woman by
an urn now a much more severe urn without a figure – the way
from Baroque-Roman classicism to Grecian classicism. –
Elizabeth Batson † 1808. Tablet with a relief of Faith, the sides
tapering, i.e. again Grecian. By *Honeybone* of Shrivenham.

In the village there is not much of note. The best house by far is immediately N of the church: PARLIAMENT PIECE, late C17, brick, of five by five bays with a hipped roof and dormers. Cross-windows of wood. Later porch. Staircase with strong turned balusters. Good GATEPIERS with arms and STABLES. The E end has a half-hipped roof and a big upright oval window. At the E end of the village on the way to the bridge THE CEDARS, modest Georgian, with a façade with two bows and STABLES of seven bays with a middle archway, gable, and lantern.

46b RAMSBURY MANOR. A perfect example of the moderate-sized brick mansion of about 1680, a parallel to Melton Constable or Felbrigg or Denham Place. The estate was bought in 1681 by Sir William Jones, a prosperous lawyer, who probably rebuilt the house at once. Brick with stone dressings. Nine by six bays and two storeys on a basement still with two-light mullioned windows. Hipped roof. The windows of the house are now all sashed but must originally have had mullion-and-transom crosses. On the entrance (E) side stair to the doorway which has a segmental pediment sheltering garlands. The window above it still has flanking half-pilasters, an echo of the 'Artisan Mannerism' of the fifties and sixties. The nine bays are designed so as to culminate in a three-bay centre projection with a pediment. Quoins at the angles and the angles of the projection. Very richly carved cornice and modillions. Garlands in the pediment. The garden (W) side is almost identical; the other sides differ considerably. To the N the two middle bays are emphasized by stone facing and a pediment and have two doorways side by side. To the S the site slopes down to the river Kennet, and so the house has here three storeys. They face a service court of three sides of a quadrangle, one and a half storeys high. Attached to the S side of the S range, i.e. facing the river, the ORANGERY, dated 1775. Five tall, narrow, arched windows and a pediment right across.

Fine entrance hall and saloon across the centre of the house. They lead into one another by a big doorway with wide-open segmental pediment on carved brackets. In the entrance hall the panelling includes one principal panel (N wall) which also still has some of the restlessness of the 'Artisan Mannerism'. The saloon has a restrained late C18 plaster ceiling, and in the 47 overmantel of the elegant late C18 fireplace some fruit and flower carving fully worthy of *Grinling Gibbons*. The axis at r. angles to these two rooms is occupied by the two staircases. Only the S staircase is original. It has strong turned balusters and a curious and ingenious plan. It rises in quite a normal way with two long flights interrupted by a short one from the basement to the main floor and up to the upper floor. But at first-floor level there is in addition a bridge towards a balcony which runs along the window wall to provide a direct communication between the NW and NE corner rooms. Strangely mannered, monumental entrance on the same floor to the corridor or passage which here runs through the centre of the house. Giant pilasters with strong entasis and a bulgy broken-up frieze. It looks *c.*1700–10 rather than *c.*1680. Good late-C18 fireplaces in some other rooms, including one on the first floor which has also an C18 Chinese wallpaper.

STABLES. Not big. Five arched bays and two solid end bays with gables. Under each gable, asymmetrically placed, an upright oval window.

GATEPIERS towards Ramsbury. Of the time of the house. Large, with sunk panels and with garlands below the top cornice. The LODGES were added in the later C18. They are like cubes of one by one bay.

The house lies beautifully by the river, and the river vista to the E is closed by a handsome five-arch brick BRIDGE also of the later C18.

CROWOOD HOUSE, 1 m. NE. Five-bay, two-storey brick house, rendered. Steep one-bay pediment. A date 1686 has recently been found on a rafter. The façade remodelled, probably late in the C18. Yet later wings. Is the porch with its pilasters even more recent?

ROMAN VILLA, 2 m. NW, between Burney and Mere Farms. A corridor villa with three bath-houses, excavated in 1914–24. It appears to have been occupied in the C2–4 A.D.

MEMBURY FORT, 2½ m. NE. A bivallate Iron Age hill-fort.

REDDISH MANOR *see* BROAD CHALKE

REDLYNCH

1020

ST BIRINUS. 1894–6 by *Ponting*. Brick with four-light windows of yellow stone set under brick arches – à la Carõe. Short shingled bell-turret.

ST MARY, 1 m. SE, i.e. in old Redlynch. Built in 1837. Yellow brick. Tall two-light Perp windows. The chancel has remained short, i.e. has not undergone High Victorian enlargements.

LODGE to Redlynch House. Early Victorian, quite large, with bargeboarded gables.

RESTROP *see* PURTON

RINGSBURY CAMP *see* PURTON

ROBIN HOOD'S BALL *see* SHREWTON

ROCHE COURT *see* WINTERSLOW

1070
ROCKLEY
1¾ m. w of Ogbourne St Andrew

CHAPEL. Nave with bellcote and chancel. Stone and flint chequer. Lancet windows.

ROCKLEY MANOR. Rendered. C18, of five bays and two storeys with a central pediment. The doorway and the window above it are tripartite. To the side a four-column veranda between two canted bays. Hipped roof.

9080
RODBOURNE

HOLY ROOD. Norman s doorway, now inside the church. In the tympanum big-leaved Tree of Life. The N doorway is Norman too, but has a plain tympanum. The sunk cross seems to be later. One N window also Norman. Late C13 E window. Two pointed-trefoiled lights and a circle in plate tracery. Good C19 SW tower with saddleback roof and a few well-composed lancet windows. Of the C19 also the baptistery between tower and s doorway. Nave and chancel in one; low. Pretty niche and canopy in the N wall. – SCREEN. Of one-light divisions. – STONE SEAT. C13? – STAINED GLASS. E window, early *Morris* work, Adam and Eve and the Annunciation. Badly preserved. The Hungerford family was connected with Rodbourne.

1080
RODBOURNE CHENEY

This is really inside the boundaries of Swindon.

ST MARY. Early C13 entrance to the s porch. One order of colonnettes. Nailhead strip in the abaci. Pointed arch. C13 chancel, to the E a group of three stepped lancet windows set close together. Otherwise mostly Perp and much rebuilt in 1848. The N aisle e.g. dates from that year, and so does the w tower, though the quite elaborate doorway (traceried spandrels)

looks genuine Perp work. Two holm-oaks to the w. Inside, the
C13 is represented by the over-restored arch which once led
from the crossing tower into the s transept. It is the only evidence of this early form of the church. – SCULPTURE. In the N
wall of the tower and the w wall of the N aisle re-set Anglo-
Saxon stones with interlace ornament, that in the tower semicircular. – STAINED GLASS. Some C14 and C15 fragments in
several windows. – PLATE. Chalice, inscribed 1814; two Patens
of the same time. – MONUMENTS. William Holcroft † 1621.
Inscription tablet flanked by columns. – Several minor Georgian tablets, e.g. Arthur Evans † 1789 with mourning woman by
an urn, and Simon Wayte † 1807, by *Reeves* of Bath.

The church is now separated from the remains of the village by a
main road. To its s MANOR HOUSE and MANOR FARM, two
rubble houses mainly of the C17.

ROLLESTONE 0040

ST ANDREW. Small, of flint and stone chequerwork. Nave and
chancel, the nave having the rare feature of – no doubt C19 –
bargeboarding to the E gable of the nave. C13 chancel; see the
N and s lancets. The nave has larger Perp windows, that on the
N side Earliest Perp. – COMMUNION RAIL. C17; thin balusters. – STAINED GLASS. Some C17 heraldic panels. – PLATE.
Cup and Paten Cover, 1576; Paten, 1694.

ROOD ASHTON *see* WEST ASHTON

ROUNDWAY 0060

A small group of BOWL BARROWS lies on Roundway Down,
including one which covered the classic Beaker burial of an
old man accompanied by a magnificent bell beaker, large copper
tanged knife, copper pin, stone archer's wristguard, and barb
and tang flint arrowhead.

½ m. W of Roundway Down is an isolated BOWL BARROW which
produced a secondary Saxon burial, contained in an iron bound
wooden coffin and accompanied by ornaments and trinkets of
gold.

Continuing w again for a further ½ m. the hill-fort of OLIVER'S
CAMP (Bromham parish) is reached. Begun as an Iron Age A
promontory fort, it was later remodelled to a univallate, sub-
rectangular plan with entrance on the E.

9060
ROWDE

St Matthew. Slender Perp w tower. The rest rebuilt by
Goodridge in 1831–3. All embattled and with many pinnacles,
those at the E end detached on the buttresses in front of the E
wall. – FONT. 1850 by *Sir Matthew Digby Wyatt*, who at the
time lived at Rowdeford House. Perp, octagonal, with alternating quatrefoils and lozenges, i.e. entirely conventional
imitation Perp. – PLATE. Chalice and Paten Cover, 1576.
Rowdeford House (now a school). The house is of 1812.
Two storeys with a parapet. Thin giant pilasters to mark the
main parts. Five wide bays, semicircular porch on paired
Ionic columns. The side has three wide bays, and the centre
is recessed. Generous staircase. Iron handrail with extremely
thin lyre motifs. Glazed at the top.
Bell Inn, St Edith's Marsh, 1 m. N. Dated 1698. Six bays, cross-
windows, hipped roof.

RUDGE FARM VILLA *see* FROXFIELD

RUDLOE MANOR *see* BOX

1050
RUSHALL

St Matthew. Perp w tower, ashlar-faced with a panelled arch
towards the nave. The rest of 1812, except for the nave SW
buttress, the E and N walls of the chancel, the latter with a two-
light window, and the chancel arch (double-chamfered, dying
into the imposts). That seems all Dec. The rebuilding was in
brick. Nave and lower chancel, plus a family chapel to the N.
Its N window is remarkable. A two-light window with a quatrefoil in bar tracery is not what one would expect as an imitation
of 1812. Yet the little fluted capitals of the shafts outside are
decidedly Georgian. – FONT. Octagonal, Norman. The bowl
of the familiar Purbeck type with two very shallow blank
arches on each side, the foot probably a re-used Late Norman
capital with upright leaves like fluting. It must have belonged
to a pier as substantial as those of Stapleford. – BENCHES.
With straight-headed, simply traceried ends. – STAINED
GLASS. Two small, strongly-coloured C15 panels in the chancel
SE window. – PLATE. Chalice, 1730. – MONUMENTS. Elizabethan panel with two squares containing shields in simple
strapwork surrounds. A band of arabesque between them. On

the l. shield the initials W.P. – Edward Poore † 1788. Tablet with, at the top, relief of a seated woman by an urn. Quite good. (BAPTIST CHAPEL. 1706.)

RUSHMORE see TOLLARD ROYAL

RYBURY CAMP see ALL CANNINGS

ST EDITH'S MARSH see ROWDE

ST MARIE'S GRANGE see ALDERBURY

SALISBURY

OLD SARUM
1¼ m. N of Salisbury

PRE-SAXON REMAINS. The first traceable structure on the site appears to be a univallate Iron Age hill-fort. A single storage pit has been located within the ramparts of this fort. Associated with this first phase of settlement are two La Tène III brooches, a bronze belt link, rotary querns, and sherds of bead-rimmed Belgic pottery. During the Roman occupation the hill became the Roman town of Sorviodunum. Traces of the town walls have been located beneath the medieval castle mound. The settlement must have been of considerable importance, as it was situated at the junction between the Roman roads to Badbury and Dorchester, Winchester, Silchester, and the Mendip lead mines.

ROMAN ROADS. The Badbury and Dorchester road leaves

Sarum on its SE side, crossing the river Nadder at Bemerton, and runs SW across the golf course. The river Ebble is crossed at Stratford Tony, and from there the road runs SW to Knighton Wood, forming the Wiltshire–Hampshire border for a mile, where it is clearly visible as a raised way 40–50 ft wide and over 5 ft. high.

The Silchester road, known as the Port Way, runs NE from Sarum to Ende Burgh (a large round barrow); from there it continues as a modern highway to Winterbourne Gunner. Beyond, it runs parallel to the railway line and enters Hampshire near Grateley.

NNE from Sarum, the Mildenhall (Cunetio) road is ill-defined at its S end, but is traceable in Savernake Forest, where it passes close to a Roman kiln site; it enters Cunetio from the S.

Little of the road leading W from Sarum to the Mendip lead mines can be traced in Wiltshire, but E to Winchester, one crosses the river Bourne at Ford, running across the Downs to Winterslow.

PAGAN SAXON SARUM is represented by finds of two combs, a brooch with scroll-work ornament, and a belt fitting – all probably of the C9 A.D.

MEDIEVAL OLD SARUM. From a distance Old Sarum appears 8a an impressive earthwork. It is hard to envisage an early medieval hill-town with a keep, a cathedral, walls and houses behind them. The site is ideally defended by nature. It falls steeply to N, S, and W. The Romans appreciated the position (*see* above) if not the site.

As one gets nearer, the impression of nothing but earthworks still remains. There is a deep ditch and then a high rampart. The area enclosed by it, i.e. the area of fortress and tower, is over 56 acres. The principal approach was from the E, as it still is. The floruit of Old Sarum is from the transfer of the see from Sherborne to Sarum *c.*1075–8 to the early C13. Under St Osmund (1078–99) the following were built: the first cathedral, the moat and mound in the middle of the site and a castle on it. There were also cross ditches N and S of the mound. Bishop Roger (1107–39) enlarged the cathedral and built the keep. However, he fell out with King Stephen and was deprived of his castle. The castle remained royal, altercations between clergy and garrison never ceased, and in the end the clergy decided to move out and start a new Sarum in the valley. An additional reason existed in any case: shortage of water on the hill. The castle remained royal and active. Much money was spent on it in the 1170s and again in the 1240s. In the C14 however interest in it decreased, and in Leland's time (1535) all was in ruins, including the cathedral. Only a chapel of Our Lady, he says, was standing.

As one enters the town from the E, there is nothing but grass hiding the area where the houses stood. Walking across one comes up to the first buildings whose flint filling of the formerly ashlar-faced walls still stands up to varying heights. The wooden BRIDGE across the ditch of the inner bailey replaces a drawbridge whose stone abutments remain. The GATE-HOUSE seems to be late C12. It has two towers with semicircular fronts. To the l. and r. small, formerly vaulted guard chambers. To the SW of the gatehouse another building. It had hearths and ovens and so was probably the BAKEHOUSE. Straight W from the gatehouse is the well and then the KEEP, not really a keep, but rather four ranges of building round an inner court which remained filled up with chalk to a higher level. The arrangement in Roger's castle of Sherborne was the same. Otherwise one would distrust so completely exceptional an arrangement. In the SE corner was the chapel, formerly vaulted. To its N a room originally with wooden posts down its centre. That it had an upper floor is proved by the spiral stair-case at its N end. Projecting to the E two deep garderobe (i.e. cess) pits. Further N another spiral stair and then, at the NE corner and projecting as far as the curtain wall, a tower. This is visible at the upper level. Here two more garderobe pits and also an oblong N room with a fireplace. To the SW of the keep was the POSTERN GATE. It was later blocked up and a more tricky passage made which, from outside, first turned N and then E, by the stairs which led to the chamber above the postern gate. To its S was a strong TOWER with a mighty battered base, and to the SE of that the C13 HALL with a stone bench all along its surviving wall.* In this part of the castle is the MUSEUM of finds, nearly all Norman and including decorative pieces identical with those re-used in the Close walls of New Sarum. By the Postern Tower and the Hall is the best-preserved stretch of curtain wall. Another is on the SE. The wall is Norman and was 12 ft thick. The wall walk is clearly visible.

The CATHEDRAL and its ancillary buildings filled the NW sector. Here nothing stands up, except a chunk of curtain walling. But most of the buildings are outlined in the turf. St Osmund's cathedral, which was consecrated in 1092, was a

* The 'new hall' is mentioned in 1247.

mere 173 ft long. It had an apsed chancel and chancel aisles
ending inside in apses too, though outside in straight walls
(cf. Caen, St Albans, and other places), and it had the most
remarkable feature of transepts with big towers over, a motif
not occurring at such an early date either in France or in Germany. The only existing example in England is Exeter, some
three generations later. The best-known examples in the
French orbit are Angoulême Cathedral of c.1110–18 and Lyons
and Geneva Cathedrals of the late C12. Bishop Roger enlarged
the cathedral considerably. When he had finished it was 316 ft
long – still not large, when compared with Westminster Abbey
or Winchester or St Paul's. He added a w façade, probably
with twin towers, and he pulled down St Osmund's E end and
replaced it by a much more spacious one. This had several
features worth commenting on. The high choir ended straight,
like that of New Sarum later, or like those of Hereford and St
John's Chester in the C12. To the E of this was an ambulatory
with three chapels. That sounds like the French scheme of
ambulatory and radiating chapels, i.e. the scheme of Tours or
Cluny or Rouen or so many others, and also of many in England.
But the English had an idea that all chapels ought to face E, and
so they tended to work out compromises between radiating and
orientated chapels (Canterbury, Norwich, St Hugh's Choir
Lincoln, Leominster, Muchelney). Bishop Roger's is the most
convincing solution. The chapels are attached to a straight-
sided ambulatory and thus simply repeat St Osmund's arrangement, except that now even the wider middle apse of the three
has a straight outer wall. That satisfied another English preference, that for straight-ended plans (cf. for the C12, e.g.,
Romsey). It is likely that the ambulatory and the chapels were
lower than the chancel; if so, that again was repeated at New
Sarum.

Bishop Roger also added a cloister. He placed it to the N,
not as usual the S, and he placed it N of his choir, not as usual
the nave. This being so, it is indeed likely that the building
immediately N of St Osmund's transept was the chapter house,
even if chapter houses ought to be in the E, not the W range of
cloisters. It would be a curious chapter house in another way as
well; for it has an undercroft, and only this remains. Twice
four bays with originally three round piers and rib-vaults. The
arrangement was caused by the fall of the site to the N.

Yet further N excavations (which are not exposed) have
revealed the former BISHOP'S PALACE. It bordered imme-

diately on the cloister and had an aisled hall running N–S, a
courtyard to its W, and a narrower range W of the courtyard.

NEW SARUM

THE CATHEDRAL

INTRODUCTION

The reasons why Bishop Poore moved from Old Sarum into the
valley have already been stated (p. 347). The move must have
been decided already shortly before 1200. Peter of Blois, a
canon of Sarum, wrote in a letter, probably in 1198–9, that he
was sorry not to be able to be present at the distribution of
plots for canons' houses, but delighted 'that you have decided
to transfer the site' from a place 'ventis expositus, sterilis,
aridus, desertus'. The papal bull of Honorius III, dated 1219,
finally authorizing the move confirms all the disadvantages of
Old Sarum. 'Let us descend joyfully to the plains, where the
valley abounds in corn, where the fields are beautiful and
where there is freedom from oppression.' Henry of Avranches
in a highly rhetorical poem calls it 'mons maledictus', where
nothing grows except 'absinthia amara', whereas in the valley
there are lilies, roses, violets, of course 'philomela', and plenty
of springs 'cristallo clarior, auro purior, ambrosia dulcior'.
In fact 'Huc si venisset expulsus de Paradiso/Exilium patriae
preposuisset Adam' (If Adam had gone here when he was
expelled from Paradise/He would have preferred the exile to
his fatherland).

Bishop Poore laid the foundation stones in 1220, one for the
pope, one for Archbishop Stephen Langton, one for himself;
and William Longespée, Earl of Sarum, and his countess Ela
laid two more. In 1225 three altars could already be consecrated,
those no doubt in the Lady Chapel and at the E ends of the
chancel aisles. In the week following their consecration the
archbishop and the king visited the church. In 1226 William
Longespée was buried in the church. Building continued at the
same uncommonly fast rate. Matthew Paris wrote of Bishop
Bingham, who died in 1246, that he *perfecit* the cathedral,
including the front and its lead-covered gable. This can hardly
be true. An indulgence was granted in 1244 to those who would
contribute money to the building; for without such money the
building could not be completed. And the consecration took
place only under Bishop Bridport in 1258, and the leading of
the roof (no doubt of the nave) is recorded only for 1266. At the

same time a mighty campanile or bell tower was added in the
NW corner of the precinct, square and heavily buttressed
below, then with a smaller square stage, in its detail much like
the interior of the crossing tower, and, above that, with an
octagonal top stage, probably of wood, and a short spire.*
The cloisters and chapter house were begun at about the same
time by Bishop de la Wyle, i.e. between 1263 and 1271, but
completed only about 1300. About thirty years later the tower
was wonderfully heightened and the spire added. The contract
for this work dates from 1334. In the C15 two low chantry
chapels were added to the N and S of the Lady Chapel: the
Beauchamp Chapel, very sumptuous inside, by Bishop
Beauchamp (1450–81), the Hungerford Chapel in 1464–77.
The spire gave cause for worry, and Bishop Beauchamp put
in the two strainer arches. In 1668, when Seth Ward, mathematician and astronomer, was bishop, *Wren*, his friend and a
fellow astronomer, made a report on its state, praised the proportions of nave width to height and of nave to aisles, the
presence of 'large planes' without too many ornaments
(which might 'glut the eye'), of windows without tracery
(for 'nothing could add beauty to light'), but criticized the
inadequate foundations and inadequate buttressing. He recommended long-term measures for the future, but for the
present only small adjustments including 'the bracing ye
Spire towards ye Top with Iron'. *Francis Price*, surveyor to the
cathedral, in his book of 1753, reported more in detail and with
quite exceptional sagacity and competence. Then came *James
Wyatt* and his restoration of 1789 etc. which has often been
called disastrous and which was indeed both ruthless and
biased. He swept away the two Perp chapels,‡ two small
porches,§ and the campanile, refurbished much of the interior,
and tidied it up with depressing orderliness. *Sir G. G. Scott*
in 1863 etc. swept away as much Wyatt as he could and replaced
it by Scott. Of his time e.g. are nearly all the statues of the
façade. Scott's iron screen and reredos in their turn were swept
away in 1959–60.

* Such campanili were not an exception, although only two – at Chichester
and at Evesham (the latter as late as *c*.1530) – survive. But there were campanili also e.g. at Westminster Abbey, Norwich Cathedral, St Augustine
Canterbury, Tewkesbury, Worcester, Romsey, Kenilworth.

‡ The decision to do so had already been taken by Bishop Shute Barrington
before Wyatt appeared on the scene.

§ One led to the N transept, the other to the S chancel aisle. For the re-
erected N porch, *see* p. 400.

We do not know who the designer of Salisbury Cathedral was. Mr Harvey pleads for *Nicholas of Ely*, a mason who was granted a messuage E of the cloister by Bishop Poore. He is the most likely first master mason. But is he also the most likely designer? *Elias de Derham*, Canon of Sarum, ought certainly to be considered seriously. Mr Harvey accepts him only as an appreciative client. But he may well have been more; for what we know of him not only establishes him as an extremely able churchman and administrator, present at Runnymede in 1215, an executor for instance after the deaths of Archbishop HerbertWalter,of Archbishop Stephen Langton,of Archbishop Grant, of Bishop Poore, of Bishop des Roches of Winchester, a personal friend of Bishop Jocelyn of Wells and Bishop Hugh II of Lincoln, but also as an artist and a man closely connected with architecture. In 1220 the shrine of St Thomas Becket for Canterbury was made, according to Matthew Paris by the 'incomparabilibus artificibus mag. Walter de Colecestria, sacrista de Sancto Albano, et Elya de Derham, canonico Salisburiensi, quorum consilio et ingenio omnia quae ad artificium thecae . . . necessaria fuerant parabantur'. It would be highly unusual for an administrator to be called an incomparable *artifex* even in an age when *faciebat* applied to buildings often means 'he was responsible for' and not 'he designed'. Now Elias was also in charge of the king's works at Winchester and at Clarendon in the 1230s, had perhaps been busy on the king's works in London already in 1199, where an Elias *Ingeniator* appears, and at Salisbury he is called 'a prima fundatione rector novae fabricae'. Rector of course may well refer to administration only, but it stands to reason that an amateur *artifex* of high standing would also take more than a business interest in the new cathedral. Of later masons a *Richard* was left one mark by the treasurer of the cathedral in 1267, and the contract of 1334 for the building of the spire is between the chapter and *Richard of Farleigh*, who must have been a man of some reputation, as he insisted on also carrying on with his commitments at Bath Abbey and Reading Abbey.

The cathedral is built of Chilmark stone, i.e. a stone quarried a mere 12 miles from the site. The building is 449 ft long outside. The vaults are only 81 ft high inside. The height of the spire is 404 ft. It leaves all other English spires behind, though not all Continental spires. The tallest of all, that of Ulm, completed only in the C19, is 630 ft.

EXTERIOR

The plan of Salisbury Cathedral is the *beau idéal* of the E.E. [12] plan. On a virgin site the designer could do exactly what he thought best, and the outcome differs in every respect from the French ideal of Chartres, Reims, and Amiens. At Salisbury all is rectangular and parts are kept neatly from parts. The Lady Chapel projects two bays. Then there are two bays of retro-choir. The high choir is seven bays long with an E transept projecting two bays and a main transept projecting three bays beyond the chancel aisles. The nave is of ten bays. A screen façade not organically growing out of nave and aisles finishes the building to the w. A tall N porch two bays deep is added, and this sticks out as straight and as detached from the rest as the two pairs of transepts and the E parts. In elevation the Lady Chapel and retrochoir are as low as the aisles.

Of all English cathedrals Salisbury is the most unified in appearance. It was built entirely in the course of sixty years except for its justly most famous feature, its spire. This, though of course far too high from the E.E. point of view, happens to be the work of a mason of the highest genius and fits the rest perfectly. The C 13 has certain motifs in common throughout which can be listed at once. The windows are lancets, mostly in pairs or triplets and nowhere excessively elongated and narrow. They are often shafted outside and mostly inside – nearly always with Purbeck marble shafts. The windows appear with and without tracery, the tracery being of the plate variety. The buttresses are characterized by a group of five closely-placed set-offs about two-thirds up. The base of the cathedral and the buttresses have also many set-offs, and at the sill-level of the windows there is yet another course with four set-offs. The top parapet is panelled with trefoil-headed panels. It rests on a frieze of pointed trefoils with a band of half-dog-tooth between.

As building went on from E to w, we start our more detailed examination at the LADY CHAPEL. Its E wall has three conse-cration crosses in encircled quatrefoils below the windows. The windows are a group of three stepped lancets, shafted (the shafts with a shaft-ring). The top of the E wall carries three crocketed gables. The side gables have two low lancets with a quatrefoiled circle in plate tracery. In the centre is a group of five stepped lancets, the l. and r. ones being blank with pedestals for statues and curved-back panels. The pinnacles are *Scott*'s. The N and s sides have pairs of lancets not shafted but only

12

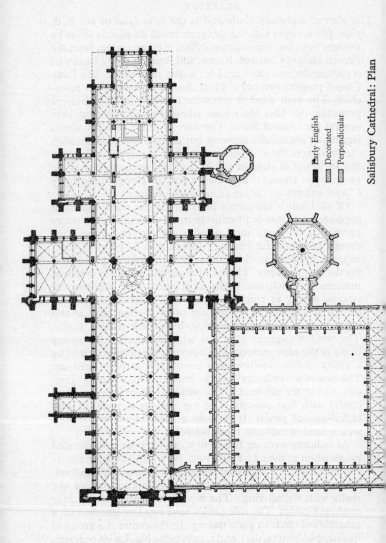

Salisbury Cathedral: Plan

Early English

Decorated

Perpendicular

double-chamfered. The chamfering of the middle post of each pair stops at the top.

The CHANCEL AISLES have their E windows as groups of three stepped lancets, shafted, the shafts with a shaft-ring, and gables like the middle gable on the Lady Chapel. The pinnacles are again *Scott*'s. The N and S walls are of four bays, identical with those of the Lady Chapel, except that in the bays closest to the transepts the chamfering of the post between the two lancets has an inner hollow chamfer.

The HIGH CHOIR has a group of seven shafted stepped lancets in the gable, with the first and the last blank, a group of five shafted stepped lancets below, again with the first and last blank and flat buttresses embracing the angles. On them are Perp pinnacles. To the N and S the High Choir has clerestory windows of groups of three stepped shafted lancets. Between the trefoil frieze and the panelled parapet there is here no dog-tooth, and that remains so throughout the clerestory. The E wall is steadied by steep flying buttresses on the N and the S side.

Now the EAST TRANSEPTS. To the E they have one pair of chamfered lancets continuing the details of the W bays of the chancel aisles and one group of three shafted stepped lancets. The N and S fronts of the transepts do not carry on the rhythm so far determining the exterior. The dog-tooth frieze breaks off at the W end of the NE and SE buttresses. Then the E aisle has on the ground floor a pair of shafted lancets continued to the l. and r., towards the buttresses, by rising half-arches, an oddly fragmentary motif, hard to explain, and harder to appreciate. It is going to puzzle us more often as we go W. Above, under the roof, is just one small lancet. The centre of the transept front has on the ground floor three lancets of the same height, but greater width for the middle one. They are triple-shafted and have fine dog-tooth in the arches. Again fragments of arches rise to the l. and r. On the first floor three pairs of smaller lancets, again the middle pair wider. Each pair has a quatrefoil circle in plate tracery over. The surrounds are shallowly moulded with hollow chamfers. A little stiff-leaf in the spandrels. The second floor has a stepped group of four shafted lancets, the centre pair again provided with a quatre-foiled circle. In the gable five stepped lancets, one and five being blank. These two have no proper arches but two rising half-arches, and two and four, though they have proper arches, have two rising blank half-arches above them. Simple polygonal

pinnacles l. and r. On the s side the design is partly obscured by
the addition of the Sacristy and Muniment Room, which seems
to date from the later C13. It is octagonal, partly of ashlar, partly
of flint with irregular stone, two-storeyed with a flat roof. In
the corridor one lancet and one blocked lancet. In the building
itself the lower windows have segmental heads, the upper ones
end straight.* The w lancets of the E transepts have consistently
hollow chamfers in their surrounds, and that now remains the
rule for the parts further w. In the tucked-away bays of the
chancel aisles between E transepts and main transepts, the E bay
has a sloping roof. With the w bay the friezes start again. These
bays and those immediately w of the main transept are not in
their original state, as the addition of the Dec spire made flying
buttresses necessary in a N–S and E–W and in a diagonal
direction. They carry square pinnacles with small blank Dec
arches and tracery. In the s transept all three flying buttresses
are of this type, in the N transept only the inner one, the outer
two being thinner and steeper (and probably later).

The E side of the MAIN TRANSEPTS is in no way different
from what precedes it, except for one minor detail: in the
clerestory the flat C13 buttresses, as they finish, do not divide
the trefoil frieze into sections, but run up into one awkwardly
elongated arch. This motif is carried on all along the nave.
The façades of the main transepts are unfortunate: as there is
an E but no w aisle, the composition is lopsided. The dog-tooth
friezes break off as in the E transepts. The E aisle front has on
the ground floor again the shafted two lancets with rising
fragmentary arches l. and r. and on the first floor instead of a
group of three shafted lancets, the same two shafts but instead
of arches three, then four, then again four rising half-arches to
follow the roof-line. The centre or 'nave' part of the transept
front is made tripartite by thin buttresses with set-offs which
rise through the ground floor and first floor. To their l. and r. are
single lancets with rising fragmentary arches only outward. In
the centre is just one lancet. On the first floor pairs with
quatrefoiled circles in plate tracery and again rising fragmentary
arches outward. On the second floor a group of five, the outer
ones blank, the middle one wider and higher and with a two-light
window with a sexfoiled circle (the first we have come across)
in plate tracery. Above one and two and four and five a large
blank pointed quatrefoil (also the first). In the gable are two

* The upper room has a renewed, octagonal central pier of wood and eight
renewed, curved, radiating braces of wood.

pairs with quatrefoiled circles and above them a big octofoiled circle (the first again). The surrounds are chamfered in the N transept, but in the S transept they have thick and heavy roll mouldings apparently of a slightly later date. The W sides of the main transepts have nothing new. The pairs of lancets, the pairs with the quatrefoiled circle in plate tracery, the clerestory triplets, the frieze and parapet all continue, and continue into the nave as well.

The NAVE clerestory has flying buttresses not evenly distributed on N and S. The more easterly ones have the Dec pinnacles, the two further to the W are thinner. Originally the C13 work had the flat buttress strips running awkwardly into the trefoil frieze which we have first met on the main transept E walls.

The NORTH PORCH is a very fine piece. Externally it continues the system of the nave, but the E and W walls are entirely blank, and the N wall has a tall and wide, richly shafted entrance. The innermost shafts are detached. One tier of shaft-rings. Richly moulded arch. On the first floor two pairs of shafted lancets with a quatrefoiled circle in plate tracery. However, the lancets now have pointed cusping in their heads (the first we have met). Small dog-tooth in the arches, a quatrefoiled circle in the spandrel. In the crocketed gable two quatrefoiled arches with shafts carrying stiff-leaf capitals (the first, except for the tower – *see* below). Inside, the porch is vaulted in two bays and has noble erect proportions. On the ground stage vigorous blank arcading with detached shafts and relatively simple stiff-leaf capitals. The arcading has pointed cinquecusping in the heads. On the upper stage each bay has two pairs of blank lancets. All shafting is detached. The capitals are moulded here. The arches again have pointed cusping. The quatrefoils in the circles are also pointed. They must still be called blank plate tracery, but come very close to bar tracery. Above in the lunettes two quatrefoiled circles and a large octofoiled one. Bits of stiff-leaf in various places. Quadripartite vaults, resting on strong shafts which stand detached from the walls and indeed cut into the ground-floor arcading, even if they form an organic part of the first-floor system. Finely moulded ribs and stiff-leaf bosses. Terribly restored inner portal. Thick shafting l. and r. The stiff-leaf capitals are of Purbeck marble, and those on the l. seem original. Trumeau of four attached shafts with four small hollows in the diagonals – a section which became popular much later. Pointed trefoil

arches. The C 19 figure of Christ in the tympanum is placed in
a large pointed quatrefoil. Above a row of four short trefoiled
arches, the shafts with stiff-leaf capitals, and one blank quatrefoiled circle over. The ribs as well as the large octofoil and the
prominent pointed quatrefoils indicate a relatively late date,
not too far indeed from cloister and chapter house. The floor
of the porch, with its simple geometrical pattern of white and
grey, could be original.

The FAÇADE of Salisbury Cathedral is a headache. There is
so much in it which is perversely unbeautiful. There are also
far too many motifs, and they are distributed without a com-
prehensible system. The façade is of the screen type, i.e. wider
than nave and aisles (which the English had already done in
Norman form e.g. at St Paul's Cathedral and at St Botolph
Colchester), and it has no tower or towers. Instead there are
two square turrets, hardly more than over-broad buttresses
at the angles, and they carry a spirelet each, hardly more than
a pinnacle, each accompanied by four corner pinnacles. In the
middle is a gable, but this has the nave width only and thus
looks somewhat stunted. That the sculpture all over the façade
is of the 1862 restoration (by *Redfern*) does not help either.
Indeed only six figures are old, and they are so over-restored
that only the Peter and Paul to the l. and r. of the great w
window can count.* Their style is decidedly C 14. Is this due to
the restorers?‡ The same question arises with regard to the
bases of the statues. Most of them have stiff-leaf brackets, but
on the lowest tier the decoration is partly by ballflower. That
again is impossible before 1300, and the façade cannot be as
late as that. Are these motifs then again due to the restorers?

The great w window is the centre of the façade, a group of
three stepped lancets, triple-shafted, the shafts with two shaft-
rings. To the l. and r. rise once more the unununderstandable fragmentary arches. Much dog-tooth. This window dwarfs all the
rest and especially the triple porch below, a French motif with
its three gables, but ridiculously insignificant, as the three together represent the nave, not the nave and the aisles. Moreover in all its details it is C 19. The side parts have no doors, just
blank arcading, the middle part five shafts on each side in the

---

* The others are the two below Peter and Paul and two in the bottom row
of the N tower.

‡ It is not known whether the façade had all its statues before the C19.
An engraving by Hollar shows twenty-two, but there is no reference to their
destruction.

jambs, two portals separated by a trumeau, filigree stiff-leaf in one order of the arch, and in the tympanum three C19 figures beneath pointed-trefoiled arches with gablets over. The portal recess is much deeper than the side recesses. The latter being left blank proves of course that the designer used the French scheme of the three portal gables expressing nave and aisles without an inkling of its meaning. The real aisle fronts also have three gables each, but they are narrower and lower. Portal with cinquecusped arch. In the middle, above the porches a gallery of saints under trefoil-headed canopies. In the aisles pairs of lancets with the usual quatrefoiled circle in plate tracery and the perennial fragmentary side arches. In addition, the square angle turrets which project beyond the aisles, and also the buttresses between nave and aisles, have two tiers of statues at this level, flanked by shafts which carry pointed-trefoiled, gabled canopies. These canopies, a new and most unfortunate motif, break round the corners. In outline they look bitten out. Also – and this makes one more doubtful about the capabilities of the designer than anything else – the buttresses project further than the turrets, and to even that out, the turrets in their inner quarter send out their own buttress to range with the other buttresses. That the niches and gables of the buttress part are cut off by the meeting with the turret part will by now hardly surprise. It applies to the other buttresses as well.

Above this level the familiar frieze of half-dog-tooth comes round, the one (much too weak) motif that tries to tie the whole façade together. Then the great W window, and alas to its side, below the fragmentary arches, statues under their canopies, two l., two r., one on top of the other. They have so little space that the canopies cannot stand on shafts. In the aisle parts this tier of the elevation is much less high, just two pairs of lancets, with the indispensable quatrefoiled circles. Dog-tooth in the arches. In the turrets on this level more statues, more shafted canopies, more gables and dog-tooth. The aisles then come out with a broad band of quatrefoiled lozenges with trefoils in the spandrels. This motif is repeated, higher up, in the centre, above the great W window and moreover cut into by the raised middle lancet of the window. At this level, in the aisles and turrets are more pairs of lancets with the quatre-foiled circles. Shafts with stiff-leaf capitals. Finally aisles and turrets end with the panelled parapet familiar from the E part of the cathedral and battlements over, and the centre ends in a steep gable. Here once again two pairs of lancets with quatre-foiled circles. Above the circles a lozenge with a vesica inside. In this a Victorian Christ in Majesty and above the vesica, again rather squeezed in, a bird in profile, probably a Pelican. Is it original? It is not in the Grimm engraving of 1779. Very much dog-tooth all around here.

As the turrets project beyond the aisles they have a visible E side, an awkward fact which spoils the view W along the nave and aisles. There is, for example, a supporting wall with a sloping-up top as a kind of prop with rising blank arches. The repetition of the clerestory triplets on the E side of the screen wall, i.e. where the façade itself pretends to have upper aisle windows, on the other hand, is a happy solution.

The idea of the Salisbury façade must be derived from Wells on the one hand, Norman towerless screen façades on the other. Wells has the display of statuary, but mighty towers as well. The effect is baffling enough, even if not quite as baffling as that of Salisbury. The Wells façade seems to have been designed about 1235, i.e. earlier than the Salisbury façade.

After so much has been said against the Salisbury façade two redeeming features deserve to be noted. There is one major motif which ties the discrepant parts of the front together. If one draws a triangle connecting the top of the great W window with the tops of the aisle W windows, the two lines will be parallel to those of the top gable. And secondly, though this is not the merit of the designer of the façade, the crossing tower and spire, seen from a distance, do not call for any greater emphasis on the W front than the spirelets of the turrets and the middle gable provide. Anything more prominent would compete, to the detriment of what must after all be considered the crowning glory of Salisbury.

So now, after pages of embarrassed criticism, we can indulge in the examination of the CROSSING TOWER and the STEEPLE. The E.E. cathedral was meant to have only a relatively low lantern tower. On top probably was a lead pyramid spire (cf. Interior, p. 366). The C13 stage of the tower, the one against which the roofs abut, has tall blank E.E. arches with depressed trefoil heads. Shafts and stiff-leaf capitals (the earliest so far in the cathedral). Then the Dec work begins. Its date, as has already been said, is 1334 etc. Ballflower frieze and blank battlements and then two tall stages. They are studded everywhere with ballflower. Tall two-light windows with circles over. In these, on the lower stage, undulating foiling, on the upper subcusped foiling. Friezes of cusped lozenges and trefoils. All these motifs are an intelligent, up-to-date restating of E.E. motifs of the cathedral. The angle buttresses start flat and set-back, but in the Dec work turn polygonal, with the same kind of fine blank arches, tracery, and gables that we have found in the pinnacles of the flying buttresses added at the same time to help carry the tower and spire.

The spire is wonderfully slender, and the solution of the problem of how to reach the octagon from the square is perfect. Short crocketed pinnacles on the buttresses, in the middles of the sides at the foot of the spire lucarnes under crocketed gables and with pinnacles, and again at the corners taller inner pinna-cles rising higher than the lucarnes. They are square, with their own angle buttresses and angle pinnacles, as it were. From a distance the effect varies. If you are inside the Precinct the pinnacles keep close to the spire and the outline is almost like that of a broach-spire, except for just the slightest barbs. If you are in the meadows to the S or W the pinnacles speak individually and form a subordinate preamble to the spectac-ular rise of the spire.

INTERIOR

The interior of Salisbury Cathedral is as unified as is the exterior. That (and *Wyatt*'s tidying-up) gives it its perfection, but also a certain coolness. The whole interior (like the whole exterior) has certain motifs in common: particularly the slender, detached polished Purbeck shafts applied wherever possible. These, in conjunction with the consistently used lancet win-dows, endow the interior with a vertical vigour needed to counteract the relative lowness of the vault and the strong stresses on horizontals, especially in the gallery. The result is poise, and so contributes to the perfection of the whole.

The LADY CHAPEL and RETROCHOIR with the E ends of the [13a] chancel aisles must be taken as one. They are all of the same height, considerably lower than the High Choir. This concep-tion Salisbury Cathedral took over from Winchester, where it had been demonstrated by Bishop de Lucy before 1204. The Lady Chapel as well as the retrochoir have narrow aisles (on the 'hall' principle), though those of the retrochoir are not at once noticed, because the chancel aisles act as more prominent, wider aisles. What distinguishes Salisbury at once from Winchester is the emphasis on the slenderest Purbeck shafts. In the Lady Chapel the piers separating nave and aisles are just single Purbeck shafts without any shaft-rings – like stove pipes, it has been said disrespectfully.* In the retrochoir there is a cluster of five shafts instead, all detached. Between retrochoir aisles and chancel aisles a similar cluster, but with stronger shafts and an extra shaft added to the inside to correspond with the detached wall shafts of the Lady Chapel aisle walls. These detached wall shafts to carry the vaulting become a recurrent motif throughout. The windows moreover also have detached shafts throughout. In the vaults thin ribs and transverse arches no wider, though of a different moulding. The w bay of the Lady Chapel has small dog-tooth in ribs and transverse arches. The w bays of the retrochoir aisles are a little irregular in shape to connect with the piers of the E wall of the High Choir.

A few further details may be noted. Most capitals – most capitals of Salisbury Cathedral – are moulded and of Purbeck marble. But the capitals of the piers to N and S between retrochoir 'nave' and retrochoir aisles have dainty stiff-leaf sprays, the earliest in the cathedral. The arches from the retrochoir to the E ends of the chancel aisles are enriched with big dog-tooth.

Against the walls of the Lady Chapel Perp niches with little fan-vaults, a foliage frieze, and cresting. In the retrochoir on the S side a fine double piscina with trefoil-cusped arches, on the N side double aumbry with shelf on triangular heads, heavily roll moulded.

The CHANCEL AISLES just carry on, though in the vaults there are now small stiff-leaf bosses. All this work so far probably belongs to 1220–5. There are five bays from E to W, i.e. to the level of the E aisles of the E transepts. The E transepts will be examined a little later. To their W the chancel aisles continue for another three bays. What is different now, and the sign of a slightly later date, is that the stiff-leaf bosses are decidedly bigger than further E.

The HIGH CHOIR has piers of beautiful grey unpolished Purbeck with black, polished, detached Purbeck shafts. The forms of the piers differ remarkably. First the E side. There are three arches. The piers consist of two strong grey shafts, just detached, and two slender black shafts to N and S. Arches with many thin rolls, those to the l. and r., i.e. those corresponding to the retrochoir aisles, a little higher than the middle one – the first of the minor oddities inside of which we have found so many outside. The reason is that the wide band of

* And the real stove pipes of the antediluvian stoves in chancel aisles and aisles call for the comparison.

mouldings is the same for the three arches and that the steeper angle of the side arches pushes their apex up higher. The arches have hood-moulds with stops consisting of two pellets, one above the other, a motif that was to become standard for a while. The NE and SE corner piers are stronger. They have four big detached grey shafts and four thin black ones. Now the N and s sides. The arches here have dog-tooth. The first pier is quatrefoil with eight detached shafts, the next octagonal with concave sides into which black shafts fit nicely. Then the piers of the E crossing, again quatrefoil with eight shafts. The motif of detached Purbeck shafts round a pier was taken over from Canterbury and Lincoln. In St Hugh's Choir at Lincoln especially they are used in front of concave sides of a pier. But both Canterbury and Lincoln have foliage capitals, whereas at Salisbury only the W piers introduce any ornamentation in the capitals. They are of the crocket type. The arches are many-moulded, and they have the pellet stops like the E end; however, only on the N, not on the s side. We do not go further W yet, but first look at the upper parts.

Salisbury still has a gallery – like Lincoln and Westminster Abbey – though the Île de France had by that time given up galleries. Moreover, the gallery of Salisbury emphasizes the horizontal particularly strongly. The E wall at gallery level has five arches, the middle one a little wider. They are thickly Purbeck-shafted, and the arches themselves are cinquecusped. The clerestory has a group of five stepped lancets. The outer bays have rising half-arches, of three curves outside, only one short one inside. The next bays have two and one, and only the middle one is a normal arch. In the spandrels stiff-leaf paterae.

The gallery has for each bay two pairs of two-light openings with trefoiled heads. They are low and much Purbeck-shafted. The two sub-tympana have foils in awkward areas, bordered by two sub-sub-arches and the sub-arch. The foils are quatre-foils, then octofoils, then again quatrefoils. In the main tym-panum a quatrefoiled circle, then an octofoiled circle which has the foils pointed, then again a quatrefoiled circle. The super-arches are excessively depressed as though the designer wanted to do everything in his power to counterbalance the verticalism of all his shafts. The foils of the circles have little knob-like cusps, and the hood-mould stops, wherever they occur, are knobs too. The vaulting shafts start only in the spandrels between the super-arches. They stand on heads and

have rich stiff-leaf capitals, much richer than the few further E.
The leaves are quite big, but arranged as only one tier. Clerestory with wall passage and stepped triplet arcading – the
Anglo-Norman tradition. Again all detached shafts. Spandrels
with stiff-leaf paterae.

The vaults are quadripartite rib-vaults on an oblong plan,
i.e. the French system of Chartres, Reims, Amiens, etc. Ribs
and transverse arches are, as in the E parts, very thin and of the
same thickness, which is not usual in C13 France. The mouldings again differ. Small stiff-leaf bosses, also in the E crossing.

The EAST TRANSEPTS are separated from the chancel – for
safety's sake – by strainer arches inserted probably in the C14.
Their date is uncertain. They stand on Chilmark piers with
attached shafts, deliberately similar to those of the C13. Small
Perp leaf capitals. Arch with many fine mouldings, and on its
apex an inverted arch, the two together performing the shoring
action. Vertical frame-like moulding and horizontal moulding
across at the level where the arches meet.

The NE and SE transepts are essentially identical. The inner
bay of the E aisle is of course identical with the W bay of the E
part of the chancel aisles. The bay has a stiff-leaf boss, the
arches have dog-tooth. The pellet-stops are present, and in fact
remain part of the system of decoration, until further notice.
The first pier of the E aisle is of the octagonal type with concave
sides and eight shafts, the next is of the type with two strong
detached grey shafts and two thin black ones to N and S (see
chancel E wall). The details differ a little. In the S transept the
SE bay has bits of dog-tooth in the window arches, the next bay
to the N in the arcade arch. The SE bay has a stiff-leaf boss, the
next has not. In the N transept the NE bay also has dog-tooth in
the windows but no boss, the next bay no dog-tooth and no boss.
But these variations are not relevant. The gallery continues
as in the High Choir, except that some of the hood-mould
stops have stiff-leaf instead of being simply knobs. The
clerestory continues too, except that there are no paterae in the
spandrels. In the aisle of the NE transept in the S wall double
piscina, in the N wall double aumbry, exactly like the pair in the
retrochoir. In the SE transept in the S wall double piscina, in the
N wall double aumbry, the former with pointed-trefoil-cusped
arches.

The S wall of the SE transept and the N wall of the NE transept
have first three big lancets of even height with detached triple
shafts and pellet hood-mould stops. However, where the

triplet ends, another arch starts and has no space to carry on, a most disconcerting conceit. We shall see more of this than we want. At gallery level there are three lower lancets, the middle one wider, and their capitals do not range with the gallery capitals, which is disconcerting again. At clerestory level, four windows but only three openings to the inside. The outer ones rise again by three half-arches and come down by only one (see E wall of the High Choir). To the W the two outer bays have single lancets delightfully detailed. Shallow niches fill the jambs, a tiny quadripartite rib-vault the intrados of the arch. The inner bays have the arches to the W parts of the chancel aisles. There is here the usual gallery opening over. Above the single lancets are paired windows with stiff-leaf hood-mould stops. The vaulting-shafts here start lower, close to the bottom of the windows. They also stand on heads. The clerestory is like that of the E side, but the shafts now have shaft-rings. The small bosses are a little bigger than those of the chancel.

Now the W bays of the chancel, i.e. the three bays W of the E crossing. They continue the system, i.e. have a pair of piers which are quatrefoil with eight shafts and one pair which is octagonal with concave sides and eight shafts. Arches with dog-tooth, gallery with two quatrefoils in circles and the big circle octofoiled with pointed foils, clerestory without shaft-rings and paterae, and vaults with bosses. The one principal difference is that these bosses are emphatically bigger and more agitated than any so far (or any after).

So we have reached the main CROSSING. The piers have five shafts to each side. On the bases are slight bits of decoration, of stiff-leaf on the SE and SW piers, of an abstract kind (or never carved further?) on the NE and NW. The arches are studded with thick C15 fleurons. A lierne-vault was also put in in the C15. It is thinly cusped. The geometrical patterns are such that the step to Elizabethan plaster patterns really is not wide. But above it is the lantern stage of the C13, originally open from below. It has very tall blank twin arches with a quatrefoil in plate tracery. The dividing major shafts are quatrefoil, the minor ones single, and both types of Purbeck marble with shaft-rings. While this stage is closed to the space below by the lierne-vault, it is open to the lower Dec stage. Between crossing and transepts strainer arches were put in in the C15. They have wide jambs with tall, narrow image niches, embattled tops, and spandrels with open tracery. In the tracery straight and nearly straight diagonals play an important part. In addition the crossing tower and spire were steadied by flying buttresses in the gallery and the clerestory wall-passage to E, W, N, and S.

Back to the tower. Inside it iron tie-rods were placed by *Wren*, by *Price*, and later by *Scott*. To see the inside of the SPIRE one must ascend high. But the climb is worth the effort. One can see the timber scaffolding put up for the construction of the spire and sensibly left standing as a steadying. It has a middle post with arms and braces. One can also see the bronze ties inserted in 1939. The stonework of the spire is 2 ft below, thinning up to 9 in. at a height of 20 ft.*

The MAIN TRANSEPTS are again nearly identical. The E arcade has first one of the octagonal piers, then piers of four strong grey shafts without black ones. Arches with some dog-tooth. In the aisle vaults small stiff-leaf bosses. The gallery has for the first bay three quatrefoiled circles, for the rest two and the big upper one octofoiled. Hood-mould stops etc. with stiff-leaf instead of plain knobs. This, it will be remembered, was the same in the E transept gallery. The clerestory shafts have shaft-rings like the W walls of the E transepts, and this now becomes standard. The S transept S and N transept N walls are very similar to those of the E transept end walls. The triple shafts of the ground-floor windows are stronger, the three arches on the gallery level of equal width, and the climbing arches of the clerestory are treated differently too. The centre here is a pair with pointed-trefoil heads and an octofoiled circle over. In the W walls are three pairs of lancets, then on the gallery level three two-light pairs with stiff-leaf hood-mould stops. The vaulting-shafts, as in the E transepts, start close to the foot of the upper windows. They stand, like all the others, on heads. The clerestory with shaft-rings as on the E side. The vaulting bosses are smaller again, not as big as in the W part of the chancel. N and S transepts are identical, except for one minute detail: one hood-mould stop on the ground floor of the S transept W wall has stiff-leaf instead of the pellets. Actually, this does represent a deliberate change, as we shall see presently. In the S transept W wall doorway to the cloister. It is of Purbeck marble. The arch is very depressed, two-centred, and stands on short vertical pieces – a Westminster Abbey motif. A similar doorway, also Purbeck, but with an arch almost flattened out to be horizontal, in the N transept W wall.

13b   The NAVE continues the system without major revisions.

* At the base of the spire is a C14 TREADMILL of 12 ft diameter, used to hoist the masonry and the timbers of the spire.

What is different is only this: the arcade piers are now grey quatrefoils set diagonally with four black shafts in the main directions, a change made no doubt under the influence of the round piers with four shafts of Westminster Abbey (and the French cathedrals). Westminster Abbey was begun in 1245. Does that date the nave, or at least its design? The shafts have no shaft-rings, except for the w responds. The piers are placed on continuous sleeper-walls (due to the swampy terrain?*) The richly moulded arches have no dog-tooth, but hood-mould stops with stiff-leaf instead of pellets, i.e. what had been begun in one bay of the w wall of the transepts. On the gallery the foiling of the circles above the openings is now as follows: it alternates between four, four, four and four, four, eight; the eight being all pointed foils with stiff-leaf decoration in the little spandrels. Stiff-leaf also for hood-mould stops and cusps. The mouldings round the foiled circles are much deeper and more subdivided, i.e. on the way from plate to bar tracery. The clerestory continues as in the main transepts, i.e. with shaft-rings. The vaulting bosses are certainly smaller than those of the w parts of the chancel, though of about the same size and type as those of the main transepts.

The w wall is again an embarrassment. How can it be that the designer cared so little for any linking with the nave walls? Did the sense of keeping part from part as isolated units, as we have seen it at work in the whole exterior, go so far that even walls inside were not seen in conjunction? The ground floor has three blank arches, the middle one much wider. They have stiff-leaf stops, and their capitals are just a little below the shaft-rings of the nave w responds. Under the middle arch is another blank arch, and under this the two real arches of the portal. Stiff-leaf stop in the middle. The string-course finishing this ground-stage at the top is not at the level of the capitals or abaci of the nave piers. The next stage has four pairs of blank arches with quatrefoiled circles over. The arches are pointed-trefoiled. Then the great w window, amply shafted. The shafts have two tiers of shaft-rings. Here again the system of the nave walls is in no way continued. The sill of the great triplet is just that painfully little lower than the floor level of the gallery.

FURNISHINGS

They are described topographically from E to W.

LADY CHAPEL. STAINED GLASS. In the E triplet C13

* For swampy it was – Philomela or no Philomela.

greyish-green glass in geometrical patterns. In the middle
window also c16 fragments. In the l. window at the bottom
some c14 glass (Annunciation*). – N windows by *Clayton &
Bell*, *c*.1901. – s windows by *Clayton & Bell*, *c*.1872.

RETROCHOIR. STAINED GLASS. s windows by *Clayton &
Bell*, *c*. 1885.

SOUTH CHANCEL AISLE, EAST PART. PAINTINGS. Presentation in the Temple by *Palma Giovane*. – St Jerome by
Ribera. – STAINED GLASS. Two windows, very good, with
white and brownish single figures, under the influence of the
Pre-Raphaelites. By *Holiday*, made by *Powell*, 1881 and *c*.1892.

NORTH EAST TRANSEPT. PISCINA (or IMMERSION
FONT?), s chapel. Perp. Panelled base with trough at the top.
Recess with diagonally set jambs. Little vault inside. Cusped
ogee arch with crockets. Straight top. – ROOD SCREEN. Part
of the original rood screen is here re-erected. Stone. Wonderfully unrestored. Five plus five shallow niches for statues of
kings (there were originally seven plus seven) and a Perp doorway in the middle. The doorway comes from the Beauchamp
Chapel. Between the niches triple Purbeck shafts, flanked by
thick stiff-leaf sprays. Big, very agitated stiff-leaf capitals,
dating the screen to *c*.1235–50. The niches have nodding
trefoiled heads with little gablets partially over. The gablets
stand on stiff-leaf stops. Arches on outstandingly well characterized heads above the gablets. In the spandrels small demi-
figures of angels with spread wings. The motif of the angels is
familiar from the Westminster Abbey transepts, but is later
there. At Westminster it was taken over from the exterior of the
apsidal chapels at Reims Cathedral, at Salisbury it is more
probably derived from work on a smaller scale. It occurs already
in the c10 illumination of the Athelstan Psalter and in stone
e.g. in a recently published fragment of *c*.1200 in a private
collection at München Gladbach. The screen has a tall, narrow
doorway with a four-centred arch, a concave-sided gable
against a panelled background, and a straight top – SCREEN.
A simple, panelled screen w of the piscina; Perp. – STAINED
GLASS. In the E aisle the s windows by *Powell*, 1870s; the N
windows by *Burlison & Grylls*, *c*.1887. – The w single lancets
by *Powell*.

SOUTH EAST TRANSEPT. SCREEN to the N. The openwork
rosewood carving is Indian and recent. – COPE CHEST. Large,

* The Annunciation comes from Mr Tower's private collection. Tower
was Kempe's partner.

semicircular. Attributed to the C13. – CHEST. Probably C13.
5 ft long. The feet were probably longer. – STAINED GLASS.
NE windows by *O'Connor*, 1859. – Then to the S *Clayton &
Bell*, *c.* 1877. – The S windows have C13 grisaille glass in
geometrical patterns.

NORTH CHANCEL AISLE, WEST PART. TAPESTRIES.
Two, recently given to the cathedral. Flemish, early C17, rather
coarse. – STAINED GLASS. Both windows by *Clayton &
Bell*, *c.*1884.

SOUTH CHANCEL AISLE, WEST PART. TWO TAPESTRIES,
as above. – STAINED GLASS. The E window by *Clayton & Bell*,
*c.*1885. – The W window by *Morris & Co.*, the amply draped
figures by *Burne-Jones*, part of a series of the hierarchy of the
angels. Of *c.*1875–80. The same composition was also woven as
tapestry (see e.g. Eton College Chapel, Brockhampton Church
Herefordshire).

CHANCEL. Scott's REREDOS and IRON SCREEN have been
scrapped, a crime against the tenets of the Victorian Society,
but the need of the C13 cathedral was indeed greater than theirs.
– STALLS. The lower parts C14. With MISERICORDS and arm-
rests decorated with heads, beasts, and foliage. The upper parts
by *Scott*, *c.*1870, as are the BISHOP'S THRONE and ORGAN
CASES. Rich and stuffy. – PAINTING of the vault. Re-done
*c.*1870 on the general lines of the C13 work. Medallions with
figures and scenes, sparse scroll ornament, and masonry lines.
The repainting is by *Clayton & Bell*. – STAINED GLASS. The
E window of the Brazen Serpent, though it looks late C16 or
early C17 Flemish in composition, colouring, and Michel-
angelesque poses of the figures, is in fact of 1781, designed by
Mortimer and made by *Pearson*.

CROSSING. PULPIT. 1877.

NORTH TRANSEPT. One more big TAPESTRY as above, but
of the late C16. – STAINED GLASS. In the E aisle N windows by
Clayton & Bell and by *Ward & Hughes*, *c.*1884. – The E
windows by *Clayton & Bell*, *c.* 1880–5 (?).

SOUTH TRANSEPT. EMBROIDERY. Altar frontal, C18,
probably Spanish. – STAINED GLASS. Of the S windows the
centre light of the top tier contains C13 grisaille glass. – Also
some in the northernmost twin window of the 'gallery' tier on
the W side.

NAVE AND AISLES. COLLECTING TABLE (N aisle). This
incorporates a MISERICORD with the story of the Virgin and
the Unicorn. It was presented to the cathedral. – STAINED

GLASS. The nave w window is largely C13 grisaille glass in the usual geometrical patterns, but it includes C15 and early C16 glass from France. – C13 grisaille glass also in the aisle w windows. – s aisle third bay from the w excellent C14 and C15 glass with whole C14 figures. It comes from the great w window. – Fifth bay from the w, 1891 by *Holiday*. – Easternmost by *Clayton & Bell*, c. 1887.

MUNIMENT ROOM. TILES on the floor of the upper room and the staircase landings, probably of c.1260. Remarkably complete and undisturbed pavement.

PLATE. C13 Chalice said to come from the tomb of Bishop Longespée, who died in 1297; Paten from the same grave; Flagon, 1606; pair of Tankard Flagons, 1610; pair of large Chalices with Paten Covers, early C17; pair of silver-gilt Patens, 1661; pair of silver-gilt Candlesticks, 1663.

MONUMENTS

The monuments are arranged topographically from E to W. Salisbury is rich in monuments, but not rich in monuments of outstanding quality. After the C14 they get in fact very few.

RETROCHOIR, from N to S. Sir Thomas Gorges, the builder of Longford Castle, erected in 1635 and very Baroque. Two recumbent effigies. Arches to all four sides, with flanking fluted pilasters. The decoration curiously Early Renaissance. At the corners large detached twisted Corinthian columns. Top with obelisks, various polyhedra, with square and hexagonal facets, pediments, and four Virtues. The very top is formed of four semicircular members like the top of an arbour. Inside, above the effigies coved ceiling with circular reliefs of the seven *dona spiritus sancti* and cherubs' heads. Many inscriptions. The scenes have been identified to varying degrees of probability: Judgement of Solomon, Sacrifice of Manoah, David at Prayer?, Sacrifices of Cain and Abel, Samson slaying the Philistines, Joseph and his Brethren, Esther, Joseph warning Pharaoh. Among the inscriptions the following are specially felicitous:

Sagax et Celer Insequitur Praedam
Constans et Fidelis Consequitur Praemium

and

Mundus mare Vita navis
Quisque navigat Mors portus
Patria Caelum Fidelis intrat.

– Bishop Wordsworth. By *Frampton*, 1914. White marble recumbent effigy on a black marble tomb-chest. – Perp tomb-chest in a recess with thin continuous mouldings. – St Osmund † 1099. Tapering black (Tournai?) marble lid of a former coffin (*see* p. 378) – Earl of Hertford † 1621, son of the Protector and his wife, sister of Lady Jane Grey. Very tall wall-monument, almost covering the E window of the S aisle. The type of monument erected at the same time in Westminster Abbey, where the tallest of all monuments is that to Lord Hunsdon † 1596. Tripartite centre. The lower side parts with two kneeling children between columns, facing the altar. Very big obelisks l. and r. The centre with the two recumbent effigies, she behind and above him. Coffered arch. Obelisks also on the side parts and curiously fragmentary bits of curved pediments with allegorical figures. Top structure in the centre with more allegorical figures and more obelisks.* – William Wilton † 1523. Tomb-chest with cusped quatrefoils and lettering and a rebus. Recess with panelling. Frieze with inscription. – Bishop Moberly † 1885. Designed by *Sir A. Blomfield*. Rich, with big gabled arch and recumbent effigy. Against the back wall big quatrefoil with four scenes.

NORTH CHANCEL AISLE, EAST PART. Bishop Bingham † 1246. Excellent Purbeck effigy under nodding pointed-trefoiled head-canopy on thin shafts. His staff overlaps the canopy. Stiff-leaf border. The effigy belongs to a mid-C13 Purbeck type of which similar examples occur e.g. at Ely (Bishop Northwold † 1254, Bishop Kilkenny † 1256). The canopy over the tomb is rebuilt, but correctly. – Bishop Audley † 1524. Large, important chantry chapel. A tall stone screen surrounds it. To the aisle it has two tall transomed windows, polygonal buttresses and pinnacles with concave sides, and many niches for images. To the chancel the composition is much more restless. The two windows are subdivided differently, the W one into a doorway and a window, the E one into a tomb-chest with a canopy and a very pretty extra canopy over with pendants and a little fan-vault inside. The whole chapel has a fan-vault as well. Against the E wall lively reredos with niches. – Roger de Mortival † 1329. Tomb-chest. Black lid; the brass is missing. Ogee arch with openwork cusping and subcusping. A clan of charming little figures reclines on it. Enormous top finial. On

---

* The wife of Lord Hertford died in 1598 and was buried in Westminster Abbey with an equally splendid monument, which round its top also has five obelisks.

top of this thin buttress canopy similar to those of Edward II at Gloucester and the Despencers at Tewkesbury. L. and r. pairs of slim openings with gables and a little Dec tracery. An original iron grille fills the main arch.

SOUTH CHANCEL AISLE, EAST PART. Bishop Kerr † 1869. By *B. Pleydell Bouverie*. Recumbent effigy of white marble. Canopy in the C13 style. – Walter Lord Hungerford † 1449. The monument comes from the Hungerford chapel, demolished by Wyatt. It was beautified by Lord Radnor in 1778. To this date belongs the thin Gothic decoration of the stone base towards the chancel. The tall sides are entirely of iron, and the cresting, though it looks stone, is of wood (?). Pretty painted ceiling inside with shields undulatingly connected by cord. – Simon of Ghent † 1315. Tomb-chest. The brass has disappeared. Wide ogee arch, filled by an original iron grille (cf. the Mortival monument opposite). Jambs with ballflower. Arch with fleuron trail in one order. Big crockets and very big finial. Buttress-shafts l. and r. – Between chancel aisle and E aisle of the SE transept Bishop Giles de Bridport † 1262. A marvellous monument of Purbeck and stone. Purbeck effigy, beardless, under a pointed cinquefoiled head canopy. Turrets to its l. and r. Two angels also l. and r. The bishop raises both hands. The effigy lies in a shrine-like architecture open in two twin openings to N and S. To the N they are of Purbeck marble, to the S of stone. They consist each of pointed-trefoiled arches and a quatrefoiled circle over. All this is pierced work, i.e. bar tracery, and the earliest occurrence at Salisbury of this important motif, some five or ten years before the cloisters, though over fifteen years after Westminster Abbey. Stiff-leaf sprays. The upper parts are of stone on both sides. Gables on dragons, small heads between the arches and the gables. The gables again with leaf sprays, just on the point of abandoning the stiff-leaf convention. Scenes from the life of the bishop in the spandrels, again earlier than in the chapter house. The scenes are unrestored. Slender figures and much relished landscape elements. Shrine-like roof as a top. On it stiff-leaf crockets and finials.

NORTH EAST TRANSEPT. Brass to Bishop Wyville † 1375. An enormous piece, the actual brass plate 7 ft 6 in. long. The composition is unique. A fantastic tower or abbreviation of a fortress, a suitable thing for so militant a bishop.* In the

---

* He obtained licences to crenellate his manors of Sarum, Sherborne (both of which he had recovered), Woodford, Chardstock, Potterne, Canning, and Salisbury House London.

Salisbury Cathedral, brass to Bishop Wyville † 1375

fortress, the bishop, a demi-figure, and below him a smaller figure of a knight on guard.

SOUTH EAST TRANSEPT. On the E side: William Lisle Bowles, the poet, † 1850. Gothic tablet, no doubt by *Osmond* (*see* below). – J. H. Jacob † 1828. Grecian sarcophagus in relief. – On the S side: Bishop Burgess † 1837. Standing wall-monument with canopy. By *Osmond*, Gothic of course. – On the W side: Dean Clarke † 1757. Astonishingly classical, without a touch of the Rococo, i.e. on the way from Rysbrack to Wilton. Below, a still-life of astronomical and geometrical instruments. This was originally above the inscription, and on top was a big urn inside an arch (Devizes Museum 1, 49). – Bishop Seth Ward † 1689. Large tablet. A bad bust at the top. At the foot a still-life in the round of mathematical instruments. – Gothic tablets to Richard Hooker and William Chillingworth, both placed by Bowles in 1836 and both by *Osmond*.

NORTH CHANCEL AISLE, WEST PART. Thomas Bennett † 1558. Cadaver on a half-rolled-up straw mat. Tomb-chest with cusped quatrefoils and shields with initials. Recess with four-centred arch, panelled. Straight top. L. and r. re-used triple Purbeck shafts. In the E jamb Crucifixus. Not a trace of the Renaissance yet. – George Sydenham † 1524. Cadaver, already on a half-rolled-up mat, which makes a date in the 1540s more likely. No tomb-chest. – Bishop Woodville † 1484. Purbeck tomb-chest with cusped quatrefoils. Much wider surround. Very broad panelled posts l. and r. Four-centred arch towards the top really straight-sided. Horizontal top. Rather plain.

SOUTH CHANCEL AISLE, WEST PART. Bishop Selcot † 1557. Tomb-chest with quatrefoils, purely Gothic still. – Bishop Davenant † 1641. Standing monument, no longer Jacobean in style. Complicated architectural setting with, at the top, a segmental pediment and two fragments of a wider segmental pediment l. and r. – Sir Richard Mompesson † 1627. Probably by the master of the Hertford Monument. Two recumbent effigies, he behind her and a little higher. Detached columns with vine wound round. Shallow back arch. Big obelisks outside, l. and r. Top with allegorical figures and obelisks. – Bishop Mitford † 1407. Alabaster. Tomb-chest with gabled niches. Recumbent effigy. Much wider surround. Four-centred panelled arch. In one of the orders martlets and very pretty columbines. In the spandrels shields with allegorical figures and arms. Top quatrefoil frieze.

38a

NORTH TRANSEPT. In the E aisle Walter Long † 1807, a surgeon. Marble tablet with Gothic details. L. and r. allegories of Science and Benevolence. It is signed by *John Flaxman*. – On the N wall: Richard Colt Hoare. By *R. C. Lucas*, 1841 (of Leonardo da Vinci fame – the wax bust). Seated marble figure with a book. Heavy chair. – Bishop Blyth † 1499. Recumbent effigy. Tomb-chest with cusped quatrefoils. Tight-fitting plain canopy with horizontal top. – On the w wall: William Benson Earle † 1796. By *Flaxman*. Big tablet with standing female figure unveiling a relief of the Good Samaritan. Obelisk background. – First Earl of Malmesbury. By *Chantrey*, 1823. Very Grecian semi-reclining figure with book. But the architectural details Gothic. – George Lawrence † 1861. By *Gaffin*. Still with a Georgian mourning woman, amazingly late. – James Harris † 1780. By *Bacon*. Seated female holding a portrait medallion. Obelisk background. – John Britton, the antiquarian, † 1857. Brass plate.

SOUTH TRANSEPT. In the E aisle: J. H. Jacob † 1862. Designed by *Street*. Ornate table tomb with alabaster and mosaic. Low coped tomb-chest beneath. Under a canopy. – Bishop Fisher † 1825. Made by *Osmond*, 1828. Tomb-chest and on it, instead of an effigy, a cushion, the Bible, and the crozier. Canopy with four-centred arch. – On the s wall: tablet to Bishop Hume † 1782, by *King* of Bath. So small and so simple. – Poore family, 1817. Already in an archaeologically accurate Perp. Triple canopy. By *John Carline* of Shrewsbury, to a design of the Rev. *Hugh Owen*. – On the w wall: T. H. Hume † 1834. Gothic tablet by *Hopper*. – Sir Robert Hyde † 1665. Black and white marble. Bust in an oval medallion; bad.

NAVE AND AISLES. Wyatt transferred the monuments from the Lady Chapel and the Beauchamp and Hungerford Chapels to the nave and lined them all up neatly on the sleeper walls between the arcade piers.* We take them from the NE to the w and back to the SE. Sir John Cheney † 1509. Tomb-chest with cusped fields. Alabaster effigy. – Walter Lord Hungerford † 1449. Two tomb-chests side by side, to appear as one very broad one. The brasses have been looted. – Sir John de Montacute † 1390. Damaged effigy of a formidable knight. The N side of the tomb-chest is of Purbeck marble and was the top of the canopy of a Hungerford monument. – Tomb-chest of a person unknown. Cusped quatrefoils. – William Geoffrey † 1558. Tomb-chest with on the N and s sides three small

---

* He no doubt interfered with the tomb-chests as well.

Salisbury Cathedral, monument to
Bishop Roger † 1139

sexfoils enclosing shields. – William Longespée the Younger
† 1250. Purbeck effigy of a cross-legged knight. One hand on
the sword-hilt, the other holds the shield up high. – Miniature
stone effigy of a bishop; C13. Pointed-trefoiled, nodding head-
canopy. Angels to its l. and r. – Tapering coffin lid of an unknown bishop, C12 or C13.

Against the w wall: D'Aubigny Turberville † 1694. His wife
died in 1704. Very tall black base with long inscription. On top
putti, a shield, and a vase. – Thomas Lord Wyndham † 1745.
By *Rysbrack*. Seated female figure (in the round) drying her
tears and holding a staff and a lyre. On the l. big urn. To the l.
of this on the ground a curious square slab with the arms of
George II, in style consciously antiquated, i.e. of *c.*1700.

s aisle from the w: black lid with tapering sides. Unknown
whom it records. – Then two effigies. The first is Bishop
Roger's. He died in 1139. It is a lid with tapering sides. The
carving is completely flat, except of the head, which is a C14
replacement. Flat leaf border. Crozier on a dragon. The slab is
of Tournai marble (i.e. imported) and may date from the mid
C12. The head is Purbeck marble. Mr Hugh Shortt has recently
pointed out the close similarity of the slab to that of St Memmie
at Châlons-sur-Marne. The leaf border and the dragon are
almost identical. – The other slab is Purbeck throughout. It
commemorates Bishop Joscelin de Bohun † 1184. The head is
bearded. The modelling is considerably rounder. The head in
an odd two-lobed surround. Inscription on the orphrey of his
chasuble: Quisquis es, affer opem, deveniens in idem, i.e.
Whoever you are, help (with prayer). You will be like me. A
much longer rhymed inscription on the rim. It starts: 'Flent
hodie Salesbirie quia decidit ensis/Justitiae, pater ecclesie
Salesbiriensis'. The whole inscription in Mr Shortt's felicitious
translation (at the same time interpretation) is as follows:

They weep today down Salisbury way, for now lieth broken
Justice's sword, Sarum's bishop and lord, yet low be it spoken,
While yet alive, the poor used to thrive – he feared not the strong
    ones,
But was a mace that could batter the face of the proud and the wrong
    ones.
Princes in hordes, dukes nobles and lords as his sires he could muster,
Bishops were three who had sat in this see, and to them he gave
    lustre.

– Tomb-chest with three cusped lozenges. – Opposite against
the s wall Alexander Ballantyne, 1783, designed by *Nicholas*

Revett. Simple but very elegant tablet. – Bishop Beauchamp
† 1481. Tomb-chest with ornate quatrefoils.* – Opposite tablet
to Edward Davenant † 1639. Already entirely classical; black
and white. – Robert Lord Hungerford † 1459. Purbeck tomb-
chest with cusped fields. Alabaster effigy. – Opposite Mary
Cooke † 1642, also classical. – St Osmund. Part of the shrine,
probably C13, with three kneeling-holes to the N, three to the
s. – Bishop de la Wyle † 1271. Perp tomb-chest with quatrefoiled panels of Purbeck marble. These come from the canopy
of the monument to Robert Lord Hungerford. Purbeck effigy
with a pointed-trefoiled nodding head-canopy. It must have
been of good quality once. – Opposite Sir Henry Hyde † 1650.
With a militantly royalist inscription. Black columns with white
Ionic capitals. – Elihonor Sadler † 1622. Kneeling figure with
columns l. and r. – William Longespée † 1226. Tomb-chest of
wood with wooden shafts carrying pointed-trefoiled arches.
This was once covered with gesso and painted. The effigy of
freestone is the earliest English military effigy. Chain mail, also
covering the one visible arm and hand. Long shield with six
lions rampant.

15a

CLOISTERS (for the architecture *see* below). Many Gothic
tablets of stone, no doubt by *William Osmond*. There are
tablets commemorating two Osmonds, one who died in 1875
aged 84, the other who died in 1890 aged 69. One classical
tablet († 1824) is also signed *Osmond*.

CLOISTERS

17a Salisbury is a secular, not a monastic cathedral, and so, while a
chapter house was needed, a cloister was not, and indeed the
Salisbury cloister has no other rooms attached to it. It was an
afterthought altogether. No provision was made for it when the
s aisle was built. It is entirely isolated from the cathedral, except
for the w side of the s transept and a corridor or branch passage
continuing the w walk to the N until it meets the aisle. To the E
of this passage is an open space, called the Plumbery. The
cloisters were begun by Bishop de la Wyle, as we have seen.
This may have been about 1270. They are of twelve bays to each
walk. In the middle of the garth are two splendid cedar trees,
beautifully framed by the broad openings of the cloister walks.
The cloisters introduce the bar tracery of Westminster Abbey
to Salisbury,‡ and with it a sumptuousness so far quite absent

---

* The tomb-chest did not originally belong.
‡ But cf. the Bridport Monument, p. 372.

from the design of the cathedral. The lancets which had dominated up to 1270, even with what plate tracery there is, emphasize height, the cloister openings breadth. They are framed by plain buttresses with plain set-offs. Each bay has two-light openings with a deeply moulded quatrefoiled circle. The trumeaus are of a centre shaft with two shafts at r. angles to the wall attached to it and two detached shafts in the direction of the wall – a subtle, wholly successful arrangement. All capitals are moulded. In the lunette above the two pairs is a large circle alternately cinquefoiled and sexfoiled. Westminster Abbey in 1245–55 had taken this type of four-light bar tracery from Amiens, where it had occurred about 1235–40. Above the arcade runs a parapet with small quatrefoiled circles, two to each bay. Only in the E wall opposite the chapter-house entrance the system of the openings is interrupted. There are here simply two large openings into the garth without subdivision or tracery. Above the N half of the E walk is the LIBRARY, built in 1445. It has straight-headed cusped two-light windows to the W, i.e. the garth, as well as to the E. Actually what happened in 1445 is that the new accommodation on the upper floor was built as long as the whole E range. The surviving N part was the Chancellor's Schools. The library occupied the S part. This was demolished in 1756, and the library moved N.

The interior of the walks is rib-vaulted throughout, with quadripartite bays and bosses. The ribs and the transverse arches have the same thickness and mouldings. The bosses are mostly stiff-leaf in the E and N walks, though there is the occasional figure-motif, e.g. biting dragons by the chapter-house entrance and mermaids further S. At the SE corner the foliage turns naturalistic and goes on being so in the S walk. The vaulting of the W walk came last. The bosses here have more human figures and heads. The style is decidedly later, say of c.1300–10, though the rib profiles do not change. At the N end of the W walk a branch runs N to connect with the S aisle of the cathedral W of the Plumbery. The walls of the cloister walks are all covered with blank arcading, echoing the openings with their bar tracery. Each bay has two arches with a big sexfoiled circle over. All shafts are detached. At the entrance to the S transept the S wall of the short passage to the entrance is canted, and the blind arcading cants with it in the same disconcerting way in which in the earlier C13 work quatrefoils were broken round corners.

There are a number of c13 DOORWAYS out of the cloister. That in the NE corner to the S transept is nine times cusped with stiff-leaf cusps and stiff-leaf in the spandrels. To its S is a second, minor doorway, cinquecusped. Where did it originally lead to? Another small doorway leads E from the SE corner. It is also cinquecusped. The entry to the cloister from the W is by a doorway at the NW corner. This has a type of arch frequent at Westminster Abbey. The arch is very depressed two-centred and stands on short vertical pieces. The doorway cuts into the blind wall arcading, though symmetrically. The same type in the doorway from the N branch of the W walk to the Plumbery, also cutting into the wall-arcading and also symmetrically. The doorway into the S aisle is cinquecusped with leaf cusps and cuts very awkwardly into the blank arcading. The exterior of the cloister ranges is very bare, without windows and only with simple buttresses, but the *leitmotif* of the parapet of blank trefoil-headed panels is preserved even here.

CHAPTER HOUSE

The chapter house, of about the same date as the cloisters,* is connected with them by a two-bay corridor. It has sexfoiled circular windows and the same small quatrefoiled circle over as the parapet of the cloisters. The chapter house itself is an octagon, with gloriously spacious windows of four lights with two quatrefoiled circles and a large octofoiled circle over. The pattern was of course Westminster Abbey, where the chapter house was apparently complete by 1253. Frieze without dogtooth and parapet. Buttresses without the multiplied set-offs. Flat roof – unfortunately. Higher stair-turret NE of the corridor.‡

The portal from the cloister into the corridor is all c19. The walls of the corridor have the same blank arcading as the walls of the cloister, except that here Purbeck shafts are used. Vault in two bays with ribs like those of the cloister and stiff-leaf bosses. The inner portal also has a trumeau. This is slender, of Purbeck marble, and consists of four shafts attached to a centre shaft. The detail is all c19. The jambs l. and r. are thickly

* Or a little later, if Gleeson White (Bell's Cathedral Series) is right in pointing out that pennies of Edward I were found below its foundation. That would give 1279 as the earliest possible date.

‡ As one looks at the exterior of the chapter house one can also see the E wall of the library (*see* above), the passage leading to it at an angle, and the projection of the fireplace.

Purbeck-shafted. Purbeck stiff-leaf capitals, restored. The two arches are cinquecusped with stiff-leaf cusps, all this also of Purbeck. The super-arch has one order of little figure niches 15b with trefoiled canopies. This also corresponds to Westminster Abbey. The little figures represent the Virtues and Vices. They are largely of 1856 (*Clutton*).

Now the interior of the chapter house itself. It is 58 ft across. The large windows make it very light. Moreover the centre pier is very slender. Circular centre with eight thin detached Purbeck shafts.* Two tiers of shaft-rings. Stiff-leaf capitals and a little stiff-leaf on the base. Vault with eight arches across and eight cells with 'triradial' ribs, i.e. ribs radiating to the centre and two corners. All ribs slender. Stiff-leaf bosses. Below the windows blank arcading with pointed cinquecusped arches. Quatrefoil Purbeck wall-shafts, and in front of them at the angles detached triple Purbeck shafts. Rich stiff-leaf capitals, some with heads, birds, animals, grotesques. More heads as hood-mould stops – these indeed most remarkable. They are of all physiognomies, types, and expressions, male and female, heads held up and leaning a little sideways, heads with the tongue out and with a distorted mouth, heads bearded and beardless, heads young and old. They carry on the tradition of the rood-screen. On the spandrels *see* below. The only disturbing element is the w wall. The blank arcading first continues one more bay, but the bay is wider and the arches hence round-cinquecusped. But the portal cuts into their mouldings. In the big main spandrel a large quatrefoiled circle with a c 19 figure of Christ. This upper part of the portal cuts into an upper blank arcading of eight bays, necessary because the corridor has that height. Consequently the w window has no space to go down as low as the others. The row of blank arches has very rich stiff-leaf capitals. Head stops, shallow spandrels with stiff-leaf, dragons, etc.

The spandrels of the blank arcading right round the chapter house have carved stories from Genesis, from the Creation to Moses, i.e. with Adam and Eve, Cain and Abel, Noah, Abraham, Esau, Jacob, Joseph. The carving was unfortunately savagely, i.e. sentimentally, restored in the 1860s, by *John Birnie Philip*. But iconographically the series remains extremely valuable all the same, a veritable picture book with any number of lively, well-observed genre details.

---

* The original top with the splendid capitals and base is now in the s w corner of the cloisters, where it looks exactly like a font.

THE CLOSE

The building of houses for the canons, choristers, etc. began at once, and C13 remains survive, though they and the later medieval remains have to be pieced together laboriously. A licence to build a wall round cathedral and houses and thus make the close a close was granted by Edward III in 1327. The open area to the W and N of the cathedral was a graveyard. Bishop Shute Barrington (1782–91) and Wyatt turfed it and thus created that smooth green expanse which goes so perfectly with the cathedral. It may well be said that Salisbury's is the most beautiful of English closes. Even Lord Torrington – he wrote in 1782 and he never writes but to nag – must admit that 'the close is comfortable and the divines well seated'. Well seated they are now too, and moreover in houses of absorbing architectural interest. The Salisbury close has more such houses than any other; that is certain.

The shape of the close is roughly a rectangle with the Bishop's Palace alone to the SE. In addition there is a NW extension, called Choristers' Green and separated from the close by the most effective island of houses, there is a SW extension, and there is a feeler to the E from the NE corner, like a street.

THE WALL. Much of the C14 wall remains, built in parts with stones from Old Sarum. The longest even stretch is along St John Street and Exeter Street (W) and turning into St Nicholas Road (S). Most of the wall is embattled. The wall-walk behind the battlements also survives. To the N of St Ann's Gate Malmesbury House (*see* p. 385) has its upper floor and a canted oriel on the wall – all C18. To the S of St Ann's Gate is a square oriel on a big curved medieval bracket. Opposite the Bricket Hospital in Exeter Street a platform on five brackets. In this stretch many small Norman panels from Old Sarum with flowers, etc. The N wall hides mostly behind the houses on the N side of the close. Behind No. 55, for example, a stretch with wall-walk.

GATES. NORTH GATE, at the S end of High Street. Perp. Four-centred arch to the N. Traceried spandrels. Quatrefoil frieze. Two small upper windows. Another panelled and quatrefoiled frieze. Battlements with shields. To the inside niche for a statue now inhabited by Edward VII. Here also fragments of Old Sarum, diaper and zigzag. – ST ANN'S GATE, St John Street. Built *c.*1331 etc. Low two-centred arch with two continuous chamfers. To the inside the arch dies into the imposts. Two-light Dec window over. Two damaged gargoyles.

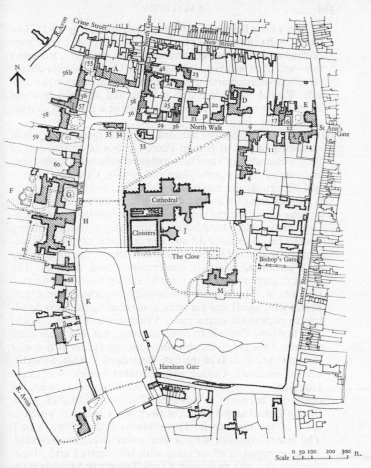

Salisbury: The Close

A. Hungerford Chantry
B. Mompesson House
C. Matrons' College
D. Theological College (No. 19)
E. Malmesbury House (No. 15)
F. Old Deanery (No. 62)
G. Training College
H. Audley House (Nos 63-4)

I. King's House (No. 65)
J. Chapter House
K. Walton Canonry (No. 69)
L. Leadenhall (No. 70)
M. Bishop's Palace (Cathedral School)
N. South Canonry (No. 71)

St Ann's Gate belongs to Malmesbury House, Nos 14–15 The
Close. – BISHOP'S GATE, Exeter Street. Also C14. Four-
centred arch with two continuous hollow chamfers. Renewed
two-light Dec window. – HARNHAM GATE. Double-chamfered four-centred arch with continuous mouldings to the outside. To the inside the arch is segmental and dies into the
imposts. Above seven corbels for a bay or a platform, but no
upper storey. Fleurons and gargoyles.

BISHOP'S PALACE, now Cathedral School. A picturesque whole
consisting of part of Bishop Poore's palace of c.1220, part of
Bishop Beauchamp's and his successors' palace of c.1460–1500,
and part of Bishop Seth Ward's of 1670–4. Of the C13 the W
end. Externally not much tells of the date, but internally there
is an important UNDERCROFT. It has six bays with two short
circular piers carrying circular abaci and heavily single-chamfered arches and ribs. Above was the Great Chamber. Bishop
Poore's hall does not exist any longer. It was 125 by 58 ft, i.e.
larger than that of Old Sarum and even that of the royal palace
at Winchester, which is contemporary and survives. The
Great Chamber was swept away by Bishop Sherlock's DRAW-
ING ROOM. The style of this certainly represents the 1740s.
Frieze with heads and garlands, somewhat rustic. Coved ceiling, an eagle in the centre panel. Venetian windows to N, S, and
W. They have Corinthian columns inside, but look bleak from
outside. Attached to the drawing-room NE corner at r. angles
the CHAPEL. This is of the C15. Buttressed N front. Straight-
headed windows. Ceiling with moulded beams. – STALLS.
Jacobean. – COMMUNION RAIL. Also Jacobean; with flat
openwork balusters. – SCREEN. With C17 and C18 parts.
Bishop Beauchamp's principal work was a hall with porch to
the E of the undercroft. This replaced Bishop Poore's hall.
The porch remains, with a fine tower over. Ashlar-faced.
Three-storeyed. Tall entrance with two-centred arch. Inner
doorway also with two-centred arch. Tracery and shields in the
spandrels of the outer entrance. Straight-headed window with
cusped lights. The tower is surmounted by a delightful stair-
turret with decorated top and spirelet. The HALL itself however has been swept away in alterations and compartmenting of
several centuries. Only the ashlar facing remains on the N side
and only the buttresses on the S side, and the two-centred arch
of the exit from the screens passage. Seth Ward, for example,
put into it his new and very effective grand STAIRCASE. It
starts in two flights and returns in one and repeats this for the

second floor. Strong turned balusters and still a solid string. Seth Ward seems also responsible for the whole S side of the centre, a homely, loveable front of nine bays and two storeys, stuccoed. Georgianized windows. Seth Ward's have stone crosses and appear in front of his staircase, in the recessed centre part of the N side (the wall here of flint and stone chequer) and in other places. Of the Seth Ward time also the doorway in the middle of the N side. The pretty Gothick porch into the C13 part, also from the N, must be Bishop Barrington's, i.e. of *c.*1790.

HOUSES IN THE CLOSE. To follow their numerical order we must start where they are least eventful: N of the Bishop's Palace and NE of the cathedral. The houses mostly are or look Georgian. Only No. 6 is Victorian Tudor. By No. 9 the street-like extension towards St Ann's Gate starts. The house faces N, into this street. Five bays, two storeys, brick. Tuscan porch with semi-circular hood. A tripartite window over. In the kitchen panelling from the choir stalls of Seth Ward. The painted-on names of the prebends can just be deciphered. The stalls were put in about 1670–5. The panelling is perfectly plain. Mid-C18 entrance hall with panelling and open pediments on Corinthian pilasters. Stair entrance of the later C17. Two arches and a rusticated square pillar. The staircase also later C17. Posts with vases. More later C17 work. Also one room with a Rococo stucco ceiling.

No. 11 has an early C18 front of five bays and two and a half storeys. Quoins, parapet curving up to the l. and r. Nice later C18 doorway, and nice minor late C18 decoration of one room. – No. 12 is nothing special externally, but inside are the remains of the Hall of the Vicars Choral. In the passage from the entrance on the r. big wooden window with cusped lights, straight-headed, late C15 or early C16. Then tall entrance arch into the screens passage. On the l. the three low and even arches into kitchen and offices. On that side two more doorways and also, accessible from the r. hand arch, a room with a fine C15 fireplace. Pedimental lintel with blank tracery. Are the architectural parts C15 too, or C14? – No. 14 is of *c.*1700. Five bays, two storeys. Doorway with pediment on fluted Doric pilasters.

Opposite, concealed by trees, MALMESBURY HOUSE hides its strikingly splendid interior. Externally it has a seven-bay ashlar façade of probably Queen-Anne date. Seven bays, two storeys. Two narrow windows l. and r. of the centre. Round the corner

13

3b a sundial dated 1749. Spacious staircase of *c*.1750. Three twisted balusters to each tread. Stucco decoration of walls and ceiling including round niches for busts. To the l. a nice Rococo room, to the r. another, simpler one. But on the first floor the library in a delightful Earliest Gothic Revival, i.e. still with many small details kept classical. Also the chimney-

54a piece is entirely Rococo. Charming bay window with leaf ribs. It all points to *c*.1750–60.* Only the ceiling looks *c*.1800 or later. On the first floor another, smaller Rococo chimneypiece in a room overlooking St John Street with an oriel (*see* Walls). In fact the upper room of St Ann's Gate belongs to the house. At the back of the garden a SUMMER HOUSE of the late C17. Three bays, rusticated wall. Pediment with cartouche and cornucopia. Panelling inside. The doors have unusual trellis glazing (cf. No. 68 The Close).

No. 16 is an odd and picturesque assembly of cottages forming an L. No. 17 is an interesting, tall, three-storeyed symmetrical brick house of only two bays. Elizabethan or Jacobean with a Victorian doorway. Large mullioned and transomed windows on ground floor and first floor, smaller only mullioned ones on the second. Inside, the whole front of the first floor is one room, with panelling, pilasters, and frieze with geometrical arabesque decoration, a plaster frieze with strapwork and figures, and a ceiling with thin-ribbed patterns. The house belonged to *W. E. Tower*, Kempe's later partner and then successor, and there is quite some *Kempe* glass about, also a coat of arms with three wheatsheaves and some C15 quarries with wheatsheaves.

No. 19 is the THEOLOGICAL COLLEGE, a large, even, late C17 house of nine bays with the first and last two projecting. Two storeys, hipped roof. Brick and stone quoins and other trim. Doorway with straight hood on moulded brackets. Good gate-piers with pineapples. Panelled entrance hall. Good staircase with twisted balusters and still a plain string. To the E Victorian flint CHAPEL, completed in 1881 by *Butterfield* – a pity. In it STAINED GLASS by *Kempe*, 1888 and 1907.

No. 20 is externally Early Georgian, five bays and two storeys, hipped roof. It was built *c*.1725. But in its E wall is the large blocked arch of a former gatehouse to No. 21, and there is medieval masonry on the N and W sides. No. 21 has a fine Elizabethan flint front with two gables and mullioned windows

* James Harris, who lived in the house, is praised on his monument in the cathedral for his great learning. The library was no doubt installed for him, and he died in 1780.

– much renewed. However, inside the entrance hall there are at once a little C15 frieze and a lamb and flag indicating that this was outer wall. Further back to the E a C13 room, probably the chapel. It has lancet windows to E, N, and (blocked) S. In one room frieze of Early Renaissance woodwork (brought in?). In another, coved ceiling with Elizabethan plasterwork. Also on the upper floor an unexplained C14 arch now close to floor level. Several C15 windows. At the NW corner a tower projects. Its basement is tunnel-vaulted.* The house was called in the Middle Ages Aula-le-Stage. In the mid C19 it was W. Lisle Bowles's (see Bremhill, p. 127), and he added the miniature porch. He also in 1830 put up the memorial in the garden to William Coxe, incorporating a tall chamfered archway perhaps from the outbuildings of the house (cf. No. 20 above).

Nos 22–5 lie back along a little lane pointing N. No. 26 is a rather gaunt four-bay Georgian house of two and a half storeys; cemented. Late C18 doorway. No. 29 has a C14 porch entrance and a later medieval doorway. – Then, facing these houses, the island between the N range of the close and the lawn of the cathedral. The houses, Nos 33–5, are nothing very special, but their very variety is an asset. No. 34 faces E with two Early Victorian bargeboarded gables. No. 35 has C16 to C17 brick and stonework to the N.

No. 36 is the corner to Choristers' Green. It is Georgian, of five bays and two storeys, with a hipped roof. Wide stone doorway with Tuscan pilasters and pediment. No. 38 has a late-C18 doorway, but inside a large wall-painting of the mid C17, a hunting scene which Mr Croft-Murray, on the strength of a comparison with Wilton House, attributes to *Edward Pierce*.‡ Then the MATRONS' COLLEGE, established by Seth Ward in 1682 and quite possibly designed or approved by *Wren*, who was a friend of Seth Ward of long standing. Low, of two storeys, with a hipped roof. Thirteen bays and projecting two-bay wings. Two-light mullioned windows with frames flat except for a slight outer moulding. In the wings dormers with circular windows. Doorway with a segmental pediment on brackets. Above, inscription cartouche with open scrolly pediment. Steep top pediment with coat of arms and garlands. Octagonal glazed lantern. Minor doorways in bays one and thirteen of the centre. The back has five gables. The chimneystacks are set diagonally and grouped. No. 48 adjoins the North Gate and has

* In the small N window STAINED GLASS, a complete, kneeling C15 figure.
‡ It was boarded up at the time of writing.

a doorway on elaborately carved brackets and a much earlier stone chimneybreast to the s. Nothing of importance opposite.
The N side of Choristers' Green starts with the STABLES of Mompesson House. They appear to be late C17. Five bays, two storeys, brick, cross-windows below, mullioned windows above. Hipped roof. Arched doorway with rusticated surround re-set. It was originally in the large archway to the l. of the house. This also has a rusticated surround. The window above the doorway is elaborately framed, with an open scrolly top. The large archway now belongs to the r. wing of Mompesson House, which is also of brick, five bays long, and has a panelled parapet. Later doorway with Doric pilasters, a metope frieze, and a pediment. Later also the lunette window and broken pediment above the archway.

48b MOMPESSON HOUSE is dated 1701 on a rainwater head. It is ashlar-faced, of seven bays, with a hipped roof. The windows to the l. and r. of the centre are narrower. Doorway with big open segmental pediment filled with garlands. It rests on brackets. The window above has side scrolls and garlands. Fine gatepiers, iron gates and iron railings. The other sides of the house are brick. Here some original glazing bars. Back doorway pedimented, but low, as it is below the staircase landing. An earlier wing runs out to the N. This still has bricks in English bond. Entrance hall with pedimented doorways. Wall paintings with recent *trompe l'œil* still lifes. Modest plasterwork. Depressed arch to the staircase. This has robust stucco on the walls and ceiling and below the staircase. Three twisted balusters, decorated at the foot, to each tread. Carved tread-ends. The stucco must be of c.1740. If the staircase is of the same date, it is conservative. On the other hand it can hardly be of 1701. The front E room also has stucco work of c.1740, and in addition a late-C18 chimneypiece. The plasterwork of the front w room is modest. The back w room has a good chimneypiece of c.1740, the back E room again modest stucco work and a late-C18 chimneypiece. From the first-floor landing short corridors run w and s. In the front room a ceiling with an eagle in the centre.

Then the HUNGERFORD CHANTRY; but there is nothing medieval left. Five bays, two storeys, parapet, brick, simple doorway with pediment. No. 55 is also C18 and also of five bays. But it has a big three-bay pediment. Segment-headed doorway. Then follows No. 56, HEMINGSBY HOUSE, and with it the w range of the Close, the range of the largest and most interesting houses, and also the houses with the finest gardens. They stretch down to the Avon, and some have superb trees. No. 56 is gabled and quite modest externally, but it has a little wing projecting on the r. and in this a C14 portal blocked. Round arch, triple shafts. Above, the former chapel, with a C14 E window and a C15 side window. The walls of the wings have hundreds of tiles, partly laid herringbone-wise. They are said to come from Old Sarum. It is possible that the portal was the entrance to the porch which led into the hall. The hall indeed exists, but it has now another porch. The entrance to this is Perp. Is it re-set? The great thing about the hall is its roof, with collar-beams on arched braces and four tiers of single-cusped wind-braces. Single-cusping of the principals above the collar-beams too. Wall plate with quatrefoils and inscriptions repeating the name of William Fideon, a Greek who had escaped from Constantinople in 1453. C17 dormers. So the hall is C15, the porch and chapel C14. The hall screen also survives, though not *in situ*. It has two entries with charming shafts and buttress-shafts. In the hall now a small Jacobean staircase with tapering square balusters. In one first-floor room linenfold panelling, very good and very complete. This however is in the attached neighbouring house, No. 56b, which was built in 1727 to replace a decayed wing of Hemingsby House. There is in fact re-used medieval masonry at the back. The front is of brick. Five bays of very large windows, a main floor on a basement, a little like an orangery. Evenly rusticated quoins, panelled parapet. Arched doorway with a surround with rustication of alternating size.

Then WREN HALL (a recent name), formerly the Cathedral School, completed in 1714. Five bays, brick, on a basement of stone with small mullioned windows. Quoins. Hipped roof. Large windows with basket arches. Doorway with an oval window over. Inside the schoolroom with its panelling and the master's seat. No. 57, BRAYBROOKE, was the master's house. It is connected with the school. Five bays, two storeys, brick, on a stone base, doorway with pediment on carved brackets. No. 58 is the WARDROBE (part of the Training College; *see* below), a very big house. Flint, brick, and stone irregularly used. Recessed centre and projecting wings, each with two gables. They have Victorian bargeboards. In the centre on the first floor a six-light window with two transoms. Below an early C19 (?) brick arcade of three Tudor arches, and behind it a large blocked C15 door surround, straight-headed. At the back in this centre part of the house, which was no doubt the medieval hall, a buttress and the chimneybreast of the hall fireplace. The N side was in that case the medieval kitchen and offices, and there are here indeed two big chimneybreasts. Inside, three rooms with mid-C18 stucco. The middle room with a fine classical chimneypiece and an eagle in the centre panel of the ceiling. The room to its s has a Rococo ceiling and fireplace, and the staircase richer Rococo stuccowork.

No. 59 (ARUNDELLS) lies far back. It has good gatepiers and gates. The house is supposed to have been built in 1749; but this cannot have been a complete rebuilding. Five bays, two storeys, hipped roof. Staircase with turned balusters and still a simple string, probably of c.1700. No. 60, the NORTH CANONRY, is the most picturesque building in the Close, pre-Reformation and C17 and very much *Sir G. G. Scott*. Flint and stone. Ashlar-faced projecting centre with polygonal angle buttresses and pinnacles. Top gable. On ground floor and upper floor a large seven-light window with transom. To the r. archway with pedestrian entrance to its l. Four-centred arch. This lies in a lower wing. Here at once a canted oriel, Scott's work. This and the following original three-light window have arched lights without cusps, a Henry VIII form. On the first floor cross-windows with finely moulded surrounds and the initials R H for Richard Hill, who lived in the house from 1672 to 1695. End buttress. The l. attachment is C18 with a Victorian front. Beneath the r. wing is a C13 undercroft with a short round pier and round abacus. The vaults do not survive. So – on the parallel with the bishop's palace – one may assume that above this was the original solar or else the original hall. The oriel would belong to its successor. But nothing of all this can be traced any longer. In the part with the polygonal buttresses at the back a blocked smallish two-centred arch. The principal room in this part is on the first floor. It has a mid-C17 wooden overmantel. At the far end of the garden, by the river, brick SUMMER HOUSE of the early C18. To the river on the ground floor two vertically oval windows. Tile-hung above. Parapet curving up to the corners.

The following stretch of the Close is dominated by the TRAINING COLLEGE. This was started in 1841 and moved to the King's House in 1851. It began to extend then. But most of the extensions are of after the Second World War. They are extensive indeed, of brick, Neo-Georgian, and architecturally insignificant (*Green, Son & Lloyd*). They are mostly between the old buildings of the Close and the river, i.e. to the N, but at the place we have now reached they come into the front. One of the new buildings, dating from 1949, lies behind the gate-piers and iron gates of the old No. 62, which is the OLD DEANERY. This had to be preserved. One finds it behind the new building. Externally it is disappointing indeed.* Flint with a cemented front with large Georgian windows. One buttress. To the s two big chimneybreasts, one stone, the other flint, and another big buttress. At the back, from the s, first a Georgian projection, then, parallel with it, a medieval one with, to the N, C15 two-light windows with cusped lights. Further N more georgianized windows. The interior shows the whole, minus the Georgian projection, to be essentially of the C13. Documents prove that the house was built between 1258 and 1274. It consisted of a hall with the solar at the s, the butteries at the N end. Of C13 details, by the porch one lancet window can be traced, and others have been found during recent repairs inside. They face E, are on the upper floor, and belong to the original hall. In the part with the C15 windows a C13 doorway too, also on the first floor. Moreover, the trussed rafter roof of the C13 still exists, with the only C13 louvre framing in the country. At the time of writing the finds have not yet been published.

AUDLEY HOUSE, Nos 63–64 (Training College), is a pair and has a plain seven-bay Georgian brick front of two and a half storeys, right on the road. – No. 65, the KING'S HOUSE, is the headquarters of the Training College. The house is large and lies back. It is of flint. The centre has on the l. a two-storeyed C15 porch with diagonal buttresses and entrances from N as well as E. The entrance arches are panelled and the porch has a very handsome fan-vault inside. To the l. of the porch one gable, to the r. two. Renewed mullioned and transomed windows replacing medieval (C13?) windows whose outline is visible. They belonged to the original hall. Old drawings of the back show one such hall window complete, of two lights with what looks like plate tracery. More evidence of the hall does indeed remain. For one thing the exit to the W, in line with the porch, survives, now inside the house. Also, the room behind the porch, to the N of it, has a Georgian screen of Ionic columns. They obviously replace the medieval hall screen. The room has a finely moulded fireplace, as has the 'parlour' to its s. And, as

* The appearance of the building at the beginning of the C19 is recorded by Buckler (Devizes Museum IX, 23).

one ascends into the roof, there is the open timber roof of the hall with cusped wind-braces. It is continued in the office direction (s) with simple wind-braces in two tiers. Then to the r. a taller brick bay was added in the late c16. Big two-storeyed canted bay window. The ground floor has one transom, the upper floor two transoms. This no doubt was a renewal of the parlour and solar of the c15. At the back of the house the brick bay shows as a tower. The windows are as large here as the bay windows of the front. Inside, the upper room has a plaster ceiling with the usual Elizabethan interlaced geometrical patterns. The College added dormitories in 1873 and the wing with the chapel (at the back) in 1899. In the chapel STAINED GLASS by *Kempe*.

From No. 68 onwards the houses face the sw extension of the Close, rougher, and with more trees. No. 68 is the stateliest c18 house in the Close, too townish almost for its location. The house is said to have been built in 1718. Ashlar-faced, but brick on the sides and at the back. Seven bays with a three-bay centre. Basement, two storeys with giant pilasters and attic above the cornice. Parapet on the attic. Front garden with gate-piers of brick and stone, iron railing and gates. Open stairs to the front door. The doorway has a segmental pediment on Corinthian pilasters. The back is of brick with stone dressings and has giant pilasters too. The back door has trellis glazing bars like the summer house behind Malmesbury House. Large entrance hall containing the staircase and a balcony round at upper-floor level. Thin turned balusters. Inlay work on the first landing. Panelling and back doorway with open pediment on fluted pilasters. The room at the back has a diagonally placed fireplace. The head in the frieze can hardly be earlier than 1730. The same is true of the plaster ceiling of the large drawing room to the l., which is 40 ft long and runs through from front to back. Small stone fireplace flanked by pilasters.

No. 69, WALTON CANONRY, is simpler. It dates from *c*.1720. Seven bays, basement and two storeys. Doorway with seg-mental pediment enclosing garlands.* Wide angle strips; parapet. Staircase with three turned balusters to the step. Back doorway with an apsed hood containing a tiny shell. Later No. 69 was the house of Constable's friend Archdeacon Fisher. That is how Constable could paint views of the cathedral from the meadows w of the close and from the gardens of the Bishop's

* The arms are those of Francis Eyre, who was tenant in 1719. His pre-decessor had been Isaac Walton.

Palace. – No. 70 is in itself now of little interest, but to its s lay
Elyas de Derham's house, the LEADENHALL, and from this
a few fragments now adorn the garden walls close to the house.
The most interesting one is a two-light window, the lights
trefoiled, and a quatrefoil in plate tracery over – i.e. a type
identical with those of the cathedral. Also one lancet and two
small circular openings. These were originally in the gable, the
lancet below the two circular windows. The stables of No. 70
have two early-c19 gate lodges. – No. 71 is the SOUTH CAN-
ONRY (now Bishop's House). Low, two-storeyed, brick, of
five widely spaced bays. Said to be of *c*.1665 with major alterations of 1778. Broken middle pediment. Only the first-floor
middle window has a little decoration. The doorway and the
roof brackets seem altered (Early Victorian? The date mentioned is after 1889, which seems too late). Behind this c18–19
front, however, is an older house. The room to the r. of the
entrance has moulded beams and a big boss. The arms are
probably those of a succentor of the first decade of the c16.
Facing these houses across the sw extension of the close are the
Harnham Gate and a few more houses. The only one needing
comment is No. 74, because it is really part of the Harnham
Gate and built immediately by its side.

THE TOWN

INTRODUCTION

New Sarum was founded with the cathedral, received its first
charter in 1227, and remained under the control of the bishops
until 1611. From 1261 the town had a mayor. Before the end of
the c13 there were three parish churches (St Thomas, St Martin,
St Edmund) and houses of the Franciscans or Greyfriars (founded
before 1230) and the Dominicans or Blackfriars (founded before
1281). The Dominicans were to the w beyond the Avon, towards
Fisherton, the Franciscans by St Ann Street and the street still
called The Friary (for remains *see* p. 410). A rampart and a ditch
to protect the town were provided in 1310. Soon after, it will be
remembered, the cathedral close received its wall. Inside the
rampart the streets form a grid, though not a regular one. It is
called The Chequers and can be assumed to go back to the c13.
Salisbury is extremely well provided with water, and in former
times suffered much from flooding. The Avon flows to the w and
s, split into three on the w side as well as to the se. The Nadder,
also split into two, comes in from the w, the Wylie from the n (at

Wilton), and the Bourne also from the N. In addition, up to 1852 the streets of Salisbury had narrow canals; Leland calls them streamelettes, Celia Fiennes rivulets. The street New Canal still bears witness to the past.

Salisbury had a flourishing cloth trade from the C15 onwards. Several merchants' houses survive (e.g. Church House and the hall of John Halle). Aubrey in 1669 still says that 'the best white cloathes in England are made at Salisbury'. The trade declined only in the C18.

CHURCHES

ST ANDREW, Bemerton. *See* p. 96.

ST EDMUND, Bedwin Street. In a spacious turfed courtyard. Completely Perp, except that the W tower was rebuilt in 1653-5, with old parts no doubt, see the W doorway with traceried spandrels. The bell-openings appear to be C19. Battlements, pinnacles. The rest of the church, except for the chancel and s chapel by *Scott*, 1865-7, is no more than the chancel and the chancel chapels of the large collegiate church of St Edmund. The church was begun in 1407 and is all of a piece. Nave and aisles, four-light windows. Only the small N aisle W doorway seems to have been of *c*.1700 originally. The N addition however dates from the late C18 and was the school. Upper windows with the typical intersected tracery. Wide, rather bare interior. Five-bay arcades. Thin piers with four shafts and four hollows in the diagonals. Arches with two hollow chamfers. Chancel arch Victorian. Good single-framed N aisle roof with tie-beams. – FONT. Octagonal, of Purbeck marble, C13. On each side two flat blank pointed-trefoiled arches. – STAINED GLASS. Panel with entertainingly painted stories from Genesis. Swiss; dated 1617 (Vestry). – MACE REST. Early Georgian, of wood. Two feet curving outward. Framework above with two columns and a segmental pediment in outline. Arms at the top. – PLATE. Paten, 1533 (it must be one of the latest surviving pre-Reformation pieces); Almsdish dated 1732; other pieces of 1685-1703 remodelled in 1867.

ST FRANCIS (R.C.), Castle Road and Beatrice Road. 1936-9 by *Robert Potter*. Red brick. Square, with a short SW tower and an apse. The details Östbergish – rather late in the day. Quite an impressive white interior, the floor of the apse raised considerably above the altar space.

ST JOHN, Bemerton. *See* p. 96.

ST MARTIN. At one end of the town. Of the Norman church

just two fragments re-set in the tower E wall. Recent excavations to the S of the S chancel chapel have shown foundations
of some Norman walling. The chancel is of c.1230. Lancet
windows, single and in pairs. In the E wall three stepped lancets
put in in 1849 to replace a Perp window. In the gable sexfoiled
circular window. Trefoil-headed piscina. The tower comes
next, built not at all in line with whatever church belonged to
the chancel, and therefore perhaps in its core earlier. Ashlar-
faced, still with lancets below and an E doorway also no later
than the late C13. The bell-openings are Dec. Parapet, recessed
spire with rolls up the edges. Immediately to the N of the tower
W side an odd lancet. The rest of the church is Perp – as far as it
is not Victorian – and uniform, except that the arcades differ
in a certain way. The nave is four bays long, and there are one-
bay N and S chapels. These were originally part of the nave
arcades. The chancel arch was propelled to the W at an unknown
date. The piers are of the familiar four-shafts-and-four-
hollows section, and the arches moulded. But the N arcade has
its E parts with round bases and round capitals, the S arcade
and the W parts of the N arcade have them polygonal. So the E
bays on the N side must be C14 Perp. The aisles were originally
lower and narrower – see the roof-line against the E face of the
tower. The present Perp windows are all renewed. In the S aisle
S wall a small Perp niche. In the N aisle corbels carved with
heads, one wearing spectacles. Good ceiled wagon roofs of
chancel, nave, and aisles – quite a South-West English impression. The W façade of the church has an ashlar-faced porch,
added, it is assumed, in the early C16. Might the front wall not
be earlier ? The vestry, placed in the NW corner, was a chapel.
– FONT. Octagonal, of Purbeck marble, with two flat trefoil-
headed blank arches on each side. – LECTERN. Brass eagle on
strongly moulded foot and shaft. The same type as at Bovey
Tracey in Devon, at St Nicholas Bristol, at Croydon, at
Cropredy in Oxfordshire, and at Wiggenhall St Mary in
Norfolk. – SCULPTURE. An alabaster relief of the Annunciation
is completely renewed. – PLATE. Chalice with Paten and Cover,
c.1575; Paten, 1620; Almsdish, 1662; Flagon and Cover,
1669; Paten, 1728. – MONUMENTS. Tomb-chest in the porch.
Flat, ogee-headed blank arches. The brasses are missing. –
Bennet Swayne † 1741. Standing wall-monument, ambitious
and Rococo. Against a black obelisk a black sarcophagus and
on it a white erection with two putti. Medallion with two profile
heads, unveiled by a third putto.

St Michael, North Bemerton, St Michael's Road. 1956–7 by
N. F. Cachemaille Day. Yellow brick, with a big apse facing the
road with a very large relief by *Kate Parbary*. Short broad
tower behind with low windows and a low pyramid roof. White
interior.

St Osmund (R.C.), Exeter Street. 1847–8 by *Pugin*. N aisle and
chapel 1894. The s aisle is original. Low arcade with stiff-leaf
capitals. Exterior with a sw tower with pyramid roof. Really
of no architectural interest inside or out. – altar in the s
chapel by *Pugin*. Ornate front with fleurs-de-lis in quatrefoils.
– stained glass. E and two s windows by *Pugin*, made by
Hardman, one of the two s windows inscribed *ex voto* of *Pugin*,
with the date 1850.

St Paul, St Paul's Road, Fisherton Anger. 1851–3 by *T. H.
Wyatt*. In the style of *c*.1300, with an asymmetrically placed
sw tower. Inside, low piers alternatingly round and octagonal.
Some of them and some arches come from the former church
of St Clement, w of Fisherton Mill. From there also the font,
circular, plain, c13. The N aisle is an addition of 1876. – For
the St Paul's Homes *see* p. 413.

St Thomas of Canterbury, St Thomas Square. Externally
the church is all c15 or later, and internally also, except for the
c13 corbel-table of the chancel, visible from inside, the chancel
aisles, and the w respond of the s chapel, semi-octagonal and
carrying a double-chamfered arch. This looks late c13. The
next piece in order of time is probably the s tower, which originally stood detached from the nave. It was under construction
in 1400–5. It has an inner porch with a two-centred entrance
arch and a vault with diagonal and ridge-ribs up to a big ring
for the bell-ropes. The ribs have long single chamfers and the
capitals are still c14 in style. The tower is in four stages
and has set-back buttresses. There is a two-light upper window
which has tall niches to the l. and r. Three-light blocked
window into the present s aisle. Two-light Perp bell-openings.
Panelled battlements and a small recessed lead-covered
pyramid roof. In 1447 the chancel collapsed. Rebuilding began
at once, at the expense of the rich merchants of Salisbury. The
chancel E window is of five lights with a transom and panel
tracery. The chancel chapel E windows are of four lights, and
to the N of the N chapel is a three-storeyed vestry. Records are
preserved telling us that William Swayne built the s chapel.
That gives a date *c*.1450.* His name and merchant's mark

* The panelling of the E walls of chancel and chapels is Victorian.

appear on the beams of the lovely roof. Very low pitch, almost flat. Demi-figures of angels on the beams. The N chapel was built at the same time. We are told that William Ludlow was responsible for the roof. But the big monument in the chapel (*see* below) has the merchant's mark of the Godmanstone family. The timber roof is identical with that of the s chapel. The arcades of four bays are also identical. Slender piers with four shafts and four hollows. Four-centred arches. The capitals with foliage and also inscription scrolls held by seraphim. One inscription records John Nichol as 'fownder of this peler'. The chapels have three-light windows, except for the E windows, which are of four lights N, of five lights S. The priest's doorway into the s chapel has a hood on heavy brackets and is panelled inside. In the vestry formerly a beam also recording William Swayne. Nave and aisles were rebuilt soon after. The aisles have four-light windows. The clerestory windows are wide, low, and of four lights. Three-centred arches. Battlements. w doorway with two-centred arch and traceried spandrels. Renewed great w window of seven lights with a transom. The aisles are nearly as wide as the nave, and the tower thus became attached to the s aisle. In the end the church, except for the tower, was a complete parallelogram. Sumptuous interior. Five-bay arcades. Thin piers with foliage capitals. The piers have a section of four shafts and four waves in the diagonals. Two-centred arches. Panelling round the clerestory. Panelling also on the w wall round the doorway. Shafts rise from the piers to help carry the timber roof. Capitals with foliage and shields. Tall chancel arch. Broad simple arches from the aisles into the chapels. They also have foliage capitals. The aisle roofs are an imitation of the chapel roofs. Extremely ornate and dainty nave roof, of Somerset type. Low pitch, tie-beams with cresting and inverted cresting below. Traceried arched braces. Tracery above the tie-beams and on the wall plate.

FURNISHINGS. REREDOS in the s chapel. 1724. Of wood, in the Wren style. Centre with open scrolly pediment and garlands. Put up when the E end of the chapel became the Eyre family vault. In connexion with the same event the IRON RAILINGS were put up, equally splendid. – ORGAN CASE. 1792, from the cathedral. Altered in 1897. – PAINTINGS. Above the chancel arch Doom, early C 16, of low quality. At the foot two saints in differently shaped niches. Above on the l. the rising of the dead, on the r. the fate of the damned and the mouth of hell. At the top Christ on the rainbow, the Virgin and St John, saints below, and a town l. and r., the most interesting part of the composition. – On the N wall of the S chapel Annunciation, Visitation, Nativity, rather primitive. The little emblems include the Garter and may refer to Bishop Beauchamp (1450–81), chaplain and later chancellor of the Garter. – STAINED GLASS. C15 fragments collected in the S chapel E window (including the merchant's marks of Swayne and Webbe – cf. Church House, p. 414), and the N chapel windows. In the vestry C15 figures. – E window, with two large figures, Victorian. – EMBROIDERY. In the vestry remains of an altar frontal with the Annunciation, letters, and double eagles; C15. – CLOCK-JACKS. Below the clock; 1582. – MONUMENTS. Tomb-chest with richly cusped quatrefoils and panelling. To a member of the Godmanstone family, later C15 or early C16. – Thomas Eyre † 1628 with wife and children, kneeling figures in the usual way. To the l. and r. big obelisks. – Christopher Eyre † 1628 and wife. Also kneeling figures.* – *Humphrey Beckham* † 1671. Wooden tablet, 'his own worke', with primitively carved religious scenes like those on overmantels.

BAPTIST CHURCH, Brown Street. 1829.

CONGREGATIONAL CHURCH, Fisherton Street. 1879, by *Tarring & Wilkinson*. Gothic, and C.-of-E.-ish, with an asymmetrically placed steeple. Canopies on the broaches, certainly an unusual motif. The style is of *c*.1300.

METHODIST COMMUNITY CHURCH, St Edmund's Church Street. 1810–11, enlarged and given its present shape in 1835. Five-bay stuccoed front with projections l. and r. Italianate windows. In the middle a later Tuscan colonnade with semicircularly projecting centre.

METHODIST CHURCH, Wilton Road. 1860. Brick and stone. Debased Italianate, with pediment across. Arched windows and a (later?) curving-forward porch.

MILFORD STREET ELIM CHURCH. Brick, terribly debased Italianate. The date 1896 shows the front moreover to be equally terribly out-of-date. The architect is *W. H. Dinsley*.

PUBLIC BUILDINGS

GUILDHALL, Market Place. The Elizabethan Council House was destroyed by fire in 1780. The second Earl of Radnor donated a new one. It was designed by *Sir Robert Taylor* and

* I owe the identification of the two monuments to Mr L. E. Tanner of Westminster Abbey.

built with some alterations by *William Pilkington* in 1788–95.
The building is stately and has few but impressive motifs. It is
of grey brick with dressings in a wild rocky rustication. As it is
today, it has a façade with a one-storey portico of six tall
Tuscan columns. Originally the centre was recessed and the
columns formed a screen in front. The alteration was made in
1829–30. Three arched windows above them, and to the l. and
r. very big arched windows. According to Taylor's design, the
windows ought to have been of the Venetian kind, but this was
not carried out. They are surrounded by thick rocky rustication. The projecting portico of the Guildhall was in the beginning on the w side. This was taken down in 1889, when cells
were built. The E side is in its original state (except for the
Venetian windows). It has a large bay window canted outside.
Inside, the Banqueting Room is along this side. The bay is
semicircular here. Restrained plasterwork. The centre of the
building is the staircase hall with a glazed round lantern. It is
divided from the entrance hall by a screen of Tuscan columns.
In the hall a re-set Elizabethan chimneypiece. – INSIGNIA.
Watchman's Horn, 1675; Candlesticks, 1743; three Salvers,
1745; Great Mace and two more Maces, 1749; Loving Cup,
1796.

COUNCIL HOUSE, Bourne Hill. Formerly Wyndham House.
On the site of the College of St Edmund founded in 1269. The
Wyndhams' house was built about 1670 and considerably
altered *c.*1715, *c.*1730, and in 1788. The s front is of nine bays
and two storeys; of brick. Parapet with balls. The first and last
bays project as wings. The centre has Gibbs surrounds to all
windows and the arched doorway. That can hardly be of
before *c.*1730. Originally the windows were mullioned and
transomed. The massive porch is yet later Georgian. Triple
Tuscan columns oddly grown together; metope frieze and
pediment. The fronts of the wings are more Baroque, of the
Late-Wren–Archer type. The main windows have heavy
basket arches, and there are horizontal oval windows above
them. Also to the centre the wings show circular recesses with
brackets for busts. In the w wall a large sham Gothic window,
probably Late Georgian. E front towards the grounds of 1788.
Two canted bay windows and a tripartite doorway. Entrance
hall in the position of a medieval hall. Fluted Doric pilasters.
Staircase with modest Late Georgian iron balustrade. The
grounds were landscaped by *R. Woods*. They border on the
one remaining part of the RAMPART of the town. In the SE

corner a re-erected c15 PORCH from the cathedral. It stood outside the N transept facing N and was removed by *Wyatt* in 1791. The spirelet and pinnacles were added when it was taken to Wyndham House in that year to be a piece of picturesque garden furnishing. It is small but ornate, and clearly of the c15. Two-centred arches to all four sides, leaf in the spandrels, fleuron framing on the surrounds. Inside a shallow lierne-vault.

POST OFFICE, Castle Street. 1907 by *W. T. Oldrieve*. Tudor.

TELEPHONE EXCHANGE, Chipper Lane, adjoining the Post Office. 1936 by *D. N. Dyke*.

NAAFI CLUB, New Street. Stately, Neo-Georgian, ashlar-faced. By *E. M. Joseph*, 1950–5.

VICTORIA PARK. Bronze STATUE of Sidney Herbert by *Baron Marochetti*, 1863. It stood until recently in front of the Guild-hall.

PUBLIC LIBRARY. 1904 by *A. C. Bothams*. Free Tudor. In 1910 the YOUNG GALLERY was added, a pretty design by Mr *Blount*.

SECONDARY MODERN SCHOOL, Bemerton. 1956 etc. County Architect *F. I. Bowden*.

ST EDMUND'S CHURCH SCHOOL, Bedwin Street. 1860 by *Woodyer*. Very Gothic.

COLLEGE OF FURTHER EDUCATION, St Martin's Lane. Begun in 1960. County Architect *F. I. Bowden*.

SCHOOL OF ARTS AND CRAFTS, New Street. 1871 by *Bothams*. Built as the Literary Institution. Gothic, with brickwork in many colours. Only three bays wide. Bargeboarded gable and two half-hipped dormers. For the Annexe *see* The Hall, New Street, p. 408.

GENERAL INFIRMARY, Fisherton Street. The centre 1767–71 by *John Wood* of Bath. Brick, seven bays, four storeys. Low, broad doorway with Tuscan columns and pediment. To the S embattled, and originally to the N too. (Inside, one ward in its original state, and also the original chapel.) Additions of many dates. The two wings added to the centre in 1845 and 1869. The large recent buildings at the back are of 1934–7.

OLD MANOR HOSPITAL, Wilton Road. *See* p. 413.

MARKET HOUSE, Cheese Market, i.e. Market Place. 1859 by Mr *Strapp*. Ashlar with rusticated piers and three archways with rusticated arches, the middle one taller. They represent nave and aisles inside. Simple iron construction. Lavish cast-iron GATES by *Hill & Smith* of Brierley Hill.

STATION (former), Fisherton Street. *See* p. 413.

PERAMBULATIONS

The medieval centre of the town is roughly oblong and bordered on the w by High Street and Castle Street, on the N by Bedwin Street and Bourne Hill, on the E by Rampart Road, and on the s by St Ann's Street and New Street. In the following perambulations sallies will however be recommended beyond these boundaries to the s and the w.

(A) *The Market Place and its immediate surroundings*

The Market Place of Salisbury is large and attractive, an oblong with a smaller oblong to its w, the N side running on flush. Both have trees along the sides, and the main part in addition another line across to frame the Guildhall. This is in the s E corner. The longest, i.e. the N side, called BLUE BOAR ROW, has at the corner of Endless Street a gabled tile-hung C15 house with a small doorway to Endless Street with handsome carved brackets.* Then two Georgian houses with parapets, one of five, the other of three bays. After that a plain group of three identical Georgian three-storey houses, brick with quoins, a good backcloth. (Behind this a timber-framed HALL built in 1444. VCH) Then LLOYDS BANK of 1869, ambitious, of Ham Hill stone, five bays, with a five-bay addition of 1901. Ground floor with pillars between the windows. They have naturalistic foliage capitals. The first floor has coupled columns with fancy capitals (egyptianizing?), the second floor segment-headed windows. In the centre on the top group of two reclining figures. Then the E side, called QUEEN STREET. The corner to Win-

* See a two-light C15 window with cusped lights on the E side.

chester Street has the pretentious LONDON AND LIVERPOOL
GLOBE INSURANCE, lavish and sham mock-timbered, 1878
by *H. Hall*. Then mostly minor Georgian things. No. 20 has
a nice canted oriel with ogee cap and a panelled parapet
curving up on both sides in each of two bays. s of No. 17 a
passage leads to the yard of the former PLUME OF FEATHERS
INN, with an ogee-trefoil-headed C15 doorway on the N side
and a picturesque outer C17 staircase. No. 8 was originally
built *c*.1450. It is known as JOHN À PORT'S HOUSE. John
à Port was a wool merchant. Timber-framed, three-storeyed,
with second-floor overhang. Two gables. Inside, one room
with Elizabethan panelling. Pilasters and frieze with abstract
arabesques. Fireplace with two allegorical figures and a very
primitive relief of the Sacrifice of Isaac in the overmantel.
Opposite, i.e. behind the Guildhall, between Fish Row and
New Canal a long house with overhang, but altered in the C18
and stuccoed. Nice iron balconies. To FISH ROW two gables.
Angle bracket set diagonally for the second-floor overhang.
Fish Row runs w behind the Guildhall. There are two C16
houses with gables here, but altered out of recognition. The
same is true of the gabled houses in BUTCHER ROW, which is
the continuation of Fish Row.

At the end of Butcher Row is the POULTRY CROSS, C15, with
the top parts of 1853. It is the one remaining of four such
market crosses at Salisbury. The Cheese Cross stood s of the s
end of Castle Street (*see* Cheese Market, below), the Wool Cross
in New Canal, Barnewell's Cross at the corner of Barnard
Street and Culver Street. The Poultry Cross is hexagonal. It
has four-centred arches with blank ogee tips and buttresses.
On each arch a statue niche with a pinnacle. Pinnacles also on
the buttresses. Big flying buttresses carry six shallow niches
and the top spirelet (cf. the Malmesbury Cross). The square in
which the Poultry Cross stands is small, and the streets around
here are intricate.

SILVER STREET continues Fish Row. At the corner opposite
the Poultry Cross a three-storeyed, gabled, timber-framed
house. C15–16. Second-floor overhang. Thin diagonal
braces. Then on the same (N) side Nos 48–52, four-storeyed,
gabled, timber-framed. At the back of one of them, towards the
churchyard, a perfect two-light timber window with ogee-
headed lights. The passage through to St Thomas's church
looks early C18. To the N St Thomas Square, not remarkable in itself but specially intricate. Back to the Market

Place by MINSTER STREET. Nos 3–5 are timber-framed and
of four storeys. Big renewed bargeboards. On the first floor
blocked windows with arched lights and small decorative
quatrefoils over. This looks *c*.1500. So does the r. oriel window.
Is it all *in situ*? Nos 7–17 are of the same time, but much
damaged. They make the best picture from St Thomas's,
where most of them are tile-hung.

The s side of the Market Place is called OX ROW. No. 6 must be
Early Georgian. Big pedimental gable with, beneath it, two
Venetian windows and a taller arched window. The w side of
this major part of the Market Place is OATMEAL ROW. The s
corner also overlooking the Poultry Cross is timber-framed and
tile-hung. Double overhang. Then a little N Nos 16–17,
Elizabethan or Jacobean, with a big two-storeyed oriel,
mullioned and transomed. The mullions and a transom also
continue blank between first and second floor.

The smaller w part of the Market Place is called CHEESE MAR-
KET. No houses of note except the Market House, *see* p. 400.

(B) *To the North and North-East*

CASTLE STREET starts from the w end of Blue Boar Row. At
once the best early C18 merchant's house, No. 1. Brick and
stucco. Only four bays, but much done to give an appearance
of grandeur. Bays one and four are flanked by giant pilasters.
Doorway in bay one, with pediment on unfluted Ionic attached
columns. Segment-headed second-floor windows, parapet –
rather a tight composition. At the back, on the first floor, a
room with a fine plaster ceiling and doorcase of *c*.1775. More
but minor plaster ceilings. Opposite the CHOUGH HOTEL, the
medievalizing façade all new, but a mid-C17 staircase with
turned balusters. Then, again on the w side, facing Chipper
Lane a neo-Tudor gatehouse, formerly giving access to a
brewery. No. 45 is early C18. Five bays, three storeys, the middle bay with narrower windows. Giant angle pilasters. Entrance
hall with diagonally set fireplace. Arches to the staircase. One
original staircase with columnar and twisted balusters, one later
C18 staircase. Splendid mid-C18 plaster ceiling in a room
added at the back. Ceiling on a raking cove. Beam across also
made part of the stucco composition. Several Kentian heads.
Over the chimneypiece Rococo ornament and naturalistic
branches. Nos 57–61 are timber-framed, but have C18 fronts.
Behind No. 61 a long plain WOOL STORE of brick, said to have
been built in 1738. Contemporary cottages face it. The factory

whose store and workers' cottages they were, was Joseph
Hinxman's. There are from other houses as well such narrow
passages to the former stores and dye vats. They had to be close
to the river. Then (79 etc.) gabled timber-framed houses.
After No. 95 the site of the former CASTLE GATE. The Royal
Arms only have been preserved. Then HUSSEY'S ALMS-
HOUSES, rebuilt in 1875. Two ranges of gabled Tudor brick
houses. Finally, yet further out, MILFORD HALL (No. 206),
Georgian, three widely spaced bays. Porch with broken
segmental pediment on oddly shaped, no doubt recent,
columns.

On the way back two turns to the E. First along Scots Lane into
BEDWIN STREET. No. 24 has a nice late C18 doorway. Then
FROWD'S ALMSHOUSES, dated 1750. Brick with brick quoins.
Nine bays, two storeys, with small, broad, widely spaced
segment-headed windows. Centre with brick quoins, a doorway
with a broken segmental pediment on intermittently rusticated
pilasters. A small Venetian window over. Octagonal lantern on
the roof. At the back brick arcade of fifteen bays. Small circular
windows on the upper floor. A little further E TAYLOR'S
ALMSHOUSES, built in 1698 and rebuilt, evidently not without
alterations, in 1886. Doorway and windows have heavily
moulded surrounds. Boldly chamfered stone quoins. Big
Dutch gable above the centre, a remarkably late use of this
motif. Yet further E, facing St Edmund's church, No. 60, again
with a nice late C18 doorway. After that on the other side the
Council House, *see* p. 399.

The second turn E from Castle Street is along CHIPPER LANE
with several public buildings (*see* p. 400) and a Georgian
terrace of originally identical houses (Nos 26–34) to SALT
LANE, where the only building of special interest is the
PHEASANT INN, of the C15, timber-framed, with an oversailing gable to the E. At the back CREWE'S HALL, the hall of
the Company of Shoemakers left to them in 1638. Timber-
framed and with no special features.

Three streets connect Bedwin Street with Salt Lane and Winchester Street further s (*see* Perambulation C, p. 405): Endless
Street, Rollestone Street, and St Edmund's Church Street.

In ENDLESS STREET from N to S. The N end actually reaches
further N than Bedwin Street, and there are several good houses
here. Closing the view to the N BELLEVUE, a simple four-bay
Regency house. Then on the E side Nos 52 and 54, two three-
storeyed brick houses of the C18 with doorways with broken

pediments on attached Tuscan columns, and opposite, No. 47, grand but rather bleak, of *c*.1820. Three storeys, cemented, with giant pilasters with sunk panels and a doorway with Tuscan columns and pediment. Then s of Bedwin Street on the E side No. 26, with a porch on clusters of very thin Gothick shafts, and No. 16, a two-bay C18 house with a two-bay pediment. At the corner of Chipper Lane the former County Hall and then PALACE THEATRE, red brick, 1888, by *Fred Bath*, ornate, in a kind of 1700-Baroque, with a long, also very lively side elevation to Chipper Lane. Two more Georgian five-bay houses, one on the same side as the former theatre, the other (No. 12) on the E side.

In ROLLESTONE STREET very little. At the corner of Salt Lane a five-bay Georgian house with hipped roof and a first floor like an assembly room. This was probably the Hall of the Weavers' Guild, who were given the house in 1784.* Then, opposite, Nos 12–14. No. 12 is early C18, of seven bays with handsome carved brackets carrying a straight hood. Staircase with three twisted balusters to each tread. No. 14 has a straight hood curving forward and resting on thin columns. This seems late C18.

In ST EDMUND'S CHURCH STREET No. 41 of 1787 (rainwater head), of seven bays and two storeys, with a parapet. No. 24 is of five bays with one of the frequent canted central oriels. At the corner of Winchester Street a specially interesting C17 house. Its C18 façade is in Winchester Street (*see* below).

(C) *To the East and the near South-East*

WINCHESTER STREET runs E from the NE corner of the Market Place. Nos 3–5 is early C18 with a parapet curving up towards the corners. The r. bay has later, minor Venetian windows. Then the CO-OPERATIVE SOCIETY, ashlar-faced neo-Tudor of 1926 by *E.J. Elkins*, and, at the corner of Rollestone Street, a nice C18 house of five bays with heads on the keystones of the ground floor. But the most important house in the street is No. 47. This dates from *c*.1675, but has an C18 front of five bays and two storeys. Mathematical facing tiles,‡ broad angle strips, late C18 door surround. To the E, i.e. St Edmund's Church Street, C17 windows, of one light with a transom (an unusual thing) and of mullion-and-transom crosses. The s part on this side has brick quoins. Both parts have the brickwork in

* Information kindly provided by Mr Shortt.
‡ A technique quite often found in the Georgian houses of Salisbury.

English bond. Further E at the corner of GUILDER LANE a
row of plain C16 timber-framed houses. Then, on the N side,
BLECHYNDEN'S ALMSHOUSES, two humble brick ranges of
one storey, at r. angles one to the other. Founded in 1683.

To the E from the S end of Queen Street (see Perambulation A)
MILFORD STREET, the E continuation of New Canal (Perambulation D). At the start the RED LION HOTEL. Façade of
1820–3. Brick, stuccoed. Four wide bays. Arch way through
two storeys. In the courtyard, on the first floor, an early C17
timber gallery, now closed. (Some C16 woodwork inside.
MHLG) Then at the corner of Gigant Street an early C18 three-
bay brick front, and in GIGANT STREET the partly early C19
brick premises of the ANCHOR BREWERY. At the corner of
PENNY FARTHING STREET, behind No. 43, what is left of
the derelict TAILORS' HALL, notably a wooden bay window
with mullions and a transom. The house itself is timber-framed
and has two overhangs. No. 42 Milford Street has one of the
nice Salisbury oriels, No. 41 opposite is timber-framed and
slate-hung with two overhangs. At the top (E) end of Milford
Street No. 88 (SWAN SCHOOL), a timber-framed C15 or C16
house with a gable to the street. Herringbone tile infilling on the
ground floor, brick infilling above. The oversailing first floor
is carried on heavy angle brackets. (Inside, in a ground-floor
room an original stone fireplace. MHLG)

Milford Street is crossed near its W end by Brown Street. Half-
way down Brown Street to the S TRINITY STREET leads to
the E, so-called after the TRINITY HOSPITAL. This was
founded before 1379 and rebuilt in 1702. Brick. Seven bays,
two storeys, hipped roof, small two-light mullioned windows
in flat surrounds. Doorway with thin open segmental pediment.
The broad flat string-course oddly rises towards it. Through an
entrance hall into the courtyard. The two are separated by an
arch of three bays. Tuscan columns; depressed arches. At the
far end of the courtyard the entrance to the chapel. Wide portal
with open segmental pediment. Tall narrow arched windows l.
and r. The chapel is orientated, which is a surprise as one
enters. Coved ceiling on a deep modillion frieze. – SCREEN
with balusters and two PEWS, l. and r. of the low REREDOS,
with miniature balusters. – Small fragments of old STAINED
GLASS. – PLATE. Elizabethan Chalice.

A little further E a group in BARNARD STREET, DOLPHIN
STREET, and PAYNE'S HILL, all close together. No. 58
Barnard Street, at the back of 117–19 Dolphin Street, has

a nice early-c18 composition of doorway and window over.
Nos 117–19 themselves look towards St Ann Street (*see* Perambulation D). They are probably of *c.*1700. Three bays, chequer brick, stone quoins. Across, at the corner of Payne's Hill,
No. 53 of the early C18. Four bays, two storeys, brick with
stone quoins. Doorway with pediment on carved brackets.

(D) *To the South and farther South-East*

Immediately s of Butcher Row and Fish Row (*see* Perambulation
A) and parallel with them is NEW CANAL, the street commemorating one of the many canals of Salisbury. New Canal
widens on its N side as if it were a subsidiary Market Place.
Facing this widening a great curiosity, a cinema with a grossly
overdone timber-framed Tudor façade of 1881 (by *Fred Bath*),
and behind this façade the substantial and memorable remains
of the HOUSE OF JOHN HALLE, a wool merchant of Salisbury
who was four times mayor and bought the land for his house
in 1467. The house was built in 1470–83 and restored by *Pugin*
in 1834. The principal survival is the hall, with a splendid open 30b
timber roof of three bays. Arched braces on figure brackets
carry the collar-beams. The braces form pointed arches. Four
tiers of delightfully cusped wind-braces also forming pointed
arches. The hall is ashlar-faced. It has to the w only one small
two-light window but to the E two large, straight-headed
transomed four-light windows and one transomed two-light
window. The lights are arched and cusped at the top as well as
below the transoms. The small doorway cuts into the southern
of the four-light windows, giving it an oddly limping shape.
So on that side was the screens passage. Yet the room to the s
of the hall has a ceiling with heavily moulded beams. The room
to the N, the entrance hall of the cinema, must have been
remodelled in the C17. It has a gallery round with flat cut-out
balusters. Splendid stone fireplace with a frieze of quatrefoils
in the hall. STAINED GLASS. A good deal of original scrollwork, well restored and supplemented by *Willement* (Dean
Woodforde). Further w, on the s side, a c15 gable with
original bargeboards, the only ones at Salisbury. The overhang
rests on heavy brackets. Opposite, a former mill, probably
early C19. One hoist. Brick, the windows with very closely set
glazing bars.

Now turn s and at last walk down the HIGH STREET. On the E
side SUTTON'S RESTAURANT, timber-framed and tile-hung,
and the OLD GEORGE HOTEL, also timber-framed. Two

pretty, irregular canted oriel windows with transoms. The house has an extremely interesting interior. On the ground floor in the room to the l. of the entrance is a big post with a bracket projecting forward to carry the overhang. The mouldings as well as the decoration with ogee-tracery and fleurons point to the early C14. On the first floor the s room has early C17 plaster friezes on the beams and a wooden overmantel of the same time. Behind, in a N wing projecting to the E, was the hall. It goes through two storeys and has a C15 hammerbeam roof with big, rather coarse heads against the hammerbeams. Arched braces carry collar-beams, and above these the triangle to the ridge is pointed-foiled. The original doorway is in the s wall at its w end. The heavy scissor-bracing is a characteristic motif also visible on the second floor. The roof here has decorated wall plates and spandrels. Two rooms with tie-beams with kingposts and four-way struts. Opposite, inside the CROWN HOTEL (in the Lounge Bar), two big traceried spandrels from a C15 roof and a fine early C13 stone head of a lady wearing a wimple. On the same side of the High Street, at the corner of Crane Street a timber-framed, tile-hung house with a second-floor overhang and, facing it, at the s corner of Wane Street, Messrs BEACH'S BOOKSHOP, also timber-framed and perhaps of the C14. Three gables and very heavy diagonal braces. Along towards the North Gate of the Close (see p. 382) nice C18 houses. No. 51 has a figure of a ram above the doorway (recent), No. 64 opposite a pretty late-C18 doorway.

Then into NEW STREET to the E. Nice Georgian houses on the s side past the School of Arts and Crafts (see p. 400). The OLD HOUSE RESTAURANT has two gables and a (not original) date 1569. One gable is of rubble and brick, the other timber-framed. Broad doorway with pediment on Doric pilasters. The NEW INN is low and timber-framed, perhaps C15. No. 33 is a stately three-storeyed four-bay house of the C18. Doorway with attached Tuscan columns, metope frieze, and pediment. Then THE HALL, now an annexe of the School of Arts and Crafts. It is a stately seven-bay brick house and was built in 1751–8. Canted oriel in the centre on Tuscan columns. Windows with keystones. At the back a room with a delicate plaster ceiling of c.1775, similar to that of No. 1 Castle Street. From here to the N in CATHERINE STREET No. 12 with another canted first-floor oriel and nice early-C19 shop windows. To the E Ivy Street into Trinity Street (see Perambulation C). Instead to the s. At the NE corner of ST JOHN STREET is the

WHITE HART HOTEL, built in the late C18 and remarkably grand for an inn of that date. Nine bays, three storeys, grey brick, with a three-bay porte-cochère on which rises a giant portico with unfluted Ionic columns and a pediment.* Nos 3–5 is timber-framed with overhang and diagonal bracing. No. 7 is the former Assembly Room of the KING'S ARMS, three bays, two storeys, with the centre window flanked by thin Roman Doric columns carrying a broken pediment. The King's Arms itself is timber-framed, of four storeys with two over-hangs. On the first floor panelling and an original stone fire-place. No. 13, at the corner of St Ann Street, is the former workshop and office of *Osmond*, the mason whom Pugin used to employ. Small, ashlar, with porch of Greek Doric columns and a tripartite window over. Opposite, on the w wide of the street, the wall of the Close (*see* p. 382).

Here the Perambulation divides. We go E first, S later. ST ANN STREET is one of the most rewarding streets of Salisbury. Nos 6–8, ST ANN'S MANOR, is a fine group to start with, No. 6 of the late C18 with a pretty doorway, No. 8 of the late C17 with low mullioned basement windows and cross-windows on the ground floor. Brick with brick quoins. The top is altered. Inside, a large back room with a grand tripartite window. Tall scagliola columns with white Ionic capitals. Niches l. and r. Opposite St Ann's Manor is No. 3, of the C15–16, timber-framed with diagonal braces. At the corner of The Friary No. 18, also timber-framed, but with C18 alterations. Then, op-posite, off to the N. BROWN STREET and at once THE PRIORY, lying a little back. C17, brick, stuccoed, but with a two-storeyed, gabled ashlar porch. This has a three-light window. The same window on the second floor of the house. The other windows seem to be Early Victorian. The house probably had gables originally. The staircase with thick twisted balusters looks late C17. The adjoining house, No. 93, has traces of late C16 or C17 windows in its S wall, but an C18 front of six bays. The window-sills are carried on small foliate corbels. Three storeys. Quoins, parapet. To the S from Brown Street and St Ann Street into THE FRIARY. The L-shaped group of CRA-DOCK HOUSE and FRIARY COURT is of the early C17. (The date 1618 is recorded in title deeds. MHLG) Mullioned windows with round filleted mullions. The room to the l. of the doorway

---

* The porte-cochère and portico appear an early-C19 addition. In the car park at the back one three-light mullioned window, all that remains of THE BARRACKS, a mansion once comprising an inner court.

has a four-light transomed window instead. In this room a little thin-ribbed plaster decoration. Friary Court was added to, on the E, in the C18, and the S front is C18 too. (C18 staircase with turned balusters. MHLG) The Friary is so called because here was the Salisbury house of the Greyfriars. Remains of it belong to WINDOVER HOUSE (No. 22), which has a Georgian front with a nice tripartite doorway and a canted oriel over. The brickwork of the front is only 'mathematical tiles' applied to a timber-framed building. Behind in the courtyard the timber-framing is all exposed and may be Jacobean or earlier. Jacobean staircase. In the back ranges two C15 roofs belonging to the friary.

No. 38 is low with an overhang, but a late C17 doorway with Tuscan columns against a rusticated background. Pediment on the columns. The l. bay is an C18 addition. It has indeed on the upper floor a coved ceiling and in the lunettes grisaille paintings of Music and Painting, probably of *c.*1775, whereas the r. part of the house has a room with Elizabethan panelling and an Elizabethan fireplace. No. 40 is now the MUSEUM. Façade of Victorian brick in the Tudor style (1863 by *John Harding*). Inside the C18 house which the museum originally was, a large circular room of 1812. Domed, with gloriously overdone stucco decoration. Pilasters with fancy capitals. Abundant vine in the frieze above the pilasters and then wreath round the centre above the coffering of the dome. No. 44, VALE HOUSE, has a late C18 doorway. Opposite, No. 49, the ST MARTIN'S GUESTHOUSE, early C18, of three storeys and four bays, with a panelled parapet, and, again opposite, No. 54 with a nice early C18 doorway. Straight hood rising into a segmental arch in the middle. Carved brackets. Nos 56–8, the former JOINERS' HALL, is the best timber-framed house of Salisbury. Late C16, first-floor bressumer with running arabesque decoration. Five-light oriel with thin mullions and transom on figured brackets. Two gables. Nos 60–66 are timber-framed too, of two storeys. No. 68 is Georgian, of five bays, with quoins and a doorway flanked by pilasters and crowned by a broken pediment. No. 82 is later C18, two and a half storeys and of brick colour-washed. Parapet. Doorway with Roman Doric columns and a horizontal hood projecting in a curve. Awkward decoration to the middle window and the middle of the parapet, probably not *in situ*. No. 84 is the end. Early C18, of five bays and three storeys. Brick, cemented. Rusticated ground floor. Three-bay projection. Doorway with attached Tuscan columns against a more closely rusticated background. Pediment. Ground-floor and second-floor windows segment-headed. First and second floor have giant angle pilasters. Panelled parapet raised in the centre to a Baroque gable with curved sides and a semicircular top. Arched windows in it.

St Ann Street is continued to the SE by ST MARTIN'S CHURCH STREET. Nos 23–35 is a row of identical late C18 or early C19 cottages. Opposite the HOUSE OF MERCY. (In the chapel *Kempe* glass of 1895–1904.)

We must now retrace our steps to the corner of St Ann and St John Streets and continue S along EXETER STREET. The precinct wall goes on accompanying us on the W side. On the E side Nos 81–82 with two very odd identical door surrounds. The details are Kentian, i.e. of *c.*1730–50, but they are certainly not *in situ*. They are probably made up of fireplace surrounds. By No. 85 fine view of the cathedral due W. No. 95 is Georgian, of five bays and two storeys with a one-bay pediment. The BRICKET HOSPITAL was rebuilt in 1895, but keeps its Adamish foundation tablet of 1780. No. 131 at the end is of washed brick, three storeys, and with tripartite windows and a porch with wide broken segmental pediment on Tuscan columns.

Nothing further S, but much if we turn W into ST NICHOLAS ROAD. The precinct wall continues on the N side. No. 4 is Late Georgian, of white brick, with a pretty iron porch carrying a canted oriel. At the corner of DE VAUX PLACE an interesting group of brick houses, now mostly of the C18 but taking the place of, and incorporating scanty fragments of, DE VAUX COLLEGE, which was founded *c.*1260 by Bishop Bridport for scholars who had migrated from Oxford. It was for twenty scholars and may well be called the earliest traceable university college in England. The N buttress of DE VAUX HOUSE and the very thick flint wall next to DE VAUX PLACE belong to the college. De Vaux House has a much pulled-about front and one pre-Reformation door, also probably altered. The oriel on brackets, two with heads, may be brought in. DE VAUX LODGE has an C18 front of three bays, segment-headed windows, and giant brick angle pilasters. Then in De Vaux Place an even terrace of early C19 houses of three storeys.

In St Nicholas Road follows now the ST NICHOLAS HOSPITAL, a fragmentary but most valuable survival of the hospital built by Bishop Bingham, probably in connexion with his new bridge (*see* below). The buildings as they are now (and as they represent Hiram's Hospital in Trollope's *The Warden*), consist of two ranges at r. angles to the road and facing one another. The l. range appears entirely Victorian, except for a small doorway with a four-centred head and a two-centred arch at the r. end. The r. range at once rouses one's curiosity by the circular piers and double-chamfered arches built into its front. These represent the dividing arcade of the originally two-naved hospital. The N nave has disappeared. At the E end were two parallel chancels. The arrangement means perhaps an original division into a male and a female ward. The s chancel has two single-chamfered lancets to the s and two to the E with a cusped octofoil in a circle above them (cf. Cathedral). Of the N chancel the two E lancets and one N lancet remain and a big piscina in the s wall, with a trefoiled head. Deep w porch and blocked w doorway into the s nave. Alterations to the hospital are recorded for 1498–1501, and a restoration by *Butterfield* for 1854 (PF).

Then immediately the BRIDGE, built by Bishop Bingham about 1230 to divert traffic from the main road to Wilton into New Sarum. The bridge crosses the arms of the Avon, the first and shorter with two cutwaters, and on the island between stood the CHAPEL OF ST JOHN. Considerable remains of this are incorporated in ST JOHN'S ISLE. They date clearly from the same years as St Nicholas Hospital. Lancet windows or traces thereof in the N, E, and s walls. In the E widely spaced group of three stepped lancets with hood-moulds. Doorway to the w with one continuous chamfer. The chapel stood precariously low by the water. Opposite, Nos 16–18, nice from outside with its overhang and tile-hanging. It is a medieval or C16 house (see the overhang) with a C17 s side (see the brickwork) and an C18 tile-hung front. The s part of the bridge is of six, the N part of two arches. Ashlar stone. The C13 appears inside a casing of 1771 visible from water level. The six arches are pointed and have double transverse arches in two orders.

(E) *To the West*

We go out by Bridge Street and return by Crane Street. In BRIDGE STREET the COUNTY HOTEL, two buildings. The l., three-storeyed, is of 1874, Italian Gothic, i.e. round-arched, like an office building in the City, the r. part Tudor of *c.*1908. Opposite a former MILL, the E part brick, probably of *c.*1800, the w part C19 medievalizing. Across the bridge and at once on the l. the CLOCK TOWER, a depressing Gothic erection in a position without distinction. It was built in 1892 on a corner of the GAOL, which dated from 1631 with Georgian additions.

In Fisherton Street nothing of note except the modest MRS HAYTER ASYLUM of 1797, a two-storeyed range of six windows and three doors, brick, cemented, with a hipped roof. Then, past the railway bridge on the l. the original Great Western STATION, by *Brunel*, 1856, humble, of brick with stone dressings, one-storeyed and just describable as Late Classical. Further out, on the other side, the ST PAUL'S HOMES, almshouses of 1860. Flint and brick bands. Two ranges connected by screen walls. Tudor style.

WILTON ROAD seems to have developed as a well-to-do suburb about 1830 to 1850. An example is No. 52, irregular, pretty, Gothick, with a semicircular projection with Tuscan colonnade on the l. Another example is THE PARAGON (Nos 182 etc.), two pairs of houses of grey brick facing each other. Opposite the OLD MANOR HOSPITAL. Of the Old Manor itself nothing seems to remain. In the forecourt a bronze FOUNTAIN of mermaids, signed by *L.J. Chavalliaud*, a French sculptor who lived in London from 1893 to 1904.

Back by South Western Road into MILL ROAD. Here the delightful group of FISHERTON MILL and the MILL RACE HOTEL, late C18 probably and at the time entirely out of town. The mill has quite sizeable premises. The miller's house has a façade of three bays and three storeys. Nice door-hood. Behind the hotel the CHURCHYARD of St Clement's church. In Crane Bridge Road the back of the General Infirmary. CRANE BRIDGE is of the C15. It has four splayed arches and four cutwaters. Widened on the S side in 1898.

At the SE corner of CRANE STREET immediately CHURCH HOUSE, a very interesting wool merchant's house, though its W front to the river and bridge is almost entirely of 1887. It is all the more picturesque for that, with stone windows, on the ground floor, half-timber work and tile-hanging. The architect was *Crickmay*. The sensational part of the house is the N range, although here also Crickmay seems to have beeen a little too busy. This range is ashlar-faced and shows to the street a C15 archway with broad continuous mouldings and a hood-mould on concave-sided stops. Original traceried door. To its r. the hall front, two four-light windows set close together, each of four lights with a transom; cusped arches, but not below the transom. As for these fine windows it must, however, be said that in illustrations of 1881 they are much smaller and have no

transoms. Then the start of parlour and solar, i.e. two small
two-light windows, one on top of the other, and then Crickmay's N side of the W range. To the l. of the archway AUDLEY
HOUSE, Georgian, of five bays and two storeys. Doorway with
pediment on carved brackets. Tall windows. However, this
Georgian building is said to replace (or conceal?) the kitchen
and office range of Church House. As one enters the courtyard,
one sees the inner side of the hall. The same coupled windows,
again larger than in the illustrations of 1881, but followed by a
bay window of five sides of an octagon. So that was the high-
table end. Overlapping the bay window a staircase projection
with a small C16 doorway and very odd cross-windows whose
transoms and lintels form very shallow pediments. Is this
Elizabethan or later? The W range shows nothing old to the
courtyard except the brickwork of the r. half. This is laid in
English bond. The S range was rebuilt of brick in 1728. Nine
bays, three storeys. It replaces a range added to the house in
1637, when it was made a workhouse. In the range one re-set
C16 fireplace with fine mouldings. Inside, the hall has a roof
with collar-beams on thin arched braces, tracery above the
collars, and two tiers of wind-braces. The wall-posts rest on
stone demi-figures of angels with shields, and their attitudes
show that the hall was from the start three bays in length. On
one shield a merchant's mark. The same occurs at St Thomas,
together with the initials of John Webbe. So this must have been
his house. The mighty chimneypiece towards the archway is
not part of the house. But where was the original fireplace,
where was the original entrance, and what is in the assertion
that the archway was shifted? Another brought-in chimneypiece (with cusped quatrefoils) in the present entrance room to
the front part, and yet another in a room on the ground floor of
the W range (also with cusped quatrefoils). Another puzzle is
the NW room, the original parlour presumably. It has a wide
twin bay window to the W of which only one of the two inner
arches is old. Is the rest correct reconstruction or Crickmay's
fancy? In this room also a big brought-in chimneypiece. The
only chimneypiece *in situ* is that above this, i.e. in the solar.
Lintel with three very big quatrefoils. Elizabethan plaster
ceiling with thin ribs. Big wooden windows to the W with
mullions and transoms.

STEYNINGS, a little to the E, is of about 1700. Five bays, wide
windows. The centre bay projects and has a doorway with
carved brackets. Staircase with a solid string and turned

balusters on it. No. 91 is pre-Reformation, but the façade is C17. It has on the ground floor two oblong bay windows of stone with mullioned and transomed five-light windows. Upper overhang and half-hipped gables. Mostly C18 windows. Porch with a broad pediment on Tuscan columns. Inside, the fragment of a C14 stone doorway, a timber roof with tie-beam and octagonal kingpost, and two plaster ceilings, one small and C18, the other (first floor, front room) large, impressive, and probably Jacobean. Deeply moulded ribs in the usual interlocked geometrical patterns and small pendants. So back to Beach's Bookshop and the High Street.

SAMBOURNE see WARMINSTER, pp. 494 and 495

SANDY LANE see CHITTOE

SARUM see SALISBURY

SAVERNAKE FOREST

2060

ST KATHARINE, ⅜ m. N of Tottenham House. Built for the second Marchioness of Ailesbury by *T. H. Wyatt* in 1861. A major church, as they were built on the large estates in those decades and as they have become a problem now. Flint, with a S tower with broach-spire, N and S transepts, and a polygonal apse. Later C13 details. Inside, the most remarkable feature is the stone screens with tracery dividing the transepts from the nave. Under the tower charming romantic vault with naturalistic leaf corbels. Much rich carving of foliage inside too. The N aisle is bricked off at the time of writing. – MONUMENT. Second Marchioness of Ailesbury † 1892, evidently by *Gilbert*. Small tablet. Stone frame and inside a bronze panel of a young woman in white and gold and a kind of stylized tree, its branches spreading in front of her face.

64

CHRIST CHURCH. *See* Cadley, p. 140.

THE WARREN, ½ m. NW. Model farm, the front consisting of three detached three-bay stone houses, the middle one more ambitious than the others. All three have low-pitched roofs and pediments instead of end-gables. Big BARN of chequered brick behind. The group is not on a map of *c.*1780 but marked on one of *c.*1820.*

* I owe this information to the kindness of the Earl of Cardigan.

KNOWLE FARM, 1 m. N. Good C18 brick house of five bays and two storeys. Three-bay pediment. Doorway on brackets. At the back a rainwater head with the date 1735. On the side two windows still have mullion-and-transom cross windows of wood and the old lead glazing. The other windows are sashed, and a number of them have kept their old heavy glazing bars.

CHAPEL OF ST MARTIN, behind Knowle Farm. Small rectangle with one blocked ogee-headed N window and the surround of the E window. No other features remain. The chapel is supposed to date from the late C13.

ROMAN ROAD. *See* Salisbury, p. 347.

SCRATCHBURY CAMP *see* NORTON BAVANT

SEAGRY

ST MARY. 1849 by *Hakewill*. Nave with bellcote, transept, and chancel. Lancet windows. – FONT. With band of triangle-headed arcading; Norman; circular. – SCREEN. Perp, with single-light divisions as usual. – STAINED GLASS. In the E window of 1849. – MONUMENTS. C13 stone effigy of a Knight (S transept) and C13 stone effigy of a lady wearing a wimple. – Rebekah Stratton † 1678. Small panel with inscription, skull, and hour-glass; very elementary. – Charles Bayliffe † 1735. Good tablet.

GATEWAY of the C14, SW of the church, through an outbuilding to the former manor house. Double-chamfered arch dying into the imposts on the S side. A little lantern or vent on the W gable. The present manor house is C18.

SEAGRY HOUSE, ¾ m. W, was destroyed by fire in 1949. It was an Early Georgian mansion. However, the four fine GATEPIERS and the wrought-iron gates remain, also Early Georgian.

THE CHESTNUTS, Upper Seagry, by the post office. Handsome house of chequer brick, five bays with a doorway carrying an open scrolly pediment.

SEAGRY MANOR FARMHOUSE, a little further S. An attachment to the dovecote has two upright oval windows, typical of *c.*1675.

SEDGEHILL

1¾ m. SW of East Knoyle

ST KATHERINE. 1844. But the tower arch seems to be later C14 and the rest of the tower C17 or C18. Porch 1763. – STAINED GLASS. In the chancel apparently by *Powell's* and probably of the 1880s.

SEEND

HOLY CROSS. A charming approach between the garden walls
of two large houses. A fine N aisle built by John Stokes, a c15
clothier (*see* below). Ashlar-faced, with gargoyles, battlements,
and pinnacles. Three-light windows, and three-light windows
also in the clerestory. In the W window moulding, inside as
well, sheep-shearing shears. Hood-mould on busts. Hood-
moulds on busts also for the straight-headed S aisle windows.
So far the features observed are all Perp. The W tower is
disappointingly low, and it is earlier, as the arch to the nave
(two chamfers dying into the imposts) shows. The chancel is
disappointing throughout. It was rebuilt in 1876 (by *A. J.
Style;* PF). Perp arcades inside, the moulding four thin shafts
and four big waves. The chancel arch is similar. – FONT. Dug
up in 1939. Octagonal, Perp, with quatrefoils in circles. –
WEST GALLERY. Parts of it now under the tower, dated 1706
and also 1726. – PAINTING. Traces of a large Crucifixion (or a
carved rood?) above the chancel arch. – PLATE. Chalice and
Paten Cover, 1712. – MONUMENTS. John Stokys † 1498 and
wife. Brasses, 16 in. long. They are duly in his N aisle. – A
number of good tablets, especially George Husey † 1741, by
Thomas Paty of Bristol (coloured marbles, woman by an urn).
Seend is full of good houses. The two best are Seend House and
Seend Green House. SEEND HOUSE is W of the church. It is
of the late c18, of six bays and three storeys, ashlar-faced, with
a two-bay pediment and a porch on pairs of Tuscan columns.
The ground-floor windows slender and arched. On the garden
side the ground-floor windows tripartite under a blank segmental arch. Two LODGES with four Tuscan columns in front.
E of the church is the MANOR HOUSE of 1768. Five bays, two
storeys, Ionic porch. Fine STABLES with Gibbsian archway and
lantern. To the w of Seend House, at the w entry to the village,
a three-storeyed brick terrace of five houses. Two-light windows. Built probably for weavers. In the village many three-
bay houses and cottages with two-light or three-light windows,
dating from various moments in the c18. They are of brick or
ashlar-faced. Near the E end SEEND GREEN HOUSE, large
and ashlar-faced, and so absolutely plain with its seven bays,
three storeys, and parapet that it looks like an institution. The
windows are of two lights, but originally had transoms, and the
mouldings of the mullions are c17 rather than c18 too. The
windows are in fact under hood-moulds connected into a

14

continuous stepped course. The porch of paired Tuscan columns on the entrance side is evidently later. So is the porch of two Tuscan columns on the garden side, placed in front of a doorway which looks *c*.1700. To the SE across a field or two the WELL of the SEEND SPA, which Aubrey mentions in 1684 as attracting much company. Yet further E than Seend Green House HILL FARMHOUSE, partly original timber-framing with brick infilling. (It retains an original cruck. VCH)

SEEND HEAD HOUSE, 1½ m. WSW. A seven-bay house of two and a half storeys, brick-faced on stone.

SEMINGTON

ST GEORGE. Mostly of 1860, e.g. the bell-turret of the type of Leigh Delamere and Biddestone. – PLATE. Cup and Paten Cover, 1579; Paten, 1697. – MONUMENTS. Bisse family, *c*.1770–5. Coloured marbles. Hardly any ornament. – James Matravers † 1799. By *King* of Bath. With the usual woman by an urn.

MANOR FARMHOUSE. Dated 1698. The windows are of two lights and have the typical stepped-back mouldings. Doorway with bolection moulding.

ST GEORGE'S HOSPITAL, the former WORKHOUSE. By *H. E. Kendall*, 1836–9. Nine-bay front with three-bay pediment and low wings l. and r. Further ranges behind. It is typical of the coming of the Victorian age how the classical and Grecian motifs get clumsy and extremely heavy.

In the main road between the church and the workhouse turnings a group of Georgian houses, especially one of about 1800 with tripartite windows and a porch of two pairs of Ionic columns.

SEMLEY

ST LEONARD. By *T. H. Wyatt*, 1875, for the Marchioness of Westminster (*see* Fonthill). Ashlar-faced, with a W tower and an unusually high stair-turret with conical spirelet. The aisle arcade capitals naturalistic. – FONT. Circular, with mouldings of the lower rim. – PLATE. Foreign Chalice, Renaissance; Almsdish, assigned to Nuremberg; Salver, 1768. – MONUMENTS. Large effigy of a Priest, later C13. Under a nodding head-canopy which stands on shafts. Badly preserved. – Lt.-Gen. Dewrance Irving Armstrong. By *Henry Pegram*, 1916. Bronze soldier with tropical helmet on a horse, the whole only about 4 ft high, i.e. curiously small considering its display in the churchyard.

CHURCH FARMHOUSE, N of the church. C17. Low range with dormers and at r. angles higher gabled part with a three-storeyed bay window. Four-light mullioned windows.

SEVENHAMPTON

1½ m. SE of Highworth

ST ANDREW. 1864 by *W. Pedley*. E.E., with quite a substantial w tower, its top stage provided with blank arcading. Nave and chancel with lancet windows – PLATE. Set, 1771.

WARNEFORD PLACE, ¼ m. SE. Of the house only the so-called Ballroom remains, early C18. It was the r. wing of a house of nine bays with a pedimented three-bay centre and a l. wing as well. Five bays, brick and stone, arched windows, doorway with pediment, reached by a two-arm staircase. The interior with pilasters etc. may be part of the remodelling of 1904. The basement is brick-vaulted, but its windows look older. The l. wing differed in fenestration and doorway from the remaining wing. The STABLES are dated 1734, a short range with lantern. The shaped gables cannot be of that date.

FRESDEN FARMHOUSE, 1½ m. NE. Elizabethan, flat symmetrical front with gabled porch. Mullioned windows. Dovecote with lantern.

SEVINGTON

1 m. SW of Leigh Delamere

SCHOOL. By *J. Thompson*, 1847, for Joseph Neeld, M.P. (*see* Grittleton, p. 233). Next to it a LODGE to the estate. The school incorporates parts of the old church of Leigh Delamere, especially the tremendous bell-turret. It is square, but was placed diagonally on the ridge of the nave at the E end so that two corners stand on heavy corbels. In each corner a battery of five shafts. Arches and a short spire. Also from the church of Leigh Delamere the C14 chancel arch used as the porch door-way, and the REREDOS of stone inside, with canopied niches.

Typical Neeld estate cottages with triangular bay windows.

SHALBOURNE

ST MICHAEL. Flint. Rebuilt in 1873, but with the use of quite a number of old parts, e.g. the Norman S doorway (one order of colonnettes with scallop capitals, zigzag at r. angles to the wall surface), the simple Transitional N doorway, two N lancets, one or some of the late C13 two-light windows in the chancel with pointed-trefoiled heads and a quatrefoil over, and also the E window of three stepped lancets, shafted inside. The recently cleaned painting of the nave and aisle roofs is by *Bodley & Garner*. The chancel roof is no longer quite their design. – FONT. Octagonal, the lead lining inside turned outside over the rim and decorated with little circles. – SCREEN. Of *c*.1875–90, by the Rev. *Thomas Hungerford Michell*, reaching right up to the roof; quite bold and original patterns in the upper parts. – PLATE. Chalice and Paten, inscribed 1663; Paten dated 1727. – MONUMENTS. Sir Francis Choke † 1562. Excellent standing wall-monument, similar in many ways to the Brydges Monument at Ludgershall, but less rich. On the other hand more dignified and less gushing. Recumbent effigy. Columns l. and r.; four-centred arch; top foliage frieze. Achievement at the top between two pilasters and two nimble putti. – Elizabeth Mayott † 1722. Standing marble figure in an arched niche. Pilasters l. and r. and an entablature curving up to the middle – in fact very typically Early Georgian.

SHALBOURNE MANOR, ½ m. SSW. Flint and red brick, with two gables and a third smaller one in front of the second and belonging to the two-storey porch. The house extends to the r. of the gable. Diagonally-set chimneyshafts at the end gables. The windows all re-done recently and the whole much restored. The bargeboards of the gables have remained untouched. Is the house basically Elizabethan?

8060

SHAW

I m. NW of Melksham

CHRIST CHURCH. 1905 by *C. E. Ponting*. Arts and Crafts Gothic with a NW tower and many pretty details. The clerestory half-timbered. The S transept front with two lancets and a circular window over remains from *T. H. Wyatt*'s preceding church of 1836–8. Interior all timber, even the piers, i.e. posts, of the arcade.

SHAW HOUSE, ½ m. SE. Fine ashlar-faced Georgian house of seven bays and two storeys, with a three-bay pediment, a doorway with segmental pediment on brackets, and a hipped roof behind a balustrade.

WHITLEY FARMHOUSE, ½ m. N. 1696. Two-storeyed, with three gables. Mullioned windows. Doorway simple, but with fine mouldings.

SHEAR CROSS *see* LONGBRIDGE DEVERILL

SHELDON MANOR
2½ m. ENE of Chippenham

8070

The house possesses an astounding late C13 porch, much too big
for the present house. The entrance arch has two continuous
chamfers, the upper window two lights and a kind of rough
Y-tracery, and the inside below is heavily rib-vaulted (single-
chamfered ribs). Angle-buttresses. To the r. of the porch C15
work, see one cusped two-light window. The rest is mostly
later C17, with cross-windows and gables. Detached a small
oblong C15 chapel with an E window with simple Perp tracery
and small cusped side windows. Very tall and old yew trees in
front of the house.

SHERRINGTON

9030

ST COSMAS AND ST DAMIAN. Small C17 church, the date
1624 on the porch. The E and W windows of the medieval predecessor were re-used, one with four-light tracery, cusped intersected, the other reticulated, i.e. *c.*1310 and *c.*1330. Straight-
headed chancel side-windows carrying on with those of the
nave: C14 *versus* C17. A similar comparison between the
chancel N doorway and the chancel arch. Inside, very complete
furnishings and fitments. On the walls PAINTED TEXTS in cartouches, dated 1630. A tablet with the date 1621 is visible when
one opens the pulpit door. PULPIT, COMMUNION RAIL,
BENCHES, all of *c.*1630. The communion rail has vertically
symmetrical balusters. – FONT. E.E., plain, with fleurs-de-lis
against the underside of the bowl. – FONT COVER. Of *c.*1630
again. – PLATE. Paten, Carolean; Flagon, 1694.

RECTORY, N of the church. Two-light windows in two storeys
plus dormers in the thatch. Probably *c.*1700.

MOTTE AND BAILEY CASTLE, W of the church. The castle
belonged to the Giffords.

SHERSTON

8080

HOLY CROSS. An impressive church with a crossing tower,
almost too tall for the rest. The tower is, except for its lowest
stage, of 1730 and was designed by *Thomas Sumsion*, quite
consciously as a Gothic tower. The battlements and square
pinnacles, all in openwork, are quite a feat of archaeology, but

the clasping buttresses, the tracery, and of course the niche give away the real date. Sumsion was paid £1 15s. 0d. for the design. The building history starts however inside. Late Norman N arcade of four bays. Circular piers, capitals with decorated trumpet scallops. Square abaci. Round, single-step arches, with zigzag at r. angles to the wall surface. The one arch on the S side led into a former transept. Norman also the famous Rattlebones, really quite a blasphemous name, as it is no doubt a saint. Norman finally some heads of a corbel table re-used in the N transept. The E.E. style is importantly represented by the crossing arches, partly resting on big and excellently carved heads, e.g. a king and a knight with a mail coif. The lowest stage of the tower outside is also E.E. To the same period, i.e. the first half of the C13, belongs the N transept, with a beautiful N group of three closely-set stepped lancets. Inside, this is shafted with detached Purbeck shafts and has some dog-tooth enrichment. It is a remarkable fact that the hood-mould still stands on Norman-looking beasts' heads of the Malmesbury type. Or are they re-used Norman pieces too? Again of the same time the N aisle, see the plain trefoil-headed doorway and a pair of lancets which have inside short shafts on stiff-leaf corbels. And E.E. also the chancel, but late C13 and drastically restored by *Ewan Christian*, whose work is the E window. After that the Perp work, as follows: S porch, two-storeyed, with panelled battlements, pinnacles, and a lierne-vault of which four panels are cusped – a Bristol idea. S aisle and S chapel embattled with straight-headed windows, except for the E window, which has a four-centred arch. The nave W window and N aisle W window are Perp too. The S chapel inside has an arch with panelled jambs. The arch itself is four-centred again. – PULPIT. Jacobean. – RAILING. To the N chapel, C16 or early C17. – PLATE. Paten, 1718; Chalice and Paten Cover, 1725. – MONUMENTS. In the N transept N wall tomb recess with cusped arch and an effigy of a Civilian, his head on a diagonally placed pillow. Mid-C13. – Another tomb recess, C14, in the N aisle, plain, with an ogee arch. – Anne Hodges † 1676. Tablet with twisted columns. On the pediment naively carved angels blowing pipes. – Joyce Hitchings † 1715. A conservative piece. She kneels in a niche with a shell arch. – Estcourt Cresswell family, late C18. An elegant work; a mourning woman by an urn, a garland above her. – William Jenkins † 1803. By *King* of Bath. Seated woman by an urn. – Richard Estcourt Cresswell † 1841. By *Sanders*. Grecian, with a praying woman.

The HIGH STREET of Sherston is very wide, like an elongated market place. Several noteworthy houses, especially No. 15, which is c16, see the arched heads of the lights of the mullioned windows; Nos 19–21, the back with good mullioned and mullioned-and-transomed windows under hood-moulds; No. 6 opposite, early c18, of three bays, with a weeny pediment and a doorway with shell-hood on corbels; the ANGEL HOTEL of 1648, with gables and mullioned windows; and No. 31, tall and narrow, also c17, and also with mullioned windows under hood-moulds. Parallel with the High Street is CLIFF ROAD with the CONGREGATIONAL CHAPEL of 1825, a plain building with a half-hipped roof, and COURT HOUSE at the corner of Court Street, with a big wooden shell-hood over the door and to Cliff Road two vertical oval windows. The house is probably of c.1700.

EASTON TOWN, ¼ m. NE, has several steep-gabled houses with mullioned windows.

PINKNEY COURT FARMHOUSE, 1 m. NE. Late c17. One front of five bays with three–two–two–two–three-light mullioned windows. Hipped roof.

BYAM'S FARMHOUSE, Willesley, 1¾ m. NNE. Early c18, ashlar-faced, two storeys, shell-hood over the door.

SHREWTON

0040

See also Maddington, p. 286.

ST MARY, ⅜ m. N of the centre of the village. By *T. H. Wyatt*, 1855, except for the short, ashlar-faced W tower and the impressive Late Norman to E.E. arcades and chancel arch. An earlier Norman church of unknown dimensions was apparently first enlarged by a one-bay chapel (NW). Square pier, a little chamfered, and with a little flat zigzag in the abacus. Then, the decision was taken to build complete arcades on both sides (and probably to lengthen the church). The work now started with the SW respond, which still has a normal scalloped capital. Then came the rest, with trumpet scallops decorated in various ways. The next was the SE respond, where E.E. leaves come in. The abaci are all square, and the arches pointed, with two slight chamfers, in the NW bay no doubt a replacement. The chancel arch followed after 1200. The very fine capitals still have traces of trumpets, but mostly leaf shapes, including proper stiff-leaf. Wyatt's church is Perp, but he added a Dec-looking clerestory and thereby dwarfed the tower. – FONT.

Norman, by *Wyatt*. – SCULPTURE. Crucifixion, probably the head of a churchyard cross. – PLATE. Chalice, early C17.

The village has an amply domed LOCKUP by the stream, right in the middle. To the S in the Wilton Road a terrace of four cottages marked by a cast-iron plaque as having been erected in 1842 for flood victims. The BAPTIST CHAPEL between the cottages and the centre, though of 1846, is still of the Georgian type. Brick, with arched windows and a pedimented doorway.

Opposite the Lockup a pretty Gothick cottage with pointed windows and a thatched roof, and a four-bay brick house with a mansard roof and on the side a porch with Tuscan columns. Then a gabled stone house with mullioned windows dated 1637 (?), and after that, to the N and NW of Maddington church, the VICARAGE, dated 1704, of flint and stone chequer, with thinly moulded window surrounds, sash windows, and a hipped roof, and MADDINGTON FARM, having as one of its buildings an early C16 range with two-light windows with round-headed, uncusped lights and an impressive roof with tie-beams and wind-braces. It is said to be connected with a grange of the Amesbury nunnery at Shrewton.

SHREWTON HOUSE, ¼ m. NE of Shrewton church. Probably of *c.*1830. Three bays, two storeys, rendered. In front of the ground floor a veranda on coupled Tuscan columns. Above it on the first floor an iron balcony. In front of the house a terrace also with an iron railing. It makes a handsome sight.

ROBIN HOOD'S BALL, 2½ m. NW. Neolithic causewayed camp with two roughly circular concentric banks and ditches. Little surface indication of the banks. Sherds of Windmill Hill ware were found in the ditches and beneath the outer bank.

SILBURY HILL *see* AVEBURY

SILK HILL *see* MILSTON

SLAUGHTERFORD

ST NICHOLAS. Small unbuttressed W tower with Somerset tracery in the bell-openings. The rest of the church, nave and chancel, virtually of the restoration of 1883. (In that year the church is called built in 1823; PF.)

FRIENDS' MEETING HOUSE. The little C17 building, in the wood behind a derelict house close to the paper mill, has collapsed.

SNAIL DOWN *see* EVERLEIGH

SOPWORTH

St Mary. A small church, drastically restored in 1871. The 'low-side' window of the chancel with its trefoil-headed rere-arch is E.E. The chancel arch (continuous mouldings) seems c 14, but is over-restored. Perp w tower, unbuttressed, with big battlements and small pinnacles. N aisle of 1871. Are the s transept s window and the vestry E window old and re-set? – FONT. Circular, c 13. Trefoiled arches on stem shafts with two shaft-rings. – PULPIT. With tall, thin Jacobean arches. – STAINED GLASS. Clearly by *Morris & Co.*, the figures designed by *Burne-Jones*. The glass represents the Three Maries. Date of death commemorated 1870.

The s end of the village is a fine sight. To the r. the MANOR HOUSE with its early c 18 seven-bay front, hipped roof, and shell-hood over the door, to the l. a late c 17 five-bay house with stone cross-windows. In addition outbuildings and barns in the vernacular.

SOUTH MARSTON

St Mary Magdalen. Simple Norman N and s doorways. Chancel of the c 13, see the one N lancet, and the E window with three stepped lancet lights. The s porch has pinnacles. So has the broad w tower. All this is Perp. By *John Belcher*, 1886, the battlements, the odd turret at the E end of the nave, the s transept, and the pretty chancel arch with nodding-ogee corbels. – STAINED GLASS. Windows of 1886 by *Clayton & Bell*. – PLATE. Chalice and Paten Cover, 1715. – MONU-MENTS. Henry Southby † 1721. Tablet with fluted Corinthian pilasters. – Anne Southby † 1770. Small urn on a bracket. Cherub's head below.

School. 1873.

SOUTH NEWTON

St Andrew. 1862 by *T. H. Wyatt*. Perp, with pyramid roof on the w tower. Chancel arch on lavishly carved corbels. Medieval the N arcade. The two E arches c 13, the w arch c 14. The E pier circular, the w pier with four canted shafts, the earlier arches with one slight chamfer and one proper chamfer, the later normally double-chamfered. – PLATE. Cup, 1576.

SOUTHWICK

St Thomas. 1899–1904 by *C. E. Ponting*. Rock-faced, Gothic, with a sw tower with playful details (shingled spike). Aisleless, with a roof with collar-beams on arched braces.

BAPTIST CHAPEL. 1815. Three by two bays, brick. The arched windows look a good deal older. By the bridge a little to the w an open-air BAPTISTERY for immersion. A pity that the rough walls, coping, and angle-posts give it such a suburban character.

THE POPLARS, by the school. Of c.1700. Three bays, hipped roof, open pediment with urn over the door.

SOUTHWICK COURT FARMHOUSE, ¾ m. NW. L-shaped, the shorter wing dated 1567. It has mullioned and transomed windows. The mullions have a tapered section ending in a fillet. Attached to the longer wing a gatehouse.

MANOR FARMHOUSE, ⅝ m. WNW. Dated 1673. Symmetrical front with three dormers.

BROOK HOUSE, 1½ m. SE. By the side of the C17 farmhouse stands a stone range of the early C16, with buttresses, windows of two uncusped lights, arranged without symmetry, and a fine roof with tie-beams, collar-beams on arched braces, and three tiers of wind-braces. The range has always been two-storeyed. On the upper floor a blocked fireplace.

SOUTH WRAXALL

8060

ST JAMES. Picturesque w tower of c.1300, see the unbuttressed but stepped-back outline, the bell-openings with Y-tracery, and the continuous double-chamfer of the arch to the nave. What gives the South Wraxall tower its point is the saddle-back roof repeated, but at r. angles, on top of the monstrously big square stair-turret. Impressive also the s porch, in one with the s chapel. Perp, straight-headed windows. This part built in all probability by the Long family (see below). In 1566 it was altered and a doorway was made carrying that date. N aisle 1823, chancel and arcade 1882. Inside, apart from the tower arch, there is only the chapel arch to observe: four-centred, on responds with the usual four-shafts-four-hollows section. – FONT. Big, octagonal, Perp. With quatrefoils. – MONUMENTS. Tall tomb-chest of the mid C15 with, on the long side, an angel and two supporter beasts *passant*. Effigy of a Lady. Long Arms (see below). – Thomas Long † 1759 and his wife † 1733. Big standing monument. Noble. Aedicule with Corinthian columns and pediment. In it on a plinth an urn.

28 SOUTH WRAXALL MANOR. The house is an outstandingly successful mixture of the C15 and the later Elizabethan and Jacobean. Moreover, what features of both periods remain are

outstanding in their own right. The owners from the early C15 have been Longs. Robert Long is mentioned in 1426 and 1433. The house is approached from the S through a GATEHOUSE with a canted oriel above the gateway. The latter has a straight lintel with rounded corners and deep mouldings. The oriel windows are transomed and the lights cusped. To its r. stretch buttressed outbuildings. Some windows with cusped lights to the N prove them to be of the C15. Past the gateway one turns r., i.e. E, and faces the hall range. This is easily recognized by its porch with deeply moulded entrance and a room over, its one two-light window, and the curious group of fireplace and bay window making the fireplace appear like a big transverse buttress. The bay window is quite low; of three lights with the small window of a room over. At r. angles to the hall range is a long, lower, further range projecting W. The E part of this (see the arch of the doorway and the cusped lights of the windows) belongs to the time of the hall, the W part is apparently of the first half of the C16.

The HALL goes up into the roof. It has collar-beams on arched braces, raking queenposts, and cusped panels instead of wind-braces. The two two-light back windows are now inside the house. The low front bay is matched by a back bay, equally low. The gallery is not original, but the doorways leading on to it are.

This nucleus is the most important pre-Reformation work at South Wraxall. The most important later work, much grander and more ostentatious, belongs to the time when Sir Walter Long was in residence. He added the large DRAWING ROOM to the N of the hall, half a floor up – Aubrey calls it the Dining Room – and gave it an enormous front window of eight lights with two transoms, turning round the corner towards the hall front with another three lights. The room is very light indeed; for it has yet another large window at the back, again of eight lights and again with two transoms. Long also added a large room SE of the hall facing E. Both rooms have gigantic stone chimneypieces, and so has the hall. The chimneypiece here carries the date 1598 and is more restrained than the others. Its overmantel is a kind of shaped gable with some strapwork. The hall screen is of the same time. It is of wood, with fluted pilasters and a handsome frieze of shells pointing alternatingly upward and downward.

The decoration of the Drawing Room can hardly be matched anywhere in lavishness. The room has a tunnel-vault with

thin ribs in geometrical patterns and a pendant, closer stucco
decoration in the lunettes, a truly colossal fireplace, over 13 ft
long, with crazy coupled caryatids l. and r. of the openings, the
figures part encased in angular bands, and in the overmantel
little niches with Prudence l., Justice r., and Arithmetic and
Geometry in the middle. Strapwork encrusts the remaining
surfaces. Opposite the chimneypiece is an unexplained deep
canted projection in the wall. No-one seems to know what is
inside it. The projection is decorated by big niches to sit in,
with shell-apses.

The wing projecting to the E, SE of the hall, to which refer-
ence has already been made, has little colonnades or loggias of
Tuscan columns on the ground floor. They probably belong to
c.1700 – see e.g. the bolection mouldings of the doorways.
Behind the cloister kitchens. Above it a timber-framed storey.
Here the so-called RALEIGH ROOM, with linenfold panelling.
To the NE of the hall is the present DINING ROOM. It has a big
Jacobean fireplace flanked by giant Ionic columns embracing
two big strapwork cartouches with inscriptions worth heeding.
The shell-headed niche to the r. and the windows with their
thick glazing bars are of course another contribution of c.1700.
Above this room is the GUEST ROOM, already mentioned for
the third outsize chimneypiece. This one has coupled columns
in two tiers, Doric below, Ionic above, and again strapwork
cartouches in the overmantel. Between them is a pretty vase
with flowers on a bracket.

To the SW of the house is an octagonal SUMMER HOUSE
with a domed roof.

MANOR FARMHOUSE, N of the former. This is an extremely
interesting building, largely a hospice of the C14. These C14
parts are T-shaped and consist of a chapel (of St Audoen) and
a hall. The HALL has a tall end window (S side) with a two-
centred hood-mould on curly stops and close to the other end,
in the angle formed with the chapel, a single-chamfered doorway. The CHAPEL has a N window with cusps, a S window
similar to that of the hall, and inside, against the E wall, the
remains of a tripartite reredos. Cinquecusped blank arches,
gables with crockets. To the N the hall was extended in the C17,
and its E wall given a new front.

By the church an attractive group: CHURCH FARMHOUSE to the
w, late C17, five bays, hipped roof, cross-windows, and the
typically high-raised moulding above the door to allow for
lighting. To the SE the Gothic SCHOOL of 1841. To the w the

LONG ARMS INN, with moulded windows, but an C18 canted bay.

At LOWER WRAXALL two houses: SOUTH WRAXALL HOUSE, three-storeyed, Later Georgian, with a semicircular portico with Tuscan columns, but otherwise plain, and MISON'S FARMHOUSE, with mullioned windows and a doorway with a four-centred head and an inscription: '1576 God save our Queen Elizabeth'.

SPYE PARK see BOWDEN HILL

STANDEN HOUSE see CHUTE

STANDLYNCH see TRAFALGAR HOUSE

STANLEY ABBEY see BREMHILL

STANTON FITZWARREN

1090

ST LEONARD. Of a Norman church on this site the apse was found in 1865. The N doorway also remains, with a tympanum surrounded by bands of saltire crosses, which is repeated in the S doorway. In the N wall one Norman window too. Chancel arch, quite high and wide, again with saltire crosses. In the chancel pillar piscina with scalloped capital. The Norman nave was lengthened to the W and the S porch added in 1891. At the same time probably the incongruous Gothic fireplace was put into the W wall. The tower stands on the N side of the church. It dates from 1631, except for the C19 pinnacles. The windows of the church are Perp and redone. In the chancel a dormer window. Old parts used in the chancel roof. – FONT. An important Norman piece, circular, with eight Virtues and Vices 11b below trefoiled arches. Above, a frieze of beaded trails and foliage. They are Largitas and Avaricia, Humilitas and Superbia, Pietas and Discordia, Misericordia and Invidia, Modestia and Ebrietas, Temperencia and Luxuria, Paciencia and Ira, Pudicicia and Libido. In addition Ecclesia and the Evil One and a Seraph with six wings. There is a similar font at Southrop, Gloucestershire. Also a fragment of a similar piece in the S wall: small bearded head of a type reminiscent of the Chichester panels, and part of a little arch with the start of an inscription. Many other architectural fragments. – ALTAR SCREEN. In the Art Nouveau taste. Carved by the rector, Canon

Masters, c.1910. – Much Victorian WOODWORK, e.g. the chancel panelling and the Pelican LECTERN. – ORGAN FRONT. With linenfold panels from a cottage at Latton. – DOOR. With blank balustrading, C17, said to come from Winchester Cathedral. – SCULPTURE. German relief of the Adoration of the Magi; the inscription records a Provost of Diessen in Bavaria and the year 1587. – STAINED GLASS. Some of 1896 and 1907 by *Kempe* (chancel s). – PLATE. Chalice and Paten Cover, 1698 (partly older ?).

STANTON HOUSE. Built in 1935 for a New York businessman by *H. W. Binns*. In the Cotswold style. By church and house a beautiful lake. Across it an artificial ruin, now mostly collapsed. It is centred on the original C14 E window of the church.

STANTON ST BERNARD

₀₀₆₀

ALL SAINTS. 1833, except for the ashlar-faced Perp w tower. The church is ashlar-faced too and has battlements and pinnacles. – FONT. Circular, Norman, with a top band of flat zigzag and a wider band below which seem to be C19. – ROODSCREEN. Low, of iron, probably High Victorian. – PAINTING, above the chancel arch, 'An apocalyptic subject.' Nothing seems known about it. It appears to date from c.1900. – PLATE. Chalice, c.1574; Paten, 1719.

MANOR HOUSE, a little E of the church. Three-bay, early C19 front of Sarsen stone, with re-set parts dated 1677, namely the doorway with a basket arch and shields in the spandrels, and two upright oval windows, typical of the date of the former house. The frieze and pediment of the doorway must be early C18. Gatepiers probably of c.1677.

STANTON ST QUINTIN

₉₀₈₀

ST GILES. Norman central tower, see the ground-floor windows and the fine w arch inside. Big leaf-capitals with volutes. Arch with zigzag. The date may be c.1125. The upper parts of the tower are of course neo-Norman, probably by *Hakewill*, 1851. s arcade of the early C13, much taller than the tower arch. Two bays, circular piers, capitals with upright crocket leaves and also with small heads. Octagonal abaci, double-chamfered arches, one arch round, one pointed. Arches with zigzag at r. angles to the wall. Hood-moulds with dog-tooth. A stone seat round the pier. The doorway is highly puzzling. It has keeled shafts with wholly Norman capitals, e.g. beasts' heads biting

into the shafts, but an arch and a hood-mould like the s arcade.
Is it made up of parts of two dates? And where does the small
round window in the N chapel w wall come from, with its pellet
band? Ornate chancel of 1888 by *Ponting*, but the Perp chancel
arch original. – FONT. Small, circular, Norman. Big knobs at
the bottom of the bowl, two tiers of flat stylized leaves above.
– SCULPTURE. Good Norman figure of a seated Christ, his
feet on a dragon. – Small Perp St Christopher in a niche, above
the doorway discussed above. – PLATE. Set, 1738.

(STANTON COURT. Built in 1780. Inside, a chimneypiece from
the manor house at Surrendell near Hullavington. *See* J.
Badeni: *Wiltshire Forefathers*.)

STANTON PARK ROMAN VILLA, ½ m. SW. One room with
painted wall plaster and hypocaust was excavated in 1910. A
number of re-used columns and capitals were incorporated in
the structure, suggesting the presence of an earlier building
on the site or near by.

STAPLEFORD

ST MARY. The Norman contributions make the church memorable, especially the tremendous round piers of the s arcade.
They are nearly 3 ft in diameter. They have scalloped capitals,
but also heads at the corners, and square abaci. One would
date this not after 1150, if it were not for the arches. They are
round and single-stepped, but have zigzag at r. angles to the
wall surface, and – a yet later motif – in the hood-moulds,
alternating with pellets – dog-tooth. It does not look an amend-
ment, and so one must reluctantly date the arcade late C12.
Norman also the clasping NW buttress of the nave and the s
doorway. One order of shafts, scalloped capitals, zigzag at r.
angles to the wall, and a roll moulding round the actual opening
of the doorway. Otherwise the church is mostly Dec, namely the
s windows, the s transept s window (reticulated tracery), the
tomb recess below it inside (moulding of two sunk quadrants),
the chancel arch, the sedilia, if they represent genuine evidence,
and the arches to the two N chapels. Perp s porch of two storeys,
and Perp clerestory. The church has a N tower, and this is Dec
below, but of 1674 above (cf. e.g. Berwick St James near by). –
FONT. Circular, Norman. Up the lower half flat leaves or
simply a motif of flat fluting. – PAINTING. Red scrolls in the
Norman arches; contemporary with the arches. – TILES. Close
to the font. – SCULPTURE. Panel with the Crucifixion, perhaps

that of a churchyard cross, under the gable. – PLATE. Cup,
given in 1678, and Paten, perhaps of the same date.

Extensive EARTHWORKS of STAPLEFORD CASTLE remain (HR).

STAVERTON

8060

ST PAUL. 1826. Low w tower with saddleback roof. The church
has windows with four-centred arches and lancet lights. The
w window with a transom. Square-ended short chancel. –
PLATE. Cup, 1577.

Higher up, parallel to the road, a terrace of three-storeyed
weavers' cottages.

Opposite the church, at r. angles to the road, another terrace of
three-storeyed weavers' cottages.

METHODIST CHAPEL. 1824, small, with pointed windows.

WYKE HOUSE. See Hilperton, p. 242.

STEEPLE ASHTON

9050

25 ST MARY. No wonder the village was known by its steeple. It is
impressive enough now; originally it had a spire on the four-
staged tower which gave a total height of 186 ft. This was
blown down in 1670. Set-back buttresses, three-light windows
in three tiers. A row of five canopied niches above the w
window. In the bell-openings Somerset tracery. Battlements
and pinnacles as a matter of course. But the rest is just as amazing as the tower. The church fairly bristles with pinnacles – a
gay and fantastical sight. The pinnacles of the aisles are polygonal and panelled, those of the clerestory are finer. There are
buttress-shafts with pinnacles in relief (in the Somerset
fashion) on the buttresses, and there are battlements with an
untold variety of gargoyles. Four-light windows, even in the
clerestory, where they have transoms. Flying buttresses at the
w and E ends of the clerestory only. Hood-moulds with beasts
and busts and heads. The chancel is lower (rebuilt, though
correctly, in 1853, by *Clutton;* PF), but also embattled and
provided with square pinnacles and at the E end the biggest
polygonal ones of all. The porches have not yet been mentioned,
though they are lavish enough too, the s porch two-storeyed,
with a lierne-vault and bosses, the middle boss depicting the
Assumption of the Virgin, the N porch meant to be two-
storeyed and vaulted. Busts to support the vault.

All this, needless to say, is Perp. It is known that the N aisle
was paid for by Robert Long, the s aisle by Walter Leucas,

both clothiers. Long's will is of 1501 and mentions the work on
the N side begun but not completed, i.e. Leland is right in
saying in 1540 that the rebuilding of the church was still 'in
the mynd of men now lyvynge'. Only the steeple was started
earlier in the C15, and the W bays of the aisles which embrace
the tower.

But the keenest surprise of all at Steeple Ashton is the
interior; for it was meant to be stone-vaulted throughout, and
that among English parish churches is almost unique (but cf.
St Mary Redcliffe, Bristol). The nave vault was executed in
wood, at once it seems; and that is a shame.* But the aisles,
chapels, and chancel have stone lierne-vaults, complicated 26a
stars with squares and lozenges and bosses. Those of the two
W bays on the S side are the best, and yet they were re-done in
1670 after the fall of the steeple; the rest are rather flat. In
the N chapel the E vault has the Assumption of the Virgin
surrounded by the Signs of the Evangelists, the W vault Christ
surrounded by Prophets and Sybils. Otherwise the bosses are
all foliage. The vaulting-shafts stand on busts again, big busts
this time which carry two canopied niches. Above the N doorway a specially big niche, carried by a bearded man and flanked
by pairs of triangular buttress-shafts (cf. Trowbridge). Niches
also l. and r. of the aisle E windows, again on busts. Busts also
at the springers of the nave vault. The timber vault has a ridge
rib with two parallel ribs all along – the motif of the Gloucester
choir in the mid C14. The tower arch is tall and panelled. There
is, oddly enough, no vault under the tower. Panelled arches also
to the W bays of the aisles and simple arches to the E of these
bays. The arcades are of four bays. Piers with a triple shaft to
the nave, single shafts in the other cardinal directions. Double
wave mouldings in the diagonals. Chancel arch and chapel
arches all of the same mouldings. Above the chancel arch a
large five-light window (the Cotswold way), now alas blocked.

FONT. 1841; imitation Perp. – STAINED GLASS. In the aisle
windows many original fragments. – E window 1868 and bad.
– PLATE. Cup and Paten Cover, 1581; Chalice, 1650; Paten
and Almsdish, 1699; Paten, 1704; Flagon, 1736; Candlestick,
late C18. – BRASS. Palimpsest plate. On the front inscription
referring to a death in 1730, on the reverse an allegorical scene
with a Frenchman, a pope, and the devil outweighed in a
balance by a Bible, Queen Anne looking on. – MONUMENTS.

* But Mr Hussey considers it possible that it dates from after the fall of the
spire in 1670.

Plenty of Georgian tablets, the best to John Smith † 1778, of coloured marbles.

MANOR HOUSE. Dated 1647. A tall, flat, symmetrical three-bay front with gables. Windows with thin architraves. Small porch with a doorway with open segmental pediment ending in little volutes. Immediately to the r., quite a surprise, a long brick GRANARY on round pillars and with two-light windows, probably late C17.

Plenty to see in the HIGH STREET, starting from CHURCH FARMHOUSE, WSW of the church; picturesque, timber-framed with brick infilling. Stone ground floor; the windows seem of c.1700. Huge stone chimneybreast. Some more timber-framed houses with brick infilling, others with symmetrical brick or stone fronts, i.e. late C17 or C18 work, e.g. No. 32 in the GREEN which has a doorway with an open pediment with a vase. In the Green side by side the octagonal LOCKUP with the customary domed stone roof and the VILLAGE CROSS, really a sturdy column of 1679, with a sundial at the top which may date from 1714. The stately house on the r. is ASHTON HOUSE. It belonged to a clothier's family called Styleman. The façade is of 1724. Five bays, two storeys, door pediment curly and open with a vase. Still cross-windows. Back range of the C20 and a Jacobean archway with strapwork on the top. Inside, the original C15 hall with open timber roof. Collar-beams on arched braces and two tiers of wind-braces. Oriel window at the back. Large C16 fireplace later inserted and cutting up the hall. The solar roof is of the same type. In other rooms heavily moulded beams.

After Ashton House and the Green, we continue first to the l. down VICARAGE LANE to the VICARAGE, which is of grey brick, C19, but has to the r. a C17 part and at the r. end a part dating back to the C14. Doorway to a porch with fine mouldings and projecting wing with a blocked upper window with tall two-centred arch. Back to the Green and along the rest of the High Street. On the r. a low, pretty, much restored timber house with brick-nogging, said to have been the MARKET HOUSE. It is not recognizable as such. Then the LONG'S ARMS, with cross-windows but an altered ground floor, and so, with several more timber-framed houses, to the end.

STEEPLE LANGFORD

ALL SAINTS. Traces of a Norman past in the chancel buttresses and the corbel-table. The E.E. style is more fully represented.

Fine chancel arch with triple responds and stiff-leaf, but also still waterleaf capitals, i.e. no later than 1200 certainly. Arch with roll mouldings. Of the same time the tower arch. The responds also triple. Upright leaves in the capitals. The arch again with roll mouldings. The upper part of the tower is Perp, and the wall was strengthened below, cutting into the tower arch. Short lead broach-spire. Dec w window, and Dec windows also in other parts. The N arcade is Dec too. Three bays, round piers, double-chamfered arches. There is in fact a consecration date of 1326 recorded. – FONT. Square, of Purbeck marble. One side has the familiar very shallow blank arches, another big zigzags, a third a motif of two rings connected by a bar. On the top in the spandrels two animal heads, a flower, and another motif. Norman. – PULPIT. Jacobean. – READER'S DESK. Made up of parts of the same type as the pulpit. Dated 1613. – SCULPTURE. Anglo-Saxon fragment of a cross-shaft. With scrolls. – PLATE. Chalice, dated 1609; Almsdish, 1694; Paten on foot, 1695; Flagon, 1768. – MONUMENTS. In the rood-stair doorway incised slab of c.1275; only 2 ft 3 in. long. On it the effigy of a forester (cf. Grovely Wood?) with a horn. – Tomb-chest with three shields in cusped fields, C15, though dated 1576. – Front of a tomb-chest with five shields in richly cusped fields; early C16. – Five panels of an Elizabethan tomb-chest with strapwork. – Joseph Collier † 1635. Portly frontal three-quarter figure with beard and bible.

OLD RECTORY, to the SE. A late C17 seven-bay front with cross-windows. At the back gables. Flint and stone chequer. Staircase with twisted balusters. A house of similar character N of the church, but two-light- instead of cross-windows.

YARNBURY GRANGE, 1 m. WNW. Date-stone 1580. With mullioned windows, the section of the mullions chamfered. Much restored and added to.

BATHAMPTON HOUSE, 1¼ m. WNW. Dated 1694. A seven-bay front with hipped roof and four fine panelled chimneys. The windows sashed, but still cross-windows round the corner. The semicircular porch with thin Tuscan columns is of course Late Georgian. Inside, a staircase of c.1740 with thin twisted balusters. But the most interesting piece inside is later and comes from Fonthill, a chimneypiece with ogee-arched open-60b ing, a grimacing face over it, and a frieze of stories telling of the misdeeds of lawyers and doctors. Even here Gothic backgrounds. Very lively and entertaining. Who carved it, and where precisely was it?

GROVELY CASTLE, ½ m. SW of Little Langford. Univallate Iron Age hill-fort. At the time of construction five bodies were deposited in the chalk rubble of the rampart; a single sherd of Iron Age A pottery was associated with one of the bodies.

CHURCH END RING and HANGING LANGFORD CAMP, 1½ m. SW. The first is a pear-shaped earthwork, connected by a ditch with Hanging Langford. The latter earthwork appears to have been occupied for a considerable period, as the finds include an early La Tène I brooch as well as Belgic pottery, a La Tène III brooch, and Roman coins.

STERT

0050

ST JAMES. The church and the MANOR FARMHOUSE, rendered a primrose yellow and with two gables, form a charming group. The little church lies at the top of a steep bank with a wide view across the Vale to the downs. The church was built in 1846 by *J. H. Hakewill* (GR). Nave with bell-turret and chancel. Hakewill kept the Perp two-bay N arcade. Octagonal pier, fleurons in the capitals; four-centred arches. – FONT. By *Hakewill*; neo-Norman. The intertwined frieze of trails with beasts and birds is quite a tour de force. – PLATE. Cup and Paten Cover, 1577.

STOCKTON

9030

ST JOHN BAPTIST. Norman N arcade of two bays. Circular pier, scalloped capitals, square abaci, slightly-double-chamfered arches. The W tower seems no later, see the flat N buttress. But the tower arch, and especially the small lancet window looking into the church, are E.E. A small lancet also in the W wall of the N aisle. E.E. also the chancel (see the lancet windows). The S arcade is early C14, as is the E arch of the N arcade. At that time the S aisle must have been rebuilt (*see* below), though its windows are later. Perp embattled clerestory. Late C16 or C17 N aisle E window, a curious combination of round-arched lights and a stepped hood-mould. Inside, the distinguishing feature of the church is the solid wall between nave and chancel, now clothed by a high ROOD SCREEN of 1910. – FONT. Circular, Norman, with a frieze of roundels at the bottom of the bowl. – TEXTILE. A piece of Elizabethan panel velvet (N aisle), given by John Topp *c.*1630. – PLATE. Flagons, 1634 and 1640; Chalice and Paten, 1681. – MONUMENTS. In a recess in the s aisle effigy of a Lady, early C14, probably the foundress of a chantry for which the aisle was built. The extraordinary thing about the effigy is that she lies on her side, but not realistically, rather as if a recumbent effigy were tipped over: see the relation of the legs to the dog at her feet and of the head to the pillow, and see also the dress on the slab itself. – Jerome Poticary † 1596 and wife. The monument is in disorder. Tomb-chest of two bays only with shields on strapwork. Heavy balusters framing them. Top parts on brackets. Brass plates against the back wall, but a piscina interfering with the composition. – John Topp † 1640. In a recess. Two arches on paired columns. Flowers with stalks and leaves in the spandrels. Recumbent effigies. The children in relief kneel behind in niches. Top with obelisk and achievement. – Rev. Samuel Fyler † 1703. Lively cartouche. – John Greenhill † 1708. Big cartouche with a skull, two putti heads, arrangements of gun barrel, pistol, measuring instruments, and the like. Two weeping putti, and an urn at the top. – David Price † 1771. White and grey marble, with a classical urn. By *J. Osborne* of Oxford.

21b

See p. 577

STOCKTON HOUSE. A fine square Elizabethan house built by John Topp, a rich clothier, faced in bands of flint and stone and crowned by three gables. The front is to the w and is entirely symmetrical. A three-storeyed porch reaches up into the zone of the gables. The entrance is flanked by Tuscan columns with vases. Above a transomed four-light window, then a mullioned one and a cresting of strapwork with a pierced ring as its centre. To the l. and r. the windows on ground floor and first floor are transomed, of four and three lights. Mullioned windows in the gables. To the s and E similarly regular compositions, of course without a porch. The N had Victorian additions, recently pulled down, except for the square water-tower. Another addition is the CHAPEL, said to date from the Commonwealth. It has two-light windows with arched lights and is connected with the house by a link, once the minister's dwelling, which has a big semicircular gable. This appendage has a flint and stone facing arranged chequerboard-wise. The interior of the house is exceptionally rich in plasterwork and fireplaces. In the HALL the plasterwork has been destroyed. Big bare fireplace, the supports of the shelf curving forward. It looks older than the rest. The mantelshelf is an importation. It has Perp panel motifs. The STAIRCASE is behind the hall. It was inserted about 1800 by *Wyatt* (James of Fonthill or Jeffry of Longleat ?).

Interesting composition to fit into a long narrow space. The stairs start in two flights, unite in a flying middle piece, and divide again to reach the first floor. In the PARLOUR an Elizabethan fireplace of stone and plaster with plenty of fretwork or arabesque motifs and four big scrolls flanking the coat of arms. Stucco frieze with strapwork and heads and thin-ribbed geometrical patterns in the ceiling. More ornate rooms on the first floor. Above porch and parlour the GREAT CHAM-·

37　BER, with a brilliant ceiling of broad bands and panels abounding in long-stalked flowers. At the junction animals, including an elephant. Large chimneypiece with coupled columns in two tiers, the lintel with a strapwork cartouche, the overmantel with, in the centre, two detached heads, like Adam and Eve. Wall panelling with fluted pilasters. In the corner a wooden LOBBY with close carving of figures and ornament. If the lobby is *in situ*, the original staircase must have come up here. One bedroom is known as the SHADRACH ROOM; for the relief in the overmantel illustrates the Three Youths in the Fiery Furnace. The scene is flanked by two outrageously big soldiers. Caryatids below. Rich ceiling with thin ribs but crowded panels. A small pendant in the middle. Another bedroom has a chimneypiece whose pilasters are rusticated. Yet another has one with the arms of James I in a strapwork cartouche. Ceiling with thin ribs and E R monograms. Was the room being done in 1603 then?

A rustic LODGE with veranda in the NW corner of the estate, on the A-road. Close to the E gates of Stockton House the MANOR FARMHOUSE, i.e. Jerome Poticary's house. It was built before he died in 1596, but mostly rebuilt in 1611. The façade seems to be late C17, see the continuous string-course. Three-light mullioned windows. Good fireplace with geometrical patterns, Elizabethan rather than later.

The village has many attractive houses which cannot be listed singly. What must be picked out is the following. Up a lane to the S and quite hidden from the road the TOPP ALMSHOUSES, founded in 1641 and built *c.*1657. Small, stone, three sides of a little forecourt. One storey and dormers. Simple front wall and gateway. Then up the parallel lane to the church and to LONG HALL, with an old timber-framed part and a fine added C18 brick front. Five bays, the pedimented middle three replaced on the first floor by just one Venetian window. Along the main road to the E the RECTORY, late C18, but with segment-headed windows. Doorway with Roman Doric demi-columns and a

broken pediment. Finally, at the E exit GLEBE FARMHOUSE,
dated 1740, yet still with dormers and three-light mullioned
(wooden) windows. Can the date apply to this façade?

BAPTON MANOR, ¾ m. E of Stockton church. Early Georgian,
of five bays with a one-bay pediment. Doorway with open
segmental pediment.

STOCKTON EARTHWORKS, 1½ m. SW. Univallate hill-fort which
has produced evidence of a considerable period of occupation,
beginning in Iron Age A times (sherds of All Cannings Cross
type ware) and continuing until the C.I A.D. (Belgic brooches,
bead-rimmed pottery, etc.).

STONEHENGE

1040

Stonehenge is probably the most celebrated prehistoric monument in Western Europe. For centuries it has excited the
admiration of countless visitors, attracting poet, novelist, and
painter. The modern visitor as a rule has some idea of what to
expect, although his mental picture is generally coloured by the
romanticism associated with the monument, so that his initial
reaction on seeing it may be tinged with disappointment.
Standing on a slight eminence, but clearly not chosen for its
commanding position, the stones appear dwarfed against the
background of rolling downland. Once within the great sarsen
circle however the massive quality of the structure is immediately apparent. The weathering of the tooled surfaces and
the mellow tones of the stones create an impression of perman-
ence, and even the fallen uprights and trilithons, half buried
beneath the turf, have the appearance of pattern and order.
Its stones have a remarkable quality of reflecting light and its
moods are as varied as our climate. Most dramatic during a
thunderstorm, the weathered stones thrown up in stark relief
take on new meaning, thrusting upwards like the very bones of
the landscape – an aspect so wonderfully observed by Turner
in his watercolour.

The site has been a target for antiquarian research and
speculation since the C17, when Inigo Jones made the first,
highly imaginative, plan of the site. This was published in 1655.
The full complexity of the place, however, has only become
apparent in recent years, as a result of a series of excavations
directed by Professor Stuart Piggott, Professor R. J. C.
Atkinson, and the late Dr Stone. Like a medieval cathedral,
Stonehenge has been subject to a number of architectural

modifications and changes. These can be divided into three
main periods, the third being capable of further division.

PHASE I. The earliest structure is that of a fairly typical Late
Neolithic henge monument. It consists of the internal bank and

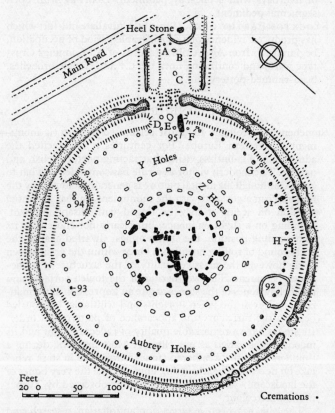

Stonehenge: Plan (From R. J. C. Atkinson's *Stonehenge*, by kind
permission of the author)

ditch, i.e. Heel Stone, Aubrey Holes, two stone holes at the
entrance, and a number of post holes in the vicinity of the Heel
Stone. The ditch, with its internal bank (a feature in contrast with the majority of the henge monuments, which

have external banks), varies from $4\frac{1}{2}$ to 5 ft in depth, and was dug as a series of individual pits later united to form a continuous, irregular, trench. The bank, encircling an area 320 ft in diameter, is much reduced by weathering and now measures only 2 ft in height but, judging by the size of the ditch, must have originally been 6 ft or more. The single entrance on the NE may have had some form of wooden gateway, as a setting of post holes was located at this point. On a line with the ends of the bank, at the entrance, were two stone holes (D and E on the plan). The Aubrey Holes, named after their finder, John Aubrey, the C17 antiquary, consist of a setting of fifty-six holes laid out in a circle immediately within the area enclosed by the bank (now marked by cement circles). These holes, containing no impressions of posts or stones, were refilled shortly after their initial digging, but were later re-opened and filled with burnt soil containing fragments of cremated human bones, bone pins, and flint fabricators. Further cremations were found in the ditch silting and in the bank. Finally to be ascribed to this phase is the undressed sarsen stone known as the Heel Stone, standing outside the entrance of the monument of Phase I.

PHASE II. The central structure of this phase is no longer visible. It consisted of a double circle of eighty-two undressed bluestones, the stone holes of which were discovered in 1954. The outer circle, the Q holes, lie between the present bluestone circle and the sarsen circle; the inner circle, the R holes, within the present bluestone circle. Although collectively termed bluestones, five different igneous rocks are represented, the commonest being spotted dolerite, rhyolite, and volcanic ash. It was finally proved in 1923 that these three main varieties of stone are exactly matched in outcrops in the Prescelly Mountains of North Pembrokeshire, and that the Stonehenge bluestones had been obtained from that region. Their transport would be effected largely by water, the final stage from the Avon being by way of the Avenue. This is a broad ceremonial way, bordered by bank and ditch, leading from the entrance of the monument. Measuring 78 ft from ditch to ditch, it is considerably broader than the Phase I entrance, a portion of the original causeway of which was filled in to bring it into conformity with the Avenue. At the same time a ditch was dug round the Heel Stone. It must have served some ritual purpose – perhaps to isolate the structure of the earlier monument – and was refilled shortly after excavation. From the entrance the

Avenue crosses the modern road and continues in a straight
line down the slope of the adjoining field to a dry valley, where
it swings eastwards and climbs between two plantations on the
skyline which hide the Old and New King Barrows. The course
then again changes, and it runs in a straight line across the
Amesbury road and beneath West Amesbury House, coming
to an end on the banks of the Avon. From Stonehenge the earlier
part of the Avenue's course can be seen by an observer standing
by the Heel Stone as two parallel lines of darker vegetation in
the neighbouring field. From the dry valley onwards its course
is visible only from the air. This second monument at Stonehenge may be ascribed to the Beaker folk, i.e. to *c.* 1800 B.C. A
number of bluestone fragments occur at the top of the primary
silting in the ditch, and Beaker sherds were recovered at the
same level.

PHASE IIIA. In this period, following the removal of the
bluestone circles, were erected the grandiose sarsen structures of
the horseshoe-shaped setting of trilithons, the lintelled circle,
the four Station Stones, and the Slaughter Stone and its vanished companion. Just within the bank on the NW and SE are
the two Station Stones, the sites of two further stones being
marked by flattened circular areas bordered by ditches on the
N. These four points appear to be connected with the process
of locating the centre of the sarsen circle. The Slaughter Stone
is a large sarsen 21 ft long, lying prone immediately within the
bank E of the causeway. This stone originally formed one of a
pair of stones flanking the entrance, the second stone being
marked only by its hole excavated in the chalk. The sarsen
circle, the most prominent feature of the site, consists of thirty
uprights supporting a corresponding number of lintels. Within
the sarsen circle lies the trilithon horseshoe of five pairs of
uprights supporting lintels. All these stones have been carefully
dressed to a rectangular form. This dressing appears to have
taken place on or near the present location of the stones, and
was accomplished by battering the surface of the stones with
sarsen mauls, many of which were found during the excavations, frequently utilized as packing for the stone holes. On a
number of stones the process of dressing is unfinished, the
surfaces being marked by a series of parallel ridges producing a
rippled effect. Each sarsen upright tapers towards the top, the
taper in a number of the stones being convexly curved to
counteract the effect of perspective. This astonishing architectural refinement – entasis – is similar to the technique employed

on columns in classical Greece. A similar awareness of perspective is apparent in the treatment of the lintels in the sarsen horseshoe, which expand slightly towards their upper faces. This feature is absent from the lintels of the circle, but these are carefully curved to conform to the curve of the circle. The lintels were secured to the uprights by means of mortice-and-tenon joints; cup-shaped depressions on the undersides of the lintels (mortices) fitting over projecting tenons on the tops of the uprights. In addition, the lintels of the circle were joined to one another by groove-and-tongue joints; a projecting tongue on one lintel fitting into a corresponding groove in the next. Both these methods of jointing are more commonly employed in woodworking than in stone. An important and recent discovery is a number of carvings executed on the faces of the sarsens of the circle and horseshoe. Most important is that on the inner face of Stone 53, consisting of a hilted dagger and four axes with expanding, crescent-shaped cutting edges and tapering butts. Similar axe carvings occur on the outer faces of Stones 3 and 4. The axes are representations of typical Early Bronze Age tools, a number of which have been found in the barrows which cluster in cemeteries around Stonehenge. The dagger, on the other hand, has no precise parallel among the weapons of the Wessex Culture barrows or indeed in Western Europe, but similar types are found in the brilliant Mycenaean culture of Greece. At Mycenae itself, in the great Shaft Graves, daggers akin to the Stonehenge carvings are included among the rich series of grave goods, and indeed the closest parallel is another carving of a dagger on a stele erected over one of these graves. The interpretation of the Stonehenge carving as a dagger of Mycenaean pattern would be in keeping with the evidence of other objects, either direct imports or copies of eastern Mediterranean objects, found in Wessex-Culture graves, attesting widespread commercial links in the C16 and C15 B.C.

PHASE IIIB. No trace of this structure is now visible, its existence being determined by the location of stone holes and inferred from the presence of dressed bluestones in the present bluestone circle and horseshoe. The Y and Z holes, a double circle of holes lying outside and encircling the sarsen circle, were dug to accommodate the undressed bluestones of the dismantled Phase-II monument, and a similar horseshoe-shaped setting of holes, in line with the existing bluestone horseshoe, was cut for the remaining bluestones, which were now dressed to shape and included at least two trilithons. Some of the dressed bluestones were erected, as they have left the impressions of their bases in the stone holes, but none of the holes for the double circle of undressed bluestones bear such impressions, and the plan was clearly abandoned before completion.

PHASE IIIC. The final phase is represented by the erection of the bluestones in their present positions. The dressed bluestone horseshoe with its two-lintelled structures of Phase IIIb was dismantled, and the tenons on the uprights were partially effaced. These dressed bluestones were re-erected on the present horseshoe plan within the sarsen horseshoe, and the undressed bluestones, with the two lintels of the dismantled trilithons, were set up in a circle between the sarsen circle and horseshoe.

There is no precise dating evidence for Phases IIIb and c, although the continuity in architectural tradition and layout suggest that they were constructed soon after the sarsen monument of Phase IIIa, and like it are the work of the Wessex Culture in the C16 and C15 B.C.

This represents the last architectural period at Stonehenge, but finds suggest the presence of later cultures on the site, particularly in the Roman period, when some deliberate destruction may have taken place, although the monument may by then have been in part a ruin.

THE GREAT CURSUS, $\frac{1}{2}$ m. N, and running in a roughly E–W direction, is an elongated rectangular earthwork of two parallel banks with external ditches 3,030 yds long and varying in width from 45 to 100 yds. Within the bank of the cursus and towards the W end there were originally two round barrows, one of which covered a Beaker inhumation. Just outside the E end is a long barrow orientated at r. angles to the axis of the cursus. Trial excavations of the bank and ditch produced little in the way of material to date the earthwork, but it is probably contemporary with the first phase of construction at Stonehenge.

THE LESSER CURSUS. A similar but smaller earthwork $\frac{1}{2}$ m. NNW of the Great Cursus.

THE STONEHENGE BARROW CEMETERIES. Clustered round Stonehenge is a magnificent series of barrow cemeteries, a number of which however are fast disappearing beneath the plough. Nearest to Stonehenge is a fine grass-covered bell barrow, lying just E of the monument on the far side of the boundary fence. The nearest cemetery is that of the Cursus Group, the majority of which are large bell barrows strung out on a line roughly parallel with the Great Cursus and lying between it and Stonehenge. A smaller group extends sw from the Lesser Cursus. Both these groups have been considerably reduced by cultivation. Looking E from Stonehenge, the belt of trees on the skyline encloses a row of magnificent bowl barrows and a single bell – the Old King Barrows. N of the Old King Barrows and separated from them by the Avenue is a further cemetery. Beginning ½ m. sw of Stonehenge are three very important groups which have yielded some of the richest burials of the Wessex Culture. Nearest of the three is the Normanton Group, many of whose barrows lie on arable land. Fine examples of bell, disc, and saucer barrows occur in this group, in addition to the commoner bowl form. Largest among the latter is the celebrated Bush Barrow, which covered the extended skeleton of a tall man buried with elaborate weapons of copper, a stone mace-head and breastplate, and belt-fastener of gold. Two pairs of bell barrows in the group share a common encircling ditch. Also within the group and belonging to an earlier period is an unchambered long barrow. sw of this cemetery is the Lake Group, consisting of twenty-six barrows, all five round barrow forms and a single unchambered long barrow being represented. Many of the barrows of this group are hidden by trees. I m. wsw of Stonehenge is the extensive cemetery of WINTERBOURNE STOKE. In addition to the magnificent unchambered long barrow with marked side ditches which gives its name to the cross-roads, there are some three dozen round barrows, mainly bowl but including examples of the other four types.

STOURHEAD AND STOURTON   7030

ST PETER. A small Perp church, except for the E window, which is of c.1310–20, if it can be trusted. Plain Perp w tower. Perp windows of four lights, in the clerestory of three. The parapets, pierced with cusped triangles and pierced with cusped lozenges, are of the time of Colt Hoare, the historian. They make the church picturesque. Internally, the arcades of four bays are a good deal older. Circular piers, circular abaci, double-chamfered arches of grey stone. The capitals are not reliable. The w tower was built into this nave. It has an arch with two continuous chamfers, as has the chancel arch. All this seems early C14.

The chancel was mostly rebuilt in 1937. – STAINED GLASS. C15 bits in the N chapel N window. – PLATE. Set given by Henry Hoare in 1723. – MONUMENTS. An uncommonly large number. Effigy of a Lady, c.1400, see the headdress, probably Lady Stourton † 1403 (N aisle). – Fifth Lord Stourton † 1536. Big tomb-chest, purely Perp, with niches, canopies, etc., but at the angles Renaissance pilasters with candelabra decoration. Two recumbent effigies. Three kneeling children at their heads, not *in situ*. – Funeral HELMS by this monument. – Henry Hoare † 1725 (who built the house). His bust right at the top. Otherwise purely architectural, tall and noble, with urns l. and r., Corinthian columns, and an open pediment. – Henry Hoare † 1785 (who laid out the grounds). White and light brown marble. An asymmetrical, i.e. still Rococo, composition of two big putti by an urn. Tall base. By *Charles Harris* of London. Rather in the style of Cheere. – Hester Colt Hoare †1785. Also a tall base, but on it a pink granite sarcophagus and at the top a black granite urn – an early use of granite. The monument was sent from Italy. – Sir Richard Colt Hoare. In the churchyard. Marble sarcophagus, purely classical, but under a Gothic canopy with pierced cusped triangle parapet. Made in Colt Hoare's lifetime. We read that he 'sibi fieri curavit' in 1819.

ORCHARD CASTLE is a motte and bailey EARTHWORK (HR).

STOURHEAD

The grounds of Stourhead are second only to Stowe in completeness and extent of picturesque layout and picturesque furnishings, and they are more compact, in that all one is intended to see is part of one sequence around a large and varied lake, half-hidden now by the splendour of the rhododendrons and azaleas, which are not part of the original planting. That planting, the damming of the river Stour, and the erection of the many buildings distributed in the grounds was begun by Henry Hoare, member of the banking family, about 1741.

51a   But the HOUSE had been built twenty years earlier by his father, also a Henry Hoare. He was married to the daughter of Sir William Benson of Wilbury House (*see* p. 510), the earliest essay in England in the revival of the style of Inigo Jones, i.e. of neo-Palladianism. Stourhead is one of the very next, and it is in a much purer Palladian. It was designed by *Colen Campbell* and built in 1721–4. The wings were added much later, in 1790–1804, and the portico, part of the Campbell design, came yet later, about 1840. The wings were designed by *Thomas Atkinson*, the portico was built by *Charles Parker*. Colen Campbell had designed Wanstead in Essex for Sir Richard Child, another banker (and a descendant of Wiltshire clothiers), in 1715, Burlington House for the earl of Burlington, the arch-Palladian, in 1719, and Houghton in Norfolk for Robert Walpole in 1721. So Stourhead is indeed very high on the list of Georgian Palladian *incunabula*.

The house faces E. It is of five widely-spaced bays with a rusticated base, one main floor, and a half-storey above. Balustraded top. The centre has a projecting tetrastyle portico of unfluted composite columns and a pediment with a raised attic behind. Two arms of a staircase lead up to it. The later wings are lower, also of one and a half storeys with a top balustrade. The view to the Downs is very fine. The centre of the house was gutted by fire in 1902, but the rooms were faithfully reconstructed from photographs. The ENTRANCE HALL is a cube of 30 ft by 30 ft by 30 ft. Coved ceiling. Door surrounds at the entrance and opposite with columns and open segmental pediments. In the lintel of the back doorway a Janus head and garlands. Fireplace with bearded termini caryatids and a tall overmantel. Open scrolly pediment.* The SALOON in the centre of the W front has a panelled ceiling and a screen of columns to the back, i.e. to the E. The doorway to this side is again a splendid piece with columns and garlands. In the over-mantel of the fireplace a painting by *Angelica Kauffmann*. Of the other rooms in the centre the STAIRCASE of two arms has a balustrade in the Wren tradition, with small leaves at the bulbous foot of each baluster and a glazed circular lantern. The terracotta reliefs are by *Rysbrack* and were bought in 1767. The LITTLE DINING ROOM has a serving alcove separated by Corinthian columns, the (N) BEDROOM a Venetian window with detached fluted pillars and another alcove. The alcove is lower than the room and has a playful rib-vault with a pendant. In the North Wing is the PICTURE GALLERY rising to full height, in the South Wing the LIBRARY, a very complete room of the early C19. It has a segmental tunnel-vault. The lunette painting is a copy of *Raphael*'s Parnassus by *Samuel Woodforde*. The lunette on the outer wall is glazed and has in stained glass the lower part of *Raphael*'s School of Athens. This is by *W. R Eginton* and *Samuel Lowe*. Overmantel with rich garlands.

* The furniture by the *Chippendales*, father and son, cannot here be described.

The plaster panel of Christ and the Money Lenders, attributed to *Grinling Gibbons*, comes from Wavendon and was originally at Ranelagh House, Barn Elms. The Wilton carpet on the other hand was made in 1803. It is in dark green and ochre with a surprisingly C20-looking, simple geometrical pattern. Much sculpture by *Rysbrack*.

What kind of GROUNDS Henry Hoare Senior visualized for his house we cannot say for certain, though the contrived contrast between cubic house and picturesque gardens at, for example, Chiswick makes it probable that picturesqueness was considered from the first. As fate willed it, Henry Senior died in 1725, and Henry Junior hesitated for a while, before the 'shifting of earth' began. The layout seems to have been decided about 1741. The whole arrangement, as it was about 1780, is known to us ideally by drawings made by the Swede Fredrik Magnus Piper in 1779. They are not only of individual buildings, but there is also a plan in which the buildings are connected by a criss-cross of lines of vision, indicating what vistas were considered when the buildings were placed.

The PERAMBULATION starts by the church and the church-yard. They have – with unmatched success – been made part of the picturesque composition. The lawn runs up to them and links them to the lake, and the Pantheon faces them challengingly. Opposite the church a terrace of C18 COTTAGES was allowed to remain. One house has an openwork parapet above its centre, picking up Colt Hoare's motif of the church. Another stands on the other side of the road, and then the castellated STABLES. All this is not on Piper's plan.

On the lawn W of the church stands the BRISTOL HIGH CROSS, given to Hoare in 1780, after it had been removed from its original site in the centre of the old town to Cathedral Green in 1733 and then stored in 1763.* The Cross dates from 1373 and consists of a tall lowest stage with shallow niches (evidently altered), crocketed ogee gables, four detached buttresses, four standing figures, originally coloured, at the next stage, then four seated figures added in 1633, and at the top a square pinnacle.

Lower down the FIVE-ARCH BRIDGE, built in 1749 and commanding views of the Rustic Cottage as well as the Pantheon.‡ By turning r. one gets to the TEMPLE OF FLORA,

* On Cathedral Green it is now replaced by one by *John Norton* of *c*.1850.
‡ Between bridge and church or cross stood in 1779 (*see* Piper) a concave structure or screen called the PORTICO.

built in 1755. This has a tetrastyle portico of Tuscan columns with metope frieze and pediment and, inside, one room. In the back wall a niche with a vase. In the l. and r. walls window recesses with busts. Below the Temple a grotto BOATHOUSE. Above the Temple and the path on a higher level originally some more small buildings.

They were reached by straight avenues from the two main *points de vue* put up in conjunction with the house, to the w the OBELISK of 1748 (rebuilt *c*.1840), which commemorates Henry Hoare Senior, to the s the STATUE of the Apollo Belvedere, no longer *in situ*.

Continuing the path by the lake, one soon reaches the place where originally a CHINESE BRIDGE went across, a handsome, curved, 100-ft structure of oak. The path, as it is now, is much longer. In the end one reaches, on the opposite side of the lake, the celebrated GROTTO, a tripartite structure which was building in 1740. In the centre the Sleeping Nymph or Nymph of the Grot, with the appropriate quotation from Pope's translation of *Huius nympha loci*. At the end *John Cheere*'s Neptune of 1751.* Tufa-lined walls, pebble floors. Framed views across the lake to the bridge and church.

The next building is a late-comer, the RUSTIC COTTAGE, not yet on Piper's plan of 1779. It has one chimney, windows with Y-tracery, and a seat in front, on genuine (?) ogee arches. Quatrefoils on the seat. Rustic furniture inside.

Further on, at the farthest distance from the house, the largest of the buildings, the PANTHEON. The Pantheon was under construction in 1753. Its designer, according to Horace Walpole, was *Flitcroft*, but, Walpole writes, the design was altered. It has a portico of four Corinthian columns *in antis*, closed bays to the l. and r. with statues in pedimented niches. These closed bays screen the junction between portico and rotunda more successfully than in the original temple in Rome. Through iron gates one enters an ante-room and then the Rotunda. Statues in niches, the principal being *Rysbrack*'s Hercules of 1756. The rest are casts from the antique, made in 1766, except for *Rysbrack*'s Flora of 1762. Relief panels above with stories of the Olympian gods by *Benjamin Carter*, 1761. Exquisitely carved frieze with bucrania and garlands.

On the s side of the lake there are no buildings by the shore.

---

* Horace Walpole in 1762 suggested as an inscription for him:
  This Stream like Time still hastens from my Urn
  For ever rolling, never to return.

Instead there is the TEMPLE OF THE SUN higher up, a rotunda, designed by *Flitcroft* after the original at Balbec which had been published by Wood in 1757. The Stourhead temple was completed in 1767. Like its original, it is a rotunda with detached Corinthian columns and an entablature curving vigorously back between each pair. Domed top. The Temple of the Sun is reached from the lake by either of two grotto passages, one a bridge above the main road from the W to the church, the other a tunnel under it. On the same plateau as the temple stood another specially famous little building, the HERMITAGE, or Hermit's Cell, or Root-House, as it displayed gnarled tree-trunks.

This ends the circuit. But there were originally several more structures, such as the Turkish Tent, the Chinese Ombrello (both where the High Cross now stands), and a Chinese Alcove, and there still are several more at greater distances. They are the following.

ST PETER'S PUMP, 1¼ m. NW of the house. C15. This was moved from St Peter's Street, Bristol, in 1765. It was placed on a grotto base. It has ogee arches, statues under round arches, and a top pinnacle.

THE CONVENT IN THE WOOD, 1⅜ m. WNW of the house. A picturesquely irregular thatched stone cottage with three turrets. (Inside, painted panels with nuns in the clothes of the various orders and STAINED GLASS from Glastonbury. *Country Life*).

ALFRED'S TOWER, 2⅛ m. WNW of the house, across the Somerset border. 1772. Of brick, triangular, with three round angle projections, one of them containing the staircase and reaching up higher than the rest. The whole height is 160 ft. The tower commemorates the victory of 879 which established the boundary of Saxons and Britons. The details of doorway, inscription plate, and statue of King Alfred in a rustic Gothick taste.

In thinking back of the whole of the grounds of Stourhead and especially the walk round the lake, the reader may agree with the writer that English picturesque landscaping of the C18 is the most beautiful form of gardening ever created, superior in variety and subtlety to the Italy of Frascati and the France of Versailles. It is also of course later, and hence could operate with a greater diversity of plants, including oriental and American species. The aim was an ideal nature, acceptable as nature (and often even today accepted as nature by the layman), but contrived with superior skill and sensibility, and of course with a view entirely to later generations than one's own. This is perhaps the most astonishing thought produced by a day at Stourhead.

STOWELL PARK see WILCOT

STOWFORD FARM see WINGFIELD

STRATFORD SUB CASTLE

1030

That is immediately below Old Sarum, on the w side, by the river Avon.

ST LAWRENCE. Early C13 chancel, see the chancel arch (one slight chamfer) and one blocked N lancet whose jamb has been exposed. Perp nave, see the demi-angels supporting the roof. The roof is a wagon roof with bosses, as is also the chancel roof. Perp the chancel E window too. The W tower was rebuilt in 1711 by 'Tho Pitt Esq. Benefactor', as an inscription in large letters tells us. It is entirely Gothic. The masonry is of flint and stone chequerwork. The windows are of two lights with round-arched heads to the lights. The chequer and the windows repeat in the nave on the N side, and the chancel E end with its bands of flint and stone also looks as if it might have been remodelled. – Much WOODWORK of c.1711, namely the REREDOS, low with an open segmental pediment and fine foliage carving, the COMMUNION RAIL with turned balusters, the centre of the SCREEN with a round arch – on the l. and r. Gothic bits are used – and the chancel PANELLING and STALLS. – The PULPIT is Jacobean and has a fine tester and an HOURGLASS. The pulpit is mentioned as in existence in 1619–20. – WEST GALLERY. Probably of c.1800. Of the three supporting arches, two are ogee. – FONT. Octagonal, C12, of Purbeck marble, with the usual shallow blank arches. – ROYAL ARMS. Lusciously carved; dated 1713. – PLATE. Whole Set, 1712.

OLD VICARAGE, also called MAWARDEN COURT. Elizabethan and Jacobean ashlar front with two projecting gabled wings. Much of this must be an early C19 rebuilding, as the recessed centre is now much narrower than it originally was. Mullioned and transomed windows. In the centre doorway with rusticated jambs. On the lintel the date 1673 and the words: Parva sed apta Domino. Whoever put this on knew his Horace. The garden side of the house is very different. It dates from Thomas

Pitt's time, i.e. *c*.1710. Six bays. Doorway with open segmental pediment. Hipped roof. Original glazing bars. Late C17 gatepiers. The elder Pitt spent much of his childhood here.

PREBENDAL HOUSE, a little to the S. 1700. With a later C18 canted bay window, the upper floor of it treated like a Venetian window. Yet a little further S PARSONAGE FARM, Late Georgian, of five widely-spaced bays and two storeys. Porch on Tuscan columns.

MANOR HOUSE, ¼ m. N. The E half C17, the W half of *c*.1900, at the back, incorporated into it, an C18 cottage. The C17 work is symmetrical. Four-light transomed windows l. and r., doorway and cross-window over in the middle. Two gabled dormers with two-light windows.

0020

STRATFORD TONY

ST MARY AND ST LAWRENCE. The C13 appears in the entrance arch to the N porch, with its roll moulding, and in the piscina of Purbeck marble. Dec chancel with three-light E window (reticulated tracery) and tall straight-headed two-light N and S windows. The chancel arch is double-chamfered and dies into the imposts. The nave must have been rebuilt in the C18. Brick with flint bands. Tall straight-headed two-light windows on the S with slightly medievalizing tops. On the N side the windows are simply segment-headed. Perp W tower, low, with pyramid roof. Perp N doorway. – PEWS, SCREENS, PANELLING, all C17, with small colonnading below the tops. – STAINED GLASS. E window by *Kempe*, 1884. – PLATE. Chalice and Paten, 1731.

STRATFORD TONY HOUSE, to the WNW. C18. Five bays, two storeys, of brick. Pedimented doorway.

ROMAN ROAD. *See* Salisbury, p. 347.

1080

STRATTON ST MARGARET

The village is largely a part of Swindon.

ST MARGARET. Small. Unbuttressed C19 W tower. Late C13 interior. Four-bay arcades with circular piers, pretty circular abaci with dog-tooth, and double-chamfered arches. The chancel arch corresponds. Aisle windows with pointed-trefoiled heads and rounded-trefoiled rere-arches (N) or depressed pointed rere-arches (S). In the N aisle two tomb recesses, ogee-arched, cusped, and with very coarse crocketing. – PLATE.

Elizabethan Chalice, *c.* 1570–5. – MONUMENTS. Tablet to Catherine Hedges † 1649. Nice and entirely classical tablet. – Thomas Read † 1748. Also a good tablet.

DOVECOTE, Pigeonhouse Lane. Square, of stone, *c.*1600.

STUDLEY *see* CALNE, p. 143 and TROWBRIDGE,
pp. 475 and 481

SUTTON BENGER   9070

ALL SAINTS. Unfortunately the church was cruelly restored in 1851 (*J. H. Hakewill*). It would be a very enjoyable church otherwise, especially the S aisle and chapel, which are Dec. The W window is tall, of three lights, with reticulated tracery and a hood-mould with oversized ballflower. Along the S side runs a fleuron frieze. The SE window has two cusped lights and an octofoil over – which is a little earlier than the W window and the prodigious E window. This is of three lights too and has reticulated tracery too, but the units are squashed rather than elongated and very richly cusped. Inside, they have plenty of ballflower. Moreover, the lower part of the middle light is blank and shows to the outside a miniature blank version of the window with buttress-shafts l. and r., and to the inside a canopied niche also with buttress-shafts, i.e. the reredos of the S chapel altar. The original piece stands on the floor in the chapel. To the r. of the window outside an enormous pig gargoyle. A pig's head also at the SW corner. Perp W tower with a niche above the W window, two-light bell-openings with Somerset tracery, panelled battlements, pinnacles, and a bell-spike in the middle. Deep Perp S porch with transverse arches carrying a stone roof. Side windows. The S arcade is of 1851. It replaces a Doric arcade. But is not the W respond, a superb Green Man, at least basically original? If so, it dated from the C13.* – FONT. Circular, Norman, the lower part scalloped. – STAINED GLASS. Chancel E probably of 1851. – EMBROIDERY. A cloth made up of a large number of saints under canopies, all from the orphreys of a chasuble. The date *c.*1500.

MANOR FARMHOUSE. At the back of the wing to the E a large blocked window with a hood-mould and a round arch, as if it were the E wall of a chapel.

RECTORY, E of the church. An older house elaborately gothi-

* The Rev. J. A. G. Haslam tells me of two more Green Men: top of the S aisle E window, outside, and SE corner of the S aisle.

cized, especially by the addition on the street front of a closely buttressed conservatory.

CAUSEWAY with semicircular arches towards the Avon – cf. Kellaways for Maud Heath's Causeway.

SUTTON MANDEVILLE

9020

ALL SAINTS. Mostly by *T. H. Wyatt*, 1862. The w tower, ashlar-faced, is earlier. But is it Perp or post-Reformation? Also, are the late C13 features of the chancel original, including the chancel arch with its triple shafts? – PULPIT. One panel is Jacobean. – SUNDIAL in the churchyard, with ball at the top. Dated 1685. – SCULPTURE. Early C13 relief of the Virgin, quite big, but alas badly battered. The figure is below a trefoil arch on shafts. The child sat in profile. Below a mysterious three-quarter figure with both arms raised to the l. (a Prophet?). – PLATE. Cup, 1576; Paten, 1646; Flagon, 1733.

SUTTON VENY

9040

ST LEONARD. In ruins. The church was of the C13, cruciform, with chamfered arches under the tower and lancets in the chancel. The N doorway is earlier, Norman, with one order of colonnettes and a big lintel. The tympanum has fallen out.

ST JOHN EVANGELIST, a little to the w. By *Pearson*, 1862, in the E.E. style. Impressive, with its crossing tower and spire and its large five-light E and w windows. Rose window in the N transept. Inside, the shock of delight to find Pearson's hallmark, i.e. a chancel and a crossing, rib-vaulted in stone. Quadripartite, i.e. more French than English, vaults. Some dog-tooth enrichment in the chancel. – LECTERN. With an eagle. Shown at the 1862 Exhibition. – PLATE. Paten and Flagon, 1790; Chalice, given in 1792.

SCHOOL. To the w of Pearson's church, also Gothic, of an even later date (1885), but with a gruesome tower. An object lesson in the range of Victorian values.

OLD MANOR HOUSE. In the middle of the house the hall of a C14 house. Simple two-light Dec windows to front and back. The two arched doorways from the former screens passage to buttery or pantry or kitchen survive (wave moulding). The hall roof has collar-beams on arched braces and one set of wind-braces. In the STABLES another window head of the same type as those of the hall. It may be from the solar or the chapel.

SUTTON VENY HOUSE. Stately early C19 house, ashlar-faced, with a central semicircular projection carrying a dome and surrounded by Tuscan columns. Lodge with portico of Tuscan columns.

At the NW entry to the village, SE of Sutton Veny House, an early C18 house of two bays, with pedimented ground-floor windows. L. and r. lower wings, the l. one with C17 windows.

SOUTHLEIGH CASTLE is a ring defensive earthwork, like a motte and bailey without the mound (HR).

SWALLOWCLIFFE

ST PETER. 1842-3 by *Scott & Moffatt*, i.e. the future Sir G. G. Scott, here however still unashamedly Norman, and at the same time equally unashamedly mixing up his Norman with non-Norman motifs, windows, for example, with hood-moulds. S tower with large twin bell-openings and higher stair-turret crowned by a conical spirelet. Narrow aisles. The arcade piers on the N side round, on the S side octagonal. – Neo-Norman FONT with intersected arches on detached shafts. – Neo-Norman stone PULPIT and READER'S DESK. Open arcading. – MONUMENT. Late C14 Knight. In the S porch, behind neo-Norman arches. It comes from the nave of the old church.

MANOR HOUSE. C17. With mullioned and transomed windows. One of four lights on the E side between two large chimney-breasts.

IRON AGE SETTLEMENT, 1 m. S, on Swallowcliffe Down. In 1925, four acres of the site were stripped, revealing 101 pits containing loom-weights, bone combs, La Tène I and II brooches, and Iron Age A pottery.

SWINDON

Swindon is the largest town of Wiltshire, not large as the cities of England go – only 70,000 inhabitants – and nowhere large to look at. It became one town only in 1900. Until then it had been two, Old Swindon and New Swindon, and although they have indivisibly grown together, to the architectural visitor they are still two. By the time New Swindon started on its career, Old Swindon had only about 2,000 inhabitants.

OLD SWINDON

HOLY ROOD, in the grounds of THE LAWN, the former Goddard mansion. The Goddards had come to Swindon from Upper

Upham in 1560. The church is a fragment, the house has gone, even CHURCH FARMHOUSE, built from stones of the church, has gone. What remains is surrounded by barbed wire at the time of writing. The chancel is roofed; of the nave only part of the arcades survives, C14, with double-chamfered arches dying into the octagonal piers. The chancel has round-arched C18 windows, but a blocked arcade of two bays to a former N chapel. This is of *c.*1300 or a little earlier. Short round pier, round abacus with a little dog-tooth decoration, double-chamfered arches. – MONUMENTS. Many tablets in the chancel, not looked after at the time of writing. The best, to Mrs Neate † 1764, is disintegrating.

CHRIST CHURCH, Cricklade Street. By *Sir G. G. Scott*, 1851, the replacement of Holy Rood. Quite big, and externally decidedly without atmosphere. Late C13 style. W tower with broach-spire. Aisles and transepts. Inside, the arches have curious details. Lush foliage capitals.

TOWN HALL, Market Square. It adjoins the old market-house of 1853. This is remarkably purely Grecian for its date. Five bays, two storeys, with giant pilasters and a three-bay pediment. The ground floor was no doubt originally open. To this in 1866 *Wilson & Willcox* added a tall Italianate tower with an open top stage with Venetian windows. The new premises extend at the back and are rock-faced.

PERAMBULATION. The MARKET SQUARE has, facing the Town Hall, a handsome three-bay brick house, Late Georgian, and attached to it on the l. a brick warehouse. This is at the corner of the HIGH STREET, in which the only building worth mentioning is the GODDARD ARMS, long and low, of chequered brick. The continuation of the High Street to the N is CRICKLADE STREET, and here, No. 42, the best house in Swindon by far. It was built in 1729 and is of five bays and two storeys, broad in the proportions. Brick with ample stone dressings, especially broad giant Composite pilasters at the angles, a broad doorway with a segmental pediment on pilasters, a Venetian window with some carving above it, a three-bay pediment with a balustrade for the rest of the roof, and big grotesque keystone heads above the windows. Below the windows brick aprons. The bow windows on the sides of the house are no doubt later. Inside a fine staircase with three slim turned balusters to each step and juicily carved tread-ends.

In WOOD STREET, running off in front of the Goddard Arms, only BOWMAKER HOUSE repays a glance, because of its pretty Late Georgian doorcase. The continuation of Wood Street is BATH ROAD. It starts, at the corner of Victoria Road, with APSLEY HOUSE, now the MUSEUM, a three-bay stone house of *c.*1830, with a Greek Doric porch. Along its older W wall runs PROSPECT PLACE, at the N end of which Nos 59–61, a rustic group of six bays, neglected at the time of writing, but quite loveable with its big segmental pediment and coarsely modelled decoration. The date may be *c.*1840–50. Immediately on in Bath Road three brick houses, each with a graceful cast-iron porch – probably of *c.*1830.

NEW SWINDON

New Swindon, as everyone knows, is the outcome of the Great Western Railway deciding to route the tracks N of Swindon and to establish repair and locomotive works. The station was opened in 1842, the works in the next year; the cottages of the new town were begun soon after. Mr Betjeman has quoted from J. C. Bourne's *History and Description of the Great Western Railway* of 1846 that 'the Company have made arrangements for the erection of three hundred houses'. More on the planning of these will be said in the Perambulation.

ST MARK, Church Place. 1843–5 by *Scott & Moffatt*. The parish church of New Swindon and the railway church, erected by the Company at a cost of £5,500. The church lies immediately W of the locomotive works. In the Dec style, with a tower and crocketed broach-spire, 140 ft high. The tower is to the NW. Spacious interior. The chancel was lengthened and altered by *Temple Moore* in 1897. – He also did the flat-fronted and prettily decorated ORGAN CASE. – STAINED GLASS. The W window apparently of the time of the erection of the church. – S chapel E by *Kempe*, 1897. – Also by him one N aisle window. – The VICARAGE to the W is probably contemporary with the church.

ALL SAINTS, Southbrook. 1937 by *Hartland Thomas*. White brick, with very elongated slender windows and a bell spirelet above the porch.

ST ANDREW, Raleigh Avenue. 1957–8 by *R. J. Beswick & Son*. With the steep, glazed front gable favoured at the time when the church was built.

ST AUGUSTINE, Summers Street, Rodbourne. 1907 by *W. A. H. Masters*. Red brick with Romanesque windows and small, low polygonal apse. No tower.

ST BARNABAS, Cricklade Road, Gorse Hill. 1885 by *J. P. Seddon*.

Rock-faced, with lancet windows. Spirelet between nave and chancel. s porch with provision for a tower, outside the s aisle.

ST LUKE, Broad Street. 1911–12 by *W. A. H. Masters*. Rock-faced with a fancy spirelet on the bellcote and oddly domestic-looking windows, in a style inspired by certain late C17 churches.

ST PAUL, Edgeware Road. 1881 by *Edmund Ferrey*. Brick; in the lancet style, without a tower. Chancel by *John Bevan*, 1883.

HOLY ROOD (R.C.), Groundwell Road. 1905 by *E. Doran Webb* (GR). Flint, with a low, broad crossing tower. A good piece of grouping.

BAPTIST TABERNACLE, Regent Street. 1886 by *W. H. Read* (perhaps with *R. J. Beswick*). Large (cost £6,000) and still remarkably purely classical, in spite of its date. Impressive giant portico of six Tuscan columns carrying a pediment.

QUEEN'S DRIVE METHODIST CHURCH, Whitbourne Avenue. 1959 by *W. H. Cripps*. Modern no doubt, but almost a caricature of motifs fashionable in the 1950s.

TOWN HALL, Regent Circus. 1889–91 by *Brightwen Binyon* of Ipswich. Cost: £9,000. Quite large. Brick, with an asymmetrically placed tower. In a vaguely C17 Dutch style.

CIVIC OFFICES, Euclid Street. 1936–8.

RAILWAY MUSEUM, *see* Perambulation, p. 460.

WALCOT BRANCH LIBRARY. 1958 by *J. L. Morgan*. A very nice little composition with the attached community hall. The group lies on one side of the shopping centre (*see* p. 460).

MECHANICS' INSTITUTION, Emlyn Square. 1892, Tudor style. (*See* also Perambulation, p. 459.)

TECHNICAL COLLEGE, Victoria Road, overlooking Regent Circus. 1956–8 by *Charles Pike & Partners*. Tall, long, modern slab. Curtain walling. At two levels two symmetrically placed loggias are inserted. In line with them on top two symmetrical tanks.

OLD TECHNICAL COLLEGE, Victoria Road. 1897 by *Silcock & Reay*. Brick, with symmetrically placed Dutch gables.

COLLEGE STREET SCHOOL. 1873. Gothic, symmetrical, yellow brick with red and blue brick trim.

PRINCESS MARGARET HOSPITAL, Okus Road. Begun in 1957 by *Powell & Moya*. The hospital is to cover about 22 acres and to have about 800 beds in the end. To the E of the low present part a high block of wards is going up. Further to the E will be more wards, and to the N a nurses' school, a nurses' hostel, etc. The first stage of *c*. 250 by 300 ft, completed in 1959, deals mainly with outpatients and casualties. The lie of the land makes this range partly single-storeyed, partly two-storeyed. The upper parts are for external, the lower for internal traffic. The architecture is very pure and precise, but saved from rigidity by the grouping and detailing, especially of the inner courtyards. Frame of reinforced concrete, faced with slate. Aluminium windows, sill-zones of white glass. At the time of going to press the second stage is under construction, i.e. the five- to seven-storey block of wards already referred to, a one-storey block for kitchens etc., another as the nurses' training school, and three-storey hostel blocks connected by covered ways.

FIRE STATION, County Road, by the roundabout. 1959 by *F. I. Bowden*, the county architect.

STATION. 1841–2. Two long buildings, 170 ft long, on the platforms. They are of stone, still in a Late Classical style and of considerable dignity. The ground floors were entirely first- and second-class refreshment rooms. All trains stopped at Swindon for ten minutes, and the catering was at first placed in the hands of the proprietor of the Queen's Hotel in Cheltenham. The upper floors of the platform buildings were a hotel. Short outer iron staircases in two arms, with very fat, cast-iron posts.

PERAMBULATION. Opposite the station the QUEEN'S HEAD, of the same time as the railway. Stone, of three bays, with a sturdy porch. Immediately W of the station are the LOCOMOTIVE WORKS. Their main entrance, leading to a long tunnel under the line, is in axis with that of the NEW TOWN. The new town was built about 1850 etc. In 1853, 243 cottages had been erected. Tradition ascribes the design to *Sir Matthew Digby Wyatt*. Swindon New Town is one of the few planned Victorian estates, small and modest and laid out without ingenuity, but planned all the same, and architecturally as orderly as is the design of the streets. The estate lies between the locomotive works and Farringdon Road and between East Street and Church Place. The streets inside this parallelogram run E–W, with one cross-axis: Emlyn Square. All houses are arranged in terraces, and all houses are of stone, which adds considerably to the dignity of the estate. Towards the outside the terraces have vaguely Elizabethan gables, towards the streets they are still just like Georgian terraces – details excepted. The centre of the estate is the MECHANICS' INSTITUTION, built in 1853–4 to the design of *Edward Roberts*, but largely rebuilt in

1892 (*see* above, p. 458). The front towards the entrance of the locomotive works has two turrets. At the back was the market hall. In Bristol Street a former SCHOOL, 1845, stone-faced too, but in the C13 Gothic style. s of the Mechanics' Institution, facing into Farringdon Road, also stone-faced the RAILWAY MUSEUM, built in the 1840s as a lodging-house for Irish workmen. Then a lodging-house for engine crews, and in the 1860s a Methodist chapel. Façade with two turrets.

The rest of Swindon is brick and has little to offer. All that deserves visiting lies outside the town proper. It can be divided between ancient and very recent.

Of ancient houses there remain the following:

WESTLECOT MANOR, off the w end of Westlecot Road. Dated 1589. The mullioned windows all renewed. Above the doorway a lintel with naive triglyphs and a hood-mould on lozenge-shaped stops.

RODBOURNE MANOR HOUSE and MANOR FARM, *see* Rodbourne Cheney, p. 343.

The C20 developments worth mentioning are:

PINEHURST ESTATE. By *Parker & Unwin*, 1919 etc., planned round a circular green.

WALCOT, E of Queen's Drive. The centre of this recent estate is The Walcot, an attractive pedestrian shopping square, by the borough architect *J. Loring Morgan*. Three-storeyed houses of pale brick with shops on two sides, the Common Room and Branch Library (*see* p. 458) opposite. Nice paving, with square flower beds and cobbled squares. Also an unusually big sarsen stone as a monument.

CHENEY MANOR ESTATE, Rodbourne. Many of the factories of this trading estate are of the kind just using the motifs fashionable at the moment. The best are SEMICONDUCTORS of 1957–8 (by *H. Stanley Smith*), with an entirely windowless aluminium front, REMPLOY of 1958 (by *E. N. Bailey & Partners*), and the more extensive works of the PLESSEY CO. by *J. Loring Morgan*.

PRESSED STEEL COMPANY. Large factory E of Gorse Hill. 1957–62 by *H. W. Weedon & Partners*.

COATE WATER. A lake 72 acres in size, formed in 1822 as a reservoir for the Wilts and Berks Canal. Close to it COATE FARM, C17, where Jefferies, the naturalist and Wiltshire writer, was born.

DAY FARM STONE CIRCLE, s of Coate. This circle, discovered

by Richard Jefferies, now consists of only nine recumbent stones.

PREHISTORIC REMAINS. Three crouched inhumation burials in flat graves, each accompanied by a long-necked beaker, were found at Okus Quarries in 1906. The same area appears to have been settled in Early Iron Age times, judging by the discovery of loom-weights in a storage pit at Okus and an Iron Age C bead rim pot in a neighbouring pit. The Purbeck and Portland stones of the quarry were probably worked by the Romans, and the remains of a Roman building were discovered in Westlecot Road in the C19. It included a small hypocaust and two small rooms with plastered and painted walls. On the site of the building were three Romano-British burials.

SYRENCOT HOUSE *see* FIGHELDEAN

TEFFONT EVIAS   9030

CHURCH. 1824–6 by *Charles Fowler*, with a steeple 125 ft tall. It is an impressive steeple, and indeed an impressive church, rising on the lawn of the Manor House. Its spire is surrounded at the foot by polygonal pinnacles. The tower windows and bell-openings have Somerset tracery. Medieval parts were used. In fact the visible masonry of nave and chancel is all old. The old w end had a bell-turret, and this was supported on an arch across from buttress to buttress above the w window, as if it had been the arch between a nave and a tower. It gives the w side an untidy look. The windows of 1825 are Perp of two and three lights. Inside it can also be seen that the N chapel is at least pre-C19. The arcade is of two bays, the piers of a Perp section (four shafts and four hollows), but the capitals typically 'debased', i.e. probably Elizabethan or C17. These details Fowler took over for his N arcade, chancel arch, and chapel w arch. – PAINTING. Sgraffito of the Angelic Choir by *Baron de Triqueti* (1804–74), in what was to be the 'Studio' style. – STAINED GLASS. Bits, whole roundels, and other pieces in all windows. – PLATE. Flagon, 1572; Cup, 1576; Paten, 1693. – MONUMENTS. Stone effigy of Henry Ley † 1574 and stone effigies of two of his sons † 1624 and † 1632. The father lies higher, and the effigy seems older indeed. But the tomb-chest in one.

MANOR HOUSE. An impressive flat front of four bays with regularly spaced four- and three-light windows, those on the first floor with transoms. Battlements at the top. A big buttress runs up the middle. Originally there were two doorways, also placed symmetrically. One room has preserved its panelling. The house seems to be early C17. Behind, Victorian outbuildings with two towers.

RECTORY. By *Scott*, 1842. Large, gabled, Tudor.

Pretty village of stone cottages by a stream.

₉₀₃₀ ## TEFFONT MAGNA

CHURCH. Nave and chancel in one; double bell niche in the gable. No chancel arch, but the chancel has a plastered ceiling (early C19?), lower than the nave roof. – CROSS SHAFT. Anglo-Saxon, with interlace, dated by Sir Thomas Kendrick late C9. – SCREEN. Perp, thin, of one-light divisions. – BELL. A late C13 bell kept on a window-sill. – PLATE. Paten of the late C15 or early C16 with the monogram of Christ; Cup, 1571.

A pretty village by a little stream. The best house is FITZ HOUSE, dated 1700, yet with its gable and four-light mullioned windows still entirely C17 in style.

THORNE FARMHOUSE *see* DONHEAD ST ANDREW

THROOPE FARMHOUSE *see* BISHOPSTONE, p. 106

₂₀₅₀ ## TIDCOMBE

ST MICHAEL. Flint and rubble. Mostly Dec, except for the short (C16?) W tower embraced by the aisles. The windows mostly ogee-headed, including the clerestory. Humble N porch of brick, dated 1675. Dec S aisle of two bays with octagonal piers and double-chamfered arches. Perp N aisle with the same features. The capital has leaf decoration. – TILES. Some in a recess in the E wall of the N aisle. – PLATE. Chalice, 1727. – MONUMENT. Thomas Rendall † 1831. Black plate, and on it an urn for him and around it suspended shields for other members of the family. By *Osmond* of Salisbury.

(MANOR HOUSE, N of the church. Five bays, two storeys, hipped roof, a one-bay pediment, and a pedimented doorway. Devizes Museum, MM)

₀₀₄₀ ## TILSHEAD

ST THOMAS OF CANTERBURY. Flint and stone, partly in chequer pattern, a custom in the houses around here as well.

Flint and stone bands are as popular. The church has a low E.E. central tower (with a curiously twice-altered s window) and an E.E. chancel. Lancets and an E window of three stepped lancets. The NW and SW lancets are small and 'low-side'. That on the S side has no glass and its original wooden shutter. Rere-arches here and in others of them of timber. The S aisle has two later C13 windows with plate tracery. The N aisle wall is of 1846, when the aisle was considerably widened. The clerestory has small quatrefoil windows, more probably Dec than Perp. Inside, earlier evidence. Norman arcades of three bays with square piers, only slightly bevelled, and completely unmoulded arches. Is that especially early or especially far from civilization? The W and E arches of the tower are E.E., with simple imposts and arches of one slight and one normal chamfer. – FONT. Circular, Norman, fluted, with bands with diagonal incisions above and below. – COMMUNION RAIL. C18. – SCULPTURE. E.E. cross-head (or boss?) found in the original N aisle wall. – PLATE. Cup and Paten Cover, 1787.

(TILSHEAD LODGE. Centre late C18 with loggia and some Venetian windows. Parapet with garlands. NBR)

THE OLD DITCH, ½ m. S. Unchambered long barrow. Nearly 400 ft long, it is the largest long barrow in England. Excavated in the C19. At the NE end an inhumation and cremation beneath a cairn of flints.

TINHEAD HILL see EDINGTON

TISBURY

9020

St JOHN BAPTIST. The largest church in its part of Wiltshire, provided with a prominent crossing tower whose upper part is a replacement after a spire had fallen in 1762. Obelisk pinnacles. That is the youngest constituent feature of the church; the oldest is the arches of the crossing, low and narrow compared with the scale which surrounds them.* Semicircular responds with three attached shafts. The shafts carry coarse trumpet-scallop capitals, intended perhaps to be carved later. The arches are pointed and have one chamfer and one half-roll each side. Quadripartite rib-vault with mouldings of one strong and two thin rolls. All this points to the ending C12, and the corbel-table outside the E wall of the N transept may be contemporary.

* Older still the four small re-set Norman capitals in the walls of the nave inside.

By the time the crossing tower received its lower stage the year
1250 was passed. Twin bell-openings with angle-shafts with
shaft-rings and Y-tracery and in the tympanum a tiny quatrefoil (W and E) or (S) a concave-sided lozenge. Of about the same
time or a little earlier the small lancet in the W wall of the S aisle,
proof of the existence of a narrow C13 S aisle. A little earlier is
the more likely answer; for the two-storeyed N porch is certainly
of the early C13. Entrance with shafts, one still carrying a
decorated trumpet capital, the other a stiff-leaf capital.
Pointed arch; lancet N window. Pointed tunnel-vault inside.
N doorway also with one order of shafts. Depressed two-
centred arch with three continuous roll mouldings. What the
chancel of the C13 was like is unknown. All the window tracery
is C19, and the E window, e.g., originally had seven, not five,
lights. The chancel was built with a separate triple-chamfered
chancel arch E of that of the late C12. The chamfers die into the
imposts. Wide and airy interior. Ogee-arched piscina rising a
little above the sill of the SE window. S transept built above a
bone-hole. The N transept was made the Lady Chapel in 1299.
After that it was no doubt remodelled as we now see it, i.e.
also in the Dec style. N window with reticulated tracery. In the
E window of three cusped, stepped lancet lights the middle
light is blank in its lower part but pierced by two simple
reticulation units. Inside, against this background, an image
niche with a coarse nodding ogee arch. The very tall niches l.
and r. of the window inside, each with space for two images one
on top of the other, are Perp. The one to the S is especially
lavishly decorated. Perp also the arcades of the nave. Four
bays. Stone piers with four shafts and four hollows. The
capitals of the shafts round and not polygonal, which makes the
later C14 a probable date. Wide double-chamfered arches
from the aisles to the transepts. Perp aisle windows, straight-
headed. W doorway and S doorway of two continuous chamfers.
W porch with stone seats. The upper part of the W front is late
C18. The ROOFS of the church (except that of the chancel) are
a delight. The nave roof, high up (on a renewed clerestory), is a
wagon roof with three (plus the two end-) pairs of hammerbeams. They have horizontal angels attached to them. This is a
C15 roof. The aisle roofs are later. They are ceiled, and the
ceilings have moulded and decorated beams (fleurons and
tracery) and in the panels St Andrew's crosses. In the N aisle
only the W half is so decorated. The E half was damaged when
the spire fell. This roof has an inscription recording Edward

Scamell and John Wakes with the year 1535, and then 1560 as the year when 'this hele (aisle) was set up' by Edward Bole and Blanche Bole. The s aisle roof is very similar, and that is dated 1616 and perpetuates the name of the donor, Lord Arundell, and of two churchwardens, one being another Edward Scamell.

FURNISHINGS. FONT COVER. C17, with Flamboyant, i.e. Gothic-Revival, decoration. – REREDOS. Presented in 1884. The design by *E. Christian*, the terracotta relief by *George Tinworth*. The surroundings are of alabaster. – COMMUNION RAIL. Made up of the dainty tracery tops of the lights of a Perp screen. – PULPIT. Jacobean, with flat arabesque carving. – PEWS. A handsome, simple Jacobean pattern. On the ends small shell-lunettes. Arabesque panels in fronts and backs. – HELM of the first Lord Arundell. – PLATE. Chalice, 1632; Chalice, 1635; two Flagons, 1685 and 1695; Almsdish, 1704.– MONUMENTS. In the N transept N wall small tomb recess. – In the s aisle re-set brasses of a Civilian and wife, *c.*1520. 25-in. figures. – Laurence Hyde † 1590 and family. Brass plate with the whole family standing.

ZION HILL CONGREGATIONAL CHURCH, Cuffs Lane. Built in 1842. A broad grey stone building with angle pinnacles, a front with stepped gable, a porch in this front also with stepped gable, and E.E. (plate) tracery in some of the windows.

CONGREGATIONAL CHURCH, High Street. Said to be of 1726. The front windows have been altered. Can the small mullioned windows and the cross-windows at the back be original, i.e. C17 survival?

PERAMBULATION. We can start by the church, the station, and the early C19 three-arch BRIDGE across the Nadder. w of the church VICAR'S COTTAGES, a row of the C17 with the upper floor of 1887. The HIGH STREET leads up the hill. It has few houses of interest. First, at the corner of Park Road, GASTON HOUSE, T-shaped, mostly late C16 or early C17, but with an early C16 window in the w front. (Big stone fireplace in the hall with carved decoration.) Higher up on the l. OLD HOUSE, with mullioned windows. At the top the street turns w, and here TISBURY HOUSE, early C19, of ashlar, three bays and two storeys. Porch with unfluted Ionic columns.

w of the Congregational Church in Cuffs Lane an early C18 SUMMERHOUSE. Arched entrance and circular windows l. and r. Heavy keystones, entirely unmoulded.

PLACE FARM. Place Farm is the remarkable survival of a grange

of the nunnery of Shaftesbury, farmhouse, barn, and outbuildings. It dates from the C14 and C15. The grange like a castle has
an outer and an inner gatehouse. The OUTER GATEHOUSE has
an archway roomy enough for wagons and a pedestrian entry.
Big buttresses and buttressed wall continuing the gatehouse.
The archway has one chamfer and one big convex moulding.
Above the pedestrian entrance a tiny two-light window. To the
yard (the 'outer bailey') two two-light windows. The INNER
GATEHOUSE leads to the house itself. This gatehouse is of the
late C15. It must have gone on to the W. It has two two-light
windows, and only one small entry passage. The HOUSE is of
the late C15 too. It runs S–N, and the N half is in a better state.
This was part of the HALL, but has later been horizontally subdivided. The hall roof has collar-beams on arched braces,
curved struts, and curved wind-braces. The fireplace is over
13 ft wide. The smoke goes out by a charming polygonal
chimneystack with a spirelet. At the S end of the house big
chimneybreast.

The BARN is also C15 work. It is the largest barn in England,
nearly 200 ft long. It is, like all the rest, of stone. Internally it is
divided into thirteen bays. Two tiers of collar-beams, the lower
ones with arched braces forming round arches. Three tiers of
wind-braces. Large porch entrances in the middles of both long
sides. The barn is thatched – 1,450 square yards of thatching, as
Mr Clifton-Taylor has calculated. Much of the walling of the
other barn is also of before the end of the nunnery.

LOWER CHICKSGROVE MANOR, 1¾ m. ENE. Elizabethan or
Jacobean, thatched, with a two-storeyed gabled porch and a
gabled r. wing. Mullioned windows.

PYT HOUSE. *See* Newtown, p. 319.

HATCH HOUSE. *See* Newtown, p. 320.

TOCKENHAM

ST GILES. Small, of nave and chancel. Bell-turret with shingled
spire. The E window is of course Victorian (restoration 1876).
C13 nave, see the S window with trefoil-cusped lights and a
trefoiled circle, and the W front with a middle buttress, and l.
and r. lancets. Inside, the bell-turret stands on old posts, and
they are flanked by (new?) timber-framed work. – FONT.
Norman, tub-shaped. Below scallops, above flat little arches. –
SCULPTURE. In the S wall W of the porch a Roman figure of
Aesculapius. – PLATE. Chalice and Paten given in 1681. –

MONUMENTS. Mrs Goddard Smith † 1726. Frontal bust in relief in a freely shaped medallion. L. and r. obelisks with black oval tablets hanging on them. – Goddard Smith's Ancestors, mid-C18. Handsome tablet of coloured marbles.

MEADOW COURT, ¼ m. W. Of brick, dated (rainwater heads) 1730. Seven bays with a three-bay pediment and quoins. Odd ornament on the window lintels. Panelled parapet. Doorway with open segmental pediment on brackets. Earlier work behind. Behind the house big SUMMER HOUSE, the size of an orangery. Five bays, brick, with tall wooden cross-windows and a hipped roof.

TOCKENHAM MANOR, 1 m. N. L-shaped manor house, the E wing of the first years of the C20, the S wing dated on the finial of the porch 1608, but perhaps a little earlier. June Badeni refers to a will of 1602 in which the house is called recently built. Two gables and gabled central porch. Inside, some panelling and wooden chimney surrounds; but the interior also much changed when the E wing was built. What remains of before the C20 includes a mid-C18 chimneypiece and some mid-C18 door surrounds. To the W of the S wing an early C18 brick addition with hipped roof and original panelling. The windows altered in the C20. Good late C18 chimneypiece. To the E of the E wing a late C17 house with two steep gables. In the gables characteristic upright oval windows. To the N of this house small C18 stables of brick. To the SW of the manor house timber-framed thatched BARN, the walls with brick infilling.

(TOCKENHAM COURT FARM. Built in two stages, both first half of the C18. J. Badeni: *Wiltshire Forefathers*)

TOLLARD ROYAL

ST PETER AD VINCULA. Much renewed, the chancel all but rebuilt, the N aisle added before 1871. In the nave two late C13 windows, one of one light with pointed trefoil head, the other of two such lights with a pointed trefoil in primitive plate tracery. The aisle was later heightened and a straight-headed Perp window set in. – PAINTING. Texts, cartouches, etc., of the C17 discovered in 1961. – STAINED GLASS. N aisle E signed by *Bertini* of Milan, 1867. More Nazarene than the English were in the sixties. – PLATE. Set of 1786. – MONUMENTS. Cross-legged Knight of the early C14, his head on pillows of unusual shape. – Robert Barber † 1686 and his wife † 1720. Marble tablet. – General Pitt-Rivers † 1900. Neo-Elizabethan.

The territory of Tollard Royal and Rushmore and of Farnham across the Dorset border is Pitt-Rivers country. A. H. Lane Fox Pitt-Rivers was a very remarkable man. He came from Yorkshire and assumed the name Pitt-Rivers on inheriting from Lord Rivers, his great-uncle. He rose to be a general, but got interested in the efficiency of rifles, then the development of rifles, then the development of weapons, the development of tools, and so in the application of the topical theories of evolution to human activities of all kinds. His London house became a museum, and he presented the collection to Oxford University in 1883. He had moved to Rushmore in 1880 and there began to study prehistory. His technique of excavation created a new standard for Britain and is still admired. He assembled another collection and made the museum at Farnham in Dorset out of it. He published five volumes on his excavations, a book on primitive locks and keys, and one on Benin art. In all he did he considered the common man and what ought to interest him and what would be of benefit to him – as we shall see presently.

KING JOHN'S HOUSE. This memorable house consists of a centre of *c.*1240 with a medieval NW addition remodelled in the later C16, a medieval SW addition of which only foundations are known, and a timber-framed E range projecting N and S. This range replaces the solar wing of the C13 house. The kitchen etc. must have been to the W. The C13 house had as its centre the hall, which was on the upper floor. This period is represented by the following features. On the ground floor two slit windows to the S with depressed arches, as nearly all the arches are. One slit window to the W as well. Also one large five-light Elizabethan window. On the first floor two of the hall windows, twin with simply moulded imposts to the responds and the intermediate shaft. Again depressed arches. Inside, seats in the reveals. The windows are not in line with those below. Nor is the small window to the W. To its r. is an aumbry. The hall is now divided into two rooms. The wooden Elizabethan chimneypiece is not part of the house. The following doorways led on to other apartments: one to the N, leading to the present staircase in the medieval NW projection – it probably always led to the staircase; one to the W near the SW corner, leading into the former SW extension; and two to the E, leading no doubt into the upper private rooms of the solar wing. The house belonged to General Pitt-Rivers, and at the time was open to the public, and not for money-making reasons.

RUSHMORE. The General's house. It is large and looks Late Georgian to Early Victorian. The interior, especially the DINING ROOM, was originally decorated by *Morris & Co*. Several canted bay windows. No fancy work externally. In the garden the large TEMPLE OF VESTA, a rotunda with Corinthian columns. Also other ornaments. Picturesque Late Victorian S and N LODGES, with half-timber work. Opposite the North Lodge the JUBILEE ROOM, really the chapel provided reluctantly by the General for his tenants. It does not look like a chapel anyway. Large double-transomed window to the S. Bargeboarded gable. Small open lantern.

LARMER GROUNDS. A larmer tree is probably a wych-elm. The larmer tree S of Tollard Royal was by tradition the tree where King John met his huntsmen. It does not stand any longer, but what remains of it is inside the pleasure grounds which General Pitt-Rivers made 'for the recreation of the people in the neighbouring towns and villages'. What that meant is that the General built a Temple in 1880 overlooking a formal pool, a house for the caretaker at the entrance in 1881 (half-timber), and then gradually six so-called 'Quarters', i.e. houses for parties to picnic in. The quarters were built in an Indian style around a central space with laurel hedges and formal paths. A bandstand was also provided, and a theatre followed in 1895, i.e. a kind of exedra. The grounds were 'open every day gratis'. The caretaker went about in a 'survival of a dress worn by the Chase (i.e. Cranborne Chase) keeper'. For picnics crockery and cutlery was offered gratis, but no alcoholic liquor was allowed. The band were sixteen workmen on the estate. They played every Sunday from three to five. For parties they had to be paid and the attendants tipped. It was a noble venture, and in 1887 15,000, in 1893 24,000 visited the grounds. After the General's death it all began to decay, but in the last ten years the present squire has taken it up again. Some buildings, e.g. the bandstand and some quarters, could not be saved. Others were repaired with pieces from those beyond redemption. The laurel hedges have grown high and are untrimmed. The pond is made picturesque and informal. The THEATRE, a classical piece built of timber, with two giant Corinthian pilasters, has a newly-painted back-cloth.* Also displayed on a rocky mound is a fine Japanese bronze horse.

ASHCOMBE, 1¾ m. NW. In a wonderfully secluded place, down

---

* The back of the exedra and the walls behind the scenes are still painted with a kind of Norman-Byzantine architecture.

from the downs into a sheltered hollow. Of the mansion of the Barbers rebuilt before 1740, and later passed on to the Arundells, only a three-bay fragment remains. But the ORANGERY is there, combined with the GATEHOUSE. The archway has a Gibbs surround on a pediment. The orangery continues it to the E: five bays and then a wing projecting by three bays and ending in a Venetian window.

2060

TOTTENHAM HOUSE
Savernake Forest

Savernake has been a royal forest ever since the Conquest. The wardens were first a sequence of members of the Esturmy family, then, from 1427 to 1675, the Seymours, then the Bruces and Brudenell-Bruces (earls and marquesses of Ailesbury and earls of Cardigan). Much of the forest was emparked by the Seymours, but Thomas Lord Bruce, Earl of Ailesbury in the early C18, made the land partly agricultural, partly commercial woodland. His son Charles married the sister of Lord Burlington, the amateur architect. Under Charles the impressive beech avenues were planted, especially the Grand Avenue, which was continued by his successor Thomas Brudenell, Lord Bruce († 1814). Of the house Aubrey in 1672 speaks as of 'a most complete pile of good architecture' replacing Wolf Hall (see p. 138), which had largely been ruined within the last two years. Then *Lord Burlington* remodelled or rebuilt this house in the 1720s and 30s, but of his efforts hardly anything remains.*

The present mansion, one of the largest in Wiltshire, was built for Charles Brudenell-Bruce, Earl (later Marquess) of Ailesbury, in 1825 by *Thomas Cundy*, at a cost (including the furnishings) of about £250,000. It consists of a main block of seventeen bays connected by quadrant wings with outer pavilions. The quadrants were embellished in 1870. The house is of ashlar stone throughout and has a basement and one and a half storeys, raised in the five-bay centre by another half-storey. To the W are wings projecting by three bays and leading on to

---

* Lord Burlington's house, as illustrated in a Buckler drawing of 1806 and in *The Beauties of England and Wales* in 1821, had a five-bay centre and angle bays with raised erections of the Wilton–Holkham–Lydiard Tregoze type. The centre had a portico of six unfluted Ionic giant columns standing above a plain ground floor. There were two wings as well. As Lord Cardigan has pointed out convincingly, one room now lying behind the main rooms of the s front still has its Burlington details, such as the door surrounds.

the quadrants, and in the centre a giant portico of unfluted Ionic columns, to the E a one-storeyed portico or veranda of four pairs of the same columns. They also repeat in the outer pavilions, of which the S one is the Orangery. The design is very restrained, and more Palladian than Grecian. The windows of the main floor have pediments.

The house is entered by a spacious ENTRANCE HALL, continued in the main axis across by the extremely tall STAIR-CASE HALL. The staircase has a cast-iron handrail and runs up to the first floor. There is a balcony all round here, and the balcony is repeated on the top floor. Large square glazed top-light. The E wall of the staircase well is arched and leads into a kind of garden loggia behind the veranda already referred to. The main rooms have excellent fireplaces, some of white marble and already turning to the ponderous heaviness of the Victorian style, others in dark coloured marbles and with bronze mounting in the Empire style. There are also fine patterned parquet floors and heavily coffered ceilings. Spe-cially interesting is the SE corner, with a small groin-vaulted lobby and a marble bathroom with a marble bath in the form of an oblong Roman urn.

STABLES. A large ashlar-faced quadrangle with a nine-bay front. The centre is a coffered archway with a lantern. The stables were designed by *Cundy* too, and built before the house, in 1818.

The GROUNDS were laid out by *Capability Brown*.

(SUMMER HOUSE, in the forest. Octagonal; now a fodder-store. MHLG) This is by *Lord Burlington*, according to a drawing at Chatsworth (John Harris), and was one of two such pavilions.

COLUMN. On the axis of the house, 1½ m. to the NW. Erected by the Earl of Ailesbury in 1781. The column is unfluted, with an Ionic capital, a drum above it, and a bronze urn at the top. *See p. 577*

TOW BARROW *see* GRAFTON

TRAFALGAR HOUSE *1020*

Trafalgar House, or, as it was then called, Standlynch, was built in 1733 for Sir Peter Vandeput, a city man whose ancestors had immigrated under Queen Elizabeth. His sister was married to *Roger Morris*, carpenter, principal engineer to the Board of Ordnance, and, as we know from Wilton and Goodwood, an architect as well. He may be regarded as the designer of the house of 1733 which is the centre of the present house. After Vandeput's death the house went to Henry Dawkins. For him *John Wood the Younger* of Bath added the wings and *Nicholas Revett* the elaborate porch. Dawkins's brother had been with Robert Wood to Asia Minor and Athens and had financed Athenian Stuart's and Revett's stay and study at Athens. Henry Dawkins too was a member of the Society of Dilettanti.

The centre of the house is a rather uncompromising block of brick with stone dressings, seven bays wide and two and a half storeys high, with the half-storey above the cornice. Both main fronts, E, the entrance side, and W, the garden side, have Gibbs surrounds to the windows. So has the E doorway. To the garden there is a three-bay pediment, and the doorway has Tuscan columns, a metope frieze, and a segmental pediment. To the entrance there is Revett's porch, hiding the centre of the ground floor. It is a complicated composition, stepping forward in the centre, where there is a pediment, and with the columns grouped in pairs. There are fourteen columns altogether, and they are of the rare Greek Doric kind, where fluting only shows right at the top and right at the bottom – imitating the unfinished late C4 columns of the Temple of Apollo on Delos. This is one of the earliest uses of a Grecian order in England* and as such memorable, even if the composition is entirely un-Grecian. The end pavilions are very substantial, three by nine bays, and two-storeyed, and are connected with the house by corridor links. The total length of the house is about 300 ft.

The interior is not of one date. The STAIRCASE alone is convincingly of 1733, large, with a spacious open well, a bold curve at the start for which the corner below was filled in, a hand-rail with three slender balusters to each tread and carved tread-ends, and a Palladian or Jonesian stucco ceiling. In the HALL as the centre of the overmantel is indeed a medallion with a bust of Inigo Jones, but the termini caryatids flanking the overmantel and the rich stucco decoration of the coved ceiling point to the forties or even fifties rather than the thirties. The hall is a cube, also a Jonesian conceit, and has giant pilasters. In the panels between them garlands under little Chinese baldacchinos. The SALOON also has giant pilasters and a Rococo ceiling. The SE room has big, continuous wall paintings crowding the whole walls above the dado. They were painted by *Cipriani* in 1766 and represent the Arts. In the NW

53a

* The very first is Stuart's Doric Temple at Hagley, which dates from 1758.

corner is the LIBRARY with a handsome chimneypiece with symbols of art and learning in the frieze.

In the end pavilions there are principal rooms too. In the s pavilion is the DINING ROOM. The broad Venetian window has cast-iron columns inside, decorated at the bottom and with figures at the top. In the N pavilion is a handsome small LOBBY with four Roman Doric columns set in the corners, *Revett* rather than Wood. The adjoining room with the Venetian window corresponding to that of the dining room has a circular centre motif in the stucco of the ceiling.

Standlynch was given by the nation to Nelson's heirs in 1814. Hence its name Trafalgar House. Of that time the Ganges Room on the top floor, with fluted pilasters and panels from the bow of the *Ganges*.

The gardens were originally laid out by *Charles Bridgeman*. CHURCH. At the bottom, close to the river, ¼ m. SW of the house, is the old church. It was built in 1677 and consists of nave and chancel only. Flint and stone in chequer pattern. Gables on big coping-stones. The windows with arched cusped lights look C19 rather than C17. The two niches l. and r. of the chancel arch must be medieval – of the C14. The W window could be C14 too. – MONUMENTS. Mrs Joan Bockland † 1689. Tablet with bow-front. Two blank columns with white capitals l. and r., open scrolly pediment with garlands. – Thomas Nelson. By *Osmond*, 1839. Standing monument in the Gothic style. Tomb-chest, recess, arch, canopy.

TROWBRIDGE*

8050

Trowbridge is the county town of Wiltshire, but that is hardly noticeable. In size, with its 15,000 inhabitants, it is smaller than it seems, with the A-road traffic stampeding through it. Its tradition goes far back. It had a castle s of the Wicker Hill–Fore Street line. The town grew along that line and expanded by a parallel line further N, now Back Street–Church Street. The two are connected by Hill Street on the W and Silver Street on the SE and embrace the church. Trowbridge is a clothiers' town, but of the cloth trade of the Middle Ages there is no visible evidence left, except of course for the church. The trade is still much in evidence. The best houses are of *c.*1700–1800, and some of them are of a startling size. In fact Trowbridge is as rich in Georgian houses as Bradford-on-Avon. In the course of the Georgian century the

---

* Information kindly communicated to me by Mr K. Rogers is marked KR. It will be evident at once how much I owe him for his help.

change took place from weavers' cottages to mills. Specific working-class housing also came in in the early C19. The population of Trowbridge grew by 3,500 between 1811 and 1821. Trowbridge is a compact town, with the church in the middle, but hidden from the main street. A perambulation will have to be conducted with circumspection to make any sense.

ST JAMES. Large and Perp throughout, if it were not for the distressing fact that in 1847–8 a restoration took place which included the rebuilding of chancel, S chapel, both arcades, and the clerestory. However, the restorers, *Manners & Gill*, seem to have copied accurately. As for the original dates, John Wykes in 1460 left goods and money to the works in hand (KR), and James Terumber, who died in 1483, left more. W tower with recessed spire. Deep W porch with battlements and pinnacles and inside a panelled four-centred tunnel-vault. Clerestory with battlements and pinnacles and three-light windows. Seven bays along the long sides. The N chapel has four-light windows and a seven-light E window, and, of course, battlements and pinnacles. Two-storeyed N porch. It has a two-centred arch with traceried spandrels and a fan-vault inside. Chancel embattled, with pinnacles. The E window is of 1846–8. The S side similar to the N side, but richer: the S porch has, for example, above the entrance a small ogee gable, flanked by buttress-shafts. Two niches l. and r. of the upper window. Stair-turret with spire. Recent vault inside. The aisles embrace the tower.

26b   The interior looks distressingly new. Five bays, slender piers with four shafts and four waves between. The N capitals octagonal and with foliage in high relief, the S capitals round and with flat foliage. Wide arches, 'lightsum', as Leland says. The same mouldings in the chancel arch and in the one-bay chapel arches and their W arches. In the N chapel, not now visible, a fine stone tunnel-vault. Between the clerestory windows niches with nodding ogee canopies flanked by coupled triangular buttress-shafts. Under the tower a fan-vault. Panelled and shafted arch to the nave. Lower panelled arches to the W bays of the aisles. Arches also from these to the E. The pretty nave roof with its gay panelling is said to be original, but restored in 1847. The latter is probably the date of the chancel roof. In the vestry a late C14 fireplace.

FONT. Octagonal Perp, big, with shields in quatrefoils. On them the signs of the Evangelists, the Cross, the Instruments of the Passion, and three sprigs (?). – STAINED GLASS (according to Mr M. J. Lansdown) mostly by *Powell*, but fragments by *Warrington*, 1848, chancel sw, and nave w and s aisle se by *Bell* of Bristol. – PLATE. Paten, 1701; Spoon, C18. – MONUMENTS. Three Norman coffin-lids, one plain, one with a staff and half-circles l. and r. (s porch), the third the most interesting. Coved, with much chip-carving and a rude cross. Inscription: Ave Maria Gratia Plena Dominus Tecum. Hic sepelitur puella nostra Acelina.* – Many tablets, ruthlessly skied, e.g. one by *C. Lewis* of Cheltenham with a Grecian Fides. – G. Crabbe, the poet, † 1832. By *E. H. Baily*. He lies on his death-bed, the Bible in his hands. Angels hover over him.

ST JOHN, Frome Road, Studley. 1858 by *W. H. Wilkins*. Nave with bellcote and chancel. Late C13 tracery, but the tracery in the E window flowing.

ST JOHN BAPTIST (R.C.), Wingfield Road. 1875 by *A.J. Scoles*. In the Dec style.

ST THOMAS, St Thomas' Road. 1868–70 by *William Smith* of Trowbridge (GR). An original design certainly, but just a little nightmarish. The exterior has many gables and in the middle a turret or flèche. The plan is nearly central. Identical transepts and short chancel, and a nave of only two bays. The wide crossing is rib-vaulted. The details are in the style of *c*.1300.

HOLY TRINITY. 1838 by *A. F. Livesay* of Portsmouth, at a cost of £6,415. Of considerable size, the parish of a growing outer Trowbridge. The style is E.E., the execution solid but clumsy. Massive s tower, transepts, big pinnacles. The interior is vaulted throughout, in plaster of course. The arcade piers are of cast iron, imitating Purbeck marble. It is really a very ugly interior, but the design needed courage.

BAPTIST CHAPEL (former; now Messrs Salter), Court Street. 1823. A large, very correct Palladian design. Rusticated ground floor. Doorway with Tuscan columns and a metope frieze. First floor arched windows. Pediment.

BAPTIST (EMMANUEL) CHAPEL, Church Street. Imposing four-bay ashlar front of as late as 1908. Tuscan porch of two pillars and two columns. Windows round-arched and tall below, segment-headed and small above. Pedimental gable.

BAPTIST (ZION) CHAPEL, Union Street. 1816. Not big. Three-bay ashlar front with two tiers of arched windows.

THE TABERNACLE (Congregational), Church Street. 1882 by *Paull & Bonella*. A surprisingly earnest and imposing church, longitudinal, with a sw tower with ogee cap. Much sheer wall.

* These lids were found on the castle site.

Relatively small windows in two tiers, all straight-headed Gothic. At the back in the same style the extraordinarily large SUNDAY SCHOOL building. Earlier Gothic screen to the street, and attached to it a former WOMEN'S INSTITUTE; c.1842.

METHODIST CHAPEL, Manvers Street. 1836 by *John Dyer*. Very large, ashlar-faced, Grecian. The porch has Greek Doric columns. Above, the Grecian style turns debased, and also gets mixed up with fluted Corinthian pilasters, a symptom of the coming of the Victorian Age.

METHODIST CHAPEL, Newtown. 1872 by *W. J. Stent*. E.E., ashlar-faced. Small, but with rather fussy motifs.

UNITARIAN CHAPEL, Conigre. 1855 by *William Smith*. Dec Gothic, quite florid. No tower. School to the l.

COUNTY HALL, Bythesea Road. 1938–40 by *P. D. Hepworth*. A long range with short projecting wings. Ashlar, Neo-Georgian, with a lantern over the centre. Not very favourably placed.

TOWN HALL, Market Street. 1887–9 by *A. S. Gooderidge*. In a wild Franco-Elizabethan style. A tower not quite in the middle of the front, and the flanking gables not quite the same.

MARKET HOUSE, next to the Town Hall. 1861 by *C. E. Davis*. Arcaded ground floor. First floor in a kind of round-arched Tuscan Trecento, but the top in the other version of the Early Victorian Italianate, the villa version.

VICTORIA TECHNICAL INSTITUTE, Castle Street. 1897 by *T. Davison*. Tall and classical, but with Baroque motifs in the centre.

COLLEGE OF FURTHER EDUCATION, College Road. 1957–9 by *D. H. P. Roberts* and the County Architect *F. I. Bowden*.

NEWTOWN JUNIOR SCHOOL, Newtown. By *T. B. Silcock*, 1900. Extremely pretty, brick and stone, symmetrical, in a domestic neo-Baroque.

PERAMBULATION

The Town Hall is a good place to start from, and the first sally shall be the best of all. Down FORE STREET and almost at once the MIDLAND BANK, Georgian, of seven by five bays, ashlar-faced, three storeys, and amazingly stately. The centre with a doorway flanked by Tuscan columns. They carry an entablature with metope frieze. Above, the window is flanked by Corin-

thian columns and carries a segmental pediment. In the middle
of the side the same motif, but with pilasters. Top balustrade.*
More or less opposite, in the bend, Nos 39–40, Victorian of
1864–5 (KR), the first floor with arched windows in a close row,
separated only by coupled columns. On the second floor they
are coupled pilasters. Then, a little further down LLOYDS
BANK, built c.1790 for Thomas Stillman, a clothier (KR), and
again so stately as to recall to mind Genoa. Seven bays, two and
a half storeys, doorway with Tuscan columns, all windows
connected by brackets with the string-course above. On the
first floor three windows have alternatingly shaped pediments.
Between them panels with garlands. Attic windows, richly
carved entablature, balustrade.

After the bend the street is called THE PARADE, and here we
find the best group of ashlar-faced houses, really a stretch of
palaces, and – as one can see better from the W than the E – at
the same time a picturesquely, not monumentally composed
group. Cobbled pavements in front. First a five-bay house of
c.1700 with cross-windows (a few are preserved) and a doorway
with a big pediment on brackets. On the side two upright ovals.
Then, stepped back, a house of c.1730, five bays plus two
narrow arched windows l. and r. of the doorway and of the
window above it. The doorway has Tuscan columns, the upper
window Corinthian columns. Staircase with twisted and very
thin turned balusters. Then Usher's Brewery, which runs
these houses and keeps them well, decided to put in a word as
well, and developed the narrow corner sticking out between
this house and the next in a typical Baroque of c.1900. The date
is 1919 (by *W. W. Snailum*). After that the most ornate house:
seven bays, three-bay pediment. Doorway with richly carved
surround and a pediment whose base curves back and whose
shanks break back. The middle window has broad, completely
flat bands of garlands down its sides. It is all a very personal
idiom. (Inside, staircase with thin turned balusters and finely
carved tread-ends. NBR) After that a late C18 house of three
bays with rusticated ground floor and a porch of two pillars
and two Ionic columns, and a five-bay house of c.1700 with
very slender windows. Doorway with Tuscan pilasters against
a rusticated background. Opposite some notable houses too,
starting with one of c.1863 which has on the first floor a
continuous row of arched windows and on the second characteristic windows – with shouldered lintels. Then a five-bay

* Mr K. Rogers writes that the house was called 'newly erected' in 1779.

ashlar front, and BARCLAYS BANK of seven bays with a doorway whose segmental pediment is on Tuscan columns. At the bottom of Wicker Hill the TOWN BRIDGE, built probably in 1777. By its side the LOCKUP of 1758, with a domed stone roof as usual. HILL STREET turns N from here. Note the KITCHENER'S ARMS, probably early C18 (anyway built and licensed by 1774; KR). A long front of three storeys, not pulled together. Windows of two lights and one light in an inconsistent rhythm (or is the l. bay an addition?). The Gothic front opposite is of 1874.* A little higher up No. 12. Five bays with a one-bay pediment. Ashlar-faced.

From one-third down Fore Street CASTLE STREET runs S. This was the area of the Castle. It was sold for development in 1814 (KR). On the l. a nice three-storeyed three-bay brick house of the late C18 – see the characteristic doorway and flanking niches. Opposite the WOOLPACK restaurant, former COURT HALL, ashlar-faced, of c.1850. Italianate, with typically Early Victorian restraint. One-bay additions carrying volutes up to the main block. Off into COURT STREET for a first introduction to Trowbridge mills. The older ones of S. SALTER'S, i.e. those of ashlar, are of c.1814 (KR). One has four bays and three storeys and broad four-light wooden windows. Segment-headed windows under the gable. The other is of seven bays and has two-light windows. Then Messrs KNEE'S, of 1828 (KR), two ranges of brick, one of eight bays and four storeys with two-light segment-headed windows, the other of eleven bays and five storeys with the same type of windows. Another apparently contemporary with it of only two storeys (MC CALL BROS) is further on towards MORTIMER STREET, by Cradle Bridge. The gable-end with segment-headed and lunette windows shows that the Georgian domestic tradition was still alive.

One last turn back to Fore Street. Two-thirds down, Manvers Street goes N and leads to an area of car parking and bus station, without any shape at the time of writing and with some debris of old houses. On the r. in what was Frog Lane the CENTRAL LIBERAL CLUB, c.1700, five bays, hipped roof, doorway with Tuscan columns, on the side still cross-windows. On top, in what was Upper Broad Street, one house of three storeys, brick and stone, with two-light windows l. and r. and a one-light window above the doorway. To its r. in what was The Conigre

* Information given me by Mr M. J. Lansdown.

a five-bay house of *c.*1700 with cross-windows. To its r. in BRITISH ROW a fine house called WESTCROFT and dated 1744. Brick with stone dressings. Five bays, two storeys, three-bay pediment. Doorway with Tuscan columns and pediment. Above a Venetian window with columns. The STABLES on the l. lead in with a beautiful ashlar-faced double curve.* That ends this sally.

Finally to the E from the Town Hall. In SILVER STREET un-eventful terraces, according to Mr Lansdown of 1862, but then a new parting of the ways: N into CHURCH STREET, on into Roundstone Street. In Church Street the NATIONAL SCHOOLS of 1842, pretty Early Victorian Early-Tudor Gothic. Then at the corner of Union Street the almshouses. But first to the end of Church Street for a look at the RECTORY, standing in its own garden. Two gables with early C16 windows (arched, uncusped lights).‡ The ALMSHOUSES are by *H. Blandford & Smith,* of 1861 (KR), and stand at the corner of UNION STREET. Ground floor of stone arcaded, upper floor a timber balcony with curious gables. Then an Early Victorian house of three bays, ashlar-faced and Palladian, except for the vermi-culated rustication. More attractive houses. The WEST WILTSHIRE LIBERAL ASSOCIATION has the house at the foot of Union and Timbrell Streets with a porch of two pillars and two Ionic columns. A Venetian window over. The most likely date is *c.*1820–30. Nos 30–35 Union Street are a nice ashlar-faced terrace of two-bay houses. In TIMBRELL STREET two more good ashlar-faced houses: No. 51 and the CROWN INN, the latter with an odd doorway, sporting a pediment not segmental but basket-arched. Opposite a terrace of brick houses, of one bay each and three storeys, minimum indeed. They were built about 1814 and catered for the new working class (KR).

Now to the E and SE. We go along ROUNDSTONE STREET. Close to the start Nos 2–3, a three-storeyed double-house with flat Venetian windows. Then a widening. On the r. the noble RODNEY HOUSE (Trowbridge Co-operative Society), three-storeyed, ashlar-faced, with a Greek-Doric porch and for the upper floors daintily carved friezes. It was built for James Selfe, a clothier, who died in 1814 (KR). At r. angles to this POLE-BARN HOUSE, first occupied in 1789 (KR), three bays, ashlar-

---

* A good deal further E in THE DOWN a pretty early C19 cottage with veranda and thick thatched roof. It may have been a tollhouse.

‡ In 1962 the decision was taken to demolish the rectory.

faced, with two canted bay windows and a doorway with Ionic columns and pediment. Venetian windows with pilasters over. The middle bay is flanked by attenuated pilasters. A little down POLEBARN ROAD a Soanian four-bay house with the typical incised Grecian ornament of Soane, and opposite it a group of pairs of little Italianate villas, ashlar-faced, of c.1845. On the r., some distance after the villas, the factory of PALMER & MACKAY. Their earlier part, easily distinguishable from the later on the strength of the experience gathered in looking at the other early mills, dates from c.1812 (KR). All brick. One range, probably not the very first, is of fourteen bays and three storeys and has segment-headed windows. Back to Roundstone Street. No. 25 is of c.1730; seven bays and two and a half storeys. The centre flanked by very slim windows. Ground floor and first floor have pilasters to flank the doorway and middle window. On the first floor a pediment on the pilasters. The detail is not carefully done. Then on the r. CHING HOUSE of 1796, an ashlar-faced three-bay house.

To the l. into THE HALVE. On the r. a three-bay ashlar-faced house (No. 13) with the lintels of the windows decorated by a motif like a printer's bracket.* After that a nice minor Georgian group (Nos 18–26) and opposite No. 5, brick, with a pretty Venetian doorway flanked by Tuscan columns. Roundstone Street is continued in HILPERTON ROAD. On the l. BELLE-FIELD HOUSE, tall and rather on its own. It appears on the map of 1803 (KR). Three bays with two-bay, one-storey wings. All the ground-floor windows of the Adam variety of the Venetian window, where the middle arch is surrounded by an outer blank concentric arch connecting the straight-headed side lights. The first and second floors with giant Ionic pilasters. Further out, typical terrace and villa development. The earliest terraces are of the 1820s. Then one can read the stages from the classical by way of the Early Victorian Italianate (windows with very elongated round-arched lights) to High Victorian fashions, Tudor, Jacobean, and Frenchy.

Finally, some postscripts on a few outlying items to the w and NW beyond the Town Bridge. In STALLARD STREET a good ashlar-faced office block (Nos 52–55) in the round-arched Tuscan Trecento. Along Bradford Road from Stallard Street and on to COCKHILL. COCKHILL HOUSE is a charming early C19 house of three bays with a Tuscan porch. It is not on the map of 1803 (KR). Further out, in WIDBROOK HILL, TROWLE

* Not in the town map of 1803 (KR).

FARMHOUSE, a townish, stylish house of *c.*1700. Five bays, two storeys, hipped roof, doorway with segmental pediment. That was one postscript. Another is an ambitious Gothic fountain in the FROME ROAD, at Studley, built *c.*1870. There is no record that original Gothic parts were used, but it looks like it. Finally, a third postscript: LADY DOWN MILL of 1838, all on its own, due N from the station, reached from Canal Road.

TRUCKLE HILL *see* NORTH WRAXALL

TURLEIGH
8060
1¼ m. w of Bradford-on-Avon

TURLEIGH MANOR HOUSE. Early Georgian, of seven bays. Doorways with bolection moulding and open pediment. At the back, however, mullioned windows. Next to the house a former chapel with arched windows, now the garage. It seems to date from *c.*1800.

UPLANDS, s of the former. Dated 1700. Typical upright two-light windows with stepped-back mouldings.

TURLEIGH FARMHOUSE, s of the former. Inside, an early C17, minor plaster chimneypiece, probably by the men who worked at Westwood Manor.

TYTHERINGTON
9040
1 m. s of Heytesbury

ST JAMES. Small medieval church, the walls only about 10 ft to the eaves. No feature earlier than the surprising little quadripartite window in the N wall, and that is hardly earlier than the C15. – BENCHES. These are old too, but also too elementary to propose a date. – COMMUNION RAIL. C18.

At the N entrance to the hamlet a four-bay stone HOUSE with a pedimented doorway in the first bay. The pediment is open. Moulded window surrounds and original gatepiers. The date probably early C18.

TYTHERTON LUCAS
9070

ST NICHOLAS. Nave and chancel; N aisle under a separate roof. The three-bay aisle is of the late C13, see the steeply trefoil-cusped doorway, the windows with Y-tracery, the E window with intersected tracery, and the arcade with octagonal piers and sparse stiff-leaf capitals. – FONT. Circular, Norman, tub-shaped. The decorative motifs of fluting and gabled arches are uncommon, and perhaps the result of re-tooling. – BELL. One of the two oldest in Wiltshire (cf. Keevil). C12, not moulded in the usual way but on a lathe.

MANOR FARM. Long front with hipped roof, late C17. The part to the l. of the doorway with symmetrically arranged mullioned windows, the part to the r. with tall cross-windows. Has there been some remodelling?

BOSMERE FARMHOUSE. Early C18. Three bays. Symmetrical arrangement of four-light mullioned windows. Doorway with a steep timber pediment on brackets.

UGFORD FARMHOUSE see BURCOMBE

UPAVON

ST MARY. Flint and stone bands. Norman chancel much restored (chancel restoration by *T. H. Wyatt*, nave restoration by *J. P. Seddon*, both 1875; PF). Are the two Norman windows in the E wall l. and r. of the Perp E window *in situ*? Was there a group of three? They would have been exceedingly widely spaced. Norman also one N window and the simply chamfered priest's doorway. The chancel arch is Norman too and was made pointed later on. Scalloped capitals, zigzag at r. angles to the wall. To the l. and r. two completely plain round-arched niches for side altars. C13 N and S arcades of four bays (N) and three bays (S). Double-chamfered arches. The S aisle was later pulled down, and the arcade remains built into the wall. But why are they not in line, and why does the fourth bay on the N side differ from the others? One can perhaps assume that this fourth bay, with semi-octagonal responds on little stiff-leaf stops, came first and corresponded to a transept, that then the S arcade was built to go as far as the existing w wall, and that finally the N arcade was provided, after the decision had been taken to build a w tower. This interpretation does not however explain why the S arcade starts a little way w of the chancel arch. The tower seems of *c.*1300, see the arch towards the nave, triple-chamfered and dying into the imposts, and see also the windows with pointed-trefoiled heads, the bell-openings with two such lights and a quatrefoil over, and the mighty angle buttresses. Oblong, not polygonal, stair-turret. – FONT. Octagonal, Norman, with an Annunciation, as remarkable iconographically as stylistically, a lion, a leopard (?), flower patterns, etc. – STAINED GLASS. E window by *Henry Holiday*, made by *Powell's*; 1917–18. – PLATE. Set, 1735. – SCULPTURE. Head of a former churchyard cross with a Crucifix, re-set externally above the W doorway.

HIGH STREET. Thatched cottages, including two timber-framed ones with brackets to support the oversailing upper floor and a bracket for a former oriel window. The ANTELOPE INN, W of the church, is Early Georgian, of seven bays and two storeys with segment-headed windows.

CASTERLEY CAMP, $1\frac{1}{2}$ m. SW. Univallate hill-fort with entrances on N, S, and W. Within the main fortifications is a slight rectangular earthwork. The hill must have been occupied before the construction of the fort. Three pits lie within its bounds; one, containing four burials, produced Iron Age A sherds, a chalk sling bullet, loom-weights, and a La Tène I brooch. The fort itself was constructed by Iron Age C peoples, their material remains including La Tène III brooches, saddle querns, and sherds of bead-rimmed pottery. The occupation probably immediately preceded the Roman invasion, as butt beakers and other Romano-British pottery forms were also represented.

UPPER UPHAM 2070
$2\frac{1}{4}$ m. WNW of Aldbourne

UPHAM HOUSE. E-shaped S front with, on the porch, the initials of Thomas Goddard and the date 1599. Just inside the angles two bay windows with mullions and transoms. Boldly shaped gables (renewed). The N front is plainer, with three straight gables, but a sumptuous coat of arms. The S porch leads into the hall, which has plaster foliage trails on beams and frieze. Remains of the screen re-used when the present dining room was made and raised. In the hall a fine, very plain, but impressive stone chimneypiece. The lintel has three big scrolls from the l., three from the r., like severely stylized waves. Another chimneypiece in the dining room. This has its opening flanked by caryatids. It was originally in the room above the hall. A large addition of 1913 to the W. This is by *Biddulph Pinchard*. Topiary in the gardens, and beautiful views towards the Berkshire downs.

ROMANO-BRITISH SETTLEMENT, $1\frac{1}{2}$ m. N of Aldbourne. The site includes baths. It has produced a number of bronze bracelets and brooches, iron spear-heads, and Romano-British coarse pottery.

UPPER WESTWOOD see WESTWOOD

9040
UPTON LOVELL

CHURCH. Small. Chancel of c.1200; see the masonry, the flat buttresses, the corbel-table, the one N lancet, and the good chancel arch. Shafted responds, pointed arch with two slight chamfers. C14 tower arch, but otherwise the tower is of the C17, and so are the long, transomed, straight-headed nave windows with round-headed lights. The date 1633 appears indeed in the roof. – WEST DOOR, also of c.1633. – PLATE. Chalice, 1684. – MONUMENTS. Late C14 effigy of a Knight, his vizor down. – Brass demi-figure of a priest, c.1460, 19 in. long.

UPTON GREAT BARROW, 1½ m. NE of Knook. Magnificent bell barrow with bank outside the ditch. Excavated by Colt Hoare, who found a primary cremation with a necklace of shale, amber, and faience beads.

KNOOK CASTLE, on Knook Down. Rectangular univallate fort with entrance on the SE.

KNOOK BARROW, 1 m. W of Knook Castle. An unchambered long barrow.

8040
UPTON SCUDAMORE

ST MARY. Unbuttressed W tower of 1750. C11 nave with mighty long-and-short NW quoins. Norman N doorway of the late C12. One order of shafts, scalloped capitals, zigzag in the arch, also at r. angles to the wall surface. The window W of the doorway, though now a lancet, may have been Norman in the first place. C13 chancel, over-restored lancet windows. Much of the church was rebuilt in 1855. Of this time the S arcade for a projected aisle. Early C14 N chapel with a two-bay arcade (round pier, round abacus, double-chamfered arches) still entirely E.E., but windows with ogee-headed lights. Perp chancel arch. – FONT. Circular, Norman, with zigzag and lozenge bands. – PLATE. Chalice, 1652; Paten, 1732. – MONUMENTS. Two effigies of Knights, late C13 and late C14. The former has stiff-leaf sprigs along the rim of the slab.

MANOR FARMHOUSE. Gabled, C17, but with the head of a C15 two-light window set to the r. of the doorway.

COTTAGE, S of the Angel Inn. Dated 1723. The window surrounds finely stepped back.

TEMPLE FARMHOUSE, a little W of the Angel Inn. C17. Symmetrical, of three bays. Two-storeyed porch with round-arched entrance. The front is tile-hung; C18 or later. Inside, a large fireplace has recently been discovered.

URCHFONT

ST MICHAEL. The church is long, and its climax is without doubt
the chancel, not high but imposing. The windows are of a
curiously indeterminate shape, but point to the Dec decades.*
Absurdly heavy buttresses, ending in saddleback roofs instead
of pinnacles. The buttresses with their roofs at the SE and NE
angles stand diagonally. A solid parapet pierced by very small
quatrefoils, and on the ridge a row of fleur-de-lis cresting. On
the N side the priest's doorway leads through one of the
buttresses, quite wide enough to take it. But the chancel is not
the earliest part of the church. The transepts are earlier, as their
end windows with cusped intersected tracery show; say of
*c.*1300. Five lights on the S side, three on the N. Embattled S
aisle. Are the W and E windows and the S doorway with a trail
of flowers on jambs and arch Dec, or are they Perp? Perp S
porch with a four-centred panelled tunnel-vault. Perp W tower,
but, judging by the odd tracery of the W window, probably at
the transition from Dec to Perp, i.e. the stage of Edington.
The tower is not high, but has tall pinnacles.

Inside, one's curiosity will of course turn to the chancel at *20b*
once; and one will be richly repaid. This is Dec indeed, as
unexpected as anything in this wilful style. It is rib-vaulted,
with ridge-ribs and liernes forming lozenges. But this description does not bring out the main characteristic. The bays are
very narrow, and the vault might better be called a pointed
tunnel-vault with a panel of quadripartite ribbing per bay
rising to the ridge from either side. The ribs are narrow and
simply single-chamfered. Bosses along the ridge and in the
intersection of each pair of diagonals. It is the pattern of the
aisles of Bristol Cathedral, where it dates from *c.*1300. Here
it may be 1320 or 1325. The ribs rise from short shafts standing
on heads. The impression is on the sombre side. Internally
again, like outside, the chancel does not chronologically come
first. The chancel arch is Early E.E., though completely
renewed – stiff-leaf capitals and also still trumpet scallops.
The three-bay arcades, like the aisles, may be Dec or Perp.
Round piers with octagonal abaci, double-hollow-chamfered
arches. The transepts we had recognized as of *c.*1300 from
outside. The two-thirds arch from the S aisle into the S transept
confirms the date. The corresponding N arch is simply double-
chamfered. Good piscina of *c.*1300. Nave roof of 1631 with
thin tie-beams, collar-beams, and meagre pendants.

* The E window is Victorian.

FURNISHINGS. FONT. E.E. On five supports; plain bowl. – DOOR to the tower; original, with tracery. – STAINED GLASS. Chancel s signed by *Wailes*, 1852; s transept E 1856, no doubt by the same. – PLATE. Paten, 1726; Flagon, 1764. – MONU-MENTS. Thomas Ernle † 1725 (s transept), very retardataire; it looks at first late C17. – Robert Tothill † 1753. Standing wall-monument with a black sarcophagus and black obelisk. Two free-standing busts; two putti outside l. and r. by *P. Schee-makers*. – James Long † 1768. Of coloured marbles, with an obelisk. By *Mauge* of Bath.

URCHFONT MANOR, ½ m. SW. Built before 1688, and one of the best houses of its type in Wiltshire. Brick with stone dressings. The garden front, former entrance side, is of seven bays and of two storeys on a basement. Three-bay projection with pediment. Mullion-and-transom cross-windows, replaced in the middle projection by sash-windows about 1730. At the same time the first-floor windows here received alternating pediments. The splendid doorway however is again of c.1685. Detached Corinthian columns carry an entablature moving up in the middle. All the detail very ornate. The side of the house is of seven bays too, and the detail seems all of c.1730. What is now the entrance side is narrower, but unaltered. Seven bays, cross-windows, doorway simply with a big bolection moulding. Inside, fireplaces with the same type of moulding. Staircase with strong twisted balusters.

Many attractive houses in the village, culminating at the green in front of the church. Here MANOR FARMHOUSE, five bays, two storeys, brick, with a pretty Chinese cast-iron porch and opposite a timber-framed, thatched house. On the main road TOWNSEND COTTAGE, timber-framed and thatched, and at the very E exit on the N side a cottage with exposed crucks.

VASTERNE MANOR *see* WOOTTON BASSETT

²⁰⁸⁰ ## WANBOROUGH

ST ANDREW. A church one does not easily forget – on account of its hexagonal tower and spire above the E end of the nave, com-peting with the more normal W tower. The hexagonal tower belongs to the principal work of rebuilding the church in the early C14. The W tower is Perp. Of the principal period the following remains. Externally the N doorway with big fleurons and trails connecting them all up the jambs, and the arch, and

See p. 578

internally the four-bay nave arcades with quatrefoil piers and double-chamfered arches, the crossing piers of the small crossing on which tower and spire rest (with triple demi-shafts), the arches leading from these W, S, E, and N, and extra arches separating the aisles from what must be called the transepts, though they do not project and are in fact narrower than the arcade arches. The quite exceptional space thus separated, a strip running N–S, is perhaps a reminiscence of the cross-space usual in English friars' churches, which, like Wanborough, as a rule have a tower on the centre of the crossing-space. The tower and spire at Wanborough are quite open from beneath, a very impressive sight regardless of whether it represents the original state or not. The tower is ashlar-faced and has straight-headed windows with a little cusped decoration, the spire one tier of lucarnes at the bottom. Perp additions are the chancel, which has straight-headed side windows, the N porch, which has pinnacles on the buttresses, and the W tower with traceried spandrels in the doorway, a three-light window, a niche above it, and bell-openings with Somerset tracery, battlements, and pinnacles. – PAINTING. C15. Entry into Jerusalem, over-laid by C17 text and scrolls. – PLATE. Chalice and Cover, 1577; Flagon, 1615; Paten or Almsdish, 1690. – MONUMENTS. Late C14 couple, of stone, damaged (S porch). – Thomas Polton † 1418 and wife. Brass demi-figures, 13 in. long (S aisle E). – Elizabethan tablet with pediment on pilasters with flower-work. Very long inscription, but no name. In all probability it commemorates Anthony Hinton † 1598 (S aisle E). – Thomas Gray † 1725. Inscription with thick leaf surround and, at the four corners, four putto heads (vestry).

DUROCORNOVIUM. 1 m. N is the probable site of this Roman town. Traces of foundations and paving slabs and a well near Covingham Farm are the only recorded structural remains. The numerous finds attest to continuous occupation from the C1 A.D. to the end of the Roman period. The site lies on the Roman road from Silchester (Calleva) to Cirencester (Corinium).

WANSDYKE see BROMHAM

WARDOUR 9020
OLD CASTLE

Licence to crenellate was granted to John Lord Lovel of Titch- 23 marsh in 1393. The castle he built is beautifully situated up a

wooded bank above a lake made in the C18, and it is unique
in its plan. Of the BAILEY in which it stands the outer walls
survive. The E FRONT of the castle itself has a recessed centre
with an archway and short projecting side wings. The hall is on
the upper floor above the archway. That promises a building of
the type of Nunney in Somerset, for which the licence dates
from 1373. But pass through the archway, and instead of finding
yourself in the open looking at just another such front as that
to the E, you are in a hexagonal COURTYARD. The ranges round

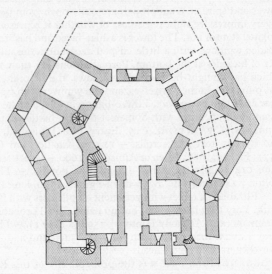

Wardour, old castle, licensed 1393

this courtyard remain only to the N and S, but stumps of walling
show clearly that a W range has existed also. The height of the
whole structure is now about 60 ft and was more. Should it be
called a keep, or a house of six sides? The question is not futile.
Nunney is a keep, but Bodiam in Sussex and Queenborough
in Kent are or were courtyard houses, the first square with a
square, the second round with a round courtyard. The first
dates from 1385 etc., the second from 1361 etc. That is the
family to which Wardour belongs.

In detail, two periods are at once discernible, Lovel's and
that of Sir Matthew Arundell, who bought the estate back in

1570 (an Arundell had held it in 1547–52) and put the date 1578 above the entrance. Entering through the archway from the E, one passes at once through an Arundell PORTAL with columns intermittently blocked. A coat of arms is above the portal, and above this the head of Christ in a niche with the inscription: 'Sub nomine tuo stet genus et domus'. Contemporary shell-headed niches to the l. and r. Of the GREAT HALL on the upper floor two tall former two-light windows give evidence. In the projecting wings are two-light mullioned windows, the lights with depressed arches – C16 no doubt, and probably Sir Matthew's, though conservative for the 1570s. The windows are on four levels and are oddly distributed (due to a spiral staircase in the SE projection). The same type of window continues along the three sides to the S, also four storeys high. There is also a minor arched DOORWAY.

As one enters the archway in the front one recognizes the springers of a fan-vault. This can hardly be of 1393, but is it as late as the 1570s? Tunnel-vaulted rooms l. and r. To the courtyard an arched doorway with big wave-moulding and smaller ones into rooms in the S and N ranges. Above, the great hall has two tall windows also towards the courtyard. The main staircase up to the hall is Arundell work and is entered by passing through a PORTAL with attached Roman Doric columns and a metope frieze. Lions' heads in the spandrels of the arch. It is a piece entirely in the mainstream of Elizabethan architecture, and it ought perhaps to be remembered that Sir Matthew in 1576 mentioned to Sir John Thynne of Longleat the presence of *Robert Smythson* in the neighbourhood, that Robert Smythson was largely responsible for work at Longleat in the 1570s and 1580s, that he was the 'Architector' of Wollaton, and that Sir Matthew was the brother-in-law of Sir Henry Willoughby, who built Wollaton in 1580–8. But his work at Wardour is minor. Most of the windows in the courtyard have the same depressed-arched lights as those to the outside, but in the W wall one Perp two-light window is revealed.

By the staircase the HALL was reached. This has a fireplace in the W wall and a fleuron frieze below the tall windows, continuing at a higher level along the N wall. Was this the dais-end, and were there windows here as well? To the S the wall is bare. On this side access must have been made to the offices. The KITCHENS were beyond, in the S range. Their enormous chimneys are unmistakable. To the courtyard they are marked by two very tall lancet windows with cusped arches. Below, on the ground floor, a room with a c16 rib-vault. In the N ranges also a large vaulted ground-floor room of three by two bays.

w of the former w range, on the outer bailey wall, is a two-storeyed Late Georgian Gothick SUMMER HOUSE. The windows have ogee heads. It is accessible from the bailey on the upper floor, from outside on the lower. Close to this outer access is WARDOUR HOUSE, unused at the time of writing. It is of indifferent late c17 architecture, but behind it, again against the bailey wall, is another SUMMER HOUSE, this one early c18, as the details of the doorway and the circular windows show.

E of the E range is a GROTTO, the work of *Josiah Lane* of Tisbury, made at about the same time as the later of the two summer houses.

To the SE, LODGE on the A30. Thick round pillars with square tops. Thatched roof.

WARDOUR CASTLE

57b The new mansion was designed by *James Paine* for the eighth Lord Arundell, begun in 1769, and completed in 1776. Rain-water heads show the date 1774. It is the largest Georgian house in Wiltshire, ashlar-faced and stern. The house consists of a main block nine by six (or five) windows and quadrant links to three-bay pavilions. The main block has a low ground floor, a *piano nobile*, and one attic storey to the garden (s), two to the entrance (N). The ground floor is rusticated with vertical tooling. The doorways in and out of the house are distressingly unstressed. The principal accents of the entrance and garden sides are on the piano nobile. They call for open outer staircases leading up to them. On the entrance side the accent is a central Venetian window with an arch over all three parts, and as the finishing touch to the whole composition a three-bay pediment. On the garden side the three-bay centre has giant Corinthian columns, coupled, single, single, single, coupled, and otherwise one arched middle window, and of course the three-bay pediment. The side parts of the façades of the centre block are given no more enrichment than pediments to the piano-nobile windows. In addition, the garden side displays coupled giant angle pilasters. That is all. The sides of the centre block are plain, except for one Venetian middle window in the E front, of the same type as that in the centre to the N. The links – quarter-circles only to the entrance, but straight to the garden – have two storeys, and below, in the rustication, arched windows in blank arches. At the top a curious form of crenellation with big balls – a Venetian motif, and as such accepted as Palladian. The pavilions are pedimented and have to both principal sides in the middle a Venetian window again like that in the centre of the N front. In addition, on the W, beyond the pavilion, is the Catholic chapel. From the garden a glimpse is obtained of a segmental lunette and a shallow apsed projection.

The ENTRANCE HALL is of course low. It has attached Roman Doric columns and a handsome Adamish fireplace of cast iron crowned by an urn. Then, immediately, the STAIR-CASE HALL opens out, the most glorious Georgian interior of 58 Wiltshire. It is 60 ft high and circular, with a diameter of 47 ft. The two arms of the staircase rise in flying, that is vertically unsupported, curves along its outer wall to the piano nobile, where a colonnade of tall Corinthian columns forms a gallery or balcony. This has in its outer walls six ample niches or apses with coffered vaults. In one of them is an organ. The columns carry a coffered dome, the coffering pattern different from that of the apses, and a glazed lantern. The N niche is singled out by coupled demi-columns; that to the S has a doorway with Ionic columns and a straight entablature.

The largest room lies to the E. It has the Venetian window referred to as the centre of the E façade and a coved ceiling. No special decoration. Altogether there is comparatively little decoration in the rooms of Wardour Castle. The centre room on the S side has a doorway with Ionic columns and a pediment, and excellent stucco work with long foliage scrolls in the oval centre, the four lunettes, and the four spandrels. In the oblong centre of the centre a copy of Reni's *Aurora* by *Batoni*. On the N side the middle room has columns in the principal doorway too, and there is a charming apsed BOUDOIR on the W side with a coffered niche and a stucco ceiling.*

In the E pavilion is the large KITCHEN, gutted at the time of writing and hence, in a Vanbrughian-Brutalist way, most impressive, and above it a handsome room with Adamish columns.

CHAPEL. The chapel built by *Paine* and lengthened by 59b *Soane* was technically a private chapel, but is the size of a very major parish church. Moreover it is so grand in its decoration that it seems to express consciously – even if designed by Anglican architects – the spirit of the Catholic *ecclesia triumphans*.

* The school which has now taken over the house has had a subsidiary staircase installed, by *Booth & Ledeboer*, and refreshingly un-period.

It was originally opened in 1776; Soane's work dates from 1788. The chapel has giant fluted pilasters along the walls, a groin-vault with penetrations, and delicate classical stucco work by *Quarenghi*. The colouring is pink for the walls, white and blue for the vault. Soane added the crossing, with an oval vault, shallow-apsed transepts, and a shallow apse with lunette windows. There is a shallow apsidal w end (ritually w) as well, with the organ gallery on fluted Ionic columns. The altar wall has coupled columns l. and r. and an apsed recess for the altar like those of the w wall, but they have Corinthian columns. – ALTAR. By *Giacomo Quinenza*, c.1775; free-standing, with a great many varieties of marble. – SCULPTURE. Small relief of the Virgin and Child with little St John, signed by *Monnot*, Rome, 1703. – PAINTINGS. In the nave five large paintings by *Gaspar de Crayer*, the sixth by *Louis de Boullogne*, 1695. – The painting behind the altar is by *Giuseppe Cades* (1750–99), a Roman painter who specialized in the imitation of the style of older masters. – STAINED GLASS. Altar lunette by *F. Eginton* representing the Trinity with cherubs in clouds. – PLATE. Silver-gilt Chalice and Paten, 1638, a recusant set; Altar Vase, 1725 (Mr Oman says probably the only surviving such vessel of before the C19); three pairs of Candlesticks by *Charles Kandler*, 1733; Censer, Paris, 1778; second Censer made in 1786 by *Kandler* in imitation of the former; Holy Water Bucket, 1793, by *John Schofield*; Cruets and Dish, 1820, by *Rundell, Bridge & Rundell*.

VESTMENTS. Cope of violet velvet, with silver lace perhaps partly late C17. – Cope of silk with woven rose-sprays in silver, white, and red. C18 or C19. – Cope of green velvet, C19. On hood and orphreys English embroidery of c.1500 (Virgin and Child, Saints). – Cope of silk; woven flower pattern on red damask ground, C18 or C19. Orphreys (Saints, Bishops) probably early C16 Flemish. – Silk Chasuble etc., of silk, woven flower pattern, silver and gold on white ground. Orphreys: gold floral scrolls. C18. – Chasuble of fairly modern white and silver brocade. Orphreys of English embroidery c.1450–75, restored (Crucifixion, St Peter, Prophets). – Chasuble of fairly modern purple velvet. Orphreys of English embroidery c.1450–75, restored (Crucifixion, Saints, Bishop). – Chasuble and Mass Set of dark purple velvet with silver lace. Late C17 or C18. – C18 veils of cloth of silver. – Set of Cope, Chasuble, etc., of cloth of silver. Fine French or English C18 embroidery. – Silk Chasuble. Woven floral pattern in gold and colours, C18 or C19.

Front orphrey: early C16 English embroidery. Back orphrey: English, or c.1450 (Saints in pairs). – So-called Westminster Chasuble. Plain red velvet perhaps C16 or C17, which is later than the early C16 possibly English embroidery applied to it (Tudor roses, fleurs-de-lis, pomegranates, portcullises). Orphreys Flemish, chiefly early C16, except for the Presentation at the top of the front orphrey. Rest of the front orphrey: pairs of saints. Back: Betrayal, Agony in the Garden, Washing of the Feet. Also arms of the Duke of Burgundy on shield, Golden Fleece, lozenge with Burgundian and English royal arms impaled (referring to the marriage of Charles the Bold and Margaret of York which took place in 1468). – Early C16 green velvet Chasuble with embroidered eagles and original sequins. Orphreys: figures under canopies. English. – Rose silk Chasuble with woven flower pattern, C18. – Several English embroidered orphreys of the C15 to C16; all very restored. – High Mass Set: Chasuble, two Dalmatics, etc., floral pattern on gold ground, C18–C19. Alb: C18 Brussels lace.* – MONUMENT. Tenth Lord Arundell † 1834. Bust on a tall pedestal.

TEMPLE, in the garden, close to the chapel. Square, with rounded portico of Tuscan columns. Decorated metopes. Circular ceiling inside.

WARMINSTER

ST DENYS. A large Perp church, very thoroughly renewed in 1887–9 by *Blomfield* at the expense of Canon Sir James Philipps, rector from 1859 to 1897. On the whole the renewal represents what was there before. Nave and aisles, transepts, crossing tower, chancel and chapels. Only the nave with clerestory was Early Georgian when Blomfield started. The Perp work comprises the crossing arches of two and four chamfers dying into the imposts and the S chancel chapel (Maudit Chapel, built in the late C15), with large four-light windows and arcade piers of the four-shaft-and-four-waves section. Blomfield also re-set from the medieval church two-thirds of a Norman arch and made it a Norman window (N transept). – ORGAN CASE. A delightful piece of 1792, from Salisbury Cathedral. Made by *England*, with a middle turret and urns on the raised angle pieces. – PLATE. Chalice, inscribed 1682; two Patens, 1706; Flagon, 1710; Chalice, 1750. – MONUMENTS. Quite a number of tablets.

* I owe this list to the kindness of Mr G. F. Wingfield Digby, who went specially to Wardour Castle to compile it.

ST LAWRENCE, High Street. C14 W tower (see the arch to the nave with two chamfers dying into the imposts) with short recessed spire. The rest a Victorian rebuilding. – FONT. An C18 baluster stem and a small bowl.

CHRIST CHURCH, Sambourne. 1830–1 by *John Leachman*. A long church. W tower with tall, heavy pinnacles. Tall two-light Perp windows. Chancel 1871 by *T. H. Wyatt*. In 1881 arcades were inserted inside to make the church more churchy (by *Vialls*; PF).

ST JOHN EVANGELIST, Boreham. 1865 by *Street*, at the expense of Canon Sir James Philipps. Tall nave with bellcote over the E wall, and low chancel. Late C13 details. The windows tall and narrow. The semicircular baptistery at the W end is an addition of 1926 by *Ponting*. Low lean-to N aisle. The organ chamber N of the chancel is screened off by a stone parapet and two cusped arches. – MOSAICS. Also by *Ponting*, in the N aisle of *c.*1911, in the chancel of *c.*1913–15. – Good group of SCHOOL and stone LYCHGATE, built in 1874.

BAPTIST (EBENEZER) CHAPEL, North Row. 1811. Brick. Arched windows with Victorian tracery. Hipped roof. The SCHOOL next to the chapel looks *c.*1845, see the elongated arched window lights.

CONGREGATIONAL (COMMON CLOSE) CHAPEL, The Close. 1840. E.E. style with top-heavy pinnacles. SCHOOL on the l.

TOWN HALL. 1832 by *Blore*. small, two-storeyed, symmetrical, restrained Jacobean. No vertical accent yet, as the Victorians would have demanded.

ST BONIFACE COLLEGE, Church Street. The college was founded by Canon Sir James Philipps in 1860. The core is a handsome house of 1796, partly with tripartite windows. At the back two canted bay windows and a tripartite arched doorway.* To this a tall, somewhat fussy neo-Jacobean building was added in 1897 to the design of *J. A. Reeve*. In 1927 followed the tall Chapel block with the Library beneath. Impressively bare walls. By *Sir Charles Nicholson*.

LORD WEYMOUTH'S GRAMMAR SCHOOL, Church Street. 1707. A stately block of seven bays and two storeys with cross-windows. The school-room on the r., the master's house on the l. In the middle arched doorway with garland over and Corinthian columns l. and r.‡ Slightly projecting bay above.

* The house is, as Mr Rogers tells me, by *David Glascodine* of Bristol.
‡ Mr Rogers informs me that, according to the Thynne MSS, it came from Longleat and was 'made by the directions of Sr. *Chr. Wrenn*'.

SAMBOURNE HOSPITAL, the former WORKHOUSE. Built in 1836. Nine-bay, two-storey front. Higher behind. The style is Latest Classical with pedimental gables.

PERAMBULATION. Warminster lies impressively close to the downs, their bare outlines and their wind-breaks of beeches. In the main street – for the town is largely one long street – one does not notice that much, but move away to the W, e.g. to the parish church, and you feel at once in the open.

The walk starts by the Town Hall, i.e. in the MARKET PLACE, and goes first E. Across Weymouth Street another Jacobean building by *Blore*, bigger than the Town Hall. The BATH ARMS HOTEL is Georgian, of eight bays and three storeys with a rusticated ground floor and a parapet.* Opposite the OLD BELL HOTEL, nicely white and black, and the ground floor colonnaded. Then an eighteen-bay terrace of plain three-storeyed houses with segment-headed windows. On the other side EVERSFIELD HOUSE, of four bays, with a double entrance in the rusticated ground floor. In EAST STREET No. 14 is dated 1767. It is of three bays with stepped tripartite (i.e. minimum Venetian) windows on the ground floor, plain tripartite on the upper floor (flat mullions).

Nothing else to the E. Now to the W from the Town Hall, down HIGH STREET. At the junction, in the yard of a house, reached from Weymouth Street, a little late C17 stone building with a horizontal oval window over the pedimented doorway. Then, at the corner of North Row, a five-bay brick house with hipped roof. At the corner of The Close the former ATHENAEUM, by *W. J. Stent*, Jacobean of 1879. Down the hill on the l. several ashlar-faced houses with nice doorways, on the r. a charming one-bay brick house with a Venetian window and a five-bay house (No. 24) with a pedimented dooorway on pilasters, a Venetian window with pilasters over, and plainer stepped tripartite windows otherwise.

Fork r. first into PORTWAY. At its end PORTWAY HOUSE, stately but rather bleak. Seven bays, three storeys, with lower three-bay wings. The doorway is reset. Above its former middle position pilasters with blocked capitals and an open pediment, and another order of pilasters without pediments. Very fine C18 railing and gates. Staircase of twisted and columned balusters. (Also Kentian chimneypiece. NBR) On the garden wall in the corner a flat-roofed brick and stone garden house. Back and fork l. into George Street. At the bottom continue along

* Refronted in 1744 (K. Rogers).

SILVER STREET. This finally takes us near the architectural centre of Warminster. On the r. at once, in Ash Walk, a nice Later Georgian house with two canted bays and a pedimented doorway with Tuscan columns. Then soon the OBELISK, erected in 1781. It has a highly incorrect top cornice for an urn. Facing the obelisk on the s side CRAVEN HOUSE, brick and stone, with two canted bay windows and a Gibbsish doorway. To the l. VICARAGE STREET. No. 6 is Early Georgian (five bays). Then the MINSTER SCHOOL, 1845–6, Gothic, with a big bay window and an openwork quatrefoiled parapet. From here into EMWELL STREET for a group of brick houses, especially that to the l. of the Weymouth Arms with its surprisingly grand pedimented doorway. On in Silver Street to No. 32, an ambitious seven-bay house with a Gibbsish doorway and a Venetian window with pilasters over. Vicarage Street now splits. To the l. is POUND STREET with some MALTHOUSES on the l., No. 24, another five-bay house, on the r. To the r. is WEST STREET. No. 12 is a three-bay ashlar-faced Late Georgian house. The COCK INN on the other side has a fine iron inn-sign.

Back to the Obelisk and at last into CHURCH STREET, the best street of Warminster. At the corner, hidden inside a garage, the former LOCKUP. Opposite TEDDINGTON HOUSE, of c.1700, five bays and two storeys, slightly moulded window surrounds. Opposite, a little further on, a brick house with a good, elaborate late C18 doorway, and another of c.1750 with a doorway with a head and a garland below the broken pediment. Then the house of 1796 which belongs to St Boniface College and opposite it BYNE HOUSE of 1755.[*] Three wide bays and three storeys with a Venetian middle window with pilasters and plain stepped tripartite windows. Then the Weymouth School of 1707, and so to the church.

BATTLESBURY CAMP, 1¼ m. ENE. Univallate hillfort with entrances on the E and NW. Nine pits were excavated within the camp in 1922. Finds included chariot-wheel nave-bands, iron tools, a rotary quern, and Iron Age B pottery.

WARNCLIFFE HOUSE see BOX

WARNEFORD PLACE see SEVENHAMPTON

---

[*] The date comes from Mr Rogers.

WEDHAMPTON
1 m. w of Chirton
0050

MANOR HOUSE. Early C18. Five bays, two storeys, hipped roof. Doorway with open curly segmental pediment with some carving inside. Iron garden gate.

WEST ASHTON
8050

ST JOHN EVANGELIST. 1846 by *Wyatt & Brandon*. Perp, with NE tower and spire, in the grounds of Rood Ashton. – STAINED GLASS. E window, mild English Expressionism. Designed by *H. Wilson* and made by *Powell's*. – MONUMENT. Walter Long † 1847 and wife. Signed by *H. Timbrell*, Rome, 1848. Young woman with baby and angels.

ROOD ASHTON is now gutted and a ruin. It was built for Richard Godolphin Long about 1808 by *Sir Jeffry Wyatville* and altered by *Thomas Hopper* in 1836. The house is on a vast scale, and most impressive in its present state. A varied castellated façade culminating in a porte-cochère tower with tall thin stair-turret. The LODGE on the road to Steeple Ashton also remains. Very picturesque, even if silly, with its big square tower and small round tower and its machicolations.

WESTBURY
8050

ALL SAINTS. All Perp, and much renewed. With an oblong crossing tower and an embattled nave. Except for the N chapel with transomed N windows, the seven-light, triple-transomed E window, and the clerestory, the church is still at the stage of transition between Dec and Perp, just like Edington near by, see the windows of three lights with two tracery units, still close to the usual reticulation, but a purely Perp top-unit (s aisle, s transept, N aisle, N transept, N aisle chapel), and see also the windows of the s chapel and of the tower. The s porch is two-storeyed with a handsome vault. Liernes in the centre make a cross with triangular ends, and this part of the vault is cusped. A niche above the inner doorway. The W window dates from 1847 (*T. H. Wyatt*; PF), as does the vestry between s porch and s transept. The W front is remarkable, with battlements rising up the steep lean-to roofs of the aisles and the less steep nave roof. The window jambs are panelled, and below the W window is a shallow porch, panelled inside and vaulted, with tiercerons and bosses. At the sw corner a turret. Tall arcade bays of four bays, with piers of four shafts and four hollows in section. The same section for the crossing arches. Those to the N and S are lower than the others. The N chapel W of the transept has a tierceron-star vault. The aisles have transverse arches with a flying-buttress-like retaining arch, both no doubt to help support the clerestory. The chancel chapels have panelled W arches. The arcades to the chancel with four piers and two waves in the diagonals. – FONT. Octagonal, Perp, with panelling and shields. – STAINED GLASS. E window and N chapel E window both of c.1848. – MONUMENTS. In the S transept Sir James Ley † 1629. Two recumbent effigies. Columns l. and r., and at the top the four cardinal Virtues. – William Phipps, Governor of Bombay, † 1748. By *Sir Robert Taylor*. With a lively bust in front of a grey back panel. – George Turner † 1768. A good conservative tablet. – Other tablets with mourning women.

HOLY SAVIOUR, Westbury Leigh, *see* below, p. 499.

TOWN HALL. 1815, built at the expense of Sir M. M. Lopes. Three bays, still open below, with Tuscan columns. Arched upper windows. One-bay pediment.

PERAMBULATION. There is not much to be picked up on the way at Westbury. The churchyard gates lead N into the MARKET PLACE. Here, besides the Town Hall, the LOPES ARMS HOTEL, in the SE corner, Georgian, low, and nicely L-shaped. Opposite, on the N side BARCLAYS BANK, earlier C18, brick, of five bays with a shell-hood. L. of the Town Hall to the E ALFRED STREET with FERNDALE HOUSE (Conservative Club), a good mid-C18 brick house of three bays with four Venetian windows. Opposite the Lopes Arms MARISTOW STREET runs off to the W. One house has a semicircular porch with Tuscan columns, the next a semicircular hood on brackets. Both are brick rendered, the second is early C18. Turn S into EDWARD STREET. On the l. LAVERTON'S CLOTH MILLS, brick, with symmetrical two-light windows on four floors. The two ranges are said to date from 1772 (Bitham) and 1784 (Angel).* Now off towards the church by CHURCH STREET. EDGAR HOUSE, Early Georgian, has segment-headed windows, No. 4 a nice carved door-hood on brackets. At the top of Edward Street turn W into WARMINSTER ROAD to see

---

* Bitham has cast-iron pillars fluted with ornamental pedestals, cast-iron beams, and brick vaults. All the rest of the buildings have plain cast-iron piers and wooden beams. It seems pertinent to report that Cobbett, visiting Westbury in 1826, wrote: 'It has cloth factories, and they seem to be ready to tumble down'. That does not inspire confidence in the reported dates.

No. 24, five-bay, early C19, Soanian, with the typical incised Grecian ornament, turn E into BRATTON ROAD to see BERES WELL, picturesque, timber-framed with brick infilling and a stone part. Then the LAVERTON INSTITUTE, 1873, brick and Gothic.

The WESTBURY WHITE HORSE is 166 ft long and 163 ft high. It was apparently made in the early C18, but in 1873 it was alas 'rectified', and now it looks a moderately correct, dispirited animal.

HEYWOOD HOUSE. *See* Heywood.

WESTBURY LEIGH 8050

Westbury Leigh is really inside the Westbury Urban District, but visually it is still apart.

HOLY SAVIOUR. 1876–90 by *W. H. White*. A serious, well-done neo-Perp job. W tower, nave with S aisle, and chancel. The S arcade is of two wide arches. The capitals are naturalistic but not overdone, the arches are interesting but not without regional precedent. Single-framed roofs, but in the chancel arched braces to high collar-beams.

In the main street a number of worthwhile houses. From E to W, No. 16a, Early Georgian, brick, with arched upper windows. No. 18a, of the same period, also with arched windows. The doorway has an open curly pediment. Hipped roof. Past the church on the l. old MALTHOUSES.

Then the BAPTIST CHAPEL of 1796. Brick, big, with two tiers of tall, arched windows. Doorway with pediment on brackets. Minister's house behind.

With that the former Apple Tree Inn at Dilton Marsh is reached, and the Penkney Chapel, *see* p. 193.

WEST DEAN 2020

ST MARY, N of Church Farmhouse. Only part of the church was allowed to remain when the new church was built. It is Dec, see the windows and the recess mentioned below. It contains an interesting series of MONUMENTS (and in addition an iron GUARD RAIL). Dec recess in the S wall with ogee arch. – John Evelyn † 1627 and family. Large kneeling figures facing one another. The children kneel below in the 'predella'. Two arches above the main figures carried by columns l. and r. – Elizabeth Tirell † 1629. Dull, small frontal bust in a recess. Open segmental pediment over. – Brass of George Evelyn

41b † 1641, aged six. – Robert Pierrepont † 1669. Large tripartite
composition. Coupled white Ionic columns l. and r. of the
centre. Open scrolly segmental pediment on them. Below, a
black niche with the white kneeling figure in profile. A fat man
and agitated drapery. An angel behind him, i.e. to the r. The
niche can be closed by two brass doors with long inscriptions in
italic letters. Below, an inscription in stone held by two putti.
The monument might well be by *Bushnell*. – Sir John Evelyn
† 1685. Excellent, white frontal bust in a black niche which can
also be closed. Iron doors. The niche stands in front of a
sarcophagus. At the top open pediment with two good reclining
allegorical figures.

St Mary. The new church is by *Pownall & Young* and was built
in 1866. Flint and red brick, with a bell-turret and an apse.
Original c12 and c13 material was used, namely a shaft with
a waterleaf capital and with another such capital as its base.
This is now the lectern. c13 mouldings in piscina and aumbry.
– c13 tiles against the back of piscina and aumbry. – plate.
Cup and Paten Cover, 1581; two Patens, 1720.

Barn of Church Farmhouse, by the old church. Brick, buttressed, of thirteen bays. Probably early c16.

Roman Villa, ne of the church. A tessellated pavement with
central floral design was found in 1741. In the c19 further
pavements and floor areas were uncovered, and excavation
revealed a bath suite, hypocausts, and painted wall plaster.
Much of the site lies across the county border in Hampshire.

2020   WEST GRIMSTEAD

St John. Recent brick w tower with pyramid roof. Nave and
aisles and chancel with a one-bay n chapel. This is the earliest
remaining part. Double-chamfered round arch on semicircular
responds. Then the n aisle arcade of two bays. Round pier and
round abacus. Double-chamfered arches. The piers are grey
stone, the arches alternatingly biscuit-coloured and brown.
The s aisle is only one bay long. The moulded capitals of the
responds are of *c*.1300. To the w of the bay a space indicative of
a former or projected s tower. Its entry, like the n doorway, is
single-chamfered. The chancel seems to be of *c*.1300 too.
Arch of two continuous chamfers, piscina pointed-trefoil-
headed, e windows a group of three stepped lancets, pointed-
trefoil-cusped. – pulpit. Jacobean, with flat arabesque
carving. – plate. Paten, 1553 (?); Cup, 1576.

WEST HARNHAM

St George. Nave and chancel are both Norman. One chancel N window, one nave N window, and the N doorway are evidence. The doorway has one order of shafts with stylized leaf in the capitals. Another nave N window is *c.*1300, as is the style of the remodelling of the chancel. Chancel arch with triple shafts and two sunk quadrant mouldings in the arch. Also lancet windows, quite Victorian from outside. Piscina with trefoil head. Dec s chapel. The arch is double-chamfered and dies into the imposts. Piscina with ogee top. The N tower is mostly early C19. Yellow brick and flint chequerwork. The W front of brick (English bond!) is part of *Butterfield*'s restoration of 1873. To the r. of the chancel arch a pointed niche with a fine WALL PAINTING of the Noli me tangere in red outline. The painting is late C13, the chancel arch a little later. Its making interfered with the niche. The chancel has a ceiled wagon roof with rough bosses. – SCREEN to the s chapel. Jacobean. – SCULPTURE. Two panels in high relief, Flemish, early C16. The Presentation and the Entombment.

All Saints, Harnham Road. 1854 by *T. H. Wyatt*.

Harnham Mill, N of St George. The miller's house is Early Victorian and tall, the mill Perp and low. Ground floor of stone and flint chequer. Windows and doorways straight-headed. Lozenge hood-mould stops. One doorway with blank tracery in the spandrels. To the N one-light window and two cross-shaped slits, probably re-set. The upper floor is of brick, an early case in the county. Inside, rough open timber roof with tie-beams and raking queenposts to collar-beams.

Further E than All Saints a pretty terrace of white cottages with rustic porches carrying hats of thatch. Yet nearer Salisbury and the medieval bridge the THREE CROWNS, timber-framed and much restored.

Harnham Hill Settlement. On Harnham Hill, W of Salisbury Hospital, is an earthwork with V-sectioned ditch, within which were a number of pits containing Iron Age A pottery, including haematite-coated ware and a few bead-rimmed (Iron Age C) sherds.

Saxon Cemetery, 400 yds NW of the hospital. Sixty-four graves were excavated in the C19. The burials comprised adults and children of both sexes and were accompanied by iron weapons, saucer brooches, and glass and amber beads. One rich male burial contained two saucer brooches, gold, bronze, and silver rings, a Roman brooch, and an iron knife.

WEST KENNETT

1¼ m. SE of Avebury

1060

WEST KENNETT HOUSE. Georgian, brick, five bays and two and a half storeys. Porch.

LONG BARROW. *See* Avebury, p. 89.

ROMAN ROAD. *See* Mildenhall, p. 313.

WEST KINGTON

8070

A pretty group of cottages by the bridge in the combe. One ascends to the church past a Gothick COTTAGE with an ogee-headed doorway and windows with Y-tracery. The church lies on the hill.

ST MARY. Unbuttressed w tower, the bell-openings of two lights with Somerset tracery, continued below a transom in blank panels, and the whole repeated blank to the l. and r., i.e. exactly as at Burton (Nettleton), at Westwood, and in other Wiltshire places and a development of Somerset elements. Panelled battlements, pinnacles. The church 1856 by *S. B. Gabriel* of Bristol. Rather bald inside, with its cream-coloured bare walls. Nave, transepts, and chancel. The single-framed roofs quite successful. – PULPIT. A delicately carved Perp piece. Crocketed ogee arches to the panels (cf. Potterne). – STAINED GLASS. Chancel by *Bell* of Bristol. – PLATE. Chalice, 1577.

WEST KNOYLE

8030

ST MARY. Perp w tower with gargoyles, battlements, and pinnacles. The rest of the church is of 1878 (by *J. Mountford Allen*; PF). – FONT. An C18 baluster font, now replaced. – PLATE. Chalice and Paten, 1727; Flagon, inscribed 1727.

WEST LAVINGTON

0050

ALL SAINTS. An interesting church with a somewhat complicated story which starts inside. The N arcade is of four bays. The first three date from *c.*1200. Circular piers, cruciform abaci, single-step arches. The capitals have stiff-leaf crockets and large, flat, single leaves. The tower is later, as it cuts into the first bay, the E parts are later, as bay four has a double-

chamfered arch. That is the form of the E.E. arches of the s
arcade. The s arcade was built at one go. Circular piers and
circular abaci. So when this was done, the N arcade was also
lengthened, the clerestory of single lancets was built, and the
chancel too. The chancel arch goes correspondingly with the
s arcade, but the rest is mostly Victorian, especially of course
the E window. However, the five s lancets are all original, as
they were covered by the later s chapel. By, say, 1250 the church
was thus complete. Next the N transept was added. The forms
look indeed later C13, particularly the N windows of three
stepped lancet lights. In fact the transept must have been
added after the clerestory was ready; for one of its windows
gives into the transept. Of the early C14 the W tower with bell-
openings of Y-tracery under ogee arches. Higher stair-turret.
Then, late in the C14 or early in the C15, the tower must have
given reason for anxiety. The arch towards the nave was
lowered and narrowed (traces of the larger one remain), and the
aisles were lengthened to embrace (and support) the tower.
Perp also the s transept, see the small blocked W doorway, the
N chapel and, at the end of the story, the s chapel, which, with
its pinnacles, is more lavish than the rest. Doorway from the
chancel to the chapel with roses. The s transept was converted into the family chapel of the Dauntseys, and at that
time the bleak, large arch with its simple pattern of Ds was
made. – PAINTING. The Virgin; tall, narrow oblong panel by
*Louis Davis, c.*1910. – STAINED GLASS. Much of the 1840s to
60s. – Chancel N, two windows by *Kempe*, of 1892 and 1907.
– PLATE. Chalice and two Patens, 1640; Flagon, 1680. –
MONUMENTS. In the s transept effigy of a Lady, probably late
C15. – Brass to John Dauntesey † 1559, a 26-in. figure.*
– Elizabeth Dauntsey † 1636. Semi-reclining figure, reading,
somewhat funny. In a black marble recess. – Henry Danvers 41a
† 1654. Of white marble. Semi-reclining figure in an elegant
posture on a sarcophagus. Above, inscription on an oval
plate with a wreath as its frame. Volutes l. and r., an open
segmental pediment and arms at the top. Quite a good piece.
– Two identical large tablets to members of the Hunt family.
They have no other figures but two putto heads at the foot of
each. Inscription plates with volutes l. and r. and a segmental
pediment at the top. That in the N aisle is to Margaret † 1729,
that in the N transept to Thomas, 1732.

* The brass is a palimpsest. On the reverse is part of a Flemish inscription
of 1518 of which the other part was re-used at Norton Disney in Lincolnshire.

DAUNTSEY'S SCHOOL. The buildings are all of brick. The original architect was *Ponting* of Marlborough, whom Marlborough College had given little of a chance. The oldest building dates from 1895 and is a long range with a central lantern. Angle pavilions at the ends. No higher than two storeys. Newer buildings behind, of no architectural interest (up to *c*.1920 architect *A. C. Martin* of Egham). The most recent additions are a science block and the chapel, both of 1957.

West Lavington, Littleton Pannell, and Market Lavington have all grown into one. The Manor House of Littleton Pannell, for example, belongs to Dauntsey's School. At West Lavington proper the following houses deserve recording.

WEST LAVINGTON MANOR in its present appearance is largely of 1908, Cotswold style, but with new round-arched features. Original details are the porch entrance with the initials of a Dauntsey † 1571 and his wife † 1559, and the mullioned windows and the arched gateway to the road. This is Jacobean and was brought in.

NE of the church humble brick ALMSHOUSES of 1831. They were founded in 1543, and some original details remain. To the E of these PYT HOUSE, Late Georgian, of three bays, brick, and then No. 48, a timber-framed house with brick infilling.

SE of the church the OLD VICARAGE, Early Georgian, of four bays, red and blue brick.

W of the church the OLD MANOR, with Georgian front with tripartite windows. However, two-light mullioned windows round the corner.

S of the church the PARSONAGE, a late C17 brick house of five by four bays, with two-light windows and a hipped roof. Further S, downhill, on the road to Tilshead, DIAL HOUSE, 1691, brick, of five bays, with cross-windows and the hood-mould over the door raised high enough to fit in a small two-light window. (Good staircase.) Opposite HUNT'S, Late Georgian, of three wide bays, the ground-floor windows under blank segmental arches. Tuscan porch.

WEST OVERTON

ST MICHAEL. 1878 by *C. E. Ponting*. In a mixture of styles: the w tower – just a little too thin to be genuine – appears to be C13, the N aisle also, the N transept a little later, the nave and chancel

Perp. Also a contrast of materials between tower and church. In the porch a decorated Norman window-head.

MANOR HOUSE, W of the church. The ground floor has some C16 details, notably the doorway with a basket arch.

LOCKERIDGE HOUSE. *See* Fyfield.

WEST PARK FIELD *see* BROMHAM

WEST WICK FARMHOUSE *see* PEWSEY

WESTWOOD

ST MARY. Splendid Perp W tower, ashlar-faced, with a prominent stair-turret crowned by a dome. The bell-openings form part of a composition of nine (three plus three plus three) lights with a transom. All this is blank except the upper three middle lights. It is an arrangement which corresponds to a whole group of Wiltshire churches (e.g. Nettleton, Devizes St James, Yatton Keynell) and is a reduction of the motifs of the Wells crossing tower and the Shepton Mallet group in Somerset. Gargoyles, tall panelled battlements, pinnacles. Tall panelled arch to the nave. The stair-turret corbels out with the nave and rests on a winged monster. The tower was built by Thomas Horton, a rich clothier who died in 1530 and is buried in Bradford-on-Avon parish church. His initials are above the entrance. Perp nave of three bays, two-bay ashlar-faced N aisle of two bays, again with battlements and gargoyles. In the aisle niches to the l. of the E window and a good ceiling, the E bay with quatrefoiled panels. The arcade piers with four shafts and four wide wavy mouldings in the diagonals. However, there is much earlier evidence as well. In the chancel a N lancet and the priest's doorway with a trefoiled head and above it the remains of a primitively carved tympanum: an incised rosette and incised lilies. This seems C13, with the tympanum perhaps originally Norman, and partly incised much later. The continuous mouldings of the chancel arch are C13 too, and so is the primitive piscina with dog-tooth decoration. – FONT COVER. Perp, ogee in outline, with crocketed ridges and a scale pattern. Suspended from an iron bracket. – PULPIT. 1607, with the usual blank arches. – SCREEN. Low; originally probably the COMMUNION RAIL. Mid-C17, with an interesting pattern of ovals into which four knobs stick out, almost meeting. – STALL FRONTS. With Perp tracery and poppy heads. – STAINED GLASS. Much Perp glass in the chancel, especially the E window with Christ crucified, surrounded by angels and the Instruments of the Passion, the angel panels on a ruby ground. The Instruments have been compared with those in the glass at Leigh-on-Mendip in Somerset. – MONUMENT. Richard Cox † 1789. Large oval plaque, with garlands along the upper half of the edge. Relief of a woman by an urn. The inscription on a scroll hanging down from the base of the relief.

WESTWOOD MANOR. A perfect Wiltshire manor house of the type of South Wraxall, quite extensive, not too regular, and with a fascinating, complicated architectural history unravelled only very recently. There are essentially four periods: c.1400, c.1480, c.1515–30, and the early C17. The second of the four periods is that of Thomas Culverhouse, the third that of the rich clothier Thomas Horton who bought the property about 1515 and died in 1530 (cf. Bradford-on-Avon), the fourth is the end of the Horton ownership and that of John Farewell, brother-in-law of the last Horton. He came in 1616 and died in 1642.

The forecourt of the house is reached by a tall Jacobean arch with a strapwork top standing against the sky. Having passed through this, one faces the projecting W wing and has the hall range on the r., i.e. the N. An E wing corresponding to the W wing has disappeared. The S part of the W wing contains the oldest surviving feature, a ground-floor window to the W with details of c.1400. It belonged to an originally detached small house. This appears e.g. from the fact that the level of this S part is lower than that of the rest of the wing. However, the oriel to the E above the room with this window has uncusped four-centred heads to its opening, and this detail is more in accordance with Thomas Horton's time than the other window.

Culverhouse probably built the S range, but the only detail of c.1480 is now the beams of the ground-floor room at its extreme W end. Thomas Horton did much more. His is especially the two-storeyed bay window close to the N end of the W wing. The room on the ground floor behind this bay window has a big fireplace of the Horton time with curly leaf spandrels, and the entrance arch to the bay is panelled, like so many tower arches of churches of the same time. The ceiling has Horton's thin beams but Jacobean motifs in the panels. In the bedroom above, to which belongs the upper part of the bay window, is a little STAINED GLASS from Horton's time (see his rebus). Culverhouse's HALL was originally no doubt open to the roof, but Farewell divided it horizontally to create his Great Chamber. So the hall is now low. It has a plain ceiling. The relatively simple wooden screen is Jacobean. At the w end is a pretty triangular LOBBY, corresponding to Farewell's rather awkward staircase projection in the corner of the hall and the w range. E of the hall, where originally the kitchen and offices must have been, Farewell inserted a small extremely ornate room, known as the KING'S ROOM. It has a plaster ceiling with deeply moulded ribs and big branches in the panels, a pendant, exuberant friezes, an overmantel with a mermaid, fishes, the fox and geese, a duck, and branches, and at the top of the wall panelling a frieze of panels painted with portraits of English kings up to Charles I. This was bought from Keevil Manor in 1910. On the first floor the *pièce de resistance* is of course the GREAT PARLOUR above the hall, with a plaster ceiling of very low pitch standing on a frieze, and below that a deep coving. The plaster ribs are thin and form geometrical patterns. In the cresting are pendants, in the coving big branches, and, in the middle of one short side, a coat of arms, along the other strapwork. The overmantel also has branches, partly set in naively detailed blank arches. More rooms with Jacobean features on the upper floor of the w wing, e.g. another overmantel with branches in blank arches in the Horton bedroom and ribbed panels of concave-sided star shape between deep beams plastered with foliage trails in the NW corner room.

An impressive C15 stone BARN stands at some distance E of the church.

At UPPER WESTWOOD two houses of importance. One is C17, with an embattled porch with fluted pilasters, the other, GREENHILL, is early C18, of five bays and two storeys with a hipped roof. Giant pilaster strips, pedimented ground-floor windows. Low gabled C17 wings of one bay, much re-done. Gateposts and garden wall. A recent stylized garden across the road.

WHADDON

1½ m. NE of Hilperton

ST MARY. Nave and chancel and stone bell-turret. The chancel and bellcote were rebuilt in 1879, and the nave was much restored. The N addition with the round-arched windows with Y-tracery is the Long Chapel, with the family vault under. A long gentle flight of steps leads down to the tunnel-vaulted chamber whose date can be read in it in large figures: 1778. What is the most valuable part of the church is hidden by the porch: the Norman s doorway, alas reconstructed and evidently not quite correctly. One order of shafts, capitals with decorated scallops, and then a remarkable lintel, segmental below, semicircular above, and decorated with beaded tendrils or trails and palmettes in several directions. The arch has excessively big and deeply moulded crenellations, obviously cut off. The blocked N doorway is Norman too, and has simple but a little unusual imposts and again a lintel segmental below. – DOOR. C14 s door with iron hinges. – PLATE. C17 Chalice and Paten Cover. – MONUMENTS. Walter Long † 1807, the *magnum opus* of *King* of Bath, magnum certainly in size, though in style both a little bleak and a little pompous. Standing monument, tripartite composition. On the side pieces in relief very slender urns surrounded by rays, in the centre long inscription, and above, to the l. and r., in the round, two long torches. Top semicircular with garlands. – Kathleen Long † 1814. By *Sir R. Westmacott.* Also a standing monument. Relief of a kneeling angel sickling corn. Another angel hovers over him. The relief represents Job v:26 ('Like as a shock of corn cometh in season'). The earliest Long monument is a brass inscription and shield of 1612.

SAXON BURIAL. *See* Alderbury.

WHELPLEY FARM *see* WHITEPARISH

WHETHAM HOUSE *see* BOWOOD

WHISTLEY FARMHOUSE *see* POTTERNE

WHITCHURCH FARMHOUSE *see* MALMESBURY,
p. 295

2020

WHITEPARISH

ALL SAINTS. Externally all Victorian (1870 by *Butterfield*; PF). Shingled bell-turret with steep pyramid roof. Nave and aisles under one big roof. Tall SE chimneystack. But in the chancel plain Norman priest's doorway and Dec low-side window. Remains of alterations in the chancel N wall. Dec w doorway and window of three stepped lancet lights, cusped. In the w wall re-set Norman bits. Inside a much more complex affair.

First the two E bays of the S aisle. Circular piers, many-scalloped round capitals (cf. Ivychurch, Alderbury), bases with corner spurs, single-step pointed arches. Then the whole N aisle, C13, with circular piers and circular abaci, but still single-step pointed arches (re-used or the restorer's?). After that the S aisle W bays, Perp, with an octagonal pier. The chancel arch is C13, but altered. Voussoirs alternatingly grey and brown. Perp E window. – PAINTINGS. St Peter denying Christ, by *J. F. Rigaud*. Night scene with lamp-light. Rigaud came to England in 1771 and died in 1810. He did decorative painting for churches, for Windsor, for the Guildhall and other places, and was an R.A. – HELM, late C16 (N aisle). – PLATE. Chalice, 1603; Paten, 1672. – MONUMENTS. Edward St Barbe † 1671. Tablet with three skulls at the bottom. – Mrs Hungerford † 1692. Almost identical.

LYNCHES, N of the church. Late C17. Brick, of six bays and two storeys, a seventh for the doorway and a horizontal window over. Stone cross-windows; flat surrounds, with a slight outer moulding. Gatepiers to the front garden.

ABBOTSTON HOUSE, ¼ m. W. Dated 1627. Brick, gabled, with mullioned and transomed windows.

COTTAGE, ¾ m. SW, at Newton, just NE of the A 36 road. Timber-framed; of cruck construction.

WHELPLEY FARM, 1 m. WNW. The flintwork walls of the former CHAPEL OF ST LEONARD remain as a chicken-house, but there are no features of interest.

NEWHOUSE, 2¼ m. SW. Called 'lately erected' in 1619. A brick house of most unusual plan. Hexagonal centre and three wings, leaving each façade with a centre and two wings projecting at an obtuse angle. Only one façade has all three parts gabled. Mullioned-and-transomed windows. The house is said to have been built as a hunting lodge for Sir Thomas Gorges of Longford Castle, another house designed on the triad principle. However, closer still to Newhouse is a house curiously called Newhouse Farm, which is near Goodrich in Herefordshire and was built in 1636. In the C18 longer and lower wings were added, and two remain, one of them with fine Rococo plasterwork inside. In the centre two staircases, one with the strong, vigorously twisted balusters of the late C17, the other, larger one with the slender twisted balusters in groups of three which belong to the C18. Rainwater heads have the dates 1742, 1750, 1762, 1764. On the stable clock is the date 1751.

EYRE'S FOLLY, 2¼ m. WNW, on the brow of Brickworth Down

with wide views to W and E. 1606. Octagonal brick tower with pyramid roof. The first floor has raised brick bands, a kind of rustication. Nearly all the windows are now blocked. The tower was probably a 'standing'.

WHITESHEET HILL *see* KILMINGTON

WHITLEY FARMHOUSE *see* SHAW

WICK HILL *see* BREMHILL *and* KELLAWAYS

²⁰⁴⁰

WILBURY HOUSE
1 m. N of Newton Toney

The great importance of Wilbury House lies less in its appearance now than in its appearance as it was first built and illustrated in *Vitruvius Britannicus*. It was designed by and built for *William Benson* in 1710. He is notorious for having been made Wren's successor in 1718, when George I dismissed Wren as a Tory and an old man, and for having failed so completely that he himself was replaced only one year later. But he is memorable as the designer of the first, not Neo-Palladian, but neo-Inigo-Jones house in England. For this is what Wilbury was, as Sir John Summerson was the first to point out. The house then had a four-column Corinthian portico of tall columns set well away from the wall, as Webb had, for example, done at Amesbury, not so far away. It was crowned by a pediment, and a hipped roof with a belvedere like Pratt's at Coleshill.

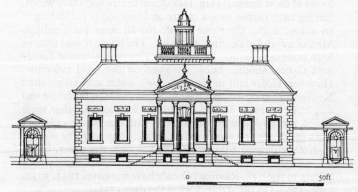

Wilbury House, as originally built by William Benson, 1710

A little later, we do not know when but can assume a date
c.1740–50, the portico was altered so that the middle interstice
became wider than the side ones and an upper floor was added.
The window surrounds are moulded like those on the ground
floor. About 1775 or so the roof was probably changed, and on
that occasion the top frieze introduced. Also wings were built
with canted fronts and unmoulded window reveals. Finally,
early in the C19, a bow was added on the w side.

The main front is to the s. It has the portico and two bays
each side. Part of the work of c.1775 is the handsome doorway,
tripartite, with elegant elongated corbels – very similar to that
at Durnford Manor. On the n side the middle three bays project
a little and there is a porch of c.1775 with Adamish Ionic
columns. Inside, the room behind the portico is splendid
indeed – but it is certainly not of 1710. The style is Kentian and
the date probably c.1740–50. Three bays, ample coffered
coving, wreath in the centre of the ceiling. Big doorcase at the
back, with Corinthian demi-columns and an open pediment.
Above the fireplace panel with putti, opposite oval panel with
a Roman emperor. L. and r. of this Rococo bands. The big
niches in the se room on the other hand could well be Queen
Anne, even if their decoration and that of the chimneypiece
look again rather c.1740. The ceiling of the sw room is restrained and specially fine. The fireplace of the late C18 was
brought in. In the sw wing the library, with original bookcases
of c.1775. The dark green and gold colour scheme is said to be
original. In the se wing in a ceiling a curious putto head with a
kind of feather cloak. This is attributed to *Burne-Jones* or Mrs
Wyndham; for Mr Percy Wyndham lived at Wilbury while
Webb built Clouds at East Knoyle for him.

Various garden furnishings need mention. First to the w of
the house in the trees a GROTTO with pointed arches in the
main room and a gangway to a back exit. Then to the n a
COLUMN of modest size commemorating Queen Victoria's
Jubilee in 1897, and to the e of this, some little distance away,
an octagonal, domed SUMMER HOUSE on a mound with a small
GROTTO in it. The summer house has pilasters with intermittent rocky rustication. An ARCHWAY s of the summer house.

WILCOT 1060

HOLY CROSS. The chancel arch is of c.1200. Semicircular, with
three detached shafts. The capitals decorated trumpet scallops
and also of the crocket type. Perp w tower; the doorway has

spandrels with big flowers and big leaves. Bell-openings with Somerset tracery. Most of the church however is the work of *A. J. Style* (PF) after a fire of 1876. – PLATE. Chalice and Paten Cover, 1664; Paten, 1708. – MONUMENT. John Berwick, dated 1574. Simple, flat substructure with three shields. Narrower superstructure with a four-centred arch and above it a typically Early Elizabethan broad frieze of very simplified big volutes and small stylized honeysuckle (?) between.

WILCOT MANOR. In Domesday, Wilcot Manor is mentioned as an excellent house, which is highly unusual. Its vineyard is mentioned too. The present manor house has gables with mulonlied windows but a front remodelled in the C18. Circular DOVECOTE.

LADIES BRIDGE, ¾ m. WSW. A surprisingly ornate bridge across the canal, dated 1808 and, according to the MHLG, by *Rennie*. Single arch with much vermiculated rustication, applied also in triangle and lozenge patterns, and flat swags, in medallions and without medallions. Part parapet, part balustrade.

By the KENNET AND AVON CANAL, to the N a nice bit of canal-erie; brick and thatch cottages.

STOWELL PARK, 1 m. NE. The completion date said to be 1813. Rendered. On the entrance side an attic with grouped chimneys. Round the corner, on the garden side, veranda of six Doric columns, arranged two–one–one–two. In the grounds STATUE of a girl by *Frank Dobson* and, across the canal, a miniature SUSPENSION BRIDGE.

WILLESLEY *see* SHERSTON

1030   WILSFORD
                     1½ m. SW of Amesbury

ST MICHAEL. Unbuttressed Norman W tower; see the herring-bone flintwork, the W doorway (one order of shafts, scallop capitals, single-step arch), and the arch towards the nave (unmoulded, on the simplest imposts) with a window over. The body of the church by *T. H. Wyatt*, 1851. Nave and chancel in one, lancet windows. The timber porch is of 1869 (by *Weaver*; PF). – CANDLESTICKS l. and r. of the altar, two fine pieces of the Arts and Crafts period. – Eight C18 SCONCES. – STAINED GLASS. Small C15 Crucifixus in a S window. – MONUMENT. Mrs Wynlayne Foster Lodge † 1922. By *Eric Gill*. Round-headed slate panel with a young woman and, on the ground, a baby. In the unmistakable, slightly Egyptianizing Expressionism of Gill.

WILSFORD HOUSE. 1904–6 by *Detmar Blow*, built with local labour and without a sub-contractor. The style is that of the local c17. Chequer flint and stone, gables, mullioned windows. Late c17 staircase with strong balusters. The woodwork, made by *Ernest Gimson*, has all disappeared.

LAKE HOUSE. This was an imposing house of flint and stone 35b chequer built by a clothier, George Duke, who had bought the estate in 1578. It fell on evil days and was reinstated with exemplary care and tact by *Detmar Blow* in 1898 'with the council of *Philip Webb*'. In 1912, it was gutted by fire and later reinstated and added to by *Darcy Braddell & Deane*. Fine front with five even gables and an embattled two-storeyed porch. Under the first and last gables canted bays, also embattled. More gables round the corner. The original house was L-shaped. The principal addition is the dining room in the SE corner. Inside the house panelling and some fireplaces acquired fairly recently and said to come from houses in Bristol. The most spectacular piece is a chimneypiece of stone with an oval relief of St George and the Dragon. Also a very restrained chimneypiece dated 1658.

WILSFORD 1050

4 m. SW of Pewsey

ST NICHOLAS. Low, modest E.E. chancel with single lancets on the N and S and a group of three stepped lancets on the E. A former N chapel had a c14 arch of two chamfers. Set into the blocking of the chapel a doorway which might be Norman. Perp nave. Good head-corbels for the roof. Perp W tower with a quatrefoil frieze at the base and a fleur-de-lis frieze below the battlements. Higher stair-turret.

WILTON 0030

Wilton in the Middle Ages had a famous Benedictine nunnery, founded by King Alfred and in the c12 and c13 probably over eighty nuns strong. Close to the nunnery a town grew up. Its plan is preserved in the present street plan. There were in addition a Dominican house founded before 1245, the Hospital of St Giles founded before 1135, the Hospital of St John Baptist founded in 1190, and the Hospital of St Mary Magdalene founded before 1307. Leland says Wilton had twelve parish churches. That may

17

be an exaggeration, but six are known to us by name in history. Of one of them a fragment survives. But the church remembered at Wilton is not one of them.

61b ST MARY AND ST NICHOLAS. Built in 1843 by *Thomas Henry Wyatt & D. Brandon* for the Rt Hon. Sidney Herbert, Secretary of War, at a cost of £20,000. The church is a *tour de force* in the *Rundbogenstil*, the round-arch style, to use a German term for a style revived particularly in Germany, first by Schinkel and then by others. It had a vogue in England in the forties, and a measure of Wilton's international prominence in the style is the fact that it was described in the *Allgemeine Bauzeitung* of Vienna. The term 'round-arch style' is appropriate; for it could take the shape of Early Christian, Byzantine, Italian Romanesque, or indeed Norman. At Wilton we are faced with the Italian Romanesque. The symptoms are unmistakable: twisted columns in the main portal standing on recumbent lions; friezes below the eaves climbing up and down them in the façade; a big rose window; an isolated campanile. The basilican appearance on the other hand is generally Early Christian to Italian Romanesque. The church is remarkably high, and the campanile reaches a height of 108 ft. It is connected with the church by a playful little gallery of richly decorated colonnettes. Rich also is the carving of the portals. The apse is lower than the chancel, has shafts reaching right up it, and incidentally faces the green of the estate. The interior is certainly monumental, with its erect proportions and its open timber roof. The proud columns have capitals carved by *William Osmond Jun.* of Salisbury. Above them a kind of triforium, of eight little arches for each bay, not at all an archaeologically correct motif. The chancel is divided from the nave by very tall black marble columns. It is groin-vaulted. There are also chancel aisles ending in apses. Their W arches have black columns too, and they are original ancient Roman pieces from the Temple of Venus at Porto Venere (C2 B.C.). The chancel aisles are divided from the chancel by a tripartite colonnade, again not a correct motif. The mosaic pavement in the chancel is by Mr *Singer*, the very Italian mosaics of chancel and apse by *Gertrude Martin*, the chancel colouring and patterning by *Willement*, the side apse mosaics by *Gertrude Martin* to the design of *Sir Charles Nicholson*. Heavy W gallery forming two sham *ambones* round the first columns. Doorways flanked by twisted columns with stone mosaic. Of the same type the CANDLESTICKS in the main and the S apse. All these columns are genuine *Cosmati* work. But the NW doorway has thick black marble barley-sugar columns instead. The PULPIT stands on a forest of black marble columns with excellently carved capitals. The upper colonnettes are again of *Cosmati* work and from the same source as those in the chancel. Sidney Herbert bought for 47 guineas at the Strawberry Hill sale in 1842 the so-called Shrine of Capoccio which William Hamilton had acquired in 1768 and presented to Horace Walpole. It dates from 1256 and was at S. Maria Maggiore. The Shrine of Capoccio had been made fit for display in Horace Walpole's chapel by *John Augustus Richter* in 1774, and some of his work ought also to be traceable. Moreover, the *Journal of the Brit. Arch. Ass.*, XV, reports that some twisted columns came from Palermo. The church ought to be investigated properly with full use of the Pembroke archives.

FONT. Of Italian marbles, more sensuous in shape than the rest. The font is called 'of ancient Italian workmanship' in *The Illustrated London News*, 4 August 1849. – PULPIT. *See* above. – READING DESK. With Flemish (Spanish?) Baroque reliefs. – DOORS. The doors have old wood panels: Early-Renaissance English (N chancel aisle), Flemish C16 (N aisle), Flemish C16 and others (W doors). – STAINED GLASS. An amazing collection of pieces from the Continent and England, starting with the wonderful panels in the apse. The centre panel, part of one large figure, comes from the clerestory of a French later C12 cathedral, the other panels are French C13 glass.* So is one group in the N apse. Also in the N apse fine early C14 angels. Then there is German C14 glass, badly preserved, in the N aisle NE window, English C15 glass in the S apse, English mid-C16 glass from the chapel of the first Earl of Pembroke's house in the S aisle SW window (kneeling donors), and German and Flemish glass in the N aisle NW window. The figure of God the Father came from Malines, is attributed to *Arnold van Nijmegen*, and belongs to a group the rest of which is at St George's Hanover Square (from Antwerp). Excellent German Pietà below. In the W rose window the glass is mostly C19, but there is also German C16 glass. In the vestry Netherlandish C16 and C17 roundels. Of C19 glass TK mentions in the N wall glass by *O'Connor*, 1853, at the SE end by *Wailes* 1847 and *Gibbs & Howard* 1882. – PLATE. Paten, 1683. – MONUMENTS. John Coffer † 1585. Small brass plate with kneeling figure (N aisle).

---

* Professor Grodecki has made it probable that a prophet in this window belonged to a scene from the Childhood of Christ at St Denis Abbey.

– William Sharp † 1626. Kneeling figures above the N aisle NW door. Children below, but the whole not in its original state. – Ninth Earl of Pembroke † 1749. Big grey base and bust on top. – Elizabeth Countess of Pembroke, by *Rossi*, 1793, with a delicate relief, partly *schiacciato*. – Tenth Earl † 1794. Designed by *James Wyatt* and carved by *Westmacott Sen*. A severe sarcophagus and nothing else. – Eleventh Earl † 1827. By *Sir Richard Westmacott*. A beautiful relief with a Holy Family and a Grecian Shepherd. Portrait bust in relief in a medallion at the top. – Lord Herbert of Lea and the Countess of Pembroke, his mother, the founders of the church, † 1861 and 1856. Recumbent white effigies on tomb-chests. Designed by *Wyatt* and carved by *John Birnie Philip*.

ST MARY, Market Place. The nave is in ruins. The arch of the W window remains, and the arcades inside, Perp, with the usual pier section of four shafts and four hollows and with four-centred arches. The chancel has a plaster ceiling of the C18, the E bay gracefully and sparingly decorated. The E window seems early C19. – Many TABLETS, e.g. John Thomas, 'an eminent Manufacturer of this Borough', † 1793.

ST PETER, Fugglestone, Salisbury Road, by the roundabout. Nave and chancel and small polygonal bell-turret. The chancel is C13, with three stepped lancets at the E end and single lancets on the sides, all over-restored. The two uncommonly wide arches between nave and S aisle also seem C13. Piers square and only slightly chamfered. Arches pointed with one slight chamfer. Narrow aisle. – The bell-turret probably C15. – – FONT. C18 baluster. – (PEWS. Remains of C17 pews with decoration along the walls.) – COMMUNION RAIL. Later C17. – PLATE. Cup, 1581; similar Cup, *c*.1630; Tankard, 1589; Silver-gilt Chalice, Italian (?). – MONUMENT. Small coffin-lid of a Lady, her hands on her breast. Re-cut face. C13; Purbeck marble.

METHODIST CHAPEL, Kingsbury Square. 1875. Red brick and stone dressings, five bays wide, like a Cinquecento palazzo front.

WILTON HOUSE. The first earl of Pembroke was granted the nunnery estate in 1544. Of his house, which was built round a courtyard, the general shape remains, and certainly the so-called HOLBEIN PORCH, now a garden ornament to the W of the S front, but originally the porch from the courtyard to the Great Hall, which lay in the N range (cf. e.g. Dingley and Deene Park, both Northants), is a typical piece of *c*.1560–70, open on three sides and with three façades. Pairs of fluted Ionic columns below, pairs of fluted Corinthian columns above. The latter frame a field with a coat of arms and two frontal portrait busts in round recesses. Top with two shell-gables. Inside a transverse depressed tunnel-vault.

As for the first earl's house itself, a good deal of the masonry must belong to it,* and also at least the outline on the most imposing side, that facing E. We have a drawing dated 1563 which shows this side as it then (i.e. at the time of the Holbein Porch) was, and this has the same tall central frontispiece with archway and tall oriel window and lantern as it has today, the same lower connecting links, and the same higher corner pavilions. Only every detail is changed. The archway – it was the main entrance up to the C19 – looks medieval in the drawing, the details of the three-storeyed oriel differ, the top is a prominent pediment – early for 1563, though preceded about 1550 at Somerset House, the Lord Protector's London house. The present frontispiece has a different archway, a different fenestration, and a different lantern, adjustments made by *James Wyatt* when he worked at Wilton. The connecting links, now with two bays of classical windows in two and a half storeys,‡ had just one five-light transomed window surprisingly high up and again top pediments; and the corner pavilions, now by Inigo Jones on the l. and repeated thus on the r., had straight gables with big chimneys and also five-light windows lower down. The windows had no arched lights and were in that respect again remarkably advanced.

Wyatt was called in by the eleventh earl in 1801. He did much to the house. He rebuilt the W range recessed by two steps in the centre and then only one-storeyed and provided with a large bay window. Inside this range a Gothic Library was contrived. It was ungothicized in the C20. Wyatt also rebuilt the N front, which originally contained the Great Hall, and made it the main entrance. To do so he raised the level of the forecourt and gave it its embattled walls. The details of the N front are a mixture of the Wyatt Elizabethan and the C20 Classical. The arms of Henry VIII, however, may well be original work of c.1544.§ The forecourt is closed to the town by

---

* See a recent opening in the SW corner of the upper cloister, i.e. outside the Single Cube Room.

‡ The balustrades were added in the C20.

§ In the N entrance hall a STATUE of Shakespeare leaning on an urn. It is by *Scheemakers*, 1743.

a splendid ARCHWAY with coupled Corinthian pilasters framing a tunnel-vaulted arch on Tuscan columns to the N and S. In the spandrels paterae with garlands hanging oddly, as if they were going to slide down any moment. On top on a stepped base the equestrian statue of Marcus Aurelius. This arch was designed by *Sir William Chambers* just before 1759 and erected on top of the hill to the S of the house. Wyatt brought it down to close the forecourt and create a worthy overture to the house. He added the two cubic LODGES l. and r. The GATES are of the C18, from Mount Merrion near Dublin. They were bought in Italy *c.*1840.

Wyatt also converted the former main entrance on the E side into a GARDEN HALL, giving it a thin plaster rib-vault,* built a large but rather bare STAIRCASE next to it (with a plain iron handrail, replacing alas Jones's 'Geometrical Staircase' i.e. staircase without any visible support for the steps – cf. the Tulip Staircase in the Queen's House at Greenwich), and improved communications throughout by taking off the four sides of the inner courtyard enough space for a CLOISTER. The cloister is two-storeyed, with a plaster tierceron-vault on the upper level.‡

The only front of the house not interfered with by Wyatt is the SOUTH FRONT. This was built by *John Webb* after a fire which had occurred in 1647-8 but on the advice of *Inigo Jones* (and according to Aubrey of Charles I, who visited Wilton every summer). Jones was over seventy-five when the commission was given. The range was built for Philip, the fourth earl, who had succeeded his brother in 1630. To the two brothers the First Folio is dedicated. Before work started on the new S range, about 1632, a large formal garden was laid out by *Isaac de Caus* in front of it. Here also the 'advice and approbation' of *Jones* are mentioned. Mr Colvin draws attention to the fact that de Caus's garden is twice the width of the present S front, and that a drawing at Queen's College Oxford shows the front the same width as the garden, with a centre motif of a portico of six giant Corinthian columns, with a wider interval in the middle and a top pediment. It can be assumed that this is an echo of Jones's design of *c.*1632, and that what was executed fifteen years later is a reduction of it. It is nine bays wide, of Chilmark stone, the bays very generously spaced, and has a semi-basement with segment-headed windows with heavy keystones, a

* In the hall four busts by *Roubiliac* and busts by *Foley, Steell,* and others.
‡ Plaques of *Coade* stone in the walls.

principal floor with the State Rooms, and an attic floor above crowned by a balustrade. The centre window is of the Venetian 43 type with a coat of arms over, flanked by very French-looking figures in shallow relief. Main windows otherwise have just straight entablatures, and the angle bays are raised by one storey into pedimented pavilions, one bay wide and two bays deep. These are entirely missing in the Oxford drawing. In these angle bays the main window has a pediment and the top window a segmental pediment. That is all. It is an extremely restrained front which does not prepare for the luxuriance inside. The originally projected centre motif would of course have given it additional grandeur. The windows in the C17 can, needless to say, not have been sashed, and one must assume stone crosses of mullion and transom. The motif of the raised angle pavilions can be traced back to Serlio (VII, 21), i.e. the principal Italian Cinquecento source book of the years before Palladio.

The s range must have been rebuilt rapidly: in 1652 Huygens could already be shown the new state rooms and admire their ceilings. Their decoration is indubitably *Inigo Jones*'s own work (see e.g. the drawings). The contrast between exterior and interior is one which Jones created deliberately. The remark is familiar which he once committed to paper, that ' outwardly every wise man carries a gravity, yet inwardly has his imagination set on fire and sometimes licentiously flies out'. As in man, so in the works of man. What Jones has thus created in the STATE ROOMS at Wilton is unique in England and can vie with the best decoration of the mid C17 in France. It is classical, but opulent, not at all strictly Palladian, but rather stimulated by the semi-classical, semi-Baroque decoration of France, as exemplified, for example, in the engravings of Jean Barbet. The greater part of the decoration is in white and gold.* The characteristic motifs are fat and compact fruit or leaf garlands – very different from the looser and more deeply undercut garlands of the Wren period – heads between garlands or swags, very large chimneypieces – too large really for the smaller of the state rooms – robust and grave caryatids flanking them on the overmantel, open pediments, triangular or segmental or even double-curved and curly at the open ends, and more generally a passion for sudden projections, broken cornices, and so on, i.e. a character not at all smooth, let alone academic. There are six state rooms, the Little Anteroom and the Corner

* But the Little Anteroom is blue, dun, and gold.

Room (both with early C19 flock wallpapers and the former with a ceiling painting by *Sabbatini*, the latter with one attributed to *Luca Giordano*), the State Bedroom (now Colonnade Room because of the bed niche divided off by two fluted Ionic columns; ceiling with *singeries* by *Andieu de Clermont*, 1735–9, far too finicky for Inigo's architecture), the Great Anteroom (curved wall towards the Double Cube Room, Ionic pilasters, ceiling probably by *Clermont*), and then the Double Cube and the Single Cube Rooms, the former $60 \times 30 \times 30$, the latter $30 \times 30 \times 30$ ft, simple geometrical relations which Inigo favoured. The panelling of the Double Cube was designed from the start to take the celebrated *van Dyck* portraits of the Herberts, culminating in the family group of the fourth Earl painted *c*.1634. The heavy cove painting is by *Edward Pierce*, the ceiling painting with heavy figured architecture very probably by *Emanuel de Critz*. In the Single Cube the dado paintings of scenes from Sidney's 'Arcadia', written, it will be remembered, at Wilton, are by *Thomas de Critz*, the cove by *Clermont*, the ceiling by the *Cavaliere d'Arpino*.* Of other interiors the two Smoking Rooms in the E range have some restrained C17 decoration. It goes with the external remodelling of the connecting links to the E, and the date is not recorded. Possibly it is of the late C17.‡

To the NW of the house the so-called ALMONRY, the one surviving fragment of the nunnery buildings. It has a doorway with fine mouldings and a shouldered lintel, apparently of *c*.1300, and a two-light ground-floor window. Close to it the simple RIDING SCHOOL, built by *Roger Morris* after the tenth Earl had succeeded in 1749. He was a great authority on equitation

The GROUNDS were landscaped between 1732 and 1738 by the ninth Earl, who may have been his own designer or may have consulted *Kent*.

ORANGERY. Probably of the early C19. Seven bays, quite simple. To the l. and r. two Ionic COLUMNS with bands of thick rocky rustication. They are of the *Jones–Webb* period.

PALLADIAN BRIDGE. 1737. Designed on the pattern of a Palladian drawing, also followed at Stowe before 1745 and Prior Park, Bath, in 1750. The design was done by the ninth

---

* A description of the furniture, largely by *Chippendale*, father and son, but also by *Kent* and others, is outside the scope of *The Buildings of England*.

‡ In a room not seen by the public and called the Hunting Room wall panels painted by *Pierce* the elder. In other private rooms some more Jonesian chimneypieces, especially one splendid one in the room to the r. of the hall on the N front (information given me by Mr John Harris).

Earl of Pembroke and his architect *Roger Morris*. The bridge is covered and consists of end pavilions with arches, attached columns and pediments, and a middle piece with a straight entablature on four Ionic columns.

(CASINO, on the hill in front of the s façade. Shortly before 1759, by *Chambers*. Tetrastyle Tuscan portico with pediment on a tall rusticated base. Inside the base the kitchen, inside behind the portico a room with a plaster ceiling.)

LOGGIA. Three arches, four attached Corinthian columns 45a carrying four busts. The date is unknown, the C17 likely. In front a tall Corinthian COLUMN of porphyry on a tall pedestal. On top an Italian Venus probably of *c.*1600. According to Defoe, the column was brought from Alexandria.

WASHERN GRANGE, by the s end of the park, a good deal s of the Palladian Bridge. Of brick, probably built in the late C17. The front is of two plus seven plus two bays. The angle bays have windows with oval windows over and a balustrade with vertically symmetrical balusters. The seven middle bays are blank arches, except for the entrance. Piers with bands of stone. Parapet with blank medallions. Inside, a courtyard with the same motif all round, except that it is transparent to the w. On the E side is a screen to hide a C14 BARN. Inside the barn a single-framed roof.

PERAMBULATION. There is not much to be looked at at Wilton, although in early medieval times it was the most important town in Wiltshire. The walk starts at the gates of Wilton House and moves along MINSTER STREET. In the trees opposite, ISLAND HOUSE, Georgian, of brick, with a porch on thin Tuscan columns. Then the PEMBROKE ARMS HOTEL, late C18, of white brick, three wide bays, segment-headed windows, porch with broken segmental pediment on Tuscan columns. The widening which follows is called KINGSBURY SQUARE. It is a green, with modest two-storeyed houses around, except for a presumptuous timber-framed pub. On by Silver Street to the MARKET PLACE. The MARKET HOUSE is of 1738, six bays, of red brick, with a heavy clock turret.* Between it and the church the COUNTY CROSS, a curious pillar, obviously consisting of parts not belonging together, including a Crucifixus, a decayed sundial, and an C18 urn at the top.‡ From the

* REGALIA. Mace, 1639; Great Mace, 1685; Loving Cup, 1693; Sergeant's Mace, 1709.

‡ On Rocque's plan, i.e. in the mid C18, a square building appears in the Market Place which is called the Carpet Workhouse.

Market Place N in NORTH STREET No. 25, a timber-framed house with an overhanging first floor on the l. and r., but not in the centre. An even line for the eaves is gained by double-curved braces, the so-called Wealden way. Then from the Market Place to the W along WEST STREET with the generous RECTORY, red brick with giant yellow brick pilasters and a curved porch on thin Tuscan columns. Late Georgian. Past the church to ST JOHN'S SQUARE and the HOSPITAL. Of this the chancel of the chapel survives, with a late C13 E window and Dec and Perp side windows, and in addition nave and N transept used as dwellings. Opposite, a five-bay house probably of the early C18. Finally down SOUTH STREET from the Market Place. Here No. 129, a *mixtum compositum*, with three gables, but a Venetian window and a doorway with fluted Ionic pilasters and a pediment. Opposite, the new MEMORIAL HALL, by *B. O. Brown*, Neo-Georgian, completed in 1938. At the end, past the bridge, No. 46, also irregular, with a doorway flanked by heavy Corinthian columns which carry an open segmental pediment, i.e. *c.*1700. Yet further S BULBRIDGE HOUSE, early C18, of brick chequer, with two-light windows. In the front garden a modest ROTUNDA with Tuscan columns and a little dome.

WILTON ROYAL CARPET FACTORY, Warminster Road. The main building must be of the later C18 or early C19. It is sixteen bays long, of brick, and has round-arched windows below, segment-headed windows above. New building of 1957 by *Robert Townsend*. With a multiple paraboloid timber roof. The building is a square of 110 ft and was erected in six weeks.

KINGSWAY HOUSE, NW of the station. The former WORK-HOUSE, 1836–7. Brick, still classical, with the usual octagonal centre.

WINDMILL HILL see AVEBURY

WINGFIELD

ST MARY. Ashlar-faced Perp W tower with stair-turret higher than the tower. The rest C18 except for the N transept, which is of 1861. Over the S porch inscription referring to a burial of 1622. But the forms look later. Nice coved chancel ceiling with rosettes. Its date is not known, but there is a date 1732 for the rebuilding of the nave. – PLATE. Paten, given in the mid C17; Chalice, Paten and Flagon, given 1749. – MONUMENTS. John

Bayley † 1665. Tablet with columns twisted not the Baroque but the Cosmati way. Open segmental pediment. – Thomas Morris † 1818. By *Reeves*. With an urn and a weeping willow.

CHURCH FARMHOUSE. Dated 1636. Gabled and with mullioned windows.

STOWFORD FARM, 1¼ m. NW. Front with three irregular gables and windows with uncusped arched lights. They are of four, three, two lights. The date probably early C16. Perhaps even earlier the gable round the corner with coping and two animals.

MIDWAY MANOR, 1¼ m. NNW. Col. Henry Shrapnel's house. He invented the shrapnel bomb in 1785. On the gateway piers shrapnel bombs and the names of battles won by their use (Waterloo, Table Bay, Chuzneemedanse, Kioze, Bidasoa, Tsage, Busaco).

WINKLEBURY CAMP *see* BERWICK ST JOHN

WINSLEY 8060

ST NICHOLAS. Lively Perp S tower, quite unusual in its composition, with the mid stair-turret and the saddleback roof – perhaps by the same team as South Wraxall. The church itself was rebuilt by *R. S. Pope* of Bristol in 1841 to the N and connected by a passage with the tower. Tallish two-light Perp windows. Short, lower chancel. The interior uninspired. – FONT. Perp, octagonal, with shields in foiled fields.

WINSLEY MANOR HOUSE. With C16 windows with arched lights. A date 1612 has recently been found inside.

CHEST HOSPITAL. By *Silcock & Reay*, 1903–4.

CONKWELL GRANGE. By *Guy Dawber*, 1907. Symmetrical neo-William and Mary, of seven bays, with a slightly recessed centre, a big hipped roof, and a r. wing. Large model farm premises.

WINTERBOURNE BASSETT 1070

ST KATHERINE. A church with excellent Dec work, in the N transept, N arcade and aisle, and the chancel. The Despensers were lords of the manor at the time. The N transept has unusually dainty detail. It was probably the family chapel. N window with reticulated tracery, a little enriched at the top. Mullions and tracery-bars finely moulded. Inside shafts with naturalistic leaf capitals. Below the window a recess, also finely moulded. It has a low broad ogee arch across half-way up and serving as the plinth for statuettes long lost. They may have been the Crucifixus with the Virgin and St John. Above the former centre figure a delightful crocketed nodding ogee arch. There was no doubt a monument in the recess. The coffin lid now kept in its place (*see* below) does not of course belong. The most astonishing detail of the transept is the arches to the N aisle and the nave. The N arcade is of baldly detailed piers and arches united by continuous mouldings. But the two arches just mentioned have towards the transept many mouldings, and in the corner, where they meet, they intersect most enterprisingly. Of the same build the N aisle doorway, close to the transept. It has one ogee arch and big fleurons in the jambs and arch. The chancel has windows with flowing tracery to the N and S and plain reticulated tracery to the E. It belongs to the transept chronologically, but is handled less lavishly. Perp W tower, ashlar-faced, with a stair-turret higher than the battlements. Tall arch towards the nave. In the nave on the S side a good Perp window with a straight head and the original iron bars and glass. – FONT. E.E., circular. With large stiff-leaf sprays and smaller single upright leaves between. – REREDOS. With re-used Jacobean bits, perhaps of domestic origin. – PULPIT. Jacobean. – READER'S DESK. Of the same details. – BENCHES. In the nave W parts. Also C17, plain and nice. – COMMUNION RAIL. Again C17. With turned balusters, carrying arches, and quite a bit of carving. – STAINED GLASS. In the head of a chancel N window bits of original C14 glass. – PLATE. Chalice, *c.*1680; Paten, 1695. – MONUMENTS. An excellent, though not too well-preserved late C13 coffin-lid with two slender figures, husband and wife, holding hands. He has a short beard. Cinquefoiled top with some sprays of stiff-leaf. – Mrs Mary Baskerville † 1724. Good tablet.

WINTERBOURNE DAUNTSEY

1030

The village starts just N of Winterbourne Earls church. THE ELMS, immediately N, early C18, of dark brick with red-brick dressings. Giant pilasters at the ends. Five bays, round-arched windows. Three dormers, the middle one with a semicircular gable. (Walled garden on the E side with pedimented entrance. MHLG)

MANOR HOUSE, also early C18. Of brick, seven bays, originally basement and two storeys, but later heightened by a third. Quoins, and for the pedimented three-bay centre quoins of even length. Rusticated door surround. All windows segment-headed. Original glazing-bars. The house has character, owing perhaps to its tight proportions. Wrought-iron garden gate.

(THE GRANGE. Early C18, brick, dark with red dressings, three storeys, giant angle pilasters, five bays, arched windows. Two-storeyed extension on the r. MHLG)

WINTERBOURNE EARLS   *1030*

ST MICHAEL. On the A-road. By *T. H. Wyatt*, 1867–8. Flint and stone bands and stone in irregular patterns. SW tower with pyramid roof. The nave and aisle Perp, the chancel E.E. – PULPIT. Jacobean, flatly carved. – STAINED GLASS. Two blackened medallions, C13 or early C14. – PLATE. Chalice, 1668; Flagon, 1777 (altered). – MONUMENTS. Slab in the porch with the indent of a kneeling figure and Perp decoration l., r., and top. – Demi-figure of a priest holding his heart in his hands. Probably early C14 (chancel).

FIGSBURY RINGS, ¾ m. SE of the Inn. Univallate Iron Age hill-fort with opposed entrances at E and W. It has produced Iron Age A sherds, including haematite-coated ware.

WINTERBOURNE GUNNER   *1030*

ST MARY. Flint and rubble. In the N wall of the nave the head of a blocked Norman window. The squat, unbuttressed W tower probably also Norman. Later pyramid roof. Early E.E. S aisle, demolished. The arcade remains inside. Two bays, octagonal pier, pointed arches with one slight chamfer. Chancel arch of the same style, but the window with the pointed-trefoiled head of course late C13. – BENCH END. Just one Jacobean one in the chancel. – PLATE. Cup, 1576; Paten and Flagon, 1792.

ROMAN ROAD. *See* Salisbury, p. 347.

WINTERBOURNE MONKTON   *0070*

ST MARY MAGDALENE. 1878 by *Butterfield*, with a number of parts of the old church, e.g. the S porch, the N doorway and part of the S doorway, both early C14, a C13 lancet in the chancel, the nave W window with its intersected tracery, a two-light Dec chancel S window, and the C16 or C17 three-light, mullioned-and-transomed nave N window. Old also the two mighty round posts which carry the renewed belfry, and old the C13 chancel arch. Typical of Butterfield the tall chimneystack at the NE end of the nave and the tile patterns inside the chancel, especially in the reredos. – FONT. Circular, Norman, with decorated trumpet scallops and zigzag. – PULPIT. With the usual blank arches of the Elizabethan and Jacobean age. Probably of 1627, the date of the iron HOURGLASS STAND. – PLATE. Chalice, *c*.1581 or later; Almsdish, 1681; Chalice and Paten, 1723.

MIDDLE FARMHOUSE, on the main road. Georgian, of Sarsen stone, two storeys, with a hipped roof. Big thatched barns, also of Sarsen stone.

₀₀₄₀

WINTERBOURNE STOKE

ST PETER. Flint and rubble. With transepts and a crossing tower. At the beginning of the history the two Norman doorways. N with one order of shafts, foliage capitals, and in the arch a frieze of saltire-crosses with appended blobs, and a frieze of zigzag. The S doorway similar but simpler. Incised in the lintel the lower half of a circle. We then turn to the crossing. The N and S arches are E.E., with tripartite respond shafts and strongly moulded capitals, S earlier than N. When the present crossing was built about 1300, these arches were considered too weak and the bigger W and E arches – with continuous triple chamfers – were made to overlap them. The top of the tower is Perp. Dec transepts, but in the S transept re-set two lancet heads probably from the E.E. transept to which the N and S arches belong. Nave W window Perp. Are the N and S nave windows of *c*.1300, because of their uncusped intersected tracery, or are they a C19 alteration? – FONT COVER. Jacobean, nice, with volutes and balusters. – PULPIT. Rich but flat Jacobean carving. – TILES. An assembly by the font.

MANOR HOUSE. Of flint and stone chequer, as are several handsome cottages in the village. The old part later C17, with tall mullioned ground-floor windows and a continuous stringcourse instead of hood-moulds. Much use is made of relieving arches. C20 additions to the l. as well as the r.

YARNBURY CASTLE. *See* Berwick St James, p. 97.

BARROWS. *See* Stonehenge, p. 445.

₂₀₃₀

WINTERSLOW

ALL SAINTS, West Winterslow. Externally mostly *T. H. Wyatt*'s building of 1866.* Inside, much that is older and of some

* He took out e.g. the music gallery, 'where Psalmody of the most unsavoury character was performed by rustics whose knowledge of singing was the very smallest' (PF).

interest. The nave before 1866 was only two bays long. The s arcade is quite Early Norman. Cruciform pier. Single-step arches. Grey stone. The N aisle is of the C13. Circular piers and abaci, double-chamfered pointed arches. The chancel arch also seems to be C13. – PULPIT. Later C17, with small figures of apostles in guilloche frames, but two in frames with Gothic details. Short fluted supports. – SCULPTURE. Head of a niche with canopy. Under this, relief of a head above clouds, held by two angels. Perp. – PLATE. Chalice, 1636; Chalice, 1692; Flagon, 1693; Paten, late C17.

ROCHE OLD COURT (FARM), 1½ m. NE. Brick range of the late C17. Six bays, two storeys. Two-light windows. The brick-work still in English bond. – Opposite BARN of the C15, weatherboarded.

ROCHE COURT, adjoining. Built in 1804 by *C. H. Tatham*. Four bays, two storeys. Ashlar-faced, quite restrained. Porch on two pairs of Tuscan columns.

FLINT MINES, ¾ m. NE of the Pheasant Inn, on Easton Down. Neolithic and Early Bronze Age flint mines, many of the shafts of which can still be traced. A number of the shafts, which are U-shaped, have been excavated. The finds, in addition to flint tools and an enormous quantity of waste flakes and cores, included antler picks and ox scapulae shovels employed in sinking the shafts.

BARROWS. Just N of the Pheasant Inn, a group of barrows including two very large bell barrows.

SAXON CEMETERIES. Two cemeteries of pagan Saxon burials on Roche Court Down, just N of the road junction at Lopcombe Corner. One cemetery of sixteen male skeletons, of which nine had been beheaded. Another cemetery of sixteen individuals, two with knives of C6 type.

ROMAN ROAD. *See* Salisbury, p. 347.

WISHFORD

0030

ST GILES. Rebuilt in 1863–4 by *T. H. Wyatt*, except the lower part of the tower and the chancel. The E wall has the original E.E. hood-mould of a group of three stepped lancets. – FONT. Circular, Norman, with columns and wild vertical strips of zigzag between. – CHEST. Jacobean, and exceptionally hand-some. – PLATE. Tazza, 1576; Flagon, 1637; Chalice, 1679; Paten, 1711. – MONUMENTS. Sir Thomas Bonham † 1473 and his wife † 1469. Tomb recess with low crocketed ogee arch and

Perp panelling behind. His effigy as a pilgrim. Hers is not in the recess. – On the floor Brasses of some of their children; the others (to make up nine) indents only. – Sir Richard Grobham † 1629 and wife. Large standing wall-monument. She is in widow's garb, he lies behind and a little above her, hands folded over the Bible. Columns l. and r., allegorical figures in the reveals of the coffered arch. – Sir Richard's HELM on the wall opposite.

GROBHAM ALMSHOUSES and HOWE SCHOOL, side by side, to the NW of the church. The almshouses were founded in 1628, the school in 1722. The one is of stone, the other of chequer brick. The one has mullioned windows and four dormers, the other arched windows and a hipped roof.

Wishford has three main streets running from the church S, W, and E. In SOUTH STREET the RECTORY, a nice five-bay brick house with stone quoins and a doorway with carved brackets. Other attractive houses opposite.

WOLF HALL see BURBAGE

1060
WOODBOROUGH

ST MARY MAGDALENE. By *T. H. Wyatt*, 1861. Nave with bell-cote and short chancel.

1030
WOODFORD

ALL SAINTS. 1845 by *T. H. Wyatt*, except for the Perp flint and rubble tower, the Perp S arcade of two bays with concave-sided pier and double-chamfered arches, and the Norman S doorway with one order of shafts, scalloped capitals, and zigzag in the arch at r. angles to the wall surface. – FONT. Perp, octagonal, heavy, with encircled quatrefoils. – WEST SCREEN, Jacobean with columns, and WEST GALLERY, Jacobean on brackets with a little stucco. – PLATE. Cup, 1576; Paten, c.1660–75. – MONUMENT. Several tablets, especially instructive a comparison (s aisle) between † 1596 and † 1759.

HEALE HOUSE, ½ m. ENE. A fine varied brick house with stone dressings. Much enlarged by *Detmar Blow* after 1894, a technically most skilful job, i.e. really unrecognizable from the original work of the later C17. The original work is at the SW end. To the E three original bays, except that the canted bay window is an addition. The centre bay projects a little and has its own quoins. Steep pediment. Doorway with a characteristic two-light opening above the door lintel. Open segmental pediment. Cross-windows. The same style and details on the sw side. Of this front however only the r. half is original. The l. half and the whole N front by Blow. The staircase is original c17 work (with vertically symmetrical balusters), but does not belong to the house. Nor does the upper panelling of the staircase hall with its round-arched and eared windows and the mythological ceiling painting. The garden has a Japanese park with a bridge made in Japan.

At NETTON the last cottage on the Salisbury Road is by *Detmar Blow* and was built about 1900. It is of cob and thatched.

LOWER WOODFORD MANOR HOUSE, ¾ m. SE. Brick; basement and one and a half storeys. Outer stair with wrought-iron railing to the doorway which has a segmental pediment.

UPPER WOODFORD. A three-bay farmhouse on the main road. By an outbuilding a handsome, gay Neo-Georgian clock-turret dated 1935. This commemorates George V's Silver Jubilee and is by *Darcy Braddell* (cf. Lake House, Wilsford).

LOWER DURNFORD MANOR. *See* Durnford.

WOODHAM HOUSE *see* WROUGHTON

WOODHENGE *see* DURRINGTON

WOODLANDS MANOR
¾ m. SSE of Mere

8030

The house consists of a c14 chapel and hall, both buttressed. The CHAPEL was always on the upper floor, originally with an outer staircase on the N side. The NE window is straight-headed but has reticulation motifs, the E window is Perp, of three lights. Wagon roof, brought in from outside, as is much of the woodwork of the house. The windows of the ground-floor room below the chapel seem to be c16 and not too late. The hall has a porch entered by a double-chamfered arch dying into the imposts. Above it a room with an Elizabethan two-light window. In the HALL itself a doorway towards the chapel which is again c14. The S windows on the other hand seem c15, one of two cusped lights, the N window corresponding to it the same, and the S window at the high-table end also of two cusped lights, but larger. The roof of the hall has arched braces up to collar-beams. 29b

The size of the braces and the height of the collar-beams alternate. Three tiers of cusped wind-braces. The gallery, and the
beam on which it stands, are again brought in. Between hall
and chapel, in the re-entrant angle a recent piece replacing a
ruinous old one. C17 windows. To the r. of the hall again later
windows, but this wing, the offices side, projects to the N as far
as the N side of the chapel, and there an enormous fireplace
survives with a lintel beam of 19 in. scantling. That must have
been the kitchen fireplace. About 1570 the chapel was converted
into principal living rooms. The lower received a fine thin-
ribbed plaster ceiling and a splendid stone chimneypiece with
thin fluted Ionic columns and the coat of arms above the opening flanked by thin decorated Corinthian columns against
which lean big, rather bare volutes. Volute motifs also in the
lintel (cf. The Hall, Bradford-on-Avon, p. 123). The upper
(chapel) room formerly had a similar fireplace, but that was sold
and is supposed to be now at Leeds Castle in Kent.

WOOTTON BASSETT

ST BARTHOLOMEW AND ALL SAINTS. A strange church now,
as restored and remodelled by *Street* in 1870, and a strange
church when it was new. It consisted originally, i.e. in the
C13, of two naves and a chancel with chapel. They were
separated by slender circular piers. Were the piers shorter than
they are now? It is likely. The W respond, though far from
precise in its message, seems to indicate a heightening too.
The piers have circular capitals and abaci, except for the nave
E pier, which has an octagonal abacus. The three-bay chapel
arcade is, judging by the mouldings of its capitals, later than the
five-bay nave arcade. The arches have two hollow chamfers
in the nave, two sunk quadrant mouldings in the chancel.
Street provided the neo-E.E. upper parts of the W tower and
all the C13-looking windows. He also added a new N aisle, so
that the church now has identical S and N arcades. The best
original external work is the façade of the S aisle. This has one
Dec window close to the E end which was formerly the NE
window. The other windows are Perp and large. Two-storeyed
embattled porch in the middle. Big gargoyles. Nice pitched
and panelled roofs in the old naves. – REREDOS. By *Street*, the
relief by *Thomas Earp* of Lambeth. – FONT. Circular, designed
by *Street*. – PULPIT. Perp, simple. – STAINED GLASS. E
window by *Hardman*. – CHANDELIER. Of brass, two tiers.

1782. – PLATE. Chalice and Paten Cover, 1631; Paten c.1674; Paten, 1691.

HILLSIDE METHODIST CHURCH, Bath Road. 1838. With pedimental gable, two arched windows below, but a porch with a fancy Gothic gable.

SCHOOL, immediately W of the former. 1858, but still with Gothick rather than Gothic windows.

TOWN HALL. 1700. Given by Laurence Hyde, first Earl of Rochester. Restored extensively in 1889 at the expense of Lady Meux. The hub of Wootton Bassett. Across the W end of the High Street. Open ground floor on fifteen stone columns. They taper considerably and have elementary capitals. Timber-framed upper floor. Open staircase with heavy balusters. The whole very conservative for 1700.

PERAMBULATION. A walk through Wootton Bassett is almost confined to the HIGH STREET, a miniature edition of that of Marlborough, 8 m. away, i.e. straight, wide, even, and un-disturbed. The trees which the Wootton Bassett High Street possesses are so cruelly lopped at the time of writing that they do not enter into the picture at all. One starts by the town hall. The houses to look for are all Georgian, and Early rather than Late. To the NW of the town hall No. 28, brick, of five bays, with a pedimented doorway. Then a group on the other side. First, the most ambitious house of Wootton Bassett, No. 141, stone, of seven bays with very long and narrow windows and with a centre raised to a semicircular gable with an arched window. Below it another arched window. Doorway with a full-blown shell-hood on carved brackets. Even quoins, also to the three-bay centre. Staircase with alternatingly turned and twisted balusters and carved tread-ends. The date must be early C18. No. 137 is of five bays, brick, with hipped dormers in the roof. Doorway with an open segmental pediment embracing an urn. The pediment is on carved brackets, as was usual at Wootton Bassett. Nice window architraves. Panelled parapet. Then the CROSS KEYS INN, dated 1742. Low, red and some blue brick, of two storeys and five bays. Central archway. Upper windows with aprons. After that back to the N side for the ANGEL HOTEL, chequered brick, of six bays and two storeys. No. 53, also brick, has a doorway with straight hood on carved brackets. No. 57 stands back from the street. It is coated with pebbledash and has a hipped roof. Five bays and two storeys, doorway with pediment on carved brackets. Queen Anne probably, but the windows altered. Spacious staircase with thin turned balusters. Then the interest of the High Street stops, and the only other house to be mentioned lies at its very E end, i.e. originally outside the town: LYME KILN HOUSE, L-shaped, of the early C18, with yet another door-hood on carved brackets. Another house originally outside is NORE MARSH HOUSE, along the street running parallel to the High Street, to its S. This is rendered and has six bays, two storeys, and a hipped roof with dormers.

VASTERNE MANOR, 1¼ m. WSW. The house has been much altered and modernized (by Sir Henry Meux). The C15 doorway and probably the small window adjoining it came from Berwick Bassett Manor House. The other doorway, smaller and daintier, is Elizabethan and goes with the splendid, large, quite simply detailed chimneypiece in what must have been the hall. Here also moulded beams with a foliage boss. The mullioned-and-transomed windows seem all new.

LITTLE PARK FARM, 1½ m. SW. A symmetrical front with two short gabled angle-projections and a gabled central porch. It looks C17, remodelled about 1700.

1060   WOOTTON RIVERS

ST ANDREW. Nave and chancel and a wooden bell-turret with shingled broach-spire. The church was severely restored by *Street* in 1862. The style remains Dec throughout. S and N doorways with deep mouldings. Above the S doorway a niche. The S porch entrance with fine bold cinquecusping, the spandrels pierced. Windows of two lights with a quatrefoiled circle in bar tracery. The W window Dec and the E window of three lights with reticulated tracery, i.e. also Dec. All windows in very deep reveals. No chancel arch at all. – FONT. Of tub-shape, with no separate stem. Decorated with quatrefoils above simply cusped panels – also Dec in all probability. – PULPIT. Stone and no doubt by *Street*. – PLATE. Elizabethan Chalice and Paten Cover.

A village with many timber-framed, thatched houses, especially MANOR FARMHOUSE, S of the church, which has however on the r. side a ground floor of stone with a four-centred head to a doorway.

9050   WORTON

CHRIST CHURCH. 1843 by *Wyatt & Brandon*. Nave and chancel and transept. Bellcote with an ogee cap. Oddly tall, slim, straight-headed two-light windows with ogee-arched lights. – BOX PEWS.

THE GRANGE. Gabled timber-framed house. Brick between the timbers. The larger part of the house is recent.

WORTON HOUSE. Late Georgian, brick, of three storeys, with two canted bay windows and a doorway with thin Tuscan columns and a pediment.

PRINCE HALL. Neo-Georgian; 1912.

WROUGHTON

ST JOHN BAPTIST AND ST HELEN. Late Norman s doorway with one order of colonnettes, zigzag in the arch at r. angles to the wall surface, and small flowers in the hood-mould. Norman N doorway with scalloped capitals to the colonnettes, but an arch, made pointed, probably later. Dec chancel with an interesting E window of five lights. The top of the tracery is a large circle with two almond shapes set in. Chancel arch double-chamfered and dying into the imposts. Fine sedilia with crocketed ogee arches. Dec also the s arcade of two bays. Octagonal piers, double-chamfered arches. But are not the bases Norman, from a previous arcade? The arcade was lengthened by a Perp bay to the w when the Perp w tower was built. The N arcade dates from 1846. Perp one-bay N chapel. – REREDOS, s aisle. A curious arrangement of a row of coarse arches with the middle one higher. They were no doubt for painted figures. – PLATE. Chalice and Paten Cover, 1576; Flagon, 1710; Paten, given in 1719. – MONUMENTS. Many tablets to members of the Benet family, e.g. Mrs Thomasine † 1645, already completely classical. Also a tablet placed in 1670, and richly decorated cartouches of † 1708, † 1712, † 1754.

WROUGHTON HOUSE, ¾ m. E of the church. C18, of stone. Five-bay front. L-shaped back of six and five bays.

WOODHAM HOUSE, ¾ m. E. White three-bay house with a nice doorway. Behind, a delightfully secluded court with a mill with tall chimney. Brick, with low, segment-headed windows.

OVERTOWN HOUSE, 1¼ m. ESE. C18. Of three bays, with a hipped roof. (C16 staircase inside. NBR)

WHITE HORSE. On Hackpen, 3⅜ m. s of Wroughton church. Cut into the turf in 1838. About 90 by 90 ft.

BARBURY CASTLE. See Ogbourne St Andrew.

WYKE HOUSE see HILPERTON

0030

WYLYE

ST MARY. Low w tower with battlements and pinnacles. The arch towards the nave is triple-chamfered. Otherwise only the E window of the chancel is old. It is a fine E.E. piece, of three stepped lancets, shafted outside, with little stiff-leaf capitals and much dog-tooth. The rest of the church was rebuilt in 1844–6. – FONT. Baluster font of 1765. – PULPIT. A splendid piece, dated 1628. It comes from the church of Wilton. At the angles balusters covered with leaves. In the panels the usual blank arches, but with trees growing in them. Back panel also with such a tree. Large tester. The stair with twisted balusters is late C17. – The READING DESK and CLERK'S DESK belong to the pulpit. – COMMUNION RAIL, late C17. Parts re-used. Alternation of twisted balusters with old-fashioned (or re-used) flat openwork balusters. – SCULPTURE. In the N aisle inside small Crucifixion, probably from a cross-head. – CHANDELIERS. One of them dated 1814. They also come from Wilton church. – STAINED GLASS. N aisle NE and NW by *Kempe*, the former of 1904. – PLATE. Gilt Chalice, hallmarked 1525, knop with angel heads, beautifully pierced stem, foot engraved with Crucifix; Cup, 1562; Cover Paten, 1569; Almsdish, 1671; Tankard, 1678; Bowl, 1781. – MONUMENT. In the churchyard good C18 iron railings round a monument no longer identifiable. The story is that it was set up by one Popjay who was of mean extraction, had left the village, but one day returned with all outer signs of wealth and ordered the monument to be made. He then disappeared and never paid for it.

The village has plenty of houses faced with flint and stone chequerwork.

In the river Wylye, close to the mill, STATUE of a draped, but mostly nude man blowing a horn; probably C18.

YARNBURY CASTLE *see* BERWICK ST JAMES

YARNBURY GRANGE *see* STEEPLE LANGFORD

0070

YATESBURY

ALL SAINTS. Externally Perp. w tower with battlements and pinnacles. Nave with battlements. Straight-headed windows. In addition the chancel of 1855, inside with a stone screen, stone pulpit, and coloured wall decoration. But there is much

older work, the Norman s doorway with one order of colonnettes and zigzag in the arch, all much renewed, and the group
of three small stepped E lancets at the w end of the N aisle. The
aisle arcade is indeed E.E.: three bays with round piers and
abaci and double-chamfered arches. There was a s aisle as well
to go with the Norman s doorway, but of that only one bay is
now visible inside. It is late C12, with round piers and abaci and
a double-chamfered round arch. One capital has a variety of
trumpet scallops, the other is moulded. Nave roof of low pitch;
tie-beams with tracery over. – FONT. Circular, Norman, with
large coarse upright leaves and a band of trails below. –
STAINED GLASS. In the s aisle E window head some original
glass. – In the E window glass probably of 1855 with the
monogram M.S. (?).

YATTON KEYNELL   8070

ST MARGARET. C13 chancel with two lancet windows. w tower
unbuttressed and below C13 too. Above Perp with fine bell-
openings of the Westwood and Nettleton type, i.e. two lights,
continued blank below a transom and the whole repeated
blank l. as well as r. Perp the rest too, including the two-bay s
arcade with octagonal piers, capitals with fleurons, and panelled
four-centred arches, and the additional E bay, which is taller
and panelled throughout. Panelled also the surround of the E
window of the aisle and that of the four-light window in the N
aisle. The church was drastically restored in 1868, by *Street*.
– SCREEN. Of stone, good, with one-light divisions with ogee
gables and a braced top frieze of foliage. – PLATE. Chalice and
Paten Cover, 1576.

MANOR. Dated 1659. Three gables, flat front, symmetrical
fenestration. Decoration with lozenge-shaped panels.

OLD FARMHOUSE, at the N end of the village. C18, with a
Tuscan porch. The BARN of the house may be late C17 or early
C18. It has to one's surprise a big, bold, shaped gable.

IVY FARMHOUSE, West Yatton. Dated 1706. Of five bays with
two-light windows, thin frames and mullions slightly stepped
back. Hipped roof.

A COTTAGE on the sw side of the road has a small C13 one-light
window.

LONG DEAN. A pretty group of mill and C18 cottages in the
combe.

ZEALS

ST MARTIN. 1843–6 by *Scott*, the future *Sir G. G. Scott*, an early work, in the Dec style, but already with a proper developed chancel. The W tower on the other hand, with a spire added in 1876, is archaeologically much less serious. It turns octagonal with angle pinnacles to cover the transition. The spire has two tiers of lucarnes. – PLATE. 'Ancient Flemish Almsdish' (Nightingale).

ZEALS HOUSE. The house is big and offers a confused picture, owing largely to ample Victorian additions. The MHLG sees medieval features in it. It ought to be studied properly. (Staircase C17 or C18. MHLG)

ALMSHOUSES. 1865. Tudor, brick, with gables.

GLOSSARY

Abacus: flat slab on the top of a capital (q.v.).

ABUTMENT: solid masonry placed to resist the lateral pressure of a vault.

ACANTHUS: plant with thick fleshy and scalloped leaves used as part of the decoration of a Corinthian capital (q.v.) and in some types of leaf carving.

ACHIEVEMENT OF ARMS: in heraldry, a complete display of armorial bearings.

ACROTERION: foliage-carved block on the end or top of a classical pediment.

ADDORSED: two human figures, animals, or birds, etc., placed symmetrically so that they turn their backs to each other.

AEDICULE, AEDICULA: framing of a window or door by columns and a pediment (q.v.).

AFFRONTED: two human figures, animals, or birds, etc., placed symmetrically so that they face each other.

AGGER: Latin term for the built-up foundations of Roman roads; also sometimes applied to the banks of hill-forts or other earthworks.

AMBULATORY: semicircular or polygonal aisle enclosing an apse (q.v.).

ANNULET: *see* Shaft-ring.

ANSE DE PANIER: *see* Arch, Basket.

ANTEPENDIUM: covering of the front of an altar, usually by textiles or metalwork.

ANTIS, IN: *see* Portico.

APSE: vaulted semicircular or polygonal end of a chancel or a chapel.

ARABESQUE: light and fanciful surface decoration using combinations of flowing lines, tendrils, etc., interspersed with vases, animals, etc.

ARCADE: range of arches supported on piers or columns, free-standing; or, BLIND ARCADE, the same attached to a wall.

ARCH: round-headed, i.e. semi-circular; pointed, i.e. consisting of two curves, each drawn from one centre, and meeting in a point at the top; segmental, i.e. in the form of a segment; pointed; four-centred (a Late Medieval form), *see* Fig. 1(*a*); Tudor (also a Late Medieval form), *see* Fig. 1(*b*); Ogee (in-

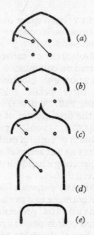

Fig. I

troduced *c.* 1300 and specially popular in the C14), *see* Fig. 1(*c*); Stilted, *see* Fig. 1(*d*); Basket, with lintel connected to the jambs by concave quadrant curves, *see* Fig. 1 (*e*).

ARCHITRAVE: lowest of the three main parts of the entablature (q.v.) of an order (q.v.) (*see* Fig. 12).

ARCHIVOLT: under-surface of an arch (also called Soffit).

ARRIS: sharp edge at the meeting of two surfaces.

ASHLAR: masonry of large blocks wrought to even faces and square edges.

ATRIUM: inner court of a Roman house, also open court in front of a church.

ATTACHED: *see* Engaged.

ATTIC: topmost storey of a house, if distance from floor to ceiling is less than in the others.

AUMBRY: recess or cupboard to hold sacred vessels for Mass and Communion.

BAILEY: open space or court of a stone-built castle; *see* also Motte-and-Bailey.

BALDACCHINO: canopy supported on columns.

BALLFLOWER: globular flower of three petals enclosing a small ball. A decoration used in the first quarter of the C14.

BALUSTER: small pillar or column of fanciful outline.

BALUSTRADE: series of balusters supporting a handrail or coping (q.v.).

BARBICAN: outwork defending the entrance to a castle.

BARGEBOARDS: projecting decorated boards placed against the incline of the gable of a building and hiding the horizontal roof timbers.

BARROW: *see* Bell, Bowl, Disc, Long, *and* Pond Barrow.

BASILICA: in medieval architecture an aisled church with a clerestory.

BASKET ARCH: *see* Arch (Fig. 1e).

BASTION: projection at the angle of a fortification.

BATTER: inclined face of a wall.

BATTLEMENT: parapet with a series of indentations or embrasures with raised portions or merlons between (also called Crenellation).

BAYS: internal compartments of a building; each divided from the other not by solid walls but by divisions only marked in the side walls (columns, pilasters, etc.) or the ceiling (beams, etc.). Also external divisions of a building by fenestration.

BAY-WINDOW: angular or curved projection of a house front with ample fenestration. If curved, also called bow-window; if on an upper floor only, also called oriel or oriel window.

BEAKER FOLK: Late New Stone Age warrior invaders from the Continent who buried their dead in round barrows and introduced the first metal tools and weapons to Britain.

BEAKHEAD: Norman ornamental motif consisting of a row of bird or beast heads with beaks biting usually into a roll moulding.

BELFRY: turret on a roof to hang bells in.

BELGAE: Aristocratic warrior bands who settled in Britain in two main waves in the C1 B.C. In Britain their culture is termed Iron Age C.

BELL BARROW: Early Bronze Age round barrow in which the mound is separated from its encircling ditch by a flat platform or berm (q.v.).

BELLCOTE: framework on a roof to hang bells from.

BERM: level area separating ditch from bank on a hill-fort or barrow.

BILLET FRIEZE: Norman ornamental motif made up of short raised rectangles placed at regular intervals.

BIVALLATE: Of a hill-fort: defended by two concentric banks and ditches.

BLOCK CAPITAL: Romanesque capital cut from a cube by having the lower angles rounded off to the circular shaft below (also called Cushion Capital) (Fig. 2).

Fig. 2

BOND, ENGLISH or FLEMISH: see Brickwork.

BOSS: knob or projection usually placed to cover the intersection of ribs in a vault.

BOW-WINDOW: see Bay-Window.

BOX PEW: pew with a high wooden enclosure.

BOWL BARROW: round barrow surrounded by a quarry ditch. Introduced in Late Neolithic times, the form continued until the Saxon period.

BRACES: see Roof.

BRACKET: small supporting piece of stone, etc., to carry a projecting horizontal.

BRESSUMER: beam in a timber-framed building to support the, usually projecting, superstructure.

BRICKWORK: *Header:* brick laid so that the end only appears on the face of the wall. *Stretcher:* brick laid so that the side only appears on the face of the wall. *English Bond:* method of laying bricks so that alternate courses or layers on the face of the wall are composed of headers or stretchers only (Fig. 3a). *Flemish Bond:* method of laying bricks so that alternate headers and stretchers appear in each course on the face of the wall (Fig. 3b).

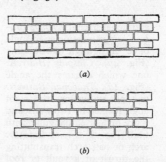

(a)

(b)

Fig. 3

BROACH: see Spire.

BROKEN PEDIMENT: see Pediment.

BRONZE AGE: In Britain, the period from *c.*1600 to 600 B.C.

BUCRANIUM: ox skull.

BUTTRESS: mass of brickwork or masonry projecting from or built against a wall to give

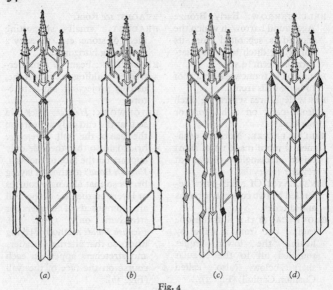

(a)   (b)   (c)   (d)

Fig. 4

additional strength. *Angle Buttresses:* two meeting at an angle of 90° at the angle of a building (Fig. 4*a*). *Clasping Buttress:* one which encases the angle (Fig. 4*d*). *Diagonal Buttress:* one placed against the right angle formed by two walls, and more or less equiangular with both (Fig. 4*b*). *Flying Buttress:* arch or half arch transmitting the thrust of a vault or roof from the upper part of a wall to an outer support or buttress. *Setback Buttress:* angle buttress set slightly back from the angle (Fig. 4*c*).

CABLE MOULDING: Norman moulding imitating a twisted cord.

CAIRN: a mound of stones usually covering a burial.

CAMBER: slight rise or upward curve of an otherwise horizontal structure.

CAMPANILE: isolated bell tower.

CANOPY: projection or hood over an altar, pulpit, niche, statue, etc.

CAP: in a windmill the crowning feature.

CAPITAL: head or top part of a column (q.v.).

CARTOUCHE: tablet with an ornate frame, usually enclosing an inscription.

CARYATID: whole figure supporting an entablature or other similar member. *Termini Caryatids:* busts or demi-figures or three-quarter figures supporting an entablature or other similar member and placed at the top of termini pilasters (q.v.).

CASTELLATED: decorated with battlements.

CELURE: panelled and adorned part of a wagon-roof above the rood or the altar.

CENSER: vessel for the burning of incense.

CENTERING: wooden framework used in arch and vault construction and removed when the mortar has set.

CHALICE: cup used in the Communion service or at Mass.

CHAMBERED TOMB: burial mound of the New Stone Age having a stone-built chamber and entrance passage covered by an earthen barrow or stone cairn. The form was introduced to Britain from the Mediterranean.

CHAMFER: surface made by cutting across the square angle of a stone block, piece of wood, etc., at an angle of 45° to the other two surfaces.

CHANCEL: that part of the E end of a church in which the altar is placed, usually applied to the whole continuation of the nave E of the crossing.

CHANCEL ARCH: arch at the W end of the chancel.

CHANTRY CHAPEL: chapel attached to, or inside, a church, endowed for the saying of Masses for the soul of the founder or some other individual.

CHEVET: French term for the E end of a church (chancel, ambulatory, and radiating chapels).

CHEVRON: Norman moulding forming a zigzag.

CHOIR: that part of the church where divine service is sung.

CIBORIUM: a baldacchino.

CINQUEFOIL: see Foil.

CIST: stone-lined or slab-built grave. First appears in Late Neolithic times. It continued to be used in the Early Christian period.

CLAPPER BRIDGE: bridge made of large slabs of stone, some built up to make rough piers and other longer ones laid on top to make the roadway.

CLASSIC: here used to mean the moment of highest achievement of a style.

CLASSICAL: here used as the term for Greek and Roman architecture and any subsequent styles inspired by it.

CLERESTORY: upper storey of the nave walls of a church, pierced by windows.

COADE STONE: artificial (cast) stone made in the late C18 and the early C19 by Coade and Sealy in London.

COB: walling material made of mixed clay and straw.

COFFERING: decorating a ceiling with sunk square or polygonal ornamental panels.

COLLAR-BEAM: see Roof.

COLONNADE: range of columns.

COLONNETTE: small column.

COLUMNA ROSTRATA: column decorated with carved prows of ships to celebrate a naval victory.

COMPOSITE: see Order.

CONSOLE: bracket (q.v.) with a compound curved outline.

COPING: capping or covering to a wall.

CORBEL: block of stone projecting from a wall, supporting some horizontal feature.

CORBEL TABLE: series of corbels, occurring just below the roof eaves externally or internally, often seen in Norman buildings.

CORINTHIAN: *see* Orders.

CORNICE: in classical architecture the top section of the entablature (q.v.). Also for a projecting decorative feature along the top of a wall, arch, etc.

CORRIDOR VILLA: *see* Villa.

COUNTERSCARP BANK: small bank on the down-hill or outer side of a hill-fort ditch.

COURTYARD VILLA: *see* Villa.

COVE, COVING: concave undersurface in the nature of a hollow moulding but on a larger scale.

COVER PATEN: cover to a Communion cup, suitable for use as a paten or plate for the consecrated bread.

CRADLE ROOF: *see* Wagon-roof.

CRENELLATION: *see* Battlement.

CREST, CRESTING: ornamental finish along the top of a screen, etc.

CROCKET, CROCKETING: decorative features placed on the sloping sides of spires, pinnacles, gables, etc., in Gothic architecture, carved in various leaf shapes and placed at regular intervals.

CROCKET CAPITAL: *see* Fig. 5. An Early Gothic form.

Fig. 5

CROMLECH: word of Celtic origin still occasionally used of

single free-standing stones ascribed to the Neolithic or Bronze Age periods.

CROSSING: space at the intersection of nave, chancel, and transepts.

CROSS-WINDOWS: windows with one mullion and one transom.

CRUCK: big curved beam supporting both walls and roof of a cottage.

CRYPT: underground room usually below the E end of a church.

CUPOLA: small polygonal or circular domed turret crowning a roof.

CURTAIN WALL: connecting wall between the towers of a castle.

CUSHION CAPITAL: *see* Block Capital.

CUSP: projecting point between the foils in a foiled Gothic arch.

DADO: decorative covering of the lower part of a wall.

DAGGER: tracery motif of the Dec style. It is a lancet shape rounded or pointed at the head, pointed at the foot, and cusped inside (*see* Fig. 6).

Fig. 6

DAIS: raised platform at one end of a room.

DEC ('DECORATED'): historical division of English Gothic architecture covering the period from *c*.1290 to *c*.1350.

DEMI-COLUMNS: columns half sunk into a wall.

DIAPER WORK: surface decoration composed of square or lozenge shapes.

DISC BARROW: Bronze Age round barrow with inconspicuous central mound surrounded by bank and ditch.

DOG-TOOTH: typical E.E. ornament consisting of a series of four-cornered stars placed diagonally and raised pyramidally (Fig. 7).

Fig. 7

DOMICAL VAULT: see Vault.

DONJON: see Keep.

DORIC: see Order.

DORMER (WINDOW): window placed vertically in the sloping plane of a roof.

DRIPSTONE: see Hood-mould.

DRUM: circular or polygonal vertical wall of a dome or cupola.

E.E. ('EARLY ENGLISH'): historical division of English Gothic architecture roughly covering the C13.

EASTER SEPULCHRE: recess with tomb-chest usually in the wall of a chancel, the tomb-chest to receive an effigy of Christ for Easter celebrations.

EAVES: underpart of a sloping roof overhanging a wall.

EAVES CORNICE: cornice below the eaves of a roof.

ECHINUS: Convex or projecting moulding supporting the abacus of a Greek Doric capital, sometimes bearing an egg and dart pattern.

EMBATTLED: see Battlement.

EMBRASURE: small opening in the wall or parapet of a fortified building, usually splayed on the inside.

ENCAUSTIC TILES: earthenware glazed and decorated tiles used for paving.

ENGAGED COLUMNS: columns attached to, or partly sunk into, a wall.

ENGLISH BOND: see Brickwork.

ENTABLATURE: in classical architecture the whole of the horizontal members above a column (that is architrave, frieze, and cornice) (see Fig. 12).

ENTASIS: very slight convex deviation from a straight line; used on Greek columns and sometimes on spires to prevent an optical illusion of concavity.

ENTRESOL: see Mezzanine.

EPITAPH: hanging wall monument.

ESCUTCHEON: shield for armorial bearings.

EXEDRA: the apsidal end of a room. See Apse.

FAN-VAULT: see Vault.

FERETORY: place behind the High Altar where the chief shrine of a church is kept.

FESTOON: carved garland of flowers and fruit suspended at both ends.

FILLET: narrow flat band running down a shaft or along a roll moulding.

FINIAL: top of a canopy, gable, pinnacle.

FLAGON: vessel for the wine used in the Communion service.

FLAMBOYANT: properly the latest phase of French Gothic

architecture where the window tracery takes on wavy undulating lines.

FLÈCHE: slender wooden spire on the centre of a roof (also called Spirelet).

FLEMISH BOND: *see* Brickwork.

FLEURON: decorative carved flower or leaf.

FLUSHWORK: decorative use of flint in conjunction with dressed stone so as to form patterns: tracery, initials, etc.

FLUTING: vertical channelling in the shaft of a column.

FLYING BUTTRESS: *see* Buttress.

FOIL: lobe formed by the cusping (q.v.) of a circle or an arch. Trefoil, quatrefoil, cinquefoil, multifoil, express the number of leaf shapes to be seen.

FOLIATED: carved with leaf shapes.

FOSSE: ditch.

FOUR-CENTRED ARCH: *see* Arch.

FRATER: refectory or dining hall of a monastery.

FRESCO: wall painting on wet plaster.

FRIEZE: middle division of a classical entablature (q.v.) (*see* Fig. 12).

FRONTAL: covering for the front of an altar.

Gable: *Dutch gable:* A gable with curved sides crowned by a pediment, characteristic of *c.* 1630–50 (Fig. 8*a*).

Fig. 8*a*

Shaped gable: A gable with multi-curved sides characteristic of *c.*1600–50 (Fig. 8*b*).

Fig. 8*b*

GADROONED: enriched with a series of convex ridges, the opposite of fluting.

GALILEE: chapel or vestibule usually at the w end of a church enclosing the porch. Also called Narthex (q.v.).

GALLERY: in church architecture upper storey above an aisle, opened in arches to the nave. Also called Tribune (q.v.) and often erroneously Triforium (q.v.).

GALLERY GRAVE: chambered tomb (q.v.) in which there is little or no differentiation between the entrance passage and the actual burial chamber(s).

GARGOYLE: water spout projecting from the parapet of a wall or tower; carved into a human or animal shape.

GAZEBO: lookout tower or raised summer house in a picturesque garden.

'GEOMETRICAL': *see* Tracery.

'GIBBS SURROUND': of a doorway or window. An C18 motif consisting of a surround with alternating larger and smaller blocks of stone, quoin-wise, or intermittent large blocks, sometimes with a narrow raised band connecting them up the verticals and along the face of the arch (Fig. 9).

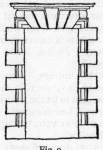

Fig. 9

GROIN: sharp edge at the meeting of two cells of a cross-vault.

GROIN-VAULT: see Vault.

GROTESQUE: fanciful orna-mental decoration: see also Arabesque.

HAGIOSCOPE: see Squint.

HALF-TIMBERING: see Timber-Framing.

HALL CHURCH: church in which nave and aisles are of equal height or approximately so.

HAMMERBEAM: see Roof.

HANAP: large metal cup, gener-ally made for domestic use, standing on an elaborate base and stem; with a very ornate cover frequently crowned with a little steeple.

HEADERS: see Brickwork.

HERRINGBONE WORK: brick, stone, or tile construction where the component blocks are laid diagonally instead of flat. Alternate courses lie in opposing directions to make a zigzag pattern up the face of the wall.

HEXASTYLE: having six de-tached columns.

HILL-FORT: Iron Age earthwork enclosed by a ditch and bank

system; in the later part of the period the defences multiplied in size and complexity. They vary from about an acre to over 30 acres in area, and are usually built with careful regard to natural elevations or promontories.

HIPPED ROOF: see Roof.

HOOD-MOULD: projecting moulding above an arch or a lintel to throw off water (also called Dripstone or Label).

ICONOGRAPHY: the science of the subject matter of works of the visual arts.

IMPOST: brackets in walls, usually formed of mouldings, on which the ends of an arch rest.

INDENT: shape chiselled out in a stone slab to receive a brass.

INGLENOOK: bench or seat built in beside a fireplace, sometimes covered by the chimney breast, occasionally lit by small windows on each side of the fire.

INTERCOLUMNIATION: the space between columns.

IONIC: see Orders (Fig. 12).

IRON AGE: in Britain the period from c. 600 B.C. to the coming of the Romans. The term is also used for those un-Roman-ized native communities which survived until the Saxon incur-sions.

JAMB: straight side of an arch-way, doorway, or window.

KEEL MOULDING: moulding whose outline is in section like that of the keel of a ship.

18

KEEP: massive tower of a Norman castle.

KEYSTONE: middle stone in an arch or a rib-vault.

KING-POST: see Roof (Fig. 14).

LABEL: see Hood-mould.

LABEL STOP: ornamental boss at the end of a hood-mould (q.v.).

LANCET WINDOW: slender pointed-arched window.

LANTERN: in architecture, a small circular or polygonal turret with windows all round crowning a roof (see Cupola) or a dome.

LANTERN CROSS: churchyard cross with lantern-shaped top usually with sculptured representations on the sides of the top.

LEAN-TO ROOF: roof with one slope only, built against a higher wall.

LESENE or PILASTER STRIP: pilaster without base or capital.

LIERNE: see Vault (Fig. 21).

LINENFOLD: Tudor panelling ornamented with a conventional representation of a piece of linen laid in vertical folds. The piece is repeated in each panel.

LINTEL: horizontal beam or stone bridging an opening.

LOGGIA: recessed colonnade (q.v.).

LONG AND SHORT WORK: Saxon quoins (q.v.) consisting of stones placed with the long sides alternately upright and horizontal.

LONG BARROW: unchambered Neolithic communal burial mound, wedge-shaped in plan, with the burial and occasional other structures massed at the broader end, from which the mound itself tapers in height; quarry ditches flank the mound.

LOUVRE: opening, often with lantern (q.v.) over, in the roof of a room to let the smoke from a central hearth escape.

LOWER PALAEOLITHIC: see Palaeolithic.

LOZENGE: diamond shape.

LUCARNE: small opening to let light in.

LUNETTE: tympanum (q.v.) or semicircular opening.

LYCH GATE: wooden gate structure with a roof and open sides placed at the entrance to a churchyard to provide space for the reception of a coffin. The word lych is Saxon and means a corpse.

LYNCHET: long terraced strip of soil accumulating on the downward side of prehistoric and medieval fields due to soil creep from continuous ploughing along the contours.

MACHICOLATION: projecting gallery on brackets constructed on the outside of castle towers or walls. The gallery has holes in the floor to drop missiles through.

MAJOLICA: ornamented glazed earthenware.

MANSARD: see Roof.

MEGALITHIC TOMB: stone-built burial chamber of the New Stone Age covered by an earth or stone mound. The form was introduced to Britain from the Mediterranean area.

MERLON: see Battlement.

MESOLITHIC: 'Middle Stone' Age; the post-glacial period of hunting and fishing communities dating in Britain from *c.* 8000 B.C. to the arrival of Neolithic communities, with which they must have considerably overlapped.

METOPE: in classical architecture of the Doric order (q.v.) the space in the frieze between the triglyphs (Fig. 12).

MEZZANINE: low storey placed between two higher ones.

MISERERE: *see* Misericord.

MISERICORD: bracket placed on the underside of a hinged choir stall seat which, when turned up, provided the occupant of the seat with a support during long periods of standing (also called Miserere).

MODILLION: small bracket of which large numbers (modillion frieze) are often placed below a cornice (q.v.) in classical architecture.

MOTTE: steep mound forming the main feature of C11 and C12 castles.

MOTTE-AND-BAILEY: post-Roman and Norman defence system consisting of an earthen mound (the motte) topped with a wooden tower eccentrically placed within a bailey (q.v.), with enclosure ditch and palisade, and with the rare addition of an internal bank.

MOUCHETTE: tracery motif in curvilinear tracery, a curved dagger (q.v.), specially popular in the early C14 (Fig. 10).

Fig. 10

MULLION: vertical post or upright dividing a window into two or more 'lights'.

MULTIVALLATE: Of a hill-fort: defended by three or more concentric banks and ditches.

MUNTIN: vertical part in the framing of a door, screen, etc., stopped by the horizontal rails.

NAIL-HEAD: E.E. ornamental motif, consisting of small pyramids regularly repeated (Fig. 11).

Fig. 11

NARTHEX: enclosed vestibule or covered porch at the main entrance to a church (*see* Galilee).

NEOLITHIC: 'New Stone' Age, dating in Britain from the appearance from the Continent of the first settled farming communities *c.* 3500 B.C. until the introduction of the Bronze Age.

NEWEL: central post in a circular or winding staircase; also the principal post when a flight of stairs meets a landing.

NOOK-SHAFT: shaft set in the angle of a pier or respond or wall, or the angle of the jamb of a window or doorway.

OBELISK: lofty pillar of square section tapering at the top and ending pyramidally.

OGEE: *see* Arch (Fig. 1c).

ORATORY: small private chapel in a house.

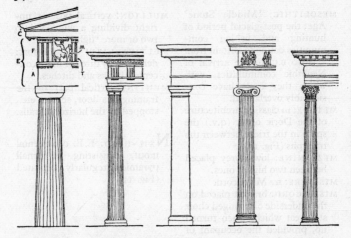

Fig. 12 – Orders of Columns (Greek Doric, Roman Doric, Tuscan Doric, Ionic, Corinthian) E, Entablature; C, Cornice; F, Frieze; A, Architrave; M, Metope; T, Triglyph.

ORDER: (1) *of a doorway or window:* series of concentric steps receding towards the opening; (2) *in classical architecture:* column with base, shaft, capital, and entablature (q.v.) according to one of the following styles: Greek Doric, Roman Doric, Tuscan Doric, Ionic, Corinthian, Composite. The established details are very elaborate, and some specialist architectural work should be consulted for further guidance (*see* Fig. 12).

ORIEL: *see* Bay-Window.

OVERHANG: projection of the upper storey of a house.

OVERSAILING COURSES: series of stone or brick courses, each one projecting beyond the one below it.

PALAEOLITHIC: 'Old Stone' Age; the first period of human culture, commencing in the Ice Age and immediately prior to the Mesolithic; the Lower Palaeolithic is the older phase, the Upper Palaeolithic the later.

PALIMPSEST: (1) *of a brass:* where a metal plate has been re-used by turning over and engraving on the back; (2) *of a wall painting:* where one overlaps and partly obscures an earlier one.

PALLADIAN: architecture following the ideas and principles of Andrea Palladio, 1518–80.

PANTILE: tile of curved S-shaped section.

PARAPET: low wall placed to protect any spot where there is a sudden drop, for example on a bridge, quay, hillside, housetop, etc.

PARGETTING: plaster work with patterns and ornaments either in relief or engraved on it.

PARVIS: term wrongly applied to a room over a church porch. These rooms were often used as a schoolroom or as a store room.

PATEN: plate to hold the bread at Communion or Mass.

PATERA: small flat circular or oval ornament in classical architecture.

PEDIMENT: low-pitched gable used in classical, Renaissance, and neo-classical architecture above a portico and above doors, windows, etc. It may be straight-sided or curved segmentally. *Broken Pediment:* one where the centre portion of the sloping sides is left out. *Open Pediment:* one where the centre portion of the base is left open.

PENDANT: boss (q.v.) elongated so that it seems to hang down.

PENDENTIF: concave triangular spandrel used to lead from the angle of two walls to the base of a circular dome. It is constructed as part of the hemisphere over a diameter the size of the diagonal of the basic square (Fig. 13).

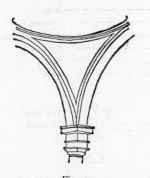

Fig. 13

PERP (PERPENDICULAR): historical division of English Gothic architecture covering the period from c.1335–50 to c.1530.

PIANO NOBILE: principal storey of a house with the reception rooms; usually the first floor.

PIAZZA: open space surrounded by buildings; in C17 and C18 England sometimes used to mean a long colonnnade or loggia.

PIER: strong, solid support, frequently square in section or of composite section (compound pier).

PIETRA DURA: ornamental or scenic inlay by means of thin slabs of stone.

PILASTER: shallow pier attached to a wall. *Termini Pilasters:* pilasters with sides tapering downwards.

PILLAR PISCINA: free-standing piscina on a pillar.

PINNACLE: ornamental form crowning a spire, tower, buttress, etc., usually of steep pyramidal, conical, or some similar shape.

PISCINA: basin for washing the Communion or Mass vessels, provided with a drain. Generally set in or against the wall to the S of an altar.

PLAISANCE: summer-house, pleasure house near a mansion.

PLATE TRACERY: *see* Tracery.

PLINTH: projecting base of a wall or column, generally chamfered (q.v.) or moulded at the top.

POND BARROW: rare type of Bronze Age barrow consisting of a circular depression, usually paved, and containing a number of cremation burials.

POPPYHEAD: ornament of leaf and flower type used to decorate the tops of bench- or stall-ends.

PORTCULLIS: gate constructed to rise and fall in vertical grooves; used in gateways of castles.

PORTE COCHÈRE: porch large enough to admit wheeled vehicles.

PORTICO: centre-piece of a house or a church with classical detached or attached columns and a pediment. A portico is called *prostyle* or *in antis* according to whether it projects from or recedes into a building. In a portico *in antis* the columns range with the side walls.

POSTERN: small gateway at the back of a building.

PREDELLA: in an altar-piece the horizontal strip below the main representation, often used for a number of subsidiary representations in a row.

PRESBYTERY: the part of the church lying E of the choir. It is the part where the altar is placed.

PRINCIPAL: *see* Roof (Fig. 14).

PRIORY: monastic house whose head is a prior or prioress, not an abbot or abbess.

PROSTYLE: with free-standing columns in a row.

PULPITUM: stone screen in a major church provided to shut off the choir from the nave and also as a backing for the return choir stalls.

PULVINATED FRIEZE: frieze with a bold convex moulding.

PURLIN: *see* Roof (Figs. 14, 15).

PUTTO: small naked boy.

QUADRANGLE: inner courtyard in a large building.

QUARRY: in stained-glass work, a small diamond or square-shaped piece of glass set diagonally.

QUATREFOIL: *see* Foil.

QUEEN-POSTS: *see* Roof (Fig. 15).

QUOINS: dressed stones at the angles of a building. Sometimes all the stones are of the same size; more often they are alternately large and small.

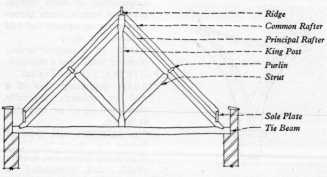

Ridge
Common Rafter
Principal Rafter
King Post
Purlin
Strut

Sole Plate
Tie Beam

Fig. 14

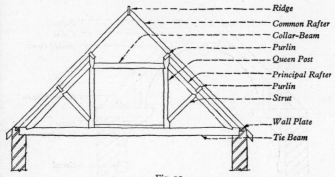

Fig. 15

RADIATING CHAPELS: chapels projecting radially from an ambulatory or an apse.

RAFTER: *see* Roof.

RAMPART: stone wall or wall of earth surrounding a castle, fortress, or fortified city.

RAMPART-WALK: path along the inner face of a rampart.

REBATE: continuous rectangular notch cut on an edge.

REBUS: pun, a play on words. The literal translation and illustration of a name for artistic and heraldic purposes (Belton = bell, tun).

REEDING: decoration with parallel convex mouldings touching one another.

REFECTORY: dining hall; *see* Frater.

RENDERING: plastering of an outer wall.

REPOUSSÉ: decoration of metal work by relief designs, formed by beating the metal from the back.

REREDOS: structure behind and above an altar.

RESPOND: half-pier bonded into a wall and carrying one end of an arch.

RETABLE: altar-piece, a picture or piece of carving, standing behind and attached to an altar.

RETICULATION: *see* Tracery (Fig. 20).

REVEAL: that part of a jamb (q.v.) which lies between the glass or door and the outer surface of the wall.

RIB-VAULT: *see* Vault.

ROCOCO: latest phase of the Baroque style, current in most Continental countries between *c.*1720 and *c.*1760.

ROLL MOULDING: moulding of semicircular or more than semicircular section.

ROMANESQUE: that style in architecture which was current in the C11 and C12 and preceded the Gothic style (in England often called Norman). (Some scholars extend the use of the term Romanesque back to the C10 or C9.)

ROMANO-BRITISH: A somewhat vague term applied to the period and cultural features of Britain affected by the Roman occupation of the C1–5 A.D.

ROOD: cross or crucifix.

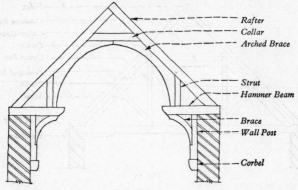

Fig. 16

ROOD LOFT: singing gallery on the top of the rood screen, often supported by a coving.

ROOD SCREEN: *see* Screen.

ROOD STAIRS: stairs to give access to the rood loft.

ROOF: *Single-framed:* if consisting entirely of transverse members (such as rafters with or without braces, collars, tie-beams, king-posts or queen-posts, etc.) not tied together longitudinally. *Double-framed:* if longitudinal members (such as a ridge beam and purlins) are employed. As a rule in such cases the rafters are divided into stronger principals and weaker subsidiary rafters. *Hipped:* roof with sloped instead of vertical ends. *Mansard:* roof with a double slope, the lower slope being larger and steeper than the upper. *Saddle-back:* tower roof shaped like an ordinary gabled timber roof. The following members have special names: *Rafter:* roof-timber sloping up from the wall plate to the ridge. *Prin-*

cipal: principal rafter, usually corresponding to the main bay divisions of the nave or chancel below. *Wall Plate:* timber laid longitudinally on the top of a wall. *Purlin:* longitudinal member laid parallel with wall plate and ridge beam some way up the slope of the roof. *Tie-beam:* beam connecting the two slopes of a roof across at its foot, usually at the height of the wall plate, to prevent the roof from spreading. *Collar-beam:* tie-beam applied higher up the slope of the roof. *Strut:* upright timber connecting the tie-beam with the rafter above it. *King-post:* upright timber connecting a tie-beam and collar-beam with the ridge beam. *Queen-posts:* two struts placed symmetrically on a tie-beam or collar-beam. *Braces:* inclined timbers inserted to strengthen others. Usually braces connect a collar-beam with the rafters below or a tie-beam with the wall below. Braces can be straight or curved (also called arched). *Hammer-beam:* beam projecting at right angles, usually from the top of a wall, to carry arched braces or struts and arched braces (*see* Figs. 14, 15, 16).

ROSE WINDOW (or WHEEL WINDOW): circular window with patterned tracery arranged to radiate from the centre.

ROTUNDA: building circular in plan.

RUBBLE: building stones, not square or hewn, nor laid in regular courses.

RUSTICATION: *rock-faced* if the surfaces of large blocks of ashlar stone are left rough like rock; *smooth* if the ashlar blocks are smooth and separated by V-joints; *banded* if the separation by V-joints applies only to the horizontals.

S ADDLEBACK: *see* Roof.

SALTIRE CROSS: equal-limbed cross placed diagonally.

SANCTUARY: (1) area around the main altar of a church (*see* Presbytery); (2) sacred site consisting of wood or stone uprights enclosed by a circular bank and ditch. Beginning in the Neolithic, they were elaborated in the succeeding Bronze Age. The best known examples are Stonehenge and Avebury.

SARCOPHAGUS: elaborately carved coffin.

SCAGLIOLA: material composed of cement and colouring matter to imitate marble.

SCALLOPED CAPITAL: development of the block capital (q.v.) in which the single semi-

19

circular surface is elaborated into a series of truncated cones (Fig. 17).

Fig. 17

SCARP: artificial cutting away of the ground to form a steep slope.

SCREEN: *Parclose screen:* screen separating a chapel from the rest of a church. *Rood screen:* screen below the rood (q.v.), usually at the W end of a chancel.

SCREENS PASSAGE: passage between the entrances to kitchen, buttery, etc., and the screen behind which lies the hall of a medieval house.

SEDILIA: seats for the priests (usually three) on the S side of the chancel of a church.

SEGMENTAL ARCH: *see* Arch.

SET-OFF: *see* Weathering.

SEXPARTITE: *see* Vaulting.

SGRAFFITO: pattern incised into plaster so as to expose a dark surface underneath.

SHAFT-RING: motif of the C12 and C13 consisting of a ring round a circular pier or a shaft attached to a pier.

SHEILA-NA-GIG: fertility figure, usually with legs wide open.

SILL: lower horizontal part of the frame of a window.

SLATEHANGING: the covering of walls by overlapping rows of slates, on a timber substructure.

SOFFIT: underside of an arch, lintel, etc.

SOLAR: upper living-room of a medieval house.

SOPRAPORTE: painting above the door of a room, usual in the C17 and C18.

SOUNDING BOARD: horizontal board or canopy over a pulpit. Also called Tester.

SPANDREL: triangular surface between one side of an arch, the horizontal drawn from its apex, and the vertical drawn from its springer; also the surface between two arches.

SPIRE: tall pyramidal or conical pointed erection often built on top of a tower, turret, etc. *Broach Spire:* spire which is generally octagonal in plan rising from the top or parapet of a square tower. A small inclined piece of masonry covers the vacant triangular space at each of the four angles of the square and is carried up to a point along the diagonal sides of the octagon. *Needle Spire:* thin spire rising from the centre of a tower roof, well inside the parapet.

SPIRELET: *see* Flèche.

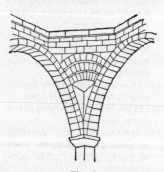

Fig. 18

SPLAY: chamfer, usually of the jamb of a window.

SPRINGING: level at which an arch rises from its supports.

SQUINCH: arch or system of concentric arches thrown across the angle between two walls to support a superstructure, for example a dome (Fig. 18).

SQUINT: hole cut in a wall or through a pier to allow a view of the main altar of a church from places whence it could not otherwise be seen (also called Hagioscope).

STALL: carved seat, one of a row, made of wood or stone.

STAUNCHION: upright iron or steel member.

STEEPLE: the tower of a church together with a spire, cupola, etc.

STIFF-LEAF: E.E. type of foliage of many-lobed shapes (Fig. 19).

STILTED: *see* Arch.

Fig. 19

STOUP: vessel for the reception of holy water, usually placed near a door.

STRAINER ARCH: arch inserted across a room to prevent the walls from leaning.

STRAPWORK: C16 decoration consisting of interlaced bands, and forms similar to fretwork or cut and bent leather.

STRETCHERS: *see* Brickwork.

STRING COURSE: projecting horizontal band or moulding set in the surface of a wall.

STRUT: *see* Roof.

STUCCO: plaster work.

STUDS: upright timbers in timber-framed houses.

SWAG: festoon formed by a carved piece of cloth suspended from both ends.

TABERNACLE: richly ornamented niche (q.v.) or free-standing canopy. Usually contains the Holy Sacrament.

TARSIA: inlay in various woods.

TAZZA: shallow bowl on a foot.

TERMINAL FIGURES (TERMS, TERMINI): upper part of a human figure growing out of a pier, pilaster, etc., which tapers towards the base. *See also* Caryatids, Pilasters.

TERRACOTTA: burnt clay, unglazed.

TESSELLATED PAVEMENT: mosaic flooring, particularly Roman, consisting of small 'tesserae' or cubes of glass, stone, or brick.

TESSERAE: *see* Tessellated Pavement.

TESTER: *see* Sounding Board.

TETRASTYLE: having four detached columns.

THREE-DECKER PULPIT: pulpit with Clerk's Stall below and Reading Desk below the Clerk's Stall.

TIE-BEAM: *see* Roof (Figs. 14, 15).

TIERCERON: *see* Vault (Fig. 21).

TILEHANGING: *see* Slatehanging.

TIMBER-FRAMING: method of construction where walls are built of timber framework with the spaces filled in by plaster or brickwork. Sometimes the timber is covered over with plaster or boarding laid horizontally.

TOMB-CHEST: chest-shaped stone coffin, the most usual medieval form of funeral monument.

TOUCH: soft black marble quarried near Tournai.

TOURELLE: turret corbelled out from the wall.

TRACERY: intersecting ribwork in the upper part of a window, or used decoratively in blank arches, on vaults, etc. *Plate tracery: see* Fig. 20(*a*). Early form of tracery where decoratively shaped openings are cut through the solid stone infilling in a window head. *Bar tracery:* a form introduced into England *c.*1250. Intersecting ribwork made up of slender shafts, continuing the lines of the mullions of windows up to a decorative mesh in the head of the window. *Geometrical tracery: see* Fig. 20(*b*). Tracery characteristic of *c.*1250–1310 consisting chiefly of circles or foiled circles. *Y-tracery: see*

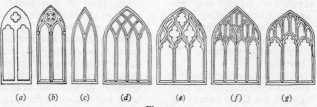

(*a*) (*b*) (*c*) (*d*) (*e*) (*f*) (*g*)

Fig. 20

Fig. 20(c). Tracery consisting of a mullion which branches into two forming a Y shape; typical of c.1300. *Intersected tracery: see* Fig. 20(d). Tracery in which each mullion of a window branches out into two curved bars in such a way that every one of them is drawn with the same radius from a different centre. The result is that every light of the window is a lancet and every two, three, four, etc., lights together form a pointed arch. This treatment also is typical of c.1300. *Reticulated tracery: see* Fig. 20(e). Tracery typical of the early C14 consisting entirely of circles drawn at top and bottom into ogee shapes so that a net-like appearance results. *Panel tracery: see* Fig. 20(f) *and* (g). Perp tracery, which is formed of upright straight-sided panels above lights of a window.

TRANSEPT: transverse portion of a cross-shaped church.

TRANSOM: horizontal bar across the openings of a window.

TRANSVERSE ARCH: *see* Vault.

TRIBUNE: *see* Gallery.

TRICIPUT, SIGNUM TRICIPUT: sign of the Trinity expressed by three faces belonging to one head.

TRIFORIUM: arcaded wall passage or blank arcading facing the nave at the height of the aisle roof and below the clerestory (q.v.) windows. (*See* Gallery.)

TRIGLYPHS: blocks with vertical grooves separating the metopes (q.v.) in the Doric frieze (Fig. 12).

TROPHY: sculptured group of arms or armour, used as a memorial of victory.

TRUMEAU: stone mullion (q.v.) supporting the tympanum (q.v.) of a wide doorway.

TUMULUS: *see* Barrow.

TURRET: very small tower, round or polygonal in plan.

TUSCAN: *see* Order.

TYMPANUM: space between the lintel of a doorway and the arch above it.

UNDERCROFT: vaulted room, sometimes underground, below a church or chapel.

UNIVALLATE: of a hill-fort: defended by a single bank and ditch.

UPPER PALAEOLITHIC: *see* Palaeolithic.

VAULT: *Barrel-vault: see* Tunnel-vault. *Cross-vault: see* Groin-vault. *Domical vault:* square or polygonal dome rising direct on a square or polygonal bay, the curved surfaces separated by groins (q.v.). *Fanvault:* Late Medieval vault where all ribs springing from one springer are of the same length, the same distance from the next, and the same curvature. *Groin-vault* or *Crossvault:* vault of two tunnelvaults of identical shape intersecting each other at r. angles. Chiefly Norman and Renaissance. *Lierne:* tertiary rib, that is, rib which does not spring either from one of the main springers or from the central boss. Introduced in the C14, continues to the C16. *Quad-*

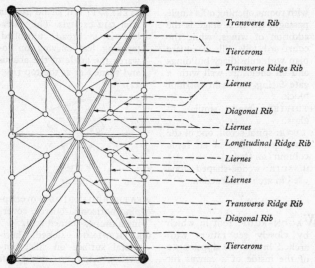

Transverse Rib

Tiercerons

Transverse Ridge Rib

Liernes

Diagonal Rib

Liernes

Longitudinal Ridge Rib

Liernes

Liernes

Transverse Ridge Rib

Diagonal Rib

Tiercerons

Fig. 21

ripartite vault: one wherein one bay of vaulting is divided into four parts. *Rib-vault:* vault with diagonal ribs projecting along the groins. *Ridge-rib:* rib along the longitudinal or transverse ridge of a vault. Introduced in the early C13. *Sexpartite vault:* one wherein one bay of quadripartite vaulting is divided into two parts transversely so that each bay of vaulting has six parts. *Tierceron:* secondary rib, that is, rib which issues from one of the main springers or the central boss and leads to a place on a ridge-rib. Introduced in the early C13. *Transverse arch:* arch separating one bay of a vault from the next. *Tunnel-vault* or *Barrel-vault:* vault of semicircular or pointed section. Chiefly Norman and Renaissance. (*See* Fig. 21.)

VAULTING SHAFT: vertical member leading to the springer of a vault.

VENETIAN WINDOW: window with three openings, the central one arched and wider than the outside ones. Current in England chiefly in the C17–18.

VERANDA: open gallery or balcony with a roof on light, usually metal, supports.

VESICA: oval with pointed head and foot.

VESTIBULE: ante-room or entrance hall.

VILLA: (1) according to Gwilt (1842) 'a country house for the residence of opulent persons'; (2) Romano-British country houses cum farms, to which the description given in (1) more or less applies. They developed with the growth of urbanization. The basic type is the simple corridor pattern with rooms opening off a single passage; the next stage is the addition of wings, while the courtyard villa fills a square plan with subsidiary buildings and an enclosure wall with a gate facing the main corridor block.

VITRIFIED: made similar to glass.

VOLUTE: spiral scroll, one of the component parts of an Ionic column (*see* Order).

VOUSSOIR: wedge-shaped stone used in arch construction.

WAGON-ROOF: roof in which by closely set rafters with arched braces the appearance of the inside of a canvas tilt over a wagon is achieved. Wagon-roofs can be panelled or plastered (ceiled) or left uncovered.

WAINSCOT: timber lining to walls.

WALL PLATE: *see* Roof.

WATERLEAF: leaf shape used in later C12 capitals. The waterleaf is a broad, unribbed, tapering leaf curving up towards the angle of the abacus and turned in at the top (Fig. 22).

Fig. 22

WEATHERBOARDING: overlapping horizontal boards, covering a timber-framed wall.

WEATHERING: sloped horizontal surface on sills, buttresses, etc., to throw off water.

WEEPERS: small figures placed in niches along the sides of some medieval tombs (also called Mourners).

WHEEL WINDOW: *see* Rose Window.

INDEX OF PLATES

INDEX OF ARTISTS

INDEX OF PLACES

ADDENDA
(JANUARY 1963)

p. 104 [Bishopstone, St Mary.] Mr J. A. Finch draws my attention to the odd little two-light window in the E wall of the porch: cusped ogee arches and an incised star in the spandrel – all rather oriental-looking. Also, Mr Finch points to the concave-triangular shape of the arches in the church, including the chancel arch.

p. 219 [Fonthill Gifford, Fonthill Abbey.] According to evidence found by Mr John Harris, Alderman Beckford's Palladian mansion was built by the architect *Hoare*, who according to Mr Colvin designed the court house at Maidstone.

p. 265 [Liddington.] LIDDINGTON CASTLE, S of the village. Earthwork with bank, ditch, and counterscarp bank (J. A. Finch).

p. 311 [Mere.] The CHANTRY HOUSE consists of a centre with a hall formerly open to the roof, a two-storeyed solar end to the W, and a six-bay service end to the E. Two chimneystacks are original. The screens passage with its three doorways (one blocked) to the service quarters also survives. Restored hall roof with collar-beams on arched braces.

p. 327 [Ogbourne St Andrew, St Andrew.] Tower, aisles, and clerestory are Perp. Mr J. A. Finch tells me of flat, shallow, presumably Norman buttresses at the E corners of the chancel.

p. 328 [Ogbourne St George, St George.] Mr Finch points out the flat, shallow, probably Norman buttress at the SE corner of the chancel and the small carved angel on the SW buttress of the tower.

p. 437 [Stockton, St John Baptist.] The tablet to John Greenhill has recently in *Country Life* been attributed to *Nost* (by Mr Bailey) and to *Thomas Davis* (by Mr Esdaile).

p. 471 [Tottenham House.] Mr John Harris draws my attention to a note in *The Ambulator*, 1811. Here it is said that the column was originally erected by George Bubb Dodington 'to the memory of his lady' at Brandenburg House, Hammersmith, and then removed by Thomas Wyndham to Tottenham House.

p. 486 [Wanborough, St Andrew.] The w tower was begun in
   1435, according to a brass plate inside which mentions
   Thomas Polton (*see* below) and other benefactors.

NOTES

NOTES

NOTES

NOTES

NOTES

NOTES

NOTES